Recreation and Youth Development

Recreation and Youth Development

Peter A. Witt and Linda L. Caldwell

Venture Publishing, Inc.
State College, Pennsylvania

Venture Publishing, Inc.
1999 Cato Avenue
State College, PA 16801
Phone (814) 234-4561
Fax (814) 234-1651

Production Manager: Richard Yocum
Manuscript Editing: Valerie Fowler, Richard Yocum, Michele L. Barbin
Cover by Echelon Design

Library of Congress Catalogue Card Number 2005930077
ISBN-10: 1-892132-57-5
ISBN-13: 978-1-892132-57-4

Table of Contents

List of Tables and Figures

Chapter 1

Chapter 2

Chapter 5

Chapter 7

Chapter 8

Chapter 9

Chapter 10

Chapter 11

Chapter 13

Chapter 16

Chapter 17

Chapter 20

Chapter 21

Preface

If you are reading this book, you must have an interest in youth. We do too, and realized through teaching courses on youth development and recreation there was a gap in the literature—very little organized information exists that addresses the growing need to increase the capacity of professionals working with youth in a recreation context to be able to more fully contribute to youth development. Thus, the goal of this book is to increase knowledge about who youth are, why they do what they do, and how to facilitate their development through recreation.

We hope you are challenged and inspired by what you read so that you undertake efforts to make a difference in youth's lives through recreation. Perhaps you will be confronted with new perspectives. We hope so, and we hope you discuss and debate these ideas, perspectives, and issues with others—that will help you learn (and make us feel good).

The book mainly focuses on issues related to adolescents. This is a critical period of development and an age group that has been underdiscussed in the recreation literature. However, to successfully understand the needs of adolescents and some of the ways to meet their needs, we must also understand some of the issues that operate in young people's lives before they reach adolescence.

Guiding Beliefs for This Book

We want to share some of the basic beliefs that guided the development of this book. Fundamentally, we believe the following:

- It is necessary to take an ecological approach to conceptualizing and developing youth services.
- Recreation is a powerful context for youth development.
- The diversity in the cultural backgrounds and experiences of young people must be understood and honored when developing programs and services.
- Adults can be powerful contributors to youth development.
- Youth can and must be meaningful contributors to their own development.
- A strategy based on promoting positive experiences through recreation is more effective than an approach solely focused on reducing problems.

- Deliberate, well-planned programs based on achieving healthy developmental outcomes are essential.
- Youth need to be educated and guided to reap healthy developmental benefits through recreation.
- We must move beyond simply counting the number of participants in our programs to a fuller understanding of why programs work (or not), for whom they work, and under what conditions they work.

Who and Context

One of the challenges with a book where chapters are supplied by different authors is to try to bring coherence to the overall work. For example, our authors used a variety of terms, including adolescents, youth, and young people. You will also notice that there are several different labels that the authors used when referring to professionals who work with young people—youth worker, recreation professional, activity leader, and program specialist. In the end, we decided that the diversity of terms referring to "youth" and "professionals" reflects the reality of the different contexts through which supports, opportunities, services, and programs are available to youth. Thus, these various terms are used throughout the book.

It is also important to understand that this book is not just about service delivery and programming. Although these are important components of the book, we adopted a broader perspective that includes leisure and recreation as important contexts—whether formal or informal—for fostering youth development.

Flow and Progression of Book

This book has a deliberate flow to it, and you will find that we try to relate the material in one chapter to ideas in other chapters. Because of this, there are at times some redundancies of basic ideas across chapters. We do this to help you to link ideas together and to avoid the book becoming a series of disparate chapters written by different authors. Although we think that most readers will want to read the book in the current order of the chapters, some may choose to only read specific chapters of special interest. We would like to suggest, however, that the material in the first section of the book is essential groundwork and provides a context for grasping some of the nuances of what comes later in the book.

The book is divided into four main sections:

- All About Youth
- Developing Youth's Potential
- Supports, Opportunities, Services, and Programs
- Diversity: Implications for Youth Development

Chapters in the first section combine to paint a picture of what youth development means, who youth are today, and the evolution and current status of youth service organizations. The second section contains chapters that describe some of the basic theoretical frameworks that examine youth development, the role of recreation as a context for youth development, and how to facilitate youth development. In the third section, authors present information about the supports, opportunities, services and programs that contribute to youth development through recreation. The chapters in the fourth section remind us of the necessity to consider the diversity of youth and the importance of context in the development of youth's potential. We end the book with a brief summary chapter.

Voices in the Book

We started out writing this book ourselves, but quickly realized we lacked the full expertise to address many of the things we thought were important to include. Therefore, we asked some of our colleagues to help us out. Thankfully they agreed to do so. When you read the bios of the authors, you will see that we were fortunate that individuals with a broad set of backgrounds and experiences were willing to contribute chapters or work with us as coauthors on chapters for the book. The material is enriched by the involvement of a number of different "voices." We owe a debt of gratitude to all of our partners who contributed to the book as authors and coauthors:

> Cheryl K. Baldwin, Jason N. Bocarro, Megan Kelly Cronan, Mary Ann Devine, Jesse M. Ellis, Arnold H. Grossman, Karla A. Henderson, Susan L. Hutchinson, Reed W. Larson, Francis Lobo, Kristi Montandon, Bill Niepoth, Corliss Wilson Outley, Daniel F. Perkins, Jennifer Skuza, and Kathrin Walker

We are privileged to know each of these individuals as colleagues and friends. We worked with each author in an effort to create material that related to the overall themes of the book. Thus, all of the chapters were edited and underwent several rounds of revisions, including the ones we were involved in as authors. We hope this improved the readability of the book.

You will notice in the book that when it is necessary to refer to the authors, the term "we" was used. The use of "we" made it easier for the book to have a common voice. This does not mean, however, that all authors are collectively responsible for any failings of the book. It would be fair to say that all the individual strengths of the book are due to the expertise of our contributors and all of the areas needing improvement or clarification are on us, Peter and Linda.

Thanks

This book was a labor of love and professional commitment on the part of many people. First, thanks go to the authors who contributed chapters to this effort. Their expertise has enabled the book to go well beyond what it could have been if "we," Peter and Linda, had tried to write all of the chapters ourselves. Thus, we thank all of the contributors for their flexibility and willingness to partner with us to make this book a reality. It was a sincere pleasure to work with them all.

We would also like to thank our colleagues who provided critical reviews for some of the chapters and made comments and suggestions that made the chapters better. In particular we would like to thank Cheryl K. Baldwin, Jesse M. Ellis, Lydia Justice, Douglas Kleiber, Reed W. Larson, Joyce Nies, Lori Palen, Daniel F. Perkins, Erin Sharp, and Kathleen Raupach.

One of our colleagues, however, deserves special mention and thanks. Megan Kelly Cronan, a graduate student at Texas A&M University, devoted countless hours to reading, editing, and commenting on most of the chapters in this book. Her insights were extremely useful, in many cases helped to focus ideas, and in all cases led to improvements in the final product. We were also fortunate that Megan played a significant role as one of the authors of two of the chapters in the book. The book would not be the same without her significant involvement.

Peter is also indebted to the Sequor Foundation which funded his endowed chair and helped support some of the research and editing for this book.

Finally, Peter would like to thank his wife, Joyce Nies, and Linda would like to thank her husband, Ed Smith, for their support, understanding, patience, and encouragement.

Peter Witt
Texas A&M University

Linda Caldwell
The Pennsylvania State University

Section I
All About Youth

In the first section of this book we will provide some of the fundamental information necessary to understand the basic principles of youth development and the status of youth today in the United States and around the world. We will also explore some of the historical antecedents to the development of youth services in the United States and the current status of some of the major youth serving organizations.

The 10 principles of youth development outlined in Chapter 1 present a dramatically different philosophy for offering youth services than the remediation of problems approach that has been used in the past. The principles not only outline the need for helping young people diminish negative behaviors but also emphasize the need to develop supports, opportunities, programs, and services (SOPS) to help young people develop the values, attitudes, knowledge, skills, and behaviors necessary to successfully navigate adolescence and become fully functioning adults. This discussion will provide a foundation for Section II of the book where we will discuss some of the ways leisure is important to development and specific approaches necessary to develop youth's full potential.

Section I includes two chapters about the status of youth today. In Chapter 2, we review some of the basic data concerning the household living arrangements that youth grow up in and the economic status of young people. This chapter also provides a review of the educational attainment and health status of youth. Together these sections remind us that many young people in the United States grow up under fairly nurturing circumstances, achieve a good education, and avoid undertaking many of the behaviors that can compromise health status. However, we are also reminded of the number of young people who grow up under difficult circumstances, fail to receive the level of education necessary to successfully function as adults, and undertake health-compromising behaviors.

Chapter 2 also contains information about how young people spend their time and how they get and spend their money. Understanding adolescent time use and the resources adolescents have to support their nonschool time activities are important considerations when developing the SOPS necessary to ensure positive youth development.

Understanding the role that different cultures play in the development of young people around the world is also important. Thus, in Chapter 3 we discuss how differing patterns of time use, gender roles, and child rearing impact the status of youth. We also discuss some dangers to children as they seek to grow up in a troubled world. Topics such as the impact of war and dislocation, land mines, HIV/AIDS, sexual exploitation, child labor, and the involvement of young people as war combatants help us to better understand the difficult circumstances children around the world face in their daily lives. Understanding these factors also helps us to understand the critical role of play and recreation for children living in these difficult circumstances.

While understanding the current circumstances of young people is critical to creating meaningful SOPS to encourage their development, it is also critical to understand the historical context that has guided the development of approaches to youth services. Therefore, Chapter 4 provides a review of the forces in the late 1800s and the first several decades of the 1900s that led to many of the approaches to dealing with young people we see today. We discuss the societal forces, such as industrialization, immigration, and urbanization, which changed the way young people were viewed and treated by society. The development of child labor laws, compulsory and longer schooling, curfews, and juvenile courts all helped to create a period between childhood and adulthood, which we now call adolescence, and led to the creation of a number of youth serving organizations that still are important players in youth development today.

Building on this discussion, Chapter 5 provides an in-depth look at some of the prominent youth serving organizations, including the Boys and Girls Clubs, Boy Scouts and Girl Scouts, YMCA and YWCA, and local park and recreation departments. For each of these organizations, we look at their history, the way they are organized, and the types of SOPS they provide for young people today.

The chapters in this section provide an important foundation for understanding the material presented in the other sections of the book, including the historical context for understanding current approaches to youth development, the necessity of developing a comprehensive set of SOPS, and the need to consider the role of diversity in the development of youth services.

Chapter 1

10 Principles of Youth Development

Peter A. Witt and Linda L. Caldwell

This book was written to help you (a) to understand how youth develop through recreation and leisure experiences and (b) to structure and provide recreation supports, opportunities, programs, and services (SOPS) to promote optimal development. To initiate the learning process, we begin the book with a set of general principles that are useful in understanding how to guide youth development. These principles have evolved over the last 20 years as practitioners and researchers working with young people have sought to define the basic SOPS necessary to enable youth to develop as fully functioning adults. These principles provide general guidance for how recreation professionals should provide SOPS to youth. All of the chapters in the book relate in some way to these principles. Specifically, Chapter 6 will describe in more detail what youth development is and Chapter 8 will continue the discussion by outlining how recreation and leisure contribute to youth development.

Let's just take a minute to briefly understand what the terms supports, opportunities, and programs mean because this will help us to articulate and to better grasp the essential nature of youth development goals and practices. The definitions for these terms come from the Center for Youth Development Policy and Research 2003 document, *What Is Youth Development?*

> ***Supports***. Motivational, emotional, and strategic supports to succeed in life. Supports can take many different forms, but they must be affirming, respectful, and ongoing. Supports are most powerful when they are offered by a variety of people (e.g., parents and close relatives, community social networks, teachers, youth workers, employers, health providers, and peers) who are involved in the lives of young people.
>
> ***Opportunities***. Chances for young people to learn how to act in the world around them, to explore, express, earn, belong, and influence. Opportunities give young people the chance to test ideas and behaviors and to experiment with different roles. It is important to stress that young people, just like adults, learn

best through active participation and that learning occurs in all types of settings and situations.

Services (and Programs). Services in such areas as education, health, employment, and juvenile justice, which exhibit (a) relevant instruction and information; (b) challenging opportunities to express oneself, to contribute, to take on new roles and be part of a group; and (c) supportive adults and peers who provide respect, high standards and expectations, guidance, and affirmation to young people.

Karen Pittman (2001), Senior Vice President of the International Youth Foundation (IYF) and Executive Director of the Forum for Youth Investment (FYI), is one of the leaders in understanding and writing about youth development. She offers a complementary view of SOPS, which is presented in **Table 1.1** (see p. 6). Notice that recreation and leisure are important aspects of opportunities and programs, and certainly implicated under supports.

Historically, SOPS stemmed from an underlying philosophy that youth had many problems and that adolescents in general were going through a period of "storm and stress." Initially, therefore, SOPS were often geared toward fixing problems or providing opportunities so that youth would avoid trouble. Fortunately, a new perspective has evolved that considers youth to be largely responsible, caring, and concerned people who are learning to navigate the world, finding out about who they are, and learning how they fit into the larger society.

Based on this updated perspective, we present a set of 10 principles that have been formulated to help move us from a conceptualization of youth as problems that need to be fixed to a broader understanding of the need to develop the full potential of all youth to enable them to develop as fully functioning adults. After we list these principles, we discuss each in detail.

10 Principles of Youth Development

1. Understand that young people are assets in the making and not just problems to be fixed.

2. Move beyond deficit-based models (addressing only problem behaviors) to models that focus on developing youth capabilities (assets).

3. Base the provision of SOPS on a vision of a fully functioning and capable adult.

4. Move beyond thinking in terms of either/or.
5. Focus on developing a wide range of knowledge, skills, and behaviors.
6. Involve adults from the family and community in fostering youth development.
7. Support youth in being essential players in their own development.
8. Design youth development supports, opportunities, and programs deliberately.
9. Bring programs to scale.
10. Sustain supports and opportunities over time.

Principle 1: Young People as Assets in the Making

If you read the daily newspaper, it is easy to get the impression that many young people are problems in their homes, at their schools, and in their communities. "Teen Arrested for Convenience Store Robbery," "Gun-Carrying Boy Detained at School," and "Teen Pregnancy Continues to Soar" are examples of headlines that appear in local papers—very often on the front page. These headlines lead many adults to assume there is a crisis among young people, that the behavior of teens is out of control, and that swift remedial and punitive actions are necessary to protect society by eliminating negative behaviors. Stories about the good things that teens are doing (e.g., going to and doing well in school, volunteering in their communities) are less often told. Consequently young people are too often seen as liabilities to be controlled rather than assets to be nurtured.

It is true that some young people get into trouble and thus require extra attention and remedial intervention to help them navigate their teenage years; however, the vast majority of young people are able to steer a fairly smooth course through their teen years with the assistance and support of parents, schools, community members, and organizations. Even for those teens that get into trouble, in almost all cases they also have strengths and positive attributes that need to be rewarded and nurtured. Some of the unique challenges and problems associated with youth are explored in Chapter 2, and the way in which youth develop resiliency to overcome these challenges is discussed in Chapter 7.

Table 1.1: Supports, Opportunities, Programs, and Services
Adapted from Pittman, 2001

Supports (main actor: the provider)
Affirmation and assistance to set and accomplish goals

Healthy relationships
- Nurturance
- Friendship

Role models, resources, and networks
- Options assessment
- Planning
- Assessing resources (financial, connections)

High expectations and clear standards
- Guidance
- Monitoring

Opportunities (main actor: the individual)
Chances to learn, earn, and contribute

Quality instruction, training, and informal learning
- Learning and building skills
- Exploration and reflection
- Expression and creativity
- Leisure and play

Challenging roles and responsibilities
- Employment and earned income
- Influence and advocacy
- Interaction and membership

Programs/Services (main actor: the provider)
Receipt of instruction in care and use of facilities

Human Services
- Educational
- Vocational
- Health/mental health
- Social
- Recreation and leisure
- Law enforcement
- Rehabilitation

Infrastructure
- Transportation
- Public maintenance
- Retail

Stable places
- Homes
- Neighborhoods
- Community meeting places

Current wisdom suggests that viewing youth in negative terms is counterproductive to helping youth develop their potential so they and their communities can thrive in the future. So, how do we change society's basic attitudes about young people? The first challenge in developing a positive approach to dealing with young people is to see them as assets, not liabilities. If we do not help young people develop their full potential, they will not be able to maximize their contributions to society and act as nurturers and supports for the generations who will come after them.

As we have suggested, the development of young people depends on a range of SOPS from their families, communities, and other institutions that touch their lives. "When supports and opportunities are plentiful, young people can and do thrive; when their environments are deficient or depleted, youth tend not to grow and progress" (Gambone & Arbreton, 1997, pp. 1–2). Thus, working from a positive perspective is essential in developing appropriate SOPS to facilitate youth's positive development.

Principle 2: Move Beyond Deficit-Based Models

Stemming from Principle 1, youth workers must use and/or develop asset-based models rather than deficit-based models to guide their practice. Deficit-based models assume that the main goal of youth work is to help a young person avoid negative behaviors—to be problem free. For example, some people might consider the goal of youth work as providing the SOPS necessary to enable a young person to avoid using drugs, being involved in a gang, dropping out of school, and becoming pregnant. However, being "problem free" may not enable a young person to develop the knowledge, attitudes, skills, and behaviors necessary to be "fully prepared" to function as an adult. Thus, enabling a young person to be problem-free is only half the story. Efforts also are needed to promote development beyond problem reduction. Karen Pittman (Pittman, Irby & Ferber, 2000) encapsulated these ideas in her seminal statement: Problem free is not fully prepared.

In addition, even if young people develop the requisite knowledge, attitudes, skills, and behaviors, they might not choose to put them into action. Thus, Pittman also argued: Fully prepared is not fully engaged (Pittman, Irby & Ferber, 2000). A young person can be fully prepared but not have the motivation or resources to use his or her knowledge and skills to practice prosocial and productive behaviors. Thus, it is possible to be problem free and still not grow up to be a fully functioning adult, and it is possible to be fully prepared and not use the skills and abilities one has in a positive manner.

This formulation of the need for both preparation and engagement is similar to the debate that emerged in the health field after World War II. Health was often defined as the "absence of illness." However, the World Health Organization (2004) now takes the view that health is "a state of complete physical, mental and social well-being and not merely the absence of disease or infirmity." Under the "absence of illness" approach, effective treatments are those that change the physical state of the body so as to eliminate the specific illness. Therefore, this approach generally involves looking for single,

very specific cause for illnesses, with correspondingly specific treatments, like antibiotics for infections, which are expected to control or eradicate that illness in most people, under most conditions. However, increasingly it is understood that for a person to achieve a reasonable quality of life, more than being free from illness is necessary. Thus, the discussion has turned to ways to enhance health through better diet, exercise, positive relationships with others, and expansion of interests and abilities. "Creating a healthy lifestyle" has been added to "reduction of illness" to become twin goals of medicine.

As we have moved beyond a "problem free" focus in youth services, other understandings have also emerged. For example, Pittman (2001) also argued (a) academic achievement, while critical, is not nearly enough and (b) competence alone, while critical, is not enough. In the first instance, to be fully prepared, individuals also need to achieve vocational, physical, emotional, civic, social, and cultural competence. In the second, it is necessary to apply one's competence by turning it into action.

Efforts such as America's Promise (http://www.americaspromise.org) and the Search Institute (http://www.search-institute.org) have emerged from the desire to move beyond deficit reduction and identify the competencies one must develop to fully function in society. America's Promise proposes a series of five promises that society should make to young people. According to America's Promise (2003), society should provide the following:

- opportunities for ongoing relationships with caring adults—parents, mentors, tutors or coaches—to support, care about, and guide youth
- safe places with structured activities during nonschool hours for both physical and emotional safety for youth
- adequate nutrition, exercise, and healthcare to pave the way for healthy bodies, healthy minds, and smart habits for adulthood
- marketable skills through effective education to help youth navigate the transition from school to work successfully
- opportunities to give back through community service to enhance self-esteem, to boost confidence, and to heighten a sense of responsibility to the community

Keeping these promises is seen as critical to positive youth development; consequently, families, schools, and community organizations are asked to define their role in meeting these promises.

The Developmental Assets model, championed by the Search Institute (2003), provides a powerful tool for identifying and building the 40 assets

(20 internal and 20 external) deemed necessary for youth to move along the pathway to adulthood. The assets model is based on research about both the protective factors that inhibit high-risk behaviors and resilience factors that increase young people's ability to function positively in the face of adversity, a concept that will be discussed more fully in Chapter 7. For example, learning resistance skills can provide protection for individuals tempted by drugs. At the same time, the availability of a strong positive adult role model in a youth program may help an individual be resilient, despite the lack of positive adult role models in the home.

Let's take a closer look at four areas that make up the 20 external assets (home, school, or community attributes that provide supports and opportunities):

1. support from family, neighbors, schools, and other adults
2. actions to empower youth
3. establishment of boundaries and expectations
4. provision of opportunities for the constructive use of time

The 20 internal assets (the attitudes and behaviors that are necessary for youth to grow up to navigate their adolescent years and function successfully as adults) are also divided into four areas:

1. making a commitment to learning
2. developing positive values
3. developing social competencies
4. creating a positive identity

Table 1.2 (pp. 10–11) displays more detail about these assets.

Studies undertaken by the Search Institute provide evidence of the relationship between the number of assets young people have and their problem or positive behaviors and attitudes. For example, 49% of young people who indicate they have 0 to 10 of the 40 assets are likely to engage in problem alcohol use as opposed to only 3% of young people with 31 to 40 assets. The same relationship holds true for being involved in violence, illicit drug use, and sexual activity (**Table 1.3**, p. 12). Conversely, 47% of young people with 31 to 40 assets succeed in school while only 8% of those with 0 to 10 assets do so. Similar percentages are found for other positive or thriving behavior attitudes such as exhibiting leadership, maintaining good health, and valuing diversity.

Table 1.2: The Search Institute's 40 Developmental Assets

External Assets

Support

Family Support—Family life provides high levels of love and support.
Positive Family Communication—Young person and his or her parent(s) communicate positively, and young person is willing to seek advice and counsel from parents.
Other Adult Relationships—Young person receives support from three or more nonparent adults.
Caring Neighborhood—Young person experiences caring neighbors.
Caring School Climate—School provides a caring, encouraging environment.
Parent Involvement in Schooling—Parent(s) are actively involved in helping young person succeed in school.

Empowerment

Community Values Youth—Young person perceives that adults in the community value youth.
Youth as Resources—Young people are given useful roles in the community.
Service to Others—Young person serves in the community one hour or more per week.
Safety—Young person feels safe at home, at school, and in the neighborhood.

Boundaries and Expectations

Family Boundaries—Family has clear rules and consequences and monitors the young person's whereabouts.
School Boundaries—School provides clear rules and consequences.
Neighborhood Boundaries—Neighbors take responsibility for monitoring young people's behavior.
Adult Role Models—Parent(s) and teachers encourage the young person to do well.
Positive Peer Influence—Young person's best friends model responsible behavior.
High Expectations—Both parent(s) and teachers encourage the young person to do well.

Constructive Use of Time

Creative Activities—Young person spends three or more hours per week in lessons or practice in music, theater, or other arts.
Youth Programs—Young person spends three or more hours per week in sports, clubs or organizations at school and/or in the community.
Religious community—Young person spends one or more hours per week in activities in a religious institution.
Time at Home—Young person is out with friends "with nothing special to do" two or fewer nights per week.

Table 1.2: The Search Institute's 40 Developmental Assets
continued

Internal Assets

Commitment to Learning
Achievement Motivation—Young person is motivated to do well in school.
School Engagement—Young person is actively engaged in learning.
Homework—Young person reports doing at least one hour of homework every school day.
Bonding to School—Young person cares about his or her school.
Reading for Pleasure—Young person reads for pleasure three or more hours per week.

Positive Values
Caring—Young person places high value on helping other people.
Equality and Social Justice—Young person places high value on promoting equality and reducing hunger and poverty.
Integrity—Young person acts on convictions and stands up for his or her beliefs.
Honesty—Young person "tells the truth even when it is not easy."
Responsibility—Young person accepts and takes personal responsibility.
Restraint—Young person believes it is important not to be sexually active or to use alcohol or other drugs.

Social Competencies
Planning and Decision Making—Young person knows how to plan ahead and make choices.
Interpersonal Competence—Young person has empathy, sensitivity, and friendship skills.
Cultural Competence—Young person has knowledge of and contact with people of different cultural/racial/ethnic backgrounds.
Resistance Skills—Young person can resist negative peer pressure and dangerous situations.
Peaceful Conflict Resolution—Young person seeks to resolve conflict nonviolently.

Positive Identity
Personal Power—Young person feels he or she has control over "things that happen to me."
Self-Esteem—Young person reports having a high self-esteem.
Sense of Purpose—Young person reports that "my life has a purpose."
Positive View of Personal Future—Young person is optimistic about his or her personal future.

Principle 3: Vision of a Fully Functioning Adult

Furstenberg (1999) suggested that to function successfully as adults, young people in American society must be given a fair chance to develop the knowledge, attitudes, skills, and behaviors that will make the successful transition to adulthood possible. However, to know where to focus our attention, we need to understand what it means to have successfully transitioned through adolescence into adulthood. Furstenberg (1999, pp. 9–10) suggested three main ideals that would indicate this successful transition. Youth should be able

- to find rewarding and remunerative employment
- to form a lasting and gratifying partnership
- to become contributors in their communities

To move toward these goals individuals must become educated to their highest potential, be able to foster a positive identity, have a personal sense of well-being and self-efficacy, and develop the habits associated with good citizenship (e.g., voting, caring, contributions to others). Thus, the goal of providing supports and opportunities for young people should be more than keeping them off the streets, entertained, and out of trouble. We must move beyond simply supplying "fun and games," to a purposeful strategy of helping young people develop the foundation they will need to fully function as adults. We discuss how recreation and leisure contribute to youth developing into fully functioning adults in a number of later chapters in this book.

Table 1.3: Relationship Between Assets and Negative and Thriving Behaviors

		Number of Assets		
Negative Behaviors	0–10	11–20	21–30	31–40
Problem alcohol use	49%	27%	11%	3%
Violence	61%	38%	19%	7%
Illicit drug use	39%	18%	6%	1%
Sexual activity	32%	21%	11%	3%
		Number of Assets		
Thriving Behaviors	0–10	11–20	21–30	31–40
Succeeds in school	8%	17%	30%	47%
Maintains good health	26%	47%	69%	89%
Values diversity	36%	57%	74%	88%
Exhibits leadership	50%	65%	77%	85%

Principle 4: Move Beyond Either/Or

Deciding whether to take a deficit reduction or developmental approach to youth development has sometimes been approached as an "either/or" decision. For example, communities may decide to invest the majority of their resources in stopping gang membership or problem drinking, while ignoring opportunities to develop assets in young people to enable them to undertake more positive behaviors. In other words, choices are made between taking a "problem free" *or* "fully prepared" approach. However, a successful system of youth supports, opportunities, programs, and services needs to undertake both the "problem free" *and* "fully prepared" approaches simultaneously. Youth development does not need to be a choice between prevention and positive development. Thus, more recent approaches to prevention see youth development as a continuum, with youth development services at one end and social control or incarceration at the other (Quinn, 1999, p. 98).

Pittman and her colleagues at the Forum for Youth Investment (Pittman et al., 2000) provided other examples of where the "and" approach is needed and superior. For example, we must

- Work to achieve quick turnarounds of negative behaviors "and" undertake efforts to develop longer-term supports for positive development.
- Promote both basic services targeted to a single issue or area of the community "and" at the same time promote efforts to strategically plan a system of services in our communities.
- Utilize youth professionals to lead and plan activities "and" ensure that youth, their parents, and other stakeholders in the community are fully engaged and involved.
- Develop new ideas into pilot programs "and" make concerted efforts to develop long-term programs, with solid funding streams.

The "and" approach is important for recreation and park providers to adopt because it suggests that models of collaboration with other services such as health agencies, schools, and quasi-public agencies (e.g., YMCA/YWCA), are important. Adopting the "and" approach reduces territoriality and keeps the focus on youth's needs and positive development. The "and" approach also suggests a good way for recreation and park providers to partner with other youth service providers. Most often recreation professionals are skilled at the promotive aspect of service—that is, what they do typically does not focus on deficits but focuses on providing opportunities for, among other things, skill development, competence, and fun. Thus, if recreation professionals partner with others who might be more focused on risk reduction, an ideal situation is created for youth development to occur. In later chapters we address how recreation and leisure contributes to youth development (Chapter 8) and we also address in more detail the concept of health promotion as an important component of risk behavior reduction.

Principle 5: Develop a Wide Range of Knowledge, Skills, and Behaviors

SOPS must be available to develop the full range of knowledge, skills, and behaviors necessary for youth to successfully transition to adulthood. While the current emphasis on academic competence is commendable and necessary, according to Pittman et al. (2000) it is not nearly enough. Young people also need to achieve vocational, physical, emotional, civic, social, cultural, and spiritual competence. These competencies set the stage for young people to be successful in dealing with what psychologist Erik Erikson identifies as three crucial challenges to be faced during the adolescent years:

1. the task of industry—learning to be productive, learning to contribute
2. the task of identity—learning who you are and where you fit
3. the task of intimacy—learning how to be with others and finding a life partner (cited on the Forum for Youth Investment website, http://www.forumforyouthinvestment.org/ideasabout.htm)

Furthermore, youth must learn to self-regulate their actions and emotions in responsible ways. People tend to take action when they believe they have some level of competence, and youth development means that youth need the opportunity to learn to take actions that lead to positive outcomes. Chapters 6, 7, and 13, in particular, address the need for self-regulation and its importance to satisfying, effective, and responsible behavior.

Principle 6: Involving Adults From the Family and Community

Parents, school personnel, youth workers in community organizations, and other adults living in local communities are critical to helping young people thrive. Thus, it is necessary to adopt an ecological approach to meeting youth needs (e.g., Bronfenbrenner & Morris, 1998). This approach advocates the inclusion of a number of different adults in the development of assets. For example, one of the ways to contribute to youth development is by setting boundaries and high expectations. This involves parents and many other adults—in families, schools, neighborhoods, and churches. People in youth-serving organizations must clearly define rules, monitor youth's behavior, and set consequences for not following the rules. In a similar manner, a wide range of adults need to be involved in the development of opportunities for youth during out-of-school time activities. Parents, for example, are critical in helping guide their children in making appropriate choices, providing opportunities for family activities, and modeling appropriate behaviors. School personnel provide after-school athletic and other programs, as do nonprofit organizations, such as the Boys & Girls Clubs and Boy Scouts, governmental entities (e.g., park and recreation departments), and faith-based organizations, such as churches.

Adults play critical roles in youth development through supporting young people in their efforts to navigate the pathways to adulthood, while still enabling youth to have real voice and power in planning, organizing, and leading programs and activities. (See Chapters 11, 12, and 13 to explore this notion further.) There is substantial evidence that "resilient children, the ones who thrive despite obstacles, typically have caring adults present and active in their lives" (Walker & White, 1998, p. 14). Caring adults can be youth program or school staff, volunteers from the community, and/or parents. In all cases, the adults who are most effective "work in partnership with young people, who see themselves as supportive friends and advocates in contrast to adults motivated to save, reform, or rescue young people from their circumstances" (Walker & White, 1998, p. 15).

The key to adult involvement in youth development is for them to provide young people with the "scaffolding" necessary to enable growth and development (Pittman et al., 2000). Youth, like an emerging building, need support during "construction development." Scaffolding refers to the framework of temporary supports provided by adults as youth develop new skills. As skill development increases, the scaffolding is gradually reduced (called "fading") until the scaffolding is no longer needed.

The right level of scaffolding, however, is critical. Youth should not be stifled by too much support nor allowed to fail due to too little support. Scaffolding is a dynamic process where the adult assesses the youth's ability to get to the next rung, and what help they will need to get there, but does not continue to help them achieve rungs they have already mastered.

To realize the full power of adults in the lives of youth, quality adult leaders must be hired, trained, rewarded, and retained. However, this is not always easy to accomplish. Many youth-serving organizations hire individuals who are too young and have too many issues themselves to be strong resources in the lives of youth. In addition, too often leaders are hired who only plan to be around for a short period of time, thus undermining the value of creating longer-term, meaningful relationships between adults and youth. In many cases, a system is not in place to develop leaders who understand the principles of youth development and know how to translate these principles into meaningful practice. Finally, staff are often not paid enough to attract and retain them to youth work. Too often we entrust responsibility for our youth to low-paid individuals who, therefore, turn over far too quickly.

One of the results of hiring "short-timers" is that youth miss out on the advantages of developing longer-term relationships with adults. Young people often have difficulty investing in a relationship they know is only temporary. For young people from families where divorce has taken place or where they cannot depend on adults to "be there" for them, transient relationships can be taken as further evidence of the lack of involvement of caring adults in their lives. Developing trust and respect takes time and requires some stability in adult-youth relationships. In some cases young people develop relationships with adults, who by leaving "break their promise" to be there for the young person, thus undermining the future willingness of the young person to invest in developing meaningful relationships.

Principle 7: Support Youth

Involving youth in the development, design, and evaluation of SOPS is critical. Adults, when possible, should work with young people, as opposed to always initiating, planning, and directing youth activities. Further elaboration of this principle can be found in Chapters 12 and 13. Youth involvement and self-determination are keys to developing supports and opportunities. Thus, young people should have opportunities

- to participate in rule making, governance, and leadership
- to form enduring, durable relationships with peers
- to feel a sense of belonging and being valued
- to make a contribution to the community

Too often youth feel that adults plan *for* them, rather than *with* them. Youth workers often forget that it is the process of participating rather than the activity itself that is most rewarding. Thus, in many youth development programs, considerable efforts are being undertaken to empower youth to take ownership and responsibility for developing and sustaining programs.

There has been a significant shift from centralized top-down decision making by youth professionals to decentralized, youth-centered decision making.

The desire for active involvement in the decisions and circumstances that impact an individual's life appears to be a basic need, sometimes called *autonomy* or *self-determination.* Consequently, preserving choice and initiative is critical to helping individuals fully engage in their surroundings. On the other hand, when individuals are overregulated or opportunities to self-determine behavior are thwarted, young people may have a tendency to become externally rather than internally motivated, resulting in a lack of interest and full engagement. Adults often overregulate the behavior of young people by doing "for" them rather than "with" them, which leads to dependence and a self-fulfilling image of young people as being apathetic or only being motivated by external factors (Deci & Ryan, 2000; Ryan & Deci, 2000). See "Foster Involvement" on page 18 for an example of processes used by one organization to foster youth involvement.

Principle 8: Youth Development by Design

In the past, the main goal of most youth recreation programs has been to provide fun opportunities to keep youth busy and off the streets. So, recreation providers have simply provided a place for young people to go and things to do when they got there. However, in concert with the youth development movement, it is increasingly critical for programmers and service providers to move beyond causal approaches focused on numbers of participants to "gym and swim" or "fun and games" approaches to deliberate approaches that emphasize planning and leading on an intentional basis (McLaughlin, 2000). Employing intentionality requires answering the question, "What do we want to happen and how are we going to make it happen?" If we plan and execute programs consciously, we can create more supports for more youth in more neighborhoods and offer the basic things young people need such as people to talk to, places to go, and opportunities for development. We can also actively help young people build the attitudes, skills, values, and knowledge that they need in a full range of areas from cognitive and vocational to personal and civic. (Pittman et al., 2000, p. 49). Chapter 10 addresses this issue in more detail.

To practice intentionality, we need to utilize a comprehensive planning model—one that moves from assessing needs, to setting goals, to developing programs to meet goals, to assessing whether goals have been met. In some cases, this planning process needs to go on at the microlevel and focus on the needs of a particular individual in a particular setting (e.g., an after-school program offered by a local nonprofit organization). In other cases, the process is at the macrolevel, including efforts to think broadly about community needs and the kinds of actions that should be taken to meet those needs (e.g., the youth summit and youth task forces as noted in the "Foster Involvement" box).

To practice intentional programming, an understanding of the dimensions of activities that make the transition to adulthood more likely to succeed is needed. At present, there is fairly good agreement among professionals that the following program elements need to be offered or created (Gambone & Arbreton, 1997):

- a sense of safety
- challenging and interesting activities
- a sense of belonging

Foster Involvement

In Richmond, British Columbia, the Youth Involved Process (YIP) was created when the agency recognized the need to shift from its traditional top-down program model. The YIP model recognized that the process of planning, facilitating, implementing, and evaluating was more important than merely participating in a program. Implementation of the YIP was designed to enhance the development of specific internal and external assets from among the Search Institute's 40 Developmental Assets. The shift from a direct delivery to youth to a facilitative role for youth was challenging for staff, because it required a change in philosophy, work plans, job expectations, and desired outcomes.

Youth summits have also become a useful way of involving young people in thinking about their own needs and planning actions to meet those needs. In some cases, cities of other jurisdictions have created community-wide task forces to help better understand the issues facing youth in the community and the kinds of supports, opportunities, programs, and services necessary to deal with these issues. The involvement of young people in these forums is critical if the outcomes and recommendations are going to be accepted and embraced by youth.

For example, the Mayor's Office in Phoenix, Arizona, sponsored a Summit on Youth entitled Youth Empowerment in Action. The summit enhanced awareness of the need for comprehensive youth programming and services and provided momentum for further action. Several city staff committees were formed to discuss youth services in response to the summit's recommendations. Phoenix Parks, Recreation, and Library Department convened an internal 29 member Youth-At-Risk Task Force to develop program priorities. Ultimately, this led to creation of the At-Risk Youth Division within the department and greater involvement of youth in the development of youth programs.

- supportive relationships with adults
- involvement in decision making
- opportunities for leadership
- involvement in community

A major report on youth development by the National Academy of Sciences (2001) lists 10 basic elements that characterize quality youth programs (see **Table 1.4**). These elements are thought to be the building blocks of quality youth development programs. Changing the way we think about the design and delivery of programs can achieve development beyond problem prevention.

Principle 9: Bring Programs to Scale

SOPS need to be offered at an appropriate level of scale and saturation to make an impact on a young person's life. Even when an appropriate system is designed, SOPS often serve only a limited number of the young people who could benefit from involvement. Sometimes youth who live in risky environments are targeted for services, ignoring other youth who could also benefit from attention. Most often, however, these latter youth are ignored or the agencies where they live are so poorly underresourced, service provision is limited. On the other hand, some parents who are economically well-to-do

Table 1.4: Characteristics of Environments That Promote Positive Youth Development *National Academy of Sciences, 2001*

1. Physical and psychological safety
2. Structure that is developmentally appropriate
3. Emotional moral support
4. Opportunities for adolescents to experience supportive adult relationships
5. Opportunities to learn how to form close, durable human relationships
6. Opportunities to feel a sense of belonging and being valued
7. Opportunities for skill building and mastery
8. Opportunities to develop confidence in one's abilities to master one's environment (a sense of personal efficacy)
9. Opportunities to make a contribution to one's community and to develop a sense of mattering
10. Strong links between families, schools, and broader community resources

suggest that services for their children are lacking, because providers assume either parents can take care of their youth's needs, or services are not necessary for this group. Thus, an important issue in youth development is finding ways to offer a critical mass of services to a critical mass of young people. We should work to ensure sufficient quantity and quality of supports and opportunities so that more young people in more neighborhoods can be served more of the time (Pittman et al., 2000).

Principle 10: Sustainability

Program sustainability is critical to program success and gaining the trust and involvement of youth. Discontinuing a successful program after two years can be unsettling for youth, staff, and parents. Program discontinuation often happens because the program in question was a "pilot project" created as a result of a grant or other one-time monies. Sporadic funding from foundation and government grants can lead to an ever-rotating series of service system components; thus sustaining programs becomes difficult. This problem tends to occur because most grants are only available for a specified period of time (e.g., three years). In addition, grants often come with the expectation that the receiving organization will make efforts to raise funds from other sources to continue programs after the initial grant period ends. While staff are sometimes successful in finding the funds to maintain programs, it is a challenging task that most personnel are not trained to do.

There are a number of reasons to try and avoid one-shot or short-term programs. First, achieving a quality program in the first year or so can be difficult. It usually takes at least a year for programs to identify appropriate staff and stabilize their service model. For young people, this may mean that the service system designed to meet their needs is a matrix of ever changing elements and personnel. This makes it hard for young people to commit to involvement, because the programs and the staff they have grown to trust move on to the next funded priority when the particular project ends.

Another reason short-term programs should be avoided is that youth development is ongoing and takes time to accomplish. Continued involvement in a program allows youth to develop skills and competence, and leads to initiative. One-shot/short-term programs can generate participants but not necessarily meaningful development. Finally, it is almost impossible to properly evaluate the effectiveness of these short-term programs to achieve longer-term objectives.

To be most effective, youth development efforts must begin early, be sustained throughout the adolescent years, and allow for skill development through participation in various levels of challenge. Programs should be comprehensive, addressing many aspects of youth development. Finally, we need to develop a system of services that are ongoing and inclusive of the variety of services necessary to meet youth's needs.

Final Thoughts

According to youth development advocates, efforts are needed to create organizations and communities that enable youth to move along the pathways to adulthood by supplying the supports, opportunities, programs, and services beyond simple problem prevention. These approaches do not eliminate the need to target specific high-risk individuals for attention, but clearly efforts should not be restricted only to youth with high risk factors or only focus on problem remediation. Central to this thinking is the idea that young people are assets in the making—with their development dependent on a range of supports and opportunities coming from their family, the community, and the other institutions that have the potential to positively impact them. When supports and opportunities are plentiful, young people can and do thrive; when their environments are deficient or depleted, youth tend not to grow and progress.

These understandings represent exciting changes in the evolution of the philosophy of youth development over the years. Unfortunately, in a number of cases, youth-serving agencies, and in particular agencies that provide recreation have adopted "the youth development language," but have in reality made few changes in their service priorities and approaches. Thus, the purpose of this book is to educate you about how to not only "talk the talk" but also "walk the walk" of youth development. Each of the subsequent chapters in this book addresses one or more of the principles in more detail and provides information that will prepare you for working with youth using a youth development approach.

References

America's Promise. (2003). Retrieved January 6, 2004, from http://www.americaspromise.org

Bronfenbrenner, U. and Morris, P. A. (1998). The ecology of developmental processes. In R. M. Lerner (Vol. Ed.) and W. Danon (Series Ed.), *Handbook of child psychology Vol 1: Theoretical models of human development* (pp. 993–1028). New York, NY: Wiley.

Center for Youth Development Policy and Research. (2003). *What Is Youth Development?* Retrieved January 6, 2004, from http://cyd.aed.org/whatis.html

Deci, E. L. and Ryan, R. M. (2000). The "what" and "why" of goal pursuits: Human needs and the self-determination of behavior. *Psychological Inquiry, 11*, 227–268.

Furstenberg, F. E. (1999). *Managing to make it: Urban families and adolescent success*. Chicago, IL: University of Chicago Press.

Gambone, M. A., and Arbreton, A. J. A. (1997). *Safe havens: The contributions of youth organizations to healthy adolescent development*. Philadelphia, PA: Public/Private Ventures.

McLaughlin, M. W. (2000). *Community counts: How youth organizations matter for youth development.* Washington, DC: Public Education Network. Retrieved January 6, 2004, from http://www.publiceducation.org/PENreports.asp

National Academy of Sciences. (2001). *Community programs to promote youth development.* Washington, DC: National Research Council, National Academy of Sciences.

Pittman, K. (2001). *Preventing problems, promoting development, encouraging engagement: Competing priorities or inseparable goals?* Retrieved January 6, 2004, from http://www.forumforyouthinvestment.org

Pittman, K., Irby, M., and Ferber, T. (2000). Unfinished business: Further Reflections on a decade of promoting youth development." In *Youth development: Issues, challenges and directions*. Philadelphia, PA: Public/Private Ventures. Retrieved March 14, 2004, from http://www.ppv.org

Quinn, J. (1999). Where need meets opportunity: Youth development programs for early teens. *The Future of Children, 9*(2), 96–116. Retrieved March 14, 2004, from http://www.futureofchildren.org/usr_doc/vol9no2art9done.pdf

Ryan, R. M. and Deci, E. L. (2000). Self-determination theory and the facilitation of intrinsic motivation, social development, and well-being. *American Psychologist, 55*, 68–78.

Search Institute. (2003). *40 developmental assets.* Retrieved November 15, 2003, from http://www.search-institute.org/assets/forty.html

Walker, J. and White, L. (1998). Caring adults support the healthy development of youth. *The Center*, 14–19. Retrieved from http://fourh.umn.edu/resources/center/center1998.html

World Health Organization. (2004). *About WHO.* Retrieved March 14, 2004, from http://www.who.int/about/en

Chapter 2

Youth Today and Tomorrow: A U.S. Perspective

Linda L. Caldwell

Consider these questions: How many youth are there in the United States? Are young people "better off" today than 20 years ago? Are they faced with more or less problems? Do they exhibit more or less problem behaviors (e.g., substance use)?

Although many adults think youth are worse off today than they were years ago, it might surprise you to know that the majority of youth in North America are relatively happy and healthy and are making good developmental progress toward adulthood. According to analysis from the Monitoring the Future Survey (Child Trends, 2005), youth have increased their participation in volunteering, and fewer report being involved in school violence, being pregnant, or smoking. Most youth are well-adjusted and on the way to successfully negotiating adulthood.

Having said that, while youth may not have as many problems as society perceives, it is still important to recognize that as youth mature and go through adolescence, they must deal with physical and emotional changes and are exposed to increased opportunities to use drugs, cigarettes, and alcohol, and engage in risky sexual behavior. Research has shown that youth who have the basic skills, knowledge, and characteristics necessary to navigate this period in their lives make the transition from childhood to adolescence to adulthood more easily than their less-prepared peers. Most youth need help from adults in acquiring these skills, knowledge, and characteristics. Essentially that is the focus of the positive youth development movement—providing supports, opportunities, programs, and services to help youth develop into well-adjusted, happy, and fully functioning adults.

Given the need to help youth develop basic skills and knowledge, many recreation professionals seek to create programs that provide youth with essential developmental assets. To successfully develop programs that have a youth development focus, recreation programmers must recognize the trends, issues, strengths, problems, and challenges faced by youth. Therefore, the purpose of this chapter is to provide an overview of adolescents in the United States. This information will serve to provide a background for the material presented in other chapters in the book. In the following sections, we discuss indicators of the current status of youth in American society, including statistics reflecting the number of people under 18, demographic profiles of these youth, discussions and descriptions of their living conditions, considerations of their health status, and general information about their educational attainment. We also discuss the ways in which youth make and spend money. For each indicator, we provide information about why it is important to understanding the current status of youth.

We think you will learn the most from this chapter if you continually ask yourself the following question: In what ways can recreation and leisure contribute to, enhance, or mitigate some of the highlighted youth strengths, problems, and issues? Keeping this question in mind will provide a way of assessing the applicability of the information and not becoming overwhelmed by the statistics presented.

A considerable amount of additional information about adolescents that we cannot address here is available. To assist you in finding additional information about youth, we provide brief descriptions of selected websites at the end of this chapter (p. 45). The list provides two types of websites: (a) websites for agencies and organizations (private and public) whose activities and services make a major contribution to improving the life possibilities of youth, and (b) websites containing some major national studies that focus on life choices and health behaviors of youth.

Present Social and Demographic Profile and Future Trends

Much of the following information was taken with permission from the Child Trends website (http://www.childtrends.org). Child Trends is a nonprofit, nonpartisan research organization that promotes and engages in scientific research aimed at improving the lives of children and youth. Child Trends is one of the major websites that brings together data from a variety of sources on the current status of youth. In cases where the information did not come from the Child Trends website, the source is noted.

How Many Youth Are There?

In 2001 there were 72.6 million youth under age 18 in the United States, which is a 40% increase in the number of children and youth from 1950 (see **Figure 2.1**). By the year 2020, that number is expected to grow another 6.3% to 77.2 million. Despite this growth, since the early 1960s children have formed an ever-smaller *proportion* of the total U.S. population, declining from 36.0% in 1960 to 26.0% in 1990, to 25.5% in 2001 (see **Figure 2.2**, p. 28). This percentage is expected to decline further to 24% by the year 2020 as families have fewer children or no children at all.

Understanding current and future population trends is critical to effective strategic planning. Society makes substantial investments in children in all areas of life, including health and safety, education and training, recreation, and social development. Tracking and predicting numbers of youth can enable these investments to be made more intentionally and perhaps more effectively.

Just knowing how many youth there are, or will be, is not enough. Given that we live in a diverse society, understanding the breakdown of youth numbers by race and ethnicity allows for better services to be offered. This is because children of different races and ethnicities often show large differences in many areas of well-being, including health, mortality, school performance and attainment, and access to family and community resources. These and similar disparities are also evident in adulthood. (See Chapter 16 for an in-depth examination of issues related to race and ethnicity.)

With that in mind, it is important to understand that the demographic profile of youth in the United States is changing and becoming more diverse. In 2003, for example, about 20% of youth had a foreign-born parent. With respect to ethnic diversity

- The percentage of non-Hispanic White children has fallen from 74% to 62% between 1980 and 2003 and it is expected to drop to 55% by the year 2020 (see **Figure 2.3**, p. 29).

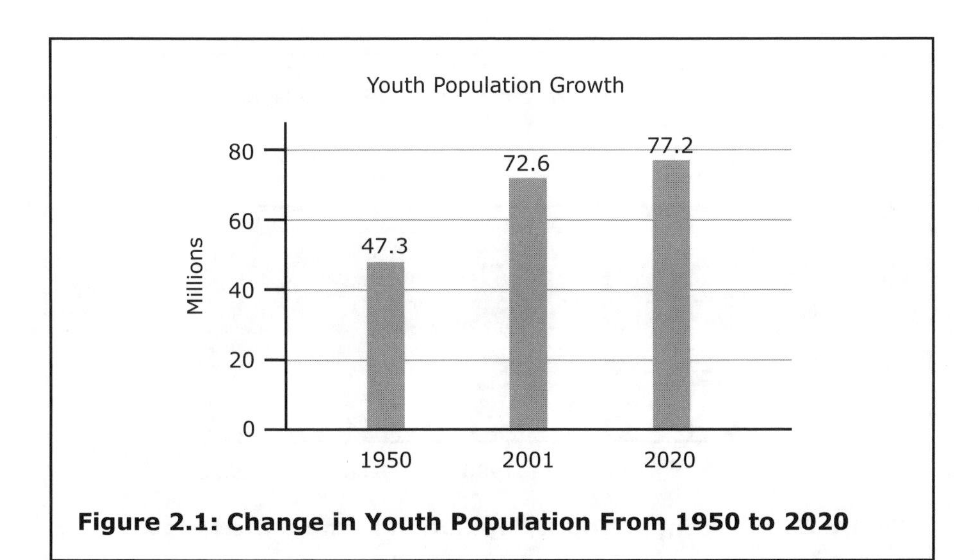

Figure 2.1: Change in Youth Population From 1950 to 2020

- The percentage of children in the United States that are Hispanic or Asian has increased steadily since 1980, and by 2020 these groups are expected to comprise nearly 29% of the entire child population.
- The percentage of non-Hispanic Black children in the United States has stayed relatively constant at about 15% since 1980, but it is expected to drop slightly to 14% by 2020.
- Non-Hispanic Asian and Pacific Islander children increased from 2% to 4% by 2001 and are expected to increase to 6% by 2020.
- Non-Hispanic American Indian and Alaska Native children have held constant at about 1% of the total child population since 1980.

Under What Conditions Do Youth Live?

Youth live in a variety of situations. The following data provide a snapshot of some of the important situational differences among youth (taken from Federal Interagency Forum on Child and Family Statistics, 2002).

Household living arrangements. Mothers and fathers both play important roles in the growth and development of children. Both the number and the type of parents (e.g., biological or step) in a household can have strong effects on children's well-being. Single-parent families tend to have much

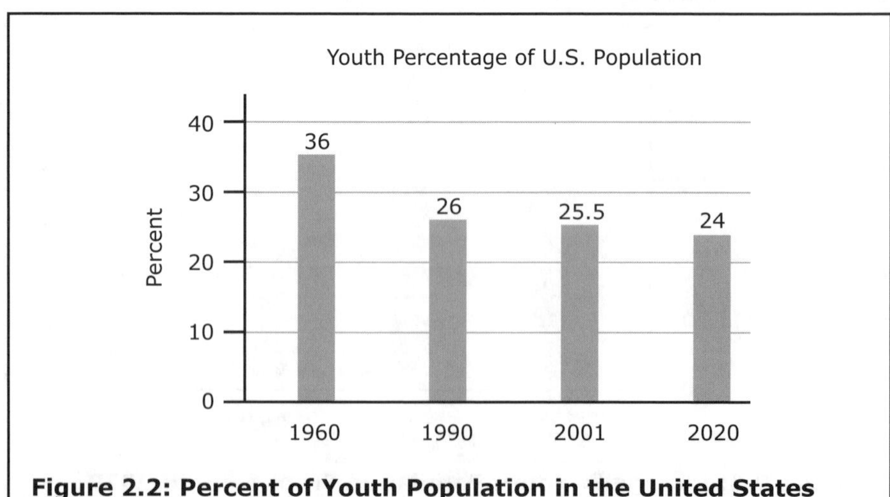

Figure 2.2: Percent of Youth Population in the United States

lower incomes than two-parent families. Recent research, however, indicates that the income differential accounts for only about one half of the negative effects of parent absence on many areas of child and youth well-being, including health, educational attainment and assessment, behavior problems, and psychological well-being.

From 1970 to 1996, the percentage of children under age 18 living with two parents declined from 85% to 68%. This percentage has now stabilized, with 69% of youth living with two parents in 2002. In addition,

- Since 1970 the percentage of children living in mother-only families increased from 11% to 23%, and the percentage living in father-only families increased from 1% to 5%.
- In 2002 the percent of children living without either parent (with other relatives or with nonrelatives) stayed fairly constant at about 3% to 4%, and 5% of all children lived in the home of their grandparents. In the majority of these families, however, one or both parents were also present.
- Most children living with two parents are living with both biological parents. However, in 1996, the most recent year for which these estimates are available, about 7% of all children lived with a stepparent.

Family composition differs by race and ethnicity. For example:

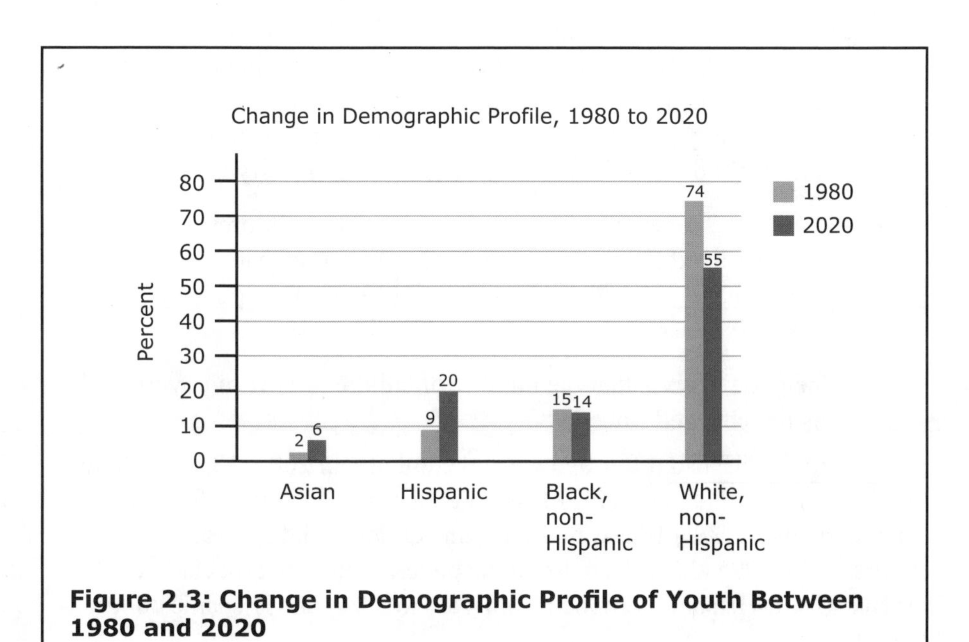

Figure 2.3: Change in Demographic Profile of Youth Between 1980 and 2020

- White, non-Hispanic children are more likely to live in two-parent families (78%) than Hispanic children (65%), and Black, non-Hispanic children (39%).

- For Black, non-Hispanic children living in two-parent families the percentage increased from 33% to 39% from 1996 to 2002.

Poverty. Being raised in poverty puts youth at increased risk for a wide range of problems. Children under 18 are much more likely than adults to be poor. For young children, growing up in poverty is associated with lower cognitive abilities, lower school achievement, and impaired health and development. For adolescents, growing up in poverty is associated with a lower probability of graduating from high school. Poor children are also more likely than other children to have behavioral and emotional problems. Finally, growing up in poverty is associated with lower occupational status and a lower wage rate as an adult. The problems associated with being raised in severe poverty (less than 50% of the poverty threshold) are correspondingly worse.

The child poverty rate in the United Sates is substantially higher—often two to three times higher—than that of most other major western industrialized nations. In 2003, a family of four with an annual income of $18,400 was considered below the federal poverty level. However, this cut-off point may be too low, since in many areas of the United States it takes roughly double this amount to provide a family of four with the basic necessities of life (e.g., food and housing). It is also critical to note the following:

- In 2001, 16% of children in the United States lived in poverty, and 7% lived in extreme poverty conditions, meaning that their parents made $9,200 or less per year (or one half of the recognized poverty level). Combined, these numbers mean that 17 million children in the United States lived in poverty in 2001.

- Just above the poverty level, 38% of American children—27 million—lived in low-income families, meaning that their parents made $36,800 or less per year (200% of the poverty level).

- The good news is that the number of children living in poverty has not changed since 1980.

Poverty levels also differ by race and ethnicity. In 2002, 13% of White, non-Hispanic children and 11% of Asian children lived in poor families, compared with 32% of Black, non-Hispanic children and 28% of Hispanic children. The 1995–2001 decrease in the poverty rate was especially evident for Black, non-Hispanic (dropped from 42% to 30%) and Hispanic children (39% to 27%).

Children are much more likely to be poor if they live in single-mother families than if they live in married-couple families. In 2002, for example, 40% of children living in single-mother families were poor, compared with 9% of children living in married-couple families. The same pattern holds whether children are White, Black, Hispanic, or Asian/Pacific Islander.

What Is the Educational Attainment of Youth?

Young adults who have completed higher levels of education are more likely to achieve economic success than those who have not. Although many jobs have minimum educational requirements, completing more years of education protects against unemployment. Further, higher levels of educational attainment lead to higher wages and income, as well as jobs with opportunities for advancement. Educational attainment is not only related to economic well-being. Adults with higher levels of education report being in better health and having higher levels of socioemotional well-being.

Since 1971, high school completion rates have risen from 59% to 87% among non-Hispanic Blacks age 25 to 29. These gains have narrowed the gap between non-Hispanic Blacks and non-Hispanic Whites from 23 percentage points in 1971 to just 6 percentage points in 2001.

The educational attainment levels of 25- to 29-year-olds in general have increased steadily over the past 30 years. For example,

- 58% of 25- to 29-year-olds completed at least some college in 2001, up from 34% in 1971.
- In 2002, 29% of all 25- to 29-year-olds had completed a bachelor's degree or higher, up from 17% in 1971.

Higher proportions of non-Hispanic Whites than non-Hispanic Blacks or Hispanics completed schooling at each level of education. Although minorities have still made great strides in overcoming the education gap, the gap itself still exists:

- Gains by non-Hispanic Blacks over the last 30 years have substantially reduced the Black-White gap for high school completion (with 93% and 87%, respectively, having completed high school in 2001).
- Hispanics have also shown gains since the 1970s, but have been unable to close the gap with non-Hispanic Whites.
- Among those ages 25 to 29, the percentage of non-Hispanic Whites who attained at least a bachelor's degree in 2002 was

four times that of Hispanics (36% compared to 9%) and twice that of non-Hispanic Blacks (18%).

A slightly higher percentage of females than males completed high school in 2001 (89% compared to 87%). However, significantly more females completed some college (63% compared to 54%) and received at least a bachelor's degree (31% compared to 26%) than their male counterparts.

What About the Health Status of Youth?

Health status can be assessed in a number of ways. In this section we will address four of the most relevant indicators of health among youth: feeling sad or hopeless; obesity, eating disorders, and physical activity; chronic conditions; and substance use.

Overall, about 87% of youth are in very good general health. Again, this varies by race and ethnicity. For example,

- White, non-Hispanic children were more likely than Black, non-Hispanic and Hispanic children to be in very good or excellent health.

- In 2001, 87% of White, non-Hispanic children were reported to be in very good or excellent health, compared with 74% of Black, non-Hispanic children and 77% of Hispanic children.

Health also varies by income level. For example, in 2001 about 71% of children in families below the poverty line were in very good or excellent health, compared with 86% of children in families living at or above the poverty line. Some specific aspects of the health status of youth are described next.

Feeling sad or hopeless. Physical health is only part of what constitutes health. Although in the United States 87% of youth report being in good health in general, in studies conducted in 1999 and 2001, 28% of students in grades 9 through 12 reported feeling sad or hopeless almost every day for two weeks or more in the previous year. This is of concern because these types of feelings are often predictors of depression and suicide.

Females are more likely to report being sad or hopeless than males (33% vs. 20%, respectively) and Hispanic youth (34%) are more likely to report being sad or hopeless for extended periods of time than are either White, non-Hispanic (27%) or Black, non-Hispanic (29%) youth. Rates are highest among Hispanic female students (42%).

Obesity, eating disorders, and physical activity. We discuss obesity, eating disorders, and physical activity together because they are intertwined.

Youth, for example, who are not physically active have a tendency to become overweight. Opposite to that, youth who have eating disorders are likely to overexercise. This is an area where much more research and attention are needed to help youth develop appropriate and healthy physical activity and eating patterns.

Obesity. Youth in America are more likely to be overweight today than in previous years—more than one in seven children was overweight in the United States in 1999–2000, triple the rate of the 1960s. This increase in prevalence of overweight children has emerged as a serious public health concern. Children who are overweight are at an increased risk of developing Type II diabetes, cardiovascular problems, orthopedic abnormalities, gout, arthritis, and skin problems. Also, being overweight is likely to negatively affect children's social and psychological development, and it has been linked to the premature onset of puberty. Moreover, the health threats posed by being an overweight child can be long lasting. Children and adolescents who are overweight are at risk of becoming overweight adults.

Although boys and girls are about equally likely to be overweight, as with many other social and demographic factors, the obesity rates among racial and ethnic groups differ significantly. For example,

- In 1999–2000, Black, non-Hispanic girls and Hispanic boys were at particularly high risk of being overweight (24% and 29%, respectively).

- Among children ages 6 to 11, Hispanic boys were significantly more likely to be overweight than both Black, non-Hispanic and White, non-Hispanic boys.

Through its *Healthy People 2010* initiative, the federal government has set a national goal to reduce the number of overweight children from a 1988–1994 baseline level of about 11% to a new goal of 5%. To reach this 5% goal, the Federal Drug Administration and the National Institutes of Health are encouraging schools and communities to educate parents and children about the importance of a healthy diet and physical activity.

Eating disorders. The obesity issue, however, is only one concern related to weight. Issues about body image are just as important. Many youth feel pressured to conform to "ideal" weight and body image standards and do so by inappropriate and often dangerous weight loss strategies that lead to eating disorders. Eating disorders are complex illnesses that rank as the third most common chronic illness in adolescent females (Society for Adolescent Medicine, 1995). In 2001, about 5% of all youth in grades 9 through 12 reported vomiting or taking laxatives to control their weight, and females were more likely to do so than were males (8% versus 3%).

Taking laxatives and vomiting to lose weight are symptoms of bulimia, one of the most common eating disorders. Bulimia is characterized by a cycle of excessive eating (i.e., binging) followed by vomiting (i.e., purging), the use of laxatives, or other means of weight control. Bulimia, like anorexia, is considered a psychological disorder, which often begins with dissatisfaction about one's body. The practices of vomiting and using laxatives can lead to serious medical problems. Self-induced vomiting, which exposes one's mouth, esophagus and colon to acidic gastric contents, can lead to oral complications (e.g., erosion of tooth enamel, swelling and soreness of salivary glands), ulcers, ruptures of the esophagus, and other health problems. The use of laxatives can cause intestinal and systemic complications (e.g., dependency on laxatives, the loss of colonic function).

Physical activity. Physical activity helps one to maintain appropriate weight and contributes to cardiovascular health, but many youth do not get the recommended amount of vigorous physical activity. As students get older, the amount of vigorous exercise they get declines. In 2001, the proportion of youth who participated in vigorous exercise dropped from 72% to 56% between 9th and 12th grade. The difference was most pronounced among females, who dropped from 67% in 9th grade to 45% by 12th grade.

Regular physical activity has both short-term and long-term health benefits. For adolescents, participation in sports, physical education classes, or other types of regular exercise helps to build and to maintain healthy bones and muscles, and control weight, and can lead to other positive psychological benefits. Adolescents who exercise also improve their long-term health. Participation in physical activity decreases the risk of developing heart disease, diabetes, high blood pressure, and colon cancer. Additionally, people who are active in their youth tend to remain active and physically fit as adults. The International Consensus Conference on Physical Activity Guidelines for Adolescents recommended that adolescents should be physically active daily and participate in vigorous physical activity three or more times a week for at least 20 minutes (NIH Consensus Development Program, 1995). However, more than one third of all high school students do not participate in this recommended amount of vigorous physical activity:

- Within all racial and ethnic subgroups, and across all grades, levels for male physical activity participation are between 14 and 25 percentage points higher than for females.

- Non-Hispanic Whites have the highest rates of participation in physical activity in 2001 (67%), with non-Hispanic Blacks and Hispanics following at 60% and 61%, respectively.

Chronic conditions. In 2001, approximately 8% of children ages 5 to 17 were reported to have activity limitations due to chronic conditions and approximately 20% of Americans currently live with one or more limitations or disabilities. These conditions may include limitations in normal physical activities due to health conditions and impairments, difficulty seeing, difficulty hearing, diagnosed learning disabilities, or limitations requiring help with bathing or showering. Boys are over 50% more likely than girls to have one or more limitations (23% vs. 14% in 2001). Families of lower socioeconomic status also report higher rates of activity limitations compared with children in higher socioeconomic status families.

Increased birth and survival rates among very low birth weight infants (who have a high risk of disability) and the increased diagnosis of attention deficit/hyperactivity disorder and asthma in recent years have led to a larger population of children with one or more disabilities. These disabilities may affect more than the diagnosis reveals. In 1997, for example, a study of children with limitations revealed that over 31% reported feeling sad, unhappy, or depressed, compared with only 17% of children without limitations. This increased level of negative emotion among children with limitations may reflect, in part, frustration with environmental barriers that limit their ability to fully engage in home, school, community, or social activities as well as the condition itself. Chapter 21 will discuss these issues in more detail.

Substance use. While youth substance abuse issues have persisted over the years, trends in this area are encouraging. Federal Interagency Forum on Child and Family Statistics, 2003 reported the following:

- In 2002, daily cigarette use among 8th, 10th, and 12th graders reached its lowest point (5%, 10%, and 17%, respectively) since the beginning of the Monitoring the Future Survey, continuing the downward trend that began in 1997 for 12th graders and in 1996 for 10th and 8th graders.

- From 2001 to 2002, the proportion of 10th graders reporting episodic heavy drinking (i.e., having at least five drinks in a row at least once in the previous two weeks) declined from 25% to 22%. Rates remained stable from 2001 to 2002 among 8th and 12th graders, with 12% and 29%, respectively, reporting this type of alcohol consumption in 2002.

- Between 2001 and 2002, illicit drug use in the past 30 days declined from 23% to 21% among 10th graders. One quarter of 12th graders and one tenth of 8th graders reported past-30-day illicit drug use in 2002, unchanged from the previous year.

Although the rates of risky behaviors are decreasing, there is still a significant proportion of youth that continues to use substances. In addition, medical science understands more about the compound affects of substance abuse. For example, cigarette smoking, an addictive behavior usually established in adolescence, is a primary preventable cause of death in the United States. More than 430,000 people die each year from tobacco-related illnesses. Additionally, youth who smoke are more likely to drink alcohol, use other drugs, and engage in a variety of other risky behaviors. They are also less likely to be physically fit and more likely to suffer from respiratory problems.

Finally, we are learning that the use of illicit drugs and alcohol is associated with many harmful behaviors and can cause both short-term and long-term health problems. In 2000, over a third of all traffic deaths among youth ages 15 to 20 were alcohol-related. Alcohol use among adolescents has been related to an increased risk of alcohol dependence in adulthood. Binge drinking can contribute to many health disorders, including cancer; liver, pancreatic, and cardiovascular diseases; and a variety of gastrointestinal problems, neurological disorders, and reproductive system disorders. Environmental risk factors associated with adolescent drinking include having alcoholic parents; a lack of parental support, monitoring, and communication; and having peers who drink.

Youth who use illicit drugs and alcohol are more likely to engage in risky sexual behavior, delinquency, and crime and to use increasingly more dangerous drugs. They are more vulnerable to coerced sexual activity. Additionally, youth using illicit drugs often have problems in school, including attendance problems and poor academic performance, and are more likely to drop out of school or be expelled. Youth who use illicit drugs are also more likely to have poor relationships with their families and peers.

Many health risks are also associated with illicit drug use. The physical problems associated with illicit drug use are numerous and vary depending on the type of drug used. Physical problems can include abnormal heart rates, seizures, kidney failure, respiratory failure, and brain damage. Additionally, youth who use illicit drugs have higher death rates than their peers because of increased risk of accidents (e.g., car accidents), suicide, homicide, and illness. Many mental health problems are also linked to illicit drug use, including depression, anxiety, paranoia, hallucinations, developmental lags, delusions, and mood disturbances. Therefore, it is important not only to recognize the signs and symptoms of adolescent substance abuse but also to have a plan of action for helping young people to overcome the problem.

How Do Youth Spend Their Time?

Leisure and recreation. In the United States, about 40% to 50% of the average nonworking youth's time is discretionary. Reed Larson, a developmental psychologist at the University of Illinois, and his colleagues have studied the time use patterns of children and adolescents for a number of years (e.g., Larson & Verma, 1999). One of the key issues they have been interested in is the breakdown of time use outside of school. In other words, they have studied how much time adolescents spend on "productive" activities (e.g., homework, chores, employment), maintenance activities (e.g., eating, transportation, personal care), and leisure. In their studies, they typically break down leisure participation into a variety of categories that include watching TV, listening to music, creative activities, talking, playing, playing games, playing sports, public leisure (e.g., leisure shopping, attending a movie, outings), and idling (e.g., doing nothing, thinking, waiting).

Larson and his colleagues not only study what North American youth do with their time but also compare their time use to that of youth in other countries. Larson estimates that North American youth have about 6.5 to 8 hours a day of free time, compared with 5.5 to 7.5 hours for European youth, and 4 to 5.5 hours of free time for Asian youth. Interestingly, all youth spend about the same amount of time watching TV—1.5 to 2.5 hours a day. North American and European youth spend more of their time in sports (30 to 60 minutes a day for North Americans, 20 to 80 minutes a day for Europeans) than East Asian youth. North American youth and European youth also spend more time in other structured leisure activities (an average of 10 to 20 minutes a day) than East Asian youth.

Remember that these are generalizations and that these statistics will again vary by race and ethnicity. For example, Larson and his colleagues also found that an urban, Black, non-Hispanic sample of 5th through 8th grade youth in Chicago showed different patterns in their time use than suburban and predominantly White, non-Hispanic youth (Larson, Richards, Sims & Dworkin, 2001):

- Over half of the waking hours of the youth in the urban sample were spent in free time and discretionary activities, and boys spent significantly more time in these activities than did girls.
- 17% of this time was spent watching TV, as compared to 13% reported in a suburban, White, non-Hispanic sample.
- Almost 10% of the Black, non-Hispanic sample's time was spent idling compared to 6.8% of the White, non-Hispanic sample.
- On the other hand, youth in the Black, non-Hispanic sample spent less time in creative activities, playing, playing sports, and engaging in public leisure.

Volunteering. Adolescents who are involved in community service or who volunteer in political activities are more likely to have a strong work ethic as adults and are more likely to volunteer and vote in the future. Youth who volunteer are less likely to become pregnant or to use drugs, and volunteering in adolescence is also related to overall positive academic, psychological, and occupational outcomes. Recent data show:

- Teenagers ages 16 to 19 in the United States are more likely than any other age group under the age of 35 to have volunteered in the past year.
- Of those who volunteer, most work with either education or youth-service related organizations (34%) or religious organizations (31%).
- 41% of teen volunteers reported that they approached the organization for which they volunteer, rather than being asked by someone else to volunteer.
- For students in 8th, 10th, and 12th grades, rates of volunteering increased in the years between 1991 and 2001. For example, among 12th graders the rates increased from 24% to 35%, and among 10th graders the jump was from 27% to 29%.
- In 2001 28% of 8th graders volunteered at least once a month, compared with 26% in 1991. Females were more likely than males to volunteer (35% vs. 24%).

How Do Youth Get and Spend Money?

Spending money. Regardless of the current economic downturn and declining employment rate among teens, youth still have access to relatively large amounts of money, and consequently considerable marketing is aimed at attracting their expenditures. Additionally, the availability of numerous media outlets makes teens an easy target for marketers. For example, based on findings from a joint Yahoo! Inc. and Carat North America study of 2,618 youth ages 13 to 24, Jupiter Research reported that on a typical day, youth had access to over 200 cable television networks, 5,500 consumer magazine titles, 10,500 radio stations, 30 million+ websites, and 122,000 newly published books (Greenspan, 2003). **Table 2.1** shows the amount of exposure youth have to various media sources.

Apparently industry efforts and studies are working, as youth are responding to these marketing efforts by spending increasing amounts of money. For example,

- The Drinks Business Review Online reported in February 2003 that between employment and what teens get from their parents, the amount of money at the disposal of youth will increase by more than 5% per year between 2002 and 2007.
- According to Teen Research Unlimited, teenagers in the United States spent $172 billion in 2001, up from $100 billion in 1995. Moreover, they estimate that the typical teenager spent $104 a week (Choi, n.d.).
- The June 2003 Harris study of nearly 3,500 participants (known as “Generation Wired”) found that 15% of youth spending is done online, and boys remain more comfortable with e-commerce than girls as they spend 1.7 times as much as girls do online. Jupiter Research expects total online spending for today’s youth to exceed $13 billion by 2006 (Greenspan, 2003).

Not surprisingly, as youth age, they spend more money. In 2003, Harris Interactive found the following three subsets of youth spenders:

- preteens (ages 8 to 12), who spend at a rate of $19.1 billion annually, or $946 per capita
- teens (ages 13 to 19), who spend at a rate of $94.7 billion annually, or $3,309 per capita
- young adults (ages 20 to 21), who spend at a rate of $61.3 billion annually, or $7,389 per capita (Greenspan, 2003)

Getting money. Where is all this disposable income coming from? According to Greenspan (2003), it is estimated that 87% of income for children under age 13 years is parent-supplied, compared to 37% of teenagers’ income.

As we discuss in Chapter 4, youth have always worked, but the rate and level of employment seems to be changing in recent years. The Children’s

Table 2.1: Youth Exposure to Media

Type of Exposure	Hours per Week
Internet (excluding e-mail)	16.7
Watching TV	13.5
Listening to the radio	12.0
Talking on the phone	7.7
Reading (excluding school)	6.0

Defense Fund (CDF) reported that only 34% of teenagers ages 16 to 19 were employed (part-time or full-time) in January 2004, marking the lowest youth employment rate for the month of January since 1965. This follows a trend in declining youth employment since 1977–1979 (United States Department of Labor, 2000).

Overall, youth ages 16 to 19 have lost more than one million jobs since January 2000, according to the Labor Department data. The same data show that, as of January 2004:

- 33.2% of male teens worked, which is the lowest percentage on record (records start in 1948).
- 34.9% of female teens worked, which is the lowest since 1972.
- 19.6% of Black, non-Hispanic teens worked, which is the lowest since 1984.
- 27.2% of Hispanic teens worked, which is the lowest on record (records for Hispanic teens start in 1994).

This drop in employment seems directly related to the 26% ($352 million) funding cut in 2002 for youth programs under the Workforce Investment Act (Children's Defense Fund, 2004).

Youth employment naturally varies by age and by whether or not school is in session. During the school months of 1996–1998, 9% of 15-year-olds were employed in an average month, compared with 26% and 39% of 16- and 17-year-olds, respectively. Youth in each age group were more likely to work during the summer, with employment rates at 18%, 36%, and 48% for 15-, 16-, and 17-year olds, respectively.

Amount of money. One would expect that when young people first enter the labor force they would be earning minimum wage. However, current population survey data indicate that earnings were above the minimum wage for most youth regardless of whether the youth were working in the summer or during school. Therefore, although the federal minimum wage was $5.15 in 1998, median earnings of 15- to 17-year-olds combined were $5.57 per hour. Earnings, however, varied slightly across sex and ethnic groups. For example, Hispanic and White, non-Hispanic males had the highest median hourly earnings. Hispanic and Black, non-Hispanic females had the lowest. Many youth report that they work mainly so that they are able to buy clothes, CDs, or a car. However, it is important to note that high school students also report working to contribute to family income and to earn money for long term goals, such as college (Galinsky, Kim, Bond & Salmond, 2005).

Concluding Remarks

Given the material presented in this chapter, if someone asked you to paint a picture of a typical child or adolescent, could you? Probably not, because there is no such person. Yet, these statistics do serve to provide us with a broad picture of some of the issues that youth face as well as their current social and demographic characteristics. These statistics also provide further evidence that race, ethnicity, and gender play important roles in understanding youth. Later chapters in this book address those issues in more detail.

As youth face the challenges of adolescence, those who acquire appropriate skills and knowledge will be most likely to succeed. Clearly some youth are growing up in less-than-ideal circumstances, faced with poverty or low-income environments and concomitant lack of social and other services associated with low-income situations. Despite that, youth are relatively healthy and happy. This state of affairs is what has prompted, to a degree, the positive youth development movement discussed in Chapter 1 and the need to think about how leisure and recreation contribute to the mitigation of risk factors and promotion of protective factors, leading to risk reduction and healthy development of youth (Chapter 7). An overarching goal of most youth-serving, general human service agencies (i.e., those that are not targeted toward a clinical group, such as those with addictions or youth who have attempted suicide) is to prevent problem behaviors from occurring or from getting worse, to promote and support existing strengths of youth, to provide opportunities and structures for youth to develop and acquire new talents and skills, and finally, to facilitate youth's engagement with life opportunities.

Although this chapter has provided a great deal of information, we have not provided information about all of the various statistics available to help understand the current status of young people. Thus, we challenge you to do some research of your own on some of these other topics, or at least keep in mind that there are other important issues facing youth in their daily lives. For example,

- We did not address gangs, but it is important to know who joins gangs, what factors make it more likely that someone will join a gang, and some of the consequences of gang membership.
- We also did not address the differing opportunities available to youth in urban, suburban, and rural environments. What is the effect of growing up in a suburban versus a rural area? Are there settings that make it easier for youth to make connections with other youth and participate in organized recreation?

- What is the effect of technology on youth? How do cell phones, personal digital assistants, virtual reality, instant messaging, and other yet-to-be invented technologies impact the lives of young people, and are these impacts positive or negative? For example, there is currently a great deal of concern about safety as a result of the Internet and the ease of communication among strangers.

The more we understand the circumstances of young people the better we will be able to develop the supports, opportunities, programs, and services necessary to help them make a successful transition to adulthood. Keeping in mind the conditions and circumstances of youth, and how they influence each other (e.g., poverty, poor health, and poor academic achievement are all linked) will enhance the ability of recreation and youth workers to purposefully plan and deliver programs that enhance youth development, no matter what the life circumstances are. In other words, what might be helpful to youth in a low-income, Hispanic neighborhood may not work as well in a suburban, non-Hispanic White neighborhood, and visa versa. We address these issues as we continue on with the book.

References

Children's Defense Fund. (2004, February 18). *Youth employment rate fell to lowest level for January in 39 years.* Retrieved March 29, 2004, from http//:www.childrensdefense.org/pressreleases/040218.asp

Child Trends. (2005). *American teens: The good news. What parents, policymakers, and program staff need to know about raising healthy, productive adolescents.* Retrieved February 16, 2005, from http://www.childtrends.org/_pressrelease_page.cfm?LID=BB240EC8-F2B5-4303-9124884842E9D389

Choi, R. (n.d.) *Youth's spending power turn merchandising tide.* Retrieved December 3, 2003, from http://www.bazeley.net/mosaic/news/archives/news

The Drinks Business Review Online (2003, February). *Youth spending power: Rising by 5% per year.* Retrieved August 15, 2004, from http://www.drinks-business-review.com

Federal Interagency Forum on Child and Family Statistics. (2002). *America's children: Key national indicators of well-being, 2002.* Washington, DC: U.S. Government Printing Office.

Federal Interagency Forum on Child and Family Statistics. (2003) *America's children: Key national indicators of well-being, 2003.* Washington, DC: U.S. Government Printing Office.

Galinski, E., Kim, S. S., Bond, J. T., and Salmond, K. (2005). *Youth & employment: Today's students, tomorrow's workforce.* Families and Work Institute. J. P. Morgan Chase. Retrieved April 15, 2005, from http://www.familiesandwork.org/Summary/yande.pdf

Greenspan, R. (2003, September 16). *The kids are alright with spending.* Retrieved February 16, 2005, from http://www.internetnews.com/stats/article.php/3077581

Healthy People 2010. (n.d.) Retrieved August 15, 2004, from http://www.healthypeople.gov

Larson, R. W., Richards, M. H., Sims, B., and Dworkin, J. (2001). How urban African American youth adolescents spend their time: Time budgets for locations, activities, and companionship. *American Journal of Community Psychology, 29*, 565–597.

Larson, R. W. and Verma, S. (1999). How children and adolescents spend time across the world: Work, play, and developmental opportunities. *Psychological Bulletin*, 125, 701–736.

NIH Consensus Development Program. (1995, December 18–20). Physical activity and cardiovascular health. *NIH Consensus Statement Online, 13*(3), 1–33.

Society for Adolescent Medicine. (1995). A position paper of the Society for Adolescent Medicine: Eating disorders in adolescents. *Journal of Adolescent Health, 16*, 476–480.

U.S. Department of Labor. (2000, November). *Report on the youth labor force.* Retrieved, March 29, 2004, from http://www.stats.bls.gov/opub/rylf/rylfhome.htm

Major Sources of Information and Major Studies of Youth

http://www.search-institute.org
Search Institute is an independent, nonprofit organization whose mission is to provide leadership, knowledge, and resources to promote healthy children, youth, and communities. To accomplish this mission, the institute generates and communicates new knowledge, and brings together community, state, and national leaders.

At the heart of the Institute's work is the framework of 40 developmental assets, which are positive experiences and personal qualities that young people need to grow up healthy, caring, and responsible.

http://www.childtrends.org
Child Trends is a nonprofit, nonpartisan children's research organization. They collect and analyze data; conduct, synthesize, and disseminate research; design and evaluate programs; and develop and test promising approaches to research in the field. Founded in 1979, Child Trends is supported by foundations, government agencies, private organizations and individual donors. Child Trends has achieved a reputation as one of the nation's leading sources of credible data and high-quality research on children. In keeping with its mission to improve the lives of children, Child Trends is committed to sharing the results of its research and analysis with those who set policy, provide services, fund programs, launch studies, and shape opinions related to children and their families.

http://www.afterschool.gov
Afterschool.gov offers one-stop access to government resources that support after-school programs. You can find information to help you understand the issues that face kids and teens or to fund, start and operate an after-school program. You don't even need to know which federal agency has the information you need—afterschool.gov searched the sites for the information requested most often and put it in easy-to-use categories. Research studies, news, and publications are added as they are released to keep you up to date on what is happening in the field of after-school programs.

http://www.ppv.org
Public/Private Ventures is a national nonprofit organization whose mission is to improve the effectiveness of social policies, programs, and community initiatives, especially as they affect youth and young adults. In carrying out this

mission, Public/Private Ventures works with philanthropies, the public and business sectors, and nonprofit organizations.

http://www.youthdevelopment.org
The Institute for Youth Development (IYD) is a nonpartisan, nonprofit organization founded in 1996 dedicated to ensuring the best possible future for America's children by promoting positive choices and behaviors.

IYD is unique in its commitment to a comprehensive risk-avoidance message regarding major risk behaviors among youth, including alcohol, drugs, sex, tobacco, and violence. Based on data showing unquestionable linkages between these behaviors, IYD promotes a consistent, comprehensive risk-avoidance message for all these behaviors. IYD believes that if parents and adults provide children and teens with consistent risk-avoidance messages, young people are capable of choosing to avoid these behaviors altogether.

http://www.nydic.org
The National Youth Development Information Center (NYDIC) is a project of the The National Assembly through its affinity group, the National Collaboration for Youth. NYDIC provides practice-related information about youth development to national and local youth-serving organizations at low cost or no cost.

Between 60% and 80% of all adolescents participate in nonschool programs. Many programs increasingly employ a youth development approach to deliver their services. They purposefully meet the needs of youth by building the competencies necessary for young people to become successful adults. NYDIC provides community programs with the information tools they need to improve their services.

http://www.theinnovationcenter.org
The Innovation Center for Community and Youth Development connects thinkers and leaders of all ages to develop fresh ideas, forge new partnerships, and design strategies that engage young people and their communities. The center helps innovative programs to become strong, sustainable ventures. They seek out community organizations around the world to find creative ideas and promising practices in the youth development field. They offer technical assistance and practical guidance to organizations that want to deepen, expand, and launch new initiatives.

http://www.childstats.gov
This website offers easy access to federal and state statistics and reports on children and their families, including population and family characteristics,

economic security, health, behavior and social environment, and education. Reports of the Federal Interagency Forum on Child and Family Statistics include *America's Children: Key National Indicators of Well-Being*, the annual federal monitoring report on the status of the nation's children, and *Counting Couples*. The Forum fosters coordination and collaboration in the collection and reporting of federal statistics on children and families.

http://www.iyfnet.org
The International Youth Foundation (IYF) is working in nearly 60 countries and territories to improve the conditions and prospects for young people where they live, learn, work, and play. Established in 1990 to bring worldwide resources to young people in need, IYF works with hundreds of companies, foundations, and civil society organizations to strengthen and "scale up" existing programs that are making a positive and lasting difference in young lives.

http://www.un.org/youth
The United Nations aims to enhance awareness of the global situation of youth and of the rights and aspirations of young people. It works toward greater participation of youth in the social and economic life of their societies. The United Nations Youth Agenda states that young people everywhere

- have aspirations and want to participate fully in the lives of their societies
- are key agents for social change, economic development and technological innovation
- should live under conditions that encourage their imagination, ideals, energy and vision to flourish to the benefit of their societies
- are confronted by a paradox: to seek to be integrated into the existing society or to serve as a force to transform it
- are also a social and demographic group at risk with an uncertain future, even though they represent society's greatest hope

http://www.unesco.org/youth
UNESCO stands for the United Nations Educational, Scientific, and Cultural Organization. In 1999, the "Strategy for UNESCO's Action with and for Youth" was drawn up to guide the organization's youth policy. It aims to empower young people, ensuring their full participation in society as equal and reliable partners. To this end, UNESCO seeks to encourage and mobilize

support within the organization, from member states, and from other partners with regard to three equally important domains:

1. young men and women's actual presence in UNESCO bodies and at all events organized by UNESCO or its partners
2. the incorporation of youth views and priorities and collaboration with young people in the launching of projects and programs in the areas of UNESCO's competence
3. the mainstreaming of youth concerns and issues into Member State's policies in order to create spaces and opportunities for the participation of young people and to give visibility to their contribution

Youth participation in UNESCO's activities was also ensured by youth forums during international conferences, such as the World Conference on Higher Education (Paris, 1998), the World Conference on Science (Budapest, 1999) and the 29th session of UNESCO's General Conference (Paris, 1999). The recommendations of these meetings resulted in concrete projects implemented in partnership between young people and UNESCO specialists in the domains of higher-education reform, prevention of HIV/AIDS, science education, promotion of the culture of peace, and volunteering, among others.

http://www.worldleisure.org/about/interest_groups/children_youth.html
World Leisure established a Working Group on Children and Youth in early 2000. Since then over 30 individuals from 14 different countries have been involved at different times and to different degrees.

The overall purpose of the Working Group on Children and Youth is to enhance the leisure experiences of children and youth worldwide by working for their right to have equitable access to leisure. The group pursues this purpose through the following objectives:

- Support and encourage relevant research.
- Identify and catalog important data related to children and youth.
- Facilitate dissemination of research findings and other useful data.
- Develop networks and partnerships with other international organizations.
- Advocate on behalf of families and local communities who seek to nurture children through leisure.

- Serve as a resource for other organizations or entities.
- Provide a context where experts may share their knowledge and support each other.
- Serve as a voice for leisure in those situations where the well-being of children is in question.

http://www.cdc.gov/nccdphp/dash/yrbs
The Youth Risk Behavior Surveillance System (YRBSS) of the Centers for Disease Control was developed in 1990 to monitor priority health risk behaviors that contribute markedly to the leading causes of death, disability, and social problems among youth and adults in the United States. These behaviors, often established during childhood and early adolescence, include the following:

- tobacco use
- unhealthy dietary behaviors
- inadequate physical activity
- alcohol and other drug use
- sexual behaviors that contribute to unintended pregnancy and sexually transmitted diseases, including HIV infection
- behaviors that contribute to unintentional injuries and violence

http://www.cpc.unc.edu/addhealth
The National Longitudinal Study of Adolescent Health (Add Health) is a nationally representative study that explores the causes of health-related behaviors of adolescents in grades 7 through 12 and their outcomes in young adulthood. Add Health seeks to examine how social contexts (e.g., families, friends, peers, schools, neighborhoods, communities) influence adolescents' health and risk behaviors.

Initiated in 1994 under a grant from the National Institute of Child Health and Human Development (NICHD) with cofunding from 17 other federal agencies, Add Health is the largest, most comprehensive survey of adolescents ever undertaken. Data at the individual, family, school, and community levels were collected in two waves between 1994 and 1996. In 2001 and 2002, Add Health respondents, 18 to 26 years old, were reinterviewed in a third wave to investigate the influence that adolescence has on young adulthood.

Multiple datasets are available for study, and more than 1,000 published reports and journal articles have used the data to analyze aspects of these complex issues. Add Health investigators hope this research will enable policymakers, researchers, healthcare providers, and educators to better understand how to protect the health of young people in the United States.

http://www.monitoringthefuture.org
Monitoring the Future is an ongoing study of the behaviors, attitudes, and values of American secondary school students, college students, and young adults. Each year, a total of some 50,000 8th, 10th, and 12th grade students are surveyed (12th graders since 1975, and 8th and 10th graders since 1991). In addition, annual follow-up questionnaires are mailed to a sample of each graduating class for a number of years after their initial participation. Reseach is funded through NIDA (National Institute on Drug Abuse) to Survey Research Center, Institute for Social Research, University of Michigan.

The Monitoring the Future (MTF) study is a continuing series of surveys intended to assess the changing lifestyles, values, and preferences of American youth. Each year since 1975, high school seniors from a representative sample of public and private high schools have participated in this study. The 2002 survey is the 12th to include comparable samples of 8th and 10th graders in addition to seniors. The study is conducted by the University of Michigan's Institute for Social Research (ISR) under a grant from the NIDA. The survey design consists of a multistage random sample where the stages include selection of geographic areas, selection of one or more schools in each selected area, and selection of a sample of students within each school. Data are collected in the spring of each year using questionnaires administered in the classroom by representatives from ISR. The 2002 survey included 13,544 high school seniors from 120 schools, 14,683 10th graders from 133 schools, and 15,489 8th graders from 141 schools (a total of 43,716 students from 394 schools).

Chapter 3

Play and Recreation in Childhood and Adolescence: An International Perspective

Francis Lobo and Bill Niepoth

Play and recreation are global phenomena. Young people engage in these activities in all countries and regions of the world. In some ways, these behaviors are similar across national boundaries and cultural identities. At the same time there are important differences. Our purpose in this chapter is to provide some examples that will give a sense of the similarities and differences in play and recreation patterns across several countries. We believe that this perspective can help youth leaders gain insights and understandings about their own at-home situations, particularly as immigration to the United States and Canada remains high.

The chapter contains three sections. The overall emphasis in the book is on youth, and we begin the first section of the chapter by presenting some views on general youth culture from the perspectives of a Swedish author and an Australian author. They provide an opportunity for the reader to consider how these views, from two different parts of the world, are similar to or different from perceptions about recreation and leisure suggested in other chapters of the book. The next part of this first section draws on two investigations involving relatively large populations of young people that reflect leisure behavior trends. Finally, we comment briefly on several studies taken from recent issues of *World Leisure Journal.* We include these as examples of the variety of topics and approaches evident at the international level.

In the second section, we use examples from several countries to present ideas about the influences of culture and cultural diffusion on recreation and play. The third and final section focuses on challenges of serving children in a troubled world. In both of these sections, we broaden our consideration to include children as well as adolescents and youth, which gives a more global picture of recreation and leisure among young people across the world.

Youth Culture and Participation Patterns

Youth Culture

Fornäs (1995), writing from a Swedish point of view, suggested youth culture is flexible, mobile, widely divergent, and constantly shifting in different directions. Youth and being young belong to the future and young people are often associated with what is new in culture. On the negative side, youth is a time period often associated with the dangers of the future. Here fear of the unknown is coupled with a culturally pessimistic diagnosis of degeneration in which the morals and norms of youth become sure signs of the sins and transgressions of modernity.

On the positive side, youth have long been associated with future hopes, promises of a new life, and progress. Young people are the adults of the future. Some of them will wield power and be decision makers. This biological, psychodynamic, social, and cultural conditioned flexibility also gives youth a strong, seismographic ability to register deep but hidden social movements and to express these in the clear language of style. But Fornäs also stated that not all young people are avant-garde innovators—many are incredibly conservative and keep a tight grip on habits and routines, possibly just because they have such an enormous need for some sort of security when both they themselves and the world around them are in a state of enigmatic flux.

Another perspective is presented by Richard Eckersley (1997), an Australian author. He paints three portraits of young people: postmodern, modern, and transformational. In the *postmodern* perspective young people are well-informed, educated, and technologically sophisticated. They are self-reliant, street-wise, enterprising, creative, and fast on their feet—keeping options open. In other words they are attuned to the postmodern world: adapted to transience, fragmentation, and pluralism; comfortable with its absence of absolutes and blurred distinctions between real and unreal; at home in cyberspace as in physical space; equipped for its abundant opportunities, exciting choices, and limitless freedoms—and its hazards and risks.

The *modern* portrait suggests most young people successfully negotiate the transitions of adolescence to become well-adjusted adults. Most cherish their families, enjoy life and are confident they'll get what they want out of it—a preferred job, travel, a partner, and eventually a family of their own. Although some youth may be turning to crime, abusing drugs, suffering depression or eating disorders, or even taking their own lives, they are a small minority and often victims of their own personal circumstances.

The *transformational* portrait reveals young people who are deeply cynical, alienated, pessimistic, disillusioned, and disengaged. Many are confused and angry, uncertain of what the future holds and what society expects of them. While they continue to work within "the system," they no longer believe in it or are willing to serve it. From this perspective, the suicidal, the depressed, the drug-addicted, and the delinquent represent the tip of the iceberg of psychological pain and distress that includes a substantial proportion, perhaps even a majority, of young people today.

Citing broad-ranging studies, Eckersley maintained that evidence of all three portraits is detectable: adaptability and resilience; conventional dreams of career, family, and happiness; and anxiety and pessimism about the future. In this chapter, our concern is with all youth in respect to play and recreation. They include those with problems; those who are problem-free but still do not have the knowledge, abilities, or skills to function as adults; and those who are fully prepared but may not be using their knowledge, abilities, and skills. The challenge, however, is with the first category—those with problems.

Participation Patterns and Commonalities

Research from the Australian Bureau of Statistics (ABS; 1993) on time, age, and gender shows that young people between the ages of 15 and 24 years have the largest amount of free time. Males have 383 minutes a day and females 350 minutes a day. Females in the 55 to 64 age group are the only ones to exceed the foregoing amounts of time with 385 minutes a day.

The ABS leisure participation data reveal that young people have generally higher participation rates than other groups in the following 17 out of 21 most popularly ranked leisure occupations:

1. watching TV/video
2. listening to radio
3. reading
4. listening to music
5. visiting friends and relatives
6. relaxing/doing nothing
7. phone calls to friends
8. exercise/keeping fit
9. dining out
10. pleasure shopping

11. swimming in home pool
12. art/craft/hobbies
13. driving for pleasure
14. indoor games
15. swimming
16. walking the dog
17. visiting pubs

Leisure occupations of gardening, entertaining, playing outdoors (around the home), and walking for pleasure were higher for other age groups. Young people between the ages of 14 and 19 years show lower participation rates in activities that require transportation or income, or where they are prohibited by law from participating. However, their counterparts between 20 and 24 years of age show higher participation than any other in the workforce. These activities include visiting friends/relatives, entertaining, driving for pleasure, and visiting a pub. There is little difference in participation rates for reading and art/craft/hobbies across age groups. Most activities in the top 10 are home-based and young people show high rates of participation. These findings have led Veal and Darcy (1996) to conclude that young people exhibit high participation rates in most activities, but as people age and family and work responsibilities increase, leisure participation declines.

Similar findings are noted in New Zealand by Laidler and Cushman (1996), who observed that young men enjoy participating in sport, exercising, running, swimming, boating, and driving for pleasure. They also stated that much of their leisure time is spent less vigorously—"relaxing and doing nothing," listening to music, and going to the pub. Favorite activities for young women are listening to music, watching TV/video, visiting friends, reading, walking, dining out, and formal sport. As in Australia, art and crafts are more popular with young women than young men. The differences in participation rates between genders and between those who have the means prompts the question whether leisure opportunities are freely accessible to all young people or whether leisure participation is shaped by structural factors of society, such as social class and gender. In the book *World Leisure Participation: Free Time in the Global Village*, Cushman, Veal, and Zuzanek (1996) noted similar participation patterns in Canada, France, Germany, Hong Kong, Israel, Poland, Spain, and the United States, although survey methodologies differed in the various countries.

Young people spread their time over many leisure activities that include the use of electronic media. In Australia, watching television was the most time-consuming and accounted for one third of the time available to teenagers between the ages of 13 and 17 years. Cupitt and Stockbridge (1996) found that this age group spent on average 2 hours and 19 minutes a day watching television. Their data also revealed that listening to the radio, cassettes, and CDs and going out were the next most time consuming activities with each taking an average of about 40 minutes a day. The proportion of time spent on electronic entertainment (53%) exceeded that spent on nonelectronic entertainment (33%). The remaining time was spent on homework (13%) using electronic and nonelectronic modes. Electronic entertainment activities included television (34%), listening to music (10%), computer/video games (5%), videos (4%), and cinema (<1%). Nonelectronic activities included going to places (10%), general play (3%), playing sport (8%), hanging around (8%), and reading, drawing or writing (4%).

Boys spent significantly more time watching television and playing sports than girls, while girls spent more time reading. Some five hours of the day were spent engaged in leisure activities and homework, with almost an hour of that period being spent doing two or more activities simultaneously, which included listening to radio, watching television, or listening to prerecorded music. Ownership of radios, cassettes, and CD players was widespread among 13- to 17-year-olds and the proportion of those who had electronic media in their bedrooms increased with age. However, more boys than girls had televisions, personal computers, and TV-linked games and machines in their bedrooms (Cupitt & Stockbridge, 1996).

The high level of ownership of media equipment, radios, cassette or CD players, and televisions was noted in 1997. Increases were observed for video games (48%), portable hand held video game systems (35%), personal computers or laptops (20%), videocassette recorders (16%), and pay television (5%). More boys than girls had televisions (45% as compared with 31%), video game systems (63% as compared with 31%), portable video game systems (45% as compared with 23%), and interactive computer game systems (55% as compared with 16%; AMR: Quantum Harris, cited in Cupitt, Nugent & Ramsay, 1998). However, the patterns of electronic media use have not remained static. In 2004 the proportion of time spent on electronic entertainment and ownership of electronic media equipment increased exponentially.

Childhood and Adolescent Leisure: Recent Research

Research on childhood and adolescent leisure is conducted in most countries around the globe. The studies summarized here suggest some ideas about youth culture in general and about participation patterns. We now want to present a few additional studies to illustrate the diversity of topics and approaches.

Pereira (2004) explored children's playground accessibility in the north of Portugal. The author saw playgrounds as important for supporting development and promoting healthy lifestyles. She surveyed 38 districts in four subregions in the north of Portugal. Almost half the districts had fewer than five playgrounds in their respective areas. In general, these were not located to best serve large numbers of children, and they had minimal equipment. Pereira concluded that children have fewer opportunities to play because of the lack of playgrounds and a reduced choice of activities because of less attractive equipment. She also noted an unequal distribution of playgrounds with more playgrounds located in economically well-to-do areas and fewer in poorer districts.

Sweatman and Heintzman (2004) conducted a study in Canada on the perceived impact of outdoor residential camp experiences on the spirituality of youth. Their research focused on 11 participants in month-long leadership programs at two YMCA residential camps. Through in-depth interviews the authors found that participants felt that camp had a positive effect on their spirituality. The camp setting played a role by providing a natural setting as an escape from urban living. Experiencing structured and unstructured time alone and with others allowed them to reflect on their lives. Consequently, the majority of participants felt that the camp experience equipped them with positive feelings that were linked to their spirituality.

Kloep and Hendry (2003) explored "paradoxes between the ideology of protection provided by adult society as part of youth socialization, and young people's perceptions of control, challenge and boredom" (p. 1). In part, the authors drew on perceptions of Scottish, Swedish, and Norwegian adolescents revealed in an earlier cross-cultural study. Kloep and Hendry observed that adults were destroying important learning opportunities for youth by caring too much, and forever organizing and overstructuring adolescents' leisure. These adult behaviors prevent adolescents from participating in decisions related to their own leisure. The overall outcomes were that adolescents often are bored and not challenged and as a result may engage in undesirable or inappropriate free-time activities. The authors offered some suggestions and broad recommendations for adults to help young people "find a balance between excitement and boredom, challenge and risk, and conformity and self-agency" (p. 1).

Canadian researchers Yuen and Shaw (2003) examined play and its impacts on the resistance and reinforcement of gender ideologies. They com-

pared the impacts of unstructured play, guided by children themselves, and structured play, where adult influence clearly is evident. Unstructured play

typically involves problem solving, negotiation, and improvisation, and provides opportunities for children to develop these skills. In this way, it may contribute to "children's ability to resist dominant views of gender as they develop ideas of their own" (p. 20), because children may feel more empowered as they develop more confidence in their own abilities.

Research conducted in Norway (Vestel, 2004) showed how leisure could improve social relations and reduce cultural differences among youngsters in a multicultural suburb in Rudenga. Through greeting and language practices, sport, love relationships, and musical practices, a cohesive community of young people, who came from widely different backgrounds, was achieved. The young people were from Pakistan, Somalia, Gambia, Morocco, Eritrea, Turkish and Iranian Kurdistan, Chile, and Spain as well as those from Norwegian-born parents. An important exception in this community of differences was the noticeable absence of young women from more conservative Muslim families.

In Israel, Aphek (2001) headed a project initiated by the Israeli Ministry of Education, where 11- and 12-year-olds tutored older adults on Internet and computer technology skills. The project was aimed at minimizing the intergenerational gap and digital divide. The rationale was that children who are familiar and comfortable with the computer and the Internet use their mastery to teach the new language to senior citizens, most of whom were quite unacquainted with electronics and keyboards. The experiment involved writing with the elders a digital mini "e-book" based on of the seniors' personal histories. The project was highly successful and for her efforts Aphek received an Israel Ford Foundation Award.

These six studies represent different topics, age groups, and approaches to research. Collectively, they suggest that the concerns of researchers are similar at the international level to those evident in the United States. What is not apparent in the summaries are details that might suggest cultural influences. We address this matter in the next section.

Cultural Differences and Diffusions

It does not take travel advertisements or television documentaries about distant lands to remind us that people in different areas frequently exhibit different behaviors, values, and ways of life. Differences can be as broad as the distinctions between western and eastern ways of thinking and living. Or they might be as specific as variations from one ethnic community to another in a large urban area or area of a country. Culture often transcends geographic boundaries, as in the case of the world's major religions.

In the following paragraphs, we examine two aspects of culture that are particularly relevant to any consideration of an international perspective: (a) cultural uniqueness as a differentiating influence and (b) the diffusion of culture as a force for encouraging common interests and behaviors. The concepts of culture, cultural influences and cultural diffusion or transmission are complex. While there is a wide and rich body of literature in these areas, we present only a few studies and points of view that illustrate cultural uniqueness and difference.

Culture as a Differentiating Influence

Hyun (1998) noted the centrality of culture and suggested that it is an influence on all play interactions among children and between children and adults. In addition, many individuals are influenced by more than one culture. In some cases, these influences are in conflict. For example, in the behaviors of adolescent immigrants, the values and traditions of the former culture encourage and may demand certain behaviors and discourage or prohibit others. At the same time, there may be strong desires to adapt to the new culture and to "fit in."

Time differences. Perceptions and uses of time are sources of influence related to culture and can have differential impacts on how time is used. A major review of cross-cultural time studies by Larson and Verma (1999) provided data on uses and availability of time, with particular reference to work and free time for children and adolescents. The review included data from populations in most regions of the world. It revealed clear differences between nonindustrial and postindustrial countries. In nonindustrial settings, youth spent large percentages of time in labor activities and unstructured leisure—by middle childhood, children typically spent more than six hours per day, and this figure rose to eight hours per day for adolescents. Not surprisingly, there were clear gender differences. Boys typically had more free time than girls, and girls typically had considerably more responsibilities for household chores.

In postindustrial societies, gender differences were less apparent. Overall, the time both boys and girls spent in labor activities was noticeably lower—typically less than one hour per day. Instead, they spent large amounts of time doing schoolwork and in media use. There were differences between East Asian youth, who typically spent more time with or near family members and doing homework, and North American adolescents, who had more free time to spend with peers in leisure activities. European youth fell in between the two patterns, and had relatively large amounts of free time, but with fairly heavy homework assignments. These differences reflect economic influences, but they also reflect parental attitudes and cultural values about such factors as work, education, the roles of females, and play.

Gender, play, and work. An extensive review of the literature on the play of African children by Marianne Bloch and Susan Adler (1994) pointed to similar differences in gender roles with respect to play and work in nonindustrialized settings. The review also pointed to the influences of such factors as parental attitudes, seasonal labor requirements, and the social organization of villages. Referring particularly to rural situations, the authors observed that play often was related, in the functional sense, to work carried out by adolescents or adults. Play might lead to work or be integrated into work. The authors also observed that definitions of work and play in rural African settings often vary considerably from those prevalent in other countries.

Socialization. Attitudes, beliefs, and traditions also vary in how a society's young are socialized. Children and adolescents must learn how to behave in the particular culture in which they live. In large measure the welfare, if not survival, of the society depends on it. Socialization in this sense involves the transmission the values, beliefs, attitudes, general skills, and understandings necessary to live in the particular society. Societies rely on various institutions to help children become socialized (e.g., family, schools, religion, government).

To the extent that aspects of socialization differ from one society or one culture to the next, different values, beliefs and behaviors will result. Some of these differences will be reflected in play and recreation. Others will be seen in things that influence these behaviors, such as the independence afforded to adolescents, the roles of women, and emphases given to competition or cooperation.

Child-rearing practices. Take, for example, the matter of child rearing. Child rearing is a socialization process. There is considerable evidence that cultures differ in the ways parents typically rear their children, and that these differences may be related to different play behaviors. Kleiber (1999) offered support for this generalization. He commented on findings of an early study by Roberts and Sutton-Smith (1962) and noted, "In cultures where there was a great emphasis on obedience, children were likely to prefer games of strategy; whereas in cultures where child rearing was unpredictable, games of chance were preferred" (p. 70).

Characteristic interactions between parents and children also vary from culture to culture. Using observations from her own studies and the work of various other researchers, Vandermass-Peeler (2002) presented several important findings that will serve as illustrations. Indonesian parents more often interacted with their children when they were infants, but in later years older siblings became the play partners (Farver & Wimbarti, 1995). Chinese mothers tended to emphasize social harmony and respect for rules (Haight, Wang, Fung, Williams & Mintz, 1999). Similarly, Japanese mothers typically gave more attention to social interactions (Tamis-LeMonda, Bornstein, Cyphers, Toda & Ogino, 1992). These tendencies were in contrast to European American mothers who typically promoted independence and self-expression. Roopnarine, Hossain, Gill, and Brophy (1994) suggested that East Indian parents played with their infants to make them happy and for their own enjoyment, as opposed to parents in western industrialized societies who were more focused on cognitive benefits.

A study by Edwards (2000) pointed to some further dimensions of parental influence. She suggested that cultural norms determine whether or not adults will encourage play behavior, depending on whether they see it as good or a waste of time. Norms also prompt adults either to attempt to preserve traditions or to encourage independence and autonomy in children. Schwartzman (1979, p. 213) observed that, in more complex societies young people seem to have more "leeway" in terms of their play and their choices of play companions. The question of how much independence and freedom parents grant probably is more of an issue in the case of older children and adolescents. In some situations where adolescents are expected to work, or in cultures where the transition is directly from childhood to adult status, the role of the parent in granting independence may be less apparent.

In recent years in the United States we have seen considerable variation in what constitutes a family. Racially or culturally mixed marriages, marriages across ethnic and religious lines, same-sex marriages, and single-parent homes are much more apparent than in past years. Each of these arrangements may have impacts on child-rearing practices that differ somewhat from traditional patterns of the past. We have not reviewed data on family characteristics in other countries, but we assume that the changing patterns are not unique to the United States. It appears that these changing models of the family also have implications for children's play (Hyun, 1998).

Tradition. A country's history and traditions are very much a part of its culture. These elements frequently influence play and recreation behavior. Children's games often rooted in the history of the group. Pan (1994) spoke of traditional games in Chinese culture, and noted that these games have been passed from one generation to the next and that they often are associated with special festivals. The author's comments on firecrackers suggest the relationship of play to myths and celebrations.

> ...during the Chinese New Year, children light firecrackers. The lighting of firecrackers is related to a myth that symbolizes the "year" as a "fierce monster." The monster usually appeared during the end of the year, injuring people. It then disappeared

> on New Year's eve. The next morning, the Chinese would say "congratulations" to each other for surviving the previous "year's" disaster. (p. 37)

Pan also identified the use of lanterns in play, kite-flying and other activities that are part of Chinese traditions.

A further observation was that these traditional activities are gradually vanishing, with the result that the Chinese government has undertaken efforts through the schools to encourage their preservation. Martin and Mason (2004) noted a similar concern in some Islamic countries, due to the influences of global media. Traditional play forms probably are vanishing in many cultures. Part of this is due to cultural diffusion, which we discuss in the next section. Part of it also seems a result of changes in the culture itself. One example is the matter of changing roles for women in many countries, which impact play and recreation. As an illustration, time spent playing with children may be diminished if more women enter the work force.

Religion. Religious faith and practice are additional sources of cultural differences. Different faiths permit or prohibit different play activities. Martin and Mason (2004) commented on this fact as reflected in Muslim contexts. They described the concepts of "halal" and "haram"—the former referring to activities that are acceptable and the latter to ones that are unacceptable. The authors observed there is variation in the extent to which these concepts influence individuals, based in part on where people live (e.g., urban or rural areas), differing social and economic conditions, and differing interpretations of the laws. A specific example will serve to illustrate a prohibition and how people may respond differently. In December 2003, the Interior Ministry of Saudi Arabia announced a ban on the importing of dolls (Associated Press, 2004). Strict Islamic law prohibits any toy that is a representation of the human figure and particularly an exposure of the female figure. The article noted that there had been a ban on Barbie dolls for 10 years previously. Apparently many Saudis did not take the ban seriously, thus necessitating a reinforcement of the existing prohibition.

Celebrations are yet another influence of religion. Often they are reasons for play and recreation behavior. Commenting on practices in India, Roopnarine et al. (1994) observed:

> . . . there are few societies in which religious and nonreligious celebrations evoke such playful participation as in India. During religious festivals such as Diwali, the festival of lights, and Holi, children engage in gleeful activities with peers and adults… In other celebrations (e.g., Janmashtami) and at Melas children enact important figures in Hindu religious philosophy through songs, dance, and mime… (p. 23)

In some countries, there are many different religions. In others, there may be only one dominant one. For example, Judaism is the official state religion in Israel. That reason accounts at least to a degree for its widespread influences on the everyday behavior of Israelis, including their free time (Leitner, Leitner & Associates, 2004). For example, buses do not operate on Friday afternoon and Saturday, the Jewish Sabbath, since schools are closed and most workers are off work. Lack of public transportation on these days limits travel by young people to recreation sites.

As another example, Wang and Stringer (2000) discussed the pervasive influence of Taoism in China. They noted that over the past 2500 years it has influenced every part of life, including leisure. Taoism has encouraged "close connections to the natural world... martial arts, traditional arts such as painting and poetry, enjoyment of cultural activities and celebrations, and tourism" (p. 33).

Cultural Diffusion

In the previous section, we illustrated some ways in which cultural differences lead to differences in play and recreation. We now want to look at some influences that promote a diffusion of interests from one culture to another.

Avedon and Sutton-Smith wrote a comprehensive text in 1971, *The Study of Games*. The authors examined games from several perspectives, including anthropology, folklore, sociology, psychology, and history. They noted that historically there have been diverging opinions among theorists about the role of games in cultural diffusion. Those who support the diffusion point of view hold that, "...games have crisscrossed many nations and cultures at various periods of history as a result of commerce, warfare, exploration, education, and a host of other reasons" (p. 62). Let's look at some current sources of diffusion and their consequences.

Marketing. Commerce may be one of the most influential forces for diffusion in today's world. Marketing of toys, video games, music, clothing, and other products influences both buying behavior and play behavior. In a 1995 article, Kline commented on the prevalence of marketing on the global scale aimed at children and adolescents. Referring to observations made by James McNeal (1987), Kline noted the following three reasons for the emphasis on marketing to children:

1. childhood is the basis for lifelong habits, formative brand images, and loyalties.
2. children are an influential market with growing power to influence parental choices.

3. children are a market segment of primary users with increasing disposable income and the power to purchase particular goods. (Kline, 1995, p. 115)

Kline suggested that multinational industries target children everywhere. He observed that "Coke, Levi Strause, McDonalds, and Disney have become the source of endless campaigns designed to 'enfranchise' youth in the globalizing democracy of the marketplace" (p. 110). A statement by a Coca-Cola executive, included in Kline's article, provides a further illustration. "There is global media now like MTV and there is a global teenager. The same kid you see at the Ginza in Tokyo is in Picadilly Square in London, and in Pushkin Square at Notre Dame" (p. 108).

Toys. Children's toys represent a specific dimension of global marketing. Barbie, Teenage Mutant Ninja Turtles, and Batman toys have been sold on a worldwide scale. Kline also commented on the worldwide popularity of the children's television show Sesame Street, and noted, "Bert and Ernie are as visible in Turkey, Israel and Germany as they are in the United States…" (p. 124). This popularity is evident not only in terms of TV watching but also in purchases of Sesame Street toys. Edwards (2000) also spoke about toys and the diffusion of interests. Referring to a paper by Rossie (1998), she noted, "…news of new playthings can spread from one child to the next, creating fashions, fads, and crazes in the local, regional, and now global cultures of childhood" (p. 322).

Television, technology, and film. A large body of literature confirms that children watch a lot of television programming and engage in activities involving other media and technology. Further comments here will add to that observation.

The time study by Larson and Verma (1999) presented data about adolescent TV viewing patterns. Estimates for North America were 1.5 to 2.5 hours per day; the estimates were the same for Europe and East Asia. Michio Takeuchi (1994) commented on television watching by Japanese children. Her data suggested that 75.6% of the children surveyed watch television during their free time, compared with 76.9% for the United States, 79.4% for the United Kingdom, 74% for France, 62.7% for Thailand, and 69.4% for Korea. These variations depend on many different factors, however, it is safe to say that television viewing is a popular activity among both children and teenagers in most countries. TV programming is a main source of diffusion of play and recreation interests among children and adolescents.

Internet use is another force for diffusion of interests. In a study of adolescent leisure in Hong Kong, Atara Sivan (2000) reported that 90% of secondary school students indicated that they used computer technology and that they "surfed" the Internet.

Music, either through televised programs and performances or the sale of CDs is another global commodity. No doubt, music available on the Internet, in either legitimate or "pirated" forms, constitutes a fairly large part of this diffusion. Teenagers who have access to computers probably constitute a sizeable part of this kind of use.

Video games represent still another vehicle for diffusion. These appear to be popular forms of play in many different countries, and content typically crosses cultural lines. Takeuchi (1994) noted the prevalence of video game play among Japanese children. She stated that 20% of all households owned a video game set. Results of a 1989 nationwide study showed that 34% of elementary school boys played video games—an increase of five times the usage reported in 1984. This was the second highest reported activity in the survey. There would be no reason to believe that this use has declined since 1989.

The popularity of U.S. movies, videotapes, and DVDs released in other countries and the prevalence of foreign films in the United States demonstrate yet another avenue for diffusion of interests. Distribution of films produced in the United States is a global enterprise. Major productions often are more profitable in overseas markets than in the United States (Smith, 2004). Many children's films, such as those produced by Disney, enjoy similar or greater popularity in other countries.

The influences of media and technology, of course, are proportionate to their availability. Many of the world's children and adolescents have very limited or no access to such resources as television, the Internet, movies, and commercially produced toys. On a broader level, large numbers face conditions daily that restrict their access to play and recreation opportunities in general.

Endangered Children and Adolescents: Challenges of Serving Young People in a Troubled World

Any focus on play and recreation at the international level would be incomplete without attention to children and youth who live under difficult circumstances. In this section we will present some information about these young people, and we will suggest some considerations in attempts to serve them.

Martin Monestier, a distinguished French author and journalist, tells us that 300,000,000 children and adolescents live daily lives of hell. In his book titled, *Los Niños Esclavos: El Infierno Diario de Trescientos Millones Niños* (in the 1999 Spanish translation), Monestier describes the impacts of war, poverty, exploitation, and other devastating conditions on young people. He writes that many children are enslaved—enslaved because the conditions they suffer are beyond their control and their abilities to escape. Lobo and Olson (2000) also commented on young people in similar circumstances and suggested:

> There is a certain irony in the image of children at pleasure as presented in contemporary leisure management and planning textbooks, and the reality of the millions of children from throughout the world for whom leisure has no practical meaning. (p. 5)

Awareness, Progress, and Unmet Goals

We know about the circumstances of these children, at least in part. We read about them in daily newspapers and see them on television. Also, much of our awareness comes from the educational and advocacy efforts of UNICEF, Save the Children, and other nongovernmental organizations. In its 2001 Annual Report, UNICEF noted positive developments in many areas. For example, overall infant mortality rates are down. Higher percentages of the world's children are being vaccinated against preventable diseases. The number of children, and particularly the number of girls and young women, who are enrolled in programs of formal education are increasing.

There are other positive indications. Yet, there is considerable evidence that much remains to be done. In 2001, UN Secretary General Kofi Annan wrote a summary report on the status of the world's children. In it he noted areas of progress but he also spoke of "unfulfilled commitments" and observed that many of the goals set by a World Summit for Children in 1990 have not been achieved. In May 2002, the UN General Assembly convened a Special Session on Children. Presentations and discussions at the Special Session confirmed what seems to be an appropriate overall assessment: In many ways, the status of children and youth has improved globally. At the same time, far too many young people continue to live in the hell described by Monestier.

Like their counterparts in less stressful situations, the children we are concerned about here exhibit a wide variety of characteristics. They are of different ages and genders. Their family situations differ. They experience different levels of health and wellness. Their cultural traditions differ. In short, they present the same diversities represented in the overall population of children and adolescents. But unlike the general population, they experience conditions that make not only leisure but also life itself difficult. We present some illustrations of some of the problems young people face, but the statistics we include do not paint the whole picture. Also, the specific numbers may have changed somewhat since the reporting dates; nonetheless they suggest the magnitude of the conditions.

War and Dislocation

The Global Movement for Children (2004), referring to a political crisis in Haiti that involved armed rebels, described the effects of war on children and families:

> …1.2 million children have already been identified as being especially vulnerable to the violence. It is becoming more difficult for children to attend school, receive medical attention, find food and shelter. Children, especially girls, living or working in the streets of urban centers are especially at risk. School attendance has dropped dramatically in most areas due to unsafe roads, lack of security in schools, and disruption of public transportation.

Other authors have documented similar effects. In her book on the *Impact of War on Children* (2001), Machel observed that in recent years wars and human rights violations have driven an estimated 20 million children from their homes and communities (p. 26). The Office of the United Nations High Commissioner for Refugees noted that in 1998 UNHCR was caring for almost 22.4 million people, most of whom were women and children (UNHCR, n.d.).

Land Mines

One specific effect of war that tragically impacts children is the residual presence of land mines. Land mines and unexploded ordinance pose serious problems in many different countries. As an example, in 1999 these devices caused 5 to 10 casualties a day in Afghanistan, only one of the approximately 80 countries where they exist in the aftermath of wars (Machel 2001, p. 105). Children are most vulnerable. They may not recognize the land mines and, because they are curious might handle them. Also, they often play in areas where there are mines. Machel provides an anecdote that illustrates this last fact.

> On 23 October 1999, Yusup Magomedov begged his mother to let him go outside to play soccer in the Chechen village of Novi Sharoi following days of confinement because of the war. A few minutes after Yusup left his house; an unexploded Russian cluster bomblet detonated and shredded his legs. Seven children died in the explosion, and at least 15 were injured. (p. 108)

The situation has improved somewhat. In the mid-1990s, a ground swell of concern led to the Convention on the Prohibition of Use, Stockpiling, Production and Transfer of Anti-Personnel Mines, and on Their Destruction. Opened for signing in 1997, the Convention became international law in 1999. At that time, 40 countries had ratified it (Machel 2001, p. 109).

HIV/AIDS

Wars and genocide have left hundreds of thousands of children without parents. The widespread presence of the AIDS virus also has decimated families. In 2000, *Newsweek* reported that an estimated 10.4 million children under 15 would be orphaned in Africa by the end of that year, having lost their mothers or both parents to AIDS (Bartholet, 2000). Fortunately, "tracing" efforts by such organizations as the International Federation of the Red Cross and Red Crescent Societies, UNICEF and other nongovernmental organizations (NGOs) have enabled some children to be reunited with remaining family members (Machel, 2001, pp. 29–30).

Of course, AIDS kills children and adolescents too. An HIV/AIDS newsletter produced by teenagers in Zambia pointed out that 50% of the new infections affect people ages 15 to 25. A comment by one of the authors summarizes the problem. "I mean if we are the future and we're dying, there is no future" (quoted in Machel, p. 41).

Abuse and Neglect

Not all of the violence young people experience comes from war. Children and youth often are victims of abuse in their own homes, or in the homes of caregivers, and victims of crime in their own communities. This appears to be true in all countries.

Data from the United States provide an illustration. Statistics from the U.S. Department of Health and Human Services indicate that an estimated 826,000 children were victims of abuse and neglect in 1999 (2001, p. 72). Children and adolescents are more likely to become victims of sexual assaults than older persons. Statistics from the year 2000 suggest that in 67% of all reported incidents the victims were less than 18 years of age. One out of seven were younger than six, and over one third were under 12 (2001, p. 72). While rates in general are declining, the problem still is very evident.

Sexual Exploitation

Child pornography and prostitution are related dimensions. In both cases, adults use children and adolescents for personal and economic gain. There have been several international efforts to address these problems, including a 1996 World Congress against Commercial Sexual Exploitation of Children. However, the problems continue to exist.

Monestier (1999) estimated that 30 million have been affected, but he observed that the actual figure might be at least double (p. 311). The vast majority are girls. A report reflecting on progress since the Fourth World Conference on Women, held in Beijing, suggested that while there is considerably more awareness,

> …many NGOs observed that the problem of trafficking is actually worsening. A combination of globalization and free market economies results in the easing of cross-border restrictions, spreading materialism, and the treatment of people, especially female children as goods or property. These factors create an atmosphere conducive to the sale, abduction and enticement of millions of girls as virtual slaves in the sex trade. (NGO Working Group on Girls, 2000, p. 15)

Child Labor

In 1997, the International Labour Office estimated that there were 250 million children and adolescents between the ages of 5 and 14 in the world labor force. Many of these young people "…work in the most abhorrent conditions which rob them of their childhood, their health, and sometimes even their lives" (ILO, 2002, p. 5). The extent of the overall problem might be much greater. Often child labor is hidden "…in underground sweat shops, brothels and other establishments or in domestic service while much more of it is in remote farms, mines and workshops." (p. 24).

The child labor problem is not confined to developing countries. It is evident in many industrialized areas as well. Moreover, it is a complex problem. Many young people work under difficult circumstances in their own families. Also, their labor outside the home often is an economic necessity. In addition, the laws of different countries vary with respect to what is legal and what is not in terms of child labor.

Youth Combatants

Yet another dimension of exploitation is the use of children in armed conflict. Machel (2001) noted that over 300,000 young people were in use as combatants in the wars that plague the world (p. 2). *Newsweek* featured an article about this problem in May 2002, the same month the UN General Assembly convened a Special Session on Children. The article observed that governmental military forces, paramilitary units, and armed opposition groups have used soldiers, often under the age of 15, in over half of the recent conflicts in more than 30 countries (Masland, 2002, p. 28). Masland wrote of interviews he conducted with four boys, ages 14 to 16, who had been soldiers in Sierra Leone. At the time, the four were attending St. Francis Primary School. Masland said that they did not stand out particularly, except for being bigger than the other fourth and fifth graders. However, he noted that on closer observation, they were different. There was some physical evidence of their experiences, including welts from incisions made by their commanders, which identified them as members of the Revolutionary United Front. What they did not show were the psychological scars brought about by being forced to participate in the brutalities of a civil war (p. 25). Teachers reported that the teenagers were doing well in school. The boys themselves spoke of their hopes for the future, including the desire to continue with their schooling.

Multiple Effects

Many problems have multiple effects. As one example, war and dislocation typically disrupt schooling. We have not spoken of poverty and hunger, but these are also serious and widespread (Lobo & Olson, 2000) and often lead to the explotation of children. In addition, natural disasters have multiple impacts. The December 26, 2004, earthquake off the west coast of Sumatra, and the region-wide tidal wave that followed it, provide a dramatic illustration. These events caused extensive damage and loss of life across much of southern Asia. A high percentage of the casualties were children and youth. In addition, the disaster left large numbers of the survivors without parents (Kher, 2005). The disruptions and confusion that typically accompany natural disasters such as this one often lead to other negative impacts beyond the immediate destruction. One problem is that people involved in human trafficking frequently use these types of situations to exploit children. Relief workers have been concerned about this potential in the aftermath of the south Asia tsunami.

Play and Recreation in Difficult Situations

Obviously, the traumatic conditions young people encounter influence their opportunities for play and recreation. In most cases, the opportunities are restricted and they may at times be nonexistent. One might wonder if children and youth who experience such conditions can even be interested in play and recreation. The answer seems to be, yes. Two examples illustrate. One is from an Associated Press news release carried in the *Honolulu Advertiser* (April 7, 1999; p. A14). The story was about the refugee movement out of Kosovo in 1999. It described the experiences of an Albanian boy named Dren, who had suffered a gunshot wound to his arm. At the field hospital where medical personnel were treating him, he asked his grandfather, "Wherever we go, do you think they will play soccer there as well?" The second is a picture that appeared in *Time* magazine's special issue on the best photos of 2002. Under the caption, "An unlikely playground," the photo shows an Afghan child swinging on a tree branch against the background of a desolate, war-torn Kabul graveyard (Boulat, 2002). Both examples point to the universal nature of play, and they illustrate children's quest for normalcy and security through play.

The Right to Play

Several international protocols and agreements deal with the rights of young people in general. Perhaps the most important is the Convention on the Rights of the Child, adopted by the United Nations General Assembly on November 20, 1989. UN Secretary-General Kofi Annan stated that it is now "the world's most widely embraced human rights instrument" (Annan, 2001) However, while it has encouraged much progress for children, it has not eliminated the problems young people face. John Brandon, writing for *The Christian Science Monitor* 10 years after the adoption of the Convention, noted this failure: "Although almost every nation in the world is signatory to this convention, its enforcement has been hollow and weak and has offered little remedy for the injustices children throughout the world are forced to endure" (Brandon, 1999, p. 9).

As Brandon noted, most of the countries in the world have ratified the Convention. Regrettably, the United States is not one of those countries. The reasons center around U.S. objections to provisions that relate to capital punishment and reproductive rights, including abortion and various dimensions of sex education (Sengupta, 2002).

The 1989 Convention includes two provisions that directly address the matters of play, recreation and leisure. These are contained in Article 31, and provide that Parties to the Convention:

1. ...shall recognize the right of the child to rest and leisure, to engage in play and recreation activities appropriate to the age of the child and to participate freely in cultural life and the arts.
2. ...shall respect and promote the right of the child to participate fully in cultural and artistic life and shall encourage the provision of appropriate and equal opportunities for cultural, artistic, recreational and leisure activity.

Two NGOs concerned directly with these provisions are the International Association for the Child's Right to Play (IPA; http://www.ipaworld.org) and World Leisure (http://www.worldleisure.org). But, in spite of Article 31 and the work of IPA, World Leisure, and other NGOs, it is apparent that not all children and adolescents enjoy the right to play.

The Importance of Play and Recreation

Considerable research in child development and the social sciences documents the benefits of play and leisure for all young people, and the importance of play and leisure in terms of development. These benefits are applicable for children and adolescents in difficult situations, no less than for any other young person. In fact, play and recreation may be more important in these cases.

As suggested earlier, participation in play and recreation may help to restore feelings of normalcy when children and adolescents are experiencing disruptions in their regular lives. Participation may provide a sense of security. It might help children and teens cope with the conditions they encounter. To that extent, it might provide therapeutic benefits. Niepoth, Hernandez, and Rysberg (2000) reviewed studies of play therapy in situations involving children who were homeless, who had experienced violence, who were abused or sexually traumatized, or who lived in situations where the parents were substance abusers. In general this research suggests the benefits from play. An additional study focused on Jewish children confined in concentration camps during World War II. Observations here suggested that play has therapeutic potential in that it allows children who have experienced trauma to relive situations and to manipulate the outcomes. This can enable them to sense control and can lead to greater feelings of safety (Eisen, 1988; Glazer, 1999).

Play also may contribute to reduction of intergroup conflict. Leitner and Scher (2000) investigated the effects of an intergenerational recreation program involving Israeli Arabs and Jews and noted positive changes in attitude after participation. Another international organization, Play for Peace (http://www.playforpeace.org) is particularly concerned with using play to improve intergroup relationships and has undertaken projects in various parts of the world.

Providing Play and Recreation Opportunities in Difficult Situations

Play is a natural activity. Typically, it occurs spontaneously. However, the benefits often depend on adult guidance and the availability of appropriate play or recreation spaces and resources. Families experiencing trauma may not be in a position to provide for children's needs beyond very basic survival and in some cases not even that. When resources and conditions permit, local organizations—municipal governments, village councils, schools, churches, youth agencies, and others—typically provide recreation opportunities. However, the abilities of local agencies to deliver services may be diminished dramatically and often eliminated by war and other catastrophic or disruptive events.

A variety of international organizations can and do play roles in these situations. NGOs like UNICEF, Save the Children, and UNHCR work for the overall well-being of children and youth. In some cases their efforts include attention to play and recreation. As one example, in 1999 Sweden's Save the Children organization operated a youth center at the UNHCR Bonga Camp for Sudanese and Uduk refugees in Ethiopia. The camp had approximately 13,000 refugees, many of whom were children and teenagers (Zook, 1999). As another example, in 2000 UNICEF worked with government entities and NGOs in the city of Fés, Morocco to set up six Child Protection Centres. In addition to health and educational programs, these Centres offered recreation activities for children and youth (UNICEF, 2001, p.10). More typically, the roles of international organizations tend to be ones of advocacy, training, providing funding and other resources, and promoting interagency cooperation.

In 2000 Lobo and Olson presented an overview of goals and assumptions for consideration by any agency attempting to provide leisure services for young people at risk. These seem relevant to the situations we have been describing in this chapter. In addition, much of the programming material presented later in the book no doubt is applicable. However, there are three further considerations that are especially important when working with children and adolescents living in difficult conditions.

The Importance of Contexts

The customs, traditions, and prevailing understandings of and attitudes toward play and recreation will influence what services an organization provides and how it goes about providing them. Information about overall social and demographic conditions, the presence and viability of other institutions and the availability of resources also is needed.

Ranjana Ariaratnam Zook, who worked as a volunteer at the UNHCR refugee camp in Ethiopia mentioned earlier, pointed out one reason for sensitivity to contexts:

> In tense situations (such as populations fleeing from fighting and aggression), it will be important for organizations providing any kind of services...to try to figure out how the different groups in power (e.g., government, rebels, different ethnic groups) will react to their efforts. Depending on how it is done, if a group of people not in favor with the ruling authority in the region is providing assistance, that could endanger the providing organization's program, or the lives of its staff members or the beneficiary population (personal communication, November 22, 1999).

Contexts also underscore the need for clear goals when working in difficult situations. Robert Rossman, who has written widely in the programming field, suggested several questions useful in this regard (personal communication, December 9, 1999):

- Are the programs being delivered as a therapy for a specific problem?
- Are they to be a diversion from the hostile environment created by the crisis?
- Are they being delivered to build resiliency to aid victims in coping with this and future crises?
- Are they being delivered to aid in a transition from an abnormal to a normal situation?
- Are they intended to create cooperation and understanding between opposing groups?

Cultural Considerations

One major contextual consideration is culture. We discussed this matter earlier in the chapter. Some brief examples serve as illustrations. Organizational staff members might modify the ways they work with children and youth based on such differing factors as religious beliefs, ethnic values and traditions, patterns of child rearing, different societal expectations for children, the practice of rites of passage from adolescence to adulthood, and others. Specific questions might arise related to gender roles. In some cultures, boys have more freedom than girls. Some discourage or prohibit boys and girls playing together. Also, it may be inappropriate for male staff members to work with female participants. Cultures may also vary in emphases placed on cooperation or competition. There may be differences in the willingness of children to display individual initiative as opposed to being part of the group.

Developmental Considerations

Other contextual matters are the psychological and developmental states of children and adolescents. Expectations that we might have from our experiences working with young people in general may not be applicable in the kinds of situations discussed in this chapter. For example, age may not be a good predictor of how a child will respond. Poor health, inadequate nutrition, and other factors might have arrested development. Surprising as it may seem, some children may not know how to play (Hyun, 1998; Niepoth, Hernandez & Rysberg, 2002).With the breakup of families and destruction of communities and villages, there may be no role models for children to imitate. If war and dislocation have destroyed normal support systems, the child might have a difficult time displaying such emotions as empathy and sympathy, which are often used in play. More incidents of acting out and violent or disruptive behavior may occur.

The Challenges

Provision of leisure services for the children and adolescents we have discussed poses a difficult challenge. The task is enormous in terms of the number of youth. The situations they are living in often make service delivery difficult, and most agencies have limited resources. But, adults in general and the field of leisure services in particular must face this challenge. We know that when young people cannot engage in play and recreation, they fail to reach their full potentials. When this happens, we lose precious resources that we cannot afford to lose. The challenges the world faces today and the ones it will face in the future depend on a citizenry whose life experiences enable them to respond effectively and humanely.

The challenge for each of us is to find ways to become involved in finding solutions. Opportunities to do so may come as a result of professional roles or in a volunteer capacity, or as one exercises voting rights, makes choices as a consumer, or engages in advocacy efforts of various kinds.

Giving young people opportunities for play and recreation cannot assure that 14-year-olds will no longer fight in civil wars, or that adults will not sell children or otherwise exploit them for economic or sexual purposes. It will not eliminate wars or land mines or sweat shops or HIV/AIDS or poverty or hunger. But, it can make the lives of children and adolescents better, and to the extent that it does, it helps them to grow and develop in appropriate ways. When that happens, we all benefit.

References

Annan, K. A. (2001). *We the children: Meeting the promises of the World Summit for Children*. New York: UNICEF.

Aphek, E. (2001). Children tutoring seniors at Internet skills: An experiment conducted at one Israeli elementary school. *Leisure Issues, 4*(2), 1–8.

Associated Press. (2004, February 15). Saudi shoppers try to comprehend ban on dolls, stuffed animals. *Chico Enterprise Record*, p. 9C.

Australian Bureau of Statistics (1993). *Australia in profile: 1991 census* (Cat. No. 2821.0). Canberra, Australian Capital Territory: Author.

Avedon, E. and Sutton-Smith, B. (1971). *The study of games*. New York, NY: John Wiley & Sons

Bartholet, J. (2000, January 17). The plague years. *Newsweek, CXXXV*(3), pp. 32–37.

Bloch, M., and Adler, S. (1994) African children's play and the emergence of the sexual division of labor. In J. L. Roopnarine, J. E. Johnson, and F. H. Hooper (Eds.), *Children's play in diverse cultures*. New York, NY: State University of New York Press.

Boulat, A. (2002, Winter). An unlikely playground [photograph]. *Time (Special Issue: Best Photos of the Year)*.

Brandon, J. (1999, November 22). The exploited child. *The Christian Science Monitor*, p. 9.

Cupitt, M., Nugent, S., and Ramsay, G. (1998). The place of electronic media in the lives of young Australians. *World Leisure & Recreation, 40*(1), 17–21.

Cupitt, M. and Stockbridge, S. (1996). *Families and electronic equipment* (Monograph 6). Sydney, Australia: Australian Broadcasting Authority.

Cushman, G., Veal, A. J., and Zuzanek, J. (Eds.). (1996). *World leisure participation: Free time in the global village*. Wallingford: CAB International.

Eckersley, R. (1997). Portraits of youth: Understanding young people's relationship with the future. *Futures, 29*(3), 243–249.

Edwards, C. P. (2000). Children's play in cross-cultural perspective: a new look at the Six Cultures study. *Cross-Cultural Research, 34*(4), 318–338.

Eisen, G. (1988). *Children and play in the Holocaust: Games among the shadows*. Amherst, MA: University of Massachusetts Press.

Farver, J. and Wimbarti, S. (1995). Indonesian children's play with their mothers and older siblings. *Child Development, 66*, 1493–1503.

Fornäs, J. (1995). Youth, culture and modernity. In J. Fornäs, and B. Göran (Eds.), *Youth culture in late modernity*. London, England: Sage.

Glazer, H. (1999). Children and play in the Holocaust: Friedl Dicker-Brandeis—Heroic child therapist. *Journal of Humanistic Counseling, Education and Development, 37*(4), 194–199.

Global Movement for Children. (2004, March). *Newsletter* item #6, electronic version, info@gmfc.org

Haight, W. L., Wang, X., Fung, H., Williams, H., and Mintz, H. (1999). Universal, developmental, and variable aspects of young children's play: A cross-cultural comparison of pretending at home. *Child Development, 70*(6), 1477–1488.

Hyun, E. (1998). *Making sense of developmentally and culturally appropriate practice (DCAP).* New York, NY: Peter Lang.

International Labour Office. (2002). *Eliminating the worst forms of child labour: A practical guide to ILO Convention No. 182.* Geneva: International Labour Office and the Inter-Parliamentary Union.

Kher, U. (2005, January 17). Orphaned by the ocean. *Time*, 30–31.

Kleiber, D. (1999). *Leisure experience and human development: A dialectical interpretation*, New York, NY: Basic Books

Kline, S. (1995). The play of the market: On the internationalization of children's culture. *Theory, Culture & Society, 12*(2), 103–129.

Kloep, M. and Hendry, L. B. (2003). Adult control and adolescent challenge? Dilemmas and paradoxes in young people's leisure. *World Leisure*, *45*(3), 24–34.

Laidler, A. and Cushman, G. (1996). New Zealand. In G. Cushman, A. J. Veal, and J. Zuzanek (Eds.), *World leisure participation: Free time in the global village* (pp. 165–181). Wallingford, England: CAB International.

Larson, R. and Verma, S. (1999). How children and adolescents spend time across the world: Work, play, and developmental opportunities. *Psychological Bulletin*, *125*(6), 701–736.

Leitner, M. J., Leitner, S. F., and associates. (2004). *Leisure enhancement* (3rd ed.). New York, NY: Hayworth Press.

Leitner, M. and Scher, G. (2000). A follow up study to peacemaking through recreation: The positive effects of intergenerational activities on the attitudes of Israeli Arabs and Jews. *World Leisure & Recreation, 42*(1), 33–37.

Lobo, F. and Olson, E. (2000). Leisure services and children at risk: Against all odds. *Journal of Park and Recreation Administration, 18*(1), 5–18.

Martin, H. M. and Mason, S. (2004). Leisure in an Islamic context. *World Leisure Journal, 46*(1), 4–13.

Machel, G. (2001). *The impact of war on children*. London, England: Hurst and Company.

Masland, T. (2002, May 13). Voices of the children: "We beat and killed people…" *Newsweek, CXXXIX*(19), pp. 24–29.

McNeal, J. U. (1987). *Children as consumers: Insights and implications.* Lexington, MA: Lexington Books.

Monestier, M. (1999). *Los niños esclavos: El infierno diario de trescientos milliones niños.* (J. Madariaga, Trans.). Madrid, Spain: Alianza Editorial.

NGO Working Group on Girls. (2000). *Girls 2000: NGOs report on progress since Beijing.* New York, NY: NGO Committee on UNICEF.

Niepoth, E. W., Hernandez, H., and Rysberg, J. (2000, July). *Leisure services for children and youth in restrictive situations.* Paper presented at World Leisure Congress in Bilbao, Spain.

Pan, H. L. (1994). Children's play in Taiwan. In L. Jaipaul, J. E. Roopnarine, and F. H. Hooper (Eds.), *Children's play in diverse cultures.* New York, NY: State University of New York Press.

Pereira, B. (2004). Children's playground accessibility in the north of Portugal. *World Leisure, 46*(1), 38–45.

Roberts, J. M. and Sutton-Smith, B. (1962). Child training and game involvement. *Ethnology, 1*, 166–185.

Roopnarine, J. L., Hossain, Z, Gill, P., and Brophy, H. (1994). Play in the East Indian context. In J. L. Roopnarine, J. E. Johnson, and F. H. Hooper (Eds.), *Children's play in diverse cultures.* New York, NY: State University of New York Press.

Rossie, J. P. (1998, January). *Toys in changing North African and Saharan societies.* Paper presented at the Culture of Toys Conference, Emory University, Atlanta, GA.

Schwartzman, H. (1979). The sociocultural context of play. In B. Sutton-Smith (Ed.), *Play and learning.* New York, NY: Gardner Press.

Sengupta, S. (2002, May 11). Goals set by UN conference on children skirt abortion. *New York Times*, p. A6.

Sivan, A. (2000). Global influences and local uniqueness: The case of adolescent leisure in Hong Kong. *World Leisure, 42*(4), 24–32.

Smith, S. (2004, March 22). Westerns: Riding into the sunset. *Newsweek*, p. 13.

Sweatman, M. M. and Heintzman, P. (2004). The perceived impact of outdoor residential camp experience on the spiritual of youth. *World Leisure, 46*(1), 23–31.

Takeuchi, M. (1994), Children's play in Japan. In J. L. Roopnarine, J. E. Johnson, and F. H. Hooper (Eds.), *Children's play in diverse cultures.* New York, NY: State University of New York Press.

Tamis-LeMonda, C. S., Bornstein, M. H., Cyphers, L., Toda, S., and Ogino, M. (1992). Language and play at one year: A comparison of toddlers and mothers in the United States and Japan. *International Journal of Behavioral Development, 15*, 19–42.

UNICEF (United Nations International Childrens [Emergency] Fund. (2001). *Annual report.* New York, NY: UNICEF Division of Communications.

United Nations High Commissioner for Refugees. (n.d.). *Human rights, refugees and UNHCR: A teachers' guide.* New York, NY: Author.

U.S. Department of Health and Human Services. (2001). *America's children: Our challenge, our future.* Washington, DC: Author.

Vandermass-Peler, M. (2002). Cultural variations in parental support of children's play. In W. J. Lonner, D. L. Dinnnel, S. A. Hayes, and D. N. Sattler (Eds.), *On-line readings in psychology and culture*. Bellingham, WA: Center for Cross-Cultural Research, Western Washington University.

Veal, A. J. and Darcy, S. (1996). Australia. In G. Cushman, A. J. Veal and J. Zuzanek (Eds.), *World leisure participation: Free time in the global village* (pp. 17–34). Wallingford: CAB International.

Vestel, V. (2004). A community of differences: Social relations, popular culture and leisure in a multicultural suburb in "Rudenga" East Side Oslo. *World Leisure, 46*(1), 46–55.

Wang, J. and Stringer, L. A. (2000). The impact of Taoism on Chinese leisure. *World Leisure*, *42*(3), 33–41.

Yuen, F. C. and Shaw, S. M. (2003). Play: The reproduction and resistance of dominant gender ideologies. *World Leisure, 45*(2), 12–21.

Zook, R. A. (1999). *Bonga Refugee Camp, Ethiopia*. Unpublished information sheet.

Chapter 4

Why and How Youth Services Were Developed

Peter A. Witt

Many of us were members of some kind of youth serving organization when we were growing up. Maybe you belonged to the Boys & Girls Clubs of America, Boy Scouts, Girl Scouts, YMCA, YWCA, or 4-H, or attended programs at your local parks and recreation department community center. Each of these organizations has a distinguished history, a history that shares common roots in societal forces and events that took place in the second half of the 1800s and the first several decades of the 1900s. In this chapter we discuss these forces and events in general, and then in Chapter 5 we discuss the specific history of some of the major youth servicing organizations and describe some of the programs they offer currently.

To begin, let's discuss some of the forces and events that led people to conclude that youth serving organizations should be created. From the mid-1800s through the early 1900s, a period of rapid transformation occurred in which an agrarian and rural society was replaced by one characterized by urbanization and industrialization. To better understand the impact of these changes on children and youth, we discuss

- the creation of a distinct period between childhood and adult status that was labeled "adolescence"
- the subsequent development of youth serving organizations to serve the developmental needs of this newly created group of young people

Understanding the origin of these organizations in historical context will help readers to understand the origin of many of the current societal attitudes about young people and the way supports, opportunities, services, and programs have been developed to meet their needs.

Societal Forces Leading to a Different Way of Viewing Young People

From the mid-1800s through the early 1900s, the United States underwent dramatic structural and economic changes, including rapid industrialization, massive immigration, migration of rural populations to urban settings, and increased urbanization. These factors greatly impacted the way youth were viewed and treated by society and laid the groundwork for the development of a variety of organizational responses to youth needs.

Industrialization

The Industrial Revolution began in England in the late 1700s and quickly spread to other parts of the world, including the United States. As it spread, it fundamentally changed the way goods were produced. Before the Industrial Revolution, goods were made laboriously with hand tools, but after the revolution, factories increasingly turned out identical products crafted by machines. These factories thrived on increased division of labor and specialization of job responsibilities. Workers became more productive; and because more items were manufactured, prices dropped, making exclusive and hard to make items available to the masses and not just the rich and elite. As discussed later, young people were central to supplying the labor that made the industrial revolution possible; however, their involvement in the production process eventually drew public attention and calls for reforms.

Immigration and Migration

In the 1800s, and particularly after the Civil War, a flood of immigrants from Europe began to arrive in the United States and settle mainly in the major cities along the eastern seaboard near their point of entry. Many people originally immigrated because of crop failures (e.g., the potato famine in Ireland), poor economic conditions, and/or religious prejudice in their home countries. Most immigrants arrived willing to work, but without the education or skills to enable them to pursue more than working-class jobs.

Between 1820 and 1880, almost 3.5 million Irish and 3.0 million Germans entered the United States. At the same time, many families, but more particularly many young people, from rural settings in the United States, migrated to the cities. Due to increases in industrialization, young people were more able to find work in the cities than they were in rural and smaller communities. In fact, the migration of rural residents was so extensive that between 1880 and

1890 almost 40% of the townships in the United States lost population to the urban centers (Library of Congress, n.d.).

Urbanization

As a result of immigration and migration, urban centers grew rapidly in population. For example, New York's population grew from 33,131 in 1790 to 312,710 in 1840, 1,206,299 in 1880, and 3,437,202 in 1900. Chicago grew from 503,185 in 1880 to 1,698,575 in 1900 and Boston grew from 362,839 in 1880 to 589,141 in 1900 (Gibson, 1998).

Increases in the population of the major cities had a number of significant impacts on urban residents, particularly members of the lower class. For one thing, cities lacked the infrastructure to deal with the rapid population increases. Housing, roads and transportation systems, and sewage treatment were inadequate. Noise and pollution increased. Working conditions were often dangerous. Due to the need for labor, increasing numbers of women and young children were employed, often working long hours at monotonous and repetitive jobs. Cities also lacked public spaces for lower-class children, adults, and families to recreate during their nonwork hours.

> The children played on the streets because there was nowhere else for them. Urban space was a commodity, an item bought and sold like any other. As the population of the cities expanded, land became more and more valuable...undeveloped land was wasteland. With space at a premium, even the backyards were too valuable to be given over to children...and were used for raising animals, vegetable gardens and storage. Indoor space was also not available for play, with what there was given over to sleeping and eating. (Nasaw, 1985, pp. 17–18)

Commercial recreation locations (e.g., dance halls, saloons, small theaters, other forms of "pleasure seeking") opened to serve the needs of workers who sought things to do during their nonwork time; however, many of these establishments encouraged prostitution and drunkenness. Unfortunately, children had ready access to these locations and their associated vices.

Middle-class children were also impacted by urban and small town life. As middle class incomes rose, parents were able to "forego the labor or earnings of their teenagers and invest instead in preparing them for success as adults" (Macleod, 1983, p. 9). Thus, schooling was prolonged:

> Although some youth involved themselves beyond school in chores or part-time work, there was still plenty of free time, creating the need for outlets to occupy time and safeguard

> parents' investment [in their children] by strengthening their sons' morality and ambition…" (Macleod, 1983, p. 9)

The main goal of parents was to help their children better themselves and lead lives that preserved middle-class values and standing. City life and the activities of lower-class youth were seen as a threat to achieving these goals.

Jane Addams, one of the foremost figures in the development of Hull House, a major settlement house in Chicago that offered community-based services for both children and adults, argued that many of the problems associated with young people were not the result of their faults or internal deficits, but were due instead to the lack of constructive outlets or opportunities. Through her work at Hull house, Addams saw firsthand the need for positive contact between youth and adults. Speaking up for the needs of immigrant and what we would now call inner-city children, Addams was concerned about the impacts of city life on young people and persons from the working class.

> The social organism has broken down through large districts of our great cities. Many of the people living there are very poor, the majority of them without leisure or energy for anything but the gain of subsistence. They move often from one wretched lodging to another. They live for the moment side by side, many of them without knowledge of each other, without fellowship, without local tradition or public spirit, without social organization of any kind. Practically nothing is done to remedy this. The people who might do it, who have the social tact and training, the large houses, and the traditions and custom of hospitality, live in other parts of the city. The clubhouses, libraries, galleries, and semi-public conveniences for social life are blocks away. We find working men organized into armies of producers because men of executive ability and business sagacity have found it to their interest thus to organize them. But these working men are not organized socially; although living in crowded tenement houses, they are living without corresponding social contact. The chaos is as great as it would be were they working in huge factories without foreman or superintendent. Their ideas and resources are cramped. The desire for higher social pleasure is extinct. They have no share in the traditions and social energy that make for progress. Too often their only place of meeting is a saloon, their only host a bartender; a local demagogue forms their public opinion. Men of ability and refinement, of social power and university cultivation, stay away from them. Personally, I believe the men who

> lose most are those who thus stay away. But the paradox is here: When cultivated people do stay away from a certain portion of the population, when all social advantages are persistently withheld, it may be for years, the result itself is pointed at as a reason, is used as an argument, for the continued withholding. (Addams, 1969, pp. 4–5)

The Age of Reform

In response to the negative consequences of these rapid structural and social changes, a social reform movement began after the Civil War and gained momentum near the end of the 19th century and into the early 20th century. The reform movement was instigated and promoted by members of the middle class who worried about the activities and morals of their own children, and who were concerned about the impact of lower class children's activities on middle class children. The efforts of these reformers were aimed at improving working conditions, making cities more livable, and ensuring that children had appropriate places to play. Their efforts led to the promulgation of child labor laws; extension of the age for compulsory schooling; and the development of curfews. A number of youth-serving organizations were also created to provide character development and/or safe environments for children and youth and to serve the needs of either middle class or working class children in urban and rural communities. Many of these organizations are still prominent today.

Many of the reform efforts were based on changing attitudes toward children. Before the early to mid-1800s, childhood led almost directly into adulthood. If children went to school, they usually dropped out by the sixth grade, and even during the school year they only attended if there was a slack period in the work they were required to do. Whether in rural settings or the cities, children in poorer families went to work as soon as they were strong enough to do physical labor, which was usually well before puberty. By the time these children were teenagers, those living in rural settings were expected to achieve a level of semi-independence through either working on the farm or being "farmed out" to other nearby farms or businesses in the city. Children of families living in the cities were also expected to begin working at an early age. In other cases, children needed to seek work because one or both of their parents were no longer living (Kett, 1977).

The presence of large numbers of working youth in the cities, both those who recently immigrated and those who came from rural settings, was not without its consequences. In factory settings, children were exposed to and potentially influenced by adults and their behavior. In addition, during their nonwork hours, youth, especially boys, were exposed to street life and to adults who were engaged in drinking, gambling, and other licentious behaviors. Girls employed in the factories often spent their evenings at the dance halls, which many believed would lead to prostitution and out-of-wedlock child bearing.

Many lower-class parents condoned their children's life on the streets as a means of supplementing family income. In New York, for example, boys might be involved in huckstering, scavenging, peddling, errand running, bootblacking (shoe shinning), horseholding, and newspaper selling (Stansell, 1987). Most of these endeavors had the potential to lead children into contact with adults of questionable character. In addition, some children had no choice but to take on these jobs as the streets were often the only refuge for youth whose parents had died or they were on their own because they had moved alone from the country to the city.

Addams felt that the widespread availability of urban pleasures was having a particularly negative impact on youth. In *The Spirit of Youth and the City Streets*, Addams (1909/1972) wrote that for boys

> it is nothing short of cruelty to overstimulate his senses as does the modern city. This period is difficult everywhere but it seems at times as if the great city almost deliberately increases it perils. The newly awakened senses are appealed to by all that is gaudy and sensual. (p. 27)

The increased involvement of youth in immoral and illegal behaviors led to efforts by social reformers to deal with the "boy and/or girl problem," although most of the initial efforts were aimed at boys.

> Lads from 14 to 21 are the busiest instigators, the most active abettors, and the most daring perpetrators of offenses against the peace and good order of society. In tumults, street fights, and riotous assemblies, in resistance to authority and contempt for law, they generally take the lead. (Brace, 1852, p. 12)

While many middle class girls became teachers and tenders of shops, unmarried working class girls, especially immigrants, were usually employed in the factories. Reformers expressed concern with the increased frequency of out-of-wedlock births, divorce, venereal disease, illegitimacy, and prostitution among this segment of the youth population. They attributed these increases to girls having their own money and to girls' involvement in nonwork discretionary time activities in the community. They also felt that work environments subjected young women to the untoward advances of fellow workers and supervisors (what today we might call sexual harassment).

Dance halls, movies, and other forms of free-time outlets were also seen as contributing to girls' sexual awakening and misconduct (sometimes leading to pregnancy). Adolescent females who had migrated from rural areas were thought to be particularly at risk due to their sheltered upbringing and lack of prior exposure to city life. "As farmers' daughters they were strong and capable of taking care of themselves in an environment they understood," but once a part of city life, she was "in constant danger…as every effort is made to demoralize her completely" (Addams, 1909/1972, p. 150).

Reformers such as Rev. Joseph Tukerman (a Unitarian minister who worked with the poor in Boston), Robert M. Hartley (founder of the New York Association for Improving the Condition of the Poor), Charles Loring Brace (founder of the New York Children's Aid Society), and Josephine Shaw Lowell (a leader in the New York Charity Organization Society) adopted the Victorian view of street life as the antithesis of the home and family being valued as the central institutions leading to a moral life (Schwartz, 2000). Middle-class families viewed children on the streets as a sign of parental neglect or lack of adult supervision and a failure to promote virtuous behavior (including diligence, sobriety, and thrift vs. indolence, intemperance, and improvidence). Thus, they felt that bettering oneself and one's children and leading a virtuous life was a matter of personal responsibility.

Other reformers blamed urban problems on structural issues, including lack of opportunity, low wages, inadequate housing, and language difficulties (Schwartz, 2000). True (1914) studied the lives of 65 youth ages 14 to 18 on the West Side of New York City and placed much of the responsibility for youthful indiscretions with the community. His comments regarding a group of working-class girls, ages 14 to 18, from the tenements on the West Side of New York City are representative of the views of many of the reformers.

> They have been brought up from babyhood in these blocks. Born in the crowded, dark tenement house, they had for a nursery the crowded sidewalk, and for a playground, the street. They had gone to the nearest school and from there to work in the nearest factory. They had seen the West Side, breathed the West Side, fed on the West Side for fourteen years or more, and had built up their adolescent ideals of the same forlorn material. That they had succumbed to unwholesome influences does not prove them to have been peculiarly weak or susceptible. Nor does it prove that their parents had been culpably delinquent in their duties. Conditions of living in the crowded city have tended to loosen the family bond, and the powerful force of neighborhood influence cannot be adequately combated by parental authority alone. The community must assume the

responsibility for the environment of its least protected members. (p. 16)

The reformers argued that the failure to demonstrate virtuous behavior was not the primary reason that individuals were and remained poor. They noted that for the poor, the laissez-faire market did not appear to reward virtuous behavior (and among the rich, nonvirtuous behavior did not often lead to poverty). They saw the poor as already essentially virtuous, but still poor. They also recognized that the vast majority of the poor wanted to improve their lot (Schwartz, 2000).

Nevertheless, most members of the working class were not looking for a handout or a free ride. Despite applying themselves to work and avoiding vice, there was little economic reward for their hard work and good behavior. Thus, virtuous behavior was threatened by societal conditions and poverty. Much of the poverty could be ascribed to "unemployment, overwork, old age, or industrial accidents" (Schwartz, 2000, p. 102).

Addams (1909/1972) even argued that structural reforms would increase virtuous behavior. For example, women involved in prostitution were viewed as virtuous, having no other way to make money if unemployed or employed at wages below a reasonable level of subsistence. Social reformers' goals were to keep lower-class children from working in unsafe factories or being involved in street life by substituting school attendance and involvement in wholesome nonschool and nonwork-time activities.

Middle-class families were also worried about the structural changes taking place in the cities. In the larger cities, the middle class sought to make boys strong and virtuous to prepare them for business and professional success. In the smaller towns, the middle class also felt threatened by what was occurring in the larger cities and sought to preserve small town values. As a result, middle-class parents undertook efforts to protect their children from working-class and urban influences by creating separate youth-serving organizations and focusing attention on character building to insure that their children would grow up with the right values and thus preserve their middle-class standing (Macleod, 1983, p. xvi).

The Creation of Adolescence

The reformers' efforts resulted in the "creation" of a period called "adolescence" that would come between childhood and adulthood. They saw this period as an opportunity for young people to avoid some of the negative influences of city life and to develop the skills necessary to become fully functioning adults (Kett, 1977). For educators, psychologists, and leading thinkers of the time, extending dependence or semi-independence further into the teenage (i.e., adolescent) years was thought to be necessary to fully develop the capacity of children to grow into fully functioning adults.

The word *adolescence* was used infrequently until the late 1800s, but became institutionalized in 1904 with the publication of G. Stanley Hall's two volume set, *Adolescence: Its Psychology and its Relations to Physiology, Anthropology, Sociology, Sex, Crime, Religion and Education.* The creation of a distinct stage of adolescence recognized that by age 11 or 12, children had moved beyond childhood, but had not yet achieved adult status. Hall saw adolescence as "a new birth, a wiping clean of the slate of childhood" (Kett, 1977, p. 217), but also a time of "storm and stress" due to the onset of puberty and young people being suspended between the worlds of childhood and adulthood. In marking adolescence as a separate stage, Hall and the reformers identified a period that would be dominated by school dependence rather than independence and work.

Experiencing adolescence was increasingly seen as a necessity to enable young people to make the transition to adulthood. Interestingly, Hall believed that if children did not naturally go through this stage, they should be forced through it. Hall, like many others of his time, saw urban life and industrialization as hostile to an adolescent's normal course of development, since it encouraged precocity (i.e., children being exposed to circumstances that forced or enabled them to grow up too quickly).

Hall advocated a balance of "freedom and control," recognizing that adolescents needed the time and opportunity to develop their full potential and the necessity of helping channel youth through this difficult period avoiding deviant and antisocial behavior. Hall also advocated making the city more like the country, with the inclusion of nature trips, playgrounds, and sports as distractions from the negative opportunities available on the streets (Kett, 1977, p. 219).

Controlling boys' time was deemed particularly necessary as they were seen as vulnerable, awkward, and easily misguided. In general, "young people stood less in need of earnest advice than of the artful manipulation of their environment" (Kett, 1977, p. 6). This led to an "ideology of protection," which included state and other organizational interventions to encourage the appropriate growth of adolescents into socially acceptable adults (Acland, 1995), including the following:

- removing children from the workplace by implementing child labor laws designed to decrease the types of work children could do and the hours they could be employed
- reforming education and extending the period over which it would be compulsory

- undertaking efforts to keep children off the streets and at home late in the evening
- creating a juvenile court system
- organizing the spare-time activities of middle-class boys and girls through adult-sponsored youth organizations

In the following sections we will discuss each of these interventions.

Removing Children From the Workplace

Efforts began in the late 1800s to institute child labor laws designed both to increase the age at which children could begin working and to control the kinds of work that young people could do. Prior to the institution of these laws, it was not uncommon for children to be employed for long hours in repetitive factory jobs under poor working conditions. At night children often served as newsies, bootblacks, peddlers, and messengers (for both legal and illegal enterprises). Night work led to boys (mainly) spending their evenings without adult supervision, but with a ready source of earned funds available to partake of "urban pleasures." Middle-class parents worried that their children would learn about sex, smoking, gambling, swearing, and drinking if they had too much interaction with lower- or working-class boys (Baldwin, 2002).

These concerns led to laws regulating the permissible hours for boys and girls to engage in the street trades, controlled the types of work children could undertake in the factories, and removed many children and young adolescents from the labor market altogether. But it was not enough to keep children and adolescents from unacceptable work and unsavory contact with adults—other activities for them to do needed to be provided.

Extending Education

Efforts were made to extend the period of education beyond Grade 6 or 8, although for many poorer and immigrant youth, they were lucky if they stayed in school that long. Extended schooling was intended to produce a more educated person but also served to delay when youth could enter the workforce.

High school was created to extend educational opportunities beyond grade 8, and over time the educational structure became more like the one today: six years of elementary school, three years of middle school and three years of high school. This structure institutionalized the separation of children into different groups based on their stage of development. Attending school also was considered a way to Americanize and to control immigrant children and to decrease the amount of time available for them to get into trouble (Sommerville, 1982, p. 196).

Compulsory education laws were developed in Massachusetts as early as 1852; Nevada (1873), Kansas (1874), and New York (1874) followed. Laws usually required school attendance beginning from age 6 or 7 through age 16 (State Compulsory School Attendance Laws, n.d.).

Compulsory education laws worked in tandem with child labor laws to curtail the uncontrolled hours available for youth to work or be involved in "unacceptable" activities. In accordance with this, school nonattendance was increasingly seen as deviant, and habitual truants could be sent to reform schools to keep them off the streets.

Implementing Juvenile Curfews

Efforts were also made to implement juvenile curfews as a means of controlling the street time of adolescents. These efforts began mainly in smaller cities in Canada and then spread to smaller cities in the United States and eventually to the larger cities. Curfews were designed to prevent children, under age 15 in most cases, from loitering on the street late at night without adult supervision. Alexander Hogeland (1884) was one of the leaders of this movement and made a case for curfews in his book, *Ten Years Among the Newsboys*. Newsies were primarily boys, usually between ages 8 and 15, who lived on the streets, maybe going to school during the day, but making their living selling newspapers for a penny a piece. They were mostly immigrants from impoverished families. As many as 30,000 deserted kids, many of whom became newsies, were thought to be living on the streets of New York City in the late 1800s, in most cases because their parents had died or their parents could not afford to care for them at home. Efforts were begun as early as 1853 to help the newsies when Charles Loring Brace set up a newsboys' lodging home in New York City (Adoption History Project, n.d.). He also developed a program, known as the orphan trains, which exported boys and girls to live in the country.

One solution to the street problem was the institution of "placing-out" programs, which involved moving wayward lower-class children to foster homes in rural areas. This movement was instigated by the Children's Aid Society of New York, under the leadership of Rev. Charles Brace. The New York Foundling Hospital also sent children west.

The orphan trains were also intended to supplement the labor pool in rural areas while removing some of the pressures for employment in the cities. However, they were mainly aimed at removing children from the streets and away from what were perceived as inadequate home environments to more stable homes with more caring adults.

Between 1854 and 1930, between 150,000 and 200,000 children were sent by train from New York to be adopted or placed in families in states as far away as Nebraska and Kansas. True orphans were sent on the trains, but children who had been "turned loose" by parents who could not care for them due to poverty were also sent. Most were children from families who were struggling to make a living in New York after having immigrated to the United States in the mid to late 19th century (Stansell, 1987, p. 313).

Two methods were used to adopt children. One method used by the Children's Aid society put children (some as old as 14) on trains with placing agents. Advance notices of "Homes Wanted for Orphans" were placed in newspapers in towns along the route. When the children arrived, they were inspected by prospective families, and if a local organizing committee and the placement agent agreed, children were "adopted" by the local family. Siblings did not have to be adopted by the same family. The agent usually made return visits to the towns to check on the welfare of the children. It was expected that children would be treated like any other member of the family, and not as indentured servants.

The other method of placing children involved Catholic families applying in advance to the New York Foundling Hospital for a particular kind of child (e.g., a two-year-old, blue-eyed, blond-haired girl). The Sisters of Charity of St. Vincent de Paul then matched requests with available children, some of whom had been abandoned in a cradle on the front porch of the hospital. Local priests in the Midwest and the South served as the liaisons between the hospital and the prospective families.

With the start of the Great Depression, the orphan trains came to an end. Prospective families found it more difficult to add another child and other means, such as foster home placement, were developed to deal with orphaned or abandoned children (DiPasquale, 2002).

Curfews were more popular in smaller cities; however, they were not supported unanimously in any setting. An 1898 *New York Times* editorial ridiculed those who advocated curfews:

> Much literature from the "curfew" cranks has reached this office, and enough of it was read to justify its wholesale disposition in—or around—convenient waste baskets. The documents sent gave enough evidence that by shutting children up in the house at nightfall juvenile crimes and misdemeanors had been made less numerous in several towns, but what of the effect? Even more effect in this direction would be produced by cutting the throats of everybody under age.

Curfews were mostly implemented when a link could be made between adopting a curfew and decreased crime. The legacy of these efforts is that in the 1990s 80% of American cities with a population greater than 30,000 had some form of juvenile curfew law (Baldwin, 2002, p. 605).

Creating Juvenile Courts

Over time there also was movement away from treating youth as adults when they committed a crime. Thus, juvenile courts were developed, beginning with Illinois in 1899 (Building Block for Youth, n.d.). In addition, youth were often prohibited from enjoying some of the same rights as adults (e.g., the establishment of a legal drinking age). Adolescence thus became a legal as well as a social category (Kett, 1977).

Reformers wrestled with many of the age-related status issues we still struggle with today, including the appropriate age when a young person can drink, drive, vote, register for the military, run for office, leave public school, or be tried as an adult. Decisions about the appropriate age to permit involvement in each of these areas reflect the need to balance the tension between youth's responsibilities for their own actions and society's responsibility to protect young people.

Instead of encouraging the popular attitude that "boys will be boys," wayward boys' activities, in particular, were more likely to be treated as delinquent acts that needed to be punished (Breckinridge & Abbott, 1912). Interestingly, juvenile courts treated "wayward" girls more harshly and differently than misbehaving boys.

> Girls who transgressed were much more likely to be removed from their homes, given stricter sentences, and longer probationary periods. The courts frequently sentenced young women to reformatories or training schools. These institutions sought to reform wayward females through resocialization in traditional female codes of conduct and often detained girls until they were of a marriageable age of 21 or older. (Abrams, 2000, p. 440)

In the 1840s the courts began to experiment with probation for young offenders in an effort to keep them out of jail. However, in some cases even minor offenders were brought under the control or supervision of the courts, thus extending control over their behavior. For example, beginning in the early 1800s, efforts were made to segregate juvenile offenders and potential juvenile offenders from adults. The New York House of Refuge, founded as early as 1825, was among the first juvenile facilities. Besides removing children from the streets, these institutions attempted to rehabilitate them and eventually return them to city life (Sommerville, 1982).

Reform schools were developed beginning in the mid-1800s for both boys and girls. These were usually in the country, state supported, and aimed at the reformation of juvenile offenders as opposed to being places of refuge for street children. Unfortunately, reform schools became dumping grounds for teenage troublemakers and felons and those characterized by "vagrancy and stubbornness" (Kett, 1977, p. 132).

Youth Serving Organizations: Their History and Current Status

This chapter has focused on the forces at work in society from the mid- to late-1800s and into the early 1900s that set the stage for the development of a number of the prominent youth serving organizations that still exist today. While some of these organizations have altered their missions in keeping with current national youth development practices, most have remained true to their original goals, but may go about meeting these goals in different ways than they did when originally created. In the next chapter we explore specific details regarding the founding and current status of some of these organizations.

References

Abrams, L. S. (2000). Guardians of virtue: The social reformers and the "girl problem," 1890–1920. *Social Service Review*, *74*(3), 436–452.

Acland, C. R. (1995). *Youth, murder, spectacle: The cultural politics of "youth in crisis."* Boulder, CO: Westview Press.

Addams, J. (1969). *Philanthropy and social progress: Seven essays.* Freeport, NY: Books for Libraries Press.

Addams, J. (1972). *The spirit of youth and the city streets.* Urbana, IL: University of Illinois Press. (Original work published 1909)

The Adoption History Project. (n.d.). *Charles Loring Brace.* Retrieved July 18, 2004, from http://darkwing.uoregon.edu/~adoption/people/brace.html

Baldwin, P.C. (2002). "Nocturnal habits and dark wisdom:" The American response to children in the streets at night, 1880–1930. *Journal of Social History*, *35*(3), 593–611.

Brace, C. L. (1852, October 15). Youthful depravity—Home influences. *Common School Journal*, *3*, 12.

Breckinridge, J. and Abbott, E. (1912). *The delinquent child and the home.* New York, NY: Russell Sage Foundation Charities Publication Committee.

Building Blocks for Youth. (n.d.). *The juvenile court: One hundred years in the making.* Retrieved July 15, 2004, from http://www.buildingblocksforyouth.org/juvenile_court.htm

DiPasquale, C. (2002). A history of the orphan trains. Retrieved June 15, 2004, from http://www.kancoll.org/articles/orphans/index.html

Gibson, C. (1998). *Population of the 100 largest cities and other urban places in the United States: 1790 to 1990* (Working Paper No. 27). Washington, DC: Population Division, U.S. Bureau of the Census.

Hall, G. S. (1904). *Adolescence, its psychology and its relations to physiology, anthropology, sociology, sex, crime, religion and education.* New York, NY: Appleton and Company.

Hogeland, A. (1884). *Ten years among the newsboys.* Louisville, KY: J. P. Morton and Company.

Kett, J. F. (1977). *Rites of passage: Adolescence in America 1790 to the present.* New York, NY: Basic Books.

Library of Congress. (n.d.). *Rise of industrial America, 1876–1900: City life in the late 19th century.* Retrieved July 18, 2004, from http://www.memory.loc.gov/learn/features/timeline/riseind/city/city.html

Macleod, D. I. (1983). *Building character in the American boy: The Boy Scouts, YMCA and their forerunners, 1870–1900.* Madison, WI: Wisconsin University Press.

Nasaw, D. (1985). *Children of the city: At work and at play*. Garden City, NY: Anchor/Double Day.

Schwartz, J. (2000). *Fighting poverty with virtue: Moral reform and America's poor, 1825–2000*. Bloomington, IN: Indiana University Press.

Sommerville, C. J. (1982). *The rise and fall of childhood.* Volume 140, Sage Library of Social Research. Beverly Hills, CA: Sage Publications.

Stansell, C. (1987). *City of women: Sex and class in New York, 1789–1860.* Urbana, IL: University of Illinois Press.

State Compulsory School Attendance Laws. (n.d.). Retrieved August 28, 2004, from http://www.infoplease.com/ipa/A0112617.html

True, R. S. (1914) *Boyhood and lawlessness: The neglected girl*. New York, NY: Survey Associates.

Untitled Editorial. (1898, July 10). *New York Times*, p. 16.

Chapter 5

Youth Serving Organizations: Then and Now

Peter A. Witt

In this chapter, we present some of the prominent youth serving organizations, including why each was created and the programs and services they currently offer. This chapter will enable the reader to better understand the current philosophies and practices of these organizations and their contributions to youth development.

The Need for Youth Organizations

Based on the concerns and issues raised in the last chapter, a number of organizations designed to organize young people's free time were developed to deal with some of youth's critical social issues that existed at the end of the 19th and early 20th centuries. Different organizations were created to serve individuals from different social classes and different locations (e.g., urban, small town, farm communities), including the following:

- ***Boys Clubs***, and eventually playgrounds, were developed to serve the needs of lower-class and immigrant children as well as adolescents in large urban centers. Reformers could have tried to either rid the city of its vices and dangers or "quarantine" the young by shielding and protecting them from the negative influences of the city. They chose the latter, since the former seemed virtually impossible (Nasaw, 1985). Therefore, efforts were often aimed at serving large numbers in a single building or space. Due to the high volume of youth served, Boys Clubs were labeled as "mass clubs."

- ***The YMCA, Camp Fire Girls, and Girl Guides*** (the precursor to the Girl Scouts) were developed to serve middle-class youth. Their primary goals were to create and/or reinforce middle-class values by keeping middle-class youth separate from those of the lower class. These organizations also existed to help develop young people's physical and moral fitness.

- ***Settlement houses*** were created in poor or immigrant neighborhoods and were usually staffed by college students. The goal was to create a community that could improve the economic prospects of community residents. In the United States, settlement houses were active in immigrant communities in efforts to create legislation providing for juvenile courts, mothers' pensions, workers' compensation, and the regulation of child labor.
- ***4-H*** began because of interest among farm families to reinforce rural family values, attachment to the land, and the agricultural skills that characterized their own lives by providing activities for children in farm and rural settings. Organized as part of the Land Grant University system, 4-H Clubs developed first for boys and then for girls in every state across the United States.
- ***Playgrounds*** were established in densely populated urban areas to provide places for kids to play, but just as importantly to keep them from being on the streets. Most cities lacked safe places for kids to play, and being on the street was often dangerous and subjected children to potentially negative influences.

In the following sections we discuss some of these youth-serving organizations. For ease of presentation and to facilitate understanding, organizations are divided into those originally intended to serve boys, those intended to serve girls, and those designed to serve both.

Boys Work

Boys Clubs (Now Boys & Girls Clubs of America)

In 1860, a Boys Club was created by female volunteers at a congregational church in the slums of Hartford, Connecticut. The first official Boys Club, however, opened in New York in 1876, and featured both meeting space and a gymnasium. Then in 1906, the Federated Boys Clubs was formed with the purpose of bringing together 74 individual Boys Clubs, the majority of which were in New England or the Middle Atlantic states.

The first Boys Clubs attempted to keep male children and early adolescents from entering a life of crime, but over time the organization evolved to serve older adolescents as well. Many of the early clubs served street orphans and doubled as homeless shelters. Wealthy philanthropists, such as railroad magnet E. H. Harriman, supported the development of clubs because they saw their potential to control the behavior of lower-class and street boys. They also saw the club's potential to create good citizens and to Americanize participants, while also increasing working-class productivity in the work place. While proselytizing was a feature of the early Boys Clubs, this was quickly dropped not only because boys tended to shy away from clubs with too much religious content but also because children came from a variety of religious backgrounds (Macleod, 1983).

Attendance at the clubs was voluntary and usually on a drop-in basis, with most clubs designed to serve large numbers of boys. Some of the "mass clubs" were so large that their primary emphasis was keeping children off the streets rather than providing meaningful contact with adults. However, even with this goal, clubs still only served a small proportion of youth in a given area of the city. The mass clubs contrasted to the group clubs often run by settlement houses. According to one Boys Club worker,

> any boy in the city could be admitted to the club. The workers consisted of a doorkeeper, librarian and superintendent. During the club session the superintendent was obliged to walk about the rooms as a moral policeman. Occasionally visitors from the various churches came to assist by playing games with the boys. Later a few industrial classes, such as carpentry, clay-modeling, word-carving, cobbling, typesetting, and other trades, were added. A penny savings bank was a leading feature of this sort of club, and occasional entertainments. Finally, with this plan, it is possible to have an exceedingly large membership. This itself is a strong feature in the minds of many. Large figures look prosperous in a report. (quoted in Forbush, 1913, p. 68)

Efforts were made to enroll boys before their teens, to keep them busy, and hopefully to build habits and interests that might later prevent them from getting into trouble on the streets (Macleod, 1983, p. 66). In a word, prevention was the major purpose of the early clubs, as opposed to the character building agendas of organizations like the Boys Scouts and YMCA. Over time, however, the Boys Club mission shifted to attracting working-class and working boys, instead of mainly street boys.

Leaders in the clubs put emphasis on activities that had the potential to attract boys as long as they obeyed the rules. The leader of a club acted only as a moral police officer and was responsible for breaking up fights and preventing equipment thefts. Thus, negative contacts with adults were avoided, but the potential positive role of adults as mentors and guides in the lives of adolescents was often lacking. This problem was compounded because in many cases boys preferred to be on their own without having adults telling them what to do, and therefore clubs were constantly fighting to keep attendance numbers up (Nasaw, 1985).

By 1911 there were 110 Boys Clubs in the United States with a combined enrollment of 108,063 youth. Most clubs rented the space they occupied, but some, with funds donated from local businessmen, bought or built their own buildings. For example, a five-story building built for the exclusive use of the Albany Boys Club in 1911, was funded by a wealthy local businessman (Nasaw, 1985).

Boys Clubs Today

Since its inception in the late 1800s, the role of Boys Clubs has changed considerably, as they now embrace a greater focus on the positive youth development of both boys and girls of all socioeconomic classes. However, some things have remained consistent with the clubs. For example, most are still located in poorer neighborhoods, many still strive to keep children off the streets, and clubs still tend to serve large numbers of individuals.

In 1956, The Boys Clubs of America celebrated its 50th anniversary and received a United States Congressional Charter. In 1990, to recognize the fact that girls are also participating in programs, the national organization's name was changed to Boys & Girls Clubs of America. Today the organization serves over 3.6 million boys and girls at over 3,300 club locations in all 50 states, Puerto Rico, the Virgin Islands, and domestic and international military bases.

Boys and Girls Clubs list seven principles that currently form the basis of their work (Boys and Girls Clubs of America, 2004b):

1. a mission of hope and opportunity, to inspire and enable young people to become responsible, productive, caring citizens
2. a focus on young people from disadvantaged circumstances
3. a unique system of informal guidance; access to safe, easily accessible, and affordable places; diverse programs and activities; and caring adults
4. creating ongoing relationships with caring adults
5. a youth development strategy, including a sense of belonging, competence, usefulness, and influence
6. a commitment to character
7. fun, interesting, and diversified experiences

Aside from offering opportunities for free choice and open recreation, the clubs also offer opportunities for youth to participate in a variety of youth development programs. The organization has been successful in getting a number of these programs sponsored by major national companies. The following are four examples of Boys and Girls Clubs national programs (Boys and Girls Clubs of America, 2004a):

- *TEENSupreme Keystone Clubs* are chartered small group leadership development clubs for young people ages 14 to 18. Keystoners elect officers, choose their own activities and plan and implement community service projects. A national charter entitles a Keystone Club to participate in regional and national Keystone conferences. The TEENSupreme Keystone Club program is sponsored by the Taco Bell Foundation.

- *Power Hour* is a comprehensive homework help and tutoring program, and is designed to raise the academic proficiency of Club members ages 6 to 12. Power Hour is sponsored by The J. C. Penney Afterschool Fund.

- *The SMART Moves* (Skills Mastery And Resistance Training) prevention/education program addresses the problems of drug and alcohol use and premature sexual activity among youth. More than simply emphasizing a "Say No" message, the program teaches young people ages 6 to 15 how to say no by involving them in discussion and role-playing, helping them practice resistance and refusal skills, developing assertiveness, strengthening decision-making skills and analyzing media and peer influence. The ultimate goal of the program is to promote abstinence from substance abuse and adolescent sexual involvement through the practice of responsible behavior.

- *FITNESS AUTHORITY*, a small-group program sponsored by The Sports Authority, Inc., promotes fitness in all youth. FITNESS AUTHORITY provides a fun-filled, motivating fitness experience for members. There is a 12-week curriculum for each of three age groups: FITNESS SQUAD, ages 6–9; FITNESS MASTERS, ages 10–14; and FITNESS ALL-STARS, ages 15–18. Weekly sessions cover every aspect of fitness, drawing on themes of sports culture and history, self-esteem, nutrition, and physical fitness. The annual FITNESS AUTHORITY Club-wide Pentathlon competition allows club members to demonstrate and test their fitness levels.

Boy Scouts

The Boy Scouts were founded in England in 1908 by Lord Robert Baden-Powell, a British general who served in India and later in South Africa. Baden-Powell was dismayed that many of his soldiers did not have basic first-aid or elementary survival skills. Therefore, he developed scouting as a "remedy to Britain's moral, physical and military weakness," a problem considered to be a threat to the British Empire.

Using small group instruction, competition, and games, Baden-Powell began training his men in the skills necessary for scouting (e.g., following a trail, giving directions, recognizing danger signs, finding food and water). He wrote *Aids to Scouting* (1899), which outlined the instructional methods he used. He eventually rewrote this book to make it more appealing to boys and scout patrols (*Scouting for Boys, 1908*); and as a result of these promotional efforts, Boy Scout troops sprang up all over England. Then, because of interest among girls, Baden-Powell's sister Agnes formed the Girl Guides.

The Boy Scouts were promoted by the middle class and quickly became popular in England. The organization did not adopt any specific church affiliation, but sought to be a "character factory" and an instrument of "social control" by inculcating the habits of obedience, cleanliness, temperance, and loyalty that would best guarantee the perpetuation of the middle class, masculinity, economic efficiency, and ultimately the survival of the British Empire (Rosenthal, 1986, pp. 6–7).

William D. Boyce, a Chicago entrepreneur and philanthropist who imported the scouting concept in the United States, established the Boy Scouts in 1910 (see *The Unknown Boy Scout*). Julliett Low started the Girl Scouts in 1912. Although there were already several other loosely structured outdoor-oriented youth organizations in the United States, some using the name "Boy Scout" and some using other names (e.g., Woodcraft Indians created by Ernest Thompson Seton; Sons of Daniel Boone founded by Daniel Beard), Boyce provided needed structure and organization to these endeavors, and recruited key youth professionals to design and operate the programs. He also provided much of the start-up funding.

On February 8, 1910, Boyce filed incorporation papers for the Boy Scouts of America (BSA) in the District of Columbia. Seton merged his Woodcraft Indians with the new organization and became the BSA's first Chief Scout (from 1910 to 1916). The purpose of the organization according to Boyce was

> …to promote, through organization, and cooperation with other agencies, the ability of boys to do things for themselves and others, to train them in Scoutcraft, and to teach them

The Unknown Boy Scout
BoyScouts.com, 1999

William D. Boyce, a Chicago newspaper publisher, was said to be visiting London when he became lost in the fog. Out of the fog a boy appeared who offered to lead him to his destination. Successfully arriving where he wanted to go, Boyce offered to tip the boy, but he refused saying that he could accept no money for his good deed. Intrigued, Boyce asked the boy about scouting and eventually the boy took him to Baden-Powell"s office and disappeared into the fog. Boyce's conversations with Baden-Powell led him to promote scouting in the United States. The boy was never identified, but a statue is erected in honor of the "Unknown Scout" in England. In the British Scout Training Center at Gilwell Park, England, Scouts from the United States erected a statue of an American Buffalo in honor of this unknown scout.

> patriotism, courage, self-reliance, and kindred virtues, using the methods which are in common use by Boy Scouts. (Boy Scouts of America National Council, 2004b)

The Boy Scouts tried to extend boyhood and to distract youth from the problems of adolescence. For example, Boy Scouts intended to short circuit young boys' sexual urges by encouraging them to participate in vigorous exercise and by keeping them working toward goals (e.g., merit badges, which mostly dealt with rural-oriented skills and interests). However, as the original efforts were aimed at young adolescents, it was often hard to keep them involved as they got older. In addition, it was thought that involving younger boys would drive out the older ones (Robinson, 1902).

Boy Scouts had its greatest presence in the North and Midwest. However, the term "Boy" Scouts was problematic in the South. Even in the North and Midwest, many older adolescents were not attracted to the scouts due to the uniforms.

Boy Scouts Today

Today, BSA provides young people with a program whose purpose is to build character, to educate about the responsibilities of citizenship, and to develop personal fitness. Scouting serves more than four million boys and girls through more than 300 local council service centers. Scouting is a volunteer organization, with nearly 3,500 professional Scouts leading, guiding, and training more than one million volunteers (Boy Scouts of America National Council, 2004a).

Boy Scouts Organization

Scouts are divided into three divisions: Cub Scouting, Boy Scouting, and Venturing. *Cub Scouts* first became part of the BSA in 1930, and is now the largest of the BSA's three membership divisions. This year-round family program is designed for boys in the 1st through 5th grades. Boys join a Cub Scout pack, which is made up of six to eight boys known as dens. Once a month, all of the dens and family members gather for a pack meeting under the direction of a Cubmaster and pack committee. The committee includes parents of boys in the pack and members of the chartered organization. First graders are known as Tiger Cubs, 2nd graders Wolf Cub Scouts, 3rd graders Bear Cub Scouts, and 4th and 5th graders Webelos Scouts. In 2001, there were 980,555 Cub Scouts, of which 786,833 were Webelos Scouts, and 562,958 Pack Leaders worked with the boys in 54,148 Packs.

Boy Scouting as a division is designed for boys who have earned the Arrow of Light Award or have completed the fifth grade. The program achieves the BSA's objectives by focusing on a vigorous program of outdoor activities. Through these activities, scouts work toward earning one or more of 120 Merit Badges. As of 2001, 1,005,592 boys were members of the Boy Scouts, with 537,685 adult volunteers and 52,425 troops.

Venturing is a youth development program for young men and women 14 to 20 years of age. Venturing's purpose is to provide positive experiences to help young people mature and prepare themselves to become responsible and caring adults. Local community organizations establish a Venturing crew by matching their people and program resources to the interests of young people in the community. The program is designed to help youth pursue their special interests, learn to make ethical choices, become program resources for the Cub and Boy Scouts and other groups, develop leadership skills, and become good citizens. Venturing programs place emphasis on learning by "doing" through high adventure activities that provide team-building opportunities (Boy Scouts of America National Council, 2004c).

The Boy Scout Pledge

On my honor I will do my best
to do my duty to God and my country
and to obey the Scout Law;
to help other people at all times;
to keep myself physically strong,
mentally awake, and morally straight.

YMCA

The Young Men's Christian Association (YMCA) was founded in London, England, on June 6, 1844, in response to the unhealthy social conditions arising in the big cities due to the Industrial Revolution. The growth of the railroads and the centralization of commerce and industry brought many young rural men who needed jobs into cities like London. George Williams and a group of fellow drapers (i.e., garment workers) organized the first YMCA with the goal of substituting Bible study and prayer for life on the streets (YMCA, 2004a).

By 1851 there were 24 YMCAs (also known as Ys) in Great Britain, with a combined membership of 2,700. The first YMCAs in North America were established in 1852, first in Montreal and then in Boston. In 1854, the first international convention was held in Paris. At that time there were 397 separate Ys in seven nations.

In the United States during the Civil War, YMCA membership shrunk to one third its size. Fifteen of the remaining northern Ys formed the U.S. Christian Commission to assist the troops and prisoners of war. Among other accomplishments, the YMCA gave more than one million Bibles to soldiers and in doing so began a commitment to working with soldiers and sailors that continues to this day through the Armed Services YMCAs.

Four years after the end of the Civil War, there were over 600 Ys. The focus of these centers was on "saving souls" by spreading the Christian religion through saloon and street-corner preaching, distributing lists of Christian boarding houses, and providing lectures, libraries, and meeting halls. In 1866, the influential New York YMCA adopted a fourfold purpose: "The improvement of the spiritual, mental, social and physical condition of young men" (YMCA, 2004a).

Many of the branches imposed an upper age limit on participation, usually around 40, but not an official lower age limit. However, up until the 1880s, younger boys (those less than 14 or 15 years) were generally excluded. Nevertheless, the YMCAs eventually started working with boys younger than 15, both because there was significant interest among younger boys and to help recruit boys to eventual membership as adults in the YMCA. This change led to the creation of Junior Departments, designed to both work with younger boys and to act as a feeder system for programs for young men.

The main focus of the YMCA shifted over time to exclusively meeting the needs of young working- and middle-class boys and men, rather than focusing on the poor like the Boys Clubs (MacLeod, 1983). In doing so, the goals of the YMCA became character formation and prevention of negative behaviors, rather than rescue and reformation. YMCA officials were worried that involving working-class and street boys would expose middle-class boys to negative influences (Macleod, 1983). Therefore, most programs charged a fee to discourage working-class and street boys from attending. They also sought to keep numbers smaller than the "mass" Boys Clubs to provide more individualized attention.

In response to growing concerns about the range of opportunities available for boys, Ys began offering exercise classes and organizing summer camps. Sports were increasingly seen as a means to promote middle-class values, such as the willingness to follow rules and strive for rewards. Thus, basketball was invented, along with other team activities such as volleyball (see **Table 5.1** for information about some of the activities invented through the Ys). Physical training became the main YMCA activity during the 1890s; and while the religious training emphasis of the YMCAs remained, the main initial attraction for many boys was the opportunity to participate in recreation and physical activities. Together these elements (i.e., sports, religion, and recreation) formed the spirit, mind, and body triangle that is the symbol of YMCAs today.

Today's YMCAs still pay considerable attention to the needs of children and youth; however, few Ys exist in poorer communities and many Y programs charge a fee. In addition, much of the Y's work is currently based on adoption of a character development and assets-based approaches (YMCA 2004a).

Girls Work

Among the reformers, girls aroused less alarm than boys, and thus work with girls began after clubs started working with boys, and was initially much less extensive. It was generally thought that girls made an easier transition from childhood to fulfilling adult expectations than boys. According to MacLeod (1983)

> They stayed a little longer in high school and a good deal longer in Sunday school. After classes each day, they mostly went straight home, whereas boys hung about on the streets. Consequently, by one contemporary tabulation, there were twenty times as many groups doing boys' work as girls' in 1910. (p. 51)

Girls work was heavily influenced by boys work, but differing expectations for each gender led to some differences in the way services were conceptualized and organized. Until about 1909, YWCAs did little work with girls under 16, but subsequently developed programs of athletics, outdoor

Table 5.1: Sports Invented by the YMCA
YMCA, 2004b

Basketball
At the request of Luther Gulick, James Naismith invented the game of basketball at the International YMCA Training School in December, 1891. Gulick needed a game to occupy a class of incorrigibles—18 future YMCA directors who were more interested in rugby and football, and didn't care for leapfrog, tumbling, and other activities they were forced to do during the winter. Gulick, obviously out of patience with the group, gave Naismith two weeks to come up with a game to occupy them.

Volleyball
Volleyball was invented at the Holyoke, Massachusetts, YMCA in 1895, by William Morgan, an instructor at the Y who felt that basketball was too strenuous for businessmen.

Football
Professional football began at a YMCA. In 1895, in Latrobe, Pennsylvania, John Brailer was paid $10 plus expenses by the local YMCA to replace the injured quarterback on their team. Years later, however, Pudge Heffelfinger claimed that he was secretly paid to play for the Allegheny Athletic Association in 1892. The NFL elected to go with Pudge's version of events.

Softball
Softball was given its name by Walter Hakanson of the Denver YMCA in 1926 at a meeting of the Colorado Amateur Softball Association (CASA), itself a result of YMCA staff efforts. Softball had been played for many years prior to 1926, under such names as kittenball and even sissyball.

Racquetball
Racquetball was invented in 1950 at the Greenwich, Connecticut, YMCA by Joe Sobek, a member who couldn't find other squash players of his caliber and who did not like handball. He tried paddleball and platform tennis and came up with the idea of using a strung racquet similar to a platform tennis paddle (not a sawed-off tennis racquet, as some say) to allow a greater variety of shots.

life, literary studies, and domestic skills to meet the needs of older girls. Luther Gulick, who along with his wife founded the Camp Fire Girls, thought it was necessary to maintain sex differences because it would be "fundamentally evil" to copy Boy Scouting. Since girls must learn "to be womanly," the "domestic fire" became the group's symbol (MacLeod, 1983, p. 51).

Both boys' and girls' workers wanted all youth to be more physically active and both saw the value of achievement awards (e.g., merit badges). However, Girl Scouts and Camp Fire Girls (and the girls-related elements of 4-H to be discussed later in this chapter) emphasized involvement in activities consistent with homemaking and volunteerism. According to one early writer, in adapting Boy Scouting

> to the psychology of the young girl it had been recognized that boys like to be boys, while girls do not like to be girls. They are fundamentally little women, and the surest way to win their interest is to open to them the pursuits of women so modified as to insure to them the rewards of achievement. (Price, 1918, p. 367)

Girl Scouts

In the United States, the Girl Scouts was founded in Savannah, Georgia, by Juliette Gordon Low in 1912. Low used her own funds to underwrite the development of the organization. (Low may have had the longest name in youth work: Juliette "Daisy" Magill Kinzie Gordon Low; extra points if you can remember this for an exam!). Juliette had married William Low, an Englishman and lived in England and Scotland for a time. After William Low's death, Juliette traveled and settled in Paris where she planned to study sculpture (Girl Scouts of the USA, 2004).

Based on the interest in scouting among girls in England, Sir Robert Baden-Powell's sister, Agnes formed the Girl Guides in 1910. "Daisy," as Low was known, became involved in this new organization and moved back to Scotland to lead a Girl Guides troop. Soon after, she returned to her birthplace in Georgia to begin a troop in the carriage house behind her home. Daisy became a strong advocate of the Girl Scouts and her promotional efforts led to the establishment of troops in many other cities. By 1915 a national organization was incorporated. The organization initially copied the uniform, handbook, and other basic principles from the British Girl Guides, but later changed these to fit the American character of the organization. The name also was changed to Girl Scouts (Girl Scouts of the USA, 2004a).

Daisy was a firm believer in letting the girls run their own troops. Adults involved in the troops were advisers, not leaders. Over time, the Girl Scouts offered national training schools for leaders, and colleges and universities offered Girl Scout leadership training courses, with some universities offering scholarships for students who were Girl Scouts.

Girl Scout Promise

On my honor, I will try
to serve God and my country,
to help people at all times,
and to live by the Girl Scout Law.

Girl Scouts Today

Today there are nearly 3.7 million Girl Scouts—2.8 million youth members and 942,000 adult members. Girl Scouting includes the following five levels: Daisy Girl Scouts, ages 5–6; Brownie Girl Scouts, ages 6–8; Junior Girl Scouts, ages 8–11; Cadette Girl Scouts, ages 11–14; and Senior Girl Scouts, ages 14–17. Girl Scouting is a values-based organization, not a religious one. While the Girl Scout Promise includes the word God, according to the Girl Scouts' website, "The word 'God' can be interpreted in a number of ways, depending on one's spiritual beliefs. When reciting the Girl Scout Promise, it is okay to replace the word 'God' with whatever word your spiritual beliefs dictate" (Girl Scouts of the USA, 2004c).

While the most visible program run by the Girl Scouts is the annual cookie sale fundraiser (love those Thin Mints!), other programs are offered that help girls to develop leadership; financial literacy; and math, science, and technology skills. Girl Scout activities also include health, fitness, and sports; environmental education; the arts; and programs that promote global awareness. Programs are designed to help girls

- develop their full individual potential
- relate to others with increasing understanding, skill, and respect
- develop values to guide their actions and provide the foundation for sound decision making
- contribute to the improvement of society through their abilities, leadership skills, and cooperation with others (Girl Scouts of the USA, 2004b)

Camp Fire Girls of America

The Camp Fire Girls of America was created in the United States just after the founding of the Boy Scouts. From its beginnings, it was intended to provide for girls what the Boy Scouts provided for boys. It was founded by many of the same people who played a prominent role in developing Boy Scouting in the United States.

The organization was founded in 1910 by Luther Gulick, MD, and his wife, Charlotte, as the first nonsectarian organization for girls in the United States. Dr. Gulick was also a leader in the YMCA movement. His wife, Charlotte Vetter Gulick developed a girls' summer camp in Maine, based on Indian lore and ceremonies influenced by Ernest Thomas Seton. The camp was called "WoHeLo," the first two letters of the words work, health, and love.

Dr. Gulick chose the name "Camp Fire" for the new organization because camp fires were the origin of the first communities and domestic life. He felt that once people learned to make and control fire, they could develop and nurture a sense of community (Camp Fire USA, 2004b).

Camp Fire USA Today

Beginning in 1975, Camp Fire Girls became coeducational. By 2001, 46% of its members were boys and the organization changed its name from Camp Fire Girls to Camp Fire USA. The organization currently serves 735,000 children and youth annually. Youth meet regularly in small groups and participate in a variety of activities. Club members have the opportunity to earn recognition items as they complete special projects.

Camp Fire USA has five core programs areas: small-group clubs and mentoring opportunities, leadership development, camping and environmental education, childcare, and self-reliance and service-learning classes. While Camp Fire develops national programs for local councils to use, Camp Fire's relative small size and autonomous council structure allow for custom programs to be developed for each local community.

Camp Fire USA sees itself as differing in several fundamental ways from scouting programs. For example, Camp Fire is coeducational, has an autonomous council structure that allows for more custom programs for the local communities, and is more inclusive, welcoming youth and adults regardless of race, religion, socioeconomic status, disability, sexual orientation, or other aspect of diversity. Camp Fire organizers also see the organization as more group- and development-oriented than other youth-serving organizations, which they view as more activity-based (Camp Fire USA, 2004a).

In 2001, Camp Fire adopted the theme "Today's kids. Tomorrow's leaders." and debuted small-group programs designed to build social skills and academic competencies for children in grades K–5. In 2002, Camp Fire launched the Community Family Club (CFC) program. CFC is a small group model that offers coeducational youth development programs for parents and children. The model is designed to increase opportunities for parents and other caring community adults to volunteer in activities that allow them to interact positively with children and teens. The goal of the program is to include at least one adult family member or a supporting adult from the community with every child who attends. The CFC offers parents a unique opportunity to find a community support group for raising their children and provides for positive family interaction, built around experiences and activities that are structured, educational, and fun (Camp Fire USA, 2004c).

YWCA

The YWCA began as a movement; its name came later. The movement began in England in 1855, and then in the United States in 1858. In each country, a small group of women were drawn together to make life better for other women. They sensed the anxiety of young women who came to cities from a supportive home base in rural areas in search of work so they could become self-supporting. Leaders of the movement recognized the unsanitary conditions, long work hours, lack of rest periods, and poor ventilation in the factory workplace. Opportunities for any type of recreation for these children were limited (YWCA, 2004c).

The first association in New York City provided a boarding house for young girls as early as 1860, and in Boston in 1868 a residence was opened for students and young workers under age 25. On college campuses in the late 1800s, young women needed meeting rooms where students could exchange ideas, conduct Bible classes, and hold parties.

Boston was the first to use YWCA as the name for its association in 1859. The first student association began its work in 1873 at Illinois State Normal University (now Illinois State University). YWCAs quickly sprang up on other college campuses and other communities. By 1875 there were 28 YWCAs and by 1890 the total student associations reached 106. As the number of associations increased, the need for centralization to share information on issues and program, and to handle reports, records, and other aspects of administration, also increased. As a result, in 1907 the National Board of the YWCA of the USA was incorporated in the state of New York (YWCA, 2004c).

The YWCA Today

Elimination of racism and economic empowerment of women and girls are the hallmark programs of the YWCA. While the individual programs found at various local associations take different approaches to these two issues according to the specific situation of the communities they serve, the goals remain the same. Local associations also address other issues, such as women's health and prevention of violence based on needs identified locally (YWCA, 2004c).

Currently, the YWCA serves approximately two million women, girls, and their families in the United States and 25 million women worldwide. The YWCA has more than 300 associations throughout the United States. The World YWCA works in more than 100 other countries. In the United States, the YWCA movement is

- the largest provider of shelter services for women and their families in the country
- a leader in violence prevention, offering programs and services to more than 700,000 women and children annually
- the country's largest nonprofit provider of child care services, with 750,000 children participating in child care and after-school programs annually
- a comprehensive employment training and placement services agency, enrolling some 100,000 women annually
- a leader in sports and physical fitness programs for women and girls
- a trusted source for breast cancer referrals, screenings, and education services
- a pioneer in the fight for social justice (YWCA, 2004c)

Girls Inc.

The Girls Inc. movement started in New England during the Industrial Revolution in response to the needs of working-class young women who had migrated from rural communities in search of newly available job opportunities in textile mills and factories (Girls Inc., 2004a). The oldest Girls Inc. affiliate, formed in 1864 in Waterbury, Connecticut, provided programs not only for young working women but also for younger daughters of mill families who had no place to gather beyond the city streets.

During the Depression, Dora Dodge, executive director of the Worcester affiliate, published an article in a national magazine that pointed out the growing needs of girls in the congested areas of American cities. As a result, a number of people responded with concerns about the problems of girls in their own communities. Dodge invited other directors of similar organizations in Pittsfield and Springfield to talk over common problems, to discuss ways of bringing about better programs and facilities, and to create publicity that could strengthen all girls' organizations. For 10 years, these three organizations maintained their informal association. Finally, in 1945, representatives of 19 organizations met in Springfield to form Girls Clubs of America. The fledgling organization had two concerns: to exchange information on programs relevant to girls and to help communities establish new centers (Girls Inc., 2004a)

Programming in the early days was focused on recreation and preparing girls for their future roles as wives and homemakers. Every local organization had courses in cooking, sewing, and knitting; some offered dramatics and swimming. By the 1970s, Girls Inc. began examining its original mission in terms of the realities of a new era. Leaders of the organization felt it was time to move the organization beyond its original role of preparing girls as wives and homemakers, considering the powerful challenges of the civil rights movement, the women's movement, the increase in women entering the workforce, and the adolescent turbulence of the time. With changing women's roles, girls needed to prepare for very different adulthoods. Concerned by the lack of knowledge about girls' issues and the inequity in funding, Girls Inc. took on the responsibility of increasing knowledge among policy makers and government officials about the needs of girls, which in turn contributed to lowering some of the legal barriers to women's full involvement in the workforce and community life. The next step was to create programs that could affect the way thousands of girls and young women make decisions about their careers, their sex lives, and their identities as adult women (Girls Inc., 2004a).

Girls Inc. Today

In many instances, Girls Inc. currently operates through local centers that girls attend after school. In other instances, Girls Inc. partners with schools or other youth-serving organizations and uses their facilities to offer Girls Inc. programs. Programs are designed to help girls develop strategies for leading successful, independent, and complete lives. The organization also undertakes research to identify pressing issues girls face and to advocate for equitable opportunities for girls. The Girls Inc. organizers believe "in a society that still delivers subtle, often unintentional messages that girls are weaker, softer, and not as bright as boys. Girls Inc. helps girls become strong, smart and bold" (Girls Inc., 2004b).

Girls Inc. programs help to foster a girl's self-sufficiency by exposing her to a range of possibilities and helping her avoid obstacles that could stand in the way of success. The organization reaches over 525,000 girls ages 6 to 18 through Girls Inc. membership organizations, neighborhood centers, partner organizations, educational products, and the Girls Inc. website. Sixty-four percent of the girls are either African American or Hispanic, 56% come from families with incomes below $20,000, and 53% come from single-parent families.

Current programs offered by Girls Inc. include the following:

- *Operation SMART* builds girls' skills and interest in science, math, and technology. Hands-on activities give girls the opportunity to explore, ask questions, and solve problems. Components of Operation SMART include Eureka!, GirlsLink, Girls Dig It, and Career Action.
- *Preventing Adolescent Pregnancy* helps girls identify ways and reasons to avoid early pregnancy. The program fosters girls' communication skills, provides basic health education, and encourages girls to plan for the future through four age-appropriate components: Growing Together, Will Power/Won't Power, Taking Care of Business, and Health Bridge. The first two components have been translated into Spanish as Crecer Juntas and Querer/Poder Decir "no."
- *Media Literacy* encourages girls to think critically about media messages and fosters their awareness of the scope and power of the media and its effects on girls and women. Girls gain media literacy skills that enhance their ability to critically examine and advocate for change in entertainment, news, and advertising media.
- *Girls Inc. Project Bold* strengthens girls' abilities to lead safer lives. Girls develop strategies for self-defense (including physical techniques), for seeking out and talking with caring adults about personal violence, and for advocating on violence issues for girls and young women. Age-appropriate components include Kid-Ability! (Kid Jr.), Action for Safety, and Taking Action (Girls Inc., 2004c).

Organizations Designed to Serve Both Boys and Girls

4-H

Character building was considered necessary by people living in rural settings just as it was for urban families. Farm families were worried by their children's increasing attraction to city life. They also were concerned that public school education did not meet the applied learning and agricultural education needs of farm youth (Reck, 1950; Wessel & Wessel, 1982). Therefore, beginning around the early 1900s, 4-H clubs became the major vehicle for organizing the free time activities of rural youth. While youth in smaller communities had some involvement with the Boy Scouts and YMCA, these programs generally failed to attract youth from farm families (Kett, 1977, p. 246).

4-H activities were more likely to involve a philosophy of producing something useful, compared to city youth groups that might attempt a "stimulation of life on a long-dead frontier" (Kett, 1977, p. 246). The movement did not have a single charismatic leader like some of the other youth movements of the time, but a number of different educators at the University and public school levels began in the late 1890s and early 1900s to develop youth clubs focused on learning agricultural skills. "Corn Clubs" began in Illinois and quickly spread to other states to involve boys in contests to determine who could grow the most and highest quality corn. "Canning Clubs" were soon developed for girls, followed by other clubs dealing with aspects of the domestic sciences. Girls also became involved in clubs dealing with agricultural production.

In most cases, young people developed a project around a particular commodity (e.g., seed selection criteria, milk testing, road improvement), or the domestic sciences (e.g., baking, sewing, basketry). Some United States Department of Agriculture (USDA) workers realized that technology and new methods could be introduced more quickly and easily by involving farm children, who would subsequently influence their parents. The Smith-Lever Act of 1914 provided federal funds for the emerging Cooperative Extension Service, which included Extension efforts by Land Grant Universities in cooperation with their respective State and county governments. This system provided an administrative and developmental home for 4-H clubs and activities.

By 1915 there were 4-H clubs in 47 states. Leadership for 4-H clubs was provided by volunteers, often a parent of one of the participants or a local school teacher. During World War I, the energies of 4-H members were devoted to raising food to support the war effort (Wessel & Wessel, 1982). The term 4-H was first used in a federal publication written in 1918.

When Congress created the Cooperative Extension Service at USDA in 1914, it included boys and girls club work. This soon became known as 4-H clubs—Head, Heart, Hands, and Health. The pledge was adopted in 1927. By 1960, more than half of 4-H participants were nonfarm youth.

4-H Pledge

I pledge my head to clearer thinking,
my heart to greater loyalty,
my hands to larger service,
and my health to better living,
for my family, my club, my community,
my country, and my world.

4-H Today

Today, 45% of 4-H participants are from rural areas and towns of up to 10,000 people, 55% are from larger cities and their suburbs, and 30% are from racial and ethnic minorities (National 4-H Headquarters, 2004).

The 4-H program combines the cooperative efforts of nearly seven million youth, 640,000 volunteer leaders, about 3,600 full-time equivalent professional staff, 105 state land-grant universities, state and local governments, the private sector partners, state and local 4-H foundations, the National 4-H Council, and the Cooperative State Research, Education and Extension Service (CSREES) of the U.S. Department of Agriculture. According to the latest figures of participating youth

- 1,634,039 were members of 99,188 clubs
- 2,401,705 were members of 116,530 special interest groups
- 3,835,772 were in 198,382 4-H school enrichment programs
- 59,910 were in 4-H individual study programs
- 23,095 enrolled in 4-H instructional TV programs
- 87,683 were in 6,627 school-age child-care programs
- 398,268 attended 4-H conducted camps

4-H has adopted the positive youth development model in designing programs and training volunteers. Youth participants are involved in a number of project areas, including citizenship and civic education, communications and expressive arts, consumer and family sciences, education and earth sciences, personal development and leadership, plants and animals, and science and technology.

Parks and Recreation Movement

Another approach to working with lower-class and immigrant boys that grew out of the 1880's youth movement was the development of play spaces and recreation programs. In most cases these programs were developed to help remove youth from the dangers and attractions of using the streets as their play space. According to Goldmark, the street is

> …the earliest, latest, and greatest influence in his life. Long before he knew his alphabet it began to educate him, and before he could toddle it was his nursery. Every possible minute from babyhood to early manhood is spent in it. Every day, winter and summer, he is here off and on from early morning till 10 o'clock at night. It gives him a training in which school is merely a repressive interlude. From the quiet of the classroom he hears its voice, and when lessons are over it shouts a welcome at the door. The attractions that it offers ever vary. Now a funeral, now a fire; "craps" on the sidewalk; a stolen ride on one of Death Avenue's freight trains; a raid on a fruit staff; a fight, an accident, a game of "cat"—always fresh incident and excitement, always nerve-racking, kaleidoscopic confusing. (1914, p. 11)

Nasaw had this to say about the danger of the streets:

> While the children played, policemen walked their beats, prostitutes solicited "johns," peddlers shouted their wares, delivery wagons squeezed down the block to neighborhood shops, and men and women clustered in small groups on the corners, in front of the shops, at the threshold of the saloons, and on their front stoops. (1985, p. 20)

The allure of street life and the lack of suitable places for children to play prompted settlement house workers and reformers

> to campaign in the newspapers, magazines, city halls, and legislative lobbies for parks, playgrounds, and after-school programs. The reformers were, no doubt, hoping to use such supervised play programs as vehicles for socialization and Americanization, but they were also genuinely concerned for the future of children who had no place but the street to play. (Nasaw, 1985, p. 22)

Adults present on the streets and looking out tenement windows could protect children from predators or dangerous situations, but they could not protect children from the many negative influences of street life. Therefore, the reformers envisioned the creation of play spaces that had adult leaders who could provide leadership and guidance. They saw the importance of getting playgrounds funded by municipal government and making the control of play a state responsibility. City governments were targeted as the major source of funding (Cavello, 1976).

Reformers saw the following three specific benefits of play in an urban-industrial society:

- providing opportunities to recapitulate the necessary stages of development, as laid out by Hall (1904)
- developing moral ideals and social interactions necessary for modern economic and political life, including the reduction of individualism and development of an orientation toward group, means-ends activities. The team was seen as the primary vehicle for immigrant acculturation and as substitute for the lack of authority of the traditional socializing agencies: family, church, schools. (Cavello, 1976, 518–519)
- encouraging physical activity and fitness and moral and social development.

Recapitulation theory. Interest in developing play opportunities for children in part grew out of an interest in recapitulation theory put forth by G. Stanley Hall. Henry Curtis, one of the founders of the Playground Association of America, completed his doctoral dissertation under Hall at Clark University in 1898. In his 1915 book, *Education Through Play*, Curtis stated play was a production of recapitulation and that almost every play-form consisted of the same physical activities that had enabled primitive men and women to survive a hostile milieu (e.g., running, chasing, hurling objects at targets). Thus, play, while fun, was an instinctual act necessary for the healthy development of the child (Cavello, 1976, p. 510).

Another view expressed by Joseph Lee (1916), who served as the President of the Playground Association for 27 years, was the necessity of prolonging childhood for children to go through all of the necessary stages of development. These stages, according to Lee, included the following:

- *Babyhood* (birth to age 3): manipulation of objects and reaching out (bonding) to mother
- *Dramatic* (up to age 6): a period of imitative play, belonging, and social solidarity

- *Big Injun* (up to age 11): self-assertive period of individualism, including rampaging and anarchistic impulses, adventure, curiosity, egoistic activity
- *Age of Loyalty* (up to about age 20): period of adolescence, desire for social cooperation, sexual urges, and moving away from parental influence, which in turn leads to bonding with peers in organized group settings, referred to as a "belonging instinct." This instinct could lead to membership in gangs as well as teams, which is seen as the modern counterpart of the tribe.

Development of group loyalties. The last stage advocated by Lee was of particular interest to play advocates. Through recreation activities, efforts were made to direct youth away from loyalty to gangs and encourage loyalty to a sport team (Cavello, 1976, p. 515). The group was seen as a way to subordinate individualism in favor of group efforts, which in turn would help participants to acculturate to the collectivist demands of work settings created by industrialization (Cavello, p. 2). The team experience could also help balance what they called "the feminine" (i.e., passive, domestic, emotional, intuitive, and self-sacrificing) with "the masculine" (i.e., aggressive, worldly, rational, empirically oriented, and self-interested) to create the ideal team player (Cavello, p. 9). The group was also a way to further democratic ideals through integration and acceptance of others across ethnic lines.

Forming groups (e.g., gangs, clubs) was seen as part of the "gang instinct," a necessary stage in the recapitulation of the history of the race, and a result of social Darwinism (i.e., the survival of the fittest). Thus, according to Gulick

> this tendency to sympathize, cooperate, and hang together would form a large factor in survival in times of famine, since the group would always be able to rob and kill the individual, and protect their respective families from external harm. Those possessed of these social feelings would be better fitted to survive than those who were purely selfish, and so, gradually, the egoistic man would be eliminated from the race…Through the steady elimination of the more egoistic, and the survival of the more altruistic, the children would inherit social capacity, and be more and more cooperative in their tendencies and actions. (1911, p. 87)

Gulick also saw the gang as a masculine social unit—the modern counterpart of the tribe:

> It is the germ out of which the club, the society, the corporation, every effective organization develops. The instinct is the chief formative element in the character of most boys, because the opinion of the gang is for them the strongest public opinion that exists. (Gulick, 1911, p. 89)

The team experience was also thought of as creating a balance between independence and dependence:

> To an extent, peer-group direction was designed as a substitute for family supervision, which play organizers thought an inept agency of discipline and social control. Advocates of play generally saw the plight of the urban ghetto youth in the darkest terms: "He ran wild in the streets which his overworked ignorant, or negligent parents sat in dark tenements unaware of his activities. For this reason play advocates perceived the peer group as a community-controlled institution providing adolescents with values and skills that were not being transmitted by the urban, especially ethnic family." (Cavello, 1976, p. 7)

Thus, peer interactions were to be managed by adult playground directors. As a result, a cadre of "professional playground leaders" was trained to organize and manage activities. Courses were offered at a number of universities, which emphasized child development and included the social and psychological sciences. A civil service test was devised and cities were encouraged to hire only play directors who passed the test (Cavello, 1976, pp. 41–42).

By 1908, over 200 cities had playgrounds, with two thirds supported by public funds. By 1917, 481 cities operated 3,940 playgrounds (Cavello, 1976, p. 45).

Fitness and social development. With the passage of child labor laws and mandatory extended school attendance, the amount of available idle time for children also increased. Work, if undertaken, did not promote physical fitness, as had often been the case in rural, agrarian settings. For young children, there were few places to play beyond the crowded tenement houses they lived in or the neighboring streets. For older children, reformers were concerned about exposure to dance halls, pool rooms, gambling, street life, alcohol, and the vagaries of adult free-time involvements, which impinged on the opportunities for social and moral development. Play advocates felt that play

> ...was a vital factor in the development of the moral faculty because it was the agency through which motor coordinations were established, perceptions sharpened, and social habits

> formed, and all these were related to will functioning. To avoid a fatigued will; that is, one susceptible to the numerous temptations inherent in city life, one had to avoid a fatigued or inadequate musculature. (Cavello, 1976, p. 517)

Reformers also expressed concern that because of declining physical fitness, fewer individuals qualified for military service. A perceived increase in nervous disorders, which they felt was related to the congestion and pace of city life, might be overcome through participation in play (Curtis, 1917).

In 1885, the first children's designated sandlot was created in Boston. The space consisted of a pile of sand surrounded by boards to demark the area. A number of efforts to promote children's play quickly followed. On April 12, 1906, the Playground Association of America (changed to the Playground and Recreation Association of America [PRAA] in 1910) was organized through the efforts of Luther Gulick (president) and Henry Curtis (secretary and treasurer), Jane Addams (vice-president), Theodore Roosevelt (honorary president), and Jacob Riis (honorary vice-president). Joseph Lee, a Boston philanthropist and play advocate, took over as president in 1909 and served for 27 years. (Lee was a member of an anti-immigration movement, but the organizers felt that he was the right person to lead the PRAA because Lee felt strongly about providing acculturation and recreation opportunities for immigrants once they were in the country). PRAA was the forerunner of today's National Recreation and Park Association (NRPA).

In 1917, Curtis summed up the five components of the play movement as follows:

1. provision of places for play where children can go during leisure time, be off the streets and away from the evil influences which they might encounter, and enable contact with trained adults

2. promotion of opportunities for play in schools, given play's critical role in development

3. development of outdoor play spaces for preschool children

4. development of public recreation opportunities

5. promotion of the rebirth of the spirit of play, balance between work and play, shortening of the workday, inclusion of vacations, and an increase in attendance at cultural events

Addams argued strongly for the necessity of public recreation opportunities for children and youth. She saw the value of parks and recreation amenities in helping to reduce delinquency and teaching citizenship.

> The fifteen Small Parks in Chicago, equipped with clubrooms, poolrooms, drawing-rooms, refectories, reading-rooms, gymnasiums, swimming-pools, and much other social paraphernalia, are, we believe, centers in which a higher type of citizenship is being nursed. Certainly the number of arrests among juvenile delinquents falls off surprisingly in a neighborhood where such a park has been established—a negative measure, possibly, but one which cannot be disregarded. As the temple of the Greeks inspired the youth's patriotism, and as the city walls conserved but at the same time limited his imagination, so, we hope, these centers of public recreation, simply because they stand for high comradeship and intercourse, will inspire American youth to a sense of political obligation, while at the same time they teach him that the kingdom of the mind is without boundary and that he may find patriotic relationship with the youth of all nations. (Addams, 1912, p. 619)

The approach taken by the Playground Association of America was summed up by their purpose statement, published in 1910:

> Dependence is reduced by giving men more for which to live. Delinquency is reduced by providing a wholesome outlet for youthful energy. Industrial efficiency is increased by giving individuals a play life which will develop greater resourcefulness and adaptability. Good citizenship is promoted by forming habits of cooperation in play. People who play together find it easier to live together and are more loyal as well as more efficient citizens. Democracy rests on the most firm basis when a community has formed the habit of playing together. (p. 73)

Parks and Recreation Today

Today parks and recreation departments (PARDs) can be found in all major cities and the vast majority of smaller communities in the United States. Depending on the community, PARDs operate parks, community centers that house programs for young children to older adults, playgrounds, swimming pools, skateboard parks, and special event facilities (e.g., amphitheaters). In many communities PARDs have more facilities and operate more programs than any other organization. Their funding comes from city, county, or sometimes regional sources. On occasion, departments have been able to secure grant funds to operate special programs.

PARDs have continued their historic mission to provide open space for play and recreation. Community centers have provided a focal point for neighborhood activities and opportunities for young people to engage in a range of out-of-school time involvements. In many inner-city neighborhoods, community centers may be the only safe place for young people to participate after school, at night, on the weekend, and during the summer.

Many PARDs provide supports, opportunities, programs, and services (SOPS) that make a meaningful contribution to the lives of young people. A number are using the Search Institute's (2003) 40 developmental assets model as the basis for program conceptualization and design. In some instances, communities have realized that not all young people who could benefit by program involvement attend community center programs. Thus, these departments have created outreach or Roving Leader programs to enable contact with nonparticipants and to encourage their participation in community center activities. A number of cities have established comprehensive approaches to conceptualizing and developing youth programs. For example, in Phoenix, the PARD has a unit of staff who work to develop model programs that can be used throughout the community and to establish partnerships with other city and state agencies to offer needed SOPS in a number of areas that might not normally be associated with a PARD. Consider the following:

- The department sponsors a curfew diversion program in collaboration with Maricopa County Juvenile Court, Phoenix Police, and New Choices of America. Instead of taking youth to a local precinct, police take them directly to the nearest community center involved in the program. Police aides then process the paperwork while recreation staff provide supervision and recreational activities until parents pick up the detainee. The program is reported to have resulted in a 50% reduction in curfew violations.

- The city council approved an increase of 25¢ per round of golf played at the city's five courses to assist in developing additional programs for youth. Funds are used for a recreation internship program that places former interns into part-time positions throughout the department. The interns participate in a 12-week work experience and are required to complete 30 hours of education-related workshops and 90 hours of field experience.

- The department was the national leader in developing an X-Tattoo Program. In cooperation with River of Dreams, a nonprofit organization, and member of the Arizona Society of Plastic and Reconstructive Services, the program provides laser removal of visible gang tattoos for at-risk youth and adults.

> The program seeks to provide participants access to productive and nonviolent futures by removing tattooed gang insignia. (Witt & Crompton, 2002)

Other communities also offer innovative programs, including Austin PARD's award-winning Totally Cool, Totally Art (an experiential art program), Chattanooga's Project Choices (a youth leadership program), San Antonio's After-School Challenge (an after-school program in cooperation with local school districts), and Arlington County's Activities in Motion (a reward program to encourage teen participation).

Summary/Closing Thoughts

Many of the issues surrounding the development of youth services in the late 1800s and early 1900s still exist today. As modern child-saving agencies and professions have developed, they have intensified their foci on treating children and families as problems, abandoning social action, and letting go of social and economic understandings of the causes of children's problems (Macleod, 1983). We are still debating whether the main focus of our attention should be on intervention programs for youth who are considered at-risk of undertaking negative behaviors or development of the potential of all youth.

We also still wrestle with the degree of protection we should afford young people and the values that should form the foundation for youth-serving programs. In many cases, the child-saving reforms of 100-plus years ago were there to preserve childhood and to promote child welfare, even though others saw it as a form of social control (e.g., preserve and promote middle-class values and Americanize immigrants). Adults and the middle class still feel threatened by immigrants, people with different value systems than their own, and those growing up in different circumstances than they did (Levine & Levine, 1970). Consequently, some youth-serving organizations still play a significant role in separating young people by class, neighborhood, and race, when in fact these organizations could be key to promoting intergroup and community understanding and tolerance.

We also are still debating the degree of professionalization necessary to deal with the needs of youth. Thus, current statements about the need to credential and otherwise authenticate youth workers reflect the same issues and concerns of over 100 years ago. For example, while speaking about the developmental period of youth services, Sommerville (1982) observed

> For the first time in history, the child's image became a matter of professional concern. Those who worked with wayward or neglected children had to keep them before the public's atten-

> tion. Only thus could they guarantee the funding needed to continue their work and their jobs. Naturally, they wanted to create sympathy for these children. This would ensure that the public's help was given in a good spirit and would tend to raise their status as well. But they could not give the impression that children were too noble, for fear that their job would seem too easy. Above all, they could not claim to be solving the problem, for then there would be a question whether they could be needed much longer. Their agencies would be threatened with closure and their staff with dismissal. On the other hand, if they could not claim some success, people would wonder if all their efforts had been wasted.

Thus, rather than claim that efforts to work with youth were being successful, professionals could claim that the problem of juvenile misbehavior was growing. In others words, despite some success, the public would need to make an even greater commitment to efforts to work with young people. Thus, permanent organizations and bureaucracies could be created and sustained. Youth-serving agencies encouraged the message that children were a growing problem, whether this conclusion was justified or not. However justified, the rising figures on juvenile delinquency became a major concern at the turn of the century and a variety of youth-serving organizations and institutional responses emerged.

The news that the problem was increasing was at variance with the image of childhood innocence, which was so prevalent. Perhaps many people keep both of these conceptions in their heads—that children were the closest thing to human perfection but that many were sadly corrupted. Thus, it was that the child experts themselves were often responsible for growing suspicion (Sommerville, 1982, p. 203).

References

Addams, J. (1912, March). Recreation as a public function in urban communities. *American Journal of Sociology, 17*(5), 615–619.
Baden-Powell, R. S. S. (1899) *Aids to Scouting for NCOs and men.* Aldershot, England: Gale and Polden.
Baden-Powell, R. S. S. (1908). *Scouting for boys.* London, England: Horace Cox.
Boys and Girls Clubs of America. (2004a). *About our programs*. Retrieved September 9, 2004, from http://www.bgca.org/programs
Boys and Girls Clubs of America. (2004b). *Lessons of hope: Time-tested principles of the Boys & Girls Club movement*. Retrieved September 5, 2004, from http://www.bgca.org/whoweare/timetested.asp
BoyScouts.com. (1999). *Boy Scout history*. Retrieved September 9, 2004, from http://www.boyscouts.com/history.htm
Boy Scouts of America National Council. (2004a). *Boy Scouts of America: National Council.* Retrieved March 31, 2004, from http://www.scouting.org
Boy Scouts of America National Council. (2004b). *Chartered organizations and the Boy Scouts of America*. Retrieved September 9, 2004, from http://www.scouting.org/factsheets/02-507.html
Boy Scouts of America National Council. (2004c). *Fact sheets.* Retrieved September 9, 2004, from http://www.scouting.org/nav/enter.jsp?s=mc&c=fs
Camp Fire USA. (2004a). *All about us: Frequently asked questions*. Retrieved September 9, 2004, from http://www.campfire.org/all_about_us/faqs.asp
Camp Fire USA. (2004b). *All about us: History.* Retrieved April 15, 2004, http://www.campfire.org/all_about_us/history.asp
Camp Fire USA. (2004c). *Campfire USA*. Retrieved September 9, 2004, from http://www.campfire.org
Cavello, D. (1976). Social reform and the movement to organize children's play during the progressive era. *History of Childhood Quarterly*, *3*(4), 509–522.
Curtis, H. (1915). *Education through play*. New York, NY: MacMillan.
Curtis, H. S. (1917). *The play movement and its significance.* New York, NY: Macmillan.
Forbush, W. B. (1913) *The boy problem*. Boston, MA: Pilgrim Press.
Girl Scouts of the USA. (2004a). *Girl Scout history.* Retrieved April 15, 2004, from http://www.girlscouts.org/about/history.html
Girl Scouts of the USA. (2004b). *Girl Scout program*. Retrieved September 9, 2004, from http://www.girlscouts.org/program

Girl Scouts of the USA. (2004c). *Girl Scouts promise and law.* Retrieved April 15, 2004, from http://www.girlscouts.org/program/promiselaw.html
Girls, Inc. (2004a). *Learn about us*. Retrieved September 9, 2004, from http://www.girlsinc.org/ic/page.php?id=1
Girls, Inc. (2004b). *Our history: From Isabel C. Stewart, National Executive Director, 1993–2000*. Retrieved September 9, 2004, from http://www.girlsinc.org/ic/page.php?id=1.1.5
Girls, Inc. (2004c). *Programs.* Retrieved September 9, 2004, from http://www/girlsinc.org/ic/page.php?id=1.2
Goldmark P. D. (1914). *West Side studies*. New York, NY: Survey Associates.
Gulick, L. (1911, July). Games and gangs. *Lippincott's Monthly Magazine, 88,* 87–89.
Hall, G. S. (1904). *Adolescence: Its psychology and its relations to physiology, anthropology, sociology, sex, crime, religion, and education* (2 vols.). New York, NY: Appleton.
Kett, J. F. (1977). *Rites of passage: Adolescence in America 1790 to the present*. New York, NY: Basic Books.
Lee, J. (1916). *Play in education*. New York, NY: McMillan Co.
Levine, M. and Levine, A. (1970). *Social history of the helping services: Clinic, court, school, and community*. New York, NY: Appleton Century Croft.
Macleod, D. I. (1983). *Building character in the American boy: The Boy Scouts, YMCA, and their forerunners, 1870–1920*. Madison, WI: The University of Wisconsin Press.
Nasaw, D. (1985), *Children of the city*. Garden City, NY: Anchor Press.
National 4-H Headquarters. (2004). *4-H history.* Retrieved April 15, 2004, from http://www.national4-hheadquarters.gov/about/4h_history.htm
Playground Association of America. (1910). Purpose. *Playground, 4*, 73.
Price, T. H. (1918). Girl Scouts. *Outlook, 118*, 367.
Reck, F. M. (1950). *The 4-H story: A history of 4-H club work*. Chicago, IL: National Committee on Boys and Girls Club Work.
Robinson, E. M. (1902). Age grouping of younger association members. *Association Boys*, *1,* 35
Rosenthal, M. (1986). *The character factory: Baden-Powell and the origins of the Boy Scouts*. New York, NY: Pantheon Books.
Search Institute. (2003). *40 developmental assets.* Retrieved November 15, 2003, from http://www.search-institute.org/assets/forty.html
Sommerville, C. J. (1982). *The rise and fall of childhood.* Volume 140, Sage Library of Social Research. Beverly Hills, CA: Sage Publications.
YMCA (2004a). *A brief history of the YMCA movement.* Retrieved March 31, 2004, from http://www.ymca.net/about/cont/history.htm
YMCA. (2004b) *Did you know?* Retrieved September 9, 2004, from http://www.ymca.net/about/cont/didyouknow.htm

YWCA. (2004c). Retrieved September 9, 2004, from http://www.ywca.org

Wessel T. and Wessel, M. (1982). *4-H, an American idea, 1900–1980: A history of 4-H.* Chevy Chase, MD: National 4-H Council.

Witt, P. A. and Crompton, J. L. (2002). *Best practices in youth development in public park and recreation settings.* Asburn, VA: National Recreation and Park Association.

Section II

Developing Youth's Potential

The foundational chapters you have just read prepare you to better understand how leisure and recreation contribute to positive youth development. Thus, the five chapters in this section address specific ways to encourage youth development through the medium of recreation.

First, Chapter 6 describes classic theories of positive youth development. These theories are compared and discussed in relation to leisure and recreation. The chapter concludes that there is no one theory that is most useful, and that all of the presented theories are important tools, along with professional knowledge and intuition, to provide SOPS for youth to successfully develop.

Chapter 7 is based on the premise that not all youth grow up in contexts where positive youth development is maximized and certain to occur. Thus, this chapter addresses the question, "How do some youth who live and develop in less than ideal circumstances mature into responsible adolescents and adults, while others succumb to the pressures in their high-risk environments and get into trouble with the police or participate regularly in unhealthy and unproductive behaviors?" The essential concepts in this chapter are risk, resilience, and protective factors.

The theories presented in Chapter 6 and the discussion of resilience and protective factors in Chapter 7 provide the foundation for Chapter 8, which describes more fully how leisure and recreation contribute to youth development and are protective factors against risk. In Chapter 8, we describe how the context of the activity, the activity itself, and the experience while engaging in the activity each independently and interdependently contribute to youth development. The chapter concludes with some essential reasons recreation is important to positive youth development.

Chapter 9 addresses how youth can be guided into developing healthy leisure lifestyles. The premise of the chapter is that it is difficult for many youth to automatically know how to regulate their free time for maximum benefit. Youth need to be educated "for" leisure, "about" leisure, and can be educated "through" leisure. Moreover, leisure education can be considered a protective factor against some risky behaviors because learning how to construct a healthy, self-regulated leisure repertoire guards against boredom and peer pressure. An example of a leisure education program for middle-school youth is described in this chapter.

The last chapter in Section II addresses how to deliberately develop programs that will maximize youth development through leisure. Chapter 10 suggests that intentionally designed programs are necessary for promoting youth development. To intentionally design programs, one needs to have a theory of why the program should work. Thus, this chapter discusses the role of theory and then describes how different types of program outcomes (e.g., proximal, distal, ultimate) can be planned for based on the use of theory. Use of a logic model to diagram the expected outcomes and underlying theory is described. This chapter makes use of a number of examples to explain the concepts presented.

As you read the chapters in this section, we hope that you gain an understanding of the theories behind youth development and how recreation contributes to youth development. We also hope you come away from this section with some specific tools of the trade that will enable you to develop intentional supports, opportunities, programs, and services that will contribute to youth development through leisure and recreation.

Chapter 6

Processes of Positive Development: Classic Theories

Reed W. Larson and Kathrin Walker

The youth had a great time at the Lawndale after-school recreation program. They wrote and produced a play, did other fun activities, and shared a great deal of hilarity. The young adult running the program, Julia Escobar, was skilled at organizing activities. She also had a special knack for making them enjoyable, and she instinctively felt that the smiles and laughter from the youth validated that she was doing things right. But Julia occasionally stopped herself and asked, is having fun enough? Is she making a long-term difference in these youths' lives? Are the youth growing from their experiences? Are they developing?

But what is development—or "positive development"—and how does it occur? The process of human change is not something any of us can readily observe, like we could watch a quilt being woven or a plant growing from a seed. It is an abstract process, unfolding over long periods of time, and partly occurring within the private thoughts and feelings of youth. We only catch glimpses. We are often only aware of development when a youth suddenly surprises us with a display of skill, wisdom, or maturity that we had not expected. For someone like Julia to facilitate development, however, it is helpful for her to have ideas about how it occurs. You need what is often called a "theory of change."

The academic field of human development has drawn on research to formulate theories of how children and adolescents grow. These theories provide concepts for thinking about the *processes* of developmental change: What happens inside youth, or in their interactions with others, that leads to this change? Each also suggests different ways of thinking about the role of program leaders, like Julia, in facilitating these processes. We are going to describe five of the most prominent "classic" theories and theoretical perspectives on human development. Each provides a useful set of ideas about how development takes place and how it can be fostered. For each theory we will present an example from our research that illustrates the applicability of the theory to what happens in youth development programs.

One of the messages of these theories is that young people have a tremendous potential for growth. Humans, especially children and adolescents, are highly motivated to develop. They have natural dispositions to learn and to grow. The enjoyment that Julia was so skilled at bringing out in the youth is related to these dispositions. The human capacity for enjoyment of challenging activities was probably shaped specifically for the purpose of helping us develop (Csikszentmihalyi, 1990). The theories we cover present development as a process in which these dispositions are activated. They describe the natural, positive dynamics of growth in young people. Indeed, the reason people in youth development sometimes add the word "positive" to development is to emphasize the goal of mobilizing these natural processes in youth (Larson, 2000).

Learning Theory: Teaching and Shaping

Many early ideas about human development, however, did not take this positive perspective. They saw development as something that adults do to young people. Adults have knowledge, which they teach to youth. Youth develop by faithfully learning what they are taught. When young people make mistakes, the teacher, parent, or coach steers them back on track. Learning is directed by a knowledgable authority.

The scientific foundation for this model is called *learning theory,* and early researchers who took this approach developed a robust science of how to shape behavior (Fester & Skinner, 1957; Hilgard & Bower, 1966). Much of this research was based on experiments with rats and pigeons, but the basic principals were found to work with humans as well. The key to learning in this model is the "reinforcements" that the teacher or trainer uses to shape behavior. If, in a specific situation, an experimental subject's behavior was followed by a reward, researchers found that the subject was likely to repeat that behavior again. If this connection between behavior and reward occurs over and over, the behavior becomes habituated—it becomes automatic in that situation.

A number of important and consistent findings emerged from this research. First, rewards are much more effective than punishment in shaping behavior. Sometimes punishment works, but other times it has unintended effects. A second finding is that progressive use of reinforcement along a sequence of steps permits the shaping of complex patterns of behavior. In the first step the learner is reinforced for performing one small component of the desired behavior, but through gradual rewards of additional components more complete behavioral sequences can be shaped. Third the teacher or trainer has to be alert that undesired behavior is not getting reinforced. For example, when a youth gets peers to laugh by doing exactly the opposite of what an adult leader wants the youth to do, that youth may be experiencing positive reinforcement for this behavior from peers' laughter.

Early proponents of learning theory, such as B. F. Skinner, saw learning as a mechanistic process that occurs the same across humans and other animals. However, current advocates of *social learning theory,* such as Albert Bandura (1986), recognize that humans are conscious beings, and their conscious awareness of this process is important. For example, the reason punishment is not very effective is that it can make people feel inept—"I can't do anything right"—so they stop trying. Or it can make them angry and resentful, so they start thinking about how unfair the situation is, not about how they can perform the desired behavior. Bandura also showed that some of the most effective reinforcement occurs through modeling and watching others. When youth see someone else being rewarded for a behavior, they may say to themselves, "I'm going to do the same thing so that I can get that reward."

We observed this developmental approach being used by a choral director, Diane, as she taught her show choir a new song. She gathers the youth at the piano and has them start singing. But they are tentative and lifeless. Diane interrupts to ask, "What'd you forget?" One youth offers, "Take a breath?" Diane has something else in mind. Several other youth offer incorrect guesses. Unable to reward someone for the right answer, Diane finally exclaims, "TO ACT!" They go through the song again, this time with more animation and arm movement. Diane praises their improvement. Then she sings a line, "Go tell it on the mountain," and nods to the youth to repeat. Diane continues, "Over the hills and everywhere," and the youth repeat again. Diane has the youth sing the two lines together, and this time youth sway to the music, and Diane praises them again. A few moments later she interrupts and instructs them not to lock their knees, and that to avoid fainting they should stand with knees slightly bent with their feet shoulder's length apart. They continue until Diane calls out two girls who are talking and sternly says their names, then "Hi!" in a sarcastic tone as if to say, "Pay attention!" The girls get back on track, and in the end, all the youth are dancing, clapping, and strolling with arms linked while singing with spirit.

This rehearsal is successful in that the youth were engaged and learning from the instruction. In a short period of time they were singing and expressing themselves much more effectively. They had also gained valuable technical knowledge from Diane, such as how to stand. Learning theory suggests that Diane was successful because she made learning rewarding. She corrected mistakes; but she used praise rather than punishment to influence the youths' behavior. The one exception was her sarcastic reproach of the two girls, which may or may not have helped them pay attention. All and all, the youth appeared to have been reinforced by the satisfaction of pleasing Diane, as well as by the enjoyment they experienced in mastering the song.

Learning theory is useful for youth development because it helps us think about what rewards youth are getting and the influence of these rewards. This approach can be a valuable means for adults to pass on knowledge and to shape youth's behavior. But it also has limits. Regardless of how positive adults are, youth are reliant on them for direction. The noted Brazilian educator, Paulo Freire (1970), argued that learners in this situation are in a passive and dependent role. They do not have ownership of the learning process, which can make them alienated and unmotivated—as happens all too often in schools. Further, they are not learning to learn on their own; they are not learning to be reflective and make decisions for themselves. By just trying to mimic or to produce what Diane wanted, these youth had limited opportunity to develop their creativity and a broad range of other skills for self-direction. Across his career Bandura became more appreciative of the importance of the active role of learners in their own development. But to best understand this active process it is helpful to turn to other theories of human development.

Constructivist Theory: Youth as Producers of Their Own Development

At the same time that Skinner and Bandura were developing their theories, other scholars were developing theories that saw young people not as passive clay to be molded, but as active clay that molded itself. Some of these scholars based their ideas on basic biology, and their theoretical approach is sometimes called the *organismic model* (Lerner, 2002). They observed that organisms creatively adapt to their environment, and that humans are particularly good at this. Humans are able to adapt by actively learning and figuring things out. Learning is as fundamental to our species as eating and breathing (Mayr, 2001; Piaget, 1967). In other words, you do not need to make young people learn, they are highly motivated to do it.

The most influential of these theorists, Jean Piaget, provided extensive observations showing how intelligent, creative, and motivated young people are as learners. Piaget believed that infants start with no knowledge at all; they do not even understand that an object exits when it is out of sight. But they learn through an active process of experimentation and making deductions from what they experience. Thus, by 6 to 8 months most infants figure out that objects continue to exist, even when hidden from view (Piaget, 1936). As this process of experimentation and discovery continues through childhood, they gradually develop a complex understanding of themselves and the world. In adolescence, they develop abstract concepts like density, mass, the self, and how social groups function (Piaget, 1965; Piaget & Inhelder, 1969).

Piaget is sometimes called a *constructivist,* because in his theory children and youth mentally "construct" these concepts through this process of active experimentation and reasoning. He saw humans as highly motivated to organize the experiences they have into concepts and theories of how the world works. One of the implications of Piaget's ideas is that young people learn best on their own or with peers—knowledge that is taught to them lacks the depth of understanding that comes from this process of figuring things out. This implies that perhaps adults should get out of the way!

This was exactly the philosophy of Mr. Baker, one of the adult advisors at a Future Farmers of America (FFA) program that we studied. He believed that youth learn by doing, including learning from their mistakes. During our research, the youth planned a day camp for fourth graders, and the mantra of Mr. Baker and his colleague, Mr. Jensen, was, "It's their day camp." So they turned all the planning over to the youth. The adults provided support, but the youth ran the meetings, generated ideas for activities, and did the grunt work. After an initial idea-generating stage, we observed the youth struggling quite a bit. They spun their wheels, and sometimes locked horns with each other. "They're driving me nuts," one girl said of her peers. But by the end, the youth reported having developed some powerful concepts about how to work on a project like this. These included insights on organizing effort, managing one's emotions, and working as a group (Larson, Hansen & Walker, 2005).

Piaget would say that this type of development is superior because it was derived from active experience. The concepts were not simply taught and mindlessly memorized. Consistent with Piaget's theory, our analysis suggested that the FFA youth's new concepts emerged directly from the challenges they had struggled with in their work (Larson, Hansen & Walker, 2005). Thus, the conflicts they experienced with other group members appeared to lead to fundamental insights about working as a group: that you cannot always have it your way, you need to pay attention to others. One girl reported learning that "everybody's gotta give and everybody's just gotta hold back a little bit." The youth's statements reflect a significant developmental change: a shift from an egocentric way of viewing the group to one that takes into account the perspective of other members and the dynamics of group functioning. The discovery of this change is consistent with Piaget's (1965) thesis that peer-to-peer interactions provide the most fruitful context for development of concepts about group processes and morality.

Constructivist theories, then, help us to think about the powerful natural tendencies of youth to develop and to organize their experiences into understanding. Research using this approach can also help us to think about what level of concepts youth are ready for at different developmental stages. But there are also limits to this theory. The youth in the FFA program struggled in the middle phase of their work. Their motivation fell and some youth stopped coming, so never benefited from the learning experience. It could also be argued that they wasted a lot of time in a state of paralysis, and the day camp was successful in the end only because the adults began to take a more active role in providing structure and direction (Larson, Hansen & Walker, 2005). Research shows that when people lack expertise in a domain, they easily get stuck or flounder in peripheral details (Rogoff, 1998), as happened here. It is possible that giving youth a lot of freedom may be helpful for learning concepts related to working with others. But it is likely to be less effective for learning, say, athletic, artistic, or other technical skills. You might have to wait a long time for them to discover these skills on their own.

So, if a shortcoming of learning theory was that it risked undercutting youth's ownership of the learning process, a risk of this model is that when learning is entirely turned over to youth they may flounder and spin their wheels. Is there a middle ground that allows knowledgeable leaders to help guide youth in an active process of learning? Lev Vygotsky (1962, 1978) and his successors conceived of developmental processes in ways that conceptualize adults and youth as partners.

Collaborative Learning: Guided Participation

A key idea for Vygotsky was that we should stop thinking of development as something that happens inside a young person's mind. While Piaget pictured development as coming from the child, Vygotsky (1962, 1978) saw it as coming from interactions between a child and other people. To understand development, he argued, our focus should not be the solitary individual, but rather on this shared interaction. Yes, children and adolescents gradually internalize what they gain from these interactions, but learning starts with the interactions, not the individual. Development is a collaborative process.

In this theoretical perspective, youth are still active producers of their development—we are not headed back to the mechanistic adult-driven theories of Skinner. But they are active in cooperation with others. In some cases these others are peers at the same level of knowledge and experience. A youth may work with peers to solve a problem and learn. We are going to concentrate on the situation where the other is an adult or an older, more experienced peer—someone in a position to provide guidance. Interestingly, adherents of this theoretical approach now often describe this guidance as taking the form of "scaffolding." Thus, while Piaget saw young people as "constructing" development on their own, this model recognizes that this construction process often benefits from scaffolds. It is important to keep in mind, however, that this is not fixed and rigid scaffolding; it is creatively adapted in response to the learner.

An experienced adult or guide can provide scaffolding for a youth's learning in multiple ways (Rogoff, 1998; Wood, Bruner & Ross, 1976). The guide may direct the youth's attention to important clues or help to simplify a task. The guide may model a behavior for a youth to learn or provide words that help lead the youth to key concepts. The guide may also provide motivational support by offering encouragement, challenging youth to stretch, or steering them away from situations that will create high frustration. This interaction between the learner and guide is a mutual process. It includes the guide making use of cues from the learner to determine what scaffolding (if any) is needed. It also includes youth requesting help from the guide when he or she wants it.

We observed this process of collaborative learning in a media arts program when the youth were starting to film their first videos. Each youth has developed a storyboard and recruited others to be the cameraperson and actors as they direct their piece. Hector is first, and has planned an animated scene in which two actors will quarrel, leaving one in tears. The youth have a lot of energy, but on the first take the filming is chaotic and actors are confused. Janna, the adult leader, steps in and asks Hector to explain the scene. When the cameraperson is confused, she refocuses him to correctly capture the progression of events. She also positions Hector next to the cameraperson so that he can see how the picture will appear in the film. For the second take, Hector is able to better direct the actors and crew on his own. When the next youth have their turns directing their videos, Janna continues to provide occasional input, but it is clear that they have learned from watching Hector and Janna's interactions. They demonstrate progressively greater abilities to think about camera angles, sound, and the development of a story. The youth had internalized the guidance they had received from Janna.

Janna provided multiple forms of scaffolding in this and other interactions with the youth. She sometimes broke a complex problem down into simpler pieces that were easier for youth to solve. Often her scaffolding took the form of posing questions. For example, she would ask, "Do you want her voice to be heard?" If the answer was yes, then, "The mic is not going to pick up from this far away. So what's the solution?" This led the youth to troubleshoot, zooming in and out, moving the camera closer and further, trying to determine what combination of lens angle and distance would optimize the desired visual and audio effects. She also provided motivational scaffolding. As one youth said, "She gives us a little inspiration."

What is notable is that Janna supported the youth's active process of learning *at the same time* that she intervened to keep the filming and the learning process on track. Unlike the show choir conductor, she was not trying to shape the youth, indeed the youth described the process as one of giving them "freedom." Unlike the FFA advisors, she intervened in ways that kept the youth's learning from getting stalled.

Maintaining the right balance of supporting youth ownership and intervention, we have found, is by no means easy (Larson, Hansen & Walker, 2005; Larson, Walker & Pearce, 2005). When do you stand back? When do you provide scaffolding? This balance may also differ according to the situation, the age of youth, and the subject matter. Research suggests that in some domains, like moral development, youth appear to grasp concepts more effectively through interactions with peers, without adults (Rogoff, 1998). Perhaps that is what we observed with the FFA's youth learning about teamwork. But for other domains of learning and development, adult assistance can facilitate youth's learning (Rogoff, 1998). We suspect that some measured degree of scaffolding from adults is helpful for most domains, especially with younger youth.

When we are talking about youth-adult relationships as a vehicle of learning, there is an additional theoretical perspective that it is critical to include. Theories of collaborative learning conceptualize support as mainly an instrumental and cognitive process. But the feelings and emotions that occur in these relationships are also important to the process of human development.

Relationship Theories: Caring Connections as a Base for Development

Humans are needy and emotional creatures. Behind our public faces, we harbor strong drives, longings, and insecurities. It often takes little to make humans—especially children and youth—feel distressed, angry, or crushed. This portrait of the human condition is the starting point for psychoanalysis (Freud, 1953, 1961) and derivative theories, such as attachment theory, object relations theory, and self-psychology (Bowlby, 1969; Kohut & Wolf, 1978; Winnicott, 1975).

These theories see close relationships with caring adults as essential to human development. Starting in infancy, the child who is fortunate has a stable parent figure (or figures) who helps her or him to manage this internal cauldron of strong drives and feelings. The stability these children get from caring relationships helps them to feel secure enough to take on new challenges. The relationship provides a secure base for development (Mahler, Pine & Bergman, 1975). In addition, children develop through the process of experiencing need or distress and being helped to address it. Over the course of many, many cycles of distress followed by patient assistance from parent figures, these youth gradually develop greater self-confidence and greater ability to regulate internal states. These children learn to do on their own what their parent figures have been doing for them. They internalize a "working model" of the caring they received.

Some children, however, do not get this consistent emotional support—or get it only sporadically. Because they cannot count on support, these children are more vulnerable to panic and careening emotions. They do not have a trusted safe base to fall back on. Furthermore, without experiencing the cycles of distress followed by comforting support, they are less likely to develop healthy means to regulate their internal drives and feelings (Benedek, 1959). They are likely to have a less effective working model that helps them to regulate emotions—or they have a dysfunctional model (Magai, 1999). For these youth and even for those who did get this consistent support in childhood, early adolescence can be a time of new emotional challenges and threats to self-esteem. It is often also a time of greater autonomy from parents, which increases the value for adolescents to have this type of caring, safe, and stable relationship outside the family.

Youth development programs are one place where young people form connections with caring adults that serve this function. Mentoring programs, which pair youth with mature adults, are often designed to provide specifically this kind of supportive relationship. Research suggests that a long-term relationship with a mentor can help youth, especially younger adolescents, by providing empathy, acceptance, and help with learning to regulate emotions and threats to self-esteem (Rhodes, 2002). In other types of youth development and recreational programs, adults cannot have this type of close one-on-one relationship with all youth. But they can provide a stable and caring environment that serves some of the same functions. They can cultivate an emotionally safe setting that provides youth the security to take on new challenges and grow (Rhodes, 2004).

The role of program leaders in providing this supportive environment is most apparent when something happens that triggers youth's emotional insecurities. In a girls' basketball team that we studied, the girls became upset and fearful when they learned that one of their members had been briefly taken in by the police for assaulting another youth. Melissa, the co-captain, was a close friend of this girl, but said that she was afraid that the girl would become angry and "beat me up." Melissa reported that rumors were flying and people's fears were getting "cranked up." No one could focus at their next practice.

The coach, Sara, responded by canceling everything else on her schedule so she could deal with this situation. She talked with the assailant's mother and decided that the girl should not be excluded from team practices. Sara, who many described as like a second mother, also made herself available to team members. Melissa had a long talk with her in which she was able to express her fears and get support. This talk, Melissa said, had a "huge" role in helping her get a hold on her fear: "I was like, 'Hello, news flash, there is no reason to be afraid of her.'" When the assailant—her friend—came to the next practice, Melissa walked up to her and gave her a hug, then "I just let her talk to me and spill her guts out and tell me her side of the story." Melissa said it still took days to fully get control of her feelings, to stop "pretending it didn't happen, accept it, and move on." But she described it as a valuable learning experience, "a taste of what real life is going to be like." She reported that the experience, including the support she received from her coach, had helped her "mature as a person."

The coach, Sara, had developed strong trusting relationships with the girls that facilitated their ability to mange and learn about emotions. Over the course of the season the youth praised her patience and commented that "She's really here for us." We were repeatedly impressed by Sara's abilities to create a caring stable environment that minimized the rivalries and strong negative emotions that frequently emerge in competitive activities. Because of this environment, the youth often seemed able to handle potentially threatening situations in very mature ways. They reported learning about their own and others' emotions. They came to recognize emotions as part of human relationships and learned to conceal, express, or "vent" them according to the situation.

The importance of these relationship theories for youth development is in helping us to think about how important relationships can be for young people. Many adherents to these theories believe that a child's core patterns of emotional regulation are laid down in the first five years of life, and one cannot expect relationships in adolescence to easily reshape them. Nonetheless, secure relationships with adults outside the family can make a significant difference in youth's development, including leading to improvements in their relationships with their parents (Rhodes, 2002, 2004).

We are also not suggesting that every program leader has to be as emotion-attuned as Sara. Indeed some researchers have downplayed this emotional dimension of program leaders' relationships with youth. Darling, Hamilton, and Shaver (2003) argued that when adult youth leaders are less emotionally engaged it makes it easier for youth to experiment and find out what works for them. And some older youth report that they have grown by learning to work with an adult whom they do not like (Dworkin, Larson & Hansen, 2003). In many cases providing a stable context for youth to work toward some goal may best address many youth's emotional needs (Darling, Hamilton & Shaver, 2003; Halpren, 2005). But even in this type of matter-of-fact relationship, the adult plays an important, indirect role in creating a psychologically safe environment that facilitates youth to engage in positive development.

We shift now from thinking about a broader level of human relationships. Theories of human development are not solely the providence of the psychologists we have covered thus far. Sociologists also have useful ideas about young people come of age within a wider arena.

Sociological Theories: Learning Norms and Acquiring Social Capital

Sociologists see humans as social creatures. Development for sociologists is a process of coming to take your place within social groups and society. Thus, development includes learning the general rules, meanings, and ways of acting for being an American or a Filipino, for example. It can also include figuring out how to act and think as a member of a given religious faith, a member of a medical profession, or a participant in a specific youth program. Whether the social group is the entire society, a community of some type, or a small group, development takes the form of learning to follow or navigate the "norms" of that group. As part of this process, one also develops a social identity as a member of that group.

These norms and identities are acquired through social interactions. Early sociological theories saw young people as passive learners of these norms, being "socialized" into society (Wrong, 1961). In this case, young people learn from watching others, being reinforced for following norms, and sometimes from being sanctioned for doing something wrong. More recent sociological theorists stress that people are often active in this socialization process (Berger & Luckmann, 1966). Of course, when a young person enters society, many rules, norms, and ways of thinking are already in place. But youth may create new meanings for old norms. Or they make create new norms, as when a recent generation of youth started downloading music from the Internet rather than buying it at a store. As youth come to accept norms, new or old, they also become active in enforcing those norms.

These sociological processes happen within youth programs. While adults may try to set the norms for the program, youth do not automatically follow them. They may modify them, adhere to them selectively, as well as create some of their own norms. Youth also have norms from the world of their peers, their families, and their families' cultures that they bring into a youth program. For example, youth from different cultural backgrounds have different frameworks for how youth and adults relate (Serpell & Hatano, 1997), which can shape their expectations for relationships with adult leaders (Villarreal, Perkins, Borden & Keith, 2003). Bronfenbrenner's (1979) ecological theory of development (which draws heavily on sociology) elucidates how different domains of young people's lives can influence each other.

In an urban arts program, Art-First, we saw a process in which youth were socialized into the world of adult artists. Many of the teachers in this program were practicing artists, and through their teaching they invited the youth into their way of thinking and doing art. One youth, Marco, explained that artists "like looking at things at a deeper perspective," and he described having adopted that way of looking himself, along with a colorful style of dressing. Marco was learning and coming to follow the iconoclastic norms of artists. Other youth mentioned the openness they had discovered in the arts world. Several said that participation in Art-First had "opened me up" or brought "me out of my shell." In fact they were sometimes now impatient with peers at school whom they perceived as having a closed way of thinking. This process of development and change was an active process in which youth acquired insider knowledge about the art world and began to place themselves in it. Through their classes each youth was also developing his or her own artistic style, which started to give them a distinct artistic identity.

Usually the norms youth learn in a program are positive. Youth acquire norms to function effectively within a community, and they develop group norms for mutual respect and responsibility. Youth at Art-First developed skills to function in the art world and learned about viable career paths in the arts. But sometimes youth bring negative norms into a program from elsewhere in their lives, and these can propagate within the program. Researchers found that Swedish youth centers were a context in which the antisocial behavior of some youth was being reinforced and passed on to other youth (Mahoney, Stattin & Magnusson, 2001). Several studies have suggested that teen boys in sports programs get socialized by other youth into alcohol use (Eccles & Barber, 1999). In neither instance is it likely that the adults in these recreational contexts directly supported these negative norms, but the ineffectiveness of the adults in promoting alternative norms may have been a factor. Although adult leaders cannot force positive norms onto a group, they can play a major role in cultivating an organizational culture that supports prosocial behavior (Eccles & Gootman, 2002).

Another useful idea from sociology is that taking one's place in society involves not only learning things but also forming relationships of exchange. To successfully enter society you need not just the competencies stressed by psychologists, but a social network. It is helpful to know people! Connections to people provide information, assistance, and connections to yet other people—what is sometimes called *social capital* (Bordieu, 1985; Coleman, 1988). For older youth, knowing the right people can help them get a job, learn about different college choices, or chose a career.

Urban youth, like those at Art-First, often know few people that provide this type of social capital (Loury, 1977; Wilson, 1987). But the adult leaders were very deliberate about connecting youth with adults who could provide it, through special events and an internship program. Indeed as the youth had ideas about going to college or pursuing arts careers, they drew on adults they had met through the program for advice and connections (Jarrett, Sullivan & Watkins, 2005).

Conclusion: Theories as Tools

It should be clear by now that none of these theories is the "right" one. Rather, each may be appropriate for different youth, situations, and developmental goals. The purpose of developmental theory is to help us to think creatively about how young people develop (Garbarino & Abramowitz, 1992). These theories (and others we have not covered) provide tools for understanding the processes of growth and what our role can be in facilitating these processes. Of course, theory alone is not enough to make you a good practitioner. Your toolbox needs to include the type of knowledge, intuition, and rules of thumb that come only from experience. But theory plays an important role in helping you think about the abstract, hard-to-see processes of change in youth.

A common theme across these theories (except early learning theory) is that development occurs through a process in which youth are active agents of their own growth. They drive development. They are not pigeons or rats who can easily be shaped by others. Rather they think, feel, and react. They pay attention to what the rewards are in a situation and they learn behaviors that help them obtain rewards that they want (Bandura, social learning theory). They actively try to figure things out by experimenting, observing, and drawing conclusions (Piaget, constructivist theory). They willingly enter into partnership with adults who can help guide their learning (Vygotsky, collaborative learning) and who provide a safe environment that allows them to take on challenges (relationship theories). They are also active members of social groups who contribute to the creation and reinforcement of social norms (sociological theories). Human growth is a natural, positive process.

A central message, then, is that development is not something that proceeds one-way from adults to youth. Adults will rarely be successful if they do not think about what youth are thinking, feeling, and relating to others. To unlock youth's natural processes of development, program designers and leaders need to listen and be attentive. They need to think about mobilizing young people's natural dispositions for growth—their eagerness to figure things out, their motivation to participate in relationships and social groups. When someone like Julia Escobar is able to facilitate youth's enjoyment of challenging activities, she goes a long way toward activating young people's potential for development.

Youth practitioners also need to think about creating a fit between what happens in the program and young people's developmental levels and needs (Eccles & Gootman, 2002). For example, some youth—particular younger ones—may have greater need for emotional support from adults, whereas other, older youth may place more importance on access to adults who can provide social capital or the type of technical guidance that Janna provides in the media arts program. In optimal situations, skilled practitioners are able to adapt a program to individual youth's motivations and developmental levels. They find a "hook" that motivates the youth, or help shape goals that allow the youth to excel (Larson, Hansen & Walker, 2005; Roberts, Treasure & Kavussanu, 1997).

A second theme, however, is that this active process of development is not easy and automatic. Piaget had a very optimistic view of young people as organisms who are highly motivated and able to grow. But other theories draw our attention to obstacles that can stand in the way of these natural processes. The collaborative learning model recognizes that youth don't have X-ray vision. They are not always able to figure out what they need to learn and how best to learn it. They can easily get off track or have their motivation stalled. Relationship theories describe how strong emotions and insecurities can easily shut down the developmental process. Sociological theories call our attention to the norms, identities, and cultural orientations that youth bring into the program from other parts of their lives, which can be opportunities or obstacles for development.

Knowledge of these obstacles helps us to think about the roles that practitioners can play. Most of the theories suggest ways in which adults can help youth navigate this obstacle course. In collaborative learning, adults are guides who provide scaffolding in the form of clues, breaking down tasks, or supporting motivation. In relationship theories, adults can provide a caring, safe, and stable emotional base that quells youths' insecurity and allows them to explore. In sociological theories, adults might play a role in cultivating norms and helping youth to develop social capital. Across all these theories, adults need to find a balance between providing guidance around obstacles and keeping youth involved as critical actors in their own development. When youth are engaged, experience ownership, and can see an unobstructed path ahead, their energy for positive development is unfurled.

References

Bandura, A. (1986). *The social foundations of thought and action: A social cognitive theory*. Englewood Cliffs, NJ: Prentice Hall.

Benedek, T. (1959). Parenthood as a developmental phase. *Journal of the American Psychoanalytic Association, 7,* 389–417.

Berger, P. and Luckmann, T. (1966). *The social construction of reality*. New York, NY: Anchor.

Bourdieu, P. (1985). The forms of capital. In J. G. Richardson (Ed.), *Handbook of theory and research for the sociology of education* (pp. 241–258). New York, NY: Greenwood

Bowlby, J. (1969). *Attachment.* New York, NY: Basic Books.

Bronfenbrenner, U. (1979). *The ecology of human development.* Cambridge, MA: Harvard University Press.

Coleman, J. S. (1988). Social capital in the creation of human capital. *American Journal of Sociology, 94* (Suppl.), S95–S120.

Csikszentmihalyi, M. (1990). *Flow: The psychology of optimal experience.* New York, NY: Harper & Row.

Darling, N., Hamilton, S. E., and Shaver, K. H. (2003). Relationships outside the family: Unrelated adults. In G. R. Adams and M. D. Berzonsky (Eds.), *Blackwell handbook of adolescence* (pp. 349–370). Maldin, MA: Blackwell Publishing.

Dworkin, J. B., Larson, R., and Hansen, D. (2003). Adolescents' accounts of growth experiences in youth activities. *Journal of Youth and Adolescence, 32*, 17–26.

Eccles, J. S. and Barber, B. L. (1999). Student council, volunteering, basketball, or marching band: What kind of extracurricular involvement matters? *Journal of Adolescent Research, 14*, 10–43.

Eccles, J. and Gootman, J. (2002). *Community programs to promote youth development*. National Research Council Institute of Medicine. Washington, DC: National Academy Press.

Fester, C. and Skinner, B. F. (1957). *Schedules of reinforcement*. New York, NY: Appleton-Century-Crofts.

Freire, P. (1970). *Pedagogy of the oppressed* (M. B. Ramos, Trans.). New York, NY: Continuum.

Freud, S. (1953). *The interpretation of dreams*. London, England: Hogarth Press.

Freud, S. (1961). *Civilization and its discontents.* New York, NY: Norton & Co.

Garbarino, J. A. and Abramowitz, R. H. (1992). The ecology of human development. In J. Garbarino (Ed.), *Children and families in the social environment* (pp. 11–33). New York, NY: Aldine de Gruyter.

Halpren, R. (2005). Instrumental relationships: A potential model for inner-city youth programs. *Journal of Community Psychology, 33*(1), 11–26.

Hilgard, E. and Bower, C. (1966). *Theories of learning.* New York, NY: Appleton-Century.

Jarrett, R. L., Sullivan, P. J., and Watkins, N. D. (2005). Developing social capital through participation in organized youth programs: Qualitatitve insights from three programs. *Journal of Community Psychology, 33*(1), 41–55.

Kohut, H. and Wolf, E. (1978). The disorders of the self and their treatment: An outline. *International Journal of Psycho-Analysis, 59,* 413–424.

Larson, R. (2000). Toward a psychology of positive youth development. *American Psychologist, 55*, 170–183.

Larson, R., Hansen, D., and Walker, K. (2005). Everybody's gotta give: Adolescents' development of initiative and teamwork within a youth program. In J. Mahoney, R. Larson, and J. Eccles (Eds.), *Organized activities as contexts of development: Extracurricular activities, after-school and community programs* (pp. 159–183). Hillsdale, NJ: Lawrence Erlbaum Associates.

Larson, R., Walker, K., and Pearce, N. (2005). Youth-driven and adult-driven youth development programs: Contrasting models of youth-adult relationships. *Journal of Community Psychology, 33*(1), 57–74.

Lerner, R. (2002). *Concepts and theories of human development* (3rd ed.). Mahwah, NJ: Erlbaum.

Loury, G. (1977). A dynamic theory of racial income differences. In P. A. Wallace and A. Le Mund (Eds), *Women, minorities, and employment discrimination* (pp. 153–186). Lexington, MA: Lexington Books.

Magai, C. (1999). Affect, imagery, and attachment: Working models of interpersonal affect and the socialization of emotion. In J. Cassidy and P. R. Shaver (Eds.), *Handbook of attachment: Theory, research, and clinical applications* (pp. 787–800). New York, NY: Guilford.

Mahler, M. S., Pine, F., Bergman, A. (1975). *The psychological birth of the human infant: Symbiosis and individuation.* New York, NY: Basic Books.

Mahoney, J. L., Stattin, H., and Magnusson, D. (2001). Youth recreation centre participation and criminal offending: A 20-year longitudinal study of Swedish boys. *International Journal of Behavioral Development, 25,* 509–520.

Mayr, E. (2001). *What evolution is.* New York, NY: Basic Books.

Piaget, J. (1936). *The origins of intelligence in children.* New York, NY: International Universities Press, Inc.

Piaget, J. (1965). *The moral judgment of the child* (T. A. Brown and C. E. Kaegi, Trans.). Palo Alto, CA: Annual Reviews.

Piaget, J. (1967). *Biology and knowledge*. Chicago, IL: University of Chicago Press.

Piaget, J. and Inhelder, B. (1969). *The growth of logical thinking: From childhood to adolescence*. New York, NY: Basic Books.

Rhodes, J. (2002). *Stand by me: The risks and rewards of mentoring programs*. Cambridge, MA: Harvard Press.

Rhodes, J. E. (2004, Spring). The critical ingredient: Caring youth-staff relationships in after-school settings. *After-school Worlds,* 145–161.

Roberts, G. C., Treasure, D. C., and Kavussanu, M. (1997). Motivation in physical activity contexts: An achievement goal perspective. *Advances in Motivation and Achievement, 10*, 413–447.

Rogoff, B. (1998). Cognition as a collaborative process. In W. Damon, D. Kuhn, and R. Siegler (Eds.), *Handbook of child psychology* (Vol. 2, 5th ed., pp. 679–744). New York, NY: Wiley.

Serpell, R. and Hatano, G. (1997). Education, schooling, and literacy. In J. W. Berry, P. R. Dasen, and T. S. Saraswathi (Eds.), *Handbook of cross-cultural psychology: Vol. 2. Basic processes and human development* (2nd ed., 339–376). Boston, MA: Allyn & Bacon.

Villarreal, F., Perkins, D., Bordon, L., and Keith, J. (Eds). (2003). *Community youth development: Programs, policies, and practices*. Thousand Oaks, CA: Sage.

Vygotsky, L.S. (1962). *Thought and language.* Cambridge, MA: MIT Press.

Vygotsky, L.S. (1978). *Mind and society*. Cambridge, MA: Harvard Press.

Wilson, W. J. (1987). *The truly disadvantaged: The inner city, the underclass, and public policy*. Chicago, IL: University of Chicago Press.

Winnicott, D. W. (1975). *Through pediatrics to psycho-analysis.* New York, NY: Basic Books.

Wood, D., Bruner, J., and Ross, G. (1976). The role of tutoring in problem-solving. *Journal of Child Psychology and Psychiatry, 17*, 89–100.

Wrong, E. H. (1961). The pitfalls of social reductionism. *Personality and Social Systems,* 113–124.

Chapter 7

Resiliency, Protective Processes, Promotion, and Community Youth Development[1]

Daniel F. Perkins and Linda L. Caldwell

In Chapter 1, we identified a shift in the way youth development has been conceptualized—from thinking of youth as problems to be fixed to thinking of them as resources to be nourished and engaged in community life. This line of thinking spawned a great deal of thought and attention about how to prevent problem behaviors, while at the same time thinking about how to promote positive development, a perspective evident in many of the chapters in this book.

One question we have not yet addressed is, "How do some youth who live and develop in less than ideal circumstances mature into responsible adolescents and adults, while others succumb to the pressures in their high-risk environments and get into trouble with the police or participate regularly in unhealthy and unproductive behaviors?" The purpose of this chapter is to examine more closely some important concepts related to understanding how youth are affected by and respond to their everyday life situations. The main concepts important to this chapter are *resiliency*, *protective factors*, *prevention*, and *promotion*. After introducing these concepts, we turn to a discussion of how youth development programs in communities can contribute to prevention and promotion efforts through an overall framework called *community youth development.*

Resiliency

In the last 25 years, service providers and social scientists have increasingly explored the concept of youth resiliency, reducing their focus on vulnerability and maladjustment. Several scholars—Werner and Smith (1992), Rutter (1985), Masten (2001), and Luthar and her colleagues (e.g., Luthar, Cicchetti & Becker, 2000)—have been champions of this approach and have devoted considerable time to studying resiliency. This shift in focus means that although it is still important to conduct programs and research that focus on negative developmental outcomes (e.g., risk behaviors), a critical emphasis now includes (a) understanding how youth adapt successfully to challenging life conditions and adversity *and* (b) providing programs that promote positive development. Recall that this was one of the principles of youth development presented in Chapter 1 (not "either/or" but "and"). The findings of resiliency research have helped make the case for providing programs that focus on positive development rather than only on negative behaviors. Clearly recreation and leisure programs fall more heavily into the positive and promotive category.

Along with the shift in focus to include the positive, researchers and practitioners have increasingly realized that youth and their environments shape each other. People and settings in their environment are not just *acting on* youth, but youth actively shape and influence things in their environment. Therefore, there is reciprocal interaction among elements in a youth's life (e.g., parents, teachers, peers, coaches, religious leaders, neighborhoods). Several chapters in this book are premised on the principle of reciprocal interaction because it is a critical component of understanding youth development, including resiliency.

Definition of Resiliency

Consider Jacinda, who is 15. She was born and raised on a farm in a rural area in Pennsylvania. Her parents make less than $20,000 per year, and she has two younger brothers. The closest town (population 1,300) is five miles away, and she is bused 45 minutes to school. Her parents smoke heavily even though they cannot afford to, and her mother is obese. Her mother really loves her children, but verges on depression and does not exhibit good parenting skills. Often, Jacinda's dad drinks too much and becomes violent toward the family dog, although he has not yet hurt Jacinda or her mother. Lately, her 14-year-old brother has been experimenting with drugs. It is summer and she feels there is absolutely nothing for her to do on the farm except help with the milking at 4:30 every morning and afternoon. Many people would consider Jacinda to be at high risk, in particular because of the many "risk factors" to which she is subjected (e.g., poverty, mother's apathy, parental smoking, and her father's drinking and violence). We will discuss all of these things in more depth, but let us first look at Jacinda resilience despite the presence of these risk factors.

According to Masten (2001) resiliency involves *competence and adaptability in the face of adversity*. In addition, resiliency requires a scholar to assess if the adaptation is "good" or "helpful." To make that assessment, scholars use criteria to assess the youth's behavior and the youth's situation based on specific societal and cultural norms within that context. For example, if Jacinda was resilient, what characteristics would she have drawn from herself and her environment? What markers would we use to assess her competence and adaptiveness in the face of her adversity?

Jacinda demonstrates her resilience in several ways. She has set life goals for herself, which include finishing high school and going on to postsecondary education (e.g., college, a two-year trade school). She has teachers and other caring adults who are supportive and facilitative of her goals. Jacinda also has set a goal that she would not become pregnant at a young age. She has learned how to make her free time meaningful by developing a low-cost hobby (e.g., making sculpture out of old farm material), which helps her cope with daily stresses. She has also learned how to put up with her father's outbursts, by calling a friend or leaving the room.

Each of the things Jacinda has chosen to do appear to be appropriate to her "farm context" and to her age. She might at some point, however, decide that talking with her friend did more harm than good—for example, if her friend was in a similar situation and their conversations started a downward spiral of depression. Or she might realize that getting up and leaving the room when her father had an outburst only made her father more angry when she returned.

While there are many definitions of resiliency, the one we employ here is borrowed from Masten (2001): "Resiliency is defined 'as a class of phenomena characterized by good outcomes in spite of *serious* threats to adaptation or development'" (p. 228).

Resiliency focuses on how people succeed despite challenges in their environments, thus programs that promote resiliency provide skills and supports that will help youth navigate and succeed when subjected to challenging circumstances.

Let us fast forward 10 years and take a look at Jacinda in her mid-20s. We see she has met her goals and in fact exceeded them. She attended veterinary school and has joined a seasoned vet in her practice in rural Pennsylvania, not far from her family. Given the aforementioned definition, we would conclude that Jacinda is resilient; she has achieved "good outcomes in spite of serious threats" to her development.

Resiliency sounds like a wonderful concept, but there are many common myths associated with it. To really understand what resiliency means, let us explore those myths.

Myth 1: All people who survive their childhood and adolescence are resilient. *All* children and youth have to cope with stress and adverse situations in their lives; thus, in some ways all people who survive their childhood and adolescence are resilient. However, not all stress or adverse situations are alike or are of the same magnitude, and some youth are at greater risk for failure than others. Thus, some people display more resiliency than others. Examining individuals who are most at risk or vulnerable is the hallmark of resiliency research. Biological risk factors, contextual risk factors, and stressful life events are what place a person at risk of succumbing to the stress or not succeeding. In sum, resiliency is displayed or detected through an individual's response to serious adversity, whether it is a stressful life event or a situation of continuous stress (e.g., war, death of a parent, abuse, poverty).

Originally, investigators emphasized the association between a single risk variable, such as low IQ or a stressful life event (e.g., loss of parent), and negative developmental outcomes (e.g., alcohol abuse, holding down a job, forming long-term relationships). Now, resiliency researchers have learned from epidemiologists and have shifted from looking at these single variables to models that involve multiple stressors that typically co-occur. For example, the literature suggests that violence (e.g., parental abuse, neighborhood killings) and poverty often co-occur (Werner & Smith, 1992), as happened in Jacinda's case.

Myth 2: Resilient individuals are completely successful in every area of their lives. Resiliency is multidimensional in nature. Thus, one may be resilient in one domain (e.g., school) but not exhibit resiliency in another domain (e.g., work, leisure). For example, Kaufman and colleagues (1994) found that approximately two thirds of children with histories of maltreatment were academically resilient; however, when examining the social competence of these same children, only 21% exhibited resiliency. Luthar, Cicchetti, and Becker (2000) suggested that one might not only exhibit competence in one area and not another but also exhibit incompetence or problem behaviors in other areas.

Jacinda was lucky because she exhibited competence in her academic work and went on to become a vet. But suppose she became a vet because she really preferred being around animals more than people. Perhaps it was even difficult for her to communicate well with the animals' owners. To make matters worse, suppose Jacinda was unable to sustain a mature loving relationship with another person. Should Jacinda be considered resilient? Our opinion is that in her career Jacinda displayed competence and resilience; however, in forming sustained loving relationship Jacinda did not display competence and needed to seek psychological counseling.

Myth 3: Resilience stems from an internal personality trait. Resiliency itself is not a personality trait, although there are personality traits that have been found to promote resiliency (e.g., humor, flexibility). Despite the contribution of these important traits, characteristics of the person's environment seem to be as important for resiliency. For example, Jacinda was in a very stressful economic and emotional situation and she had drive, intelligence.

However, without a teacher who took a vested interest in her over a sustained period of time, it is unlikely she would have fared so well. Perhaps she would have continued on to further education, but the teacher helped direct her attention to veterinary sciences and supported her choices and decisions. Thus it took both personal and environmental factors to create resiliency in Jacinda's resiliency.

The degree of resistance to stress varies over time according to one's circumstances (e.g., Luthar et al., 2000; Masten, 2001; Rutter, 1985). Furthermore, resistance to stress in an individual is relative, not absolute. Indeed, no human is invulnerable or unbreakable, or able to conquer any level of stress. If we fast forward 10 more years in Jacinda's life, we see that she is clinically depressed. Although she got help with her relationship issues, got married, and was happy for about five years, it did not work out because her husband became an alcoholic and she is in the process of a divorce. Even though she had done very well for a while, circumstances in her life in her mid-30s were too much for her to handle. Unfortunately, this circumstance is a common phenomenon and researchers have come to realize that the definition of resilience must acknowledge a history of success while also implying the possibility of succumbing to future stressors (e.g., Masten & Garmezy, 1985; Rutter 1985; Werner & Smith, 1992).

Myth 4: Resiliency is rare. Most children and youth are resilient in the face of adversity. For example, in most studies approximately 70% of children who were living in extremely adverse situations were found to be resilient. These include children and youth who were sexually abused (Wilkes, 2002), were placed in foster care (Festinger, 1984), were in gangs (Vigil, 1990), lived in families where mental illness was present (Beardslee & Podoresfky, 1988; Werner & Smith, 2001), were born to teen mothers (Furstenberg, Cook, Eccles, Elder & Sameroff, 1998), and grew up in poverty (Vaillant, 2002). In a study designed to learn about how resilience lasts over time, Werner and Smith followed nearly 700 at-risk individuals, one-third of which had multiple risk factors, from birth to adulthood and found that the children grew increasingly like their counterparts who did not have risk factors. Moreover, in adulthood (age 32 and again at age 40) only 20% of these children who were high-risk previously (i.e., possessing multiple risk factors) were doing poorly (e.g., chronic financial problems, domestic conflict, violence, substance abuse).

In another study, Romanian children who were reared under severe deprivation in an institution were found to catch up developmentally in terms of physical and cognitive abilities once they were adopted into families (Ames, 1997; Rutter and the English and Romanian Adoptees Study Team, 1998). As noted by Masten, "the capacity for developmental recovery when normative childrearing conditions are restored is amazing" (2001, p. 233). Indeed, Werner and Smith (1992) noted that resiliency research results are evidence of the *self-righting tendencies* that move youth toward normal adult development under all but the most persistent adverse circumstances.

Nevertheless, while resiliency is not rare, it is not guaranteed. That is, a substantial minority (about 30%) of youth do not recover from adversity and cannot be considered resilient. Masten (2001) stated, "Resiliency does not come from rare and special qualities, but from the everyday magic of ordinary, normative human resources in the minds, brains, and bodies of children, in their families and relationships, and in their communities" (p. 9). Those individuals that do bounce back from adversity have connected to parts of their environment that provide support, encouragement, and opportunities that nurture their development.

In Summary: A Model of Resiliency

As we have described, understanding resiliency involves an examination of the link between the person and the demands and challenges of the context, and understanding the factors and processes that will either promote or subvert adaptation. Resilient individuals are well-adapted in spite of serious stressors in their lives. They have the environmental supports to help them cope with these stressors. The balance between a person's own traits that support adaptability, environmental supports, and the level or severity of stress are what are important in detracting from or promoting resiliency. **Figure 7.1** displays a representation of this balance.

There is a time element involved in resiliency as well. That is, resiliency is a process that occurs over time, and the cumulative effect of life events and situations is important. Time is also important because although adversity may exist in a youth's life initially, other challenges or supports might happen over time that either add to or reduces the stress. These challenges and supports include things such as being placed in foster care, moving to a new neighborhood, or having a mentoring relationship. The arrows in Figure 1 represent the multiple interactions among stressors in the environment, environmental supports, and personality traits. Thus to understand or promote resiliency means we cannot focus on a single aspect of a youth's life—a holistic approach must be taken. One must look at the multiple contexts that comprise a youth's world.

There are many implications of this model for youth-service professionals because they offer important services under the "environmental supports" component of the model. Coordination among agencies and services (e.g., parks and recreation departments, YMCAs, 4-H youth development programs, schools, human services agencies) and working with parents are means by which the holistic approach to service provision is achieved. This coordination, coupled with adopting a risk prevention and community youth development perspective, create a context for resiliency. We discuss what youth-service and community-service providers can do to promote resilience in more detail later in this chapter, but next we turn our attention to understanding what constitutes both risk and protective factors in a young person's life.

Risk and Protective Factors and Processes

What factors (e.g., events, situations) and processes (e.g., becoming educated, playing on a summer basketball league) contribute to or thwart an individual becoming resilient? Researchers have broken these factors and processes into two categories: (a) risk factors and processes, and (b) protective factors and processes.

Risk factors and processes are defined as individual or environmental hazards that increase an individual's vulnerability to negative developmental behaviors, events, or outcomes, such as alcohol and drug abuse, early unprotected sexual activity, delinquency and violence, and school failure (e.g., Masten, 2001; Werner & Smith, 1992). Examples of risk factors include poverty, violent neighborhood, parental style characterized by inconsistent discipline and lack of warmth, extreme shyness, and lack of socioemotional control. Jacinda's situation was filled with risk factors and processes. However, it is important to understand that the presence of risk factors and processes does

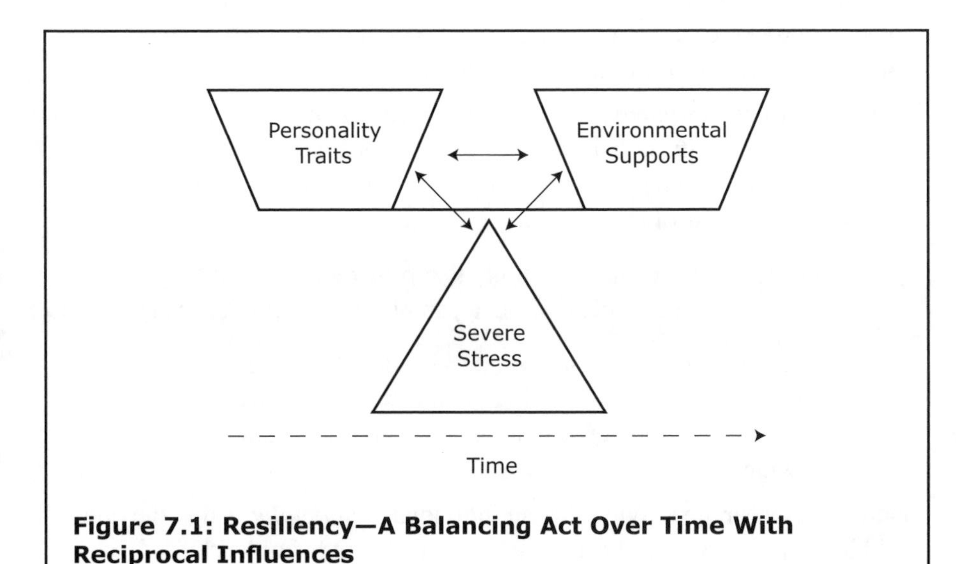

Figure 7.1: Resiliency—A Balancing Act Over Time With Reciprocal Influences

not guarantee that negative outcomes will occur; rather, it simply increases the probability of their occurrence (e.g., Masten, 2001; Werner & Smith, 1992).

The probability of negative outcomes varies as a consequence of the presence of protective factors and processes. Protective factors and processes buffer, modify, or ameliorate an individual's reaction to an adverse situation that, in ordinary circumstances, would lead to maladaptive outcomes (Kumpfer, 1999; Werner & Smith, 1992). Protective processes are incorporated into the multiple levels of adolescents' contexts and enable them to overcome adversity. They are the processes that occur in the "personality characteristics" and "environmental supports" blocks of Figure 1. According to our definition, a protective process is *primarily* evident in combination with a risk factor. Some protective processes and factors do not have a strong effect on resiliency in low-risk populations, because for these individuals resilience is not an issue in the first place. They do, however, contribute to youth development, which we discuss in more detail subsequently. The effect of protective factors and processes is magnified in the presence of risk (Rutter, 1987; Werner & Smith, 1992).

Types of Protective Factors and Processes

What factors and processes in life have been shown to be protective and promote resiliency? There have been a couple notable studies that help to answer this question. In their longitudinal study of a cohort of children from the island of Kauai, Hawaii, Werner and Smith (1992) described three types of protective processes that emerge from analyses of the developmental course of high-risk children from infancy to adulthood:

- *dispositional attributes* of the individual, such as activity level and sociability, at least average intelligence, competence in communication skills (e.g., language, reading), and an internal locus of control

- *affectional ties* within the family that provide emotional supports in times of stress, whether from a parent, sibling, spouse, or mate

- *external support systems*, whether in school, through a youth program, at work, or at church, that reward the individual's competencies and determination, and provide a belief system by which to live

Finally, the researchers found that an individual's *hopefulness* that the odds could be surmounted was a central positive factor in his or her live.

Using the ecological model (Bronfenbrenner, 1979) as her framework, Bogenschneider (1998) concluded there are protective factors and processes in each level of a youth's environment (or ecosystem):

- individual level—well-developed problem-solving skills and intellectual abilities
- familial level—a close relationship with one parent
- peer level—a close friend
- school level—positive school climate
- community level—required helpfulness (e.g., as it occurs when the adolescent is needed to bring in extra income or help manage the home) and a positive relationship with a nonparental adult (e.g., neighbor and teacher)

What protective factors and processes did Jacinda have in her environment? She knew her mother loved her very much, she had at least one good friend she could confide in, she was creative and had a good leisure hobby, and she had strong support and assistance from her teachers. Imagine if none of these existed for Jacinda? Would she have been resilient? Probably not. A question you might be asking now is how many of these protective factors and processes are necessary, and are some better than others? These are excellent questions but there are not good answers yet; more research is needed to better understand how risk and protective factors and processes influence each other.

Protective Processes and Factors for All Youth

In this book, of course, we are interested in promoting the development of all youth, even though we take care to explore youth from a variety of contexts and address a number of characteristics (e.g., race, ethnicity, ability, sexual orientation). Therefore, although we noted earlier that a specific protective factor or process is most often apparent in combination with a specific risk variable (e.g., Jacinda's physical and/or emotional withdrawal from negative situations), some protective processes have universally positive influences on all youth. Thus, some protective processes have a direct effect in enhancing adolescents' positive development regardless of their risk level. So even if a youth is facing little adversity, these protective processes enable him or her to thrive or do even better. In her comprehensive review, Bernard (2004) noted three environmental protective processes, in particular, that are found to significantly promote and foster the positive development of all youth. These universal protective processes include (a) caring relationships with nonparental adults, (b) high expectations, and (c) opportunities for participation, contribution, and recognition. These three protective factors and processes can be exhibited at multiple levels of the youth's context (e.g., family, school, youth programs, neighborhood). The more contexts that provide these processes the more likely it is that the youth is going to succeed. This relationship is just as valid for youth with many risk factors as for those without risk factors.

Caring Relationships With Adults

Since resiliency research began, caring relationships with nonparental adults has been to found to be essential for youth overcoming adversity (Perkins & Borden, 2003; see also Chapter 10). Of course, the role of the parent(s) is critical to the positive development of youth; however, the socially toxic and chaotic environment that surrounds some youth like Jacinda cannot be addressed within families alone. Caring relationships with nonparental adults provide a frame of reference and a model for how one is supposed to act. Nonjudgmental love and mentoring are the characteristics of these caring relationships. Rhodes (2002) found in her analysis of the Big Brothers/Big Sisters program that duration of the relationship is also an important factor to consider. One of the alarming findings from a study by Rhodes (2002) was that relationships between mentor and youth mentee less than six months in length tended to inflict more damage than good on the youth and contribute to a lack of continuity and stability in the youth's life. Moreover, Masten found that these relationships seem to be most needed during times of transition such as the transition into high school, which is exactly when we first were introduced to Jacinda.

Caring relationships with nonparental adults are important for all youth and, according to the report from National Research Council and the Institute of Medicine provide, "an environment of reinforcement, good modeling and constructive feedback for physical, intellectual, psychological [and emotional], and social growth" (Eccles & Gootman, 2002, p. 96). But recreation professionals and others who work with youth must understand that the relationships must be long-term to be effective, *and* that harm can be done if relationships are not of sufficient duration.

High Expectations

High expectations from parents and nonparental adults and within youth's environments (e.g., school, youth programs, and neighborhood) provide a consistent, predictable message and address the sense of safety and structure that all youth require—all of which are important protective factors and processes. For these high expectations to be absorbed by youth, they must be coupled with the warmth and responsiveness found in caring relationships as previously noted. For example, Blum and Mann Rinehart (1998) found that when parents have high expectations of their youth's academic success this lowered youth's level of emotional distress and the likelihood of their using cigarettes or engaging in violent behavior.

Another example is provided by Rutter and colleagues' classic examination of student outcomes in different types of school contexts in some of the most improvised areas of London; this example is described thoroughly in their book *Fifteen Thousand Hours* (Rutter, Maughan, Mortimore, Ouston & Smith, 1979). The researchers found significant differences in students' rates of academic attainment, delinquency, and behavioral disturbance, even after controlling for family risk factors, which they attributed to differences in school context. Teachers in successful schools (in comparison to nonsuccessful schools) emphasized academics, established clear expectations and regulations, encouraged high levels of student participation, and provided alternative resources (e.g., library facilities, vocational work opportunities, art, music, extracurricular activities). Moreover, the National Research Council and Institute of Medicine report on youth programs highlighted the importance of clear rules about acceptable behavior while in the program and monitoring of behavior by staff, even when youth are elsewhere (Eccles & Gootman, 2002). Thus, youth program staff who are communicating with a youth's school to monitor behavior as well as establish a clear message of expectations across settings should have a positive impact on those youth.

Opportunities for Participation, Contribution, and Recognition

Opportunities for participation, contribution, and recognition are critical universal protective processes for youth living in high-risk environments, as well as for youth not facing extreme adversity. As described in Chapters 6 and 7, many developmental benefits are gained through participation in and engagement with one's environment. In terms of protective factors and processes, opportunities for participation, contribution and recognition enable youth to address several of their needs, including the ability to have a sense of belonging, sense of mastery, and sense of generosity and mattering (Brendtro, Brokenleg & Van Bockern, 1990; Eccles & Gootman, 2002). A sense of mattering is created when a youth is efficacious—that is, a youth has an opportunity and feels competent to do things that make a real difference in their social world (Eccles & Gootman, 2002). For example, youth's participation in family activities, school extracurricular activities, youth programs, and other group activities provides a thread of connectedness that addresses youth's need for belonging and recognition. For youth with challenging home lives to be resilient, it is important that they have a place, if not multiple places, where they can go to feel comfortable, to fully engage, and to be recognized for their skills and talents (Werner & Smith, 1992).

Moreover, through these activities and experiences youth are tied to positive social norms (Eccles & Gootman, 2002) that assist them in understanding society's expectations. A sense of mastery is developed through participation in autonomy-granting activities or experiences that are engaging, challenging, and interesting and promote a range of competencies and skills. Chapter 8 will reveal that these experiences, labeled "flow" experiences (Csikszentmihalyi, 1997), involve high levels of goal-directedness, concentration, and intrinsic motivation. Through participation in these experiences youth engage in discovery processes about their skills, talents, and interests because they have opportunities to problem solve, make decisions, and work with others. The power of these activities comes from the "voice" and "choice" that youth are afforded within the school, youth program, and community contexts (see Chapter 13). Indeed, according to Larson (2000), structured voluntary youth activities provide a rich context for flow activities to occur, which ultimately can foster the development of initiative.

Finally, both resiliency research and youth development research have found that opportunities to contribute or to "matter" within one's context are linked with successful outcomes in adolescents (Eccles & Gootman, 2002; Villarruel, Perkins, Borden & Keith, 2003). For example, Werner and Smith (1992) found that resilient youth were often required to look after younger siblings or take over tasks usually done by an adult. They called this phenomenon *required helpfulness*. The key is that these chores are not just to help out around the house, but they are necessary for household (if not human) functioning. By engaging in acts to help others, youth gain a sense of generosity and self-worth, as well as an opportunity to overcome the egocentric thinking so prevalent in adolescence. Youth involved in making contributions are reframing their self-perceptions as well as other adult's perceptions of them from being a problem to be solved and a receiver of services to being a resource and provider of services (Bernard, 2004).

In addition, youth have so few opportunities for recognition, especially youth in risky environments, that youth service providers should structure ways to make sure youth are recognized by their peers and the community for their contributions. Recognition is very powerful and motivating to youth. Providing them with opportunities to contribute is explicitly demonstrating the concept that individuals are *producers of their own development* and shapers of their communities. According to the Carnegie Council on Adolescent Development (1995), one of the most powerful strategies for enriching the lives of youth is to enlist their energies in improving their own homes and communities.

Promotion and Prevention Through Community Youth Development

The results of numerous longitudinal studies and other resiliency studies have provided critical information to the field of youth development. Specifically, by identifying universal protective processes, researchers and practitioners have gained important information for understanding what youth need in terms of opportunities and supports from different levels of the youth's context, including designing and implementing programming for youth development.

Society expects young people will grow up to be adults who are healthy contributing members, as outlined in the vision of a fully functioning adult (see Chapter 1). For youth to become competent, contributing, adult members of society, they need opportunities and support from their communities to develop important personal and social assets (see **Table 7.1**, p. 162). These assets can also be thought of as protective factors and can be grouped into the "five Cs" identified by Lerner and his colleagues:

1. **Competence** in academic, social, emotional, and vocational areas
2. **Confidence** in whom one is becoming (identity)
3. **Connection** to self and others
4. **Character** that comes from positive values, integrity, and strong sense of morals
5. **Caring** and compassion (Lerner, 2002, 2004; Lerner, Fisher & Weinberg, 2000)

However, from a community youth development perspective, there is a sixth C, **Contribution** (Lerner, 2004; Pittman, 2000). By contributing to their families, neighborhoods, and communities, youth are afforded practical opportunities to make use of the other five Cs. These six Cs clarify and provide some guidance to the positive youth development framework.

Table 7.1: Personal and Social Assets That Facilitate Positive Youth Development Aligned With the Six Cs of Positive Youth Development
Adapted From Eccles and Gootman, 2002

Asset Category (Six Cs)	Individual Assets
Physical Development (Competence)	Good health habits Good health risk management skills Knowledge of essential life skills
Intellectual Development (Competence)	Knowledge of essential vocational skills School success Rational habits of mind—critical thinking and reasoning skills In-depth knowledge of more than one culture Good decision-making skills Knowledge of skills needed to navigate through multiple cultural contexts
Psychological/ Emotional Development (Competence, Confidence, Character, Caring/ Compassion)	Good mental health, including positive self-esteem and self-regard Good emotional self-regulation skills Good coping skills Good conflict resolution skills Mastery motivation and positive achievement motivation Confidence in one's personal efficacy Planfulness—planning for the future and future life events Sense of personal autonomy/responsibility for self Optimism coupled with realism Coherent and positive personal and social identity Prosocial and culturally sensitive values Spirituality or a sense of a larger purpose in life Strong moral character A commitment to good use of time
Social Development (Connection, Caring/ Compassion, Contribution)	Connectedness—perceived good relationships and trust with parents, peers, and some other adults Sense of social place/integration—being connected and valued by larger social networks Attachment to prosocial/conventional institutions (e.g., school, church, nonschool youth programs) Ability to navigate in multiple cultural contexts Commitment to civic engagement

More recently, practitioners (Hughes & Curnan, 2000; Pittman, 2000) and researchers (Villarruel, Perkins, Borden & Keith, 2003) have advanced the field of youth development by integrating positive youth development and community development to address the need for a broader, more holistic approach to increasing protective factors and thereby helping to promote resiliency. *Community youth development* is defined as

> ...purposely creating environments that provide constructive, affirmative, and encouraging relationships that are sustained over time with adults and peers, while concurrently providing an array of opportunities that enable youth to build their competencies and become engaged as partners in their own development as well as the development of their communities. (Perkins & Borden, 2003, p. 6)

Park and recreation departments, as well as other youth-serving agencies that create and promote recreation opportunities, are an important part of community youth development.

Community youth development means promoting processes that provide *all* youth with the critical elements needed for successful development and engagement in their communities, regardless of their level of risk. So while resiliency focuses on youth at high risk or in adverse situations, community youth development focuses on what all youth need to thrive and become engaged partners in their own development and the development of their communities.

The community youth development framework involves a two-prong strategy for providing an atmosphere that fosters fully functioning youth. The first and most explicit strategy involves the *promotion* of universal protective processes and the six Cs. These processes and the six Cs address the personal and environmental assets need by youth as outlined in the seminal book by the National Research Council and the Institute of Medicine (Eccles & Gootman, 2002; see Table 7.1).

The second strategy involves an implicit understanding and goal within the community youth development framework that *prevention* of risk behaviors among youth and decreasing of risk factors or processes in their environment are necessary if youth are to thrive. The second strategy is important and necessary; however, it is insufficient without simultaneously addressing the first strategy.

Concluding Remarks

Youth programs, especially recreation programs, have a critical role to play in the promotion of resiliency, creating universal protective factors and processes, the six Cs, and ultimately in the promotion of personal and environmental assets (see Table 7.1). They also have an important role in preventing youth's engagement in risk behaviors and mitigating or eliminating risk factors and processes. As discussed in Chapter 8, leisure and recreation contexts and experiences provide excellent settings for developmental experiences to occur, if programmers and service providers are deliberate in how they go about providing these opportunities and services.

Ironically, however, while the need for structured environments to help guide children's development has been a major focus of public attention, policy, and research over the last decade (Eccles & Gootman, 2002; Roth & Brooks-Gunn, 2003; Tolman & Pittman, 2002), public commitment to supporting youth development tends to weaken as youth grow older and their needs grow more complex. The "developmental imperative" for youth addresses this state of affairs by suggesting that young people need and deserve the following:

1. early and sustained investments *throughout the first two decades of life*
2. supports *throughout their waking hours*
3. investments that help them achieve a *broad range of outcomes* (Tolman & Pittman, 2002, pp. 21–22)

The developmental imperative calls on us to consider the full range of youth's time, particularly time spent out of school, as crucial to ensuring positive youth development.

References

Ames E. W. (1997). *The development of Romanian orphanage children adopted to Canada.* Final report to the National Welfare Grants Program: Human Resource Development Canada. Burnaby, British Columbia, Canada: Simon Fraser University.

Beardslee, W. and Podorefsky, D. (1988). Resilient adolescents whose parent have serious affective and other psychiatric disorders: The importance of self-understanding and relationships. *American Journal of Psychiatry, 145*, 63–69.

Bernard, B. (2004). *Resiliency: What have we learned?* San Francisco, CA: WestEd.

Blum, R. W. and Mann Rinehart, P. (1998). *Reducing the risk: Connections that make a difference in the lives of youth.* Minneapolis, MN: Division of General Pediatrics and Adolescent Health, Department of Pediatrics, University of Minnesota.

Bogenschneider, K. (1998). What youth need to succeed: The roots of resiliency. *Wisconsin family impact seminars briefing report: Building resiliency and reducing risk: What youth need from families and communities to succeed* (pp. 1–16). Madison, WI: Center for Excellence in Family Studies, School of Human Ecology, University of Wisconsin.

Brendtro, L. K., Brokenleg, M., and Van Bockern, S. (1990). *Reclaiming youth at risk: Our hope for the future.* Bloomington, IN: National Education Service.

Bronfenbrenner, U. (1979). *The ecology of human development: Experiments by nature and design.* New York, NY: Cambridge University Press.

Carnegie Council on Adolescent Development. (1995). *Great transitions: Preparing adolescents for a new century.* New York, NY: Carnegie Corporation.

Csikszentmihalyi, M. (1997). *Finding flow: The psychology of engagement with everyday life. The masterminds series.* New York, NY: Basic Books.

Eccles, J. and Gootman, J. A. (2002). *Community programs to promote youth development.* Committee on Community-Level Programs for Youth. Board on Children, Youth, and Families, Commission on Behavioral and Social Sciences Education, National Research Council and Institute of Medicine. Washington, DC: Sage.

Festinger, T. (1984). *No one ever asked us: A postscript to the foster care system.* New York, NY: Columbia University Press.

Furstenberg, F., Cook, T., Eccles, J., Elder, G., and Sameroff, A. (1998). *Managing to make it: Urban families and adolescent success.* Chicago, IL: University of Chicago Press.

Hughes, D. M. and Curnan, S. P. (2000, Winter). Community youth development: A framework for action. *CYD Journal, 1*, 7–13.

Kaufman, J., Cook, A., Arny, L., Jones, B., and Pittinsky, T. (1994). Problems defining resiliency: Illustrations from the study of maltreated children. *Development and Psychopathology, 6*, 215–229.

Kumpfer, K. L. (1999). Factors and processes contributing to resilience: The resilience framework. In M. D. Glantz and J. L. Johnson (Eds.), *Resiliency and development: Positive life adaptations* (pp. 179–224). New York, NY: Kluwer Academic/Plenum Publishers.

Larson, R. W. (2000). Toward a psychology of positive youth development. *American Psychologist, 55,* 170–183.

Lerner, R. M. (2002). *Adolescence: Development, diversity, context, and application.* Upper Saddle River, NJ: Prentice Hall.

Lerner, R. M. (2004). *Liberty: Thriving and civic engagement among America's youth.* Thousand Oaks, CA: Sage.

Lerner, R. M., Fisher, C., and Weinberg, R. (2000). Toward a science for and of the people. Promoting civil society through the application of developmental science. *Child Development, 71,* 11–20.

Luthar, S. S., Cicchetti, D., and Becker, B. (2000). The construct of resilience: A critical evaluation and guidelines for future work. *Child Development, 71*, 543–562.

Masten, A. S. (2001). Ordinary magic: Resilience processes in development. *American Psychologist, 56*, 227–238.

Masten, A. S. and Garmezy, N. (1985). Risk vulnerability and protective factors in developmental psychopathology. In B. B. Lahey and A. E. Kazidin (Eds.), *Advances in clinical child psychology*, (Vol. 8, pp. 1–52). New York, NY: Plenum Press.

Perkins, D. F. and Borden, L. M. (2003). Risk factors, risk behaviors, and resiliency in adolescence. In R. M. Lerner, M. A. Easterbrooks, and J. Mistry (Eds.), *Handbook of psychology: Vol. 6 Developmental psychology* (pp. 373–394). New York, NY: Wiley.

Pittman, K. J. (2000, March). *Grantmaker strategies for assessing the quality of unevaluated programs and the impact of unevaluated grantmaking.* Paper presented at Evaluation of Youth Programs symposium at the Biennial Meeting of the Society for Research on Adolescence, Chicago, IL.

Rhodes, J. E. (2002). *Stand by me: The risks and rewards of mentoring today's youth.* Cambridge, MA: Harvard University Press.

Roth, J. and Brooks-Gunn, J. (2003). What exactly is a youth development program? Answers from research and practice. *Applied Developmental Science, 7,* 94–111.

Rutter, M. (1987). Psychosocial resilience and protective factors. *American Journal of Orthopsychiatry, 57*, 316–331.

Rutter, M. (1985). Resilience in the face of adversity: Protective factors and resistance to psychiatric disorder. *British Journal of Psychiatry, 147*, 598–611.

Rutter, M. and the English and Romanian Adoptees Study Team (1998). Developmental catch-up and deficit, following adoption after severe global early deprivation. *Journal of Clinical Psychology and Psychiatry, 39*, 465–476

Rutter, M., Maughan, B., Mortimore, P., Ouston, J., and Smith, A. (1979). *Fifteen thousand hours*. Cambridge, MA: Harvard University.

Tolman, J. and Pittman, K. (2002). *Toward a common vision: Naming and framing the developmental imperative*. Washington, DC: Academy for Educational Development.

Werner, E. and Smith, R. (1992). *Overcoming the odds*: *High-risk children from birth to adulthood*. Ithaca, NY: Cornell University.

Werner, E. and Smith, R. (2001). *Journeys from childhood to midlife: Risk, resiliency, and recovery*. Ithaca, NY: Cornell University Press.

Wilkes, G. (2002). Abused child to nonabusive parent: Resilience and conceptual change. *Journal of Clinical Psychology, 58,* 261–278.

Vaillant, G. (2002). *Aging well: Surprising guideposts to a happier life from the landmark Harvard study in adult development*. Boston, MA: Little, Brown, and Company.

Vigil, J. D. (1990). Cholos and gangs: Culture change and street youth in Los Angeles. In R. Huff (Ed.), *Gangs in America: Diffusion, diversity, and public policy* (pp. 146–162). Thousand Oaks, CA: Sage.

Villarreal, F. A., Perkins, D. F., Borden, L. M., and Keith, J. G. (2003). *Community youth development: Practice, policy, and research*. Thousand Oaks, CA: Sage.

Endnote

1. This paper was supported by The Penn State Agricultural Experimentation Project Number 3826.

Chapter 8

Recreation and Youth Development

Linda L. Caldwell

In this chapter we address the general question, "What makes recreation and leisure an important context for fostering youth development?" In other words, how do recreation and leisure contexts contribute to youth development and why might these contexts sometimes be more effective in promoting development than work or school? You might recall from previous chapters that development occurs when youth have opportunities to increase competence, bond with peers and adults, experience self-efficacy, discover who one is (i.e., identity), develop positive beliefs about the future, experience the ability to be self-determined, and be recognized for one's accomplishments. These are often called *developmental outcomes.*

We discussed many of the essential features of supports, opportunities, programs, and services (SOPS) that generate positive developmental outcomes for youth in Chapter 1, but we present them again here because they are important to understanding the material in this chapter. To guide our discussion, we will use the eight essential features of positive developmental settings identified in the report *Community Programs to Promote Youth Development* (Eccles & Gootman, 2002). These are listed in **Table 8.1** (p. 170).

These features of positive youth development programs may be purposefully created through staff planning and actions. For example, staff can deliberately design activities and use intentional leadership approaches that help teach young people the critical skills they need to grow into successful, fully functioning adults. To ensure these features are designed into programs and effectively carried out, staff should be trained, and standards and assessment tools should be developed, to create a blueprint for action and for monitoring progress. Recreation and leisure programs and activities provide excellent contexts for facilitating developmental outcomes because they naturally contain many of the features that promote positive youth development.

Table 8.1: Essential Features of Positive Youth Development Settings

Physical and psychological safety. Safe and health-promoting facilities; practices that increases safe peer group interaction and decreases unsafe or confrontational peer interactions

Appropriate structure. Clear and consistent rules and expectations; firm control, continuity, and predictability; clear boundaries; and age-appropriate monitoring

Supportive relationships. Warmth, closeness, connectedness, good communication, caring, support, guidance, secure attachment, responsiveness

Opportunities to belong. Opportunities for meaningful inclusion, regardless of one's gender, ethnicity, sexual orientation, or disabilities; social inclusion, social engagement, and integration; opportunities for sociocultural identity formation; support for cultural and bicultural competence

Positive social norms. Rules of behavior, expectations, injunctions, ways of doing things, values and morals, obligations for service

Support for efficacy and mattering. Youth-based, empowerment practices that support autonomy, making a real difference in one's community, and being taken seriously. Practices that include enabling, responsibility granting, and meaningful challenge. Practices that focus on improvement rather than on relative current

Opportunities for skill building. Opportunities to learn physical, intellectual, psychological, emotional, and social skills; exposure to intentional learning experiences; opportunities to learn cultural literacy, media literacy, communication skills, and good habits of mind; preparation for adult employment; opportunities to develop social and cultural capital

Integration of family, school, and community efforts. Concordance, coordination, and synergy among family, school and community

Setting the Stage for Understanding the Power of Recreation and Leisure Contexts

The information just presented sets the stage for returning to the question posed at the beginning of the chapter: "What makes recreation and leisure an important context for youth development to take place?" That is, just how does recreation and leisure promote the developmental outcomes identified previously? To begin to think about these questions, imagine Kaylia in four different contexts. She is solving a problem in each one:

- At work: Kaylia is trying to figure out how to maximize space on shelves so she can display more magazines at the bookstore where she works.

- At school: Kaylia is working on a mathematical word problem.
- At home: Kaylia is trying to figure out how to rearrange her bedroom so that she can have better access to her computer.
- At play: Kaylia just hit a ball in a pick-up softball game and the ball went down the storm drain and she and her teammates cannot reach it.

Each of the situations represents a place or context where youth development can take place: work, school, home/family, and leisure. Think about the inherent qualities in each situation. What elements in each environment are likely to contribute to youth development? And more important to this chapter, how can what happens in a leisure or recreation context contribute to youth development? To answer that question, it will help if we understand what actually goes on in recreation and leisure settings.

Before we go further in our discussion, we need to clarify the way the terms free time, recreation, and leisure are used in this chapter. These terms are often used interchangeably among the general population, but for practitioners and researchers it is useful to make a distinction among the terms. For our purposes, *free time* is considered unobligated time in a youth's life; it is usually time other than school and doing chores. Often free time is filled with recreation and leisure activities, but not always. We will use the words *recreation* and *leisure* interchangeably for the purposes of this chapter, although often recreation is considered to be activity-oriented and leisure is considered to be a more relaxed and restful state.

It is important to our discussion to note that when free time is used for meaningful recreation and leisure, it is more likely that positive development will take place. Conversely, positive development is less likely when free time is empty of meaningful activity (i.e., when one is just filling time). Thus, free time may lead to less than positive development, and at times unhealthy behavior. For example, boredom in leisure, substance use, and feeling stress in leisure are examples of potentially unhealthy and problematic experiences that may lead to unhealthy developmental outcomes. We have addressed some of these issues in Chapter 7 and will discuss them more fully in Chapter 9. For now, however, our focus is on the positive developmental opportunities gained through leisure and recreation.

To understand how recreation contributes to youth development, it is essential to appreciate that recreation is *more than just participating in an activity*, although as we discuss, the *activity* itself is important. It is also necessary also to understand the *experiences* (e.g., feelings, attitudes) that accompany doing the activity and the *context or "container"* in which the activity takes place. **Figure 8.1** (p. 172) provides a diagram of these elements.

In this figure, you can see that experience is a part of the activity, and the activity and experience are embedded in a context, such as the ones Kaylia was in at the beginning of the chapter (i.e., work, recreation, school, and home). *Recreation contributes to youth development when the right elements of context, activity, and experience exist.* Although all of these elements influence each other and are interdependent, we discuss each of them separately in the following sections.

Leisure (compared with school, family, and work) is important to development because it affords many unique opportunities to gain developmental outcomes. Think back to Kaylia solving problems in the different contexts. Although she would reap developmental outcomes in each context, in the recreation context Kaylia was engaging in intrinsically motivating and self-determined behavior. She wanted to play softball because she enjoyed it. It is this intrinsic interest coupled with the ability to be self-determined that many researchers think is most motivating to people, thereby contributing to healthy development. Situations rich in the ability to be self-determined and intrinsically interested also foster skill development, competence and self-efficacy, positive identity formation, and a sense of belonging (among other things).

We will now delve into each of the elements and factors presented in Figure 8.1 to learn more about how recreation and leisure contribute to youth development.

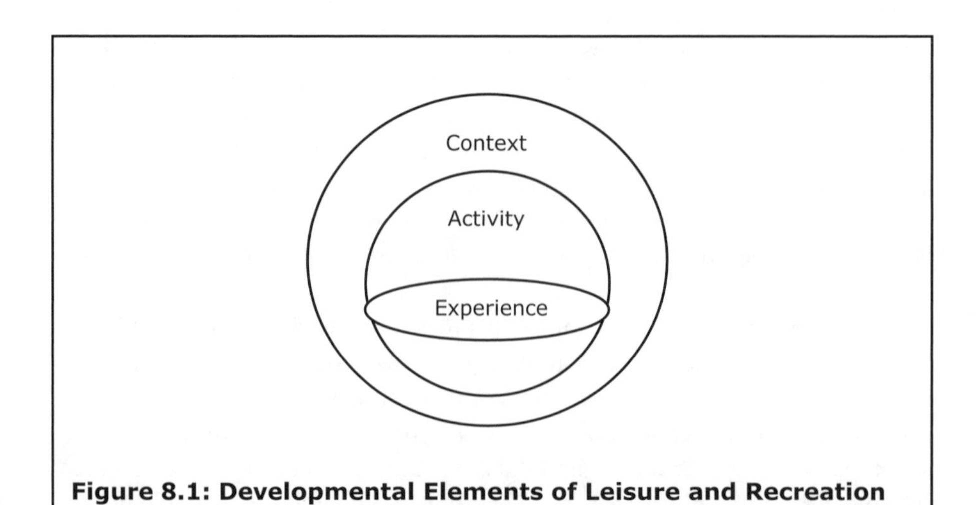

Figure 8.1: Developmental Elements of Leisure and Recreation

Developmental Elements of Recreation and Leisure: A Closer Look

Context

All activities and behaviors take place within specific contexts (e.g., work, school). Contexts include all of the elements or things within the environment that surround and can influence behaviors in a particular setting. As depicted in **Figure 8.2**, the elements in a recreation context that have a bearing on development include the following:

- opportunities
- amount and type of supervision and type of structure (i.e., informal or formal)
- adult support and guidance
- peers (e.g., how many, who)
- physical and psychological attributes (e.g., built or natural environment, physical and psychological safety, clean or dirty)

These contextual elements are crucial because they shape the experiential qualities of engagement that can contribute to positive developmental outcomes. There is no magic formula that determines how much and what combination of elements needs to be present to promote healthy development. A person's age, gender, culture, and past experience all influence the impact and importance of these contextual elements. For example, as youth

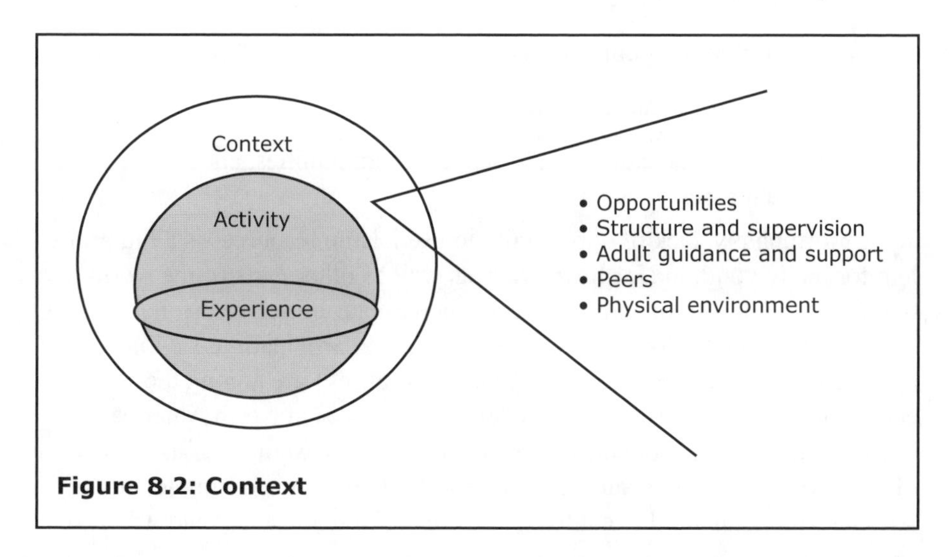

Figure 8.2: Context

get older, they need less direct supervision and more opportunity to make their own choices and shape their own experiences. Greater autonomy will in turn contribute to developing self-determination and self-efficacy. In the following sections, each of the elements associated with context is discussed.

Opportunity. Contexts provide opportunities for development to occur. Within a context, opportunity may be thought about in two different ways:

1. Opportunities may include the whole constellation of leisure activities and chances for participation that are available to a youth in his or her life. That is, opportunity means the *option to use resources*. Opportunities may also exist in one's home, community center, church, school, and so on. The opportunity to participate in a wide range of leisure experiences is important because youth need exposure to and the ability to experiment with a wide range of activities in order to find those that they are interested in and intrinsically motivated to pursue.

2. Opportunities also refer to aspects embedded in the leisure context or setting that contribute to the acquisition of positive developmental outcomes. *Leisure opportunities provide possibilities.* For example, they allow youth

    - to have choice and voice (e.g., participating in rule and decision making)
    - to feel a sense of belonging and mattering
    - to explore one's identity and gender roles
    - to be challenged
    - to develop competence
    - to form durable relationships with adults
    - to become connected to schools, communities, and churches

Unfortunately, lack of opportunity to use leisure resources is a big problem for many youth in North America, as well as other parts of the world (e.g., see Chapter 3). In addition, even when opportunities are available, some youth cannot afford the associated costs of participation. Living in poverty and/or living in rural and even urban settings are among the biggest causes of lack of opportunity to use leisure resources in North America.

Reed Larson and colleagues (2001) provided an example of how lack of resources influence leisure engagement. In their Chicago sample, urban African American youth went to school only 5.75 hours a day and watched

TV for 17% of their free time, compared to suburban youth in the same area who went to school 7 hours a day and spent 13% of free time watching TV. Thus, the youth in the urban sample spent significantly more time involved in "idle" activities and "hanging out" than youth in the suburban schools. The differences in time use may have been because the urban schools and the communities in which they were situated were underresourced. Concerns for personal safety may have also contributed to the differences in the time use statistics.

According to Lerner, Freund, De Stefanis, and Habermas (2001), it is very important in resource-restricted contexts to help youth learn to develop leisure interests and goals that are in the realm of the possible. That is, recreation staff (and other adults) should help youth to cultivate interests that they can pursue within the parameters (i.e., limitations and opportunities) of their immediate environment. For example, teaching urban youth how to snow shoe in central North Carolina would not make a lot of sense.

Lerner and associates (2001) also suggested that if interest development and activity selections are limited at an early age, acquisition of important life skills may be thwarted. Thus, a variety of leisure resources and opportunities for participation must exist, and youth must be guided in their activity choices so they will find interesting and worthwhile things to do. In these resource-restricted contexts in particular, it is all too easy for youth to claim "but there is nothing to do!" Although there is an element of truth to the claim, youth can be guided into finding "hidden opportunities." Or, when hidden opportunities do not exist, they must be created. In these circumstances, caring adults who understand the importance of leisure opportunities are especially important for helping youth discover and create opportunities for engagement. A process called *leisure education* is one way this can occur, and is discussed in Chapter 9. Adults may also need to become advocates for increasing the available opportunities in the community.

Choice and voice. A critical facet of opportunity is the amount of personal choice youth are able to exercise within their chosen leisure activity—Are there opportunities to be self-determined and to voice one's opinions? Experiencing choice and voice are important to positive youth development as they may lead to interest development, initiative, identity formation, feelings of self-efficacy, intrinsic motivation, a feeling that one matters, and accepting responsibility for decisions.

Let us take a moment to identify some commonly used terms when discussing choice and voice: intrinsic motivation, self-determination, autonomy, and self-regulation. *Intrinsic motivation* is engaging in a behavior because one wants to for the inherent enjoyment, interest, and pleasure of the activity. Intrinsic motivation is fundamental in meeting three basic human needs:

competence, autonomy, and relatedness (e.g., Ryan & Deci, 2000). Often intrinsic motivation is contrasted with extrinsic motivation or amotivation; these are all terms we use throughout the book.

It is important not to confuse intrinsic motivation with *autonomy*, *self-determination*, or *self-regulation*. These terms all have slightly different meanings, depending on whom you ask. (If you take a social psychology or developmental psychology course, you may learn more about these terms.) For our purposes, these terms share an underlying meaning, which is important to understanding how youth voice and choice works. Consider this: Having complete choice or control over one's actions is rare, even in a leisure context. For example, you probably do things in leisure more often because you know it is good for you (i.e., it serves a purpose, such as physically active leisure) or because someone else has asked you to join them in an activity, than because of the inherent pleasure of the activity.

Thus, in some way, your behavior is externally motivated rather than completely internally motivated. In these cases, can one have autonomy or be self-determined? Yes, as long as the actions are *self-endorsed*. That is, behaviors are enacted because they fit in with one's value systems, one's beliefs, and one's desires. Consider that even though Kaylia was not inherently interested in rearranging her room to get better access to her computer, she did agree with the idea and knew it was for a good purpose, thus it was self-endorsed and she experienced self-determination.

Although leisure contexts do not always provide for total self-determination or autonomy, of all of the other contexts in a youth's life, they do maximize the probability that self-determination will occur. Thus, one of the reasons Kaylia may gain good developmental outcomes from her softball experience is that she and her peers had the opportunity to exercise choice and to be self-determined. Being part of the decision-making process helps young people to take ownership of the experience and to maintain intrinsic motivation and interest. The ability of Kaylia and her friends to exercise their choices is also important because if their choices do not work out, it is their failure and they can learn from the experience. If their choices are successful, they also learn.

Youth choice does not operate in a vacuum, however, and so the right amount of adult guidance and support is important. Promoting choice and voice is a delicate balance of a youth wanting to do an activity, feeling one "should" do an activity and being guided into an activity. As you can imagine from the discussion on self-determination and autonomy, it can be a challenge for adults to provide the right amount of guidance and support.

Supervision and structure. The amount of supervision provided by adults is also an important contextual element of recreation and leisure. Depending on the circumstances, adults may supply too much, too little or just the right amount of supervision. Think of Kaylia and her friends trying to solve their problem in the pick-up softball game. How was the absence of adult supervision beneficial to their development? With no adults around, they had to work together. Probably one of the girls took a leadership role, or maybe they shared leadership. No doubt they learned how to work together and cooperate, not to mention how to retrieve the ball.

Now, what if the context had been completely structured and organized by adults with no input from Kaylia and her friends? Under these circumstances, the context might have inhibited opportunities to try out skills and could have spoiled the girls' ability to exercise control over the environment. For example, imagine if a coach was supervising Kaylia and her friends. She may have told the girls what to do to get the ball, and in the process perhaps thwarted their opportunity to develop intrinsic interest and problem solving skills. (As an aside, this provides an example of why many youth sports coaches are undergoing training on how to foster youth development through coaching, in addition to helping youth learn to play the game.)

We previously mentioned that the amount and type of supervision is related to age. In general, older youth require less supervision. However, if they are participating in risky leisure activities such as whitewater river kayaking, or are learning skill-based activities that require coaching, the level of supervision should go up. Thus, in addition to age, the type and level of guidance also relates to the activity. Although skill-based and/or risky activities will require the right mix of coaching, high expectations, and relevant feedback to youth, older youth will still need more opportunity to make decisions in these contexts. We return to this discussion when we discuss the role of adult guidance and support.

Professionals in the field have become quite interested recently in identifying the appropriate level of structure and/or guidance in young people's leisure involvements. One question of interest is whether or not structured versus unstructured activities impact positive youth development in different ways. There is not a simple answer to this question, but we will try and understand the question and its related elements.

On one hand, there is compelling evidence that structured activities such as hobbies and sports do more to contribute to development and positive adjustment for children and adolescents than unstructured activities and environments (e.g., Eccles & Barber, 1999; Mahoney & Stattin, 2000; McHale, Crouter & Tucker, 2001). For example, Darling, Caldwell, and Smith (2005) found that participation in school-based extracurricular activities binds students to school-related values, such as good academic performance and high academic aspirations.

On the other hand, too much structure can have its downside. For example, in a 2002 *Newsweek* commentary, Anna Quindlen reflected on the need for less scheduled time for children and youth:

> It is not simply that it is pathetic to consider the lives of children who don't have a moment between piano and dance and homework to talk about their day or just search for split ends—an enormously satisfying leisure-time activity of my youth. There is also ample psychological research suggesting that what we might call "doing nothing" is when human beings actually do their best thinking, and when creativity comes to call. Perhaps we are creating an entire generation of people whose ability to think outside the box, as the current parlance of business has it, is being systematically stunted by scheduling. (p. 76)

Psychologist David Elkins has long been concerned about the "overbooked child." In a recent *Psychology Today* article, he quotes Diane Ehrensaft as saying

> Middle-class children in America are so overscheduled that they have almost no "nothing time." They have no time to call on their own resources and be creative. Creativity is making something out of nothing, and it takes time for that to happen. (2003, p. 2)

Elkins concluded that overscheduled children are more likely to be stressed, and less likely to engage in important childhood activities, such as playing in a natural, creative way.

Along the same lines, an organization called Putting Family First has been advocating that people slow down and find time to not only enjoy family life, but also relaxing leisure time. The organization's Web site features a study done by William Doherty of the Family Social Science Department at the University of Minnesota that found that between 1981 and 1997 there has been a major decline in unstructured, free time for 3- to 12-year-olds. He found that over this 16-year period there was also a 50% decrease in outdoor activities such as walking, hiking, and camping. At the same time, Doherty found that participation in structured sports more than doubled (from 2 hours 20 minutes to 5 hours 17 minutes per week). He also found that passive, spectator-based leisure (excluding TV and other "screen time") increased almost six fold, from 30 minutes to over 3 hours per week.

Adult guidance and supervision. The role of adult guidance and supervision is an important part of the context of an activity and is closely related to the amount of supervision and type of structure in an activity. In fact, caring adults are so important that two other chapters in this book are devoted to parents and youth workers. As leaders, coaches, and facilitators, adults have a considerable responsibility for shaping and providing for healthy and developmentally productive leisure experiences for youth. The following provides some insight into why this is important.

A colleague of the authors worked at a teen center in Vermont. One of the active citizens in the community (a coalition member) wrote in April 2004 to a Vermont representative about the importance of adult leadership at the teen center:

> It is this familiarity that young people need to feel stable and properly grounded. Sometimes, family situations are such that the people of the Teen Program are the closest thing to family that a kid has. This "service" to the young person, if you will, can almost only be provided by an entity that is neither school, nor family, someone who plays the role of outsider and insider at the same time, someone safe, someone neutral. (Kathleen Raupach, personal communication, July 5, 2004)

This citizen's remarks reinforce the importance of supportive relationships by caring adults in a recreation environment. Caring adults promote the following:

- a sense of belonging
- psychological safety
- competence
- feeling one matters
- opportunities for skill building
- feeling of connection with the community

Providing the right mix of guidance and support depends in part on the age of the youth—that is, guidance and support need to be developmentally appropriate. If there is too much guidance and adult control, there is danger that youth will become extrinsically motivated; that is, they may begin to focus on the external rewards for participation (e.g., trophies, popularity) or feel that participation is obligatory. Extrinsically motivated youth typically become apathetic toward their recreation involvements, and therefore their interest and participation are unlikely to be sustained. This may explain why there is such a drop off in participation in formal sports and other recreational activities as youth get older (e.g., Caspersen, Pereira & Curran, 2000). Over time, young people's need for choice and voice grows dramatically, and adult-led sports or other activities usually do not have opportunities for youth to express these needs.

What youth do need as they mature are adults who can facilitate, encourage, and support their efforts; help them to process their failures; and celebrate their successes. All of these supports will contribute to youths' ability to establish emotional and behavioral autonomy from parents and other adults as part of the developmental process.

Youth also need adults who will keep them accountable for their actions and instill a sense of responsibility into leisure choices and engagement. Similarly, adults who set high but realistic standards and work with youth to achieve those standards contribute to youth development. One way adults can work with youth to develop responsibility and reach high standards is through high-quality instruction and coaching. This provides youth the opportunity to gain skills and develop competence. Without proper guidance, youth may choose to participate in activities that provide little challenge, opportunity for initiative development, or meaning.

It should be noted here that adult guidance and support should also include shared fun. Adults should not always just sit on the sidelines and watch and coach—having fun with adults is an important protective factor for youth.

Finally, one of the critical reasons adult supervision and guidance is important is that it affirms to youth that they matter. Youth who feel that they are important and worthy of attention are in much better positions to reap the developmental benefits of leisure. As youth try to figure out who they are (i.e., identity development), the supportive feeling that they matter to someone removes some of the need constantly prove themselves in unauthentic ways (e.g., posturing violence when that is not really an option one cares to exercise).

Peers. Peers are a very powerful contextual force in adolescent's lives and can exert both positive and negative influences on behavior (e.g., trying a new skill, smoking cigarettes) or experience (e.g., feeling competent, lonely).

On the positive side, peers who support another youth's attempts to try out a new activity can promote confidence and self-efficacy. For example, in a study by Culp (1998), girls described how their friends (and family) supported their attempts at new outdoor activities, and that helped them develop confidence and competence. On the other hand, peers can also have a negative influence. Some girls in Culp's study reported being inhibited from choosing to participate in outdoor recreation activities because they were concerned their peers would react negatively (e.g., they might be ridiculed).

Peers can also use gentle (or more active) coercion to get their friends to participate in negative and/or unhealthy behaviors. Partying is a particularly vulnerable free time context where peer pressure can lead to involvement in risky activities. Not surprisingly, peer pressure has been linked to drug and alcohol use and engaging in unprotected sex. Zaff and Moore (2002) suggested that regardless of having a negative or positive influence, peers tend to self-select groups to hang out with and these groups are self-perpetuating.

Thus, youth whose friends drink and smoke are more likely to do so than if their friends do not drink and smoke, regardless of the partying context. Learning ways to deal with peers in a social leisure setting is therefore an important developmental skill for youth to learn and practice.

Other aspects of peer influence are part of a leisure and recreation context. As youth get older and begin romantic relationships, they may become unduly influenced by their romantic partner and may possibly give up their interests to support or in favor of their partner's interests. It is also likely that romantic partners will develop some new joint interests. This process of negotiation of mutual interests and support of individual interests is a valuable life skill and a critical part of youth development.

Youth's leisure, because it is predominantly social, is a critical context for developing social competence and emotional regulation. Peers have the ability to act as excellent role models to each other through modeling social and emotional competence as well as new skills (Zaff & Moore, 2002). In these cases, peers promote positive social norms and feelings of belonging, which are important to positive youth development. For example, interacting with others may require youth to learn how to lead and how to follow. They also learn basic social skills and the necessity of paying attention to other people's feelings and interests. In a study by Dworkin, Larson, and Hansen (2003), one of the benefits to interacting with peers in more structured activities was the ability to control anger and anxiety and to stay focused on the activity at hand.

Leisure is also a fertile context for youth to interact with others who are "different" from themselves and to understand and appreciate those differences. Dworkin, Larson, and Hansen (2003) found that adolescents reported that interacting with peers who would normally be outside their existing network was one of the most important benefits to participating in structured, formal, youth-based activities. Youth who participate in these types of activities tend to have broader types of friends than youth who do not (Dworkin, Larson & Hansen, 2003).

Physical environment. A final aspect of a recreation and leisure context that contributes to developmental outcomes is the *physical environment*, which includes both outdoor and indoor settings. Outdoor and natural environments often provide participants with challenges. Imagine Kaylia and her friends being caught in a severe thunderstorm as they were trying to retrieve the softball. The challenge of retrieving the ball would have been increased and perhaps higher level problem-solving skills would have been required, including an assessment of safety issues. One of the reasons outdoor challenges contribute to youth development is that youth may learn to generalize skills and attitudes formed in facing them to daily life situations. For example, a youth who develops confidence in her ability to navigate Class II (slightly difficult) rapids in a kayak after weeks of practice may be able to transfer that ability to persevere to understand the Spanish language. That claim, however logical, is not yet well-documented by research, although Mahoney, Cairns, and Farmer (2003) suggested that as skills increase and one overcomes one type of challenge, new and more challenging goals are set. They believe that this process may carry over from recreational activities to other settings, such as work or school.

Besides challenges inherent in some activities done in the out-of-doors, there is evidence that the aesthetics of an environment is important. For example, some interesting research out of the University of Illinois Human-Environment Research Laboratory has demonstrated how important green environments are to adults and youth living in public housing in urban areas. For example, Taylor, Kuo, and Sullivan (2001) found that the symptoms of children with Attention Deficit Disorder (ADD) are relieved after contact with nature—the greener the setting, the more the relief. Taylor, Kuo, and Sullivan also found that the greener and more natural a girl's view from home, the better she scored on tests of self-discipline. This finding is important, they note, because a girl who is self-disciplined is more likely to do well in school and avoid unhealthy or risky behaviors. Boys, on the other hand, showed no link between test scores and nature near their home. Both of these studies, and more, can be found at http://www.herl.uiuc.edu.

Finally, environments and spaces that are youth-focused and designed are particularly compelling to youth and provide safe places to experiment with developmental issues such as competence, identity, and gender roles. On the other hand, environments that are unsafe, run-down, sterile, or "school-like," are not likely to encourage youth participation and engagement, thus preventing potential development to occur. We explore these notions further in the chapter on teen centers (Chapter 15), which can be important developmental contexts for youth development.

So far our discussion about the elements of recreation and leisure has focused on contexts, which sets the stage for development to occur. Leisure in particular is an important context for youth development because it promotes self-determined behavior and the development of intrinsic interest. In leisure, with appropriate structure and supervision, relationships can be formed with caring adults and peers, and opportunities to learn skills and develop competence are available. In a leisure context, youth are likely to feel that they matter and belong. But now we shift our focus to the activity that goes on in the context and explore how the activity itself can contribute to positive youth development.

Activity

Activity has a broad meaning and includes "idling," hanging out, or daydreaming, as well as more structured events, such as sports or the visual or performing arts. As we have just discussed, activities take place in context, and thus the elements of an activity and the elements in the context mutually influence each other. Not all activities are equal; some are better than others at producing healthy outcomes and positive affect. A Carnegie Council on Adolescent Development (1992) report about the risk and opportunities of free time for youth termed the "better" activities *high-yield activities*. As indicated in **Figure 8.3**, these activities typically

- are goal-oriented and/or creative and expressive in nature
- require discipline and focused attention
- offer challenges to overcome
- build skills and increase one's level of competence
- require persistence, commitment, and continuity to participation over time

On the whole, activities that have these characteristics tend to produce the best experiences for youth and contribute to their long-term health and development, although in some instances high-yield activities can also be associated with stress and anxiety, and possibly eventual boredom. Many of the conditions we have just discussed contribute to a condition that Mihaly Csikszentmihalyi (1990) labeled *flow*, which is discussed in greater detail under "experience."

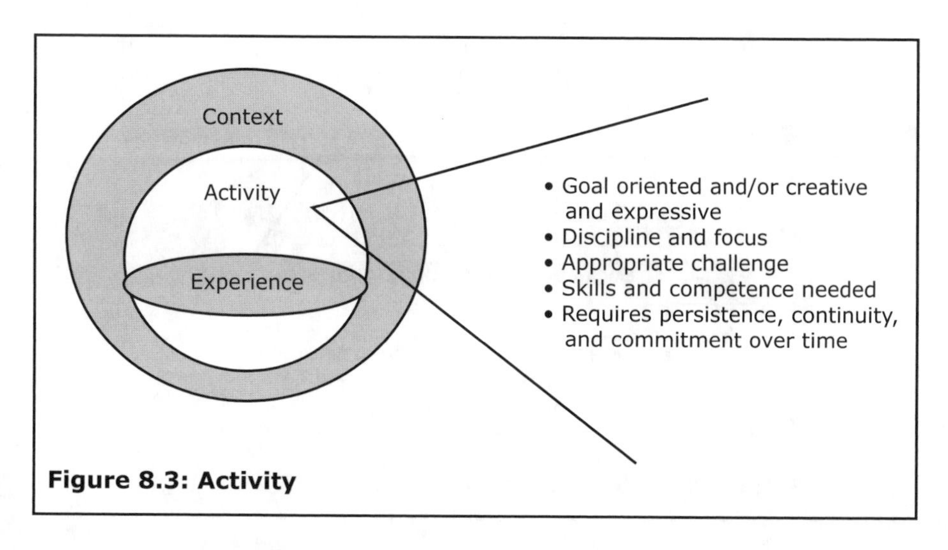

Figure 8.3: Activity

Just what are high-yield leisure activities? **Figure 8.4** presents a "leisure pyramid" (similar to the food pyramid with which everyone is familiar). The pyramid suggests that a healthy "leisure diet or repertoire" should be built on active and/or creative engagement with one's environment. High-yield activities that allow youth to manipulate or construct their own experiences, such as participating in sports, singing in a choir, playing a musical instrument in a band or creating an art project, should be the foundation of one's leisure repertoire. These activities can be done alone or with others, but they have the highest probably of containing the elements of high-yield activities identified here.

A couple of developmental outcomes in particular should be addressed here. First, these high-yield activities tend to be self-determined and intrinsically interesting to youth. Larson (2000) linked being self-determined with *initiative*, which he called a "core quality of positive youth development" (p. 170). Initiative essentially means that youth are motivated to get engaged in activities and to maintain interest. This increases voluntary, self-generated attention, which not only fosters intrinsic motivation and persistence in interesting activities but also cultivates a sense of mastery and responsibility over and for one's life.

A second developmental outcome related to high-yield activities is that of goal-setting and future perspectives. High-yield activities tend to require realistic goal-setting. Research has shown that youth who set goals in a recreation and leisure context are more likely to report having a positive future

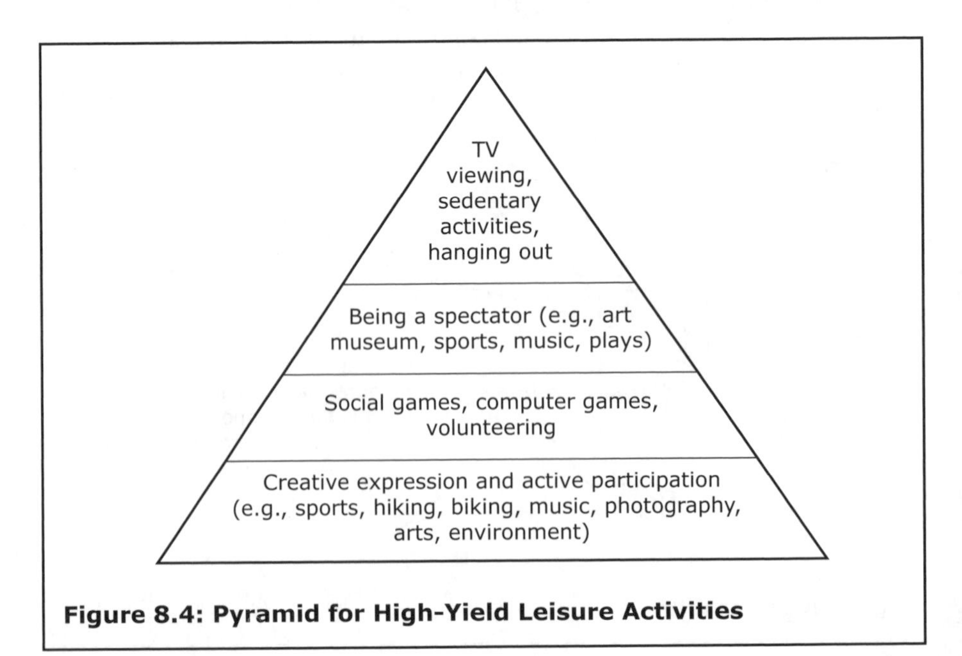

Figure 8.4: Pyramid for High-Yield Leisure Activities

perspective (i.e., a positive outlook on one's future prospects), which is critical in making the transition to adulthood (Sharp, Coatsworth & Palen, 2005). Although we focus a great deal in this book on the importance of intrinsic motivation, we make the somewhat nuanced point here that goal-oriented activities, sometimes called *identified* motivation (see Ryan & Deci, 2000), may not be entirely intrinsically motivated. That is, although the activities may be inherently interesting, youth engage in these activities for some type of purpose or goal beyond "just being really interested" or "just doing it because it is fun." We previously called these *self-endorsed* activities and they are also activities that promote many healthy developmental outcomes.

The next rung of the pyramid contains computer and other games. These are closely related to "creative and engaged" activities, but typically do not contain quite the degree of "high-yield elements" as the activities on the first rung of the pyramid. There are recently some interesting computer games that require youth to be physically active, which is a definite plus.

We place volunteering here too, although depending on the degree of commitment and nature of the position, it may be better situated on the first rung. Leisure opportunities cultivate the means for youth to volunteer and to become connected to their schools, communities, and churches. "Giving back" and "making one's community better" can not only be a powerful endeavor for youth and contribute to one's personal sense of accomplishment but also contribute to a larger *sense of community* and belonging to something "bigger than myself."

As we move up the pyramid, activities become less engaging. Spectating at either sports or cultural arts, while exciting and temporarily engaging, does not require the viewer to be fully engaged or to use as many skills as activities represented on the first two rungs of the pyramid. The level of challenge to the spectator is usually minimal. In addition, one's personal level of challenge and skill does not appear to increase over time.

Several of the most common leisure activities among adolescents are TV viewing, talking on the phone, and/or instant messaging. In most cases, these would be considered "low-yield" activities. Interestingly, TV viewing is usually done because there is nothing else to do. Youth report being bored and apathetic while watching TV, although watching TV in a social setting (with friends or family) can make a greater contribution to development than watching alone. We should also acknowledge the educational value of some TV programming, but our point is that a leisure lifestyle characterized by a large proportion of time devoted to TV viewing is not healthy.

Just hanging out also appears on the least developmentally productive rung of the pyramid. Connecting with peers is an important social aspect of life, but a steady diet of socializing and watching TV does not fully contribute to meaning and engagement in one's life.

We have already described a number of feelings associated with participation in activities. For example, high-yield activities are more likely to be associated with feelings of competence and positive affect, while low-yield activities are more likely to produce feelings of boredom and apathy. To fully understand the ways in which recreation and leisure contribute to youth development, we will look more closely at the experiential aspects of leisure engagement.

Experience

There are many types of experiences youth can have as a result of what they do in their leisure time (**Figure 8.5**). These experiences may be positive (e.g., being interested, enjoying oneself, feeling competent) or negative (e.g., feeling bored, anxious, stressed). The way a youth typically experiences his or her leisure is more important than an occasional response to an activity. If, for example, one is bored occasionally there is usually little cause for alarm. But a being in constant state boredom or apathy suggests a problem, and can be a risk factor for substance use and other risky behaviors. Chapter 9 will discuss this issue in more detail.

Fortunately, most youth do not regularly experience boredom or other negative emotions in leisure. The nature of the leisure context (e.g., providing opportunities for self-determination and intrinsic motivation) as well as the nature of the activity (e.g., need for focused attention and appropriate challenges) promotes many positive experiences. There is a need, however, to understand that negative emotions can occur and it is just as important to

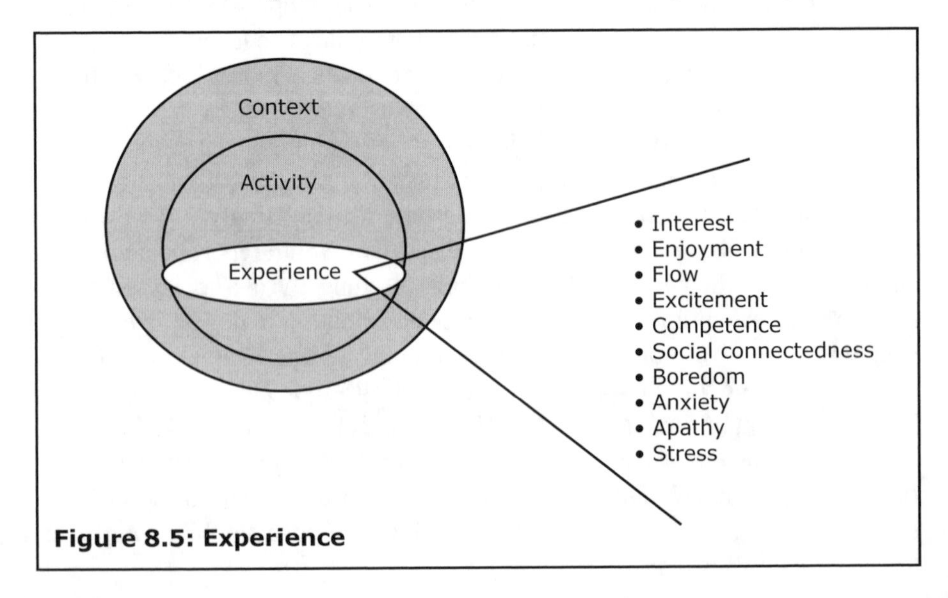

Figure 8.5: Experience

understand the causes of these negative experiences (e.g., low-yield activities, too much adult structure and guidance). As noted previously, appropriate guidance and support from parents and other adults can help youth avoid negative experiences and gain positive ones.

There are three important experiences that can occur in leisure and that are important to youth development: interest, intrinsic motivation, and flow. *Interest* is the opposite of boredom and is important to cognitive growth. Having to focus one's attention to the task at hand promotes brain activity. Interest is also associated with physical benefits, such as a decreased heart rate (Hunter & Csikszentmihalyi, 2003). Finally, interest fosters *intrinsic motivation* by serving as an internal source of compulsion to engage in activity because "it feels good." Being interested has been linked with joy, competence, and tension release (Izard, 1991).

Interest and intrinsic motivation are also linked with the experience of *flow* (e.g., Csikszentmihalyi, 1990), which contributes to positive youth development outcomes such as initiative, self-efficacy, and competence. Flow includes the following nine main elements easily achieved in a recreation or leisure activity:

1. clear goals
2. immediate feedback
3. optimal balance between skill and challenge
4. merging of action and awareness
5. being unaware of surroundings
6. no worry of failure
7. experience of time is distorted
8. lack of self-consciousness
9. the activity becomes self-guiding

Activities on the first levels of the leisure pyramid in Figure 8.4 are more likely to produce the conditions under which flow can occur than those at the top.

One of the important things about flow, as well as other positive leisure experiences, is that these types of experiences are internally rewarding (e.g., one feels competent, interested, excited) and have the potential to generate future participation. That is, when these rewards are regularly received from an activity, youth strive to continue participating (Delle Fave & Bassi, 2000) to get more of these rewards—and the more rewards, the more one is motivated to sustain participation. This sets up a chain of developmentally positive outcomes and processes. For example, the more that flow-producing activities are sought and experienced, the more youth will have to problem solve and overcome challenges to continue their participation. Youth will also have to learn to increase both skill level and challenge in an appropriate ratio such that the optimal experience of flow is maintained—that is, they learn to self-regulate, a critical developmental process.

There are many other experiences linked with recreation and leisure. Positive emotions such as love, excitement, joy, serenity, and peacefulness are experienced in leisure. Of course negative emotions such as stress, anxiety, and hate are also experienced in leisure. Although we do not know a lot right now about exactly when those emotions occur (i.e., for whom and under what conditions), there is some promising new research from a neuropsychological perspective that might help us understand better how emotions occur in leisure and how they connect with positive developmental outcomes. Also important will be learning how to prevent negative emotions from occurring.

Summary and Concluding Remarks

From a developmental perspective, recreation and leisure facilitate acquisition of a number of positive benefits. As noted, high-yield leisure is more likely to occur with the right mix of contextual elements, activity, and experience. If the appropriate opportunities, context, and activities do not exist or are not developmentally appropriate, youth will either be unable to reap the developmental benefits of leisure, or they will disengage from their leisure activities. As youth mature, issues of identity, intimacy, sexuality, and responsibility start to predominate their thoughts. Competence and social bonding are always important developmental issues for youth.

Other chapters in this book will help you to think through how to provide a developmentally appropriate mix of contextual elements, activities, and experiences to foster developmental outcomes. Not all youth learn to select activities that give them the greatest chance of experiencing positive developmental outcomes. As we have emphasized, adults and peers need to play a role in promoting interest development and assisting in the selection and persistence of recreation involvements.

As you continue through the book we hope that you will keep in mind how and why leisure is important to positive youth development. By becoming engaged with peers, family, and community through recreation and leisure, youth can reap enormous developmental benefits. In sum, leisure is an extremely fertile context for development because it

- provides for self-determined behavior
- supports intrinsic motivation, interest development, and persistence of interests
- increases the ability to experience positive emotions and self-regulate emotions
- facilitates decision making and planning skills
- increases interaction with peers, adults, and the community in meaningful ways
- contributes to identity development

We hope that you have gained a better understanding of the power of leisure to contribute to positive youth development.

References

Carnegie Council on Adolescent Development. (1992). *Task force on youth development and community programs. A matter of time: Risk and opportunity in the nonschool hours.* Washington, DC: Author.

Caspersen, C. J., Pereira, M. A., and Curran, K. M. (2000). Changes in physical activity patterns in the United States, by sex and cross-sectional age. *Medicine and Science in Sport and Exercise, 32*, 1601–1609.

Csikszentmihalyi, M. (1990). *Flow: The psychology of optimal experience.* New York, NY: Harper and Row.

Culp, R. H. (1998). Adolescent girls and outdoor recreation: A case study examining constraints and effective programming. *Journal of Leisure Research, 30,* 356–379.

Darling, N., Caldwell, L. L., and Smith, R. (2005). Participation in school-based extracurricular activities and adolescent adjustment. *Journal of Leisure Research, 37,* 51–77.

Delle Fave, A. and Bassi, M. (2000). The quality of experience in adolescents' daily lives: Developmental perspectives. *Genetic, Social, and General Psychology Monographs, 126*, 347–367.

Doherty, W. J. (2004). *Overscheduled kids, underconnected families: The research evidence.* Retrieved April 13, 2004, from http://www.familylife1st.org/html/research.html

Dworkin, J. B., Larson, R., and Hansen, D. (2003). Adolescents' accounts of growth experiences in youth activities. *Journal of Youth and Adolescence, 32*, 17–26.

Eccles, J. S. and Barber, B. L. (1999). Student council, volunteering, basketball, or marching band: What kind of extracurricular involvement matters? *Journal of Adolescent Research, 14*, 10–43.

Eccles, J. and Gootman, J. A. (Eds.). (2002). *Community programs to promote youth development.* National Research Council and Institute of Medicine Committee on Community-Level Programs for Youth, Board on Children, Youth, and Families, Division of Behavioral and Social Sciences and Education. Washington, DC: National Academy Press.

Elkins, D. (2003, January/February). The overbooked child: Are we pushing our kids too hard? *Psychology Today, 36*(1), 64–69.

Hunter, J. P. and Csikszentmihalyi, M. (2003). The positive psychology of interested adolescents. *Journal of Youth and Adolescence, 32*, 27–35.

Izard, C. E. (1991). *The psychology of emotions.* New York, NY: Plenum Press.

Larson, R. (2000). Toward a psychology of positive youth development. *American Psychologist, 55*, 170–183.

Larson, R. W., Richards, M. H., Sims, B., and Dworkin, J. (2001). How urban African American youth adolescents spend their time: Time budgets for locations, activities, and companionship. *American Journal of Community Psychology, 29*, 565–597.

Lerner, R. M., Freund, A. M., De Stefanis, I., and Habermas, T. (2001). Understanding developmental regulation in adolescence: The use of the selection, optimization, and compensation model. *Human Development, 44*, 29–50.

Mahoney, J. L., Cairns, B., and Farmer, T. (2003). Promoting interpersonal competence and educational success through extracurricular activity participation. *Journal of Educational Psychology 95,* 409–418.

Mahoney, J. L. and Stattin, H. (2000). Leisure activities and adolescent antisocial behavior: The role of structure and social context. *Journal of Adolescence, 23*, 113–127.

McHale, S. M., Crouter, A. C., and Tucker, C. J. (2001). Free-time activities in middle childhood: Links with adjustment in early adolescence. *Child Development, 72*, 1764–1778.

Quindlen, A. (2002, May 13). The last word. *Newsweek*, 76.

Ryan, R. M. and Deci (2000). Self-determination theory and the facilitation of intrinsic motivation, social development, and well-being. *American Psychologist, 55*, 68–78.

Sharp, E., Coatsworth, D., and Palen, L. (2005). *Developing a future perspective in adolescence: Relations with identity exploration through activity participation*. Paper presented to the 2005 Society for Research on Child Development biannual conference, Atlanta, GA.

Taylor, A., Kuo, F., and Sullivan, W. (2001). Coping with ADD: The surprising connection to green play settings. *Environment and Behavior, 1*, 54–77.

Zaff, J. F. and Moore, K. A. (2002, October). *Promoting well-being among American's teens: An executive summary of adolescent development research reviews completed for the John S and James L. Knight Foundation.* Retrieved from http://www.childtrends.org/files/knightexecsumm02.pdf

Chapter 9

Educating For, About, and Through Leisure

Linda L. Caldwell

In previous chapters, we examined the importance of leisure and recreation as contexts for youth development. Not all young people, however, automatically know how to maximize their involvement in leisure experiences and to reap the developmental benefits of participation. For example, many youth do not know how to choose meaningful and personally interesting leisure activities in which to participate, despite the availability of recreation programs in their communities. In addition, even when organized programs exist, youth may spend much of their free time watching TV, playing video games, or engaging in negative or risky behaviors and activities.

Another problem related to maximizing development through recreation is that many youth live in environments where opportunities to participate in organized activities do not exist. Youth living in underresourced rural or urban areas are particularly vulnerable to a lack of opportunities to participate in recreation activities. At the other extreme, some youth are so "programmed" that they have something to do every afternoon and evening. It might be soccer practice one night, piano another, and so on. Moreover, parents may tightly structure and supervise leisure at young ages. Consequently, just at the time youth reach the age where they are developing autonomy from parents and are faced with increasingly larger blocks of free time, they are often unprepared and ill-equipped to select and participate in meaningful activities independently.

Engaging in too much activity and feeling bored when not constantly on the go are conditions that reflect what Kleiber (1999) calls an *activity bias.* This bias occurs when a young person feels he or she must always be busy, and relaxation and down time are signs of an unproductive and unworthy person. These conditions also reflect the wariness parents and adults have about youth hanging out and participating in unstructured situations. At first glance, it may seem contradictory to advocate for the value of both structured and unstructured time for adolescents; however, as we have seen in the previous chapters, appropriately challenging structured activities, as well as time for "puttering," reflection, and self-expression, are critical to healthy human development. In addition, appropriate levels of structured and unstructured activities contribute to a needed balance between social and individual activity.

What are the consequences if a young person perceives there is nothing to do, if there are no resources or opportunities, or if their leisure is too controlled or jam-packed? Any of these circumstances may lead to stress, boredom, or even a feeling of alienation. In addition, young people may experience a certain "lack of authenticity" in their leisure if they feel that they are not engaged in self-chosen and interesting activities.

Leisure education is a useful way to help youth to deal with some of the issues just identified and to learn to take responsibility for finding or creating interesting things to do in leisure time. In accordance with this notion, researchers have suggested that youth who learn to take charge of their leisure experiences are at less risk for engaging in socially maladaptive and unhealthy behaviors. For example, the *National Survey of American Attitudes on Substance Abuse VIII: Teens and Parents* (2003) concluded that stress, boredom, and money were predictors of substance use by youth. Perceptions of boredom also have been linked with other problem behaviors, such as higher rates of dropping out of school, vandalism, and obesity.

In addition to reducing risk behaviors, leisure education can contribute to positive development by enabling youth to learn basic skills and to increase their levels of competence. They can learn how to gain knowledge about themselves (i.e., identity development) and the world by participating in leisure.

In short, youth need to learn how to make their leisure experiences satisfying, how to freely choose and initiate activity, and how to maintain activity involvements in the face of challenges for long-term benefits. In other words, they need to learn how to do more than just fill time. Thus, teaching youth how to maximize their leisure experiences; avoid boredom and stress; and develop, plan for, and maintain their interests is a worthy risk-reduction endeavor.

Leisure Education Defined

Leisure education is not a new concept. The Greeks recognized that leisure was intricately intertwined with education. The Latin word *schole* essentially means "employment of leisure time to study and learn" and is linked to the English words *school* and *scholar*. Implicit in the definition of schole is the "freedom to choose" to participate in leisure activity. Classical Greek scholars partook in leisure activities (including the humanities, such as drama and debate) to achieve personal excellence in many aspects of life, such as increasing physical performance, acquiring knowledge, and philosophizing. Occurring in both natural settings and gymnasia, schole was important to physical, mental, and cognitive health.

Today, leisure education can be thought of as the modern manifestation of scholè. It is possibly because of the ways schole was manifested in classical times that there are a number of ways to view contemporary leisure education. Douglas Kleiber is a scholar who has been studying leisure education since the early 1970s. He maintains that informal education, which occurs in leisure, is closely tied to human development mainly because of its ties to intrinsic motivation (Kleiber, 2002). He also suggested there are three forms of leisure education: education through and in leisure, education for leisure, and training for leisure education, which he calls education about leisure (Kleiber, 2004).

Each of these forms of leisure education is important and each can contribute to positive youth development. Nevertheless, the various forms are intertwined and share common foundations. A basic tenet of all leisure education is that leisure is freely chosen activity that promotes and enhances personal growth, transformation, and development. Responsible action is a key ingredient. Let us take a closer look at each form of leisure education.

Education Through Leisure

The basic premise of the *education through leisure* perspective is that one learns about oneself and the surrounding world through participation in leisure. Thus, we learn "in" leisure. This type of leisure education tends to be informal and personal, and is closer to the schole that occurred in natural environments.

Today, any type of environment (not necessarily the natural environment) in which leisure occurs is a context for leisure education. Thus, by participating in a whitewater rafting trip, for example, a youth might learn about personal strengths she did not realize she had, and/or she might learn about the way people used to run logs down the rapids in the 19th century. Or if a youth visits an art museum in Paris with his parents, he may learn the connection between art and religion during the Renaissance, or perhaps be inspired to express himself through art. In these cases, leisure is a context for education.

Education for Leisure

A second way to view leisure education is *education for leisure.* In this form of education, one learns to be prepared to participate in leisure through skill building (e.g., learning to play chess), knowledge acquisition (e.g., learning a bus route to get to the recreation center, learning how to overcome boredom), and attitude development (e.g., valuing leisure, understanding the benefits of appropriate leisure involvements). Formal programs that teach youth activity or leisure skills (e.g., soccer, pottery) are examples of education for leisure and are often provided by public park and recreation departments and not-for-profit agencies such as the YMCA or YWCA. Of course parents, other adults, and peers also teach activity skills. In many ways this is analogous to the learning that went on in gymnasia—learning leisure skills to be able to fully participate in chosen leisure activities.

Education for leisure also occurs as part of a formal program designed to teach youth about how to use their leisure time in personally fulfilling and responsible ways. This form of leisure education tends to be curriculum or program-based, and later in this chapter we provide an example of a curriculum designed to teach youth about self-determination, boredom reduction, initiative, responsible planning, and decision making. A number of therapeutic recreation programs and some school-based programs currently offer this form of leisure education.

Training for Leisure Education

A final approach to leisure education is most commonly associated with tertiary education and is the form of education in which you are engaged right now. That is, you are *learning about leisure* so that you can go out and engage in some form of leisure education or recreation service provision. Worldwide, there are many postsecondary professional preparation curricula and programs that have leisure and recreation as a subject.

Although colleges and universities are the ones most often thought of as training grounds for people interested in facilitating leisure in others, recreation and park departments, YMCAs/YWCAs, and community recreation centers are also involved in this type of education. Counselor-in-training programs at camps are another setting in which leisure education takes place.

Parent programs that teach parents how to manage, support, and facilitate their children's leisure education are another example. A community center in Vermont, for example, runs an ongoing series, Parents Night Out. The focus of this program is to provide education to parents about raising their children, and most topics either directly or indirectly relate to use of free time. Thus, "Creating Limits that Work (Hopefully!!) Part 1 and Part 2," deals with how to negotiate and set limits for teens in the summer, a time when teens want freedom to sleep in late, stay up late, and hang out with friends (Raupach, personal communication, May 2004). Another program in this series is "How to Help Your Teenager Make Reasonable Decisions."

The innovative Parents Night Out program is important, as there is increasing parental interest in learning positive parenting practices that will support their child's development through leisure. Thus, parental training is timely and should be considered. Chapter 11 addresses in detail the role of parents in helping youth develop through recreation.

School-Based Contexts of Leisure Education

We have suggested that leisure education occurs in a number of different contexts, both formal and informal. In the United States, therapeutic recreation is the area that has predominantly used formal, program-based leisure education to meet the needs of both children and adults with disabilities (e.g., Dattilo, 1999, 2000, 2002). The history of school-based leisure education programs is spotty. Stemming from the Greeks, the idea of leisure education in the schools had a strong voice in the American John Dewey, who in 1916 argued that schools should be educating youth for the wise use of leisure time. In 1918 one of the National Education Association's seven cardinal principles of education was "to educate for worthy use of leisure time." Thus, between 1910 and 1930, thousands of school systems established extensive extracurricular activities and programs, including sports, publications, hobbies, and social and academic experiences.

Unfortunately, Dewey's ideas have been largely ignored, although some leisure and recreation professional organizations and scholars have maintained an interest in school-based leisure education. For example, in 1966 Charles K. Brightbill wrote *Educating for Leisure-Centered Living*, which he revised and updated in 1977 with Tony Mobley. Now let us take a look at some of the more prominent school-based leisure education programs that have existed or do exist today.

Lighted Schoolhouse Projects

One of the first leisure education based efforts in schools used the concept of "lighted schoolhouses," meaning that schools would be used as locations for community members to gather and participate in supervised recreation. The first effort, in Milwaukee, Wisconsin in 1911, came about in response to the rise of youth gangs and an increased inflow of immigrants, who enjoyed physical games, dance, art, and socializing but had nowhere to go to participate in them (American Association for Leisure and Recreation Task Force on Leisure Education, 2002). These efforts were the impetus for the creation of other Lighted Schoolhouse Projects in places such as Chicago, Los Angeles, and Michigan.

A more recent version of the Lighted Schoolhouse was developed in Texas in 1989. This joint effort by a YMCA and an alternative education program shelter for homeless children sought to provide after-school supervision for youth from 3:00 p.m. to 9:30 p.m.

Florida State University's Scope and Sequence Model

Leisure studies faculty at Florida State University developed the Scope and Sequence Model in the 1970s in cooperation with Florida State Department of Education personnel as a response to the growing interest in leisure education by the National Recreation and Park Association's Society of Professional Recreation Educators (SPRE). The scope and sequence model was based on the National Policy Statement on Leisure Education (SPRE, 1972) and the curriculum contained a set of objectives for a leisure education program that could be integrated into other subjects (e.g., reading) from prekindergarten through high school. Six categories were included: self-awareness, leisure awareness, attitudes, decision making, social interaction skills, and leisure activity skills.

NRPA's Leisure Education Advancement Project (LEAP)

Another response to the interest in leisure education in the 1970s was the National Recreation and Park Association's Leisure Education Advancement Project (LEAP). This project led to the development of a comprehensive curriculum for youth in kindergarten through Grade 12, and like the scope and sequence model, was designed to be infused into the existing curriculum for that grade. Specific objectives of LEAP were for children

1. to recognize the use of leisure as an avenue for personal satisfaction and enrichment
2. to know the array of opportunities available in leisure time
3. to understand the significant impact that leisure time has and will have on society
4. to appreciate natural resources and their relationship to discretionary time
5. to make decisions regarding their own leisure behavior (Lancaster & Odum, 1976)

Despite these exemplary programs, leisure education in the schools has evolved sporadically, and recent budget cut-backs have eliminated many extracurricular arts and music programs. As we write this book, we hesitate to say the tide is shifting, but we are hopeful that over the coming years school-based leisure education programs will increase. One reason to be hopeful is the increasing prominence of after-school programs (see Chapter 14). Leisure education programs may also be recognized as appropriate during school time if research demonstrates that leisure education contributes to valued educational goals (e.g., preventing dropping out, enhancing academic achievement) as well as to risk reduction in other behavioral domains (e.g., substance use).

Although the interest in leisure education has spawned the development of some promising programs, to date few programs have been developed on a strong theoretical foundation. Likewise, extensive evaluation of leisure education efforts is limited. This is the primary reason it has been difficult to connect leisure education to valued educational and human developmental outcomes. Recently, however, a leisure education program has been developed which shows promise as a means to increase positive leisure behaviors and ultimately to reduce negative behaviors. In the following sections we describe the theoretical basis of the program and then provide some details about the program itself.

TimeWise: Taking Charge of Leisure Time

TimeWise: Taking Charge of Leisure Time (Caldwell, 2004) is a new school-based, leisure education curriculum. The program helps youth to be prepared as well as get fully engaged with their environments through leisure and recreation. *TimeWise* teaches youth to use their leisure time in healthy and productive ways by helping them, among other things, analyze current and develop future leisure interests. Initially, *TimeWise* was developed to help prevent substance abuse by middle-school youth and was funded through a grant from the National Institutes of Health National Institute of Drug Abuse (NIDA). However, *TimeWise* can be easily adapted to other groups to prevent other problem behaviors, such as obesity. It can also stand alone as a leisure education program for youth without being used as a prevention program.

A unique aspect of this program is that it takes a positive approach to prevention, not a problem-focused approach. Teachers are increasingly drawn to approaches that focus on both developmental issues (e.g., development of interests) *and* negative behavior (ideas we discussed in Chapters 1 and 7). In fact, *TimeWise* is currently being used with sixth graders in the Harrisburg, PA School District for these very reasons.

Before discussing the specific ways the program was designed, we will provide some in-depth discussion about some of the issues the program is designed to address. Because the program is based on theory, it is more likely to be effective.

Boredom and Its Negative Impacts

Boredom, while seemingly simple to understand, is actually a complex phenomenon caused by many factors. Boredom can be fleeting (i.e., a state) or more pervasive (i.e., a trait). Although reasons for experiencing boredom in leisure are numerous, reasons that resonate most with adolescents are "I don't have anything to do" or "I have to do it." Other reasons for boredom are the lack of stimulating activities in which to participate, repeatedly participating in the same activities, hanging out with the same peers, or participating in activities that present too little challenge. Three theories or sets of theories can help us understand the causes and consequences of boredom: understimulation theory, social control or resistance theories, and the forced-effort theory. Each of these is discussed next.

From a psychological perspective, the *understimulation theory* (e.g., Larson & Richards, 1991) provides one means for understanding boredom. This theory suggests that boredom is caused by a mismatch between one's skill and the challenge at hand. You have no doubt experienced boredom for this reason. Consider a 15-year-old boy, Roger, who has developed a good bit of skill playing chess. Suppose his parents decide to go on a vacation with another family that has a 13-year-old boy (Mateo) who is just learning the game. If the boys play chess with each other a few times, Roger is likely to feel understimulated (i.e., his skills are greater than the challenge) and thus bored. Boredom through understimulation can also result from (a) a lack of awareness of stimulating things to do in leisure (Iso-Ahola & Weissinger, 1987) and (b) a lack of intrinsic motivation, in particular self-determination, to act in ways that can alleviate boredom (Iso-Ahola & Weissinger, 1987; Weissinger, Caldwell & Bandalos, 1992).

Boredom from an *understimulation* perspective may be dependent on age. For example, younger youth may not have the cognitive ability to identify how they can restructure their situation (i.e., ways to change the circumstances) to alleviate boredom. As youth grow older, they usually develop the capacity to temper or regulate their interactions with their circumstances (Elliott & Feldman, 1990). In the example just provided, if Roger was 17, he may have been able to figure out how to restructure the chess game to give himself more of a challenge, while still providing the right amount of challenge to Mateo.

A second set of theories relates to *social control or resistance*. As youth grow older, they develop emotional and behavioral autonomy from parents. That is, they begin to rely more on their peers for support and to make some of their own decisions about how to manage their free time. This desire to be "grown up and independent" is often at odds with parents, who tend to continue to monitor their child's actions, especially at early adolescent ages (e.g., 14 and 15). In turn, some youth may perceive monitoring as overly controlling. In this case, boredom may be the result of resisting external control (Larson & Richards, 1991). Consequently, the adolescent may disengage psychologically and experience boredom (Eccles et al., 1993). This type of boredom may also produce a standard means of communication (e.g., apathetic responses such as "whatever") that turns into a routine aspect of youth culture.

Finally, the *forced-effort theory* of boredom (Larson & Richards, 1991; O'Hanlon, 1981) indicates that boredom occurs when youth have to attend to or focus on tasks that are repetitive and are perceived as routine. Thus, youth might experience boredom when parents, teachers, or coaches require too much routine and/or monotonous practice. In this case participation may become extrinsically motivated. Thinking back to Roger's interest in chess, suppose his parents thought he was good and wanted him to get better so they arranged for him to take classes two nights a week and wanted him to practice two other nights a week. Although Roger might have initially liked chess, he may feel that his parents' schedule for him is too much effort and that practicing is not very interesting. In this case, something that he enjoyed initially might become boring if he has to spend so much time practicing.

Boredom and motivation are intricately tied to each other. Youth who are intrinsically motivated (i.e., do things for internal as opposed to external reasons) are much less likely to experience boredom because they are interested in what they are doing. They engage in preferred activities because they like and enjoy them, regardless of the presence of other rewards like winning a race or exercising to lose weight. Significantly, they can often figure out how to alleviate being bored through some purposeful action.

On the other hand, youth who are extrinsically motivated tend to experience more boredom. It is important to note that this type of boredom occurs not only because of parent or adult structure but also when peers exert influence on a young person to participate in activities in which they are really not interested. For example, Tamara might report being bored when she goes with a friend to a rock concert because even though she likes concerts, she really didn't want to go to this one, and just went to be nice to her girlfriend (Brake, 1997).

Another form of motivation highly connected to boredom is *amotivation*, or a lack of motivation. In this case, youth might participate in an activity, but there is no clear reason why they are doing it and as a consequence they are just going through the motions. In particular youth often report being bored when hanging out with their friends because they are doing so based on a perception that there is nothing else to do. Here, hanging out is the default option. Amotivation has been linked to lack of initiative and negative behaviors such as substance use.

Interest and Initiative

The opposite of boredom is interest, and consequently leisure education for youth should address not only how to avoid boredom but also how to develop interests. Kleiber (1999) suggested there is a logical progression of interest development. **Figure 9.1** represents this process.

1. First, *experimentation and exposure* can lead to interest development.
2. Through either being intrinsically motivated, or internalizing (i.e., personally endorsing) a more external form of motivation, *interest can be sparked.* This is one reason leisure education is important...it facilitates the desire to experiment and become exposed to different forms of possible leisure.
3. Once interest is developed, *skills are learned.*
4. After skills are learned, *competence is developed.*
5. As one achieves a level of competence, *one becomes committed* to the activity and engages in it as a long-term pursuit. For some, this becomes a form of *serious leisure,* where one is wholly absorbed by the activity and devotes significant amounts of time, energy, and money into participation.

Going back to the chess example, suppose Mateo saw a Harry Potter film and was exposed to the idea of chess. His parents noted that interest, and bought him a chess set with which to experiment. They told him that they would buy the chess set only if he promised to practice (or play) twice a week. Even though that was external motivation, Mateo endorsed the idea and agreed. Over time, he developed skills and felt very competent about his ability to play more challenging games. The next year in school, he joined the chess club and committed to practice matches and playing regularly in tournaments. Although his parents could not pick him up after school once the chess matches were done, Mateo figured out a system of rides and bus routes that would enable him to continue his interest.

This process of interest development and engagement is sometimes termed *initiative.* According to Larson (2000), initiative occurs when an interest is developed, a preferred activity is selected, and constraints to participation are overcome, thus allowing sustained involvement in the activity. Sustained participation that allows for appropriate challenges and skill development is an excellent way to develop feelings of personal competence.

The ability to sustain participation in an activity, however, is often challenged by various constraints and resource limitations (e.g., lack of stamina, money, or social support) that can affect leisure participation negatively by preventing participation; reducing the frequency, intensity, or duration of participation; or reducing the quality of experience or satisfaction gained from the activity (Jackson & Scott, 1999). Leisure education, therefore, should address constraints to participation and help youth learn to develop solutions to overcoming constraints, if possible.

What Works for Some Doesn't Work for All

Things are a little more complicated than what we just presented, however. For example, not all programs work for all youth in the same way. Thus, when adopting programs it is important to ask, "For whom does this work and under what conditions?" Let us look at several examples of research findings that might help us create programs that are sensitive to individual differences.

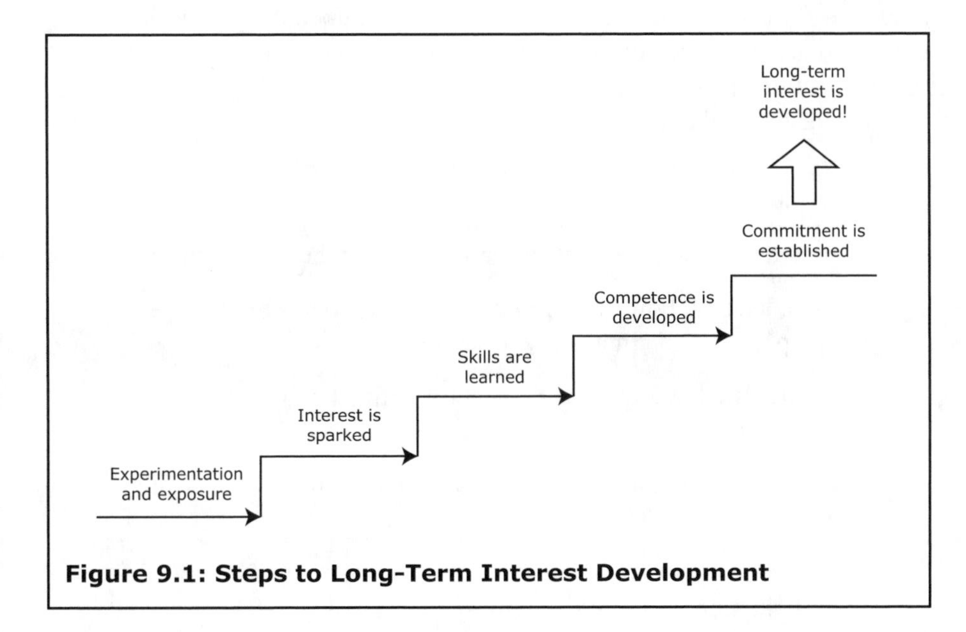

Figure 9.1: Steps to Long-Term Interest Development

Some research has examined the effect of parents' roles in a child's level of motivation and boredom. A study by Caldwell and Smith (2004) examined whether parents who were knowledgable and interested in their youths' leisure activities helped youth who were not very intrinsically motivated to become less bored (and more interested) in their leisure. Their results indicated that youth with low levels of amotivation (i.e., they *were* motivated) had low levels of boredom, and it did not matter that much how much support parents gave them. Because youth were intrinsically interested in what they were doing in free time, they were not bored. On the other hand, youth with moderate and high levels of amotivation *benefited* from their parents knowledge. Amotivated youth whose parents were knowledgable and interested in what they did in their free time reported lower levels of boredom than youth whose parents were uninterested and knowledgable. Thus parents provided that "extra push" to help youth become less bored, but only for amotivated youth. More research is needed to understand these individual differences.

Findings from the Caldwell and Smith (2004) study provide one example of the importance of paying attention to individual differences when developing programs. We will provide additional evidence related to this point when we discuss the evaluation of *TimeWise.*

The *TimeWise* Curriculum

TimeWise is comprised of six core lessons (approximately 12 sessions) and six advanced skill-builder lessons targeted at middle-school youth. The six advanced skill-builder lessons can be conducted immediately after the six core lessons are covered or used as "booster" sessions in subsequent years. As we mentioned, it was originally designed to prevent substance use among youth by enabling them

1. to determine personally satisfying and meaningful leisure activities and interests
2. to understand the benefits of participating in healthy leisure
3. to understand how one's motivation affects one's experience and participation in healthy behaviors
4. to alleviate boredom and to increase optimal experience in leisure time
5. to learn how to take responsible action to participate in desired activities
6. to identify and to overcome constraints that get in the way of participation in desired activities

One of the strengths of the *TimeWise* curriculum is that it has a strong theoretical foundation (e.g., using the theories of boredom, interest and initiative described in the previous sections). This theoretical foundation provided not only a compelling rationale for the curriculum but also guidance on how to design each lesson—essentially, we put theory into practice, which is what we will describe next. Basing *TimeWise* on theory also helped us know what we needed to measure in the evaluation to determine if *TimeWise* was effective.

TimeWise Theory of Intervention

To use theory to develop *TimeWise* and to guide its evaluation, we first had to map out exactly how helping youth learn the six things just identified would decrease substance abuse, which was the long-term or *distal outcome.* This is called specifying the theory of intervention or theory of action (see Chapter 10). By using theory and research findings, we identified leisure-related risk and protective factors (e.g., boredom, interest, and initiative) that needed to be addressed through the curriculum. In planning the curriculum in this way, we increased the probability that engaging youth in intervention activities would decrease their levels of risk factors and increase their levels of protective factors (e.g., decrease boredom). **Figure 9.2** (p. 206) diagrams why we thought the program would work.

Often the way in which a program influences outcomes is depicted in a logic model, and **Figure 9.3** (p. 207) shows the general logic model for *TimeWise*. (A more detailed look at logic models will be presented in Chapter 10.) This logic model specifies that the intervention influences a number of short-term (i.e., proximal) outcomes that in turn influence the long-term outcomes. In particular, the short-term or proximal outcomes of the intervention are as follows:

- *Behavioral.* Increased participation in preferred leisure activities; increased participation in healthy, balanced leisure; and increased involvement with an activity over time.

- *Affective.* Decreased perceptions of being bored in leisure; increased perceptions of leisure being meaningful, interesting, and satisfying; and increased personal responsibility for managing leisure time.

- *Cognitive.* Increased perception of ability to restructure boring situations, to analyze one's free time, to identify and overcome constraints, to plan and make healthy decisions, and to become aware of leisure resources.

Thus, if youth who participated in the *TimeWise* program experienced increased protective factors or decreased risk factors (i.e., the program produced a proximal or short-term outcome), we believed youth would be healthier and engage in less substance use.

Once the theoretical basis for the curriculum was specified and the logic model developed, the next step was to design the specific activities of the curriculum to achieve our outcomes. Of course, this meant specifying lesson goals and student outcomes for each lesson. Again, having theories guided us in determining appropriate lesson goals and student outcomes. **Table 9.1** (pp. 208–209) contains information about the six core lessons. It identifies the main goals we hoped to achieve in each topic and briefly describes the theoretical rationale for the development of each lesson.

The first column of **Table 9.2** (pp. 210–211) provides specific *student outcomes* from the boredom and interest lesson,[1] followed by an identification of how those outcomes will be accomplished through the *lesson activities*. We did this so we could "unpack" the curriculum into chunks and link each activity with a desired outcome. Doing this gives us good insight into understanding specifically why and how each element of the program is related and works.

The second column contains the items we used on our pretests and posttests to measure whether or not the intervention changed behaviors, attitudes, and cognitions as we had hypothesized (i.e., level of boredom/interest; ability to restructure a boring activity; and development of new, interesting activity).

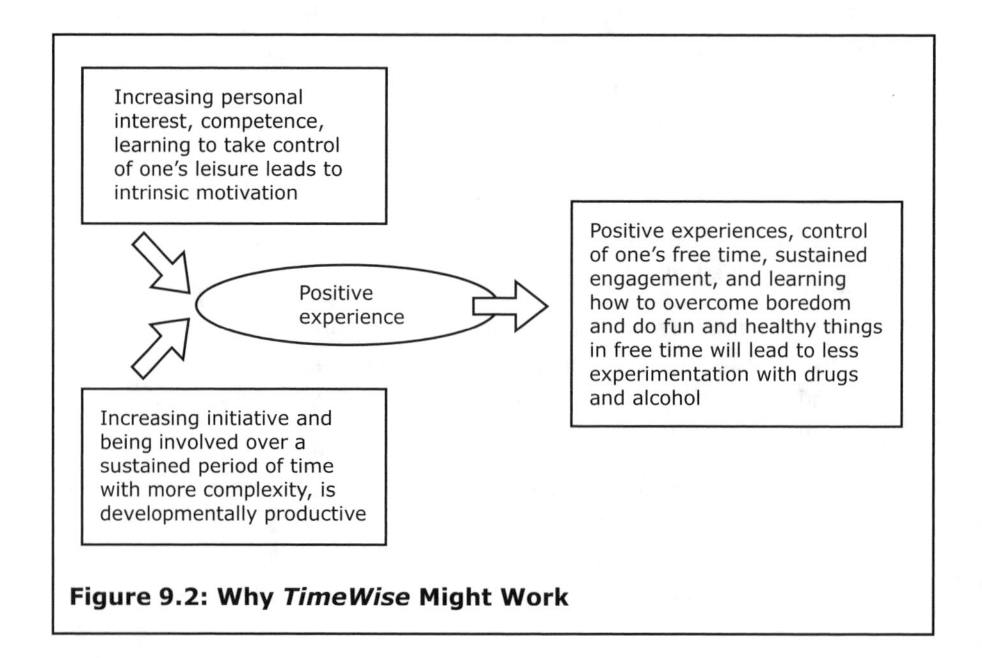

Figure 9.2: Why *TimeWise* Might Work

That is, what outcomes did the curriculum produce? In doing this, we built in the evaluation of the curriculum at the same time as we were developing it, making sure we "knew where we were going and knew how to get there." Because the program and evaluation were based on theory, it was easier to describe why things worked (or didn't). In other words, if risk factors were reduced (e.g., high boredom) and protective factors increased (e.g., interest), we could explain how the program worked to prevent initiation of substance use. Then we were able to construct the rest of the lessons in the *TimeWise* curriculum in a similar manner.

Let us now take a brief look at each of the core lessons. Each lesson contains two related subtopics, identified in Table 9.1.

Lesson 1: Exploring leisure activities. In the first lesson students identify the kinds of things they do in their free time and reflect on the benefits (e.g., physical, mental, spiritual) they receive from their activities. Students are encouraged to reflect on their activity choices and consider the possible healthy and unhealthy consequences. Students complete a four-day time diary (two weekdays and two weekend days) for homework, which is referred to throughout the six lessons.

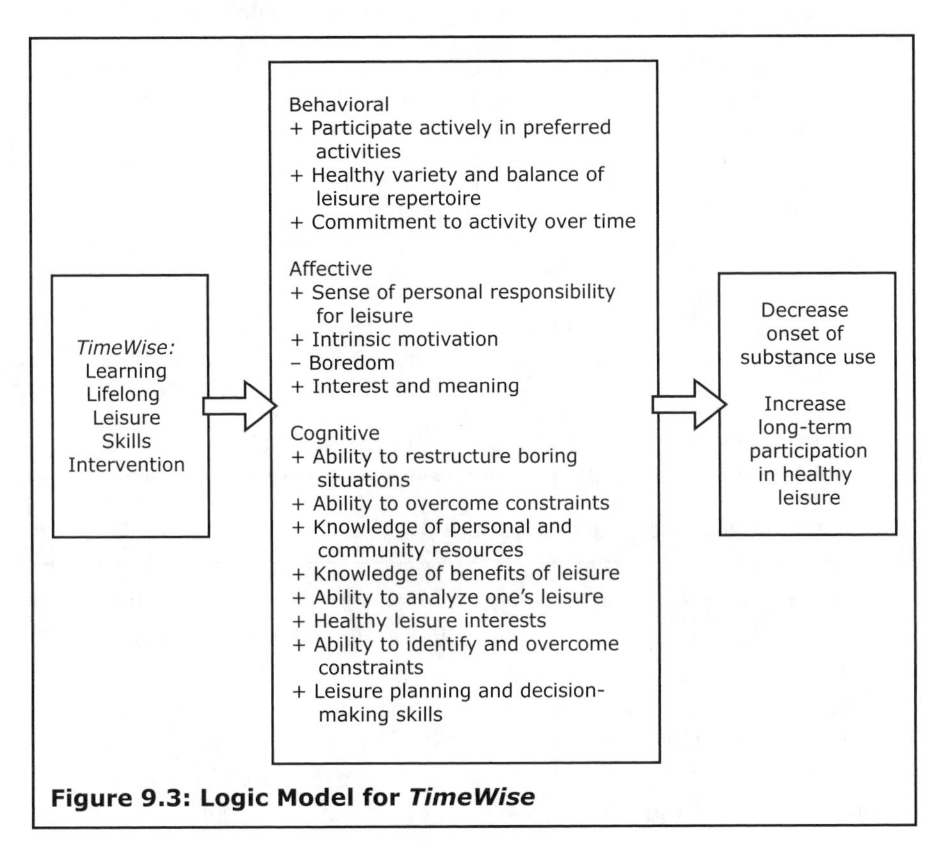

Figure 9.3: Logic Model for *TimeWise*

Table 9.1: *TimeWise* Core Curriculum and Theory

Lesson 1: Exploring Leisure Activities
Subtopics: Taking Charge of Leisure Time, Benefits of Leisure
Goals: To help students identify the kinds of free time activities they do and the benefits they get from their participation, to help students summarize and analyze their current leisure activity profile, and to instill a sense of responsibility for leisure activity choices.
Description and Theoretical Foundation: This lesson sets the stage for subsequent lessons by getting the students to become self-aware of what they do in their leisure and to recognize that there are many benefits associated with participating in leisure activities. They also learn that there are many ways to spend leisure time that are unhealthy and do not provide benefits.

Lesson 2: Checking Out My Motivation
Subtopics: Types of Motivation, Motivation, Feelings, and Benefits
Goals: To help students understand why they participate in leisure activities and summarize and analyze their leisure time.
Description and Theoretical Foundation: This lesson is primarily based on intrinsic motivation and the theory of self-determination (e.g., Ryan & Deci, 2000a, 2000b; Vallerand, 1997). Beyond becoming self-aware, the lesson moves students to become more intrinsically motivated in their leisure (if needed) rather than acting because they are amotivated, externally driven, or driven by the need to fit in or be popular with their friends (i.e., introjected motivation).

Lesson 3: Beating Boredom and Developing Interests
Subtopics: Dealing With Boredom, Finding New Interests
Goals: To help students learn what makes activities boring and interesting and helps students identify a repertoire of new leisure time interests that will augment their existing activities.
Description and Theoretical Foundation: Optimal arousal and boredom (e.g., Caldwell, Darling, Payne & Dowdy, 1999; Csikszentmihalyi, 1990; Mannell & Kleiber, 1997) are two of the concepts behind this lesson. Two other main concepts are intrinsic motivation (e.g., Ryan & Deci, 2000a; Vallerand, 1997) and initiative (e.g., Larson, 2000). Finally, the concept of personal constraints is used in this lesson. Attitudes and stereotypes that prevent one from developing or even thinking about a potential interest are discussed.

Lesson 2: Checking out my motivation. Students learn that healthy use of free time requires balancing what one *has to do* with what one *wants to do* and that is a complex and dynamic process. Thus, students are introduced to amotivated, and externally and internally motivated, reasons for engaging in leisure activity. The lesson emphasizes the importance of doing activities because of a real interest in the activity (i.e., intrinsic motivation) or because the activity serves a future purpose, such as learning to play an instrument to

Table 9.1: *TimeWise* Core Curriculum and Theory *continued*

Lesson 4: Making an Action Plan
Subtopics: Overcoming Obstacles, Accessing Resources
Goals: To help students learn to make plans and to take action in carrying out their leisure interests and to help students learn to overcome constraints and obstacles that might get in their way of carrying out their action plan.
Description and Theoretical Foundation: The theoretical impetus for this lesson stems from the work on initiative development (Bronfenbrenner & Morris, 1998; Larson, 2000) and development as action in context (Silbereisen & Eyferth, 1986; Silbereisen & Todt, 1994). Building from the previous lessons, where youth discover what their interests are and why having long-term interests are important (e.g., avoiding boredom), here youth learn to actively construct their own free time in ways that are meaningful and interesting to them. Knowledge alone is not sufficient; this lesson helps them begin to plan, problem solve, and to make decisions about their own leisure time.

Lesson 5: Managing Daily Leisure
Subtopics: Variety and Balance, Finding a Balance
Goals: To help students learn to take responsibility for their daily leisure time so that they have variety and balance in what they do, and are prepared for unexpected leisure time.
Description and Theoretical Foundation: Lessons learned here help students negotiate things that happen when they have unstructured time or encounter periods of being bored. Also in this lesson, youth learn the need to have a variety of activity types and friends in their repertoire, and a balance of how they spend their time on a daily and weekly basis.

Lesson 6: Putting It All Together
Goals: To help students integrate the material in the previous five lessons, to analyze leisure scenarios, and to facilitate student application of material to their own lives in the future.
Description and Theoretical Foundation: This lesson helps students integrate the five previous lessons, and therefore all theories that have provided the foundation for the curriculum are used in this lesson. The lesson is designed to help students analyze a scenario, integrate material, and problem solve.

get into the school band (i.e., identified motivation). In contrast, situations associated with acting because one has nothing else to do (i.e., amotivation), has to (i.e., external motivation), or is driven by the need to fit in or be popular with their friends (i.e., introjected motivation) are also discussed.

Lesson 3: Beating boredom and developing interests. Lesson three teaches students to understand what makes something boring and what makes something interesting so they can avoid or reduce boredom by choosing to

Table 9.2: Outcomes, Activities, and Measures for Beating Boredom and Developing Interests

Student Outcomes and Intervention Activities	Research Measures/ Proximal Outcomes
1. Demonstrate knowledge about what boredom is, what the negative consequences are, and how to overcome boredom. a. Define boredom and interest. b. Complete the "Boredom and Interest Add a Sentence Story" and discuss what makes something boring or interesting. c. Complete the "I'm Bored..." activity and describe ways to overcome boredom. d. Discuss difference between having long-term and short-term interests	For me, free time just drags on and on. Free time is boring. I usually don't like what I am doing in my free time, but I don't know what else to do. I almost always have something to do in my free time. My free time activities are very interesting to me. I do a lot of activities even though I'm not really interested in them.
2. Demonstrate personal value of avoiding boredom and developing interests. a. Discuss why boredom is a negative emotion. b. Discuss why it is important to have long-term interests. Write a song or poem about overcoming boredom.	
3. Shape peer norms that value avoiding boredom and developing interests. a. Using Overhead 6.1, "What Makes Something Boring or Interesting," discuss with their peers how they feel when they are bored. b. Discuss with peers why it is important to avoid boredom and to develop healthy long-term interests. c. Complete the "I'm Bored..." activity and discuss with their peers positive ways to overcome boredom.	

participate in personally interesting activities. As part of this lesson, attitudes and stereotypes that constrain one from developing or even thinking about a potential interest are discussed and role-plays are used to identify when one

Table 9.2: Outcomes, Activities, and Measures for Beating Boredom and Developing Interests *continued*

Student Outcomes and Intervention Activities	Research Measures/ Proximal Outcomes
4. Demonstrate skills for recognizing interest and boredom and avoiding boredom. a. Complete the "I'm Bored..." activity and list concrete ways to overcome boredom (Use Overheads 6.2 "Avoiding Boredom" and 6.3 "Interest!").	In my free time, I know how to turn a boring situation into something that is more interesting to me. I know how to keep up my interest in my free time activities. I can make things more fun for myself in my free time.
5. Believe in ability to develop personal interests and avoid boredom.	*In the last 6 months,* I learned a *new* activity. I developed an interest in a new activity that I do on a regular basis. I've made a new friend (or new friends) through my free time.

is being constrained by a stereotype. Also in this lesson youth learn specific ideas about how to restructure boring situations.

These first three lessons are preparatory for the "action" orientation of the next three lessons. In lessons four through six, students learned about planning skills and resources that will enable them to pursue desired leisure interests.

Lesson 4: Making an action plan. Lesson four directly deals with planning and decision-making skills, as well as overcoming interpersonal and structural constraints to preferred activity participation. Here youth learn to actively construct their own free time in ways meaningful and interesting to them. Students select one or two activities that they would really like to pursue from the list of possible interests they developed in lesson three. The lesson begins with a discussion of the planning process and youth apply the process to their situations. We also guide youth through exercises that increase their awareness of things to do in and around their communities.

Overcoming constraints theory is an important topic for this lesson. After encouraging students to think of a number of things that interest them in the previous lesson, they narrow the range of alternatives to focus on the most doable activities given resource and other possible constraints.

Lesson 5: Managing daily leisure. This lesson extends the previous lesson by helping youth learn to manage the unplanned or unexpected events that occur in free time, including negotiating things that happen when they hang out with friends. Also in this lesson youth learn the importance of having a variety of activity types and friends in their repertoire, and a balance of how they spend their time on a daily and weekly basis. Students read scenarios about youth who have balanced or unbalanced leisure, and place activity icons on a balance beam to represent the fictitious youth's leisure repertoire. Then students "fix" the fictitious youth's repertoire by adding or subtracting activity icons.

Lesson 6: Putting it all together. The last lesson in the core is a synthesis of concepts learned across all lessons. Students engage in a review session, and then choose among a number of exercises (e.g., collage, poetry, writing) to express what they learned in *TimeWise.*

To complete the picture of the curriculum, the Advanced Skill-Builder Lessons include the following:

1. Educating Others About Leisure
2. Making Decisions and Taking Risks
3. Achieving Flow
4. Managing Stress and Becoming Mindful
5. Friendships and Leisure
6. Leisure and Change

We constructed these lessons in the same way the core lessons were developed.

Evaluation of *TimeWise*

So how effective was the curriculum in reducing the initiation of substance use? To evaluate the effectiveness of *TimeWise,* a three-year, quasi-experimental design was used. Nine school districts in central Pennsylvania participated in the evaluation; four received the *TimeWise* program and five served as comparison schools. Grade 7 students were given a pretest in the fall of 2000. The program was implemented in the four rural school districts in the spring of 2001 (six core lessons provided), 2002 (when students were in Grade 8; Advanced Skill Builder Lessons 1 and 2 provided), and 2003 (when students were in Grade 9; Advanced Skill Builder Lessons 3 through 6 provided). At the end of each spring semester, students were given a posttest.

The study found that *TimeWise* did a very good job overall of influencing the proximal outcomes (e.g. leisure-related outcomes, such as decreased boredom, increased planning, and decision-making skills), and results are promising in showing that the program ultimately influences some types of substance use (Caldwell, Smith, Ridenour & Maldonado-Molina, 2004). In general, students who participated in *TimeWise* reported being less bored and more interested in their leisure, were more intrinsically motivated and less amotivated, had more initiative, and were better planners and decision makers. Boys, but not girls, who had *TimeWise* were more aware of leisure opportunities, smoked less cigarettes at the last posttest (2003), and were less likely than comparison group boys to use marijuana. The developers of *TimeWise* are currently trying to understand this gender difference. Perhaps you have some ideas.

These results are promising when we take into consideration the typical developmental trajectory of youth's problem behaviors. As youth get older, they are more likely to engage in substance use, so it is promising that the *TimeWise* curriculum led to decreases in some forms of substance use among boys. Also of note, some of the outcomes were evident only after the core part of the curriculum was given (i.e., the first six lessons) and not after the Advanced Skill Builder Lessons in Grades 8 and 9. This suggests that to be even more effective, the delivery of the program needs to be intensified. That is, we need to determine which of the activities or topics were more effective and provide more curriculum time to (or develop other activities about) these topics. This is a very important finding, and one of the reasons that research and evaluation is so important. We found we were very successful after the first year, but some of the effects decayed over time. Despite that, youth who were in *TimeWise* did benefit in terms of preventing some forms of substance use, and increasing their leisure skills, knowledge, and attitudes. More research is planned for this program, and the findings will be used to update the curriculum and make it even stronger.

Summary and Conclusions

This chapter focused on leisure education and how and why it contributes to youth development. Three basic types of leisure education were discussed: education through leisure, education for leisure, and training for leisure education. We focused mainly on the education for leisure domain. Next we described several leisure education programs and used the *TimeWise* curriculum to examine how leisure education can be used to reduce risk and to promote positive development. We also used information about the *TimeWise* program to demonstrate the need for theory-driven and evaluated leisure education programs and to demonstrate what a deliberately designed program entails.

Leisure education has always held a great deal of promise to contribute to youth development. We sense the time is right again to push this type of agenda. Perhaps in your work with youth you will discover new ways to promote and facilitate education for and through leisure. Perhaps you will also be engaged in training for leisure education. We urge you to be deliberate in your efforts to develop programs—and always evaluate your efforts. The more evidence garnered about how, when, for whom, and under what conditions leisure education works, the more likely it is that leisure education will be seen as a valued contribution to youth development.

References

Brake, S. B. (1997). *Perspectives on boredom for at risk adolescent girls.* University Park, PA: The Pennsylvania State University.

Brightbill, C. K. (1966). *Educating for leisure-centered living.* Harrisburg, PA: Stackpole.

Brightbill, C. K. and Mobley, T. (1977). *Educating for leisure-centered living* (2nd ed.). New York, NY: John Wiley & Sons.

Bronfenbrenner, U. and Morris, P. A. (1998). The ecology of developmental processes. In R. M. Lerner (Vol. Ed.) and W. Danon (Series Ed.), *Handbook of child psychology Vol 1.: Theoretical models of human development* (pp. 993–1028). New York, NY: Wiley.

Caldwell, L. L. (2004). *TimeWise: Taking charge of free time.* Scotts Valley, CA: ETR Associates.

Caldwell, L.L., Darling, N., Payne, L., and Dowdy, B. (1999). "Why are you bored?" An examination of psychological and social control causes of boredom among adolescents. *Journal of Leisure Research, 31,* 103–121.

Caldwell, L. L. and Smith, E. A. (2004, March 11–13). *Role of leisure mediators in preventing substance use among adolescents: A longitudinal analysis.* Paper presented at the Society for Research on Adolescents, Baltimore, MD.

Caldwell, L. L., Smith, E. A., Ridenour, T., and Maldonado-Molina, M. M. (2004, May 28–30). *Changing levels of intrinsic and extrinsic motivation through the TimeWise: Learning lifelong leisure skills program—Preventing the initiation of substance use.* Paper presented at the Society for Prevention Research, Quebec City, Quebec.

Csikszentmihalyi, M. (1990). *Flow: The psychology of optimal experience.* New York, NY: Harper and Row.

Dattilo, J. (1999). *Leisure education program planning: A systematic approach* (2nd ed.). State College, PA: Venture Publishing, Inc.

Dattilo, J. (2000). *Leisure education specific programs.* State College, PA: Venture Publishing, Inc.

Dattilo, J. (2002). *Inclusive leisure services: Responding to the rights of people with disabilities* (2nd ed.). State College, PA: Venture Publishing, Inc.

Dewey, J. (1916). *Democracy and education: An introduction to the philosophy of education.* New York, NY: Free Press.

Eccles, J., Midgely, C., Wigfield, A., Buchanan, C., Reuman, D., Flanagan, C., and MacIver, D. (1993). Development during adolescence: The impact of stage-environment fit on young adolescents' experiences in schools and in families. *American Psychologist, 48*, 90–101.

Elliot, G. R. and Feldman, S. S. (1990). Capturing the adolescent experience. In S. S. Feldman and G. R. Elliott (Eds.), *At the threshold* (pp. 1–13). Cambridge, MA: Harvard University Press.

Iso-Ahola, S. E. and Weissinger, E. (1987). Leisure and boredom. *Journal of Social and Clinical Psychology, 5*(3), 356–364.

Jackson, E. L. and Scott, D. (1999). Constraints to leisure. In E. L. Jackson and T. L. Burton (Eds.), *Leisure studies: Prospects for the twenty-first century* (pp. 299–321). State College, PA: Venture Publishing, Inc.

Kleiber, D. A. (1999). *Leisure experience and human development: A dialectical interpretation*. New York, NY: Basic Books.

Kleiber, D. A. (2002, January 12). *Taking leisure seriously*. Paper presented at the Pacific Rim Conference on Leisure Education, Honolulu, HI.

Kleiber, D. A. (2004). *Specifying the serious and casual while clarifying purposes for leisure education*. Paper presented at the International Conference on Leisure Education, Cologne, Germany.

Lancaster, R. A. and Odum, L. L. (1976). LEAP: The leisure education advancement project. *Journal of Health, Physical Education, Recreation, and Dance, 47,* 47–48.

Larson, R. (2000). Toward a psychology of positive youth development. *American Psychologist, 55* 170–183.

Larson, R. W. and Richards, M. H. (1991). Boredom in the middle-school years: Blaming schools versus blaming students. *American Journal of Education, 99*, 418–443.

Mannell, R. C. and Kleiber, D. A. (1997). *A social psychology of leisure.* State College, PA: Venture Publishing, Inc.

National Survey of American Attitudes on Substance Abuse VIII: Teens and Parents National Center on Addiction and Substance Abuse. (2003, August). Retrieved from http://www.casacolumbia.org/Absolutenm/articlefiles/2003_Teen_Survey_8_19_03.pdf

O'Hanlon, J. (1981). Boredom: Practical consequences and a theory. *Acta Psychologica, 53*, 53–82.

Pesavento, L. C. (2002). Leisure education in the schools: A position statement presented to the American Association for Leisure and Recreation Task Force on Leisure Education. April 8–12, San Diego, CA.

Ryan, R. M. and Deci, E. L. (2000a). Self-determination theory and the facilitation of intrinsic motivation, social development, and well-being. *American Psychologist, 55*, 68–78.

Ryan, R. M. and Deci, E. L. (2000b). Intrinsic and extrinsic motivations: Classic definitions and new directions. *Contemporary Educational Psychology, 25*, 54–67.

Silbereisen, R. K. and Eyferth, K. (1986). Development as action in context. In R. K. Silbereisen, K. Eyferth, and G. Rudinger (Eds.), *Development as*

action in context: Problem behavior and normal youth development (pp. 3–16). New York, NY: Springer-Verlag.
Silbereisen, R. K. and Todt, E. (1994). *Adolescence in context: The interplay of family, school, peers, and work in adjustment.* New York, NY: Springer-Verlag.
Society for Professional Recreation Educators. (1972). *National policy statement on leisure education.* Ashburn, VA: National Recreation and Park Association.
Vallerand, R. J. (1997). Toward a hierarchical model of intrinsic and extrinsic motivation. In M. P. Zanna (Ed.), *Advances in experimental social psychology* (pp. 271–360). San Diego, CA: Academic Press.
Weissinger, E., Caldwell, L. L., and Bandalos, D. L. (1992). Relation between intrinsic motivation and boredom in leisure time. *Leisure Sciences, 14*, 317–325.

Endnote

1. We use the boredom and interest development lesson as an example since we have focused on the theory behind boredom and interest in this chapter.

Chapter 10

Deliberate Programming With Logic Models: From Theory to Outcomes

Cheryl K. Baldwin, Linda L. Caldwell, and Peter A. Witt

So far in this book we have identified many positive outcomes that accrue to youth as a result of their participation in recreation and leisure. For example, young people can enhance their skills, increase friendships, learn to get along with each other, and decrease negative behaviors. Recreation professionals know this to be true, right? But imagine yourself trying to explain to someone in city government, a foundation, a school district, or a nonprofit agency exactly what happens to young people as a result of their participation in a recreation program, and further, explaining how and why it happens. This chapter gives you some important tools to construct a sound argument for your programs. We introduce you to principles of theory-based programming and explain a strategy that uses a logic model to identify the what, how, and why of effective programming.

Recreation professionals have a long history of needing to justify their programs. In Chapter 4, we discussed the origins of many of the youth serving organizations that developed in the late 1800s and early 1900s to reduce crime, to increase socialization, and to help young people enter effectively into adulthood and to be better citizens. Youth services became positioned in people's minds as a means for dealing with critical social issues that had come about due to the Industrial Revolution, migration of people from rural environments to the cities, and a large influx of immigrants into the major cities.

Unfortunately, today, recreation is not as widely viewed as an arena for dealing with social issues. Over time, recreation and park professionals strayed from the philosophy of providing services to meet the needs of youth and many tended to focus on "fun" as the main outcome. As a result, funders and other stakeholders (e.g., politicians, school personnel, parents, participants) often have viewed recreation as simply "fun and games"—discretionary activities that are nice for young people to do, but which hold little potential for dealing with critical social issues. Part of the problem is that professionals providing recreation services have not always been able to articulate the "business they are in" in terms of issues that matter to funders and other stakeholders (Crompton & Witt, 1997).

Today, the most successful programmers and managers design programs to produce outcomes to help them position recreation as a necessary service for accomplishing critical social goals (e.g., decreased crime, increased safety of children who otherwise might be on the streets or return to empty homes during the nonschool hours), educational goals (e.g., better test scores, graduation from high school), and behavioral goals (e.g., decreased destructive behaviors, including drug use and involvement in early and/or unprotected sex). To accomplish this positioning, funders and stakeholders must be able to see recreation as a means for accomplishing social outcomes that are important to society. Thus, it is necessary for recreation service providers to find ways to explain in terms that resonate with stakeholders the "business that we are in." Evidence of success must be provided so that recreation services can be considered beneficial to dealing with youth issues, just as are the police, schools, and the juvenile justice system.

One of the reasons programming for specific outcomes has increasingly become important is that those providing financial support to youth programs are looking at their funding as social investments (Firstenberg, 2003). In addition, there is the general expectation that youth development workers should be held accountable for the claims they make about the benefits of their programs. As such, funders are usually only willing to support programs that provide a good return on their investment and thus are increasingly interested in information that demonstrates that programs do indeed achieve their intended outcomes (Reed & Brown, 2001).

Luckily, there is scientific evidence of the effectiveness of programs to produce valued outcomes. Youth development researchers are increasingly exploring the impact of young people's involvement in school-based and community-based after-school, night and weekend programs, extracurricular activities, and informal involvements, including "hanging out" (Delgado, 2002; Eccles & Gootman, 2002; Hansen, Larson & Dworkin, 2003; Noam, Biancarosa & Dechausay, 2003). However, for recreation workers to offer valued programs and to effectively engage in collaborative efforts with other service providers, they need to learn to explain (a) what they are trying to accomplish, (b) how objectives will be achieved, and (c) what evidence exists that the program outcomes have been accomplished. The rest of chapter will explore tools for accomplishing these goals.

The Role of Theory in Program Development

Just offering a program is not enough to make claims that it is of benefit to young people; today programmers must be able to demonstrate that their programs are designed to meet their intended outcomes. When programmers take the steps necessary to demonstrate that their programs are relevant and effective and they provide theoretical explanations and evaluations of how their programs achieved the targeted goals, a program is considered *evidence-based.* A useful way to develop evidence- or outcome-based programs and to evaluate their effectiveness is to base programs on theory. Theory is important because it can explain and link what is done in the program with specific outcomes. For example, in Chapter 9, the developers of the *TimeWise* leisure education program were able to provide a model of how and why boredom led to negative consequences and to identify specifically how the program was going to decrease boredom and increase interest among youth.

Theory-based programming uses established social science theories and empirical evidence as the basis for program decisions and claims about program outcomes. Theories are used because they provide explanations or forecasts about how selected program activities and experiences will lead to particular participant outcomes. Recall in Chapter 8 we discussed developmental outcomes of leisure and recreation experiences, as well as factors that influenced those outcomes. The reason we could make those claims is that theory and previous research provided that information.

Of course, many programmers have vast experience designing and developing programs and have developed strong beliefs and expectations about how these programs impact participants. Particular ways of structuring and carrying out programs may even be so common that they are generally accepted as *best practices.* Unfortunately, even with acknowledged best practices, it is often difficult to describe the expected outcomes, explain the processes by which the outcomes were expected to be achieved, and determine whether the outcomes were actually achieved.

What we advocate in this book is the need to develop programs and to evaluate their effectiveness based on known linkages between program elements and desired outcomes. By using a theory-based approach to program planning, programmers can meet the demand of funders for evidence that monies are being used to make a difference and avoid "fuzzy thinking" about what they expect to happen in a program. They are also less likely to make unsubstantiated claims about program outcomes after the program is completed.

In sum, the ability to understand, assess, and apply theory is fundamental to quality programming. Ideally, theories should guide the development of programs, explain what one expects to occur as a result of a youth's participation in programs, and serve as the basis for gathering evidence on whether program goals and expectations are achieved.

Theory-Based Programming: An Example Using Logic Models

In theory-based programming, theory, program components, and outcomes are all linked. That is, a program is viewed as a series of successive steps with theory supporting the links between each of the steps. An initial example of program using this framework is provided in **Figure 10.1**; it is referred to as a logic model. (Note, in the literature there are many types of logic models, and although different terminology is used, the process and the intent of each is the same.)

The logic model in Figure 10.1 represents a situation where programmers are interested in offering an after-school recreation program that helps youth complete their homework. This model makes it clear that there is a logical sequence of events that occur. Provision of homework assistance related activities and knowledgable staff lead to participants completing their homework. But children getting their homework done might not be the ultimate desired outcome. **Figure 10.2** is a restatement and extension of the homework assistance program model; it includes proximal, distal, and ultimate outcomes for young people participating in this after-school program. Let's continue the example so the meaning of these terms is clear.

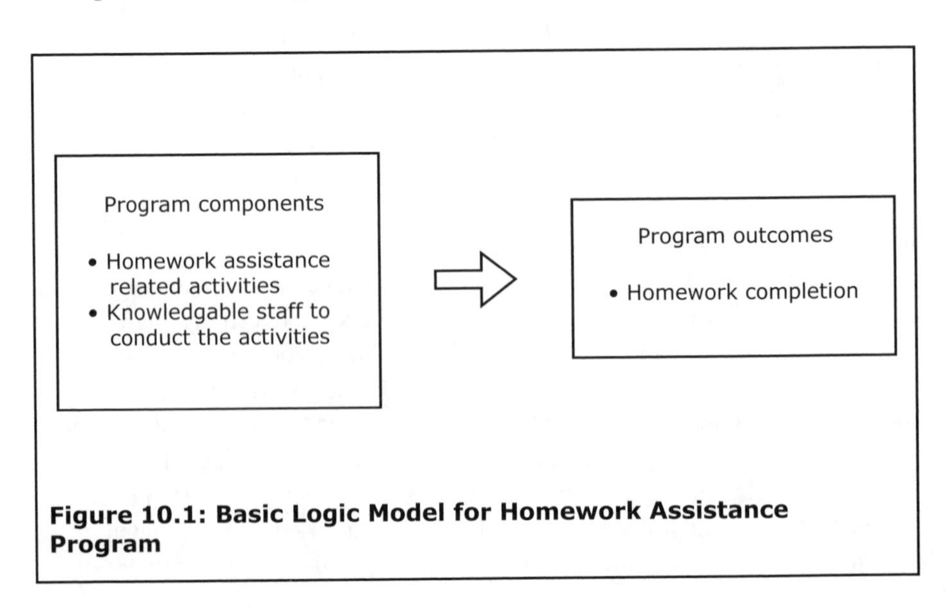

Figure 10.1: Basic Logic Model for Homework Assistance Program

In the current case, although staff are offering homework completion assistance activities, they probably are not doing so just so students can complete their homework. Homework completion is just a short-term or near-term outcome of the program; many researchers use the term *proximal outcome.* It is the first step in achieving other outcomes. In this case, as a result of students completing their homework, staff hope that over the longer term youth will improve their academic abilities enough to raise their grades and pass standardized achievement tests. This type of outcome is termed a *distal outcome* and is something that happens further out in time. It is the next step in achieving a broader outcome. Here, ultimately staff are not just interested in students raising their grades and test scores. As a result of completing homework (i.e., proximal outcome), and then raising their grades and test scores (i.e., distal outcome), staff want students to graduate from high school and be able to support themselves via employment, the *ultimate outcome* of the program. In other words, events happen in a time series, with a series of causal relationships between each of the events or outcomes. Thus, the more complete version of Figure 10.1 is the model displayed in Figure 10.2.

Note how the boxes in Figure 10.2 are numbered, beginning with Box 1 for the ultimate outcome box on the far right and working back to Box 4 for the program components on the far left. In constructing these types of models most people start by identifying the ultimate outcome that they are seeking to achieve. That is, they ask themselves, "What is the eventual contribution (i.e., ultimate outcome) I want my program to make?" There are a number of ways to choose this outcome, and we discuss them later in the chapter. For now, however, it is important to understand that "working backward" is important

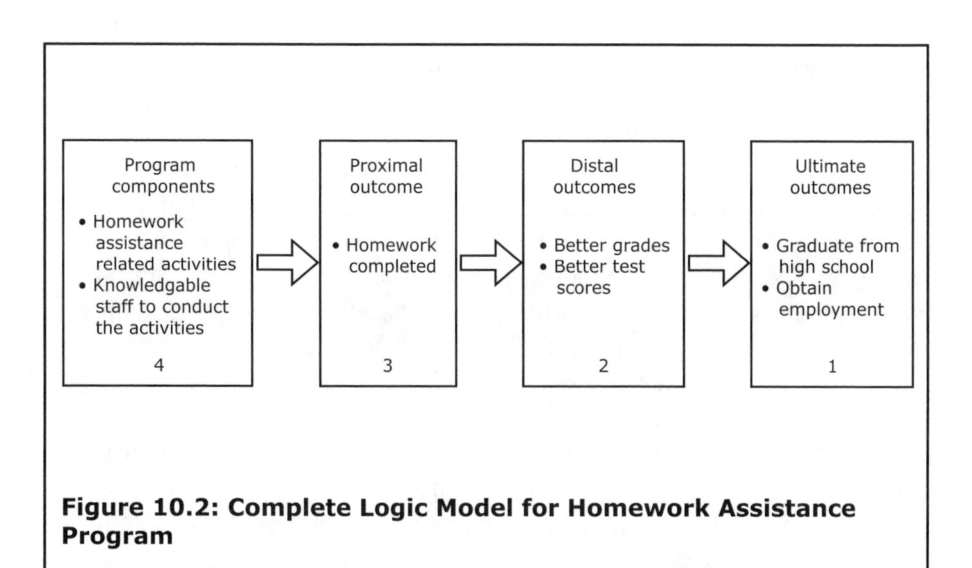

Figure 10.2: Complete Logic Model for Homework Assistance Program

because it is the clearest way to identify what the program is intended to accomplish. Sometimes it is not possible for a recreation programmer to provide evidence of meeting this ultimate outcome, but it is included in the model to indicate the potential value of the program.

In the current case, there are several reasons we might want to target academic success as an ultimate outcome and include a homework completion component as part of an after-school recreation program. For example, the assumption that parents are always available and able to help children with their homework may not be true. In some communities, parents lack the educational foundation to deal with the content of their children's homework. Even if parents have the ability, many work one or more jobs and may not be available to assist their children. In addition, in some cases parents simply shirk their responsibility to help. In each of these cases, it is detrimental to the child and to society at large to not make some kind of homework assistance available. The program itself is developed to achieve the desired outcomes. Remember, "Any old program does not accomplish any old objective." Good planning is intentional, thoughtful, and purposeful.

Theories of Intervention and Explanation

Now that you understand a logic model representation of a program's components and corresponding proximal, distal, and ultimate outcomes, let's discuss the role and contribution of theory more specifically. Two types or levels of theory are used to construct a logic model (West & Aiken, 1997). First, a *program theory or theory of intervention* is used to explain how the program components lead to the program outcomes (e.g., how Box 4 in Figure 10.2 leads to Box 3). Second, a *theory of explanation* explains *why* there are linkages between the distal, proximal, and ultimate outcomes (e.g., how Box 3 links to Box 2 and Box 2 links to Box 1).

In the homework assistance program, the program theory represents how *what happens in the program* produces the desired proximal outcome. Specifically, it is necessary to have a time for students to complete their homework (i.e., program component). In addition, tutoring or assistance by adults who have the ability to motivate students, answer questions, and provide positive rewards for successful homework completion is also provided (Box 4). By providing the program components of time and assistance, students should be able to complete their homework (Box 3).

Theories of explanation help us to link the program to proximal, distal, and ultimate outcomes. In the case of the homework assistance program, research suggests that children who complete their homework are more likely to get higher grades and higher standardized test scores. In turn, theory also suggests that students with higher grades and higher test scores are more likely to graduate from high school and to get better paying jobs.

Now that you have the idea, let's look at another example. In this next example we incorporate specific research studies that support a program designed to prevent smoking. The citations used substantiate the logic model and provide support for the connections between the program components and outcomes.

Smoking prevention. The ultimate outcome of interest in this smoking prevention program example is being a nonsmoker. In adolescence smoking cigarettes is a risk factor because in addition to the more immediate (i.e., proximal) health consequences (e.g., decreased lung capacity), it is often considered a "gateway drug" to undertaking other risk behaviors (e.g., marijuana use). These health consequences are of concern to society and this concern has led to support for programs designed to prevent adolescent smoking.

A number of social influence theories provide an explanation of the factors that influence adolescent smoking. In particular, social learning theory (i.e., the theory of explanation in this example) indicates that role models influence an individual's beliefs and behavior (Bandura, 1986). Applying social learning theory to adolescent smoking, the explanation of why some adolescents smoke is as follows. For adolescents, influential role models are peers. When a youth's peers smoke they project an image that smoking is a normative behavior and provide access to smoking (Baker, Brandon & Chassin, 2004; Petraitis, Flay & Miller, 1995). Youth who desire to associate and be liked by these peers are more likely to begin smoking. Those youth who are better able to manage their need for association with peers and who can deflect appeals or pressuring messages from their peers to smoke are less likely to become smokers. In short, research studies using social learning theory have found that one factor predictive of adolescents smoking is susceptibility to peer influence (Derzon & Lipsey, 1999).

Therefore, if a program's ultimate outcome is to deter smoking, then program activities that develop skills in managing peer influence should increase the participant's resistance to peer influence and ultimately deter smoking. Are there any leisure or recreation activities or programs you can think of that would deal with managing and resisting peer influence?

Imagine this scenario: A park district's youth director has been asked by the local health department to be involved in a community-wide effort to prevent youth from smoking. Based on evidence gathered from an annual youth risk behavior survey, it appears that this mid-size town's youth report smoking at greater rates than similar-size towns. The youth director decides to start relatively small and focuses on the agency's youth council. Twice a year the members of the youth council participate in special topic workshops.

The latest workshop focused on health and wellness. During the workshop youth were involved in cooperative recreation challenge activities focused on peer-related social skills and role played typical social situations. These cooperative activities placed youth in challenging situations where, among other things, they tried to persuade one another to do something he or she really didn't want to do, including smoking. The content of the discussion surrounding these activities was on individual thinking and assertive responses, which form the basis for successfully, but politely, deflecting peer influence.

Figure 10.3 illustrates the program logic model of how the wellness workshop affects the ultimate outcome of preventing smoking. The program theory indicates that participation in the cooperative challenge activities increases youth's ability to respond assertively. The theory of explanation indicates that assertive responses reduce one's vulnerability to peer influence. In addition, research indicates that youth who have a lower likelihood of being influenced by peers are less likely to become smokers.

The youth council's health and wellness workshop provides another example of how explanation and program theory are combined in an overall program logic model. Again, the value of constructing these types of models is that they specify the causal pathways of change and explain how programs affect behaviors and outcomes.

Using Theory and Focusing on Outcomes

Let's take a moment and briefly reflect on what we've covered about theory-based programming. So far in this chapter we have provided two program examples. The ultimate outcomes, high school graduation and smoking, are

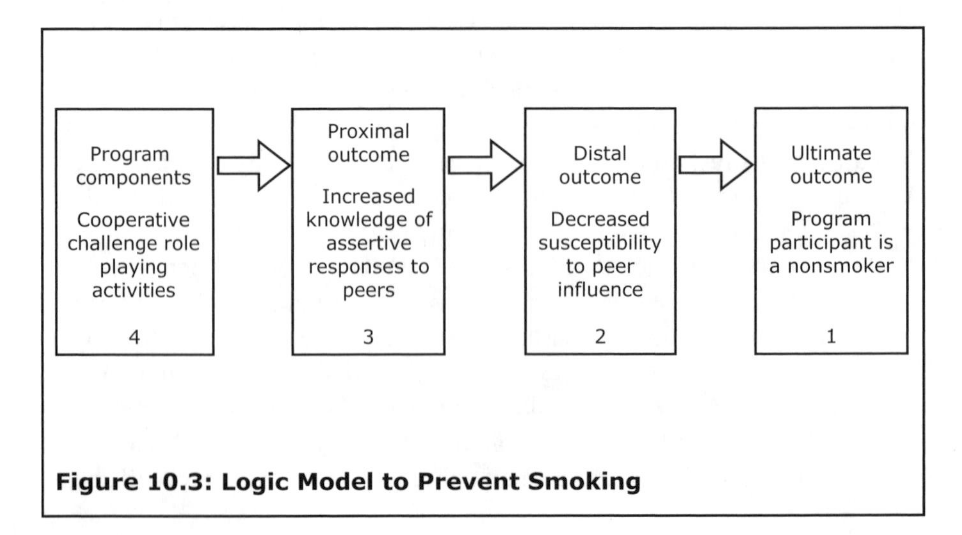

Figure 10.3: Logic Model to Prevent Smoking

protective factors—they reflect outcomes that society deems important. As ultimate outcomes they represent the end goal or purpose for each of the respective programs. To demonstrate that these programs can achieve these outcomes, we used theory-based programming and program logic models to explain exactly how these programs led to specific outcomes. The logic models illustrated the successive steps as "logically" time ordered: program components leading to proximal, distal, and ultimate outcomes. These successive steps model how the program activities produced new skills, which in turn led to outcomes that led to achieving the ultimate outcome. In addition, theory and research were used to justify the linkages across the successive steps.

You may want to look again at the model of the *TimeWise* program presented in Chapter 9. It is another, even more complex logic model of a leisure education program. As you can see programs can vary in many ways, but what is important is the soundness of the underlying logic of how the program works. As you can see, adopting this approach will do a lot to demonstrate why recreation programs and experiences contribute to positive youth development and deter risk.

Constructing a Theory-Based Program: An Example

Let us look at one more example of a program, and build it from the desired ultimate outcome back to the program that will help us to achieve it. In this example, we'll present a bit more information on how you might go about constructing your own program logic model using the principles of theory-based programming.

First, you must determine the ultimate outcome of your youth development program. As we have discussed elsewhere in this book, selection of outcome(s) will reflect things associated with healthy youth development. Which developmental assets you seek to promote with your program will depend on a number of factors related to your community and your agency. It will also depend on what you know about developmental assets and adolescent risk factors, so reading as much as you can about these is a good place to begin.

After you select an ultimate outcome you will further search the social science literature to gain as much information as possible about the desired ultimate outcome and the theories explaining how it might be achieved. A good place to begin this search is to consult the literature for a *very specific definition* of the ultimate outcome. A good definition helps in the measurement of the outcome, and helps distinguish it from other behaviors with which it might be confused. For example, consider the issue of youth being bored during their free time, a risk factor addressed in the *TimeWise* program discussed in Chapter 9. Without adequately defining boredom and understanding its theory, we could have confused boredom with apathy. These two concepts are related but not the same. Had we not been clear about what we meant when we used the term *boredom,* it would have been much more difficult to influence boredom, and to evaluate the effectiveness of our program. Finally, a specific definition of boredom allowed us to state specifically what we meant when we talked with others about the program.

Additional information that you would gather from the social science literature is evidence of the *key determinants* of the ultimate outcome. In the recreation youth council health workshop program example, susceptibility to peer influence was a determinant or predictor of adolescent smoking. Determinants are factors that explain the ultimate outcome and will be found within a theory of explanation.

For example, if your ultimate outcome is self-esteem, then the literature will include discussions of the factors that predict low and high levels of self-esteem. Looking at the literature is critical because research sometimes leads to conclusions that differ from common or folk knowledge. For example, in regard to self-esteem, a common belief is that participation in a program that helps youth feel good about who they are increases their self-esteem. However, research does not support this belief (Harter, 1999). Rather, to change self-esteem, activities need to focus on increasing competencies in domains of importance, like school, peers, and athletics. Additionally, enhancing a youth's peer and parental support positively affects self-esteem (Harter, 1999). Competencies, along with peer and parent support, are key determinants of self-esteem, and thus are factors a recreation-based program would try to affect.

The literature may also include insights about the consequences and importance of a particular behavior or attitude. For example, findings from research studies on self-esteem indicate that low self-esteem during adolescence is associated with depression (Harter, 1999). Understanding this connection helps to explain why enhancing a participant's self-esteem is important. It will also help alleviate misunderstandings. For example, high self-esteem is often credited with solving a wide range of problems, however, these claims have not always been substantiated (Kohn, 1994). Therefore, using the literature to understand what is and is not connected to the ultimate outcome is of utmost importance. Again, the more evidence you have supporting how your program works, the stronger your argument for your program will be.

To sum up, the value in reading the social science literature is developing a specific definition of the targeted outcome, understanding a theory that explains what affects the outcome, and identifying empirical evidence of a link between one or more determinants and an ultimate outcome. These elements of the theory of explanation are then used to gain insight into what kinds of program experiences will affect the key determinants. The process of identifying and describing an ultimate outcome and its determinants is illustrated next.

Developing Autonomy

Development of autonomy is one of a number of important developmental tasks youth face during adolescence. Consequently, a park district's youth workers decided to develop a program designed to increase youth autonomy (the ultimate outcome). Therefore, they formed a youth council, which meets regularly at one of the park district's community centers. The council provides input on youth programming that the park district provides and annually sponsors a special event for children and families. Under the guidance of the youth workers, the youth manage all aspects of the event, including its planning and implementation. In principle, this should be an opportunity for youth to develop ownership of the event.

What were the steps in developing this program and what is the logic model? First, staff needed to understand exactly what they meant by autonomy, so they consulted the literature to understand autonomy theory and specifically define it.

Defining Autonomy

According to Steinberg (2002), autonomy reflects self-governance, with governance conveying a personal sense of responsibility. Ryan and Deci (2000) view autonomy as a basic need central to a person's overall well-being. They conceptualize autonomy as acting in a self-determined manner, which is characterized by experiencing what one does as volitional. An autonomous individual sees his or her actions as motivated by one's own interests, beliefs, and values rather than things external to the self, like parental or school rules, rewards, and pressures (Deci & Ryan, 1985).

For adolescents, autonomy has often been defined as independence from one's parents, but based on the aforementioned definitions, this is only partially accurate. While autonomy does encompass some behavioral independence from the supervision of parents or other adults in authority (Silverberg & Gondoli, 1996), it is not simply acting without direct adult supervision, nor is it rebelling against parent and adult authority. Rather, it involves depending on and staying connected with others while one also maintains his or her own sense of individuality (Collins, Gleason & Sesma, 1997). In contrast, nonautonomous individuals avoid acting in a purposeful manner, exercise irresponsible independence, over rely on others, and view their actions as caused by forces external to the self.

After the staff better understood what autonomy was and was not, they needed to find out what clues they could get from the literature that would help them to design their program and to understand why, if certain program elements were put in place, it should work.

Autonomy Theory

In their review of the literature, staff found that autonomy develops when those in authority, such as parents, teachers, and coaches, support self-initiated behaviors and give youth choices in regard to what transpires in the home, school, or extracurricular program settings (Frederick & Ryan, 1995). Other adult actions that are supportive of autonomy are giving informational feedback in a noncontrolling manner and being able to view things from the youth's perspective (Grolnick, Deci & Ryan, 1997). Autonomy is also reflected in a youth's decision-making skills, including the ability to think ahead, to seek support, to assess outcomes associated with alternatives, and to negotiate with peers as well as adults (Collins, Gleason & Sesma, 1997).

The outlined determinants can help youth workers design a program that would enhance autonomy. For example, activities that foster youth being able to make personal contributions to a program and decisions about what happens in a program, social interactions with peers, and the quality of the relationship with program leaders are all theorized to affect autonomy.

Based on an understanding of the theory, a somewhat complex logic model for our hypothetical youth council special event program is presented in **Figure 10.4**. In some cases, more complex models are necessary to fully understand how programs and outcomes are related. Let's explore the autonomy logic model in some detail.

Autonomy Program Logic Model

The logic model illustrated in Figure 10.4 has three main distal outcomes thought to influence the ultimate outcome of autonomy: youth's sense of choice, negotiation skills, and decision-making skills. These distal outcomes are influenced by proximal outcomes that are a direct product of the program components. Thus, leadership and planning and managing an activity influence youths' perceptions of autonomy through how leaders interact with youth (e.g., nature of feedback) and how the program elements encourage behaviors such as expressing personal ideas. These links are specified both from a theoretical understanding of choice, as well as by deduction.

Deduction (also known as professional judgment) is sometimes necessary if there is insufficient information in the literature to completely justify a

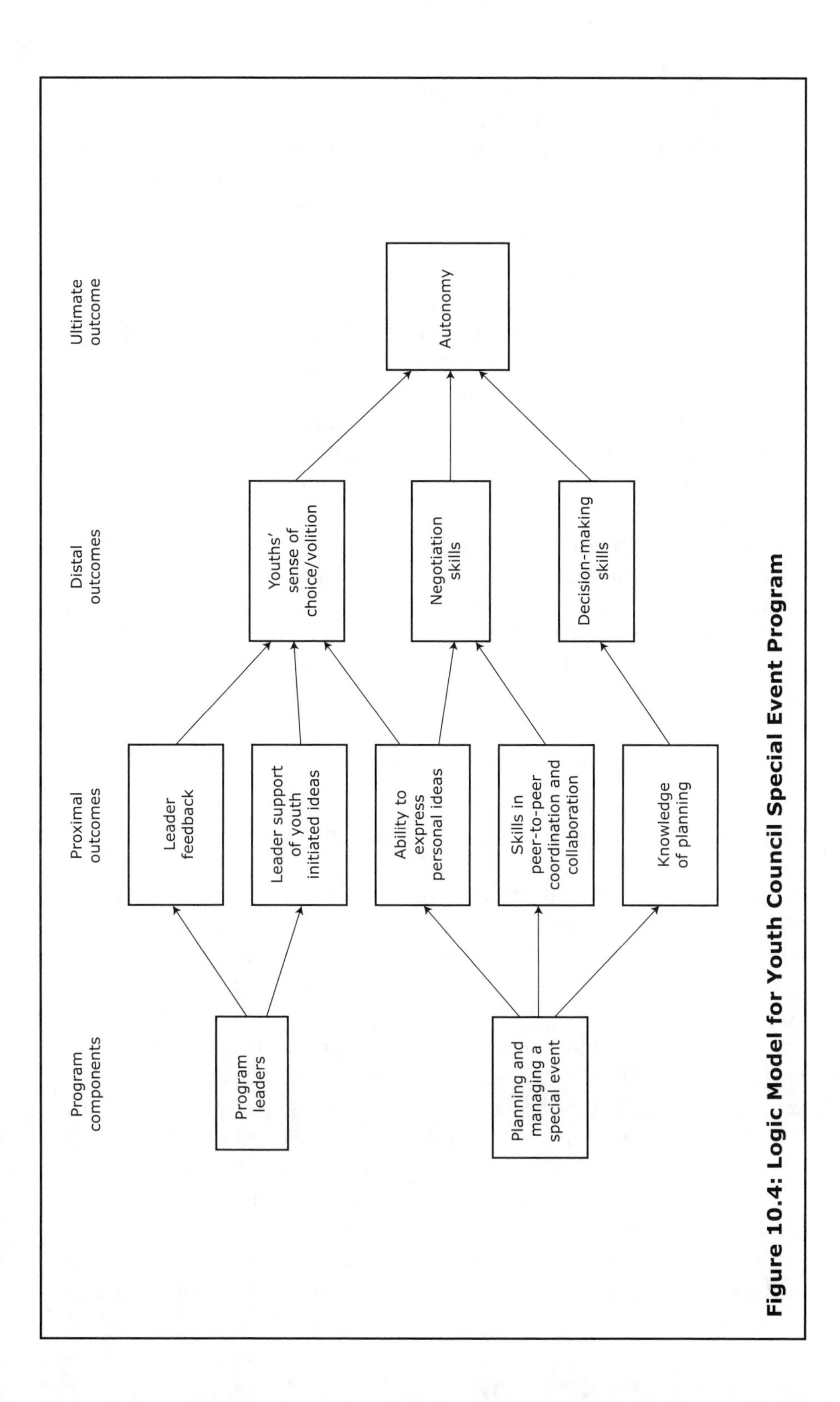

Figure 10.4: Logic Model for Youth Council Special Event Program

particular link. For example, it is a logical premise that being able to exercise and to express one's ideas and beliefs is a prerequisite skill to feeling a sense of choice/volition. As a result, this link was incorporated in Figure 10.4. It would be optimal if logic models could be primarily based on theory and empirical evidence and less on deduction; however, theory and research may not yet have clearly addressed all aspects of desired outcomes and what it will take to bring them about.

Recall that sense of choice is associated with seeing oneself as an important cause of what one does, as opposed to just responding to options provided by those in authority. Based on autonomy theory, at least two aspects of adult leadership are important: the degree to which leaders give informational rather than controlling feedback and the degree to which they support youth initiated ideas or points of view. When these leadership characteristics are present, we expect youth to feel they have a great deal of volition or choice in doing what they do.

Planning and managing the special event creates a platform whereby youth develop abilities to express their personal ideas, to increase their knowledge of planning, and to improve their skills in peer-to-peer coordination and collaboration. If the program components produce these theorized proximal effects, they should subsequently foster the distal outcomes of enhancing youths' sense of choice/volition, decision-making, and negotiation skills. If all of the distal outcomes are affected, then the ultimate outcome of youths' sense of autonomy should also be increased.

Developing the Program Theory

While the connections between the proximal, distal, and ultimate outcomes are driven by the explanatory theory, the links between the program components and proximal outcomes are sometimes less evident and require an analysis of the processes and elements of the program components. The links between the program components and the proximal outcomes are based in part on understanding the kinds of activities or program features that affect the proximal and distal outcomes. In our current example, the program components were the leaders (i.e., leadership style) and the event (i.e., activities). When designing this program, it was necessary to determine which elements were thought to influence the proximal outcomes. While the explanatory theory indicated that all of the proximal and distal outcomes influenced autonomy, knowing how and whether the recreation program leaders and participation in planning a special event affected the proximal outcomes was another matter. As you can see, it is important that you think about these activities before a program is designed so these connections are built into a program deliberately. Unfortunately, this type of planning does not always happen. Too often, the way programs are designed has little to do with desired outcomes.

It may help to think of the program components as things that could be changed or manipulated. For example, instead of planning the special event, the youth could have been involved in leading games for preschool children. In a deliberately planned program, the outcome is the main focus and drives what kinds of things are included in the program for the youth. In the current case, the main goal was to increase autonomy through a recreation youth leadership experience. Thus, the park district event is important because it is a real-life leadership experience for the youth and it was selected because it provides an ideal way to empower youth. In terms of autonomy development, having a role in running the event is likely superior to simply running games at the event because the event experience would provide more ways for youth to make more decisions and develop negotiation skills.

Issues in the Development of Theory-Based Programming

The program logic model illustrated in our autonomy example also provides an opportunity to discuss several issues regarding theory-based programming and the construction of logic models. If one reflects on all the activities and experiences that are a part of developing and running a special event, why were only the leadership and one activity included in the model? This question illustrates the challenge of representing a program in a relatively easy to understand model. The program logic model is conceptual, meaning that there is some degree of abstraction between the model and everything that happens to carry out a program. It is unlikely that a logic model will provide detail about all that happens in a program experience. However, leaving out some details may make the model easier to comprehend. Even in the *TimeWise* intervention model provided in Chapter 9, much was left out to present a more accessible model of a complex program.

If you are in a situation where you are working with an existing program that doesn't have a logic model, the process of developing a program logic model will help to identify the implicit beliefs that program staff have about how the program works (Funnell, 2000; Rogers, 2000). Reviewing these implicit beliefs may reveal that different staff members have different interpretations of a program's purpose and benefits as well as how the activities work. Constructing a logic model can strengthen the quality of a program by making sure all stakeholders share a common understanding of the program and its impacts. Thus, constructing a logic model helps one to move from implicit to shared explicit beliefs about the relationship between program design and outcomes.

Weiss (2000) suggested that when constructing a program logic model staff should focus on the most salient (i.e., important) and enduring (i.e., lasting) aspects of the program experience. In the special event example the salient features were dictated in part by the nature of autonomy (i.e., the ultimate outcome). It is completely plausible that the same special event management experience could produce other important outcomes (e.g., community attachment) and in that case an alternative model would describe the relationship between other aspects of the program experience (e.g., levels of bonding to peers and nonparental adults).

There is a tendency for recreation program planners to think about everything that happens in the course of a program and to create long lists of benefits. Focusing on the most important and most enduring benefits should, at the very least, help programmers to scale back long lists of desired outcomes to those deemed most important and most connected to the program activities.

Finally, youth program directors supervising existing programs often focus on schedules, program details, and logistics. They may have difficulty summarizing the program in a conceptual logic model and may be tempted to create a flow chart of what happens when. With practice, these theory-based programming skills can be developed and programmers will find natural ways to conceptually carve up the program experience into distinct components and corresponding outcomes.

Before we discuss evaluating an outcome-based program, it might be useful to ask a few reflective questions. Do all of the programs offered by a parks and recreation department have to have outcomes? Don't some youth choose to participate in activities simply because they value being on a team or doing a recreational activity like swimming or skateboarding? Moreover, can all outcomes be predicted? In the course of carrying out a recreation program, program staff will happen upon many teachable moments. These impromptu discussions and reflections with youth can have powerful impacts that may not be prespecified through a logic model. Thus, depending on the situation, logic models should be used as a guide to make sure that desired outcomes are achieved, but should not unduly limit the range of impacts that a program might actually produce.

The Role of the Program Logic Model in Program Evaluation

A logic model also serves as the basis for systematic program evaluation by specifying the types of outcomes that are expected to occur as well as the pathways to those effects. However, in most cases, to conduct in-depth evaluation, it is necessary to have considerable resources, individuals with research methods expertise, and a large number of program participants (Donaldson, 2001; West & Aiken, 1997). The goal of these large-scale evaluation studies is both to demonstrate that a program produced outcomes and to examine how the program produced those effects. An example of this type of evaluation effort was described in Chapter 9 for the *TimeWise* program. Evaluation studies of this magnitude are not yet common practice in youth recreation settings due to lack of funding and understanding among professionals of their value and necessity. Thus, in this chapter, it may be more helpful to concentrate on the aspects of the logic model that can readily be assessed by program staff.

In the early stages of establishing theory-based programs and outcome evaluations, programmers should focus on the underlying assumptions and theory linking the program components and proximal outcomes. Recall that in theory-based programming, theory and research evidence are used to represent a program as a series of successive and linked steps. Because the logic model supplies predictions about what happens in a program, it may be useful to begin the evaluation process by assessing these steps and assumptions. For example, are the participants reporting and describing their experience in a manner consistent with the outcomes specified in the model? If the initial elements of the program logic model (i.e., program components and proximal outcomes) are found to be lacking, then it is likely that either the program will not have the predicted outcomes or that some other program components may be accounting for the observed outcomes.

For our autonomy development example, both the way program was led and the program activities used were hypothesized to affect the proximal outcomes. Thus, it is appropriate to ask the participating youth to rate the leaders' feedback style and support of youth initiated ideas and comments. Additionally, systematic observations of the staff by qualified individuals not associated with the program could be used to help evaluate whether staff demonstrate these behaviors. If leaders do not receive high scores on their feedback style and support, it would challenge the basic assumption underlying the program logic model and would suggest a need for staff training or rethinking the importance of these characteristics for this particular program.

Youth could also be asked to report or describe their experience in the program. In this case, it would be important to analyze the extent to which youth felt that the program activities required the kinds of things represented in the proximal outcomes. For example, youth could be asked to report the extent to which the program experience provided or required them to use their personal ideas. Note that the focus of this statement is not on the youth's level of ability to express their ideas, but rather whether they feel that expressing opinions characterized their experience. The same question would be asked regarding peer-to-peer coordination and collaboration as well as planning. This evaluation strategy would facilitate determining whether the programmers' beliefs about the salient features of the program match the experience that youth actually have in the program.

Additional information can also be gathered by asking youth to complete open-ended questions about their experience and the elements of the experience they thought were important. Program staff may be surprised to find that youth identify as important program components staff had not considered. For example, Fetterman and Bowman (2002) evaluated an experiential science education program for high school youth and found that the youth reported "fun" as an important element of the program while the staff had not considered this in their program model. An additional benefit of analyzing the program components is to ensure that claims about outcomes are consistent with the types of experiences that youth have in the program.

To summarize, program staff need to develop a data collection strategy based on the program logic model that systematically measures both outcomes and program processes. The examples described here illustrate information that would help programmers to make decisions about a program. Rather than asking the youth if the program was beneficial, the evaluation strategy proposed here is to closely examine fundamental beliefs about how the program works. While a more sophisticated outcome evaluation process may require some outside support, program staff can and should gather important information about the key hypotheses underlying the program logic model.

The Future of Theory-Based Programming

As societal interest in youth's free-time activities continues to grow, the need for quality programming also increases. Based on the information provided in this chapter, whether a program is judged to be of high quality will be defined by whether the program produces important outcomes. As this chapter has illustrated, theory-based programming and evaluation are fundamental aspects of designing programs that positively affect youth. The quality of programs depends on a programmers' ability to effectively construct and manage programs based on theory and evidence of program outcomes. Adopting theory-based programming strategies will help recreation programmers position their programs as important services, but there are also many questions yet to be answered.

The challenge that confronts recreation youth development program planners is to determine what kinds of recreation program activities (i.e., components) really do affect specific types of valued proximal, distal, and ultimate outcomes. For example, does planning a recreation special event increase a youth's level of autonomy? Does volunteering to lead children's games at recreation special events also increase a youth's level of autonomy? Additionally, we must begin to better understand whether program activities work well for both girls and boys, urban and rural, and White, Hispanic, and Black youth. As the number of theory-based programs and outcome evaluations increases, programmers will need to continue to keep abreast of the growing body of knowledge in youth recreation programming. We hope this chapter has provided you with the tools to effectively begin to address these challenges.

References

Baker, T. B., Brandon, T. H., and Chassin, L. (2004). Motivational influences on cigarette smoking. *Annual Review of Psychology, 55,* 463–491.

Bandura, A. (1986). *Social foundation of thought and action: A social cognitive theory.* Englewood Cliffs, NJ: Prentice Hall.

Collins, W. A., Gleason, T., and Sesma, A. (1997). Internalization, autonomy, and relationships: Development during adolescence. In J. E. Gursec and L. Kuczynski (Eds.), *Parenting and children's internalization of values: A handbook of contemporary theory* (pp. 78–99). New York, NY: John Wiley & Sons.

Crompton, J. L. and Witt, P. A. (1997, October). Repositioning: The key to building community support. *Parks and Recreation, 32*(10), 80–90.

Deci, E. L. and Ryan, R. M. (1985). *Intrinsic motivation and self-determination in human behavior.* New York, NY: Plenum Press.

Delgado, M. (2002). *New frontiers for youth development in the twenty-first century: Revitalizing and broadening youth development.* New York, NY: Columbia University Press.

Derzon, J. and Lipsey, M. (1999). Predicting tobacco use to age 18: A synthesis of longitudinal research. *Addiction, 94,* 995–1006.

Donaldson, S. I. (2001). Mediator and moderator analysis in program development. In S. Sussman (Ed.), *Handbook of program development for health behavior research and practice* (pp. 470–496). Thousand Oaks, CA: Sage.

Eccles, J. S. and Gootman, J. A. (Eds.). (2002). *Community programs to promote youth development.* Washington, DC: National Academy Press.

Fetterman, D. and Bowman, C. (2002). Experiential education and empowerment evaluation: Mars Rover educational program case example. *Journal of Experiential Education, 25,* 286–295.

Firstenberg, P. B. (2003). *Philanthropy's challenge: Building nonprofit capacity through venture grantmaking.* New York, NY: The Foundation Center.

Frederick, C. M. and Ryan, R. M. (1995). Self-determination in sport: A review using cognitive evaluation theory. *International Journal of Sport Psychology, 26,* 5–23.

Funnell, S. C. (2000). Developing and using a program theory matrix for program evaluation and performance monitoring. In P. J. Rogers, T. A. Hacsi, A. Petrosino, and T. A. Huebner (Eds.), *Program theory in evaluation: Challenges and opportunities* (pp. 91–101). San Francisco, CA: Jossey-Bass.

Grolnick, W. S., Deci, E. L., and Ryan, R. M. (1997). Internalization within the family: The self-determination theory perspective. In J. E. Gursec and L. Kuczynski (Eds.), *Parenting and children's internalization of values:*

A handbook of contemporary theory (pp. 135–161). New York, NY: John Wiley & Sons.

Hansen, D. M., Larson, R. W., and Dworkin, J. B. (2003). What adolescents learn in organized youth activities: A survey of self-reported developmental experiences. *Journal of Research on Adolescence, 13,* 25–55.

Harter, S. (1999). *The construction of the self: A developmental perspective.* New York, NY: Guilford Press

Kohn, A. (1994). The truth about self-esteem. *Phi Delta Kappan, 76,* 272–283.

Noam, G. G., Biancarosa, G., and Dechausay, N. (2003). *Afterschool education: Approaches to an emerging field.* Cambridge, MA: Harvard Education Press.

Petraitis, J., Flay, B. R., and Miller, T. Q. (1995). Reviewing theories of adolescent substance use: Organizing pieces in the puzzle. *Psychological Bulletin, 117,* 67–86.

Reed, C. S and Brown, R. E. (2001). Outcome-asset impact model: Linking outcomes and assets. *Evaluation and Program Planning, 24,* 287–295.

Rogers, P. J. (2000). Program theory: Not whether programs work but how they work. In D. L. Stufflebeam, G. F. Madaus, and T. Kellaghan (Eds.), *Evaluation models: Viewpoints on educational and human services evaluation* (2nd ed., pp. 209–232). Boston, MA: Kluwer Academic.

Ryan, R. and Deci, E. L. (2000). Self-determination theory and the facilitation of intrinsic motivation, social development, and well-being. *American Psychologist, 55,* 68–78.

Silverberg, S. B. and Gondoli, D. M. (1996). Autonomy in adolescence: A contextualized perspective. In G. R. Adams, R. Montemayor, and T. P. Gullotta (Eds.), *Psychosocial development during adolescence* (pp. 12–61). Thousand Oaks, CA: Sage.

Steinberg, L. (2002). *Adolescence* (6th ed.). Boston: McGraw-Hill.

Weiss, C. H. (2000). Which links in which theories shall we evaluate? In P. J. Rogers, T. A. Hacsi, A. Petrosino, and T. A. Huebner (Eds.), *Program theory in evaluation: Challenges and opportunities* (pp. 35–45). San Francisco, CA: Jossey-Bass.

West, S. G. and Aiken, L. S. (1997). Toward understanding individual effects in multicomponent prevention programs: Design and analysis strategies. In K. J. Bryant, M. Windle, and S. G. West (Eds.), *The science of prevention: Methodological advances from alcohol and substance abuse research* (pp. 167–209). Washington DC: American Psychological Association.

Section III

Supports, Opportunities, Programs, and Services

In this section we discuss some of the specific supports, opportunities, programs, and services (SOPS) critical to youth development. While the list of such SOPS is extensive, we concentrate on the role of parents, community-based mentors, youth leaders, and young people themselves as critical elements in a comprehensive approach to youth development. We also discuss two important settings for youth development: after-school programs and teen centers.

Chapter 11 discusses the power of positive parents in maximizing youth's potential. After reviewing parenting styles, beliefs, and practices, we discuss the ways that parents can influence adolescents' use of free time and the value and role of family time in youth development. Finally, the chapter discusses the need for positive parenting programs and national strategies for strengthening families.

Other adults—such as teachers, recreation leaders, coaches, and neighbors—are also necessary to help supplement the role of parents in youth development. Thus, the critical role of nonparent adults from the community is discussed in Chapter 12. Of particular importance, this chapter discusses the need for adult leaders to focus on developing positive, productive relationships with young people through recreation activities. Thus, programs and activities become a means for adults to attract and to engage young people. While from the participant's point of view, a program may center on having fun, relationship-based programming has the potential to use recreation as a setting for dealing with a wide variety of issues in a young person's life. The chapter discusses some of the characteristics of adults who adopt a relationship-based approach and some of the challenges to adopting this approach to programming.

In Chapter 13, we describe the developmental necessity of involving young people as critical actors in their own development. Among the means for doing this is the value of enabling young people to play a major role in planning and developing needed SOPS. Thus, programming is done with, not for, young people and the development of "voice" is a critical outcome in its own right. The chapter describes some of the ways to increase youth voice, including establishing an environment for trust and using other more informal and formal methods of increasing youth voice.

The final two chapters in this section deal with important settings for youth development. Over the last 15 years there has been an explosion of interest in and the development of both after-school programs and teen centers. Understanding the goals, associated programming, and issues related to each of these settings is critical to the development of a community-wide approach to youth development.

Chapter 14 provides information on the needs driving the development of after-school programming, including concerns about safety of children during the after-school hours, the desire to increase opportunities for decreasing negative behaviors and increasing thriving behaviors, and an interest in using the after-school hours to increase educational attainment. We discuss some of the critical issues that programs must deal with to be successful, such as staffing, quality of programming, transportation, recruitment of participants, and parent involvement. The need for program evaluation is also emphasized as a vehicle for both continuous program improvement and demonstrating to funders and other stakeholders that programs are worthy of continuing support.

Finally, Chapter 15 discusses the value of teen centers, including the value of enabling teens to have "a place of their own," with age-appropriate activities and a strong commitment to teen voice in the development and implementation of SOPS issues at the center. This chapter also discusses some of the critical issues associated with developing centers, including the development of teen-friendly facilities, finding and retaining quality staff, and developing and maintaining community support. We also discuss ways to attract and retain teen participants.

Overall, this section provides useful information for those seeking to develop SOPS for young people. Chapters emphasize the importance of parents, other adults, and youth themselves in program development and provide guidance to those seeking to develop programming in several specific types of settings.

Chapter 11

The Power of Parents: Positive Parenting to Maximize Youth's Potential

Susan L. Hutchinson and Cheryl K. Baldwin

Consider these scenarios:

> Mariah's mother chats with her daughter's friends as they hang out on the porch, deciding where they want to go to cool off one hot summer evening. She's not afraid to let Mariah go off with her friends, including boys, because she feels she really "knows" all Mariah's friends.
>
> Rachel is interested in theater, so her mother helps her to search for a theater camp she can attend in the summer, with the hopes this will help her feel more confident to try out for her school's drama club the next school year.
>
> Lisa's father is doing the laundry. He glances over Lisa's shoulder to see who she is "talking" with on the computer as she sends an instant message to her friends.
>
> Roxie has been playing the piano. She wants to quit and take up playing the drums instead. Her parents have told her she has to stick with the lessons for the rest of the year. If she still wants to quit then, she can. However, if she chooses to take up the drums, she is also responsible for earning the money to pay for them.
>
> For the first time, 13-year-old Faith is allowed to go to the mall with her friends. They are even walking the mile there and back on their own. Her mother says that a large reason Faith is permitted this level of independence is that she has shown, over time, her willingness to follow the rules in other situations where she had some personal freedom.

From our perspective, each of these is an example of "positive parenting practices" linked to healthy adolescent leisure behavior. Parental involvement, parental monitoring, parental structuring, and autonomy support are types of parenting practices that have been demonstrated to be important for maximizing youth's potential in and through leisure activities. The purpose of this chapter is to introduce you to what positive parenting looks like and to provide examples of the kinds of innovative initiatives being introduced in communities to promote positive parenting and shared family time. As you read through the chapter, think about your experiences with your own parents and other adult caregivers. What kinds of things did they do to support your free-time activities and family fun? Conversely, do you know kids whose parents were so restrictive or uninvolved that the kids just wanted to rebel? Although many of you may not be parents yet (or may never be), it helps to think about the ways adult caregivers might make a difference in maximizing the potential of the youth you will work (and play) with in the future. Parents and caregivers can be a very important part of recreation programming, either directly or indirectly.

Positive Parenting

When you think about positive parenting of adolescents, what does that mean to you? Is it the mom who is willing to learn to play a computer game with her son…even if he is "too cool" be seen in public with her? Is it the dad who sits at his daughter's soccer game…even in the pouring rain? Do these examples still "fit" when you think that the parent might be a single parent, or that the family is made up of two same-sex parents? While we talk generically about positive parenting in this chapter, keep in mind that we are not differentiating between single-parent or two-parent families, between same-sex or heterosexual parents, or between families headed by a biological parent and those headed by extended kin (e.g., aunts, uncles, grandparents) or adoptive and foster parents. This chapter is premised on the assumption that positive parenting refers not to a particular type of relationship, but rather to the quality of the interactions and actions of adult caregivers who create conditions or contexts for optimal growth of children both within and outside the home.

Although peers become increasingly important to adolescents, parents do remain the most important influence in adolescents' lives (Collins, Maccoby, Steinberg, Hetherington & Bornstein, 2000). Increasingly there has been a focus on the important role that parents and families can play in youth's lives, particularly to protect them from risk factors, such as poverty or peers who engage in unhealthy behaviors. It makes sense then that what parents believe about leisure and what they do to foster development of their adolescents' leisure interests, skills, and behaviors can promote positive development and reduce the risk of engagement in risk behaviors. In fact, there is strong evidence that positive parenting plays an important role in preventing risky behaviors (e.g., smoking, drinking) and conversely that poor parenting practices have been linked with substance use.

Parents have an extremely challenging job! They must not only provide for their child's health and well-being but also create the appropriate conditions or family environment in which the child can develop to his or her fullest capacity. Doing this is called *parenting,* which is described in terms of parents' personality (i.e., their parenting style or personal disposition), what they believe, as well as what they do (i.e., their parenting practices) to socialize their children. Each will be described briefly next.

Parenting Styles

When you think of your own parents, parents of friends, or other adults you admire, think about the way they interacted with you and their own or other kids. What did they do (or not do) to set an emotional tone for their interactions? In other words, what was their *parenting style* (Darling & Steinberg, 1993)? Did you ever encounter parents who seemed more like drill sergeants or employers than parents? Were they cold, overly demanding, or overcontrolling? How did their children feel or behave as a result of their interactions? Did they feel they could confide in their parent(s) if something was wrong or express their personal likes and dislikes? Did the kids you know comply with this type of parenting or did they rebel? People like this are often said to use an *authoritarian* parenting style. There is evidence that low levels of parental warmth and high levels of harsh discipline are associated with adolescents' association with deviant peers (e.g., Ary et al., 1999), depressive symptoms (Sheeber, Hops & Davis, 2001), substance abuse (Moon, Jackson & Hecht, 2000), and risky or antisocial behavior (e.g., Caldwell & Darling, 1999; Dishion & Andrews, 1995). For example, Caldwell and Darling found that adolescents who perceived their parents to be overcontrolling experienced higher levels of boredom and rebellion in the free-time context than adolescents who perceived their parents to be encouraging and supportive.

Did you ever spend time with or observe parents who set firm limits and had really clear expectations, but were also fair, responsive, and warm? This is called an *authoritative* parenting style (Baumrind, 1991), and this kind of interaction between parents and adolescents is considered to be the "single most important family protective factor" (Moon, Jackson & Hecht, 2000, p. 374) for substance use (along with parents' expectations their adolescent will not drink or use drugs). Some studies have demonstrated that adolescents who perceived their parents to be firm but fair and warm exhibit fewer problem behaviors, lower levels of personal distress, and higher academic achievement than adolescents who felt their parents were neglectful (Lambourn, Mounts, Steinberg & Dornbusch, 1991).

At the other extreme are those parents who are more *permissive* in their parenting style and who, as a result, provide little structure and low expectations regarding their adolescents' free-time use. You might see a permissive parenting style in parents who just want to be their son or daughter's best friend—the parents may want so much to be liked, or they may not really care, that they will not establish clear rules or expectations, nor follow through on them. Finally, you may know of parents who, because of work, family problems, health issues, or their own mental or psychological problems, are unable to "be there" for their children. These types of parents are termed *neglectful*. There is some evidence that adolescents whose parents use authoritative parenting practices engage in fewer delinquent or risk behaviors in the free-time context than adolescents whose parents are permissive or neglectful (Caldwell & Darling, 1999; Mahoney & Stattin, 2000).

Parental Beliefs

Parents' beliefs serve as sources of influence on the development of their adolescents and are foundational to the practices parents use to manage their adolescents' or family's free time. As Sigel and McGillicuddy-DeLisi (2002) suggested, "Parental beliefs affect children's development through parental behaviors, either by fostering attitudes in the children through expectations, encouragement, and the like, or through interactions that create different learning environments for children within the context of the family" (p. 489). As you can imagine, parents' beliefs—about physical activity, health, drugs, alcohol, and leisure—have a major influence not only on the messages parents communicate to their children about what is important but also on the rules and structures they put in place in their family life. So, for example, if one parent believes that homework and chores are the most important things for her son to do in his free time, then she will communicate this not only in what she says but also by what she does and gets him to do. Likewise, parents who believe that shared family time is important will "invest" time and money into making sure they get to do fun activities with their family (e.g., by scheduling a family games night even when they have busy work lives, by buying board games). To the extent that parents invest time and money in their adolescent's extracurricular activities or in activities that promote shared family time, then they are communicating their beliefs about the importance of these activities.

Of course, parents' beliefs about what they feel they can comfortably let their adolescent do (or not do) are also shaped by their beliefs about adolescent development. According to Bosma, Jackson, Zijsling, and Zani (1996), parents adjust their expectations regarding the freedom adolescents can or should assume for decision making according to age-graded standards associated with perceptions about normative development. For example, parents may register their son for soccer "because it is good for him" when he is 10, but leave the decision to him about whether or not to join when he is older. Although this example seems straightforward, there do seem to be some gray areas where parents experience dilemmas about what is or is not the right thing to do. For instance, a parent may have no problem letting her daughter go for a sleepover with girls *and* boys at age 10, but may struggle to permit the same thing when her daughter is 12 and starting to be more interested in boys. Often in these situations the extent to which parents have come to trust their adolescent's decision making will influence their willingness to let their child do potentially riskier activities.

In our own work with parents and adolescents (Hutchinson, Baldwin & Caldwell, 2003), we found that parents' beliefs shaped the permission and support they gave to their adolescents' free-time activity choices. These beliefs were based on their own perceptions of priority activities, the benefits of certain leisure activities as well as generalized expectations about age-appropriate and socially acceptable behavior. Parents' beliefs and expectations guided parenting practices associated with establishing and enforcing rules and boundaries for free-time use. Once these parameters were established, the adolescent was relatively "free" to operate within these guidelines.

Parenting Practices

Parenting practices are what parents do to take action or establish structures to follow through on their beliefs or goals for their adolescents. The ideal practices are both *promotive* and *preventive*, and have been referred to as *family management* practices (Furstenberg, Cook, Eccles, Elder & Sameroff, 1999). Family management refers to "the executive role that parents play as managers of children's daily worlds" (Larson, Dworkin & Gillman, 2001, p. 145). It refers to things that parents do to "orchestrate, instruct, discipline, provide support, and supply important physical and psychological resources to their children" (Larson, Dworkin & Gillman, 2001, p. 145), including their investment in and support of their adolescent's free time activities.

In a recent study focused on how single parents effectively support their adolescent's constructive use of leisure, for example, Larson and colleagues (2001) found several family management practices that characterized well-functioning families, including time devoted to child-supportive activities (e.g., organizing family schedules, buying art supplies), family routines, and firm (i.e., authoritative) parenting. Interestingly, they found that family routines were also significantly positively related to the adolescents' time spent in constructive activities. As it relates to adolescents' leisure, *promotive* parenting strategies would include a parent's role in structuring their adolescents' activities, strategies used to foster development of special skills or talents, spending time with their adolescent doing activities, and providing developmentally appropriate opportunities for autonomy development (Grolnick, Deci & Ryan, 1997; Furstenberg et al., 1999).

Preventive parenting practices are the efforts by parents to reduce their child's exposure to risks. As it relates to the free-time context, preventive parenting practices include consistent discipline, efforts to monitor what their adolescents do in their free time and with whom, the ability to forecast situations associated with greater risk, and the ability to identify strategies to protect their adolescent against perceived risks. For example, there is evidence that adolescents with parents who monitor their free-time activities are less likely to engage in risk behaviors in their free time than adolescents who are largely left to structure their free time on their own (Mahoney & Stattin, 2000). As it relates to both promotive and preventive parenting practices, we expect that parents' understanding of their adolescent—"who they are," what they like and dislike, how they respond to certain situations—will be important in promoting the development of their adolescent's leisure skills and abilities and in protecting them from risky situations.

Parental Influences Over Adolescent Use of Free Time

Parents who are involved in their children's school life, from volunteering in the classroom, to checking on what homework needs doing, to ensuring they have access to the needed resources (e.g., library books and Internet access), are pivotal in ensuring the academic success of their children. However, only recently has attention been given to the impact of positive parenting practices on adolescents' free time activities. Several studies have emphasized the importance of parental support for children's continued involvement in structured leisure activities (Csikszentmihalyi, Rathunde & Whalen, 1993; Fletcher, Elder & Mekos, 2000). Parental warmth, parental trust, and parental support of activity participation have been found to strengthen adolescents' involvement in community (Fletcher, Elder & Mekos, 2000) and structured activities (Mahoney & Stattin, 2000).

In our own work (Hutchinson, Baldwin & Caldwell, 2003), we were interested in the ways that positive parenting practices shaped the self-determined leisure behavior of young adolescents (ages 13 and 14). In a qualitative study with 17 families (both single-parent and two-parent), we found that the parents used a number of practices to structure, regulate, and support their adolescents' use of free time. **Table 11.1** (pp. 250–251) outlines the categories associated with positive parenting practices in the free-time context.

First, we found that parenting practices extended from the parents' global beliefs and expectations associated with the free time context. These beliefs defined not only what parents saw as their role as parents of an adolescent but also what they believed they could legitimately expect of their adolescent regarding his or her free-time use. Parents enacted their beliefs by establishing and communicating rules that set general parameters for their relationship and for the adolescent's free-time use, and strategically monitoring their adolescents' activities.

Many of the parents instituted specific strategies for monitoring activity involvement that varied depending on the type of activity and the extent to which it was a "problem" for the adolescent to self-monitor. Monitoring strategies were particularly apparent as the parents talked about their adolescents' activities surrounding television, telephone, and computer use as well as spending time with friends. To the extent that parents felt they could "trust" their adolescent's judgment about friends, the parents let their adolescents be more autonomous in the pursuit of spending time with friends. If friendships were potentially problematic, then parents imposed even stricter rules regarding the adolescent's interactions and activities with these friends.

In addition, we found that all the parents in our study provided a range of resources that structured and supported their adolescents' use of free time, including time, money, space in their home, and transportation to free-time endeavors. Despite busy schedules, most parents took their son or daughter to lessons or games and would try to stay to watch them practice or compete. Parents talked about helping with homework; providing for sleepovers; regularly going to the library; buying books, lessons, videos, and sports equipment; getting a computer and computer games; or investing time in leadership roles within their child's organization (e.g., Scouts, coaching a sports team).

Finally, we found that for the most part parents wanted their adolescents to be more self-determined and autonomous. They enacted this belief by encouraging self-initiative, minimizing the use of controls, and acknowledging the adolescents' interests and motivations. In addition, there was evidence that parents' trust of their adolescent was pivotal in their willingness to provide opportunities for more self-directed leisure behavior. Those parents who appeared to exude a sense of confidence and trust in the adolescent's preferences, decisions, and time use also described the ways in which they were

Table 11.1: Positive Parenting Practices Associated With Adolescents' Free-Time Use

Positive Parenting Practices	**Examples**
Parents' Beliefs and Expectations	
General expectations for activity engagement	House rules Priority activities (e.g., homework) Follow through on commitment to activity
Communicating rules and expectations	Family meetings
Reinforcing rules and expectations	Provide explanations or rationale for expectations about certain activities
Enforcing rules and expectations	Non-negotiable rules Threatening to take away a preferred free-time activity or privilege

increasingly allowing their adolescent to have more control over how and with whom he or she spent his or her free time. This is not to say that these same parents did not experience dilemmas about appropriate action—they did. However, the parents who expressed that they "trusted" their adolescent also appeared to believe that their child had acquired a set of skills, had adequate resources, and the ability to use free time constructively. Therefore, they expected and trusted some situational independence.

While our study focused on biological parents of adolescents, it does seem these positive parenting practices are consistent with the kinds of interactions and structures of support that we would hope all adult caregivers, formal or informal, would use in their interactions and actions with children and adolescents. However, we're sure you can all think of the parents who dropped their kids off at the playground or pet store only to show up hours later, or who screamed at their kids when they didn't get a soccer goal. At the end of the chapter we describe programs and initiatives that are designed to promote better parent-child relationships and to strengthen families. While most families are not in crisis, all can benefit from learning strategies that enable them to become more effective in structuring the free time context for success for children and adolescents.

Table 11.1: Positive Parenting Practices Associated With Adolescents' Free-Time Use *continued*

Positive Parenting Practices	Examples
Parents' Practices	
Parent-directed activity engagement	Make decisions about activity involvement for their adolescent Require activities, based on beliefs about importance of having leisure-related skills
Situational redirection	Redirect how spending time
Activity as a means of control	Require participation in an activity as a means of controlling problem behaviors
Guided activity engagement	Offer alternative choices or solutions
Limit setting and strategic monitoring	Limit computer use and with whom one spends time
Providing resources	Invest in positive individual or shared family activities. Create time, provide money, in home space, equipment, lessons, etc.
Developing skills and interests	Strategic provision of resources to support new activity pursuits
Structuring opportunities for greater autonomy and responsibility	Facilitate choices Encourage self-management (e.g., personal responsibility for planning and coordinating free time schedules)

Shared Family Time

The belief that shared family time between parents and children is good, at least as it relates to child and adolescent outcomes, has achieved almost mythic proportions in North American society. For the most part, parents see family time as important to creating a sense of family togetherness. To that end, family leisure has been almost universally viewed as a context for family bonding, cohesion, and adaptability. In fact, some researchers have found that time spent together and appreciation for each other were highly correlated with perceived family strengths in two-parent families (e.g., Greeff & Le Roux, 1999). Other researchers found that parents intentionally seek to create family activities that fulfill important values or goals associated with family togetherness and communication and that provide benefits of a healthy lifestyle for their children (Shaw & Dawson, 2001). As Shaw and Dawson suggested:

> The main purpose [of family activities], from the parents' point of view, was not simply spending time together and enjoying each other's company. Rather, it was about using that time together to develop a sense of family and to teach children about values and healthy lifestyles. (p. 228)

Outside the recreation and leisure field there has been considerable interest in the importance of family routines and rituals for helping family members stay connected to each other. Summarizing findings from a review of over 30 studies of family routines and rituals, Fiese and associates (2002) determined that rituals can contribute to individual physical or mental health and development, strengthen family relationships, contribute to stability of family functioning, support family cohesion in times of transition, and foster the transmission of values.

A recent study that examined shared family activities following divorce (Hutchinson & Afifi, 2004) found that family routines such as eating meals together were necessary for creating and sustaining continuity and stability in family life, particularly in the face of the multiple changes they experienced. Family rituals also helped to create (or re-create) what it meant to be a family. For many of the adolescents and parents we interviewed, it was the everyday activities like eating together, playing games, going for walks, watching television, or just "hanging out" or "having fun together" that signified caring, comfortableness, and a sense of belonging and stability within their family. Irrespective of the form the activity took, spending time together was central to "being a family."

The Dark Side of Parental Involvement

The risks experienced by children and adolescents—from teen parenting, to gangs, to exposure to violence, to neglect and child abuse, often have their roots in the family. Many of these social problems have been attributed to the breakdown or weakening of the family. While more time together is often assumed to be a solution for the breakdown of family life, shared family time is not always good or beneficial for parents *or* children.

The ideologies associated with family time put great pressures on parents to create magical experiences for their children (Daly, 2001). At the same time, however, many parents are time pressured, leaving them feeling exhausted and guilty about the lack of quality time they have been able to carve into their daily lives. This is often worse for women, who assume the burden of responsibility for organizing and managing daily life, including family activities, events, and outings, and in single-parent families, where some parents have to work long hours to financially support their families. Moreover, bickering between siblings or parents, differences in opinions between parents and adolescents over how they should spend their time together, and parents (or children) venting their own feelings of frustration and stress may result in tension, disappointment, and disillusionment rather than the idealized goal of togetherness. At its extremes shared family time may be a context where abuse—of children or spouse—may occur (Samdahl, 2002).

There are other factors that also illustrate the "dark side" of some parents' involvement in their children's activities. Excessive pressures to "perform" and overscheduling of extracurricular activities can lead to low self-esteem, excessive anxiety, and "burnout" that may result in lifelong avoidance of these same activities parents want their children to do because they are "good for them." Parents who lash out when their children are not obeying them, who neglect their children to indulge in their own self-gratifying interests (e.g., leaving their children alone at home while they go to the bar), or who mistreat their children under the guise of "just having fun" (e.g., throwing a child who doesn't know how to swim into the pool, hurtful wrestling or tickling) illustrate the dark side of family togetherness.

One particularly troubling trend is parental violence associated with youth sports. While violence is often considered a natural part of some team contact sports (e.g., ice hockey, football), there has been disturbing evidence of increased violence among parents (Heinzmann, 2002; Murphy, 1999), sometimes termed the "little league parent syndrome" (Docheff & Conn, 2004, p. 63). In both the United States and Canada there have been recent reports of parents attacking coaches, other children, and other parents. As Docheff and Conn noted, "The parents of millions of youth participating in organized sports today threaten coaches, assault referees and hurt kids… There are many examples that seem to indicate that parental behavior is, in fact, out of control at youth sporting events" (p. 63). Sadly, in Reading, Massachusetts, for example, one father killed another over differences in opinion over who got the most "ice time" during their 10-year-old sons' hockey games. Overidentification or overinvestment by parents in their adolescents' activities is often at the heart of parents' misbehavior within youth sports. Docheff and Conn suggested the following six reasons for this increased parental violence:

1. parents living vicariously through their children
2. parents who hold visions of fame for themselves and their child
3. the possibility of securing a college scholarship or other material reward
4. family values associated with winning and status
5. professional sports players who model violence in professional sports
6. a "win-at-all costs" attitude

When you think about recreation programming designed to promote youth development or family benefits, it is clear that it may be important to do more than just bring parents and children together in recreation or leisure contexts. In fact, if the quality of the parent-child interactions is not good, then a recreation activity can become one more place where children or adolescents feel uncared for. In the next section we describe programs designed not only to address problems and risks faced by youth but also to strengthen and enhance family life.

Positive Parenting Programs

A variety of efforts are underway in communities across North America to develop programs, educational strategies, and resources that will promote better parent-child relationships, decrease family conflict, and improve parental involvement and monitoring. While many of these efforts are designed to promote adolescent health and well-being and to strengthen family functioning, some are also designed to combat or decrease the chances that adolescents will engage in risky behaviors. As Kumpfer and Alvarado (1998) suggested "Many family intervention researchers believe that improving parenting practices is the most effective strategy for reducing delinquency and associated problem behaviors" (p. 3). In this section, we review three major types of parenting and family initiatives relevant for recreation providers to consider as they plan for greater involvement by and with parents in their programming for youth: parent and family interventions, national initiatives to strengthen families, and examples of community strategies and programs.

Parenting and Family Interventions

A large number of effective family-focused prevention programs target a variety of family needs and types, such as foster or adoptive families, single-parent families, ethnic families, and inner-city families. As discussed previously in this book, prevention focuses on the enhancement of individual and family life in addition to the reduction of risk. Parent and family prevention programs vary with regard to whether they are a universal program designed to increase family protective mechanisms (e.g., warmth, monitoring) in a general population, a selected program, designed for a more high-risk population, or an indicated program designed for those families currently in crisis.

While many prevention programs target either youth or parents separately, there is increasing interest in programs that target parents and adolescents together. Several family researchers have argued that interventions need to target the total family to strengthen the family and to create lasting change (Kumpfer & Alvarado, 1998; Molgaard, Spoth & Redmond, 2000). A combined family skills training program has been found to be more effective than a youth-only or parent-only program. One example is the *Strengthening Families Program*, which has been designed for families with teens (ages 10 to 14). It is a seven-week program designed to bring parents and adolescents together with the goal of reducing substance abuse and other problem behaviors. Each week the parents and adolescents participate in a separate one-hour education session, followed by a second hour doing supervised family activities. There is evidence that this kind of program can make a difference. Youth who have participated in the program have reported less substance use, fewer conduct problems, and better resistance to peer pressure. Parents were better able to show affection and support and to set appropriate limits (Molgaard, Spoth & Redmond, 2000).

Family skills training programs are gaining in popularity because they provide structured activities to help parents and children practice skills or strategies learned in a supportive and enjoyable environment. Family skills training programs are more effective than a program that provides education but no opportunities for learning and practicing skills (Kumpfer & Alvarado, 1998). In other words, while education programs may increase knowledge or awareness they may have little effect on behavior change.

Although there is a concern that new programs will be poorly attended or experience retention problems, higher rates of retention are possible if transportation, child care, and meals are provided (Aktan, 1995). In addition, the program must be tailored to the developmental stage of the child. However, attention to the program content, length or target group is not enough. The quality of the instructional staff or recreation leaders is critical. Program leaders who use strong communication skills, who exhibit warmth and empathy, who are open and willing to share, who are sensitive to family and group processes, who demonstrate dedication to and concern and care for families, who are flexible, and who have a sense of humor will be better able to retain family participation and produce better results.

Family skills training programs are in keeping with many community recreation agencies' missions to promote health and well-being. Efforts to build collaborative programs between social service agencies and community recreation providers may actually enhance both the sustainability of and transfer of learning from these prevention programs. Many of the reasons programs fail to continue after an initial grant helps to get them started is that they are often "stand-alone programs" not integrated with other youth-serving and social service programs and services in a community. Even if resources were not available to staff to implement a family skills training program within a recreation facility, providing opportunities for peer-led support or discussion groups would be beneficial at a minimum. Providing parents with opportunities to ask and discuss questions about child rearing with other parents who face similar issues and dilemmas can provide much needed support—emotional (relief that others are in the same boat), social (i.e., emerging friendships), and instrumental (i.e., shared child care resources).

National Initiatives to Strengthen Families

As indicated previously, across North America there has been increasing concern about the breakdown or weakening of the family, and this concern has been reflected in national policies and initiatives to strengthen families. Although the words recreation or leisure are rarely used in these discussions, the value of bringing parents and their children together for positive interactions and enjoyment, cannot be understated. Two examples of the power of recreation or leisure for strengthening families will be highlighted here.

Putting Family First is a national grassroots organization that was initiated by community leaders in Minnesota in the late 1990s, after a talk by Bill Doherty (1997) on the topic of family time and family rituals. His inspiration and practical thinking is reflected in his book *The Intentional Family: Simple Rituals to Strengthen Family Ties.* After his talk, a model of family civic engagement was created, and a town meeting was held in which parents addressed as a community the problem of declining family time. Parents and community leaders created a community action group to make family life a higher priority. These efforts resulted in the *Putting Family First* initiative. They have developed a book, *Putting Family First: Successful Strategies for Reclaiming Family Life in a Hurry-up World*, and literally hundreds of activity ideas and resources for strengthening families (see **Table 11.2**) For more ideas and resource information, see the Putting Family First website (http://www.puttingfamilyfirst.org).

Another important national initiative is the *National Fatherhood Initiative* (NFI), which was founded in 1994 to confront the problem of father absence. NFI's mission is to improve the well-being of children by increasing the proportion of children growing up with involved, responsible, and committed fathers. Several useful resources have been developed and are available to individuals and organizations that want to promote more involvement by fathers. Again there are hundreds of possible ideas for creatively promoting opportunities for increasing fathers' involvement in their children's lives (see **Table 11.3**, page 258).

Recreation or youth-serving organizations can serve as catalysts for bringing together concerned adults in communities to begin to create community-driven projects or initiatives to respond to concerns about the lack of positive opportunities for teens to interact positively with parents or other adult caregivers in their lives. In the final section of this chapter, we address a number of other possibilities for bringing youth and adults together to benefit adolescents and families as a whole.

Table 11.2: Putting Family First Program Ideas

- National Grandparents Day
- National Stepfamily Day
- National Eat Together With Your Children Day
- National Eat Together Week
- National Family Week
- National TV Turn Off Week
- Conversation starters
- Creative mealtime ideas
- Resources to enhance family traditions and rituals
- Designing a school district calendar titled "Celebrating Family Involvement"
- Creating a Putting Family First Seal, awarded to community groups and organizations with a demonstrated commitment to supporting family life
- Establishing a family day
- Building partnerships with area faith-based organizations
- Creating a "popcorn quiz" to promote conversation between kids and their families
- Establishing "family-to-family" parent action groups
- Entering a "glitterized kitchen float" in a community parade

Table 11.3: National Fatherhood Initiative Program Ideas

- "10 Ways to be a Better Dad" brochure
- "Fatherhood Today" newsletter
- e-advice column
- e-bulletin board where fathers can communicate with other fathers by posting questions and answers about the various situations
- Training programs across the United States targeting fathers experiencing a diversity of life circumstances (e.g., Long-Distance Dads, a program for incarcerated fathers; Deployed Fathers and Families, a program for fathers in the military)
- National Summit on Fatherhood
- National Father's Day

Creative Community Recreation Programs and Initiatives

Communities around the country are already taking steps to address the problems outlined earlier regarding parents' misbehavior within youth sports. For example, the National Recreation and Park Association (NRPA) and the National Alliance for Youth Sports (n.d.) have developed a comprehensive educational program titled *Time Out! for Better Sports for Kids*, which is focused on changing the culture of children's sports. In other communities parents and guardians are being required to sign a "Code of Conduct" regarding their behavior or to participate in "Silent Saturdays" (where no yelling or cheering is allowed at a game) as ways to minimize problems of parental misbehavior (National Youth Sports Safety Foundation, n.d.). Similarly, youth sports teams are holding preseason orientation meetings with parents and sportsmanship classes to improve parents' understanding of the goals of the sports program. In addition, some community recreation programs are removing scoring from games played in younger leagues or instituting "enjoy the game" programs to prevent parents becoming upset over the outcomes of their children's games (Docheff & Conn, 2004).

Many of you may already be familiar with several different types of programs currently offered through community recreation and youth-serving agencies designed to promote positive parent-child interactions. Parent and toddler play programs, water exercises with babies, or kinder-gym types of programs are often designed to promote positive interactions and play between parents and young children. However, once children are old enough to participate in organized sports, opportunities for organized shared activities dramatically decrease.

Commercial recreation providers are also getting into family programming with family challenge events at their resorts, and an amusement park is often one place where parents and adolescents can share in the thrills of a recreation adventure. Likewise, all-inclusive family camping or adventure vacations are increasingly being designed for families who want to spend time together but don't want to have to do all the work of planning and organizing a trip. For those of us with more modest budgets, family swims, family games nights, family skates, family festivals, daddy-daughter or mother-son events, family fun nights, and community service days are other ways that recreation providers can create opportunities for adolescents and parents to enjoy shared family time.

Some recreation programmers are also starting to address the needs of at-risk families through the development of family-focused leisure education programs. Brigham Young University students and professors, for example, have developed an innovative outdoor challenge programs for families. By having families work together to solve difficult physical and mental challenges (e.g., building a fire, hauling a cart wagon), they hope that problem-solving tasks will foster mutual respect and shared decision making.

In a unique six-week program for families at-risk, a family leisure education program was designed and implemented by therapeutic recreation undergraduate students from Penn State University at a local youth center. The *TimeWise* leisure education curriculum, described in Chapter 9, was modified to address the needs of parents and adolescents within this risk group. Because the families were experiencing high levels of conflict, the parent and adolescent sessions were implemented separately. Given that we were working with street-wise adolescents who saw evenings as their *free* time, not time for more school, it was important to modify the *TimeWise* curriculum by adding in more experiential (and fun) activities.

The focus of the parent program was to help the mothers to think about how they could better structure their own, their adolescents,' and their family's free time. However, they also had long-standing (and in many cases, unhealthy) patterns for dealing with problems and conflicts that could not be changed in six weeks. Nonetheless the parents indicated that the program was a good reminder of how important it was that they take better care of themselves, so they could have the strength to deal with their children's ongoing issues. Two of the parents prepared the meals that the families ate together with the students before moving into separate teen and parent leisure education sessions facilitated by teams of two undergraduate students (the younger children were cared for by another two students). A family fun night was the "reward" for participating in the program.

These are just two of a number of different possibilities for infusing learning and skill building in the context of organized family activities. Talking with parents and youth in your community is a great place to begin not only to generate event or program ideas but also to foster parent and youth involvement to make these ideas happen.

Summary

The purpose of this chapter was to introduce the different ways parents can foster their adolescents' development through leisure and can create leisure-related opportunities for family togetherness. Recreation programmers are in a particularly powerful position to design comprehensive programs that attend to the entire range of developmental outcomes of the child (i.e., cognitive, behavioral, social, emotional, physical, and spiritual) by promoting the benefits available to the child and family through and in recreation and leisure activities.

A warm and supportive parenting style, parents' beliefs in the value and importance of healthy leisure activities, and promotive and preventive parenting practices are all important ingredients of positive parenting to maximize youth's potential. As the saying goes "The family that plays together, stays together." Whether the focus is on youth activities or the family as a whole, and regardless of the make up of the family (e.g., single-parent, dual-parent) or the extent to which the family is at-risk, the provision of opportunities for parents to be positively engaged with their adolescent can make a significant difference in the health and well-being of the adolescent and the family as a whole.

References

Aktan, G. (1995). Organizational framework for a substance use prevention program. *International Journal of Addictions, 30*, 185–201.

Ary, D. V., Duncan, T. E., Biglan, A., Metzler, C. W., Noell, J. W., and Smolkowski, K. (1999). Development of adolescent problem behavior. *Journal of Abnormal Child Psychology, 27*, 141–150.

Baumrind, D. (1991). The influence of parenting style on adolescent competence and substance use. *Journal of Early Adolescence, 11*(1), 56–95.

Bosma, H. A., Jackson, S. E., Zijsling, D. H., and Zani, B. (1996). Who has the final say? Decisions on adolescent behaviour within the family. *Journal of Adolescence, 19*(3), 277–291.

Caldwell, L. L. and Darling, N. (1999). Leisure context, parental control, and resistance to peer pressure as predictors of adolescent partying and substance use: An ecological perspective. *Journal of Leisure Research, 31*(1), 57–77.

Collins, W. A., Maccoby, E. E., Steinberg, L., Hetherington, E. M., and Bornstein, M. H. (2000). Contemporary research on parenting: The case for nature *and* nurture. *American Psychologist, 55*(2), 218–232.

Csikszentmihalyi, M., Rathune, K., and Whalen, S. (1993). *Talented teenagers: The roots of success and failure.* New York, NY: Cambridge University Press.

Daly, K. J. (2001). Deconstructing family time: From ideology to lived experience. *Journal of Marriage and Family, 63,* 283–294.

Darling, N. and Steinberg, L. (1993). Parenting style as context: An integrative model. *Psychological Bulletin, 113*, 487–496.

Dishion, T. J. and Andrews, D. W. (1995). Preventing escalation in problem behaviors with high-risk young adolescents: Immediate and 1-year outcomes. *Journal of Consulting and Clinical Psychology, 63,* 538–548.

Docheff, D. M. and Conn, J. H. (2004). It's no longer a spectator sport. *Parks & Recreation, 39*(3), 62–71.

Doherty, W. J. (1997). *The intentional family: How to build family ties in our modern world.* Reading, MA: Addison-Wesley.

Fiese, B. H., Tomcho, J., Douglas, M., Josephs, K., Poltrock, S., and Baker, T. (2002). A review of 50 years of research on naturally occurring family routines and rituals: Cause for celebration? *Journal of Family Psychology, 16*(4), 381–390.

Fletcher, A. C., Elder, G. H., and Mekos, D. (2000). Parental influences on adolescent involvement in community activities. *Journal of Research on Adolescence, 10*(1), 29–48.

Furstenberg, F. F., Cook, T. D., Eccles, J., Elder, G. H., and Sameroff, A. (1999). *Managing to make it: Urban families and adolescent success.* Chicago, IL: University of Chicago Press.

Greeff, A. P. and Le Roux, M. C. (1999). Parents' and adolescents' perceptions of a strong family. *Psychological Reports, 84*(3), 1219–1224.

Grolnick, W. S., Deci, E. L., and Ryan, R. M. (1997). Internalization within the family: The self-determination theory perspective. In J. E. Grusec and L. Kuczynski (Eds.), *Parenting and children's internalization of values: A handbook of contemporary theory*. New York, NY: John Wiley & Sons.

Heinzmann, G. S. (2002). Parental violence in youth sports: Facts, myths and videotape. *Parks & Recreation, 37*(3), 66–76.

Hutchinson, S. L. and Afifi, T. (2004). *The family that plays together fares better: Examining the contribution of shared family time to family making following divorce*. Paper presented at the National Parks and Recreation Association Leisure Research Symposium, Reno, NV.

Hutchinson, S. L., Baldwin, C. K., and Caldwell, L. L. (2003). Differentiating parent practices related to adolescent behavior in the free time context. *Journal of Leisure Research, 35*(4), 396–422.

Kumpfer, K. L. and Alvarado, R. (1998, November). Effective family strengthening interventions. *Juvenile Justice Bulletin, Office of Juvenile Justice and Delinquency Prevention*. Washington, DC: U.S. Department of Justice.

Lamborn, S. D., Mounts, N. S., Steinberg, L., and Dornbusch, S. M. (1991). Patterns of competence and adjustment among adolescents from authoritative, authoritarian, indulgent, and neglectful families. *Child Development, 62*, 1049–1065.

Larson, R., Dworkin, J., and Gillman, S. (2001). Facilitating adolescents' constructive use of time in one-parent families. *Applied Developmental Science, 5*(3), 143–157.

Mahoney, J. L. and Stattin, H. (2000). Leisure activities and adolescent antisocial behavior: The role of structure and context. *Journal of Adolescence, 23*, 113–127.

Molgaard, V. K., Spoth, R. L., and Redmond, C. (2000). Competency training: The Strengthening Families Program for parents and youth 10–14. *Juvenile Justice Bulletin, Office of Juvenile Justice and Delinquency Prevention.* Washington, DC: U.S. Department of Justice.

Moon, D. G., Jackson, K. M., and Hecht, M. L. (2000). Family risk and resiliency factors, substance use, and the drug resistance process in adolescence. *Journal of Drug Education, 30*(4), 373–398.

Murphy, S. (1999). *The cheers and the tears: A healthy alternative to the dark side of youth sports today.* San Francisco, CA: Jossey-Bass.

National Alliance for Youth Sports. (n.d.). *Time out! for better sports for kids.* Retrieved from http://www.nays.org/intmain.cfm?cat=12&page=71

National Youth Sports Safety Foundation. (n.d.). *Sport parent code of conduct.* Retrieved from http://www.nyssf.org/sportparentcodeofconduct.html

Samdahl, D. M. (2002). *Leisure and domestic abuse: Insights from autobiographies of survivors*. Paper presented at the National Parks and Recreation Association, Leisure Research Symposium, Tampa, FL.

Shaw, S. M. and Dawson, D. (2001). Purposive leisure: Examining parental discourses on family activities. *Leisure Sciences, 23*, 217–231.

Sheeber, L., Hops, H., and Davis, B. (2001). Family processes in adolescent depression. *Clinical Child Psychology and Family Review, 4*, 19–35.

Sigel, I. E. and McGillicuddy-DeLisi, A. V. (2002). Parents' beliefs. In M. H. Bornstein (Ed.), *Handbook of parenting: Being and becoming a parent* (Vol. 3). Mahwah, NJ: Lawrence Erlbaum.

Chapter 12

The Power of People: Relationship-Based Programming

Jason N. Bocarro and Peter A. Witt

Faith Evans, an educator from Colorado, recounted a story about an experience she had while waiting to register at an outdoor education conference. A woman started calling out across the room, "Mary Faith, Mary Faith." Faith knew that this was someone from a long, long time ago since she hadn't been called Mary Faith in probably 30 years. She turned around to see a woman in her 30s with a little girl about 8 or 9 years old. "Mary Faith, I knew it was you." She ran up to Faith and put her arms round her. Faith was incredibly embarrassed by the woman's show of affection, especially because she had no idea who this woman was. Faith did what most of us would do...she pretended she did, telling her it was great to see her. Still she had no idea who she was, hoping the mystery woman would give her clues to their former relationship. After a few moments, the woman exclaimed that Mary Faith was her favorite camp counselor and had an amazing impact on her life. Through their former relationship, the woman explained, Faith taught her many lessons she lived by. Gosh, thought Faith, that was all those years ago and I was just a camp counselor...You just don't think about having that much of an impact on a child's life over a couple of summers. She turned to the little girl (this woman's daughter) and asked the little girl her name. The little girl looked up and replied, "Mary Faith...I was named after you" (Evans, 2003).

Faith Evans' story provides evidence of the power of relationships established through youth development and recreation programs. Relationships with youth take many forms, but the long-term impact of these relationships may be profound and last well beyond involvement in a particular program. In this chapter we discuss the importance of relationships established between youth and adults and their role as critical components of youth recreation programs. Crucial factors necessary for making these relationships successful are also discussed.

Creating meaningful and productive relationships between young people and adults is a significant element of every model that addresses the factors necessary for helping young people grow to be successful adults. Furthermore, understanding why and how relationships contribute to youth development has been the focus of a number of research studies. Some findings from these efforts include the following:

- Studies of mentoring programs, such as Big Brothers/Big Sisters, have recognized the importance of relationships established between adults and young people, with recreation settings often serving as the environment for developing and sustaining these relationships (Tierney & Grossman, 2000).
- Herrera, Sipe, and McClanahan (2000) found that over 90% of mentors felt "close" to their mentees—a bond which provided mentees with evidence of the mentors commitment and strong support.
- Strong relationships between mentor and mentee are more likely to positively impact youth's lives (Grossman & Johnson, 1999), and positive relationships with adults are related to lower rates of substance use and exposure to violence for youth (Scales & Leffert, 1999).
- Strong relationships with teachers also result in stronger connections to school and increased academic performance.
- Positive relationships with nonfamily adults are increasingly critical. Since 1960, young people's contact with parents has been reduced by 10 to 12 hours per week (Scales & Leffert, 1999).
- In a 1997 study of adolescent health, strong adult relationships were one of the strongest predictors of teenagers avoiding high-risk behaviors (Resnick & Bearman, 1997). This study supported previous research that found that children who formed a bond with at least one adult were more likely to exhibit healthy behaviors at 18 years old (Werner, 1989). In both of these cases the adult was not necessarily a parent, but included adults from school, the community, or a religious institution.

Relationship-Based Programming

Relationship-based programming (RBP) encompasses more than teaching skills and involves more than constructing settings in which young people can have a good time. Staff demeanor, a positive attitude toward youth, and the quality of relationships between participants and staff are critical for creating a successful programmatic atmosphere. This is important because atmosphere, rather than the activities themselves, helps to differentiate successful from unsuccessful youth development programs (Roth & Brooks-Gunn, 2003). Moreover, a wide array of programmatic offerings and good facilities are usually less important than how well the participants and staff interact. When staff establishes good relationships with youth, more opportunities exist for positively impacting youth attitudes and behavior. For example, Roth and Brooks-Gunn (2003) illustrated how important it is for program staff to give youth individual attention, to act in culturally appropriate ways, and to be willing to give youth both choice and responsibility. These programming essentials create an environment which resembles "a caring family where knowledge and supportive adults empower adolescents to develop their competencies" (p. 172).

Relationship-based programming differs from traditional activity-based programming in several ways. In particular, relationship-based programs move beyond just keeping youth involved in activities, entertained, and off the streets by creating additional objectives (e.g., building strong ties between youth workers and youth). Relationships such as these may be the catalyst both for attracting youth to programs and for keeping them involved once they have joined.

Youth programs should follow this model by deliberately focusing on developing nurturing adult-youth relationships. This is certainly true of recreation-based programs, which provide a rich context for developing supportive and caring relationships, something particularly important for youth living without a strong family support system (Gilligan, 1999), but critical to all youth regardless of their family situation.

Adopting a Relationship-Based Programming Framework

Three main elements are critical to adopting a RBP framework within youth programming:

1. encouraging involvement in programs
2. implementing programs that address other facets of a child's life
3. building relationships with members of the extended family

Each of these will be described in the following sections.

Encouraging Involvement in Programs

Earlier discussion in this chapter noted it is important to move beyond a focus on activity provision to one that also includes cultivating relationships among youth and staff. Although activities are important, youth can be turned off or on to a program or activity based on their interactions with program staff. For example, some children drop out of sports because of a bad relationship with a coach or teacher. Indeed there is a growing recognition that coaches of youth sports programs need better training that goes beyond the technical aspects of the game and includes information about youth development and how to build effective relationships with children (Smith & Smoll, 1997). Following are two examples illustrating the success of the Austin (TX) Park and Recreation Department's initiative to establish relationships between youth workers and young people to increase their involvement in sport and recreation programs (Bocarro, 2001). As part of this initiative, recreation youth workers were assigned to roles as outreach workers (Roving Leaders) across the city.

Robert was one of the recreation workers assigned to work in a predominately Hispanic community where many of the females did not participate in sports. Robert was determined to promote female athletics and thus set up female-only sports teams. His philosophy was straightforward:

> I don't want to knock the kids or anything, but our teams are always made up of scrubs, the kids who are never going to win a league, they may never even win a game, but we make sure that when we lose a game our kids aren't mad. They are just happy that they got to play. It's about teaching them teamwork, good spirit and having fun and getting a chance to participate. And we achieved that.

As a result of Robert's efforts, participation by girls increased dramatically in various sports, predominately because their disappointment with losing was offset by the fun many of the girls had and the supportive atmosphere that Robert had created within that program.

In another instance, a recreation youth worker described how a 15-year-old female participant signed up for an outdoor fishing trip despite insisting she had no interest in fishing. Once on the trip she admitted that her involvement was motivated through being able to spend quality time with this particular youth worker.

Implementing Programs That Address Other Facets of a Child's Life

Successfully building relationships may be time-consuming and require youth workers to become involved in a child's life beyond their participation in programs. This may mean responding to opportunities to help young people deal with school, personal, and family-related issues. Some of Bocarro's (2001) research illustrated how a recreation youth worker might form a partnership with school counselors and teachers and act as a liaison between youth who have already dropped out or are about to drop out of school, as was the case with Jose.

Jose was an intelligent 17-year-old Hispanic male, living at home with his mom, dad, and younger brother. Jose had lived in several different public housing complexes, and had attended three different high schools in less than 18 months. Both he and his sister eventually dropped out of high school and Jose began working full-time at a computer company. Jose spent a year enrolled in a charter school while working, but that did not work out either and he dropped out again. According to Jose:

> I hated it there…It was hard, because I thought it was gonna be good but I went there for, like, one year, the first year, it was totally different. The kids that enlisted were fighting and cussing and the teachers never could teach so you couldn't never learn nothing and so I dropped out of there.

Jose resumed working at the computer company, which offered a full-time night job with benefits. However, before the beginning of the next school year, he recognized the importance of obtaining his high school diploma. He stated:

> I figured that I needed to hurry up and get my high school diploma 'cause I'm going to be 18 already in October and so I want to graduate this year. And basically I feel like I just need to get it over with. I understand that a high school diploma is an important thing.

Negotiating the high school system can be very confusing, particularly for a family with little experience with the education system, such as Jose's. Once Jose made the decision to go back to school, Robert, a recreation youth worker who had developed a relationship with Jose as part of his outreach work, took Jose and his mother to the high school and helped him enroll. Jose found the traditional school setting hard and, despite considerable support from Robert, he quit again after three months. A few weeks after dropping out, the courts decided to fine him for not going to school. Robert testified on Jose's behalf in court and stopped the situation from becoming worse by clearly explaining all the circumstances. The court decided the best path for Jose would be to attend a GED program on the other side of town. With Robert's help, Jose saved enough money to buy a car and was able to get himself to the program.

This example illustrates the importance of relationships that provide a context for recreation youth workers to have major impacts on various facets of youth's lives. As Jose's story shows, recreation youth workers' relationships with youth can contribute to youth development by helping to prevent situations from reaching extreme proportions, reminding youth of the importance of education, and facilitating action (e.g., making regular school visits, talking to teachers, sitting in on classes). Because it is easier to develop long-term and trusting relationships with youth in recreation and leisure programs than in most other contexts in a youth's life (e.g., school, work), recreation youth workers have many opportunities to positively influence youth.

Building Relationships With Members of the Extended Family

Developing rapport with members of a child's immediate and extended family facilitates successful relationship-based programming. Building meaningful relationships with family members as well as youth may aid a youth worker in helping a young person to navigate difficult personal and family issues. These relationships may also help youth workers to understand why a particular youth may be acting in a certain positive or negative way.

The knowledge gained through contacts with family members may guide a youth worker's approach to working with a youth who seems to be having difficulties, or developing programmatic activities for a particular child. Further, when youth workers successfully develop relationships with parents, they are then able to act as resources for a family and subsequently help to solve problems that may be affecting all of the family members.

Despite the desirability of building relationships with parents, this process is difficult and time-consuming, and requires a considerable amount of face-to-face contact. Additionally, not all parents want to engage in a relationship with a recreation youth worker. In activity-based programs, common in recreation departments, contact with the family is often minimal and most of the communication is through letters taken home by the child or via telephone calls. This common approach to parental involvement presents a challenge to recreation youth workers who wish to build relationships with family members, especially when time is limited. When dealing with difficult issues, face-to-face contact is more effective and, in certain cases, the only way to build relationships with extended family members.

The following example from Bocarro's (2001) research demonstrates some possible implications of relationship building:

Loretta, a 13-year-old child enrolled in a park and recreation program, was often distraught by her mother's serious drug problem. Loretta's feelings often impacted her mood, her behavior at school, and her interactions with her peers. One of the city's recreation youth workers was able to pick up on this problem during informal conversations with Loretta, and due to the positive relationship that he had built with the child's mother over the past year, was able to refer the mother to agencies that could help her address her drug problem. The mother subsequently improved, which in turn made a difference in Loretta's situation and in her subsequent behavior.

Although many of the examples provided thus far have been about youth who lived in problematic environments (e.g., a mother with drug addiction) or who were experiencing problems (e.g., dropping out of school) it should be stressed that all youth benefit from relationship-based programming. Indeed, this fact is one of the major principles of youth development presented in Chapter 1: All youth, no matter how involved or uninvolved their parents are, need relationships with other caring adults. As we mentioned, recreation and leisure experiences and activities are contexts where relationships can be built and maintained with youth and in most cases, with family members. Next we describe ways to build these strong relationships.

Relationship-Based Programming in Practice: Building Relationships

Before we talk about how to develop relationships, let us briefly look at the types of relationships that can be developed between youth and adults in recreation and other activity settings. In particular, three types of relationships have been identified by the research (e.g., Morrow & Styles, 1995; Walker & White, 1998):

Counterproductive relationships. It may be destructive to a young person's development when youth workers allow their personal biases to influence their relationships. Remember Jose from a previous example? An example of a counterproductive relationship would be if Jose's youth worker had a personal belief that most Hispanic boys who dropped out of school were no good and did not possess the cognitive skills to complete the requirements for a high school diploma. Youth workers who do not manage their personal biases are often seen as judgmental and belittling authority figures who do not take into account youth's needs and desires.

Prescriptive relationships. These relationships develop when youth workers have preconceived goals that frame the context of the relationship. Often youth workers see themselves in the role of the rescuer and view their task as improving and reeducating youth, a perspective we discussed in Chapter 1 as not only "old school" but also detrimental to a fully prepared and engaged youth. Although this approach may be well-intentioned, it leaves little room for youth input. Imagine if Faith had "pushed" her camper into taking swimming lessons because swimming was "good for her." It is doubtful Faith would have had the lasting impression and influence that she had if that had been her approach. In this mode of operation, any reluctance and reticence on the part of youth is seen as a challenge to the youth workers' authority and evidence that there is something wrong with the young person's attitude.

Developmental relationships. This type of relationship develops when youth workers devote themselves to establishing a strong connection to youth before addressing other goals. They work with youth in a respectful manner, concentrating on developing trust while being careful not to impose their own ideas and values as a condition of the relationship. These types of relationships often transcend ordinary day-to-day interactions. All of the examples provided so far in this chapter illustrate this type of relationship.

While recreation youth workers at one time or another probably exhibit each of these relationship types, the goal of most youth workers is to build relationships with youth that are developmental in nature—that is why they are in a "people profession."

What are the characteristics of individuals who are skilled at developing relationships? There is no question that developing relationships comes naturally to some people, but for most people it is a skill to be developed. A couple of studies, in particular, help to answer that question. In their landmark study of neighborhood-based organizations, McLaughlin, Irby, and Langman (1994) identified talented youth workers, termed *wizards*, who were successful in developing relationships and making a difference with youth. In all cases positive outcomes were due to the relationships between youth and these wizards, and, in almost every instance, relationships were developed and sustained through recreation experiences. These wizards all shared the following five broad characteristics. They

- saw genuine potential in youth, not pathology.
- were youth-centered.
- were confident in their own abilities to make a difference
- felt an obligation to give back to their community or society.

- displayed unyielding authenticity in all their interactions (i.e., they kept it "real").

Other research has suggested an additional set of important characteristics essential to helping youth workers develop effective relationships with youth (e.g., Bocarro, 2001; Bocarro & Witt, 2003; Seligson & Stahl, 2003). They should

- be multifaceted and flexible.
- be hands-on.
- exhibit commitment and consistency.
- be patient and empathetic.
- establish mutual caring and respect.

Multifaceted and Flexible

As we discussed in Chapter 8, recreation programs and activities are excellent contexts for development to occur. However, to successfully implement programs and activities, youth workers need to be flexible and multifaceted in how they interact with young people.

For example, youth may use a recreation or leisure context to experiment with gender roles, to work on their identity (e.g., who am I?), or to practice emotional and social self-regulation. Because these developmental processes take work, recreation youth workers have to react to the developmental issues that surface. This means that a relationship-based youth worker may have to play a number of different roles ranging from coach, to mentor, to teacher, to friend, depending on the circumstances of the young people with whom they are working, and the developmental needs at hand. Being dogmatic in approach and thinking there is only one way for a situation to be handled goes against relationship-based programming and makes no contribution to youth development.

Hands-On

Successful youth workers are those who interact with youth and participate in activities, while those who are less successful often remain on the periphery and take on the role of disciplinarian. (However, successful youth workers also recognize the necessity of establishing appropriate disciplinary boundaries.)

Being hands-on in this context does not necessarily entail being "good at" activities, just a willingness to be involved. Thus, one of the keys to developing relationships is the ability and willingness to facilitate interactions with kids. To accomplish this outcome, youth workers need to be playful, young at heart, and energetic, and to demonstrate enthusiasm. They must rely more on personal resources than physical or extrinsic resources (e.g., good facilities), and know when to "get their hands dirty" by playing and interacting with youth.

Commitment and Consistency

Being committed to making a difference is another critical aspect of relationship-based programming. Full youth worker commitment means that no matter how challenging the situation, the youth worker takes necessary steps to figure out a solution.

Several common conditions exist which may threaten commitment and consistency in relationship-based programming, including budgetary constraints, lack of equipment, and lack of supervisory support. Youth behavior may also present a challenge—that is, often when youth are perceived as troublemakers who need too much individual attention they are dropped from programs because it is easier than dealing with the problem, or because other parents or other youth complain. However, being committed means understanding circumstances in children's lives and the underlying reasons for their negative or inappropriate behavior. It also means developing a strategic plan for addressing the issue and finding ways to maintain commitment to the program.

For example, Vanessa was a child who had experienced a number of adults coming into and going out of her life. Thus, she mistrusted anyone who said they were there to help her or be her friend. She consistently used bad language and was aggressive with new staff. Vanessa explained that this was her way of testing them. Successfully working with Vanessa required commitment and consistency on the part of her youth worker.

Being consistent is critical because it allows workers to earn and maintain a child's trust and respect. For example, it is essential that youth workers avoid breaking appointments or promises they have made to young people. Many youth who have experienced broken promises from other adults in their lives may perceive that a youth worker may only be around for a short time, making it difficult for children to forge healthy relationships. Providing consistency, therefore, establishes a platform on which a trusting relationship can be built.

One youth worker renowned for his consistency described why commitment and consistency were so important in particular to the teenage boys with whom he worked. He was critical of youth workers who were consistent and committed when things went well in a child's life, but who, when circumstances became more demanding, pulled away. His philosophy was that commitment demanded a youth worker to be present through both good and bad times.

Patient and Empathetic

Being patient and empathetic is critical to building relationships with youth. Part of being patient and empathetic includes learning to be nonjudgmental, forgiving, and willing to deal with problems—even when changes take longer than desired. They must also subjugate their own needs and put youth's needs in focus. Relationships that are developmental rather than prescriptive tend to adhere to the philosophy of "meeting youth where they are" rather than expecting them to be where the youth worker wants them to be. Movement toward a goal (e.g., school attendance) requires both parties to be on the same page initially. This is facilitated by a relationship characterized by patience and empathy. For example, one youth worker discussed how he worked on building relationships with his group of boys, rather than simply worrying about how badly they were doing at school. He was particularly adept at recognizing the issues youth were facing, and discussed the need to take things slowly, however frustrating this might become:

> I think of myself as a positive influence, but hopefully I'm not necessarily another person in their face trying to beat it over their head that this is the way it's supposed to be or that type of thing, but just to approach things with a little more patience. Not to just hit them with, "This is how it is, this is what you're going to do, and this is how it's best." I mean just more of the approach of just being able to come down to their level and let them take it as slow as they need to or at a pace that they think is comfortable.

This approach may require youth workers to be less judgmental. For example, one recreation outreach worker pointed out that when he started working with a group of youth using inappropriate and foul language was common. If he had tried to reduce their use of foul language too quickly, and before he established rapport with the group, it would not have worked:

> My kids really have bad mouths. The way I deal with that is that when that kid respects you, he or she is going to catch themselves and say, "Oh I'm sorry Mister or I'm sorry Miss" or something. That's what you want. You don't want to be so much about rules that they are like, "Oh you're just another one of those guys out there trying to change me." You want

> them to come on their own terms to respect you and to respect what you are trying to do for them and that's the point that I'm at with a lot of the kids.

Mutuality

Recognizing that relationships are a two-way street is important. Children mold us as much as we try to mold them, and interactions with young people impact our own development. This means that *mutual* respect, trust, and liking need to occur. A healthy relationship may be difficult to maintain when one person cares about the relationship more than the other.

For example, two university students, Amanda and Katy, worked at an after-school enrichment program serving predominately low-income youth ages 8 to 18. The program was situated next to some low-income housing. One day Amanda noticed a 16-year-old girl from the housing projects, Rochelle, hanging around. She invited her to come along to help her work with some of the younger children. Rochelle explained that she was not interested as she did not like "school stuff." However both Amanda and Katy persisted and began sharing some of their personal stories with Rochelle to build up a degree of trust. In return, Rochelle began opening up and coming to the program on a regular basis. Rochelle felt that her relationship with Katy and Amanda was a two-way connection, and therefore she felt comfortable sharing some of the issues she was facing in school, which included being written off by teachers and being teased by other students about her weight.

A couple of caveats should be stated here. First, it is important to recognize that in reality, relationships may be one-sided, not only at first but also over the long term. Therefore, it is part of one's professional outlook to expect that not every child will like you. It is, however, one's professional obligation to try and to persist. Second, it is also important to realize that although a professional's needs may be met as a secondary outcome to a relationship (e.g., a recreation youth worker feels needed or competent), one's needs are always subordinate to the youth's needs.

Challenges to Adopting a Relationship-Based Programming Perspective

Several challenges exist for programs wishing to adopt a relationship-based programming perspective. One challenge was noted in Chapter 1: many programs are not sustainable and fizzle out after a year or two. Another challenge is high staff burn-out rates. Maintaining the funding to sustain programs has been identified as a debilitating issue by a number of youth development experts (e.g., Dryfoos, 1990; Lerner, 1995; Schorr, 1988) and too often insufficient attention is given to developing a long-term plan for maintaining program funding and staffing (Pittman, Irby & Ferber, 2000).

Lerner (1995) described some of the consequences of short-term programs that parachute in and out of communities. He pointed out that when programs shut down, communities often feel less hopeful and empowered than before the program existed. Thus, although there may be improvement in the lives of children and families, the inability to sustain programs may result in residents' feelings of loss, disappointment, or even exploitation and anger.

Another related challenge is one of sufficient dose. Just like the right amount of penicillin taken over the right amount of time is needed to cure an infection, the amount of time and length of duration youth spend with youth workers is critical. Programs that last for only a short period of time probably have less impact than those that are able to sustain involvement over a longer time period. Too often policymakers like to see relationship-based initiatives as "a quick fix" rather a commitment to long-term involvements (Royse, 1998). However, little research has been done to determine the correct dose of relationships for different youth in different contexts. That implies that what might be a good dose for some youth may not be the correct dose for others, depending on life circumstances and personal characteristics. Thus, programmers must carefully take account of individual differences when designing programs.

A final challenge is that often staff do not receive adequate training, ongoing support and supervision, or public recognition. All three of these components are important to maintaining staff morale. Huebner, Walker, and McFarland (2003) observed that there is an unspoken assumption that anyone can work with youth. Instead, we need to think more systematically about the ways in which programs can better train their staff to work with youth by embracing the important principles of a positive youth development framework. Understanding how relationships with youth are formed and developed is critical, as the intentionality of building relationships with youth will be lost if all programmers are not on the same page. Therefore, preservice and in-service training would make a significant contribution to relationship-based programming efforts.

Conclusions

There is a growing recognition that people are the most critical aspect of any youth program. A report by the Carnegie Council on Adolescent Development (1992) stated:

> Youth serving agencies, religious youth groups, sports programs and parks and recreation services and libraries all report that the adults who work with young people in their systems, whether serving on a paid or voluntary basis, are the most critical factor in whether a program succeeds. (p. 87)

Thus, creating meaningful relationships between program staff and participants is more important than the particular activities in which young people are involved. Developing close relationships with an unrelated adult through out-of-school time programs is a significant factor in youth development. However, this happens too rarely, and when it does, relationships may not be sufficiently close or positive.

Recreation youth workers are in a prime position to develop relationships due to the contextual and experiential elements of leisure and recreation. Being intentional about developing relationships will make facilitating youth development through recreation easier and more effective. This requires skill development through practice and training as well as adopting a perspective that simply focuses on the activity.

References

Bocarro, J. N. (2001). *Mobile beacons: Roving leaders and the communities they serve*. Unpublished doctoral dissertation, Texas A&M University, College Station, TX.

Bocarro, J. N. and Witt, P. A. (2003). Relationship based programming: The key to successful youth development in recreation settings. *Journal of Park and Recreation Administration, 21*(3), 75–96.

Carnegie Council on Adolescent Development. (1992). *A matter of time: Risk and opportunity in the out of school hours*. New York, NY: Carnegie Corporation of New York.

Dryfoos, J. G. (1990). *Adolescents at risk: Prevalence and prevention*. New York, NY: Oxford University Press.

Evans, F. (2003). Kurt Hahn address, 2001 AEE international conference. *Journal for Experiential Education, 25*(3), 357–362

Gilligan, R. (1999). Enhancing the resilience of children and young people in public care by mentoring their talents and interests. *Child and Family Social Work, 4*, 187–196.

Grossman, J. B. and Johnson, A. W. (1999). Assessing the effectiveness of mentoring programs. In J. B. Grossman (Ed.), *Contemporary issues in mentoring*. Philadelphia, PA: Public/Private Ventures.

Herrera, C., Sipe, C. L., and McClanahan, W. S. (2000). *Mentoring school-age children: Relationship development in community-based and school-based programs*. Philadelphia, PA: Public/Private Ventures.

Huebner, A. J., Walker, J. A., and McFarland, M. (2003). Staff development for the youth development professionalism: A critical framework for understanding the work. *Youth & Society, 35*(2), 204–225.

Lerner, R. M. (1995). *America's youth in crisis: Challenges and options for programs and policies*. London, England: Sage.

McLaughlin, M.W., Irby, M. A., and Langman, J. (1994). *Urban sanctuaries Neighborhood organizations in the lives and futures of inner-city youth*. San Francisco, CA: Jossey-Bass.

Morrow, K. V. and Styles, M. B. (1995). *Building relationships with youth in program settings: A study of Big Brothers/Big Sisters*. Philadelphia, PA: Public/Private Ventures.

Pittman, K., Irby, M., and Ferber, T. (2000). Unfinished business: Further reflections on a decade of promoting youth development. In *Youth development: Issues, challenges and directions*. Philadelphia, PA: Public/Private Ventures.

Resnick, M. D. and Bearman, P. S. (1997). Protecting adolescents from harm: Findings from the national longitudinal study on adolescent health. *Journal of the American Medical Association, 278*(10), 823–832.

Roth, J. L. and Brooks-Gunn, J. (2003). Youth development programs: Risk, prevention and policy. *Journal of Adolescent Health, 32*(3), 170–182.

Royse, D. (1998). Mentoring high-risk minority youth: Evaluation of the Brothers Project. *Adolescence, 33*, 145–158.

Scales, P. C. and Leffert, N. (1999). *Developmental assets: A synthesis of the scientific research on adolescent development*. Minneapolis, MN: Search Institute.

Schorr, L. B. (1988). *Within our reach: Breaking the cycle of disadvantage*. New York, NY: Doubleday.

Seligson, M. and Shahl, P. J. (2003). *Bringing yourself to work: A guide to successful staff development in after-school programs*. Boston, MA: National School-Age Care Alliance.

Smith, R. E. and Smoll, F. L. (1997). Coaching the coaches: Youth sports as a scientific and applied behavioral setting. *Current Directions in Psychological Science, 6*(1), 16–21.

Tierney, J. P. and Grossman, J. B. (2000). *Making a difference: An impact study of Big Brothers/Big Sisters*. Philadelphia, PA: Public Private Ventures.

Walker, J. and White, L. (1998). *Caring adults support the healthy development of youth*. Minneapolis, MN: 4-H Cooperative extension, University of Minnesota.

Werner, E. E. (1989). High-risk children in young adulthood: A longitudinal study from birth to 32 years. *American Journal of Orthopsychiatry, 59*(1), 72–81.

Chapter 13

Increasing Youth Voice

Jesse M. Ellis and Linda L. Caldwell

In the "Lisa vs. Malibu Stacy" episode of *The Simpsons* (Oakley, Weinstein & Lynch, 1994), a new talking Malibu Stacy doll is unveiled for the holidays. The doll is programmed to recite phrases such as "I wish they taught shopping in school" and "Thinking too much gives you wrinkles." Ever the activist, Lisa Simpson mounts a campaign to change the doll's banter to something a bit less demeaning and sexist. But the company would not even listen to her. Lisa finally finds an audience with Stacy Lavelle, the original creator of Malibu Stacy, who agrees with Lisa and finances a new line of dolls—Lisa Lionheart—with sayings such as "Trust in yourself and you can achieve anything." The new line bombs. Only one little girl bought a new doll, but that was enough for Lisa to believe she had done well. She did not need to change the world, she just needed someone to listen to her and take her ideas seriously.

Lisa's desire to be listened to and taken seriously is echoed by youth everywhere. Over the past two decades, researchers and youth leaders have recognized that giving youth a voice in decisions that affect their lives and environment improves the quality of youth programs by influencing important aspects of development.

Researchers have defined youth voice in several ways. For some, voice is considered an opportunity to provide one's perspectives on social issues (Anderson, Evans & Mangin, 1997). Others have regarded voice as being consistent with courage—the willingness to express one's opinion regardless of how one expects it to be received (Rogers, 1993). Formulating one's ideas, understanding one's audience, and expressing oneself through meaningful dialogue and effective communication are hallmarks of youth voice. For the purpose of this book, we define voice as the perception that one's opinions are heard and respected by others—particularly adults (Ellis, 2001).

There is some connection between youth voice and empowerment. For example, youth who feel empowered by community center staff could spark a dialogue between center management and participants about whether the center's operating hours are appropriate. Voice is not the power to make changes or decisions alone (e.g., youth opting to keep the center open until 3 a.m.), but is based on the importance of involving all impacted parties in decisions (e.g., a discussion about the pros, cons, and consequences and jointly making a decision to keep the center open until 10 p.m.). In the end, what is important is the opportunity and ability of youth to communicate and the expectation that the message will be seriously considered.

Why is voice important for youth? There are several developmental reasons voice is important. As you recall from previous chapters, self-determination and autonomy are critical aspects of leisure and healthy development for adolescents. The ability to formulate and articulate ideas to others is an essential aspect of developing one's autonomy and forming one's identity. Some researchers have considered that empowerment through voice development is a culturally sensitive method of increasing competencies in children of color (Tucker & Herman, 2002). As well, you will read in Chapter 21 how important youth voice is to the inclusion of youth with disabilities into community recreation programs. We discuss developmental implications of youth voice in more detail later in the chapter.

Supporting youth voice is also important for effective community programming. The call for youth involvement in the program planning process comes from many program providers—those in the recreation and parks field as well as those who provide community health promotion programs. These professionals recognize youth involvement as an important element of successful programming to promote youth development, and research has supported this contention (Catalano, Berglund, Ryan, Lonczak & Hawkins, 2002).

One of the reasons youth voice is important is that it is key to establishing a connection between young people and the community (Calhoun, 1992) and reducing community-based problem behaviors. For example, in a study of youth basketball teams, the existence of opportunities for youth voice was correlated with increased protective factors, self-control, self-respect, and reduced delinquency behaviors (Heath, 1994).

The Innovation Center for Community and Youth Development and the National 4-H Council (Zeldin, McDaniel, Topitzes & Calvert, 2000) have integrated the programmatic and developmental benefits of youth voice into a theoretical framework. The framework indicates that synergistic decision making between adults and youth leads to programming that helps youth develop; the combination of effective programming and involved decision makers (both youth and adults) strengthens the effectiveness and salience of what a community can offer youth. The Innovation Center's study shows that youth engagement provides significant benefits for adults and the organization as a whole. The Forum for Youth Investment (2004) takes it one step further, suggesting that youth involvement is an important part of not just individual and organizational change, but of community development.

Youth voice is considered so important that a recent Kellogg Foundation request for proposals *required* that grant applicants have a board of directors with youth representatives and that proposals include letters of support written by youth. In sum, practitioners, researchers, and funders alike recognize the value of enabling youth voice.

Developmental Benefits of Youth Voice

Youth voice can have tremendous programmatic benefits, including increased attendance, customer satisfaction, and program quality. However, voice is not just a programmatic issue. Voice can play a key role in promoting outcomes related to the health and overall development of youth.

Several key studies have shown the importance of voice. One of the primary researchers of youth voice is the linguistic anthropologist Shirley Brice Heath. As we discussed in Chapter 8, leisure is often viewed as a context for learning. Heath's (1994) research is consistent with this perspective and has centered on how youth from marginalized or vulnerable backgrounds make use of out-of-school time as a context for learning. In particular, she has been interested in the linguistic and cognitive development of young participants that sustained their membership in programs and helped them to gain knowledge and skills. She examined youth leadership and initiative in identifying and solving what they see as community problems. A prize-winning documentary about her work, ARTSHOW, documents the business laboratory and learning environments of several youth-based community arts groups in the United States. (Information about ARTSHOW and an accompanying resource guide is available through Partners for Livable Communities, http://www.livable.com.)

In another example, Heath (1996) followed a youth basketball team whose players were given the opportunity to set the direction of the team. In these cases, players set up tournaments, ran practices, and scheduled travel. Heath found that as players' voice developed, they became more able to express themselves and more confident that coaches and other adults respected what they were saying. Moreover, their sense of responsibility developed as well. According to Heath, responsibility acted as a protective factor for these youth, and as a result they gained a stronger sense of self-respect and were able to avoid participating in the negative behaviors that dominated their lives previously.

The concepts of initiative (e.g., Larson, 2000) and self-determination (e.g., Ryan & Deci, 2000) previously discussed in Chapters 7 and 8 are closely linked to voice. Initiative development implies action by youth to identify an interest and to develop a plan to further involvement or participation. When youth have a voice, they are more likely to be able to advocate for the resources needed to make their interests become reality. Self-determination, or agency, is a key aspect of initiative and is particularly important to developing voice. A youth with voice feels more authentic in his or her actions if he or she expects adults to respect these opinions. Youth must feel a real ownership of their opinions and be ready to defend them. The ability to develop an informed opinion and to recognize it as one's own rests in the attainment of self-determination and leads to the development of voice.

Another theory of development that underlies the importance of voice is captured in one of the stages in the moral development adolescents go through as they mature. In Kholberg's social contract morality stage, adolescents begin to realize greater freedoms and responsibilities (Gallatin, 1985). Youth recognize that as they transition from adolescence through adulthood, adolescence is an important period to learn to take advantage of opportunities to express themselves and learn to be responsible in their actions. For example, as youth grow into and through adolescence, they may be permitted to stay out past curfew providing they have a good reason to do so and receive permission. A teen in this situation is likely to quickly develop a voice, one that will let him or her express a confident reasoning on why he or she should be permitted to stay out late. Having a voice is "both a way to engage in active self-transformation and a rite of passage where one moves from being object to being subject" (hooks, 1989). In other words, the development of voice coincides with the development of a sense of self. Identity development allows youth to gain self-understanding, to find their place in the community, and to articulate that place.

How is voice developed? While no published model of voice development exists, Belenky, Clinchy, Goldberger, and Tarule's (1997) framework for "knowing" can be useful as a framework for voice development. According to the framework, youth first obtain knowledge as *received knowledge*, with most knowledge gained from external sources: "If Mom says the sky is blue, it must be blue." As youth get older, knowledge becomes *subjective*, and truth becomes a personal experience: "I see the sky is blue, so it must be." The next phase of knowing is *procedural knowledge*, where subjective knowledge is joined by a consideration of multiple perspectives: "I see a blue sky, but my big brother said it is just the way the atmosphere makes light look. Maybe it's really black, but I still think it looks blue." Finally, youth in the *constructed knowledge* phase are able to reconcile multiple sources of information to make an informed, yet individual, decision: "While the sky appears blue, I have learned about light refraction and understand that it is really colorless and looks black in the absence of light." This process mirrors voice development as youth strive to find their own opinions and ideas and effective methods of presenting and defending them. Adolescents are at an integral developmental stage where they are prepared to speak up for themselves and to advocate for their wants, needs, and rights. Recreation specialists are in a unique position to take advantage of these emerging abilities.

Youth Voice as an Outcome of Programming

Youth voice is important to recreation programming for three reasons. First, because of its importance to youth development, programs can be designed so voice can be an ultimate or distal outcome in itself (see the discussion on levels of outcomes in Chapter 10). That is, programs can be designed specifically to increase youth voice. Second, the expression of voice can be considered a proximal outcome that is thought to lead to something else, perhaps community engagement and attachment (Ellis, 2001). Finally, youth voice has programmatic benefits. That is, it can be used by programmers to develop better programs and to increase attendance. We discuss this final role of youth voice in the next section. Now we answer the question, "How do we measure voice, or tell if youth have developed it?" Several ways have been proposed.

One of the authors (Ellis, 2001) developed and piloted a scale (**Table 13.1**) to measure voice. The scale includes items related to whether youth perceive

Table 13.1: Youth Voice Scale
Ellis, 2001

1. People listen to my opinions.
2. People respect my opinions.
3. If I believe in something enough, I will make sure people hear what I have to say.
4. If people will not listen to what I have to say, I usually just give up.
5. I understand many of the problems facing my community.
6. I take both sides of a controversial issue into account before I form an opinion.
7. I am able to adjust the way I speak and present myself in order for others to understand me better.
8. I can have an impact on my community by voicing my opinions.
9. I learn about myself by voicing my opinion.
10. I can explain to others why something is important to me.

that adults listen to and respect their opinions, the ability of youth to adjust messages to different audiences, and their ability to independently formulate opinions. Youth can respond to the items using a typical 5-point Likert scale from 1 (strongly disagree) to 5 (strongly agree). The scale was designed for use with adolescents and incorporates many of the theoretical aspects of voice discussed earlier, including self-determination, self-efficacy, understanding of the audience, knowledge, and courage.

Other techniques to measure voice include Heath's (1994) systematic linguistic method of observation (i.e., qualitative method) to understand when youth had voice. She observed that as participants became more confident in their ability to effectively communicate with adults, their tone and expressions of confidence increased, along with other linguistic developmental indicators. Recreation specialists would probably not want to implement such in-depth evaluation procedures. However, many key indicators, such as how one presents oneself to adults, are easily observable through these means.

Programmatic Benefits of Youth Voice

Encouraging the development of voice among young participants has benefits for programmers as well. Youth workers have much to gain through soliciting participants' opinions. Youth voice can be a vehicle for needs assessment, quality assurance and evaluation, and marketing and public relations. Voice can even be seen as a component of a program, and built into program development and implementation. We briefly examine each of these next.

Needs Assessment

While many methods of assessing needs exist, the original and most effective means is to ask participants and potential participants what they want and provide avenues for input that are perceived as genuine by participants. In other words, structuring and providing opportunities for youth voice helps the programmer to understand what youth want. By providing programs and activities that youth actually want and in which they will be actively involved can be an excellent way to boost and to ensure continued attendance. Furthermore, demonstrating that potential participants have an interest in a program is attractive to program funders and decision makers.

Recall in Chapter 2 we discussed the tremendous and increasing buying power youth have. As youth's ability to make purchases grows, they become accustomed to learning to be good consumers by shopping around for the best price and quality. They are also learning they have become a "marketing niche" and that companies develop products just to please them. Youth are therefore aware that, as consumers, their opinions matter. Thus, it is no surprise that programmers who sincerely seek and listen to youth voice are the most successful.

Quality Assurance and Continuing Quality Assurance

Youth should be actively consulted regarding the development of programs and youths' reactions to programs are critical. Although quantitative data and questionnaires are important ways of gathering information, soliciting feedback through systematic procedures can also yield useful information. Many programmers employ an evaluation process after every session where they assess the degree to which participants enjoyed a program. This system often results in honest, constructive feedback. Furthermore, the "personal touch" of asking youth their opinions, and listening and making changes based on the feedback they provide, invokes a sense of ownership. A young person who is candidly asked for an honest opinion about a program will be more likely to recognize that the program truly is designed with his or her interests in mind, which leads in turn to increased commitment to the program and longer retention.

Voice can be used to clarify program goals, objectives, and priorities. Youth often participate in programs for reasons other than the benefits outlined by programmers. Think back to your youth: Did you go to recreation programs because you had fun or because your self-efficacy increased? Both are important goals that can coexist, but it is more likely fun is a primary motivator to youth. Programmers, however, might be surprised at the other needs youth would like addressed through recreation programming.

The following is an example of how youth can use their voice to elaborate on what they expect to get out of a program or activity. A recent customer satisfaction survey conducted by the Fairfax County Department of Community and Recreation Services (CRS) asked teen center participants to identify which of a list of benefits they received from participation. The questionnaire also asked which of the listed benefits they most *wanted* to receive. As shown in **Table 13.2** (p. 288), responses to the two questions indicated that what youth most wanted was not what youth were getting. In this case, the department was able to redefine its priorities and programming standards in response to the survey results and provide programming that did a better job of targeting self-esteem development, the number one priority as stated by the program participants.

Public Relations

Participants given a voice in operating a program will be more likely to feel it is their program. And when youth have ownership of a program, they are more likely not only to attend but also to recommend the program to their peers. Word-of-mouth has always been the most effective means of sharing information about programs. Youth who feel strongly about a program are most likely to proactively inform others.

How to Increase Youth Voice

The developmental and programmatic benefits of increasing youth voice are certainly compelling. If recreation specialists use appropriate methods for stimulating voice, it is hard to imagine there could ever be "too much" voice. Encouraging voice can only serve to enhance the ability of a program as it strives to meet the social, educational, emotional, and cognitive needs of its participants. For most youth, voice does not necessarily come naturally—it is learned as they mature, and it is learned most effectively by interactions with supportive adults in contexts that facilitate voice development.

Recreation is a key and unique forum through which adults can encourage, enable, and support youth voice. As a context, recreation is characterized by opportunities for choice, voice, and personal responsibility (see Chapter 8). These factors are operative in these settings more so than in any other context in an adolescent's life. Thus, recreation programmers can facilitate positive development through increasing and providing opportunities for voice through deliberate recreation and leisure programming.

Table 13.2: Responses From Fairfax County Community and Recreation Services Customer Survey

	Teen Center Participants' Rankings of...	
Benefit	Importance of Benefits	Benefits Obtained
Self-esteem	1	3
Leadership abilities	2	5
Health	3	1
Socialization/interaction with peers	4	2
Involvement in the community	5	6
Knowledge of county services	6	4
Understanding of various cultures	7	7

Special attention is required to ensure that what is supposed to be voice does not evolve unintentionally into youth feeling that they are only afforded token input in a process controlled by adults. In Chapters 1 and 8 the concepts of supports and opportunities were discussed. Supports include appropriate encouragement and assistance from staff; quick hit solutions and responses when problems arise; recognition of youths' efforts, including public recognition of youth-directed activities; a focus on issues of importance to youth; and means to include diverse voices. Opportunities include providing varied audiences, chances for accomplishment both through doing and contact, and gender- and age-specific activities.

As previously noted, for voice to develop, youth must perceive that adults respect their opinions and value their ideas. In other words, promoting voice entails more than speaking; it also requires listening. Even elementary-age children are able to detect when an adult is truly paying attention to them. Recreation specialists serious about encouraging the development of voice must be prepared to listen to and respect the opinions and ideas of their participants. This includes providing an appropriate amount of encouragement and support, and promises and follow-through.

Voice Through Doing and Contact: Establishing an Environment for Trust

Ellis (2001) suggested two pathways for youth to develop voice. The first pathway is *voice through doing*. In Ellis' study, participants in youth-directed recreation programs developed self-efficacy by successfully initiating and participating in recreational activities of their own choice and design. Ellis suggested that the sense of accomplishment gave youth a feeling that their ideas had merit and were respected by recreation program leaders. Therefore, recreation specialists can create opportunities for voice development by allowing participants to be as self-directed as possible and recognized for their achievements and competencies.

A second pathway is *voice through contact*. Ellis (2001) examined this pathway in traditional, adult-led programs. He suggested that, in most cases, voice was developed as a result of frequent contact with adults in the program who respected youth's perspectives and opinions. Remember that in Chapter 1 the presence of caring, interested adults was identified as a key protective factor for youth. When these adults are present in a program, relationships can be formed between adults and youth that can contribute to youth voice. This is especially true if there is mutual respect and youth have the opportunity to make meaningful decisions within the activity. Thus, in most cases employing competent adults in a youth program goes a long way toward the development of voice.

Recreation programmers often engage with many different types of people during the course of their work. Youth participants also should have the opportunity to speak with different audiences, such as community leaders, politicians, other service providers, educators, police officers, peers, and parents. These opportunities will help participants to increase their skills and begin to expand their voice beyond the walls of the recreation center. Understanding that audiences differ helps youth to refine their messages and to vary tone and approach to fit the situation.

Until an environment of trust is established, programmers likely will have to continuously support youth by urging them to use their voice. A trial-and-error period may be necessary to find the circumstances under which youth feel comfortable expressing themselves. As discussed in the chapters in Section IV, youth of different cultures, religions, genders, and ethnicities may respond to the opportunity for voice differently. Recreation programmers need to be sensitive to these differences in their efforts to promote voice.

Open and frank discussions where adolescents' views are taken into account are rare in community settings and schools, and participants may be wary of new and unfamiliar attempts to solicit and listen to their opinions. Recreation specialists probably will benefit by explaining what the outcomes of the idea-sharing are expected to be. Youth who understand that their comments will be used to improve the program, develop proposals, or market the center will be more willing to participate. If they feel that exhibiting voice would lead to negative consequences, youth will avoid providing input.

Once youth start to speak up, they will require *support*. Adults can help by confirming the validity of comments, suggestions, and questions. Recreation programs are perfect settings for the embodiment of the idiom, "The only stupid question (or idea or comment) is the one that is not asked." Recreation specialists can also work with participants to identify resources that help them to form and to defend their ideas. For example, if a participant wants to bring a vocational training program to the teen center, a recreation specialist can work with the participant to identify individuals and organizations that could provide such training. Working with the youth to make their arguments more thorough and convincing can develop a greater sense of confidence to speak their mind.

As participants gain more opportunities to develop voice, programmers will find more of the ideas to be doable, and implementation of youth-initiated activities and ideas will increase. This increase will result in the enhancement of participants' sense of program ownership. However, it is imperative that staff be up front with participants, explaining the processes for implementation and the likelihood that suggestions and ideas will be incorporated and acted on. For example, is youth input used to *inform* decisions or to *make* decisions?

One of the best ways to gain the trust of participants—to demonstrate their ideas are respected—is to act on their input. Recreation specialists can enact *quick hit solutions and responses* to selected ideas to show participants their ideas are not being ignored. If after-school program participants ask for a checkers tournament, and it can be accomplished with reasonable programmatic adjustment, programmers should take advantage of the situation and schedule a tournament as soon as possible. As a result, participants will recognize their ideas are listened to and have merit. As a result, they will be more apt to continue expressing their ideas and opinions.

Finding ways to recognize the efforts and contributions of participants is key to increasing voice. Such recognition can take many forms. Fairfax County Community and Recreation Services hosts an annual recognition ceremony for youth who positively contribute to the agency. The ceremony is well-attended by local politicians and the agency's senior management. Teen centers highlight within their program schedules those activities that were youth-initiated. In addition, youth are often involved coauthoring articles for local publications and designing posters and flyers for events and activities. This involvement makes it clear to participants, their peers, and others in the community that youth are an integral part of the center's operations.

Finally, adults can help to focus voice development to issues of concern to youth. Capitalizing on interest and motivation is an effective way to increase participation in voice development activities. They must also embrace diversity to ensure that the opinions of all participants regardless of background or ability are heard. For example, boys and girls have some similar interests and priorities, but in other cases they differ from each other—partly defined by biological differences, partly by sociological differences. The same is true for youth of different age groups. Therefore, to help develop and promote voice, some gender-specific and age-specific opportunities are needed. Girls' groups can focus on issues of relevance to girls. Segmenting the participant population is not intended to segregate, but rather to give all participants an opportunity to comfortably speak out in front of others going through similar experiences, with similar interests, and facing similar issues.

We have just presented some general ideas of how to increase youth voice. Next, we discuss informal, casual methods that can be used once or a few times to increase voice as well as more formal, systematic methods. We also discuss what some professional organizations do to help increase youth voice.

Casual, One-Time, and Periodic Methods

Increasing youth voice does not always have to involve formal and systematic efforts. More informal and periodic methods that are easily implemented and can also provide useful feedback and contribute to increasing youth voice.

One of the authors (Ellis) once led a violence prevention program for sixth graders as part of a recreation center's program offerings. After each session, he would ask the participants what they liked and didn't like about the program. He also asked youth to offer suggestions on how to improve the program. One of the participants once asked, "Instead of spending all this money to teach kids why they shouldn't fight, why not just buy us all bulletproof vests?" As quirky as this question was, the young man was very serious, and Ellis was able to make two key inferences from this inquiry:

1. In this participant's mind, the program was on some level slow and tedious. It seemed like a lot of work to create a society free of violence and he was in favor of a less time-intensive solution. Perhaps more interaction and movement-based activities would have helped to break up the more tedious lecture and video portions of the program.

2. Despite the young person's cynicism, at least some of what had been taught had gotten through. The nature of his question indicated that he realized two of the basic tenets of the program: (a) youth are commonly targets of violence and (b) eliminating violence is a long process—just because he participated in the program, he will not be free from violence immediately.

This simple means of giving youth a voice in the program provided feedback relative to both the participants' feelings about the program and the program's effectiveness. All that was required of the program leader was to sincerely listen and to provide clarifications as necessary. While the suggestion was not likely to be implemented, the program leader made sure to validate the comment by promoting a short discussion of the merits of the argument, discussing the insight into the problem that the question demonstrated, and—rather than immediately dismissing the comment—explaining why it did not completely conform to the ideal taught in the lesson.

Less formal needs assessments, such as idea-sharing sessions, also can be beneficial. Perhaps the most effective way to get programming ideas from youth is to simply ask them informally or while one is engaged in some activity with them. Food is also a good way to motivate for both participation and conversation. If you can walk away with one idea that can be used, finding ways to solicit input and ideas is worth it.

Another way to help youth develop voice and to increase their investment in a program is to insure them a certain amount of decision-making power. Occasional, even spontaneous allocations of power can demonstrate to participants that their ideas and opinions are valued and have a place within the program. Promoting youth decision-making power can be accomplished in a variety of ways. For example, opportunities for group choice of activities can be included as part of an otherwise structured program. A portion of the monthly budget could be set aside for a group of participants to decide how to spend it; or when older participants are upset because younger kids are trying to join their basketball game, the older participants can be asked to help craft a set of rules that maximize participation, challenge, and fairness for everyone.

Ongoing and Formal Methods

We previously mentioned the value of a needs assessment to provide valuable programmatic input. Needs assessment also can help give youth voice. Not only are needs assessments a formal way to solicit youth opinion but also they provide a more comfortable means for some youth to share their opinions. That is, by completing a written questionnaire youth who are less inclined to speak up in a group setting can be given an opportunity to express their views. For example, a needs assessment survey response by one youth suggested crocheting classes be offered and led to a new program that doubled female participation.

Other formal needs assessment techniques can help prioritize ideas. As an example, we employed the nominal group technique (NGT) with a group of sixth graders to identify recreational after-school preferences. At first many of the "expected" ideas were generated, including daily field trips to theme parks and go-kart racing. But the NGT process allowed for participants to narrow down their suggestions, and in the end, it was clear that the youth preferred an informal place to hang out, receive homework help, and participate in a variety of sports and games—a much more doable proposition.

One of the most popular formal means of giving youth voice is through representation on advisory and decision-making councils. Many organizations that provide recreation programs are governed by a board of directors or overseen by an advisory council. The number of youth-serving organizations with youth representation on their boards is growing. In these cases, young board members serve as information conduits to the board as a whole, by providing "real" perspectives on youth issues and problems, and programs that would meet youth needs. From their involvement with these councils, youth also carry away with them an understanding of organizational and real-world constraints and can serve as a powerful vehicle for interpreting the program and its issues to all participants.

Other programs maintain separate councils made up entirely of youth. Youth-only boards can supplement youth representation on adult boards when the adult board is concerned mostly with finances, major fundraising, and other business, rather than issues related to facility use and programming. If youth are included on a board or council, it is important to ensure that the business of the council is relevant to the youth who are actually being served. Inclusion on a council provides a formal "ownership" opportunity for youth and can serve as a means of improving programming not only by gaining participants' insights but also by reaching out to target populations and assuring them that programs strive to meet their real needs and wants. Youth know when they are "token representatives" and like anyone, tend to resent that tokenism, often by not participating or becoming cynical.

One drawback to councils is the time youth may need to dedicate to participation. In addition, participation may require transportation and lead to reduced time with peers and involvement in other pursuits. When these situations occur, an alternative that still develops youth voice and enables youth direction in programming is to form youth-based committees focused on specific projects. Project-focused committees enable recreation programmers to tailor experiences to the youths' interests and capitalize on their enthusiasm. For example, consider the following:

- If a participant expresses an interest in a basketball tournament, he or she could be asked to help plan and implement the tournament.
- Committees could be formed to handle decorations, deejay selection, and refreshments for a scheduled dance at the center.
- Many school systems now include community service as a graduation requirement. Program participants could help to identify local needs or issues of interest to them and then design and implement service projects to address those needs.

The key to success with such committees is to enable the youth to set the direction and to make the major decisions on their own, or with a small degree of adult guidance or input. The majority of the decision-making power should lie with the youth because the results are much more focused on individual events, activities, or projects as opposed to overall program or facility operation, as in boards and councils. When a higher level of adult involvement is required, youth can still serve in various leadership or supporting roles for specific projects.

A popular form of encouraging youth voice is through speak-outs and youth forums. These one-time or occasional events are formatted much like traditional town hall meetings. There may be a guest speaker (either youth or adult) discussing a topic of relevance to those in attendance and food and a band (or some other form of entertainment) to encourage participation. But the identifying feature of these forums is the opportunity for youth to express their opinions and ideas. For example, an "open mic" could be used to enable input from any youth who wishes to address the entire gathering, or participants might be broken into smaller groups to facilitate more participation and discussion or to address a variety of issues in a shorter amount of time.

Youth forums can have multiple purposes. Decision makers can use the forums as a type of needs assessment to gauge youth concerns and interests. Programmers can use forums to develop program ideas. In addition, well-conducted and publicized opportunities for input can showcase the organization as one in touch with the community and responsive to youth needs.

Examples From Youth and Professional Organizations

Several national organizations have taken an interest in the role of adults in youth voice development and instituted policies that mandate youth involvement in provision of services. One of the 10 Youth Development Worker Competencies created by the National Collaboration for Youth (2005) is "involves and empowers youth." The standard states that all youth workers should be able to involve participants in the development of programming and encourage leadership development among youth. In *Grading Grown-Ups 2002*, the Search Institute (Scales, Benson & Mannes, 2002) reported that nearly half of all adults and youth surveyed ranked "seeking young people's opinions when making decisions that affect them" as a "most important" action that adults can take to relate to youth. (The same survey indicated that less than 40% of adults actually seek out youth opinions.)

In another example, the National 4-H (2005) sponsored hundreds of community-level forums as part of a 2001 National Conversation on Youth Development. These discussions involved elected officials, youth workers, school representatives, and youth. All participants had time to voice their concerns and opinions on the issues that face youth in the early 21st century and how 4-H could help address those needs. The national organization as well as local 4-H groups used the results of the discussions to help focus their programming priorities.

The National Recreation and Park Association (NRPA) has also sponsored youth forums around the country as a part of their NRPA National Youth Congress program (NNYC). The NNYC, originally created to develop young people's interest in the recreation and parks profession, includes a Youth Town Hall Forum. The forum is a way for youth in the community to voice their concerns on issues ranging from violence to how young people spend their free time. These forums enable recreation specialists to better understand and program for their constituents and enable young people to recognize how recreation organizations are able to address real issues facing youth, not just offer "fun and games."

In a final example of youth forums, the Fairfax County Department of Community and Recreation Services (VA) sponsors youth speak-outs, organized by the department's Teen Services unit. The speak-outs are held monthly at each of the department's teen centers. The sessions are designed to gain programming ideas, to gauge youth concerns on community issues, to expose youth to resources, and to recruit participants to the centers' teen councils. Each speak-out has a theme, which can range from field trip suggestions and planning to job resources to human rights. A typical event begins with a guest speaker or staff presentation to clarify the issues and resources available to local teens. After the presentation, participants have an opportunity to voice their concerns on the issue and to offer suggestions for ways the teen center could better address the issue or link participants to local resources. Center staff observe these interactions to help identify participants who could fill leadership roles on teen councils and committees.

Final Comments and Concluding Remarks

Youth programs are often expected to lead to acquisition of developmental (e.g., increased self-determination) and behavioral (e.g., reduced delinquency) outcomes. If young participants are deciding or influencing program content and format, does their input negatively impact the ability of programs to achieve these objectives? The short answer is no. With careful guidance, youth will naturally create programs that support these outcomes. As an example, if teens are asked for their input on a delinquency prevention program, a common idea might be to offer Scared Straight, the program that sends kids into jails in an effort to intimidate them from undertaking negative behaviors. These types of programs are very popular among youth because of their dramatic appeal; however, research has demonstrated the ineffectiveness of such programs. A responsible recreation specialist would negotiate with participants to help them learn the elements of effective prevention programs so they could make an informed decision about needed program content, to couple with their understanding of what teens might find interesting. In the end, the teens would be able to present a more informed decision that could lead to better implementation of their ideas.

Voice is important to nurture. With the right supports and opportunities, the leisure context is a fertile arena for enabling youth to develop voice. The numerous methods for developing voice presented in this chapter can be useful depending on the local circumstances. Finding the right fit for a program drives the decision of which methods to use. Idea-sharing sessions might work well for determining activities in a drop-in setting, while a teen council could be beneficial when choosing service learning projects. Regardless of method, voice development should be encouraged as a means for achieving several key developmental outcomes. The key to proper voice development lies in providing appropriate support and opportunities, distinguishing between voice and empowerment, and reconciling participants' desires with the mission of the program.

References

4-H. (2005). *Conversations: Summary of national report.* Retrieved August 5, 2005, from http://www.4hcentennial.org/conversations/main.asp

Anderson, K. P., Evans, C., and Mangin, M. (1997). The lost voice of the adolescent male. *Journal of Instructional Psychology, 24*, 14–23.

Belenky, M. F., Clinchy, B. M., Goldberger, N. R., and Tarule, J. M. (1997). *Women's ways of knowing: The development of self, voice, and mind* (10th Anniv. ed.). New York, NY: Basic Books.

Calhoun, J. A. (1992). Youth as resources: A new paradigm in social policy for youth. In G. W. Albee, L. A. Bond, and T. V. C. Monsey (Eds.), *Improving children's lives: Global perspectives on prevention* (pp. 334–341). New York, NY: Sage.

Catalano, R. F., Berglund, M. L., Ryan, J. A. M., Lonczak, H. S., and Hawkins, D. (2002). Positive youth development in the United States: Research findings on evaluation of positive youth development programs. *Prevention and Treatment, 5.* Retrieved August 5, 2005, from http://journals.apa.org/prevention/volume5/pre0050015a.html

Ellis, J. M. (2001). *Youth-directed recreation: A model of voice and community attachment.* Unpublished master's thesis, The Pennsylvania State University, University Park.

Forum for Youth Investment. (2004, May). From youth activities to youth action. *Forum Focus, 2*(2), 1–3.

Gallatin, J. (1985). *Democracy's children: The development of political thinking in children.* Ann Arbor, MI: Quod.

Heath, S. B. (1994). The project of learning from the inner-city perspective. In F. A. Villareul and R. M. Lerner (Eds.), *New directions for child development: No. 20. Promoting community-based programs for socialization and learning* (pp. 25–34). San Francisco, CA: Jossey-Bass.

Heath, S. B. (1996). Ruling places: Adaptation in development by inner-city youth. In R. Jessor, A. Colby, and R. A. Schweder (Eds.), *Ethnography and human development: Context and meaning in social inquiry* (pp. 225–251). Chicago, IL: University of Chicago Press.

hooks, b. (1989). *Talking back: Thinking feminist, thinking black.* Boston, MA: South End Press.

Larson, R. W. (2000). Toward a psychology of positive youth development. *American Psychologist, 55*(1), 170–183.

National Collaboration for Youth. (2005). *Youth development worker competencies.* Retrieved August 5, 2005, from http://www.nydic.org/nydic/documents/competencies.pdf

Oakley, B. and Weinstein, J. (Writers), and Lynch, J. (Director). (1994). Lisa vs. Malibu Stacy [Television series episode]. In J. L. Brooks (producer),

The Simpsons. Los Angeles, CA: Fox Entertainment.
Rogers, A. G. (1993). Voice, play, and a practice of ordinary courage in girls' and women's lives. *Harvard Educational Review, 63*, 265–295.
Ryan, R. M. and Deci, E. L. (2000). Self-determination theory and the facilitation of intrinsic motivation, social development, and well-being. *American Psychologist, 55*(1), 68–78.
Scales, P. C., Benson, P. L., and Mannes, M. (2002). *Grading grown-ups 2002: How do American kids and adults relate? Key findings from a national study.* Minneapolis, MN: Search Institute.
Tucker, C. M. and Herman, K. C. (2002). Using culturally sensitive theories and research to meet the academic needs of low-income African American children. *American Psychologist, 57,* 762–773.
Zeldin, S., McDaniel, A. K., Topitzes, D., and Calvert, M. (2000). *Youth in decision-making: A study on the impacts of youth on adults and organizations.* Madison, WI: University of Wisconsin-Madison Innovation Center for Community and Youth Development and the National 4-H Council.

Chapter 14

Developing Quality After-School Programs

Peter A. Witt

Widespread Support for the Development of After-School Programs

In the last 10 years there has been tremendous growth in the number of after-school programs available for children from preschool through high school. Support for development of programs is widespread among a variety of groups, including the public at large, schools, and law enforcement officials. For example, a September 2003 telephone survey of 800 registered voters age 18 or older nationwide found the following (Afterschool Alliance, 2003):

- Nearly 9 out of 10 voters are concerned that children are unsupervised after school with too much unstructured time. Half are very concerned. Voters are equally concerned about children and teens. Voters' concerns about children cluster into a supervision dimension and a safety dimension.
- 9 out of 10 voters agree that children, including teens, need some type of organized activity or a place to go after school every day. Voters show great concern if children have no place to go after school.
- 8 out of 10 voters agree that after-school programs are an absolute necessity. Across party lines, after-school programs are seen as a necessity.
- More than half of voters say there are not enough after-school programs available to children and teens.
- Voters show a commitment to after-school programs through good and bad economic times. Voters say they are willing to use taxpayer money and even to pay more in taxes to support such programs.

- Voters want to see all levels of government make a commitment to after-school programs. They would like the federal, state, and local levels to set aside specific funds for after-school programs.
- Voters worry that if no new funds come to the programs—as a result of reduced federal funding or because of budget problems in the states—programs will have to reduce their services or close their doors.
- Voters do not want to see after-school programs become an extension of the school day and do not believe that improving test scores should be the primary goal of the after-school programs. Focus group respondents also make it clear that improving test scores cannot be the sole purpose of programs. Voters want to see children in after-school programs offered hands-on learning opportunities, recreation, community service, and creative activities that inspire them to learn and grow.

In another survey of school board presidents conducted by the National School Boards Association (2003), four out of five (82%) of the 821 responding presidents indicated that they currently have an after-school program in their district. Some of the major findings of the survey included the following:

- 83% say it is essential or very important that after-school programs continue in their district.
- Board members believe the main goal of after-school programs should be raising student performance, with 80% saying that it is essential or very important.
- Board members with after-school programs give them high marks in providing services that directly impact classroom achievement. (82% say their programs do a good or excellent job of assisting students who are struggling academically.)
- 52% foresee that their after-school programs will have to be reduced somewhat or even cut entirely in the next few years due to proposed funding cuts.

America's police chiefs also see the need to increase the provision of after-school programs (Mastrofski & Keeter, 1999). Based on data compiled by the National Incident-Based Reporting System, juveniles are more likely to commit violent crimes on school days compared to nonschool days, and on school days crime goes up dramatically when school gets out, with one in five violent crimes committed by juveniles occurring between 3 p.m. and 7 p.m. (Sickmund, Snyder & Poe-Yamagata, 1997). These hours correspond to the period when adolescents are the most likely to be without adult supervision.

During these hours kids are most likely to become victims of violent crime, to be killed by household or other accidents, to get hooked on cigarettes, and to experiment with drugs. Evidence also suggests that teens are most likely to engage in sexual intercourse and girls are likely to become pregnant during these hours. This is also a key time period for kids of all ages to get hooked on video games that too often provide training for violent behavior (Newman, Fox, Flynn & Christeson, 2000).

In 2002, 1,178 individuals from a nationally representative list of chiefs of police, sheriffs, and prosecutors were surveyed to gauge their attitudes about the provision of after-school programs. Approximately 85% of the respondents believed that "providing quality educational child care programs for preschool-age children of low and moderate income working parents will help children succeed in school and significantly reduce crime and violence when the children grow up." Respondents also indicated the strategies they felt would have the greatest impact in reducing youth violence and crime. Seventy-one percent of the respondents placed "providing more educational child care programs for preschool age children and after-school programs for school age youngsters" at the top of the list. "Hiring more police officers to investigate juvenile crimes," "prosecuting and jailing more juveniles as adults," and "installing more metal detectors and surveillance cameras in schools" were rated as the top priorities by 14.9%, 12.1%, and 2.3%, respectively (Fight Crime: Invest in Kids, 2002).

Given the importance of after-school programs, it is troubling that while mayors indicate that program capacity is growing, cities still estimate that of children needing after-school care only about 35% are actually enrolled in programs. In other words, there is a need to increase program slots to meet the need and demand for programs (United States Conference of Mayors, 2003).

Why After-School Programs Are Strongly Supported

Although after-school programs are created by a variety of organizations, have a variety of goals, and serve a range of children, the rationale for programs can be grouped into three categories: (a) safety issues and the growing need for child care, (b) the value placed on decreasing negative behaviors and increasing thriving behaviors, and (c) interest in using the after-school hours for improving educational achievement.

Safety Issues and the Need for Child Care

In their landmark 1992 study, the Carnegie Council on Adolescent Development found that the transition to adolescence has become more difficult because of the increasing number and accessibility of dangerous alternatives for time use when young people are not in school. This is especially troubling when coupled with the uneven availability of safe and healthy activities with enough appeal to attract and to hold the attention of young people.

Shifts in family and community life also increase the need for after-school programs for younger children (Halpern, Deich & Cohen, 2000; Newman, Fox, Flynn & Christeson, 2000). Welfare reform has led to the need for safe places for children to be while parents are working (Reno & Riley, 2000). Most parents feel less stressed knowing that their children are in a protected environment. Leaving younger children at home to be watched by older children is not a satisfactory arrangement and denies older children time to "just be kids."

Currently over 28 million school-age children have parents who work outside the home, but only about six million children from kindergarten to Grade 8 participate in after-school programs (Bureau of Labor Statistics, 1997; U.S. Department of Education National Center for Education Statistics, 1999). Thus, after-school program slots for children who potentially are in a self-care situation after school need to be increased. While the exact number of children in self-care has been difficult to estimate, the 1995 Survey of Income and Program Participation (U.S. Census Bureau, 2005) estimated that the percentage of all children in self-care (defined as spending 10 or more hours per week alone) was 7.2% for children 5 to 11 years old, and 16.4% for children 12 to 14 years old. For both age groups, children are more likely to be left alone if they are in single-parent families where the parent works and/or they come from lower income families (Kerrebrock & Lewit, 1999).

As children get older, they increase their autonomy and the significance of friends and peers grows. Thus, it should be expected that as children grow older, they spend some time caring for themselves with no adult present. However, for some children self-care has been associated with several negative outcomes. Self-care children have been found to be more lonely (Quay, 1992), anxious, and headstrong; to be more likely to have peer conflicts (Vandell & Ramanan, 1991); to be less likely to complete their homework (Long & Long, 1989); and to have poorer emotional well-being (Vandell, Posner, Shumow & Kang, 1995) than children who either have adult care after school or attend structured, supervised after-school programs. Self-care children tend to be more involved with peers, have more contact with deviant peers, and boys have poorer parent-adolescent relations (Galambos & Maggs,

1991). Children who "hang out" after school are most susceptible to peer pressure, followed by those children who go to a friend's house, followed by those children who go home (Steinberg, 1986).

Decreasing Negative Behaviors and Increasing Thriving Behaviors

How young people spend their nonschool hours can have a significant impact on their propensity to participate in negative behaviors and lessen the likelihood of their participating in thriving behaviors. When young people have nothing positive to do and nowhere to go, the odds are high they will find things to do and places to go that negatively influence their development and futures (McLaughlin, 2000). Consider the following:

- On weekdays, about one third of 8th graders, one fourth of 10th graders, and one fifth of 12th graders watch four or more hours of television (Child Trends Data Bank, 2002a). However, if they had other things to do after school, more than half of teens (54%) say they would not watch so much TV or play video games (Penn, Schoen & Berland Associates, 2001).
- The more violence children watch on TV, the more likely they are to behave in aggressive or harmful ways toward others, to become less sensitive to others' pain and suffering, to be more fearful of the world around them, and to increase their appetite for violence in entertainment and in real life (American Academy of Pediatrics, 2001).
- Considerable evidence suggests that students who do not spend time in constructive out-of-school activities are more likely to be involved in negative behaviors. In one study, students who did not participate in after-school activities were 49% more likely to use drugs and 37% more likely to become teen parents than those who spent as little as one to four hours per week involved in after-school activities (University of California at Irvine, 2001).
- Lack of physical activity, along with a poor diet, can lead to significant health problems. Obesity during childhood, or an increase in obesity from childhood to young adulthood, is a strong predictor of blood lipid and blood pressure levels during young adulthood. Obese individuals tend to have greater LDL cholesterol and blood pressure levels and lower HDL levels

than lean individuals. Participation in sedentary activities, such as television viewing and computer games, can negatively impact the physical activity levels of young people. Physical activity tends to decrease with age and is lower for females than males (Child Trends Data Bank, 2002b).

Increasing Opportunities for Educational Attainment

A third impetus for increasing after-school program opportunities is the current national interest in boosting educational attainment. There is a widespread belief that to raise achievement test scores, the time children are involved in educational activities beyond the school day must be increased (Newman, Fox, Flynn & Christeson, 2000). The lack of scholastic support and/or role models available to some children in their homes provides further impetus for the development of after-school programs. Supporters hope that over time after-school programs will decrease the number of school dropouts and increase school attendance, grades, and standardized test scores.

Research supports the connection between after-school participation and positive educational and life-skill outcomes. For example, participation in after-school programs is positively associated with better school attendance, more positive attitudes toward school work, higher aspirations for college, better work habits, better interpersonal skills, reduced drop out rates, higher quality homework completion, less time spent in unhealthy behaviors, and improved grades (Clark, 1988; Hamilton & Klein, 1998; Huang, Gribbons, Kim, Lee & Baker, 2000; McLaughlin, 2000; Posner & Vandell, 1994, 1999; Schinke, 1999; U.S. Department of Education, 1998).

In many after-school programs, recreation is thought of as the hook that attracts children to become involved. However, simply involving children in fun and games is not viewed as sufficient for increasing educational achievement. Thus, in many settings, particularly when school personnel are involved, efforts are made to enrich recreation activities by using them as tools for purposive learning. In addition, students are either provided with tutoring or given the opportunity to complete homework by themselves or with assistance from program personnel. Tutoring is also common when children's parents have a low level of educational attainment themselves and/or low English language skills, both of which might deny children the opportunity to receive help at home with assigned homework.

In all cases, the provision of caring adult leaders and purposely planned enrichment activities are critical program elements. Appropriate controls against deviant behavior and the absence of negative peer influences have been cited as contributing to positive learning experiences for children (Jessor, 1992). After-school programs can make an important contribution by offering program elements that bridge between risks that are inherent in the child's environment and the consequences that may occur as a result of subsequent behaviors (Witt, Baker & Scott, 1996; Witt & Crompton, 1997).

Overemphasis on student learning and achievement may potentially undermine or diminish achievement of other critical after-school program goals, such as development of decision making skills, increased physical activity, or opportunities for self-expression. To overcome this problem, Alexander (2000) recommended the viability of project-based activities that combine the best of play and academics as an alternative to a strict adherence to after-school becoming simply more school.

Halpern (1999) further warned that after-school programs need to avoid just being a place where improvement in something tangible is sought. He noted, "It will be difficult for school-age programs to create the psychological space children need if there is too much pressure to serve instrumental purposes" (p. 93). Many community organizations operate on the principle that children need a break from formal learning and the chance to just be kids. However, focusing solely on safety and recreation may not meet the requirements of parents and school personnel anxious to give increased attention to means for boosting educational achievement.

Stakeholder Issues

Stakeholders differ on which after-school objectives to emphasize. Larner, Sippiorli, and Behrman (1999) noted that children want competence, relationships, and autonomy; parents want their children to be supervised and in an enriched environment; and the public at-large wants prevention of risk behaviors and improved academic performance. Teachers may be interested in programs mainly as a means for extending the school day and thus improving test scores.

Thus, a central issue in after-school program design is the balance among stakeholders' views (Baker & Witt, 2000). For example, Larner and colleagues (1999) noted, "Because the new resources are public dollars, they are linked to policy goals that are salient to the voters and elected officials. But, after-school programs will succeed only if they also appeal to parents and children" (p. 17). Given the potential for tension between competing agendas, partnerships are needed between service providers and other stakeholders that can give full voice to the differing views of what constitutes an after-school program.

However, creating synergy between differing program agendas is not always easy. Programs created as a means for increasing academic performance may begin to look primarily like more school, whereas mass programs with high participant-to-leader ratios may look more like free play.

Sources of Funding

After-school programs are supported by a variety of sources.

- In Fort Worth, Texas, Fort Worth After-School offers after-school programming at 52 sites (47 elementary school and 5 middle schools) using equal monies from the city's crime control district and school district funding. The program serves about 2,600 children per day, at a cost of approximately $850 per child per school year.
- The Boys & Girls Clubs offer programming using a combination of locally raised dollars, corporate and individual donations, user fees (limited) and federal dollars.
- The 21st Century Community Learning Centers are funded through approximately $1 billion dollars in federal monies, with an expectation of some local match, and a community plan for sustaining the program after the initial three-year grant period.

In general, programs are being offered using some combination of user fees, state and local property tax, sales tax or income tax dollars; corporate or other donated dollars; or school district funding. The infrastructure developed for supporting after-school programs differs in each community. In some communities, a number of unrelated service providers operate—no cohesive plan or vision of the kinds of services needed in the community exists. In other communities, community organizations, schools, and government participate in a process to assess community after-school program needs and then develop an interrelated set of services, utilizing a number of different kinds of providers, to meet the identified needs.

Some of the federal sources for after-school programs include 21st Century Community Learning Centers (U.S. Department of Education), Community Development Block Grant Funding (U.S. Department of Housing and Urban Development), and Title I funding (U.S. Department of Education). A number of foundations have also provided significant funding, including the Charles Mott Foundation.

Selected states have also provided additional monies for after-school programs (e.g., California, Maryland, Texas). In addition, nonprofits (e.g., Boys & Girls Clubs) have received set aside funds in the federal budget for the expansion of programs. Many of the country's major cities and school boards have also increased funding. However, budget cutbacks in the early 2000s have led to cuts in most sources of funding, especially funding from the state and local levels.

In most cases, the cost per child is between $1.90 and $2.50 per hour, but some programs for private day care might go as high as $5.00 to $7.00 per hour. The smaller the staff to participant ratio, the more game or free play based the program, and the more programs rely on part time, temporary, nonprofessional workers, the lower the dollar per hour cost will be. However, when programs have higher staff to participant ratios, pursue academic improvement or other targeted goals, and hire specialized staff (e.g., teachers), the hourly cost will be higher. In the first case, the program may be using college students who are paid only slightly more than minimum wage, while in the latter, teachers might be hired at close to their school day hourly rate.

Program Content and Structure

Activities differ widely from one after-school program to another. Differences may be a function of program goals, the philosophy of the program provider, the available facilities, program funding, and the expertise of program staff. Programs may also differ in the amount of choice between activities that participants are afforded and the amount of time devoted to offered activities. In general, most programs contain opportunities for participants to get a snack, complete their homework or receive tutoring, and participate in one or more recreational or enrichment activities. For elementary age children, programs are usually more structured, with children receiving less choice about the activities in which they wish to participate. As students enter middle school, it becomes increasingly important to afford participants a range of activities and considerable choice about the activities they wish to participate in on a given day.

Many after-school programs place emphasis on the arts, music, and drama, activities that too often are absent from the test-score driven school curricula. Some programs for middle and high school students offer a series of "classes" that participants can sign up for and participate in over a specified number of weeks. These activities provide students with an opportunity to broaden their experiences and to participate in activities that match their interests. Offering physical or sports activities is also critical so participants can have time for exercise as well a break from activities that involve sitting and less physical energy expenditure. Exercise can also contribute to physical health and lower rates of obesity.

To be successful, participants must have a say in which programs are offered. Choice and voice creates ownership (as discussed in Chapter 13). Student surveys, focus groups, and attendance at existing programs (i.e., "voting with their feet") are all useful ways to gage student interest.

Program attendance is a critical challenge with after-school programs. Efforts should be made to retain participants in the activity over the specified session to avoid their dropping in and out of activities and disrupting the experiences of other participants. Doing this also assures that students have some continuity to what they are learning and adequate exposure to learn skills and develop competence.

The method of delivery of after-school programs varies by provider and setting. However, in most cases, more emphasis is placed on hands-on, experiential learning than is found during the regular school day. Experiential learning may include a number of different approaches, including project-based learning, adventure education, and apprenticeships (Miller, 2003). Many programs are involving students in service projects (i.e., service learning) designed to reinforce the idea of giving to others, volunteering, and making a difference in their community.

Issues in Program Development

A number of issues arise when trying to create quality after-school programs. How these issues are handled will make a significant difference in the short-term and long-term success of a program.

Unrealistic Expectations for Early Program Success

Too often stakeholders have higher than warranted expectations for early program success. They expect strong evidence at the end of even the first few months that outcome objectives, such as improved test scores, are being achieved. Thus, program organizers need to distinguish between short-term and longer-term objectives and do a good job communicating with stakeholders about what outcomes the program should be held accountable for over the short term and longer term. For example, programmers of most new programs have all they can do to get programs up and running in the first year, including identifying sites, hiring and training staff, and recruiting or selecting participants. The expectation for the first year may be that all of these tasks were completed successfully, that a certain number of children were served, at a particular cost per hour, and that participants and their parents thought highly enough about the program to consider signing up again and/or recommending the program to others. In subsequent years, there can be greater emphasis on accountability for meeting program outcome goals.

Politics of Competing With Private Providers

Both for-profit and nonprofit program providers often question the use of city, state or federal funds to develop after-school programs. For-profit programs question the use of governmental funding to compete for the same clientele they may be trying to serve. In most cases, if for-profit providers are willing to offer the same type of programs that government or foundations are willing to support and charge participants at the same or lower rates than government or grant-funded programs, then private funders should be the ones offering the programs. However, this is often not the case. For-profit providers usually have to charge more than government or grant-supported programs, and may not be able or willing to plan programs that meet the goals envisioned by stakeholders.

Both for-profit and nonprofit after-school program providers are concerned about the use of governmental funding by schools and other governmental agencies to develop programs that compete with those they are already providing. Schools and other governmental agencies can often provide services at no cost or a reduced fee, and often do not have to count fixed costs and overhead, like buildings and electricity, and sometimes program administration, as part of their expenses. On the other hand, for-profit and nonprofit providers must consider all costs and have a hard time competing when governmental services are, in essence, subsidized.

The usual solution to these problems is for governmental agencies seeking to boost the number of available after-school program slots to work cooperatively with private sector and nonprofit providers to facilitate delivery of the needed services. For example, Fort Worth After School gives principals at each of its 52 sites the option of using a nonprofit or for-profit provider from an approved provider list. Approved providers annually must apply to be on the list and are accepted if they demonstrate that they can provide the desired kind of program within certain cost parameters. Consultation and joint planning with all potential parties as the program design is being formulated can help avoid many political and coordination problems.

Staffing

Staffing after-school programs with qualified individuals can be problematic. Most after-school programs depend on part-time staff. Some nonprofit agencies do employ full-time staff to operate recreation centers, YMCA, or Boys & Girls Clubs facilities. But even in these cases, part-time staff will have to be hired to serve youth during peak hours. Finding qualified part-time workers who are willing to work for low wages can be a challenge. High school or college students or those not seeking a full-time job are often the only adults available. Low wages add to the problem of attracting and retaining experienced "professionals" for these positions.

The lack of qualified staff has led some school-based programs to hire teachers from the school site to work in the after-school program. These teachers are often paid at or near their hourly school-day pay rate. Involving teachers is seen as particularly necessary in situations where academic improvement is one of the main programmatic goals. Paying teachers at a reasonable pay rate, however, is the exception to how after-school program workers are usually remunerated. If youth development is as critical as discussed in previous chapters, it is strange that we assign such low economic rewards to those who would undertake this important work with our children.

Another issue related to quality staffing is the type and amount of training that youth workers receive. Hiring college students who are fun to be around and are perceived to be good with kids is important, but they still need a rigorous and ongoing training program if program goals are to be fully accomplished. Thus, training should include knowing the program's rules and procedures as well as content on intentional programming (i.e., purposely developing activities to achieve desired outcomes; see Chapter 10). Leadership techniques, including how to deal with young people who exhibit challenging behaviors, are also critical elements of a training program. Finally, training needs to take place on a continuous basis and not just be part of a concentrated several day, preprogram event. In most cases, staff should be paid to attend training events.

As a final point, efforts need to be made to screen out potential hirees who are unwilling to commit to a reasonable period of involvement with the program. Individuals who are hired need to commit to working all nine months of a school-year program. After-school programmers staffing their programs should make sure student workers understand the need to be available even when they have finals and that they are expected to arrange outside commitments so that they can meet their work obligations and expectations.

Continuity of staff is important for several reasons. First, as we have described previously in this book, young people need caring adults to be part of their lives. Youth become reticent to invest in meaningful relationships if they know that staff may be short-timers. Thus, in staff hiring, employing individuals who are likely to break a promise to a child (i.e., work for a while, but then disappoint participants by breaking bonds when other personal needs arise) should be avoided. Second, a constantly rotating staff makes it difficult to create a cohesive approach to working with young people and makes it difficult to provide the same in-depth training to those employed during the year as was provided for individuals employed at the beginning of the year. Finally, inconsistent staffing patterns make it more difficult to achieve the deliberate outcomes (e.g., academic competence, development of social skills) set for the program.

Parental and Community Involvement

Involving parents and other members of the community in defining program goals, supporting and assisting the program, and evaluating the impact of the program is critical to program success. As we described in the section on stakeholders, perspectives on program needs, content, and indicators of success vary. A well-run program attempts to meld these varying perspectives into a cohesive whole.

In addition, many program goals can only be accomplished if there is a reasonable level of parental involvement. For example, if the program has a strong homework assistance component, it is critical that parents are involved during nonprogram hours in assisting their children to the full extent they are able. Working with parents to adopt similar behavior management strategies may be important for merging program and nonprogram expectations.

For a program struggling to find sufficient funds to run or expand, involvement of parents and other community members is vital. Parents, employees of a local business, and other community volunteers may be able to supply support through volunteering their time, providing monetary donations to the program, or helping to work with funders to reinforce the importance of the program and its outcomes. In some communities, local businesses donate the time of their employees by allowing them to work a few hours a week in a program on company time. These volunteers may be able to provide knowledge that does not exist within the regular staff in a particular program area. For example, a local businesswoman may share her expertise with students about how to organize a fundraising event. Incorporating volunteers from the community also demonstrates to program participants that people in the community value them and care about what happens to them.

Communication

Communication among all stakeholders is critical to program success. For example,

- Staff need to talk with each other about successes and problems, with the idea of building a team that can work toward continuous improvement.

- Information needs to be provided to parents about the kinds of experiences their children are having in the program and whether programs goals are being met.
- If the program is school-based, staff need to maintain communication with the school principal and classroom teachers to insure support for the program and to maximize access to equipment and facilities.
- The community needs to know about the program and be given opportunities to understand the value of the program and see the good things that young people in their community are doing.

Regular meetings, newsletters, and posters are good ways to promote communication. In addition, programs should invite stakeholders to observe the program and should plan special events to showcase the participants and their activities to its various constituencies. Having the school principal, business leader, or city council member observe a special program may help to build stakeholder support. Undertaking this kind of public relations only when grants need to be renewed does not build the kind of partnerships necessary for long-term program sustainability and enhancement.

Bringing Programs to Scale

While a number of after-school programs have been developed in the last 10 years for children of all ages, the demand for participation exceeds the number of slots in existing programs. Many good programs are only able to serve a small proportion of the children who could benefit from participation. For example, the Fort Worth After School program has 2,600 slots. However, there are over 32,000 students at the 52 sites, and thus the program is only serving about 8% of the potential demand. Even if one assumes that one half of the children have other quality after-school involvements, this still would leave over 13,500 students without viable program alternatives. Thus, school and/or community leaders need to develop slots in existing programs and to create additional programs to serve the potential demand. Pittman, Irby, and Ferber (2001) have set a goal of serving 80% of children in a community with some nonschool time supports, opportunities, programs, and services. In almost all communities, the system as currently constructed comes nowhere near achieving this standard.

Sustaining Programs Over Time

Program sustainability is a critical issue. As we discussed in Chapter 1, many programs are funded by one-shot grant monies, and as a result may exist for a few years and then go out of existence, only to be replaced by the next *programme de jour.* Most new after-school program money that has recently been put on the table has come as a three-year grant, with the expectation that program providers will find other funds to sustain the program after the initial grant money runs out. However, when organizers of these programs approach other funders to obtain the next round of funding, they often find that the funders are more interested in funding another experimental or new program model rather than supporting already developed models with strong evidence of success. Part of this problem is that after-school service providers have not documented the outcomes achieved, leaving them vulnerable to discontinued funding.

The more established youth development organizations have an easier time sustaining funding. Many, such as the YMCA, Boys & Girls Club, and Girl Scouts, have developed more sustainable funding streams, have developed packaged programs that can be branded and which attract corporate support, and use volunteers to cover some portion of the program costs. However, much of the infrastructure and programming in the after-school market has been supported with unstable dollars. For example, funding through government is often subject to political expediency rather than an assessment of real needs. So, while there is a growing constituency of parents who understand the need for and value of after-school programs, their support is not always matched by continuous funding streams.

Luckily, the issue of after-school programs is so important to parents and other stakeholders that they are willing to advocate strongly for new funding, and provide strong opposition when attempts are made to cut existing funding. For example, federal attempts in 2003 to cut back on the $1 billion annual investment in the 21st Century Community Learning Centers program were met with intensive lobbying by grant recipients from across the country. The involvement of 6,800 rural and inner-city public schools in 1,420 communities across the United States, along with the involvement of other public and nonprofit agencies, organizations, local businesses, postsecondary institutions, and scientific/cultural and other community entities, insured a broad-based constituency that advocated for continued funding.

Transportation

Transportation is a critical issue for many after-school programs. In some cases, no bus service is provided when the program ends and parents are not always able to pick up their children at the end of a program day. If children have to walk home, especially when it is dark or children have to walk through what are perceived as unsafe neighborhoods, parents may have children take the bus home when school is dismissed and thus the children (especially those of a younger age) may miss out on attending the after-school program. Providing additional bus service at the end of the after-school program can be expensive, but it is critical to insuring that the program is accessible to all children. For middle and high school students, the catchment area for programs is larger and buses thus become even more of a necessity.

In addition to funding buses to take children home at the end of the program day, money for buses for field trips should be built into after-school program budgets. Field trips can provide added variety and enrichment to programs and help children feel less "trapped" at after-school program sites.

Snacks

Providing a healthy and nutritious snack is a necessity for most after-school programs, particularly those that operate from the time school gets out until children go home for dinner. By three o'clock, it has been three hours or more since children have had lunch, and another three hours until they will have dinner. Thus, most programs supply some kind of snack at the beginning of the after-school program. If the after-school program is run under the auspices of a school district where at least 50% of students are eligible under federal standards for free or reduced-price meals, the program will be eligible to receive funding under the National School Lunch Program of the United States Department of Agriculture. Some state-funded after-school programs can receive state funding for snacks, whether schools or nonprofit organizations operate them. After-school snacks are an excellent way to introduce children and youth to healthy eating. Concerns about obesity have made this need salient, and programs should strive to make sure snacks are nutritious.

Participant Recruitment and Retention

Given the other possibilities youth have after-school, including doing nothing and hanging out, after-school programmers must often compete for young people's time to keep them from choosing other potentially attractive activities that do not have the same potential for positive youth development.

Recruitment issues differ depending on the age of children participating in the after-school program. For most elementary school age children, parents sign their children up to participate. Thus, recruitment efforts need to be directed mainly at parents. For older elementary school children and middle school children, children begin to have a major say in whether they will attend a particular after-school program, or once in a program, whether they will remain or drop out.

Recruiting middle and high school youth, especially those who would most benefit from participation, can be challenging due to the range of formal or informal alternatives (e.g., soccer leagues, hanging out with friends) youth have for after-school involvement. In addition, peers make a big difference in whether children participate. Programs can develop a negative reputation or not be seen by opinion leaders as the place to be during the nonschool hours. In addition, because older youth often have a choice about participating, the quality of the program leaders and activities make a bigger difference than they might for younger children whose parents are making enrollment decisions based on convenience, cost, and how well the program seems to be run. Consequently, programs serving middle and high school age youth need to develop marketing plans to attract participants. Marketing efforts need to build on the fact that many young people will prefer just hanging out if they don't have a positive image of a program and its leaders and activities. While young people are anxious to have a safe place to go where they will receive personal attention, they will vote with their feet if they perceive that offered programs do not meet their needs.

A related problem is getting middle school students to attend on a regular basis. Where elementary school students may be signed up by their parents for five days a week, middle school students, even if registered, might only attend a couple days a week or even more sporadically over the year. One study of 10 after-school programs found that middle school youth attended only about 50% of the days they were scheduled to attend, while elementary school children attended over two thirds of the time (Grossman et al., 2002). Programs for middle school students must consider the growing autonomy and changing interests of teens over time (Herrera & Arbreton, 2003). To effectively recruit teens, especially those who most need the supports and opportunities represented by the after-school programs, program staff need to reach out to teens at school and in the community. A number of teens can be enticed to participate once they get to know the staff and feel comfortable that programs will have leaders and activities they like. In addition, attracting opinion leaders may create the "buzz" that a program is the place to be.

Schools keep parents informed about the after-school program in the same way they provide other kinds of school-related information. Independent programs often forge a partnership with the district to promote recruitment.

Letters, flyers, and announcements in local newspapers are simple recruitment tools. Materials can be supplied to local employers for dissemination—doing this may also spark program support.

Parental Involvement in Programs

Getting families involved is a critical component of many after-school programs. Since many parents work during the time after-school programs are offered, finding ways to involve them after work during the early evening hours should be undertaken. The 21st Century Community Learning Centers program was conceived with the goal of making schools the hub of community activity and involving parents in programs that support their children as well as providing programs that facilitate increased parenting, academic (e.g., to work toward obtaining a GED), and language skills.

Getting parents involved, however, can be challenging. Parents may feel disconnected from the programs and services that serve their children or not see the value of their involvement. After-school programs have used a variety of ways to try to increase parental involvement. A key principle is talking with parents about their needs and interests and then building programming and involvement efforts around what parents think is important as opposed to what professionals think is important for parents. Gaining input from parents who are already involved is important for gaining the involvement of other parents. Focus groups with these parents can help provide useful information about what programs and services it will take to recruit other parents.

Food and door prizes can be powerful enticements for getting parents to attend meetings or support events. Parents also enjoy watching their children performing or making presentations. For example, a family dinner theater might be offered, where teens perform a play for parents after a meal (which other teens might be involved in preparing, setting up, and serving). Activity and game nights may also be useful as ways of encouraging parent involvement. A student participant awards night may also encourage parent attendance, creating the opportunity to talk to attending parents about other activities that could be developed or are already available. Getting ministers to "spread the word" about programs and parent involvement during a Sunday service, and involving local opinion and business leaders and community volunteers in providing information and encouraging participation may also be useful. In addition, getting the local media to provide publicity about the program and note accomplishments of children attending the program are means for creating positive news about the program among parents and other people in the community.

In summary, being sensitive to barriers parents face or disincentives for participation are critical. When designing programs and services, attention needs to be given to issues such as transportation, child care, language, cost (free or low-cost is usually a necessity!), and activity location (e.g., where parents work, attend church on Sunday).

The Necessity of Program Evaluation

Many programs evaluate their effectiveness or impact mainly by compiling information on the number of youth they serve and whether participants and parents are satisfied with the program. Too often, however, little effort is made to determine if program outcome goals are being achieved.

In an age of accountability, evaluation is critical for garnering support from funders and other stakeholders. Continuing funding often depends on the program organizers' skill at supplying an annual program evaluation that demonstrates appropriate levels of attendance, program satisfaction, and whether program goals have been achieved. With the scarcity of funding for after-school programs, funders tend to favor granting funds to organizations that are willing to develop processes that can lead to the information necessary to document program achievements and continuously improve program design and delivery.

To help you to understand the need for and value of after-school program evaluations, you should look at a compilation of after-school evaluation results collected by the Afterschool Alliance and posted on their website (Afterschool Alliance, 2004). The following are some examples of evaluation study findings listed on the Afterschool Alliance website:

- Evaluations of LA's BEST show that program students' attendance improved once they began participating in the program. That improved attendance led to higher academic achievement on standardized tests of math, reading, and language arts. In addition, language redesignation rates favored LA's BEST students when compared with non-LA's BEST students.
- The evaluation of the New York City Beacons program concluded that "the vast majority of youth (85%) reported that it was 'always true' or 'mostly true' that they felt safe at the Beacons."
- Parents whose children participated in after-school programs sponsored by The After-School Corporation said that the program helped them to balance work and family life: 94% said

the program was convenient, 60% said they missed less work than before because of the program, 59% said it supported them in keeping their job, and 54% said it allowed them to work more hours.

Formative or Process Evaluation

The two basic kinds of evaluation are (a) formative or process evaluation and (b) summative or outcome evaluation. *Formative* or *process evaluation* looks at the adequacy of factors such as program management, staff hiring and training, personnel procedures, budgeting, availability of needed equipment and supplies, and program space. To undertake this type of evaluation, programs will develop a set of standards and then evaluate the extent to which the program as delivered is meeting the standards. In addition, participants, parents and staff are usually asked to supply ratings of program quality (e.g., "The program has staff who give me help when I need it," "The program has good facilities.") and their level of program satisfaction (e.g., "Would you sign up for the program again?"; "Would you recommend the program to another family?"). Collected information is used to determine whether the program is being well run, but most importantly to provide information that can lead to efforts to continuously improve the program.

Information should be collected on the number of individuals participating in a program (including information about the number of registrants and their demographics, and rates of program participation and dropouts). This information will help program leaders to assess whether individuals from the intended target group are being served and if participants like the program well enough to continue attending. In addition, if participants can choose among a variety of activities during a different time period, attendance data can be used to determine the degree to which participants want to participate in particular activities.

Formative evaluation also includes monitoring the fidelity of program delivery: To what extent does actual program content match what program organizers intended to offer? For example, if the program advertises that it will offer homework assistance, but time is not set aside for youth to complete their homework and staff is not available to answer questions and provide assistance, then the program is not being "true" to its advertised intentions.

Summative or Outcome Evaluation

Summative or *outcome evaluation* helps program organizers to collect information to determine whether programs are achieving desired outcomes.

For example, if one of the program objectives is to increase academic performance, to what extent has the program contributed to better grades or achievement test scores? Or, to what extent is a program being successful in its efforts to decrease particular negative behaviors (e.g., smoking or drug use) and increase positive behaviors (e.g., the ability to work constructively in a group setting or developing the skills necessary to participate in a particular activity)?

For both formative and summative evaluation, a variety of data collection strategies can be used, including surveys of participants, parents, teachers, staff and other stakeholders; program observations, interviews, focus groups, case studies; program attendance data analyses; and analyses of the cost per hour of participation. Each of the methods has its strengths and drawbacks. For example, surveys are inexpensive to administer, but may not be able to provide in-depth information about why participants responded with a particular rating for a particular question. On the other hand, interviews can provide more in-depth information, but interpretations of interviewees' responses can be subjective. A number of websites provide excellent resources for learning more about evaluation methods and provide examples of evaluation surveys and actual evaluation reports (cf. Geiger & Britsch, 2004; Little, DuPree & Deich, 2002; Witt, 2004).

Increasing Park and Recreation's Role in Offering After-School Programs

Park and recreation departments currently meet some of the need for after-school programs. However, in many cases, park and recreation departments have been left out of the after-school program discussion or relegated to a fun and games, service provider role. Most park and recreation departments have been unable to position themselves as major players when educational goals are put forth as the dominant rationale for creating after-school programs. In some cases, where recreation departments have had a chance to become involved in after-school program efforts, they have steadfastly insisted that they are not in the education and/or tutoring business, and that kids should not have to spend after-school time involved in educational/enrichment activities. In other cases, recreation departments have not wanted to run programs at school-based sites, fearing that they would not get sufficient credit for being involved or that the program would be dominated by school personnel.

In addition, voluntary nonprofit sector organizations, like the Boys & Girls Clubs, YMCAs, YWCAs, or Police Athletic Leagues, have better positioned themselves as providers of after-school programs. Being niche organizations, with more limited target markets than park and recreation departments, these organizations are better equipped to command community attention and support for the specialized services they provide. They often concentrate energy and resources on at-risk target groups and many of these organizations have undertaken more cooperative efforts with schools.

Park and recreation departments have also been subjected to shrinking budgets and the subsequent need to offer programs on a fee-for-service basis has led to the demise of some programmatic efforts for those who cannot pay for services. Park and recreation departments need to recognize societal expectations and the forces driving the need for after-school programs if they are to become a significant player in the after-school program movement. Luckily a number of departments are meeting this challenge. For example, San Antonio and Phoenix are involved in multisite after-school programming in cooperation with local school districts and other governmental and nonprofit agencies.

The Future of After-School Programming

The public is very interested in creating and sustaining after-school programs to protect children during the critical hours between when children get out of school and parents get home from work. The lack of family financial resources to provide quality after-school experiences, the desire to use after-school time to improve academic performance, and the utilization of the nonschool hours as opportunities for other areas of youth development are other reasons for creating after-school programs. While many programs currently exist, too few slots exist in current programs. Ongoing efforts need to be made to increase available funding to sustain and to expand existing programs and to create new programs as necessary. It is also critical that programs provide evidence that they are effectively spending their funds and accomplishing the outcomes they were designed to achieve.

Ultimately stakeholders will not base decisions about program success on the reported amount of fun participants say they experience. The ultimate utility of programs will be based on the extent to which they deal with critical issues, such as

- providing meaningful alternatives to activities that promote risk behavior for young people during the dangerous period from 3:00 p.m. to 7:00 p.m.
- helping young people to do better in school and not drop out
- enabling young people to develop to be fully functioning adults

While fun and enjoyment are necessary to keep youth involved, they are not the primary goals of most programs. It is important to develop programs that enrich the after-school hours and are more than just recreation or efforts to keep young people safe and off the streets.

References

Afterschool Alliance (2003). *Summary of findings from the 2003 national voters poll*. Retrieved January 6, 2004, from http://www.afterschoolalliance.org/poll_2003_oct.cfm

Afterschool Alliance. (2004). *Backgrounder: Formal evaluations of afterschool programs*. Retrieved August 1, 2004, from http://www.afterschoolalliance.org/press_archives.cfm

Alexander, D. (2000). *The learning that lies between play and academics in after-school programs.* The National Institute on Out-of-School Time. Retrieved June 15, 2004, from http://www.niost.org/publications/learning_article.pdf

American Academy of Pediatrics. (2001). Children, adolescents, and television. *Pediatrics, 107*(2). Retrieved June 15, 2004, from http://www.aap.org/policy/re0043.html

Baker, D. A. and Witt, P. A. (2000). Multiple stakeholders' views of the goals and content of two after-school programs. *Journal of Parks and Recreation Administration, 18*(1), 68–86.

Bureau of Labor Statistics (1997). *1997 annual average figures from the current population survey.* Washington, DC: U.S. Department of Labor.

Carnegie Council on Adolescent Development. (1992). *A matter of time: Risk and opportunities in the nonschool hours*. New York, NY: Carnegie Corporation of New York.

Child Trends Data Bank. (2002a). *Education and skills/behavior that affects learning/watching television.* Retrieved February 18, 2005, from http://www.childtrendsdatabank.org/indicators/55watchingtv.cfm

Child Trends Data Bank. (2002b). *Overweight children and youth.* Retrieved May 23, 2004, from http://www.childtrendsdatabank.org/indicators/15overweightchildrenyouth.cfm

Clark, R. (1988). *Critical factors in why disadvantaged children succeed or fail in school.* New York, NY: Academy for Educational Development.

Fight Crime: Invest in Kids. (2002, August). *National law enforcement leadership survey*. Retrieved January 6, 2004, from http://www.fightcrime.org/reports/nationalkidspoll2002.pdf

Galambos, N. L. and Maggs, J. L. (1991). Children in self-care: Figures, facts, and fiction. In J. V. Lerner and N. L. Galambos (Eds.), *Employed mothers and their children* (pp. 131–157). New York, NY: Garland.

Geiger, E. and Britsch, B. (2004). *Out-of-school time program evaluation: Tools for action.* Seattle, WA: Northwest Regional Education Laboratory. Retrieved August 1, 2004, from http://www.nwrel.org/ecc/21century/publications/ost_tools.pdf

Grossman, J. B., Fellerath, V., Juovy, L. Z., Kotloff, L. J., Price, M., Raley, R., and Walker, K. E. (2002). *Multiple choices after school: Findings from the Extended Service Schools Initiative*. Philadelphia, PA: Public/Private Ventures.

Halpern, R. (1999). After-school programs for low-income children: Promises and challenges. *The Future of Children, 9*(2), 81–95.

Halpern, R., Deich, S., and Cohen, C. (2000). *Financing after-school programs.* Washington, DC: The Finance Project. Retrieved May 23, 2004, from http://www.financeproject.org/financing_afterschool_programs.htm

Hamilton, L. S. and Klein, S. P. (1998). *Achievement test score gains among participants in the foundations schoolage enrichment program*. Santa Monica, CA: RAND Corp.

Herrera, C. and Arbreton, A. J. A. (2003). *Increasing opportunities for older youth in after-school programs*. Philadelphia, PA: Public/Private Ventures.

Huang, D., Gribbons, B., Kim, K. S., Lee, C., and Baker, E. L. (2000). *A decade of results: The impact of the LA's BEST after-school enrichment initiative on subsequent student achievement and performance*. Los Angeles, CA: University of California at Los Angeles, Graduate School of Education & Information Studies, Center for the Study of Evaluation.

Jessor, R. (1992). Risk behavior in adolescence: A psychosocial framework for understanding and action. In D. E. Rogers and E. Ginzberg (Eds.), *Adolescents at risk: Medical and social perspectives* (pp. 19–34). Boulder, CO: Westview Press.

Kerrebrock, N. and Lewit, E. M. (1999). Children in self-care. *The Future of Children, 9*(2), 151–159.

Larner, M. B., Sippiroli, L., and Behrman, R. E. (1999). When school is out: Analysis and recommendations. *The Future of Children, 9*(2), 4–20.

Little, P., DuPree, S., and Deich, S. (2002). *Documenting progress and demonstrating results: Evaluating local out-of-school time programs.* Cambridge, MA: Harvard Family Research Project. Retrieved from http://www.gse.harvard.edu/hfrp/content/projects/afterschool/resources/issuebrief3.pdf

Long, L. and Long, T. J. (1989). Latchkey adolescents: How administrators can respond to their needs. *NASSP Bulletin, 73*(514), 102–108.

Mastrofski, S. D. and Keeter, S. (1999). *Poll of police chiefs*. Washington, DC: Fight Crime: Invest in Kids. Retrieved May 23, 2004, from http://www.fightcrime.org

McLaughlin, M. W. (2000). *Community counts: How youth organizations matter for youth development*. Washington, DC: Public Education Network.

Miller, B. (2003). *Critical hours: Afterschool programs and education success*. Boston, MA: Nellie Mae Education Foundation. Retrieved from http://www.nmefdn.org/uimages/documents/critical_hours.pdf

National School Board Association. (2003). *School board survey: After-school programs—82% say programs enhance academic skills*. Retrieved January 6, 2004, from http://www.nsba.org/site/doc.asp?TrackID=&SID=1&DID=11852&CID=654&VID=2
Newman, S. A., Fox, J. A., Flynn, E. A., and Christeson, W. (2000). *America's after-school choice: The prime time for juvenile crime, or youth enrichment and achievement.* Washington, DC: Fight Crime, Invest in Kids. Retrieved from http://www.fightcrime.org
Penn, Schoen & Berland Associates. (2001). *Telephone interviews with a national sample of 500 teens, 14 to 17 years of age*. Washington, DC: Author. Retrieved from http://www.ymca.net
Pittman, K., Irby, M., and Ferber, T. (2001). *Unfinished business: Further reflections on a decade of promoting youth development*. Retrieved May 5, 2004, from http://www.forumforyouthinvestment.org
Posner, J. K. and Vandell, D. L. (1994). Low-income children's after school care: Are there beneficial effects of after-school programs*? Child Development, 65*, 440–456.
Posner, J. K. and Vandell, D. L. (1999). After-school activities and the development of low-income urban children: A longitudinal study. *Developmental Psychology*, 25, 868–879.
Quay, L. (1992). Personal and family effects on loneliness. *Journal of Applied Developmental Psychology, 13*(1), 97–110.
Reno, J. and Riley, R. W. (2000). *Working for children and families—Safe and smart: Making the after-school hours work for kids*. Washington, DC: U.S. Department of Education.
Schinke, S. (1999). *Evaluation of Boys and Girls Clubs of America's educational enhancement program*. Unpublished manuscript.
Sickmund, M., Snyder, H. N., and Poe-Yamagata, E. (1997). *Juvenile offenders and victims: 1997 update on violence*. Washington, DC: National Center for Juvenile Justice.
Steinberg, L. (1986). Latchkey children and susceptibility to peer pressure: An ecological analysis. *Developmental Psychology, 22*(4), 433–439.
United States Conference of Mayors. (2003). *After-school programs in cities across the United States.* Retrieved March 23, 2004, from http://www.usmayors.org/uscm/uscm_projects_services/education/afterschoolreport03.pdf
U.S. Census Bureau. (2005). *Survey of income and program participation.* Retrieved April 14, 2005, from http://www.bls.census.gov/sipp
U.S. Department of Education National Center for Education Statistics (1999). *National household education survey.* Washington, DC: Author.
U.S. Department of Education, Office of Educational Research and Improvement, National Center for Education Statistics. (1998). *National education*

longitudinal study of 1988: A profile of the American eighth grader. Washington, DC: U.S. Government Printing Office.

University of California at Irvine. (2001). *Evaluation of California's after school learning and safe neighborhoods partnerships program: 1999–2001.* Retrieved March 23, 2004, from http://www.cdc.ca.gov/ls/ba/as/executivesummary.asp

Vandell, D. L. and Ramanan, J. (1991). Children of the national longitudinal survey of youth: Choices in after-school care and child development. *Developmental Psychology, 27*(4), 637–643.

Vandell, D. L., Posner, J., Shumow, L., and Kang, K. (1995, March). *Concurrent, short-term and long-term effects of self-care.* Poster presented at the biennial meeting for the Society for Research in Child Development, Indianapolis, IN.

Witt, P. A. (2004). Dr. Peter Witt's web-based publications. Retrieved August 1, 2004, from http://www.rpts.tamu.edu/faculty/Witt/pubs.htm

Witt, P. A., Baker, D. A., and Scott, D. (1996). *The protective factors scale.* Unpublished manuscript. Texas A&M University, College, TX.

Witt, P. A. and Crompton, J. L. (1997). The protective factors framework: A key to programming for benefits and evaluating for results. *Journal of Park and Recreation Administration, 15*(3), 1–18.

Chapter 15

Teen Centers: A Place of Their Own

Kristi A. Montandon, Megan Kelly Cronan, and Peter A. Witt

Over the past several decades, a number of teen centers and spaces have been developed in communities across the United States. From small towns to big cities, recreation departments and other providers are working to facilitate opportunities for teens to have a "place of their own."

Ray Oldenburg (1999) likened teen centers to a "third place." Oldenburg developed the third place concept after studying the role of the pub in England as a place where friends can gather outside of work or home life and socialize. The TV show *Cheers* represents this type of place. It is a place where individuals can go unannounced, and yet be guaranteed that they will know people there as well as interact with a wide range of other individuals regardless of age, ethnicity, or socioeconomic background. According to Oldenburg, a third place supplies a location where one can experience a sense of neutrality, good conversation, accessibility, and familiarity. In short, third places can build community.

For youth, a third place would be a location other than home, school, or work—contexts we compared to leisure contexts in Chapter 8. Over the past several decades communities across the country are recognizing the value of this type of setting for teens, by creating third places for teens to "hang out," by developing teen centers ranging from full-service "homes away from home" to places simply offering weekend activities. These centers may operate in stand-alone facilities, or they may consist of dedicated space for teens inside a larger community recreation center. Some teen spaces and places may only belong to teens during specified time periods and then be used by others when teen activities are not being offered.

While facilities will differ from center to center, most will likely have a lounge area with a television, usually with video games capability. The lounge also usually contains board and table games, including Foosball, air hockey, and pool tables. Many centers also have multipurpose rooms or gyms that can be used for sports, dances, or other large group activities, and increasingly centers have computers with Internet access for participants to use. In some cases, centers will have kitchen facilities, snack bars, or vending machines; music practice rooms; a quiet area for homework help; and outdoor areas for recreation and sports participation.

The purpose of this chapter is to discuss a number of issues related to teen centers. We begin with a discussion of the rationale for the development of teen centers and then provide information on some of the issues and problems that centers must deal with to remain relevant and open.

The Rationale for Teen Centers and Programs

In Chapter 4 we discussed the impetus and origins of youth services in the United States during the late 1800s through the early 1900s. The desire to provide safe places for young people to congregate with peers was one of the major rationales for the development of programs and facilities for youth. Youth workers sought to provide safe places to keep young people off the streets and away from negative influences on their lives, such as alcohol and prostitution, as communities provided little for youth to do and few places beyond the streets were available for youth to play.

During this time period, in addition to providing safe environments for youth, program organizers had a broad range of other purposes. For example, some programs provided opportunities for immigrant youth to learn English or a trade, involved youth in what today we would call "character education," taught individuals how to work in a group, and otherwise promoted and inculcated American values.

Interestingly, many of these historical factors continue to operate today. In most communities, safety and the reduction of negative behaviors are still major rationales for the development of teen centers. For example, over the last few decades, the increase in drug use, violence, gang membership, school dropout, and other negative behaviors among youth led concerned citizens to rally around the need for teen centers as safe and secure places for youth to spend their out-of-school time. Recently, a police chief told one of the chapter authors, "Teen centers can be an effective way to pen teens up, and every hour teens spend at a teen center, they are avoiding some alternative negative behavior."

This represents one substantial and common reaction to why youth programs, and teen centers in particular, are important. Indeed, delinquent activity in the communities surrounding a center often decreases during its hours of center operation. However, centers created over the last 10 to 20 years have also sought to promote the wider youth development agenda. Thus, besides keeping kids off the streets and attempting to diminish teen involvement in negative behaviors, centers have recognized Pittman's adages discussed in Chapter 1: Problem free is not fully prepared, and fully prepared is not necessarily fully engaged.

To meet this wider youth development objective, centers are making efforts to promote youth involvement in the design of facilities and programs and to move beyond the provision of activities designed to simply occupy time to also include those that help young people move constructively along pathways to adulthood. Consequently, at many teen centers a wide range of opportunities, supports, activities, and programs are offered to enable teens to develop the knowledge, attitudes, skills, and behaviors they need to grow up fully prepared and fully engaged.

Depending on the center, we might see youth participating in a teen council that suggests relevant activities and helps to develop the rules and procedures used in the center. We might also see a bulletin board (more likely a Web site) with posted jobs available to teens and job application workshops to help teens apply for the jobs. Teen issue discussion groups, visual and performing arts groups, and opportunities to undertake service projects, go on field trips, and participate on sport teams might also be options. In some teen centers, academic support is provided in the form of homework assistance. An excellent example of a diverse set of activity offerings would be the programs offered by teen centers in Fairfax County, Virginia. Located throughout the county are nine teen spaces and centers with clever names such as The Cave, The Basement, The Attic, The Chill Spot, The Mix, The Zone, The Hideaway, The Net, and the Reston Teen Center. All of these venues offer different activities. You can go to the Chill Spot for billiards, darts and board games or to The Attic for arts and crafts, poetry club, cooking corner, and mentoring. The most comprehensive programming is at the Reston Teen Center. Activities there include peer mediation; modeling, theater, book, and dance clubs; movie madness; and many others. Teen councils provide input regarding center operations and activities, and a city-wide teen advisory council provides input regarding teen issues for Fairfax County as a whole.

Program directors for centers oriented toward youth development make an effort to hire staff or use volunteers who can be positive role models for young people. Thus, they hire staff who not only serve a preventative function (i.e., keep kids safe and out of trouble) but also serve as mentors who promote ways that youth can actively and appropriately engage with their environments and provide support and assistance with homework and other life challenges faced by youth. The Exit Teen Center in College Station, Texas, for example, provides tutoring for teens during the school year if they request help with homework or other school activities (see Box, pp. 332–333).

The EXIT Teen Center

The EXIT teen center opened in 1999 and is sponsored by the City of College Station, Texas, and paid for from the city general fund. The center was intended to give teens a place of their own, off the streets and "away from their worries." Kids and parents had also complained that there was nothing for teens to do in the community.

Teens are attracted to The EXIT mainly by word of mouth, but The EXIT has also found other ways to encourage teens to attend. For example, the local schools have agreed to include a reading of current activities at the center during their daily announcements, The EXIT staff visit schools at lunch to pass out pizza to spread the word, local radio stations provide PSAs, and school principals spread the word that the center offers a good program. Barriers to teen attendance at the center include peer pressure and a past problem of the center being perceived as unsafe.

The EXIT focuses mainly on 7th to 9th graders and discourages high school students from attending under the philosophy that older teens have jobs and organized sports opportunities, and the parents of younger teens would be worried by the presence of older teens.

The EXIT used to attract only middle- to upper-class White youth from the surrounding area. However, the ethnic makeup of the center is now more representative of all ethnic groups in the city, as efforts have been to attract children from other groups in the city. For example, The EXIT runs a joint program with Lincoln Center, a traditionally African American youth center located in another part of the city. Each facility honors the memberships of the other facility, and the Lincoln Center provides a bus to The EXIT several days a week. During the summer, attendance at The EXIT may vary from 30 to 60 teens depending on whether Lincoln Center teens are in attendance. During the school year, The EXIT hosts approximately 45 teens during the day. During both the school year and the summer, approximately 100 teens attend night-time activities.

The center is open Monday through Thursday from 3:00 to 7:00 p.m. and Friday from 3:00 p.m. to 11:00 p.m. during the school year, and Monday through Thursday 12:00 to 7:00 p.m. and Friday 12:00 to 11:00 p.m. during the summer. The EXIT also holds special events almost every Saturday night. The center's 4,000-square-feet building was built to be a teen center, but is available for other activities when teens are not using it. Its annual budget is $177,000. The center makes approximately $8,000 from rental fees, a small annual membership fee, and field trips. The majority of the funds are used for staffing, trips, and food.

The EXIT is staffed with one full-time Recreation Supervisor and 12 part-time staff members (almost all college students). Part-time staff start at $6.30 an hour and are selected through an extensive interview process which involves being observed during a Saturday night activity program and participating in live scenarios with the teens. The teens, along with the director and current staff, decide who will be hired.

The EXIT Teen Center *continued*

Volunteers work at the center, but only three per day are allowed to work to make sure that they are actually interacting with the kids and not clumped together talking. Most of the volunteers are from the local university.

The EXIT has a teen council called TAB (Teen Advisory Board), which consists of eight teens. Originally 32 teens were part of the TAB and were instrumental in advocating for building the center and then helped with decisions about the building. After the center opened, the group disbanded because they felt that their work was done. However, TAB was revamped and sponsored a highly successful 7th and 8th grade prom and summer kickoff.

While drugs and alcohol are not problems at the center, the teens are at the age when they start to be curious about drugs and alcohol. They may think using drugs or alcohol might be cool and may want to know if teen center staff uses them. (The official policy is for staff to say that they have not used any substances.) The center staff deal with children whose parents are divorcing, are too busy for their kids, or inflict emotional or verbal abuse on their children. The center staff also deal with typical middle school "drama."

Lack of parental support is a common problem for The EXIT, while lack of community support, lack of space, and recruiting youth are also issues. The community's positive perceptions of the center include that it is a safe and fun alternative for kids and that staffers serve as positive and educational mentors. The community's negative perceptions of the center include the thought that too much "hanging out" may lead to sex and drug use.

The youths' positive perceptions of the center include that trips are "cool," staffers make it "fun," and it's better than hanging out at home. Negative youth perceptions include that there is too much supervision and that the rules are "stupid."

At one time the center was taken over by the "skater" tribe, but now the director feels that the kids who come represent a wider variety of cliques and groups. The EXIT hosts programs such as Teen Talk, which is a teen lecture series where the teens decide the topics they want to discuss. Past programs have included ER doctors and EMTs, search and rescue dogs, college recruiting, future careers, sex, drugs, alcohol, summer jobs, and things they need to do in school to prepare for the future. Experts are invited to come to the center and hold discussions on the topics of interest. Pizza is served at the talks and Academy Sports and Outdoors provides prizes. Approximately 10 sessions, lasting about one hour, are planned annually. If teens attend all the talks they get to go to a water park for free. The EXIT also hosts Saturday night activities for teens including dances, lock-ins, movies/DVDs, and pool. Evaluations are conducted at the center, including teen demographic data and attendance, teen program quality, and teen satisfaction surveys. One concern is that the center does not currently have a gym, which limits activity options. However, the center has adequate outdoor space that can be used for physical activities.

To illustrate the transition of centers from places designed to diminish risk factors to places that promote the full youth development agenda, consider the development of Bomberger Teen Center (Dayton, Ohio). The center was originally created in the early 1990s after several instances of young people being killed and robbed by other youth. These incidents resulted in the community convening a Teen Summit that brought teens and adults together for a day of workshops and brainstorming to develop ideas for creating a safer community environment for everyone. The participants broke out into small group sessions, and one of the groups proposed the need for a teen center. The city commissioners approved the idea and redirected funding to refurbish an old warehouse to make the center a reality. Teens were then involved in the process of making decisions regarding the design of the center and program offerings at the center. The result was a center that offered opportunities for developmental benefits to accrue by providing teens with opportunities to explore their identities, develop leadership skills, feel a sense of belonging, feel psychologically and physically safe, and have choice and voice.

Of course simply gathering teens at a single site and getting them to regularly participate may not achieve positive developmental goals. For example, Mahoney, Stattin, and Magnusson (2001) studied the impact on juvenile crime of Swedish boys' participation at a recreation center. Their study found that frequent participation at the center was related to higher rates of juvenile offences and higher rates of persistent offending. The study authors argued that negative consequences may result when youth who are exhibiting problem behaviors (and perhaps are already engaging in risky behaviors, such as alcohol use) hang out in centers with little structure, little adult supervision, and few youth development opportunities. In these cases, drop-in centers breed problem behaviors because youth who are engaging in risky behavior tend to negatively influence their peers behaviors. Thus, the study highlighted the need for centers to be more than places for teens to hang out and the importance of supplying an appropriate level of structure and guidance to create a positive youth development atmosphere.

Developing and Sustaining Teen Centers

Often, when first conceived by community members and recreation staff, teen centers are popular ideas and receive financial and other support from the community for their development. It is often a challenge, however, for teen center staff to maintain this initial positive momentum. As a result some teen centers close soon after their development. This is an important issue to address and raises a number of questions: Why do some centers succeed and others fail? How do successful centers operate, maintain funding, and attract and retain quality youth workers? How do centers attract and retain teens? Few studies have looked at these issues specifically as they relate to teen centers, although there is some guidance in the youth development literature about the characteristics that separate successful centers from unsuccessful ones.

Among the studies that have been conducted in an effort to answer these questions is one by Baker, Hultsman, and Garst (1998). This team conducted an in-depth evaluation of programs and services offered by the Thunderbirds Teen Center in Phoenix. In addition, in 1999 another such study was conducted by Witt, Towers, and Fox who conducted surveys and interviews with a broad sample of teen center staff from across the United States. Their study provided information about why communities had created teen spaces and places and the characteristics of successful centers.

The authors of this chapter have continued the Witt, Towers, and Fox study by collecting additional information about the status of approximately 20 current teen centers. Surveys were distributed and interviews conducted with teen centers nationwide and in Canada. They asked about the founding, sponsorship, and everyday maintenance of the facilities. They interviewed center staff about teen center finances, types of programs offered, and the degree to which the centers encouraged teen voice. These additional interviews and surveys helped to further tap into the wealth of experiential knowledge that practitioners have about the issues and problems associated with developing and operating teen centers.

In the next section of this chapter, information from both the surveys and interviews conducted cover some of the specific steps centers need to take to be successful. These steps include the need

- to create and to maintain quality and youth friendly facilities (e.g., lack of space, poor design)
- to design a plan to recruit teens to participate
- to attract and train staff to facilitate youth development
- to develop a consistent funding stream
- to foster and maintain community support

Centers can be vibrant and viable to the extent that they can successfully deal with each of these issues, but flounder and perhaps close if they don't successfully respond to each challenge.

Creating and Maintaining Quality Facilities

Lack of a facility or quality space is a problem for a number of teen centers. Space problems may take many forms, making it difficult or impossible to provide separate spaces for teen activities and restricting the ability of teen programmers to provide the activities desired by teens. The lack of appropriate space contributes to youth having a negative perception of the center and feeling that it is not teen-friendly or welcoming. For example, if teens are forced to share space with younger children, or if activities can only be offered during less desirable time slots, their interest in the center may quickly wane and the teen program itself will suffer

The quality of a teen space is another factor in determining a teen program's success. In some cases, funding constraints may result in centers having to use "hand me down" buildings and facilities left over after allocations of space for other purposes. Indeed, some teen centers occupy buildings that are old and in need of repairs or structural work, making it difficult to fully adapt these facilities as quality teen spaces. While updating existing buildings is often desirable, renovations to older buildings may be expensive. As a result, teen center staff have to cope with adjusting teen center programs and services to the design of the available space.

Even when the overall space is useable for teen programs, design features may create safety or supervision issues. Some common design concerns include the following:

- *Appropriate location of bathrooms.* Place bathrooms entrances and exits in plain sight for easy monitoring by staff, primarily for safety reasons. It is advisable to avoid building bathrooms in a closed hallway or at the back of the building.

- *Locations of doors to the outside.* Like bathrooms, locate doors to the outside of the teen center in locations that can be easily monitored by center staff, enabling them to more easily keep track of when teens are exiting or entering the building.

- *Openness and flow of space.* Allow easy visibility of more than one space by a single person and facilitate good lines of sight for monitoring teens and their activities when designing the layout of the teen center.

- *Availability of computer and wall outlets.* Sufficient electrical outlets and the capability to hook up to the Internet are essential to a well-equipped teen center. In older buildings, the wiring and cable or telephone access may not be compatible with what is needed to offer quality computer access.

- *Teen appropriate furnishings and equipment.* Use furnishing and equipment of an appropriate size and design for teens. When space is shared with younger children, chairs and tables, etc. may not be perceived by teens as appropriate for their use. When space is renovated, it is critical to create a teen-friendly environment, and not a space that appears to be a recycled "little kids" center.
- *Adaptability of equipment.* Provide equipment adaptable for use by both younger and older teens. For example, in some gyms the basketball hoops are adjustable for younger players. Teens love to dunk the basketball and lower hoops may enable shorter and/or younger players to achieve success. Other accommodations can be made for persons with disabilities.
- *Graffiti proof paint and surfaces.* Use materials that can either prevent graffiti or make for easy removal (including walls, floors, tables, and other surfaces).
- *Quiet space.* Centers should contain space where teens can just sit and "chill." They need spaces to hang out. Some teen centers have designed coffee bars in the center itself or created teen lounges.
- *Drama and music area.* Teens make good use of a space where they can practice and play their instruments alone or in a band. The space should be sound-proof to avoid conflicts with other activities going on in the center. A stage area will also facilitate drama productions and band performances.
- *Sound.* Include sound panels, essential for noise control, throughout the center, especially in gyms and other areas designated for large group activities.

Attracting and Retaining Teens

As young people move through their teenage years, they often gain more discretion over how they use their time. In other words, while, parental perceptions of programs may make a difference in whether teens are encouraged, discouraged, or forbidden from attending programs, teens join parents as major stakeholders in the programs they attend and thus teen's opinions and ideas have to be given more credence if programs are going to attract and retain teens once they have started attending.

Teens gravitate toward high-quality programs that they perceive as meeting their needs. While most existing teen centers do not have problems attracting teens to their sites, examining the ways teens find out about teen centers and how this affects their perceptions of the centers is useful to know. Teen center programmers should use several means to inform teens about programs, including formal mechanisms (e.g., mailings, flyers, announcements in schools) or informal methods (e.g., word-of-mouth). These methods are described in the next few sections.

Formal Methods of Getting the Word Out

Formal methods of attracting teens include flyers and radio ads. Although potentially effective in some situations, flyers typically do not attract a lot of attention because they aren't usually posted in places where teens will pay attention to them or because so many flyers compete for attention, teens may not read all of them. Flyers tend to work best for informing teens already in a program about upcoming special events rather than as a means for attracting new participants.

In addition, formal advertising is often not worded or designed in a teen-friendly manner. Efforts need to be made to avoid advertising that has "adult sounding" messages. Thus, teens should be involved in developing flyers, radio ads, or school announcements. For example, The Admiral Boorda Youth and Teen Center in Washington State encourages teens to help design flyers for upcoming dances. Teens are organized into marketing teams and provided with the supplies necessary for designing effective flyers and signs. In one instance, the teens chose to use graffiti-style writing and symbols from hip hop culture in their advertising for a dance and took the initiative to distribute the flyers themselves. Attendance for this particular dance was almost three times greater than any previous dance event the center had hosted.

Information about center events should also be targeted to parents, who need to be assured that they are sending their teens to a safe and supervised place with positive programs. Thus, it is important to encourage local newspapers to write positive stories about the center and its activities, and to work with school district personnel to include information about the center in the school's communications with parents. Getting good publicity is essential and doing so means that the teen center directors and staff must work closely with newspaper reporters and staff from other media outlets to promote the positive aspects of center activities. A systematic approach to getting media attention (e.g., weekly contact at a specific time) is very effective, as is inviting reporters to events or creating opportunities for media representatives to talk directly with the youth organizers or participants. In most cases, the more positive the media exposure, the more parents will appreciate the teen center's presence in the community.

Another formal method of involving parents is to encourage them to participate in a group or advisory committee for the center. These groups provide input regarding center funding, staffing, and activities. For example, some centers choose to have a "parent's night" and invite parents to visit the center, provide feedback, and meet center leaders. These types of events are helpful for increasing parents' comfort levels with the center and its activities. Moreover, if these parents are opinion leaders in the community, their involvement and endorsements may serve to protect the center when problems or negative perceptions arise.

Another example of involving parents comes from Dayton, Ohio, where a group of adults and business leaders has formed a teen advisory board. The board's three major functions are (a) soliciting the opinions and concerns of the teens from the Dayton area, (b) raising funds for the center, and (c) providing a political voice for the teen population.

Informal Methods of Getting the Word Out

The most powerful way to attract and to retain teens is through word-of-mouth. Teens who are having a good experience will tell and bring their friends and otherwise spread a positive message about what is happening at the center. However, if teens are not having a good experience, what they tell others may negatively influence both recruitment of new participants and retention of current participants. Even the transmission of a single negative story among friends can influence their future participation.

All centers develop an image or reputation, whether it is deserved or not. For example, the word on the street may become that it isn't cool to attend the center, that most of the participants belong to one certain group (like "the skaters" or "the preps"), or that the "wrong kinds of kids" attend the center. The groups of teens perceived as attending the center may be out-of-favor with other groups of teens in the community and therefore other teens may avoid attendance due to fears of being associated or mixing with "undesirable" or "out-of-favor" teens. Parents, as well as teens, buy into these perceptions and as a result may discourage their children's attendance at the center.

In addition, teens can develop negative perceptions of a teen center when they feel too controlled and/or feel they have no say in what goes on at "their" center. Teens might also feel that they have "aged out" of the need for the center, because among other things

- Changes in program content and formats are not adjusted to their developmental needs at a particular age.

- They begin work and have less time for outside activities.
- They establish romantic relationships and begin forms of dating not supported by a group context like the teen center.

In all of these cases, teens may tell others that they no longer enjoy going to the center, even when they enjoyed participating at the center when they were younger. This mixed-message may negatively influence younger teens from becoming interested in trying the center out, thus squelching the interests and participation of the next generation of teens.

Consequently some form of damage control is warranted—both with teens and parents—should negative perceptions of a teen center arise. With teens, it sometimes makes sense to work on recruiting individuals with a high profile in the community to attend programs at the center. For example, to attract teens to programs at The Second Mile in Pennsylvania, Penn State student athletes are recruited to drum up business. Many youth love being able to interact or identify with athletes, making this an effective promotional strategy. Teens' positive experiences interacting with these individuals may help influence more youth to attend and send a general signal to other teens that the center is a cool place to be.

Finally, teen center staff can recruit teens by establishing relationships with them through participation in school functions or meeting up with teens where they congregate in the community. Some communities (e.g., Austin, Texas) have established Roving Leader programs through which recreation and park department staff work the streets to make contact with teens who aren't currently attracted to their center and programs (Bocarro & Witt, 2002). Interacting with teens in their own territory or social spaces may be important to develop respect and trust, which the leaders can then utilize as a platform for inviting teens to participate in more formal facilities and programs (King, 2000).

Developing Specific Means for Attracting and Retaining Teens

Offering quality programs and ensuring teen voice (see Chapter 12) in all aspects of a center's design and operation are critical to attracting and retaining teens. In addition, several other strategies can be pursued to attract and retain teens, including the following:

- Design a reward system to attract first-time participants and those motivated by extrinsic rewards. For instance, teens can earn credits toward participation in special event programs by recruiting more teen center members or taking on specific roles at the center. Baker, Hultsman and Garst (1998) even suggested offering a small gift as an incentive for first time participants. This approach will provide a means for getting teens to attend and give them a chance to experience firsthand the activities being offered at the center.

- Enforce teen-friendly rules and procedures. Teens should understand that other teens have had a significant role in their design and enforcement (e.g., teen committee to review infractions and consequences). Teens will also be more encouraged to attend a center if they perceive that rules are enforced fairly and uniformly.
- Provide transportation from school to the center and/or from the center to teens' homes, especially at night when it is dark. Parents of younger teens are often concerned about their teens walking home, especially if it is dark or they have to pass through unsafe neighborhoods. One way to ease transportation problems is to locate centers near secondary schools to avoid needing transportation to get teens to the center after school.
- Take into account differing needs of younger versus older teens, males versus females, and persons from different cultural or ethnic backgrounds. Teens will be more attracted to the center if they feel the programs have been designed with their needs in mind and the center is staffed by people who understand their needs.

Of course, attracting teens to attend a center is only half the battle. Baker, Hultsman and Garst (1998) noted that many participants are attracted to centers but then discontinue participation after just a few visits. Thus, strategies also need to be developed to retain teens once they have shown some interest in the activities at the center. Luckily, utilization of all of the strategies we just mentioned for attracting teens can also be effective ways to retain them. In addition, there are several other strategies that can be used to keep teens returning to the center, including the following:

- Initiate aggressive efforts to improve "first contact" with new teens at the center (e.g., provide a guided tour and orientation, increase staff awareness of the need to make new teens feel welcome, assign new participants a teen peer mentor who can help provide an entree for them into center activities).
- Make sure teens feel ownership in what goes on at the center. For example, provide opportunities for youth input about what

goes on at the center, and in particular provide a chance to voice concerns that can translate into needed changes.

- Participants and staff can contact center "drop outs" to better understand their reasons for leaving and if possible undertake steps to deal with the issues that may have caused a teen to quit.

Providing Access at Critical Times for Teens

Many teen centers are open after school five days a week, into the early evening, and even on weekends. However, some centers close as early as 6:00 p.m. on weekdays and are closed on weekends, while others might be only open at night during the school week. Some of these differences in scheduling are due to budget limitations, but often they occur because the varying needs and desires of teens are overlooked. Thus, staff should listen carefully when teens express a desire to have centers open more days and longer hours. Staff should remember that it is just as easy for a teen to be unsupervised, unstructured, and unproductive at night or on the weekends as it is for them to need a place to go after school.

In addition, summer programs may prove to be just as popular and worthwhile as those offered during the school year. While many teens are considered old enough to be home alone during the summer, many do not know how to constructively use their time and therefore spend the summer just hanging out, watching television, and perhaps getting into trouble. Furthermore, younger teens are not eligible for summer employment and are in need of quality teen experiences.

Summer is also a good time to run in-depth activities sponsored by a teen center (e.g., summer camps, field trips, opportunities that promote volunteering and service learning). For example, some of the teen centers run by the Cincinnati Recreation Commission provide an Adventure Camp each summer designed to meet teens' desire to explore their community. Every day during the camp teens are driven in a van to a different place around the city (e.g., stores, museums, amusement parks). This program strives to keep teens active and involved, and provides teens with access to places and situations to which they may not otherwise have been exposed. Thus, not all teen center sponsored programs have to take place at the teen center.

Offering a Variety of Activities to Meet the Interest of Diverse Teens

In developing supports, opportunities, activities, and programs at teen centers it is important to remember that not every teen wants to skateboard or play basketball; some would prefer to receive homework assistance, participate in visual or performing arts programs, participate in other sports, or just hang out talking to friends, watching TV, or playing video games. If given the opportunity, most teens will participate in several different activities and desire various levels of adult and organizational structure. Thus, working with teens to identify and provide a variety of activities helps to attract teens from a broad cross-section of the community.

Teen centers also need to provide programs and activities that reflect the differing interests of girls versus boys (see Chapters 18 and 19), youth from different cultural and ability groups, as well as youth with different sexual orientations (see Chapters 16, 17, 20, and 21). For example, single-gender programs are important because they provide separate arenas for girls and boys to discuss personal or sensitive subjects in a gender-safe environment. A teen center in Austin, Texas, offers a weekend retreat for young adolescent girls. Girls are able to play sports without having to "show-off" for the guys, go makeup free without worrying about what others might say, and discuss dating and other issues of interest.

Teens feel more comfortable when they can demonstrate competence, and offering activities that allow youth with differing levels of ability to feel competent is important. For example, in another community, several levels of sports leagues are provided. Individuals who do not have the skills to participate in top-level sports teams can join teams that participate in leagues against young people with similar levels of ability.

Centers also need to provide more than just recreational activities for teens. For example, other supports and opportunities that deal with concerns about health, pregnancy, rape, drug prevention, educational improvement, and vocational aspirations are important city center components. Seattle (WA), for instance, developed a Teen Life Center, which provides office space for organizations that offer some of the aforementioned services for teens. This approach enables teens to have a "one-stop shopping" location to obtain needed services and allows providers to deal with teens in a more holistic manner.

Finally, centers need to continue to upgrade their activities and facilities to keep up with what is currently popular among teens (e.g., climbing walls; computers with Internet access; video games; weight room facilities; a skate park that accommodates boarders, bladers, and BMXers; music rooms for jam session of local bands; high adventure programming, including outdoor recreation).

Teen Voice

A common theme in implementing each of the approaches to attracting and retaining teens is teen voice, which was discussed in some detail in Chapter 13. Recall that voice may be facilitated through involving youth in teen councils, teen advisory boards, or surveying teens about what they want to have offered at the center and securing their suggestions for how to improve existing programs. Enabling teens to be at the forefront of program planning and development creates a teen-friendly atmosphere, one in which teens feel welcome and in which they feel they have a reasonable amount of ownership and control. Teen involvement in designing and staffing teen centers is crucial to draw teens into a program and keep them involved over time.

Once youth are involved and indicate their desires, adults must be ready to assist them in carrying out these desires. For example, in one community, teens expressed an interest in having a skate park next to the teen center. It would have been easy for the center supervisor to simply assign a staff member to research skate parks, look at other communities with skate parks, build the park, and then develop a set of rules and procedures necessary to run the park. Instead, teens were involved in the research process and, with adult supervisors, developed and presented proposals to City Council for the building and funding of the park. Teens then helped design the park once funding was approved, and even participated in the skate park construction. As a result, the teens felt personally invested in the park, and when it opened, they undertook much of the supervision of the park and provided self-regulation efforts to protect the park from vandals and unauthorized uses.

In another case, The City Limits teen center in Silverdale (WA), undertook special efforts to incorporate teen voice into everyday center activities. When the recreation director received some unexpected funding, all department managers met to discuss how the money should be distributed. The teen center manager knew that the teens wanted new sports equipment and wanted to undertake renovations in certain areas of the center. She also knew that it would help create a sense of ownership and a powerful learning experience if teens spearheaded efforts to garner and secure the funding. As a result, the teens developed an Oprah Winfrey type show where participants spotlighted the center's shortcomings and interviews were conducted with center participants. In addition, the teens filmed dilapidated areas of the building and some of the run-down equipment. This whole tape was then presented to a department-wide funding allocation meeting.

Involving teens in the need-identification process at this center proved to be successful and the department allocated money for building and interior renovations and new equipment. However, teen voice and involvement in this particular center did not stop with this success. Ultimately the teens became involved in planning for the renovation. They met with engineers and interior designers, and even studied equipment catalogs. They also helped with the paint and carpet choices, gave input into needed design changes and even renamed the building. The teen's involvement led to an overall increase in awareness about the costs of supplies and the processes needed to renovate and improve the facility. The building renovations were completed in 1993, and with the full help of the teens it has remained untouched by vandalism and graffiti.

Although teen voice is a necessity, some staff may be initially hesitant to fully involve teens. Developing and implementing teen voice can be seen as time-consuming. In addition, staff may not understand the importance of self-determination and teen voice in promoting youth development. However, involving teens as essential players in the determination of their own future will help centers to attract and retain participants and to achieve their youth development objectives.

Finding, Training, and Retaining Quality Staff

Recruiting, training, and retaining good staff are critical to the success of a teen center. Good staff is the most important ingredient to make teen centers attractive places for teens to attend. However, to be successful, staff must *want* to work with teens, be *good* at working with teens, and be *willing* to work with the same teens over an extended period of time. In some cases, hiring staff who live in the local community or who might have attended the center when they were younger is wise since these people are more likely to identify with the problems and issues participants face on a daily basis.

However, no matter how carefully one goes about the staff selection process, not all staff hired will be ideal for the job. For example, when a new center opened in one community, the first director was an employee already working in the park and recreation department in an administrative capacity and had experienced no direct involvement with young people. As it turned out, this person did not have the skills to work with teens, and after several rocky years running the center he admitted that he did not even really like children! Luckily, the department responded by reassigning the individual to a position where interaction with teens was not necessary.

While this example is probably (and hopefully!) the extreme, it is not surprising to find that some teen center staffers work just because the hours are convenient or because it was easy to get hired. Thus, it is important to continually monitor and assess employees to make sure that they are a continuing fit for the teen center environment. Furthermore, center directors should provide in-service coaching and training on a regular basis. Luckily, most staff members who work at teen centers understand the importance of the work they are doing, have the ability to work with teens, and are willing to continue efforts to upgrade their skills.

In addition to recruiting and retaining quality staff, recruiting and retaining volunteers provides needed staff to fulfill day-to-day staff duties and provides additional role models for teens. However, a number of center directors report problems recruiting and retaining volunteers. In these cases, centers should consider recruiting volunteers from existing community service organizations. Critical to the successful involvement of volunteers is developing procedures that treat volunteers as if they were staff, with firm expectations for meeting their responsibilities, and the implementation of a plan to recruit, train, reward, and "fire" volunteers if they are not meeting performance expectations. Volunteers should be required to go through the same type of background checks required of paid staff. In addition, volunteers need to be respected as just as much as paid staff are. Volunteers should not be used for the grunge work that no one else wants to do. Finally, volunteers need to be willing to make long-term commitments so that teens can build relationships with them.

Staff Training and Pay: Keys to Longevity

In addition to recruiting qualified staff, three other issues are important to the entire staffing experience: training, pay, and longevity. Simply identifying and hiring individuals who have an interest in and some skill and experience working with teens is insufficient for retaining staff and assuring successful programming. Staff training is an ongoing need and appropriate pay must be provided to assure little turnover of staff.

The staff training process itself should, at a minimum, include information about center procedures, policies, and rules. Equally important is providing information about positive youth development, ways to engage and work with teens, how to promote youth voice, and how to consistently and fairly handle discipline. Training should also instruct employees (and volunteers) about how to work with teens without putting themselves into negative situations, such as those involving inappropriate physical contact or questionable joking. For example, in Fairfax County (VA), they have compiled a 66-page training manual for Teen Services. The manual is divided into five sections. The first section includes an organizational chart of teen services and explanations of the current teen services program design. In section two the procedures for planning, implementing, and evaluating teen services are presented. The third section covers working with the teens and the importance of communication, while the next section covers the need for and processes to be used for injury reports and other instances where documentation is necessary. The final section deals with job performance expectations for staff and volunteers. In this section, information is presented about the need for staff to act responsibly and ethically at all times and to have an understanding that they will be dealing with teens from diverse cultural backgrounds and teens with varying needs and interests.

Staff need considerable time to absorb new information and to gain appropriate skills. All staffers need to recognize that teens are able to discern which staff members successfully work with teens and will tend to gravitate toward these staff members. Teens will encourage friends to come to programs so that they, too, may interact with these staffers. On the other hand, staff who have not developed the needed knowledge and skills may have less than optimal dealings with teens and may even cause teens to leave the program.

Pay level is another important issue to address when staffing a teen center. It is distressing that society often pays the people who work with our most important assets—our children and future leaders—at such a low level that good youth workers often can not afford to keep working with youth. While many youth workers are making a living wage, in many cases, especially with part-time staff, the pay level is not sufficient to attract qualified, long-term staff. Whether full- or part-time, too often good youth workers must move up to a supervisory position to achieve a living wage.

Low pay can lead to job dissatisfaction, which can impact a program's participants, and may ultimately lead staff to leave the profession. Low pay may indeed be one of the main causes of turnover. Many teen staff can no longer afford to keep their jobs once they begin to have families. This presents a problem for the worker, and also because, as we noted in Chapter 1, it is critical for young people to develop sustained relationships with caring adults over a considerable period of time. Therefore, when youth workers take jobs only to support themselves until something better comes along, or are forced to leave because of low pay, not enough working hours, or lack of benefits, their leaving creates a revolving door that fails to attract and retain teens to the program. High turnover of youth workers can reinforce teens' perceptions that adults do not care about young people. In other words, it is often difficult for young people to trust a youth worker if they think that youth workers are transient in their lives. Ultimately, as we have discussed previously, lack of trust is detrimental to youth because the consistency and reliability of adult mentors is something that all youth need.

Developing and Maintaining Community Support

Teen center staff rely on community support to develop and to sustain them over time. Community support may include funding for a building or renovation of existing space as well as the provision of adequate budgets for staffing, equipment, supplies, field trips, and so on. Teen center support is usually contingent on an agreement between funders, opinion leaders in the community, parents, and teens that the center is a necessary investment and serves its intended purposes.

Support is also contingent on community members' perceptions of who the center serves and how well a center is run. Community support is complex because different stakeholders have different criteria for what constitutes center success. For example, government officials may be primarily interested in the extent to which center programs decrease negative behaviors of teens in the community. School administrators are also interested in this outcome, but may also judge a center's success by the degree to which teen participation positively influences teens' school performance. Parents, on the other hand, may just want a safe place for their children to hang out and participate in programs with the "right" group of children. Finally, teens judge success by the quality of the programs, the amount of voice they are afforded in the day-to-day operations of the center, the degree to which they are safe at the center, and the quality of the interactions they have with center staff. Varying stakeholder perspectives require center staff to carefully design communication strategies for informing the various groups about the center, its purpose and programs, and the impact that the center's programs are having on the community.

Differing perceptions of success lead to transient support for funding from the various stakeholder groups (e.g., parents, nonprofit agencies, city officials). For example,

- A negative incident at a center may raise deep concerns among civic leaders about the value of a center.
- School personnel may think that teens are spending too much time just hanging out at the center and too little time being involved in activities that can reinforce or increase academic performance.
- Parents may judge that undesirable children (e.g., those with problem behaviors) are attending the center and therefore either want their behavior controlled or want them banned from the center.

For these reasons, working with all stakeholder groups is critical to the long-term support and success of a center. Community leaders, school officials, and parents need to have avenues for learning what is going on at the center and have input into center operations. And, as already discussed, teens need to have voice in all aspects of the daily life of the center (e.g., teen councils).

For the other stakeholders, involvement as part of a community advisory committee is crucial. An advisory committee acts as a conduit through which community concerns or issues can be channeled and helps to buffer negative perceptions. The advisory committee can also be an advocate for funding. If the committee is made up of government officials, parents, school officials, and representatives from other youth serving organizations in the community, it can play a significant role in both protecting the center from undue criticism and providing a forum through which concerns and issues can be channeled.

Center staffers can also undertake other actions to help manage the community's impressions of the center and increase center support. For example, art displays or musical performances by center participants could be undertaken with community leaders and parents invited. These types of events enable outsiders to see first hand the positive things that are happening at the center. In addition, newsletters, short performances at community meetings, youth council presentations to stakeholder groups, and encouraging local newspapers to write positive stories about a center are also useful for building support.

For example, in Fort Collins (CO), the Youth Activity Center (YAC) had initial problems with community perceptions of its programs and who the center was serving. Some teens involved in a juvenile rehabilitation center were using the YAC and this caused some parents to wonder if it was safe for their teens to be using the center. As a result, YAC staff work hard to market the positive programs and make sure that the newspaper provides stories about major events. The center also undertakes several efforts to attract participants. For example, they developed "Club 56" for fifth and sixth graders to get them using the center one Saturday a month. The students are brought to the center by their parents and both students and parents spend the day doing activities. This helps to build a relationship between the parents and the staff.

Funding and Support Sources

Many centers are largely funded through dedicated city or county general funds. However, other centers depend on receiving some combination of general funds, grant funds, and/or earnings from annual fundraising efforts, such as golf tournaments. Fees (e.g., small yearly membership fees or daily use fees for particular activities or programs) are often charged, although many center directors are reluctant to charge fees, especially if it will discourage attendance from various segments of the teen population. If collected, user fees are usually used to offset the cost of field trips, special events, and daily upkeep of the facilities.

Almost all center directors report they do not have enough funding to fully support desired programs or the development or renovation of needed facilities. In addition, sustaining existing funding, especially from grants, can be a problem. There are, however, possible avenues of funding—grants available to teen centers include grants from the Juvenile Justice Department, 21st Century Community Learning Center Grants, or Community Development Block Grants. Centers affiliated with the Boys & Girls Clubs of America have also been able to develop corporate support through companies such as Nike, Taco Bell, and Circuit City.

In-kind contributions (e.g., equipment, supplies, space, utilities) to centers are also useful. For example, volunteers can provide "no-cost" staffing for activities and programs, with local businesses and service organizations serving as good sources of volunteers. Interestingly, some businesses are now giving employees paid release time to work as tutors, coaches, and activity leaders with various youth serving organizations. In other cases, businesses and service organizations may be a good source of program specific funding for supplies or equipment and may even support building or renovation costs, especially if the business name can appear above the door.

Center directors whose programs are sponsored through municipal funds often have a problem securing foundation or corporate funding because there is a perception that these centers have a ready source of additional funding from the municipalities' tax base. Thus, most foundation and corporate funds go to nongovernmental, nonprofit program providers. These providers usually have strong support groups that enable them to apply for and to receive funding.

Unfortunately, where centers receive municipal funding, funding from year to year is volatile if the tax base goes down or the community needs funding for what are deemed more basic services. Thus, supporters of teen centers need to maintain ongoing efforts to convince government leaders that teen centers are indeed part of a community's basic services. Developing a sound case that the program is serving its purposes is therefore vital. To do this, providing outcome evaluation data becomes critical.

Indicators of Effectiveness

Evaluation is critical if stakeholders are to have the information necessary to make reasoned judgment about a center's programs and services. Evaluation should include several different components, including the following:

- *attendance and demographics*, including information about frequency of participation, the types of activities that draw the most interest, and demographic breakdowns of participants (e.g., age, gender, ethnicity, school attended)
- *cost per participant*, including the cost per participant hour or per participant per year
- *program quality*, including participants' and parents' ratings of the quality of facilities, leaders, program offerings, center management, and availability of information about the center
- *program satisfaction*, including information about whether participants will sign up again for the program, tell their friends to join the program, and how much participants like the program
- *program outcomes*, including information about positive changes in values, attitudes, knowledge, skills, and behaviors that can be attributed to center participation

Most teen centers do collect some form of attendance data and undertake program quality and satisfaction surveys. However, centers often do not do enough to answer stakeholders' questions about the impact centers are having on negative and positive behaviors of teens (e.g., the value added of teen centers' programs and services to youth development; see Chapter 9 to review how to do this). Center staff can usually supply significant anecdotal evidence of their impact, but do not undertake organized studies of outcomes associated with teen involvements in the center. As a result, they may not be able to fully satisfy stakeholder demands for impact data. At the same time, many centers are not collecting information that could lead to program improvement (e.g., year-to-year changes in attendance, program satisfaction, program impacts). These types of data are also essential when center directors seek to justify funding requests to government, foundation, or corporate organizations.

Part of the reason studies are not undertaken is that they can be costly and time-consuming to design and carry out. In addition, program personnel may not have the expertise to undertake such studies. Unfortunately, in an age of accountability, center staff need to find ways to improve their ability to document outcomes. Working with college and university professors and college students who are interested in evaluation can be a good way to help center staff conduct viable evaluations. Often students need to complete honors, masters, or doctoral theses and they may be interested in working with teen center staff on evaluations as part of these projects.

Conclusions

The basic reasons for the development of teen centers have not changed much over time. The good news is that there is still considerable interest in developing new teen centers or upgrading existing facilities. For example, in June 2004, Gaithersburg (MD), approved a $2.4 million budget for construction of a new youth center. The facility will be 7,500 square feet with game, arts and crafts, and computer rooms. The center will feature a 30-foot–high indoor rock climbing wall that will be located in a tower/lobby area in front of the building. The development and construction of the new center was deemed necessary for several reasons. For example, the existing center was too small to serve the number of participants and lacked some of the basic facilities needed to offer the desired range of activities (e.g., gym space for basketball and other activities). Additionally, the existing center was located away from the area of town where most teens live. Thus, the new center will be located between the two existing middle schools, making it more accessible for a wider number of teens.

There are a number of key ingredients, (e.g., staffing, recruitment, programming) to developing and maintaining a successful teen center. Communities have had varying degrees of success with teen centers, but in most cases with careful attention to the issues discussed in this chapter, teen centers can be viable over the long term. Center staff who fail to pay attention to basic issues of youth development, fail to develop and sustain stakeholder support, and fail to develop successful teen recruitment and retention strategies may struggle and even close. In addition, particularly for older teens, if centers are just another venue for adult surveillance and control of teen activities, teens will probably resist attending. Thus, developing youth voice, ownership, and reasonable control will be critical to whether teens attend or continue to attend a center. If these elements are not present, teens may seek their own self-controlled places to interact with friends and otherwise hangout.

References

Baker, D., Hultsman, J., and Garst, B. (1998). *Thunderbirds Teen Center program evaluation*. Retrieved July 10, 2004, from http://www.prr.msu.edu/baker/thunderbirdreport.pdf

Bocarro, J. and Witt, P.A. (2002). Reaching out/reaching in: The long-term challenges and issues of outreach programs. *Journal of Park and Recreation Administration*, *20*(3), 65–80.

King, K. (2000). From the precipice: Recreation experiences of high-risk adolescent girls. *Journal of Park and Recreation Administration*, *18*(3), 19–34

Mahoney, J. L., Stattin, H., and Magnusson, D. (2001). Youth recreation centre participation and criminal offending: A 20-year longitudinal study of Swedish boys. *International Journal of Behavior Development*, *25*(5), 509–520.

Oldenburg, R. (1999). *The great good place*. New York, NY: Marlowe Company.

Witt, P. A., Towers, E., and Fox, J. (1999). *Teen centers: A place of their own.* Retrieved July 10, 2004, from http://www.rpts.tamu.edu/faculty/Witt/centers.pdf

References

Section IV

Diversity: Implications for Youth Development

So far in this book we have discussed youth in general ways, suggesting that developmental processes and programmatic issues apply to all youth. In general, this is true. But we know that great diversity exists across people, across groups, and within groups. This makes it challenging to understand, predict, and plan for human behavior. In addition, diversity sometimes makes it challenging to design the SOPS that will meet everyone's needs. Often, members of the dominant group's needs are addressed, while those of marginalized groups are ignored. There may be an economic reason for this (e.g., not enough money to provide services to all so the majority is served) or an attitudinal reason (e.g., the belief that people in nondominant groups do not want these services). However, none of these reasons is acceptable. The chapters in this section provide a number of perspectives to help you to understand differences, needs, and desires of diverse groups. You may be challenged or even uncomfortable with what you read. Actually that is good, and we encourage you to express your opinions in class and to listen carefully to the discussion to help you better understand how you can provide a recreation context for development of diverse groups of young people.

Before you delve into the chapters, let us make some observations and discuss some of the challenges to meeting needs of diverse youth. Youth workers in nonclinical settings need to group people to plan and program, as it is impossible to individually tailor each and every program to individual needs. But as soon as we start grouping, we tend to ignore differences, and making assumptions at a group level becomes a habit. We act as if all young people have the same needs and desires. When we talk about characteristics of a group, we think everyone in that group is the same. Of course that is not true. On the other hand, when we start recognizing differences, we tend to make value judgments about those differences. Differences become good, bad, and neutral. At times, differences become so pronounced or we perceive so many of them that there is a tendency to exaggerate what exists.

The purpose of this set of chapters is to explore differences rather than to explore similarities. This is not because the types of youth discussed in these chapters are different from anyone else, but it is to help us understand how to better serve unique groups and to celebrate those differences. Chapter 16 provides a foundation for understanding how youth culture, race, and ethnicity are important to understand when developing SOPS. How various cultures view developmental issues is discussed, such as identity development, interdependence, religion and spirituality, family, and communication styles. The chapter ends with the presentation of a cultural model for recreation programming.

In Chapter 17 the unique experiences of immigrant youth are discussed. We provide some insights into the processes of acculturation and assimilation, and discuss the role of recreation and leisure in these processes. How gender influences and is influenced by leisure and recreation is a topic that has received increased attention in the past two decades. Until recently, little attention has been paid specifically to boys and men. Thus, Chapter 18 deals directly with unique aspects of girls' leisure, and Chapter 19 presents the unique developmental and recreation needs of boys. In all of these chapters, guidance and suggestions for youth workers are provided.

Chapters 20 and 21 explore the leisure and developmental needs of two other unique groups of youth: lesbian, gay, and transgendered youth; and youth with disabilities. In both chapters, we describe historical and conceptual insights into youth who can be classified in these categories. We also provide specific guidance and or principles to help us to more effectively work with and serve these youth.

As you read through these chapters, keep in mind that we single out differences because we value them. We encourage students and recreation professionals to understand how to better serve unique needs without reducing differences to stereotypes.

Chapter 16

The Role of Culture in Recreation Programming for Youth

Corliss Wilson Outley

A walk through an old growth forest reveals a multitude of plants and trees. Each of these floras will vary in form, blossoms, leaves, and size, yet all share the same basic needs of good soil, adequate water, and sunlight. However, the type of soil, amount of water, and degree of sunlight required for continued growth varies plant by plant. In addition, the same species may grow differently in different contexts—hemlock trees grow in open fields or in dense forests, in rich soil and poor soil, and in New York as well as in Maryland.

Like flora, youth are diverse and possess both common and unique needs. Moreover, young people grow up in both diverse and similar cultural contexts, interacting with their environment in ways that may enhance or diminish their development. Thus, in this chapter we discuss the importance of culture as an aspect of youth diversity and the way that culture impacts youth development.

Following our discussion of the role of culture in youth development, we want to use this information to discuss the role of recreation in the lives of youth of color. As service providers, recreation professionals must be sensitive to similarities *and* differences between and across cultural groups—one size program does not fit all. Similar to the forest, youth within the community all share basic needs, but cultural differences may mean that they will differ in the types of programs that best support meeting those needs. Thus, program providers need to be sensitive, knowledgable, and understanding of the varying cultural practices that enhance the positive development of diverse groups of youth. In addition, programs must be consciously tailored, focusing on the concerns, priorities, needs, and resources of each cultural group.

Anthropologists, sociologists, and other scientists interested in human life and behavior have many ways of defining culture. **Table 16.1** (p. 358) displays some examples of these definitions. From these definitions it becomes clear that culture is not a rigid set of behaviors, but rather a framework through which people's behaviors and individual characteristics are filtered. Additionally, culture is not reborn with each generation but instead consists of shared knowledge passed from one generation to the next.

Table 16.1: Selected Definitions of Culture

An integrated pattern of human beliefs, values, behaviors, and institutions shared by a distinct group, the inhabitants of a region, or the citizens of a nation.

from *Living With the Future in Mind*
http://www.state.nj.us/dep/dsr/sustainable-state/glossary.htm

Shared knowledge, behavior, ideas, and customs of a group or groups of people.

from *MuseumLink Illinois*
http://www.museum.state.il.us/muslink/behind/htmls/gloss.html

The attitudes and behavior that are characteristic of a particular social group or organization (e.g., "the developing drug culture" or "the reason that the agency is doomed to inaction has something to do with the FBI culture").

from *WordNet*
http://www.cogsci.princeton.edu/cgi-bin/webwn

The accumulated habits, attitudes, and beliefs of a group of people that define for them their general behavior and way of life; the total set of learned activities of a people.

from *USINFO*
http://usinfo.state.gov/products/pubs/geography/glossary.htm

The beliefs, traditions, habits, and values controlling the behavior of the majority of the people in a social-ethnic group. These include the people's way of dealing with their problems of survival and existence as a continuing group.

from *International Technology Education Association*
http://www.iteawww.org/ACT/ACT_Pages/ACT_Glossary.html

The complete way of life of a people: the shared attitudes, values, goals, and practices that characterize a group; their customs, art, literature, religion, philosophy, etc.; the pattern of learned and shared behavior among the members of a group.

from *Dig: The Archaeology Magazine for Kids*
http://www.digonsite.com/glossary

People from different ethnic groups, racial groups, and nations are thought to possess a unique culture. Likewise, people living in rural or urban areas also are thought of as possessing a unique culture. Cultural groups may be found among students, academics, or others who share similar and uniquely defining characteristics. This chapter will focus on culture and leisure as it is manifested within various racial and ethnic groups, and in particular among youth of color.

Our discussion of race and ethnicity is complicated by two important considerations:

- First, *members of a racial or ethnic group do not necessarily behave in the same way*. Socioeconomic status, gender, age, education, employment, discrimination, family, and community can all influence behavior within a particular cultural group.
- Second, *individuals may differ in the degree to which they choose to adhere to a distinct set of cultural patterns*. Some people have a high degree of cultural identification and adopt, embrace, manifest, and transmit most of the common and defining characteristics of a particular group. Other people have a low degree of cultural identification and adopt, embrace, manifest, and transmit few of those defining characteristics. Still others have no cultural identity at all.

These considerations make it very challenging and perhaps inappropriate to talk about "cultural characteristics." Because not everyone in a given cultural group embraces or possesses the same common characteristics, generalizations may lead to misunderstandings, faulty assumptions, unwarranted expectations, and/or stereotyping. But how else can we begin to learn about differences unless we talk about them? The important thing to keep in mind when reading this chapter, and in fact all of the chapters within the diversity section of this book, is that there are just as many, if not more, differences within a cultural group as there are among the various groups we will be discussing.

Consider, for example, the following scenario: People often consider university students to be a cultural group that possesses unique and common characteristics. Therefore, if you asked students and professors, or watched movies or commercials depicting student life, you would see and hear about common perceptions of students as people who stay up late, party a lot, engage in binge drinking, and do not have a lot of money. But does that describe you and your friends? Does it describe everyone who is a student? Of course not. Even among college students, there are many differences. Thus, we should not expect the same behavior from all people in a particular cultural group.

Nonetheless, there is something to be learned by looking at some of the concerns, issues, and contexts that characterize youth from the four largest ethnic minority (i.e., cultural) groups found in North America: African Americans, Hispanic Americans, Asian Americans, and Native Americans. (We will refer to this whole group of youth as *youth of color*.) Choosing which characteristics to describe for each group was a challenge in writing this chapter since we did not want to fall into the trap of painting a false picture or setting up negative expectations, as in the college student example. Thus, we turned to several different definitions of culture to provide us with guidance, and decided to address values and characteristics such as religion, language, and family structure which were common to each group.

Again, remember that our depiction of characteristics of specific groups should not imply that all youth within a particular minority group are alike. And additionally, it is important to understand that being a person of color does not automatically make one "at risk."

Context Is Everything

In this next section we discuss the impact of community on the development and reinforcement of culture. As you have seen, culture is a complex matter. Generally, culture can be thought of in terms of shared beliefs, knowledge, and values. It consists of what we feel, learn and do; who we spend our time with; memories of and preferences for smells, tastes, sounds, and feelings; and even the images and stories that we cherish. Culture is the resource individuals unconsciously draw on as they interpret information, solve problems, assess themselves and others, plan for the future, and locate themselves within time and space.

Culture occurs in context. Just as context has an influence on how flora grows, context is important to understanding youth of color and their attitudes and behaviors. Cultural understanding must be grounded in an awareness of the historical experiences of individuals, groups, and nations. For example, to understand young people we must address their experiences with racial, ethnic, linguistic, or religious oppression and/or the opportunities for privilege (Nsameng, 1992) and how these experiences are understood, remembered, and processed by different individuals and groups. As Bronfenbrenner (1970) reminded us, "Development never takes place in a vacuum; it is always embedded and expressed through behaviors in a particular environment" (p. 27).

Spencer and Markstrom-Adams (1990, p. 304) furthered our understanding of the interplay of persons and the environments in which they live:

> For many minority youth, transient models of self or identity development (a) ignore socioeconomic developmental processes, (b) assume homogeneity among group members, (c) overlook patterns of coping and adaptation, (d) fail to link unique ecosystem or multi-leveled environmental experiences with life course models (which integrate historical, sociocultural,

biological and psychological components with behavioral response patterns), and as a consequence (e) ignore the opportunity of furthering or broadening the knowledge extant on risk and resilience for youth whose normative experiences require ongoing adaptive coping strategies as a function of race, ethnicity and/or color.

Traditionally, youth of color have been underserved or inappropriately served by both government-funded social service systems (e.g. health and education) and the private and nonprofit sector (e.g. the YMCA and Boys & Girls Clubs). Additionally, providers of recreation and leisure services too often have inadequately addressed culturally based perceptions and behaviors, such as value orientation, ethnic identity, social capital supports (e.g., caring adults or peers who provide positive role models), biculturalism issues, language and acculturation, religious beliefs, and family structure. However, recently attempts have been made to address these shortcomings by devising culturally appropriate approaches to developing and offering programs and services. For example, Outley and Floyd (2002) called on recreation service providers to recognize that many youth of color are adversely affected by poverty, geographic isolation, environmental degradation, violence, and crime, resulting in a lack of adequate programs and services. Therefore, it is important to understand the importance of the cultural context and how it may influence the types of programs that youth living in a particular environment want and need.

As noted in Chapter 2, the number of adolescents in the United States is on the rise, and so too is the number of adolescents of color. Additionally, it is important to recognize that many youth of color currently live in low-income families and generally do not fare as well as youth in more affluent families in terms of economic security, health, and education. This statistic is important to address since it is widely recognized that youth living below the poverty line are more likely to have difficulty in school, to become teen parents, and, as adults, to earn less and to be unemployed more frequently than those above the poverty line.

Diversity of Youth: Their Backgrounds and Issues

In the following sections, we briefly describe the more common experiences, cultural practices, and beliefs of five cultural groups: African Americans, Hispanic Americans, Asian Americans, Native Americans, and bicultural and multicultural youth.

First, we provide some background information on each group, including salient historical and sociodemographic information. This information offers insight into contextual elements and forces that shape youth development and the provision of recreation services. It is important to keep in mind that some youth are what is often called *first generation,* meaning that they moved with their parents from another country to the United States. Or, for example, youth might be *third generation,* meaning that they live in a family that has lived in the United States for three generations. These distinctions are important because a youth's degree of acculturation and assimilation may play a major role in their cultural lives and consequently in their development as youth. We address issues of acculturation and assimilation in greater detail in Chapter 17.

African American Youth

The African American population was, until recently, the largest minority group in the United States. In recent years, however, the number of Hispanics has surpassed that of African Americans. African Americans are mostly concentrated in the South and in large metropolitan areas, such as Chicago, Detroit, and Los Angeles.

Of all the cultural groups in the United States, African Americans are unique in regard to how some of them arrived here. While some African Americans entered the United States as free men and women, the majority were brought here against their will and sold into slavery. Thus, most demographers recognize three distinct African American ethnic groups: those born in America, those born in the Caribbean, and those born in Africa.

A "traditional" socialization of African American youth focuses on instilling cultural pride, or "self as a Black person," in each individual (Hill, 1999). Cultural pride is considered an important adaptation and survival mechanism for existing within a predominately White European society. Even for youth of color from higher socioeconomic backgrounds, racism and discrimination remain primary barriers to acceptance and participation in the larger community. To combat this, youth's healthy development requires support from family members to help them interpret and manage complex racial or cultural experiences outside the home.

Hispanic American Youth

Hispanics are now the largest minority group in the United States and comprise about 13% of the population. The Hispanic youth population has grown from 9% of the total population in 1980 to 16% in 2000. This growth rate surpasses that of any other group, including non-Hispanic Whites. Hispanics include immigrants with roots in different Spanish speaking countries and regions, including Mexico, Puerto Rico, Spain, the Caribbean, and Central and South America. Each of these countries or areas has its own unique sociopolitical history. Individuals from these countries have their own immigration and settlement patterns and acculturation rates. Currently, Hispanics of Mexican origin encompass the largest group in the United States, followed by Puerto Ricans and then Cubans. A large number of Central and South American Latinos also currently live in the United States.

Many people view the Hispanic population as monolithic, but in fact it is very diverse in terms of educational patterns, religious views, socioeconomic status, and language or dialect spoken. For example, some Hispanic Americans speak only English, others may speak only Spanish, while many others are bilingual. In addition, many different terms are used to describe the Hispanic population. The preferences for particular terms may vary by region within the United States and by country of origin. For example, the terms *Chicano* and *Mexican American* are used mainly in California, *Latin American* or *Latino* in Texas, *Mexican* in Arizona, *Cuban* and *Puerto Rican* in Florida, and *Spanish American* in New Mexico. Terminology used to identify individuals of Hispanic descent may be further complicated by their race (e.g., Black Puerto Rican) and the different racial designations used in other countries (e.g., someone who is "Black" in the United States may be "White" in Brazil because variations in skin tone are interpreted differently in different countries).

Asian American Youth

Like the Hispanic population, the Asian American population is one of the fastest growing ethnic groups in the United States, with numbers projected to reach 40 million by the year 2050. Immigration from Asian countries (as opposed to increases in population due to births) will account for nearly 75% of the increase. The Asian American population includes immigrants having origins in the Far East, Southeast Asia, or the Indian subcontinent (e.g., Cambodia, China, India, Japan, Malaysia, Thailand, and Vietnam). The majority of immigrants, however, come from three geographic regions: East Asia (China, Japan, and Korea), Southeast Asia (Burma, Cambodia,

Indonesia, Laos, Malaysia, the Philippines, Singapore, Thailand, and Vietnam), and South Asia (India, Pakistan, Sri Lanka, Bangladesh, Bhutan, and Nepal). The experiences of people from each of these areas are shaped by unique cultural characteristics, as well as the historical, sociopolitical, and economic conditions of their native countries.

In general, Asian Americans and other cultural groups reside in ethnic communities where they are able to concentrate their economic, social, and cultural resources. "China Town" in New York is an excellent example of this phenomenon. The 2000 Census indicated that over half (51%) of the Asian population lived in just three states: California, New York, and Hawaii.

However, it is important to recognize that profound interethnic and intra-ethnic differences exist between subpopulations. Intracultural differences may result from regional concentrations; migration patterns, degree of accultur-ation, and length of time in the United States; and education level, language, ethnic identity, and cultural values. Understanding the diversity of individu-als within this overall group is therefore key.

Asian immigrants, like many other immigrant groups, have faced and continue to face racism, prejudice, and stereotypes. For example, the popu-lar media has glamorized Asian Americans as the "model minority"—hard working and academically successful. These sorts of cultural myths have caused many Americans to view Asian Americans as a threat, although in reality little is actually understood by the general public about their cultural traditions, beliefs, or customs.

Native American Youth

Native Americans and Alaska Natives make up just 1.5% of the population in the United States (U.S. Census Bureau, 2001a). Due to these small numbers, many native peoples strive to maintain their tribal and cultural identities. As a result, some Native American youth continue to foster their tribal identities in an attempt to remain separate and distinct from other tribes and ethnic groups.

Over 500 distinct tribal groups exist in the United States and Native Americans reside in every state and every major city. Nevertheless, Native Americans remain an invisible group within American society, one that is often thought of as "extinct" or completely assimilated in "modern America." These are of course myths as Native Americans, like other ethnic groups, vary in their level of assimilation. On one end of the spectrum are those indi-viduals and groups who retain a traditional lifestyle and on the other end are those who participate in and identify with the mainstream culture. Individuals may place themselves on varying points within the spectrum throughout their lifetimes and according to specific events. For example, one individual or family may live a very westernized life and yet return to the tribal lands each year to participate in a Pow Wow and study traditional ways. Native American youth in particular may feel the pull both of traditional life, wanting to learn oral history, songs, dances, and ceremonial activities and yet also wanting to adopt urban fashion styles and music.

Multiracial/Bicultural Youth

According to Holmes (1995), the 1990 Census showed that nearly two million children lived in homes where parents were from different races. By 2000, over six million people, or nearly 2.5% of the population, were counted as of mixed race heritage, with children under the age of 18 years comprising 42% (U.S. Census Bureau, 2001b). International adoptions have also led to an increase in multiracial or bicultural youth.

Multicultural families often attempt to form traditions that merge their varying cultural backgrounds. Youth who are part of families from two different cultural backgrounds often seek to identify and embrace both cultures. The merging of traditions allows for increased biethnic identity and appreciation.

Traditionally it was believed that multicultural youth had more problems because of the need to "choose" a race with which to identify (Wilson, 1987). Due to this assumption, families would often try to rely on one set of cultural practices to the exclusion of the other(s). Recent research, however, illustrates that multicultural children do not have more problems than uniracial youth. In fact, individuals who grow up in biracial households may actually have a broader view of culture than their uniracial peers. This broader view of culture allows for a greater appreciation of minority group cultures, and results in increased language skills and the ability to identify multiple aspects of a social situation (Thornton, 1996). Despite the apparent advantages of a biracial upbringing, discrimination and racism against youth with multicultural backgrounds still exists, as some members of U.S. society feel that biracial households and intermarriages threaten traditional family values.

Celebrating Differences, Recognizing Similarities

Next we describe the ways that these cultural groups differ among each other and from "mainstream" culture as well as how they are similar. Obviously in this chapter we cannot discuss all of the salient similarities and differences in-depth, so we have chosen to address some of the key factors that contribute to and support cultural identity.

The Role of Identity in Development

Identity refers to an individual's sense of self as a unique person. Changes in one's identity may occur throughout the lifecycle; however, major identity changes and experimentation are often most notable during adolescence (as discussed in Chapter 6). For youth of color in particular, personal identity is intertwined with cultural identity. From a psychosocial point of view, striving for a unified and integrated sense of self facilitates the definition of and movement toward achieving personal goals. Identity also promotes the constructive integration of the individual into society. Therefore, identity development may be a more pressing issue for minority children as they are often confronted with the recognition at an earlier age that they are of a "different" ethnicity than their majority counterparts and therefore must find unique ways to deal with this situation (Smith, 1991).

The concept of ethnic identity will also prove useful to our discussion, and should help us to better understand identity development for youth of color. *Ethnic identity* refers to one's cultural ancestry or ethnic group membership (Steinberg, 1996). It is important because it provides a sense of belonging to a community and historical continuity with one's ancestors. For youth of color, developing a positive sense of ethnic identity along with an overall personal identity is an important task (Steinberg, 1996). Youth of color may choose various strategies for going about this; however, scholars have identified the following four major strategies youth often use for dealing with their ethnic identity development:

1. *mainstream or assimilation*, where one aligns oneself with the majority culture, norms, and traditions at the expense of one's own group

2. *strong-ethnic identification or separation,* where one is aligned with the traditions and values of the culture of family origin and rejects the majority culture

3. *marginality,* where one aligns with the majority culture but feels estranged

4. *bicultural*, where one identifies with two ethnic groups within one society, such as that of the mainstream and that of one's own cultural group (Phinney, 1990; Steinberg, 1996)

Bicultural competence provides the greatest advantage for development, because both one's own cultural group and the mainstream culture are made accessible and this enables one to develop a larger set of utilizable skills and knowledge. However, no matter which strategy youth choose, ethnic identity formation is a complex process involving the interaction of contextual (e.g., socioeconomic status) and developmental (e.g., family) factors. For example, the ethnic identity formation process will be different for a Hispanic American youth growing up in an inner city barrio while being raised by a single mother compared to a Hispanic American growing up in the suburbs in a middle class, two-parent household. For youth of color, ethnic identity formation may be inhibited or influenced by their skin color, language differences, behavioral patterns, cultural values and norms, parents' experiences, social stereotypes, and fears concerning perceived discrimination (Spencer & Markstrom-Adams, 1989).

Developmentally, the family is often a major force in the identity formation process because it provides its children with their first experiences as members of a particular ethnic group. By taking an active approach to ethnic socialization, parents may act in ways that help speed up the early stages of ethnic identity development. This is accomplished within many families of color through the introduction of cultural history and traditions at an early age to instill ethnic pride. This review of cultural history may occur at family gatherings (e.g., Sunday dinners) as well as during national events such as Black History Month or Hispanic American Month, and cultural events like Pow Wows. Steinberg (1996) suggested three themes that must be taught: (a) understanding one's own culture, (b) getting along in mainstream society, and (c) dealing with racism.

Next we discuss traditions, characteristics, and values of cultural groups that help to maintain and shape cultural identity. We categorize our discussion according to the basic values, religion, family relationships, language, and communication that commonly exist within these cultural groups. These characteristics are important for recreation service providers because they help professionals to develop culturally appropriate services for youth of color.

Cooperation and Interdependence

Interestingly, all of the cultural groups focused on in this chapter stem from cultures that place a great deal of importance on what is called *collectivism.* Collectivism means that a group works toward a common goal through the use of cooperation (Bandura, 2001). Although a bit different conceptually, the term *interdependence* is often used to describe this type of cooperative effort. Interdependence is often contrasted with *independence*. In reality, individuals *and* cultural groups both possess degrees of independence and interdependence. Context will help to define the extent to which people or groups exhibit these traits.

Most research suggests that the groups identified here both value and exhibit collectivism and interdependence more than western culture or Anglo Americans (Oyserman, Coon & Kemmelmeier, 2002). Given that youth of color live within a culture currently dominated by Anglo Americans, a challenge is for them to learn to live in circumstances that may value independence over interdependence.

One example of how cultures transmit values to youth and help them celebrate their own uniqueness is the celebration of Kwanzaa. Kwanzaa is a uniquely African American celebration that focuses on the traditional African values of family, community responsibility, cooperative economics, and self-improvement. Kwanzaa is neither political nor religious, and despite some misconceptions, it is not a substitute for Christmas. Kwanzaa is simply a time of reaffirmation of culture for African American people—a seven-day celebration of their ancestors and culture. Kwanzaa, which means "first fruits of the harvest" in the African language, Kiswahili, has gained tremendous acceptance since its creation in 1966 by Dr. Maulana Karenga. Kwanzaa is now celebrated by over 18 million people worldwide.

Dr. Karenga created Kwanzaa so that the Nguzo Saba (i.e., seven cultural values specific to African Americans) could be celebrated and formed into a philosophy of Afrocentrism. The seven principles found in the Nguzo Saba include the following:

1. ***Umoja*** (Unity)—to strive for and maintain unity in the family, community, nation, and race

2. ***Kujichagulia*** (Self-determination)—to define ourselves, name ourselves, create for ourselves, and speak for ourselves instead of being defined, named, created for, and spoken for by others

3. ***Ujima*** (Collective work and responsibility)—to build and maintain our community together and make our sisters' and brothers' problems our problems and to solve them together

4. ***Ujamaa*** (Cooperative economics)—to build and maintain our own stores, shops, and other businesses and to profit from them together

5. ***Nia*** (Purpose)—to make collective our vocation of building and developing our community to restore our people to their traditional greatness

6. ***Kuumba*** (Creativity)—to do always as much as we can in the way we can to leave our community more beautiful and beneficial than we inherited it

7. ***Imani*** (Faith)—to believe with all our heart in our people, our parents, our teachers, and the righteousness and victory of our struggle

Each day of Kwanzaa is dedicated to one of the seven guiding principles and is discussed by family members and friends. The seven-day celebration begins the day after Christmas and ends on New Year's Day with a feast. Kwanza represents the ongoing processes by which African American culture continues to evolve. Visit http://www.officialkwanzaawebsite.org for more information.

Religion and Spirituality

Religion and/or spirituality play a significant role in each of the cultural groups we are discussing. For example, the majority of Hispanic immigrants are Roman Catholics, but each country of origin has its own distinct form of Catholicism influenced by its history and culture. Consequently, it is important to recognize that religious differences exist among Hispanic youth. Youth with Mexican heritage, for example, may place great importance on Our Lady of Guadalupe—a blending of native religions and Spanish Catholicism. Our Lady of Guadalupe is similar to the Roman Catholic Virgin Mary and serves both as a patron saint and the "Virgin Mother" of Mexico.

In countries where there is a significant African and/or native people's heritage (e.g., the Caribbean region), Catholic symbols are combined with the deities and rituals of the native and African populations. For example, Puerto Ricans and Cubans often practice Santeria, which is a fusion of Catholic saints and African orishas (e.g., gods and goddesses). Similar fusions of Catholic and African deities led to the establishment of additional new religions such as vaudou (commonly referred to as voodoo) in Haiti and camdomble in Brazil. These religious symbols may influence youth's belief systems and cultural identity.

Religion and spirituality have traditionally been a source of strength within the African American community as well, regardless of denomination or even regular attendance at religious services. From its inception, the African American church has been a place where community members learn empathy for others and offer a helping hand when needed. Many churches provide a range of social services (e.g., financial assistance, housing, child care, neighborhood development) to the community to help support families, as well as child, youth, and community development. Marriages, births, and deaths are sanctified within the church to acknowledge the importance of these events to the community. For Black youth, establishing a strong spiritual core may help support the development of a healthy identity and effective ways of coping with the sometimes oppressive or overwhelming challenges in their lives.

Many traditional Asian cultures have been influenced by the doctrines and philosophies of Confucianism, Taoism, and Buddhism. Each of these three philosophies has different emphases; however, together they have evolved into complementary beliefs and practices. For example, incorporated into all three philosophies is the belief that individual achievement and success are based on the moral worth and good deeds not only of oneself but also of one's ancestors. Thus, departed ancestors are honored as they assist their relatives in this world. This practice allows for the continued maintenance of positive relationships with living relatives as well as those who have departed. In addition, all emphasize human relations are inclusive rather than exclusive; maintaining harmony with nature, with others, and within oneself must be achieved; and an individual must adhere to heart-oriented (e.g. a contemplative, spiritualistic focus) versus mind-oriented (e.g., an analytic, materialistic focus) values.

The aforementioned religions and practices have all been influenced by the belief systems that they have come in contact with throughout history (e.g., Christianity, Islam, Shamanism, Neo-Confucianism). For example, many African Americans were not originally Christians but converted or combined their traditional beliefs or practices with Christianity as a result of their contact with missionaries and their experiences as slaves in the United States. Acculturation has also impacted other groups of immigrants as well. For example, a large number of Koreans converted to Christianity on arrival in the United States.

In many traditional Native American religions, the spiritual is an integral part of everyday life. At the center of most spiritual beliefs is a deity referred to as the "Great Spirit" or "the Creator." The belief that all things are interconnected is a core concept and is frequently heard in tribal stories, songs, and dances.

Family Relationships

At the root of many family relationships across all groups is the notion of interdependence. However, interdependence is often more prominent in families of color. Usually this is manifested through extended kin (individuals related by blood ties) and fictive (i.e., nonkin) families. For example, an African American family may be defined as a group of people who care for each other even if they do not live in the same house or are not related by blood (Billingsley, 1974). Mirroring the custom in many African countries, these extended family members are often referred to as "brother" or "sister" even when there is no familial relationship. Strong family ties and loyalty to the family are also dominant aspects of Hispanic, Asian, and Native American cultures.

Hispanics, African Americans, Asian Americans, and Native Americans often place great value on the role of the extended family in raising youth. Extended family networks serve a number of important functions. Having a multitude of caring adults in one's life means that youth will have access to several mentors to guide them through the turbulence of childhood and adolescence. For example, for many Hispanics, extended family, godparents or even fictive kin take an active role during rites of passage such as marriages, baptisms, confirmations, and qinceañeras (i.e., traditional coming of age ceremonies for 15-year-old girls). Familial support systems also exist beyond these significant life events as family members often help each other on a daily basis with babysitting, child care, child rearing, or even finances. A final function of being raised in an extended family is that it promotes a respect for the elderly—an important value in most of the groups we have been discussing.

When interdependence is promoted across a family network, many decisions made concerning the family are undertaken with the advice, assistance, and consent of older family members and community elders. Individual independence is respected but it is to be offset by the belief that mutual interdependence in solving problems and reaching goals is a more valued way of life. Typically, within the family, youth are socialized to seek group consensus instead of pursuing an individual decision. For example, Native American youth are taught not to draw attention to themselves but to emphasize the group's successes. Unfortunately, people outside Native American culture may view this type of behavior as passive or noncompetitive (i.e., weak) rather than a characteristic of a collective culture.

Asian cultures value the family as the basic social unit and recognize that it serves as the connection between the individual and general society. Similar to African American, Native American and Hispanic families, the values traditionally emphasized in Asian culture include loyalty, mutual obligation, interdependence, and reciprocity. Individuals are expected to promote and protect the welfare and reputation of the family and to put the family's goals above their own goals.

Families also differ in the roles assumed by husbands and wives in the household. For many youth of color in the United States, family parenting methods and responsibilities may be based on traditional approaches they've brought with them from their country of origin. For example, in traditional Asian culture and in many cultures from the Middle East, the immediate and extended family is organized by patriarchal roles. In other words, the father is seen as the head of the household and makes many of the decisions regarding the family. This is in direct contrast to many African American and Hispanic families, which have become more egalitarian, with husbands and wives sharing household responsibilities, decision making, and parenting.

Another difference between families is that within a traditional Asian family, the strongest ties within the family may be between the parent and child, and not between spouses. Like parents in many cultures, Asian parents often are willing to sacrifice their needs for the sake of their children or the family. In turn, however, parents expect children to obey unquestioningly and to be loyal to the family.

Other differences, including parenting styles and expectations, exist across cultures. In terms of parenting style, many African American and Asian parents believe in an authoritative parenting style—setting clear limits and disciplining children in such a way that enables them to understand family and societal rules (see Chapter 10). Many Asian families believe that a child's behavior is a direct reflection of their parents and their parents' child rearing capabilities. Additionally, during the adolescent years of many Asian children, they are often expected to care for younger siblings as well as to model adult-like behaviors. This expectation creates a sense of responsibility among youth and is believed to maintain and enhance familial relationships. In addition, Asian youth may be rigorously trained on how to act properly toward others. Parents may also seek to minimize the amount of outside or western influences on their children in an effort protect their exposure to non-traditional values.

Language and Communication

Across cultures, language and communication styles are important ways of expressing and celebrating one's uniqueness. Additionally, language and communication are defining elements of a culture. Whether a family has recently settled in the United States or been here for one or more generations has considerable impact on what language is spoken in the household. For many youth of color English is their dominant language, while many parents may still rely on their native language. For example, in first generation families, the children and youth often act as interpreters for family members. In a number of instances, parents don't want their children to speak their native language lest the children be identified as foreigners.

Among Asian Americans and Hispanic groups, language depends on the family's country of origin. For example, although Portuguese, English, and French are spoken in Latin America, the main unifying language is Spanish. However, dialects of Spanish spoken by Hispanic immigrants may differ based on their country of origin, native indigenous idioms, or customary rates of speech. The dialect of Spanish spoken may also vary depending on how long a person has been in the United States.

Likewise, not all Asian people speak the same language. In fact, hundreds of languages are spoken by people belonging to strikingly different Asian cultures. The multiplicities of dialects also differ within countries and regions. As an example, the national language of China is Mandarin, and 70% of the population speaks Mandarin as its first language. In fact, Mandarin is one of the top three most widely spoken languages in the world. (The other two are English and Hindustani.) However, the Sino-Tibetan language family, to which Mandarin belongs, includes many "dialects" (e.g., Cantonese, Shanghai, Fukienese). Interestingly, however, Chinese written language is uniform. Therefore, while two speakers of two dialects may not be able to understand each other orally, they will understand each other's writing perfectly.

In the 1940s, slightly more than 1,000 separate Native American languages were in existence (Washburn, 1975). Of these languages, many are still "living" in the United States today, with Cherokee, Chocktaw, Yupik, and Navajo among the most commonly spoken. Unfortunately, while some native languages are thriving and finding new and younger learners, many are in great peril. For the same reasons that many minorities do not speak their native languages, many young native peoples choose not to learn their traditional language. Languages such as Apache-Kiowa, Chinook, and Coeur D'Alene have fewer than 20 speakers still living. Countless other native languages have become extinct. However, efforts to preserve native languages are being undertaken. For example, the four corners area (including the Navajo and Hopi reservations) is serviced by KTNN radio, "The Voice of the Navajo Nation," which broadcasts many programs in Navajo. Articles and websites have been published praising the station for helping to keep the Navajo language alive (Peterson, 2003).

African Americans speak a wide variety of dialects. Variations in languages may depend on the speaker's education and/or the geographic region where they live or were raised. In addition, depending on the situation, African Americans may choose to speak quite differently or exhibit varying skills by "talking local." For example, while surrounded by other youth of color, African American youth may speak in a unique form of "slang" or "hip-hop." However, the formality of their language may change if they are in the presence of adults who are not from their culture or if they are outside their neighborhood or in unfamiliar territory.

Current verbal communication styles for African American and Hispanic youth have at times been controversial. The impact that Ebonics and hip-hop have had on the culture has been debated in the media and in academic circles. Several authors (e.g., Kelley, 1997; Wilson, 1991) recognized hip-hop street culture as a symbol of identity among African American and Hispanic youth. In this context, hip-hop expresses identity through styles of dress, dispositions, verbal choices, and a syncopated walk. Some scholars stress that hip-hop is a coping mechanism that may be used to ensure personal survival in what youth perceive as an oppressive White society.

Hip-hop language fuses American pop culture, consumerism, urban America, current events, poetic verse, simile, and sports jargon. Originally an African American and Hispanic creation, hip-hop utilizes and influences the development of dialects like Ebonics and Spanglish. The culture is empowered through words that, when taken out of context and reinserted into "standard English" or "official Spanish," transfigure the English and Spanish languages. Today, hip-hop language, a form of resistance and empowerment by youth across the globe, has been infused into everyday American culture and has traveled all over the world. Some of these terms have now been adopted in the mainstream media (e.g., 24-7, all-day hustle; bling-bling, expensive jewelry of material possessions; and crib, a place of residence). See http://www.wordiq.com/definition/hip_hop_slang#relationships for more examples.

Serving Youth of Color: The Cultural Model of Recreation Programming

Building Cultural Competency

We just reviewed a few similarities and differences among cultural groups, recognizing that the generalizations do not apply to every member of a particular group. In the following sections, we explore some of the implications of these similarities and differences for the provision of recreation services and present a model that may be useful for recreation professionals serving youth of color through recreation programming.

The projected increase in the number of racial and ethnic persons of color will require increases in services and programs, and in a number of cases, a rethinking of how these opportunities are designed and presented. To successfully provide services for persons of color, recreation professionals will need to create opportunities within the appropriate cultural framework. Thus, many current practices will need to be reexamined and perhaps modified.

In general, professionals working in parks and recreation settings must become more culturally competent—but what does that mean? *Cultural competency* is defined as a set of behaviors, attitudes, and policies that enable a system, agency, or professional to work effectively in cross-cultural situations (Isaacs & Benjamin, 1991). Thus, developing cultural competency requires the integration and transformation of knowledge about specific racial and ethnic groups of people into specific standards, policies, practices, and attitudes used in appropriate cultural settings to increase the quality of services.

The implementation of services based on cultural competency requires an understanding of culturally based strengths, assets, resources, and desires of specific groups rather than imagined or perceived problems or risks. Both veteran and new recreation staff must discard old stereotypes, myths, and negative connotations regarding various ethnic groups and instead build relevant culturally based knowledge and awareness. This process may prove difficult, as some professionals in the field may not have been trained to consider cultural beliefs and practices, and in some cases they might not recognize the necessity of such training. Additionally, the difficulty of providing such training is further complicated by the lack of cultural diversity among professionals, academics, and advocates in the parks and recreation field.

Many youth of color live under stressful circumstances. Thus, well-planned and intentional recreation programs are important to assist these youth to successfully make the transition to adulthood and become fully functioning adults. Well-trained program staff can provide an atmosphere in which youth feel supported and empowered. For many youth of color, recreation professionals can supplement the adult support received within the home and at school or provide a primary support system that is not available elsewhere.

Agencies and organizations conducive to creating culturally competent programs and services adhere to certain values and principles, including the following:

- acknowledging culture as a prevailing factor in shaping behaviors, values, and institutions
- understanding when the values of mainstream groups are in conflict with those of diverse cultural groups
- respecting the culturally defined needs of a particular community
- acknowledging and accepting that cultural differences exist and have an impact on how services are delivered and received
- viewing natural systems (e.g. family, community, places of worship) as primary mechanisms for individual support and development
- recognizing that the concepts of individual, family, and community can differ across cultural groups

- respecting cultural preferences that value process rather than product, and harmony and balance within one's life more than achievement
- recognizing that to deal with a dominant society primarily of European descent (i.e., White), people of color have to be at least bicultural, which in turn creates its own set of behavioral issues

These beliefs and values must be infused within the agency or organization to enable the department and its staff to become more culturally competent. In addition, although the model is framed for racial/ethnic cultures, services for other marginalized groups (e.g., seniors, persons with disabilities, gays and lesbians, homeless, immigrant populations) can also be developed based on these same principles.

Obstacles to Developing Cultural Competency

Even in communities and among people who are sincerely striving for cultural competence, there are very real obstacles to overcome. One such obstacle is the fact that cultural beliefs and values are so much a part of our day-to-day reality that we take them for granted and may fail to realize how much they shape our thoughts and interactions. This unconscious cultural "baggage" influences our perceptions, responses, and ultimately our behavior, even when we believe we are acting in culturally competent ways. Indeed, one's culture forms a lens through which everything is viewed. Most people are so accustomed to these lenses that they fail to realize how their perceptions and decisions may be distorted. This very lack of awareness may be a barrier to the formation of good intercultural relationships.

A second obstacle to achieving cultural competence is that diversity is often not reflected in organizational leadership and management structures. For example, the cultural makeup of the "powers that be" might not be representative of the cultural makeup of the people actually being served. In addition, tensions between different cultural groups in society continue to present a barrier to intercultural relations. Thus, reaching an agreement among different racial groups about priorities and needed services is often difficult or impossible. As a result, these groups are unable to present a united front when trying to bring about systemic change. The end result is that the racial conflicts taking place in other parts of the community, state, nation, or world are often played out in schools, community centers, and other places where people of different cultures come together.

Related to this obstacle is a third factor, a phenomenon sometimes called *competing oppression* (Goldenberg, 1978). Competing oppression refers to the collective history of a given cultural group involving wrongs done to them and the tendency for these wrongs to be viewed as greater than anyone else's wrongs. The belief that "My oppression is worse than your oppression" tends to negatively affect the ability of people of diverse cultures to interact and work with one another.

All of these obstacles require investments of time and effort to overcome. However, over time obstacles can be overcome and cultural bridges can be built. Following are some guidelines that can assist in the development of culturally sensitive recreation programs for youth of color.

Guidelines for Developing Cultural Competence in Recreation Programs

Recreation professionals must develop the cultural competence to work with youth of color. In addition, behavioral and institutional changes will be needed to translate intellectual understandings into program design and implementation. These changes are necessary to give "voice" to youth of color and to provide services and programs that meet their developmental needs. Three principles are critical to implementing recreation programs for youth of color. Each principle has several related ideas that will help recreation providers to enact the principle.

Principle 1: Maximize Youth of Color Engagement

Build awareness and interest in recreational programs among youth of color. Many youth of color feel that recreation professionals do not show them respect, or do not reach out to young people to encourage their participation. In other cases, youth of color may view program staff as intimidating and not worthy of trust.

Organize cultural groups for participation. Many youth of color participate in programs with partners or groups. If youth have to "go it alone" because they receive little support from family and friends they are more likely to drop out or not participate. While this is true for all youth, it is particularly more important to youth of color, in part because of their more collective and/or interdependent perspective.

Create and nurture youth councils comprised of youth of color. These councils will guarantee that their voice will be heard and enable them to assist in the planning and evaluation of programs and services. This type of youth engagement allows for building trust. Opportunities to feel valued and to have a sense of belonging are essential.

Vary the types of programs and how they are delivered. Traditional methods of playing ball in the gym will not continue to hold the interest of today's youth. This is especially true for youth of color. Alternative programs may include pop culture activities (e.g., break dancing, salsa dancing lessons) and/or specific cultural programming (e.g., rites of passage programs) with delivery methods including but not limited to experiential, hands-on activities, and technology (e.g., photography, hip hop/pop sound recording studios, Web page development).

Develop a youth mapping program to galvanize attention to community issues among youth of color and the adults in the community. By investigating and mapping the resources available to youth in the community, youth can gain skills in communication, critical thinking, and community needs assessment. (See http://www.communityyouthmapping.org for more information.) In turn, adults in the community begin to see youth of color in a new light and learn how to trust and respect them. This also can lead to civic engagement, where young people become actors for social change within their own communities. The mapping process can also help to identify service gaps and lead to proposals to fill in the gaps.

Principle 2: Build Awareness and Support Within the Community

Increase the community's knowledge concerning the role of recreation in the development of youth of color. The public should be informed of the challenges faced by youth of color. The public should also be made aware of the commitment that recreation organizations must have to address these issues. Efforts should be made to help people understand that programs must deal with the assets of youth of color and not just their problems.

Build the capacity of recreation providers by utilizing community resources and leaders. Recreation programmers should meet with community leaders from the various cultural groups to be served and initiate talks about cultural competence and the staff competencies needed to successfully relate to communities and young people of color.

Form adult community advisory boards. These advisory boards should be made up of representatives of various cultural groups who provide input on the best ways to design programs and services to meet the needs of the community's young people. This type of collaboration allows the community to acknowledge and to put into practice their commitment to their youth. In addition, by maximizing community awareness, program benefits will be reinforced by family, peers, and the community. This approach could be a major challenge because community norms may not value the skills and behaviors that youth of color are trying to adopt.

Assure that diverse people are depicted on program flyers, brochures, and websites; place ethnic art in the recreation facilities; and identify cultural resources within the community. Recreation staff should develop a recruitment and retention program to attract youth of color and make the programming environments user friendly. Park and recreation departments should also make greater efforts to ensure that persons of color are hired as summer staff and recruited into full-time positions after graduation from high school. In addition, efforts should be made to make persons from diverse cultures welcome by appropriate displaying art and other related cultural symbols.

Allow community leaders to assist in examining the strengths and weaknesses of the youth serving agencies through periodic formal and informal assessments. The inclusion of community leaders and members in the evaluation of programs and services will allow staff to use the knowledge of community members to understand community needs and to design activities to improve local circumstances. Doing so also provides a feeling of community ownership of the assessment process and increases trust in the results. Finally, by involving community leaders in the assessment and creating a sense of ownership and trust in the process, it will be easier to establish priorities for action so that immediate benefits can be realized.

Principle 3: Train Staff to Be "Culturally Sensitive" Mentors

Mentoring has become the buzzword in many programs that serve youth. Many professionals believe that by ensuring that youth have a positive adult mentor, youth will be able to overcome many of the social and economic barriers they experience. One issue that arises when selecting mentors is whether caring adults have to be similar to the youth they are serving. This issue is compelling particularly since adult volunteers and professionals also tend not to be diverse. A recent study by Public/Private Ventures indicated that while 50% of the children and youth in mentoring situations belong to a racial or ethnic group, only 15% to 20% of adult volunteers working with youth of color belong to such groups (Public/Private Ventures, 2002). This dramatic difference between the availability of adult mentors for youth of color results in many youth having to wait until mentoring programs are able to match based on demographic backgrounds or must rely on cross-race matching of youth and adults.

Why is matching of adults and youth from similar backgrounds important? Several researchers suggest that programs that match mentors and professionals with youth based on gender and racial/ethnic backgrounds provide an opportunity to foster cultural relationships grounded in the cultural experience of the youth (Flaxman & Ascher, 1992; Kunjufu, 1985). These researchers argued that race is an important social construct within society and only those with the same cultural background can assist youth of color in dealing with issues and problems. The use of mentors from outside the community can convey to youth of color that no caring local adults are available to serve as role models (Kunjufu, 1985). Further, having mentors from the community allows for the development of the mentee's cultural identity without outsiders imposing (intentionally or not) their cultural values.

However, cross-race matching does have some benefits. For example, cross-race mentoring can begin to bridge cultural differences and provide a platform for true diversity (Public/Private Ventures, 2002). Providing mentors from different cultural backgrounds, who are trained to be culturally sensitive and understand their mentee's cultural heritage, can contribute to breaking down racial barriers and to an increased appreciation of cultural diversity (Flaxman & Ascher, 1992).

Public/Private Ventures (2002) provided two approaches for increasing cultural sensitivity, which can be applied to mentors who work with youth from different cultures or races than their own:

- *Assess personal biases and values.* Everyone's personal values stem from their upbringing, spiritual beliefs, and sense of morality. These values must be examined carefully to better understand where they came from and their impact on personal perceptions and actions. This process can help individuals become more nonjudgmental about the values that others, particularly youth of color, may have.

- *Understand the differences between the culture and heritage of particular groups.* This can be accomplished by an immersion in the distinct culture or heritage of the youth being served. Additionally, recreation professionals should ask the youth themselves to teach others about their culture, or have adults in the community teach about their heritage.

Conclusions

Recreation programming for youth of color presents many challenges but also many opportunities. Each cultural group has unique strengths, assets, and needs, and by acknowledging these differences we can provide better services to individuals from diverse backgrounds. The diversity of cultural groups within our society creates special challenges for recreation providers and requires professionals

1. to examine their own knowledge of and attitudes about culture
2. to strengthen their skills in working in cross-cultural and multicultural situations
3. to develop culturally appropriate models of programs, services, and interventions appropriate for the sociocultural and ecological context in which behavior develops and occurs

Recreation professionals should be proactive in pursuing culturally competent programs and services. To optimize positive opportunities for human development, contextually and culturally responsive environments must be constructed, and specific attention directed toward developing programs relevant to youth of color's life and community experiences.

References

Bandura, A. (2001). Social cognitive theory: An agentic perspective. *Annual Review of Psychology, 52*, 1–26.

Billingsley, A. (1974). *Black families and the struggle for survival: Teaching our children to walk tall.* New York, NY: Friendship Press.

Bronfenbrenner, U. (1970). *Two worlds of childhood: US & USSR*. New York, NY: Russell Sage Foundation.

Flaxman, E. and Ascher, C. (1992). *Mentoring in action: The efforts of programs in New York City*. New York, NY: Institute for Urban and Minority Education.

Goldenberg, I. (1978). *Oppression and social intervention: Essays on the human condition and problems of change*. Chicago, IL: Nelson-Hall

Hill, S. (1999). Afri*can American children: Socialization and development in families.* Thousand Oaks, CA: Sage.

Holmes, R. (1995). *How young children perceive race.* Thousand Oaks, CA: Sage.

Isaacs, M. and Benjamin, M. (1991). *Towards a culturally competent system of care, Volume II: Programs which utilize culturally competent principles*. Washington, DC: Georgetown University Child Development Center, CASSP Technical Assistance Center.

Karenga, M. *Kwanzaa*: *A celebration of family, community, and culture*. Retrieved July 29, 2004, from http://www.officialkwanzaawebsite.org

Kelley, R. (1997). *Yo' mama's disfunktional: Fighting the cultural wars in urban America*. Boston, MA: Beacon Press Books.

Kunjufu, J. (1985). *Countering the conspiracy to destroy Black boys*. Chicago, IL: African American Images.

Nsameng, B. (1992). *Human development in cultural context: A third world perspective*. Newbury Park, CA: Sage.

Outley, C. W. and Floyd, M. F. (2002). The home they live in: Inner city children's views on the influence of parenting strategies on their leisure behavior. *Leisure Sciences, 24,* 161–179.

Oyserman, D., Coon, H., and Kemmelmeier, M. (2002). Rethinking individualism and collectivism: Evaluation of theoretical assumptions and meta-analyses. *Psychological Bulletin, 128*, 3–72.

Peterson, L. C. (2003). *Tuning in to Navajo: The role of radio in native language maintenance*. Retrieved from http://jan.ucc.nau.edu/~jar/TIL_17.html

Phinney, J. (1990). Ethnic identity in adolescents and adults: A review of research. *Psychological Bulletin, 108*, 499–514.

Public/Private Ventures. (2002). *Same-race and cross-race matching* (Technical Assistance Packet #7). Philadelphia, PA: Author.

Smith, E. J. (1991). Ethnic identity development: Toward the development of a theory within the context of majority/minority status. *Journal of Counseling and Development, 70*(1), 181–188.

Spencer, M. B. and Markstrom-Adams, C. (1990). Identity processes among racial and ethnic minority children in America. *Child Development, 61*(2), 290–310.

Steinberg, L. (1996). *Adolescence* (4th ed.). New York, NY: McGraw-Hill.

Thornton, M. C. (1996). Hidden agendas, identity theories, and multiracial people. In M. P. P. Root (Ed.), *The multicultural experience: Racial borders as the new frontier* (pp. 101–120). Thousand Oaks, CA: Sage.

U.S. Census Bureau. (2001a). *Overview of race and Hispanic origin.* Retrieved August 9, 2004, from http://www.census.gov/population/www/cen2000/briefs.html

U.S. Census Bureau. (2001b). *The two or more races population: 2000.* Retrieved August 9, 2004, from http://www.census.gov/population/www/cen2000/briefs.html

Washburn, W. (1975). *The Indian in America.* New York, NY: Harper & Row.

Wilson, W. (1987) *The truly disadvantaged.* Chicago, IL: University of Chicago Press.

Wilson, W. (1991). Public policy research and the truly disadvantaged. In C. Jencks and P. Peterson (Eds.), *The urban underclass.* Washington, DC: The Brookings Institution Press.

Chapter 17

Understanding the Experiences of Immigrant Adolescents: Acculturation Is Not the Same as Assimilation

Jennifer Skuza

Khat moved to the United States from Cambodia about two years ago. He had just turned 15 years old. Prior to moving to the United States, Khat and his family lived in a village, outside of the capital city Phnom Penh, which still felt the effects of the Vietnam War and the former Khmer Rouge reign of terror that lasted from 1975 to 1979. Most of the people in his village were farmers. They would go into the capital city in search of work during the dry season when farming was impossible. Schools near his village were unable to attract and retain qualified teachers. Other than work, there was simply little to do. Although the schools were poor and the village lacked basic resources, his family and neighbors valued education and interdependence. After years of planning and preparation, Khat and his family moved to St. Paul, Minnesota, to join other relatives who had lived there since 1976. Khat experiences acculturation every day since moving to the United States—a process embedded in the everyday lives of immigrant adolescents.

Migration and immigration are worldwide phenomena of huge proportions. Considering the resulting changes for millions of people, it is quite surprising how little we know about the experience of growing up as an immigrant youth and about the process of creating a new life in a new country. Indeed, understanding the phenomenon of acculturation and the process of adjusting to a new or different culture provides a key entry point into understanding the broader experiences of immigrant youth living in the United States. However, it may be difficult to put acculturation into perspective because it is a pervasive, dynamic, vast, and complex phenomenon experienced differently by each individual.

First- and second-generation immigrant youth constitute 20% of the children growing up in the United States. Therefore, their healthy development has fundamental long-term implications for our society. Immigrant youth undergo a host of changes that may have lasting impacts on their development.

Their journeys follow complex paths, and variations exist in their life courses, the levels of difficulty they experience, and the eventual outcomes. While some youth thrive through acculturation, others struggle to find their balance. Immigrant adolescents, for instance, are likely to experience the conventional challenges of adolescent development as well as the challenges of adjustment in two distinct cultures; the more dissimilar the cultures, the greater the challenge. As discussed in Chapter 16, identity development not only is an important developmental task of adolescence but also is compounded by developing an ethnic identity. For immigrant adolescents, especially new immigrants, the combining of two cultures may be a challenge to personal and ethnic identity development. It is in identity that adolescents base their sense of self and vision for their lives. Identity incorporates adolescents' choices for themselves, their priorities, and the guiding principles by which they make decisions.

Deepening our understanding of the factors that influence the development of the burgeoning immigrant youth population is essential. For example, leisure and recreation environments provide important contexts where immigrant youth may thrive in their development. In fact, these informal environments are often the only places where immigrant youth can flourish, as you will read later in this chapter. Therefore, appropriate leisure and recreation opportunities, services, supports, and programs are important factors that may contribute to the healthy development of immigrant youth. As indicated earlier, understanding the phenomenon of acculturation provides a key entry point into understanding the broader experiences of immigrant youth living in the United States.

Acculturation and Assimilation

An understanding of acculturation begins by establishing what acculturation itself is and what it is not. For instance, acculturation is often understood as being the same as assimilation when in fact acculturation and assimilation are two very different experiences. *Acculturation* refers to the cultural adjustment one undergoes as a result of moving from one cultural context to another. It is a neutral term. Acculturation does not prescribe the direction of change nor does it place value on the types of changes that occur. For example, in Khat's case, he quickly made some friends when he moved to the United States. Instead of Khat becoming more independent and making decisions on his own like his friends did, they adopted his perspective of interdependence and made decisions more collectively as a group. Thus, Khat changed his friends…not the other way around.

Assimilation is different. It suggests that changes occur in a stipulated pattern: nondominant culture[1] changes to the dominant culture,[2] and right or not, greater value is placed on these assimilative changes. This would have happened if Khat's new friends would have influenced him to the degree that he no longer conferred with his family in his own decision making (a practice he had adopted previously). These differences have significant implications on how we understand the experiences of immigrant adolescents.

The intent of this chapter is to offer an opportunity to develop a deeper appreciation for and greater understanding of the experience of acculturation as it is lived by immigrant adolescents. In the first section, we defined problems created when acculturation is understood as being the same as assimilation. While there has been some theoretical movement toward an understanding of acculturation, in many ways this process of understanding acculturation as a lived experience has just begun. The next section presents findings from a study that describes the experience of acculturation as it is lived by immigrant adolescent females from Mexico. These findings provide an indication of what acculturation is actually like for one group. Lastly, this chapter concludes with implications for the field of youth development. But before turning to the theoretical perspectives, we define key terms.

Definition of Terms

When discussing acculturation, it is important to reach a common understanding of some of the key terms and concepts.

- *Acculturation* is the experience of adapting to a new or different culture. Acculturation is a common phenomenon found in the experiences of immigrants—as well as among the experiences of refugees, indigenous peoples, sojourners, international students, guest workers, and asylum seekers.

- *Assimilation* refers to the cultural absorption of a nondominant person into a dominant culture.

- An *immigrant* is someone who voluntarily comes into a new country with the intention of settling as a permanent resident.

- A *refugee* is different from an immigrant because a refugee by definition possesses a well-founded fear of persecution for reason of race, religion, nationality, membership in a particular social group, or political opinion. Therefore, fear, rather than a voluntary action, is the motivation behind his or her move to another country.

- *Settling* (i.e., moving to live permanently in the country) is another key distinction that separates immigrants from others (e.g., international students, guest workers, sojourners) who temporarily move to another country.
- Lastly, *culture* is defined as being more than values, customs, artifacts, and institutions (as discussed in Chapter 16). It is a way of being; thinking; organizing knowledge; reasoning; problem solving; valuing the future, past, or present; and relating to others (Mestenhauser, 1998). This definition serves as a framework for how culture is viewed in this chapter. Next, we turn to the theoretical perspectives that have influenced our understanding of acculturation.

Theoretical Perspectives of Acculturation

Various theoretical perspectives have been advanced by those studying acculturation. The classical perspective of acculturation was presented by Redfield, Linton, and Herskovits (1936, p. 149) who determined, "Acculturation comprehends those phenomena which result when groups of individuals having different cultures come into continuous firsthand contact with subsequent changes in the original cultural patterns of either or both groups."

So in this definition, although acculturation is a neutral term that suggests change may take place in either or both groups, in practice acculturation tends to induce more change in one of the groups, typically the acculturating group. Moreover, acculturation is typically studied in the context of the individual—rather than the context of a group—and individuals are known to vary greatly in the degree to which they change.

Although the concept of acculturation has been widely used, it has been criticized because its original meaning (as indicated previously) has been lost and it has become synonymous with assimilation. Assimilation suggests that a person from the nondominant culture should change to be like the dominant culture, rather than from dominant to the nondominant culture—thus, perpetuating the assumption that acculturation and assimilation are the same thing. This view prescribes a single directional change for acculturation and gives little room for the process to be understood as a multidirectional phenomenon. It also assumes the dominant culture's superiority (e.g., being independent is better than being interdependent).

Scholarly attempts to measure acculturation have aided in a clearer understanding of the term, although many variations of its definition exist. For example, some psychological models of acculturation are based on a simplistic binary (i.e., two-part) conceptualization. That is, acculturation occurs when cultural identification with the society of settlement increases and identification with the society of origin decreases. For example, in the case of Khat, his progress in acculturation could be marked by an increase in his use of the English language and a decrease in his use of central Khren, the national Cambodian language. These models assume that acculturating individuals will become culturally similar to the society of settlement, emphasizing that movement into the society of settlement will occur. Models based on a binary conceptualization perpetuate the false belief that change only occurs to immigrants and not to people in the society of settlement. These models also assume that immigrants become fully absorbed into the dominant culture—an assimilative assumption.

Other models are more realistic and mirror many reciprocal avenues of change. These multidimensional acculturation models account for several dimensions in the acculturation process (e.g., Mendoza, 1984; Olmedo, Martinez & Martinez, 1978; Szapocznik, Scopetta, Kurtines & Aranalde, 1978). These dimensions could include language and loyalty, whereby language may be lost in the acculturation process but loyalty to one's society of origin persists. Although multiple dimensions (e.g., language, loyalty, relationships) are recognized, these models still assume that people will be somewhere between cultures on each dimension.

Orthogonal acculturation models specify that identification with one culture may be independent of identification with another, which adds flexibility and a greater range of outcomes (e.g., Cuéllar, Arnold & Maldonado, 1995; Oetting, Swaim & Chiarella, 1998). In this case, Khat could identify with the Cambodian culture and United States culture at the same time. Thus, orthogonal models allow individuals to identify with one or more cultures without assuming a loss in any one culture. In turn, any pattern of monocultural, bicultural, or multicultural identification is possible. Although such models are an improvement on capturing variations in the acculturation experiences, more sophisticated theories are still needed to suit the complexity of the phenomenon.

While far from exhaustive, our review of these perspectives offers general theoretical underpinnings that have influenced our understanding of acculturation. The progression of theorizing has moved from simplistic and generalized understandings to understandings that offer greater complexity and flexibility. However, there is still a tendency to define acculturation as assimilation, which limits an understanding of how an immigrant experiences and influences his or her new environment. This approach also limits the ability to view acculturation as a multidirectional and multidimensional experience and, in terms of immigrants, diminishes the cultural worth found in the society of origin.

In the next section, we describe the experiences of acculturation for one group of immigrant Latina adolescents (i.e., females who identify their heritage with Latin American countries) who moved from Mexico to the United States.

Acculturation for Immigrant Youth

What is the experience of acculturation like for immigrant adolescents? This is an important question because understanding this phenomenon—as it is lived daily—is one of the most important entry points into understanding the broader experiences of immigrant adolescents. Despite the magnitude of this phenomenon, only in the past two decades has research begun to focus on immigrant youth experiences. Prior to that, most acculturation research was based on adult experiences, making it difficult to grasp what this experience is like for immigrant adolescents.

Because of the need to understand acculturation of immigrant youth, and the lack of prior research on the topic, I undertook an investigation that used a phenomenological methodology (Skuza, 2003). That is, without any prior understanding of the theory that I was testing, I interviewed six immigrant adolescent Latinas who were experiencing acculturation. I was able to use their words to describe how they experienced their daily lives to better understand what acculturation was and how it occurred. The girls were 18–19 years old and had lived in Minneapolis and St. Paul, Minnesota, from 3 to 11 years. By creating such a large year span, I was able to include preadolescent and adolescent periods in the study participants' lives. The interviews were conducted in English and Spanish.

The findings are best described by first looking at the general structure or meaning of acculturation as a whole. Next, I describe constituents, or the essential parts of meaning, of acculturation (see **Table 17.1** for a complete list of constituents). These will give you an indication of how acculturation is experienced in the context of one group of immigrant adolescents.

The General Structure of Acculturation

> In Mexico, a familiar way of being had been established and had served as a guide throughout daily life. Upon immigration, what was once familiar no longer existed and other ways of being had to be learned to meet the demands of new cultural contexts. Acculturation was now at the forefront of everyday life accompanying all life activities. It touches the core of one's humanity—that is, one's cultural way of being.

> Acculturation is marked by responses to being in a new cultural context, which requires a constant stream of bodily energy to offset the mounting fatigue. Acculturation is not easy; instead, it is just the opposite—a complex experience that requires effort on the part of the acculturating individual. Over time, the level of difficulty lessens as deftness, confidence, relationships, and perspective evolve. Eventually, a settling in occurs whereby the acculturating individual's way of being includes what was learned from life lived in Mexico and in Minnesota. (Skuza, 2003, p. 79)

What stands out for you as you read this description? Perhaps the primordial nature of acculturation is apparent to you. Maybe you were struck by the notion of a "bodily response to fatigue" from acculturation. Yet, this general depiction also shows that acculturation is a pervasive and complex experience that accompanies all other life events, requiring tremendous amounts of energy on the part of the acculturating individual. The depiction shows that over time, the level of difficulty lessens as competencies and relationships evolve. Consequently, acculturation progresses much more slowly without such supports and opportunities (similar to protective and risk factors and processes in Chapter 6). In time, the acculturating girls' cultural way of being included what was learned from life in both Mexico *and* the United States.

Constituent Descriptions of Acculturation

Like a biologist gazing through a microscope at one human cell, examining the smaller parts of acculturation offers a focused view into the phenomenon's

Table 17.1: Constituents of Acculturation
Skuza, 2003

- Fatiguing experience requiring a constant stream of bodily energy
- Individual and familial endeavor
- Being confined by space or parental expectations
- Enduring loneliness caused by seemingly insurmountable language barriers
- Feeling diminished by stigmatizing cultural generalizations
- Finding relief and protection in relationships
- Feeling worse and then feeling better about oneself with increased competencies
- Living bodily and relationally in Minnesota and living relationally in Mexico

depths. To help us further understand the meaning of acculturation, we now describe it in terms of its eight constituents of meaning.

Fatiguing Experience Requiring a Constant Stream of Bodily Energy

One notable constituent of acculturation is that it is a fatiguing experience that requires a constant stream of bodily energy. The degree of energy required by acculturation fluctuates depending on the demands of any given situation. It is not an experience one can take a break from or just turn off; instead, it is an omnipresent phenomenon that accompanies all other life events. Immigrants may not get something to eat or find their way around town without dealing with their new culture. Therefore, acculturation often manifests itself in bodily fatigue, signaling that a physical and psychological toll has been taken. This is shown by one girl as she recounted how she felt after living in the United States for nine years:

> Because here, I have a feeling of lifeless. I never had negative thoughts before…I felt like…I got anxiety often. I couldn't stand…and I felt like I wanted to die. Like I wanted to die, to disappear. It takes all my energy. And, I felt that. I feel that… and it doesn't erase for a long time. It keeps it there. Like, when I talk about it, you notice that I get angry. I get mad.

Feeling "lifeless" points to the fatigue endured in acculturation. The demands of acculturation drained her by tapping physical and emotional resources. Points were reached where death and disappearance seemed more desirable over the constant drain of acculturation. The fatigue was marked by a growing anxiety as if the girl was trapped in a metaphorical downward spiral. Eventually, the once anxiety-ridden emotions were replaced by anger. To make it through the challenges of acculturation, bodily energy was needed to fuel the inner strength necessary for perseverance, and at times to simply cope with the difficulty of being in a new cultural context.

Individual and Familial Endeavor

For the girls in this study, acculturation was both an individual experience and a collective family experience. The girls were part of families whose lives were intertwined, affecting each others' acculturation in various ways. This process was positive in situations where family members provided support and encouragement for each other. It was also onerous in situations where the acculturation dilemmas of some relatives would compound the problems experienced by other individuals in the family.

Problems associated with having to translate for adult family members seemed to be a common problem for the Latinas we interviewed. Some girls felt burdened by the extent of the translation and the stressful conditions under which the translation occurred—not necessarily the fact that they had to translate. The translation dilemma is one example of how an individual's experience of acculturation is intertwined with, and compounded by, the acculturation issues of others in their family. One girl reiterated a time when she had translated for her uncles in their attempt to buy a car:

> They are going to buy a car, I am going to go up there and ask the guy—"Yeah, how much is the car?" And they go, "Well, you didn't do this right!" And I am like… I get so frustrated. That is just me. Until the day I get an attitude because they are like, "You didn't tell him about this!" And I am like, "Was I suppose to tell him? You are suppose to tell me." I was learning English and they are doing this to me. And inside of me I am like ahhhhhhhh! And my uncles… I felt an obligation to do it. Yeah. And then my mom, if we didn't do it, she was like, "Do it, do it. You have to do it. You have to do it for your uncle because he is your uncle." Whatever. "You have to give him respect."

This adolescent was responsible not only for translating for her uncles but also for negotiating a large financial transaction. Pressure was put on her as her uncles pushed her to get the best deal possible. Struggling with her own language limitations, she now had the extra responsibility of using her emerging language skills in this difficult and unfamiliar situation. However, she had to help since she felt obligated and pressured to help her uncles. In another example, the positive side of family is shown in acculturation:

> Because I had my family. And because my cousin was there [in school]. Even though the both of us struggled. Both of us had the same weight. None of us had the whole weight against us, the whole school, against you. There was two of us. I could always share what was going on. I always had somebody… that helped me.

For this girl, acculturation was a struggle; however, struggling together with her cousin offered comfort and security. She was able to confide in her cousin and together they could protect each other in school, and this helped to ease the burdens of acculturation.

Being Confined by Space or Parent Expectations

The Latina girls also felt confined by space and parent expectations. Some girls longed for the freedom to move about in their communities as freely as they once had done in Mexico. They had plenty of space in Mexico, including the walking distance between their family home, school, city plaza, church, and the homes of numerous friends and relatives. This large amount of space allowed for childhood freedom and independence to flourish. In Minnesota, the spatial boundaries were dramatically reduced. In their new home, they could not easily get to community places (e.g., parks, schools) or visit friends and relatives living in the area because of the driving distance. Also, the girls' parents felt their new urban neighborhoods were unsafe and therefore placed restrictions on where their girls could go. Essentially, the boundaries were limited to the perimeters of home. In stark contrast to the space and freedom the girls had experienced in Mexico, in Minnesota the girls were confined, and as a result they felt restless, agitated, and trapped.

Some of the girls also felt confined by the gender role expectations placed on them by their parents. They felt their parents unfairly applied rules (e.g., dating, curfew, use of discretionary time) on them because they were females. The girls understood that their parents worried for their safety and therefore were being watchful and protective of them; however, the parents' expectations collided with the girls' need to develop and experience a sense of independence. This type of confinement created greater inner tension than that of spatial confinement and had more dire consequences (e.g., continuous parent-daughter arguments, running away, skipping school). The daughters attributed these consequences to their need to break free from the gender role expectations held by their parents.

Enduring Loneliness Caused by Seemingly Insurmountable Language Barriers

Underlying an immigrant's acculturation is the communication process, of which language is a part. After all, communication is a central and fundamental mode of human learning and expression. You will recall from Chapter 15 that language and communication are important and defining aspects of culture. Language is especially critical for an immigrant who comes from a language base different from that of the society of settlement. Remember Khat? He spoke central Khren, the national Cambodian language, and some French, but he also had a grasp of the English language. He learned some basic English from NGO (nongovernment organization) workers in his village. So, in addition to his high aptitude for languages, he also had an introduction to the language before moving to St. Paul and transitioned quite well into fluency (although he may have had difficulties understanding slang words and other informal means of communication).

Many immigrant youth, however, are exposed to a new and foreign language they have never heard or learned before. For the Latina girls I studied, enduring feelings of loneliness caused by seemingly insurmountable language barriers emerged as a predominant challenge of acculturation. One reason for this was that the girls had initial expectations of how well they would understand and grasp English—and this expectation was unrealistic. The gap between reality and expectation was filled with feelings of loneliness that heightened to varying levels, and enduring these feelings became critical to the process of acculturation.

The girls expressed loneliness in two ways: social isolation and personal isolation. *Social isolation* was the result of being unable to adequately communicate with people in English. Especially in the beginning of their acculturation, the girls only felt confident speaking with other Spanish speakers in Spanish, which stunted the development of their wider social network. Moreover, the girls felt like outsiders because they were not able to converse proficiently in English with peers and teachers. Also, in many classroom situations, they felt lonely because they were the only or one of a few Spanish speakers in a particular class. Language became a social barrier.

Related to social isolation, *personal isolation* refers to the loneliness experienced when the girls were alone with their emotions, and it is an inner isolation that results in feeling disconnected from the self. In this case, a deep sense of self-consciousness replaced the loss of personal comfort brought on by language barriers.

In the classroom context, especially, the girls felt increasingly self-conscious, afraid, anxious, lonely, and eventually isolated by language barriers. The girls' grades suffered, and at the same time, they were feeling like outsiders among their peers. The pressure of being a student, coupled with limited English skills, placed the girls in a particularly vulnerable position. Eventually, they lost faith in themselves and discounted the importance of their own life experiences. This loneliness caused them to feel estranged from others, and even more detrimentally, estranged from their own sense of self. Without a strong social network, the personal isolation was perpetuated further and compounded the sense of loneliness felt in acculturation. The following text excerpt depicts the two types of loneliness felt in a classroom context:

> I feel uncomfortable because I was the only Spanish speaker who was there. Alone. I was the only Mexican person in the class. I am, right now I am the only Mexican person. It kind of, you don't exist there. They, of course, the teachers know that you are there, but you never ask. I don't ever ask question or

> anything. I usually read the book, do the homework, but that's it. I learn by myself. I don't have anyone who says, in my own language, help me or, "Do you understand this?" It's like, I don't have a friend to talk with. It is hard. That's hard because sometimes there are things that you really don't understand anything and you don't have the person to say, "Do you understand?" [Interviewer: So what do you do?] I try and solve the problem by myself. If I can't, nothing. I take a bad grade. That is what I do. I know that it's uncomfortable, but I am used to it. I know I can ask questions, but I feel, I don't feel good to do it. I don't feel like myself anymore. That effort that it takes me to speak out in class is too much.

Not only did this girl feel alone in the classroom, but she also felt *non-existent* in the classroom—an essentially silent and invisible way of being. This deep-seated sense of loneliness diminished her human qualities and contributed to both social isolation and personal isolation. Feeling like one does not matter is a painfully isolating experience. After all, young people, like all people, need to know that who they are and what they do matters. Also, as the only Mexican student in the classroom, this girl was culturally different from others and spoke from a different first-language base. These differences impeded her ability to reach out to others. Feeling silenced and lonely, she opted to deal with her schoolwork alone, which left her even more isolated and diminished her possibilities for learning.

Feeling Diminished by Stigmatizing Cultural Generalizations

Prejudice and discrimination based on culture, class, race, gender and language were at the root of the cultural generalizations experienced by the Latina girls. Such attitudes and actions left the girls feeling diminished—as if they were less human—regardless of whether the attitude or action was intentional or unintentional. The girls indicated that the stigmatizing cultural generalizations made them feel like outsiders and like they were inherently associated with a negative stereotype by virtue of being Mexican.

To illustrate some of the attitudes experienced by these girls, the following text excerpt presents a verbal exchange and its diminishing effects on this one Latina:

> It was kind of hard for us [group of Mexican friends] to get along with other kids when they would get mad at us for talking Spanish. And I would get mad too. And I was defending

> myself because they did some pretty bad stuff. And oh a lot of like, "You should go back to your country! I am going to call immigration!" And I would be like, "Go ahead! I am legal in this country and you cannot kick me out! Call them! I am not afraid of you!" And stuff like that. I was mad. On the inside it felt worse, like I didn't belong. Unwanted.

This Latina also described how she and other Mexican friends banded together for protection against threatening peers. She was constantly in the position of defending herself from those who diminished her dignity through threatening and diminishing statements. She looked to her Mexican peers for protection against those who elected to exercise their positions of power. Knowing how to protect oneself emotionally and physically became a basic necessity in each school day.

Finding Relief and Protection in Relationships

Human relationships were essential to alleviating the demands of acculturation for the girls interviewed. As discussed previously, acculturation required a constant stream of energy, and throughout the process the girls faced challenging and difficult times. Relationships, in part, alleviated the difficulties by providing safety and comfort. The girls characterized these relationships as having mutual emotional involvement and genuine sense of care, and even more notably, the other person in the relationship possessed an empathetic quality of understanding the uniqueness of being an immigrant. These relationships—whether with a parent, friend, youth worker, or teacher—offered the support necessary for the girls to persevere in acculturation. For example, one girl described her relationship with her father:

> Like my dad encouraged me to keep going and never give up so I can get whatever I want. And because there was other people who were like encouraging me to be, like better. And I think that helped me too. Because I was feeling like, ah, there were some who care about me. Yeah. And so, I started doing better. And that is when it [self-esteem] went up. Like, I think of it as I was sleeping and then suddenly I wake up.

Her father's encouragement gave her the support necessary to make it through the difficulties of acculturation. She took stock in this relationship and recognized the important role it played in her life. This steadfast relationship with her father added to her confidence and eventually to the successes she found in her acculturation.

Feeling Worse and Then Feeling Better About Oneself With Increased Competencies

After moving to the United States, the girls experienced an erosion of their self-worth. After time passed, however, gains were made with the help of increased language skills and competences necessary to navigate through their new cultural contexts. Increasing their language skills was important. Once the girls developed a grasp of the English language, other competences began to flourish. As a result, the girls felt better about themselves and began to experience optimism in their eventual ability to live well in a new culture. One girl expressed the positive consequences of her emerging competence:

> Yeah, I got used to being here. And my parents gave me a sense to get around and to adjust. I got to know friends and I know other people and I know their culture…and I am used to doing what you guys do. Like to have my time counted. Now I get it. I feel better.

For this girl, developing other competencies in addition to language skills helped ease the process of acculturation. She grew more relaxed and became more comfortable with her new cultural surroundings as her competence increased.

Living Bodily and Relationally in Minnesota and Living Relationally in Mexico

Acculturation is also characterized as an existential experience. That is, the Latina girls lived bodily and relationally in Minnesota, while still living relationally in Mexico. The following excerpt illustrates living bodily and relationally while acculturating in Minnesota:

> I don't know. I was kind of depressed or something. Trying so hard to make friends here. While, I was missing something without me knowing. It is becoming a little bit more clear. Like being homesick or something. It is not very much of being homesick for Mexico really. It is the way Mexico is. It is the way the town runs like. And the way you have that freedom to run around without worries.

This girl described a lingering depression that seethed beneath the surface awaiting acknowledgment by her—the person experiencing it. Caught up in the flurry of acculturation, she became absorbed in making friends and finding a social place for herself. She was living both bodily and relationally in Minnesota. Yet, during this time, deep within herself, she also felt the loss of not being in Mexico. In this case, living relationally was extended to her relationship with how her life had been lived in Mexico. Thus, acculturation is not a neat package of life events that occurs at the onset of immigration. Instead, it is a fluid process of being in two cultures at the same time.

Implications for the Field of Youth Development and Recreation

These eight constituents of acculturation point to areas that recreation and leisure service providers can address to ease the acculturation process. For example, efforts could be made to help new arrivals in this country to learn how to deal with stress and bodily fatigue. In addition, incorporating caring adults and working to foster healthy relationships in service activities could ease some of the difficulties found in acculturation. Leisure is an important developmental context, and here in particular an excellent context in which to help young people develop friendships and feel they matter.

Students, practitioners, and researchers alike may benefit by reflecting on how they may make a positive difference in the lives of immigrant adolescents—one segment of the broad youth population. In the next section, we discuss some of the other implications of the acculturation constituents for people who work or wish to work with immigrant adolescents.

Learning Environments

In recent years, attention has been given to the need for culturally relevant and responsive approaches to youth development. There is a growing realization that practice needs to change to better reflect and serve the changing face of communities. Building intentional learning environments is one way to address the need for culturally relevant and responsive approaches to youth development.

Formal and informal learning environments may happen anywhere at anytime. Besides schools, recreation centers, campgrounds, after-school programs, faith-based centers, and parks are just a few settings that may provide learning environments. The most powerful learning environments are intentionally youth-centered, competence-centered, and assessment-centered (McLaughlin, 2000). In these environments, young people know they matter and are central to all that happens in the program or classroom. They also can learn new, relevant, and challenging things, and they have clear knowledge of when they excel and why they need improvement.

One of the most powerful learning environments occurs in community-based programs, and not necessarily in schools. These environments provide physical and emotional safety, trusting relationships, clear rules and consequences, responsibility of place and program, access as needed, and social capital (McLaughlin, 2000). For the Latina adolescents we have been discussing, these informal learning environments were important. For example, one girl described her fondest memory as an overnight field trip to an environmental camp taken with peers and an adult adviser from a neighborhood organization. Here, she easily made friends with her peers, individuals she never would have spoken to in school or in her neighborhood. In this learning environment, she also developed a trusting relationship with the adult adviser. She had fun teaching her peers and the adviser Spanish words, she learned about environmental issues, and she relaxed and forgot about the troubles she was experiencing in school. The other participants in the study described similar experiences.

Understanding the importance of informal learning environments leads to another point about social segregation. Even multicultural settings, like many urban schools, do not provide the necessary environment for adolescents to develop interpersonal and intercultural relationships among their peers. This is unfortunate, because finding relief and protection in relationships is one way for immigrant adolescents to ease the discomfort of acculturation. Using an example from the interviews, a 16 year-old Latina adolescent shared the following:

> It is kind of funny. You go to a classroom. You see mostly all White kids hanging out together and all the minority groups hanging out with each other. Even though the teachers try and separate you. You can't. You just kind of get into this group. And the White kids. Very rarely do you get to hang out with them a lot. Unless you know them from ______ [name of the "token White girl"] and you say hi to them. But you are not as close to them as you are with your little minority group.

Social segregation is a prevalent issue among adolescents. Recreation and other informal learning environments are among few places where the immigrant adolescents have a chance to truly get to know peers who are outside their segregated friendship boundaries (e.g., the adolescent Latina who participated in the environmental camp).

Perhaps, by building intentional opportunities for *all* youth to get to know each other in *all* learning environments, a greater number of healthy intercultural relationships could be fostered among young people. Thus, it is important for practitioners and researchers to consider the factors that could contribute to youth development in such learning and recreation environments.

These factors could include emphasizing the value of informal learning, facilitating time for mutually respectful communication to get to know culturally diverse peers, and designing activities and methods intended to reduce social segregation. After all, having fun together is a great way to reduce social and cultural barriers.

Community-based programs develop learning environments that typically occur during out-of-school time. Nonschool hours can lead to increased risk or opportunity for youth depending on how the time is used. Unfortunately, adolescents typically have fewer out-of-school time programs available to them because too often a heavy emphasis on academic achievement overshadows informal learning opportunities, as discussed in Chapter 13. In turn, adolescents not involved in school activities may have fewer organized youth development opportunities available to them. This is unfortunate because out-of-school time programs offer prime opportunities for adolescents to truly get involved in their own development through recreation. This is especially important to those who are not otherwise thriving in school. These programs also offer unique opportunities for immigrant adolescents—a break in the day when one has the chance to be himself or herself, sort things out, pursue an interest, or find camaraderie.

Practitioner's Way of Being

McLaughlin, Irby, and Langman (1994) used the phrase, "First you find a wizard," to introduce a chapter on effective adults who work with youth (p. xv). Adults who possess special qualities that make them successful in working with great numbers of young people are called *wizards* (as discussed in Chapter 12). Adult wizards not only possess certain characteristics, but they have a certain way of being. Wizards know themselves well, are deliberate in how they relate to others, and have certain assumptions about the worth of all people that filter their thoughts and feelings about others. In one of the interviews, a girl described the educators she found helpful:

> Not all of them. Yeah, just the ones who know them, who understand the difference. The difference between coming here and living here. They are the only ones who understand the culture maybe, but, at least that there is a difference in cultures. They make all the difference in school for me. It helps so much, having them there.

The wizard educators described in this quotation possess an empathic openness to understanding the uniqueness of being an immigrant. They did not treat all youth in the same way, ignoring the differences that may exist. In race relations, this attitude is called color-blindness, whereby race is treated like an insignificant factor that does not affect people. The equivalent term culture-blindness could be applied here if the uniqueness of being an immigrant is disregarded. The educators, who chose not to ignore culture and possessed an empathic openness, were sensitive to cultural differences, and integrated this sensitivity into how they related to this girl. In doing this, they extended themselves and made it their responsibility to check in and find out where this Latina needed help in her learning. As a result, this immigrant felt comforted and understood by these educators. Another Latina talked about how one educator worked through language issues:

> And then, I just kind of, got to know the teacher, and he was nice. And so I asked him for help. And he said, "Yes, whenever, you want, you ask me for help, and I will help you. If you want to stay after school, I will stay with you." And yes he is a nice teacher, yeah. And he speaks like Italian and those languages and so he, he told me that's it is. "Okay that you speak to me in Spanish because I am going to try and understand you because I have some Italian and French and those are similar to Spanish. So I am going to try and understand you." And so, yes, he is nice. Yeah.

These observations have implications for all practitioners working in the field of youth development. The educator's approach was welcoming and nurturing and consequently played a key role in fostering a relationship that supported this acculturating Latina. He reached out and engaged this young person, encouraging her to ask questions in Spanish while *he* took the burden of attempting to understand *her*. Think of the amount of time this adolescent spent in the classroom struggling to understand what others were saying. With this special educator, such dilemmas were reversed and she finally had an opportunity to relax in her first language.

Summary

Youth development literature focuses on the strengths youth need to succeed in their lives. Services, opportunities, and supports foster a full range of developmental pathways that may support the growth of youth, regardless of the obstacles they may be facing in their lives. However, to begin fostering positive developmental pathways one must understand the experiences of young people. For immigrant adolescents, acculturation provides a key entry point into understanding their experiences. By uncovering the complexities of this phenomenon, all of us—students, practitioners, and researchers—may develop a deeper understanding of acculturation and what it means to immigrant adolescents. This understanding will enable us to build connections and adequately address positive development pathways in ways meaningful to immigrant adolescents.

References

Berry, J. W. (1997). Immigration, acculturation, and adaptation. *Applied Psychology: An International Review, 46* (1), 5–68.

Cuéllar, I., Arnold, B., and Maldonado, R. (1995). Acculturation rating scale for Mexican Americas-II: A revision of the original ARSMA scale. *Hispanic Journal of Behavioral Sciences, 17*(3), 275–304.

McLaughlin, M. (2000). *Community counts: How youth organizations matter for youth development.* Retrieved April 18, 2001, from http://www.publiceducation.org.

McLaughlin, M., Irby, M., and Langman, J. (1994). *Urban sanctuaries: Neighborhood organizations and the lives and futures of inner city-youth.* San Francisco, CA: Jossey-Bass.

Mendoza, R. H. (1984). Acculturation and sociocultural variability. In J. L. Martinez, Jr. and R. H. Mendoza (Eds.), *Chicano psychology* (2nd ed.). Orlando, FL: Academic Press.

Mestenhauser, J. (1998). International education on the verge: A search for a new paradigm. *International Education*, 68–76.

Oetting, E. R., Swaim, R. C., and Chiarella, M. C. (1998). Factor structure and invariance of the orthogonal cultural identification scale among American Indian and Mexican American youth. *Hispanic Journal of Behavioral Sciences, 20*(2), 131–154.

Olmedo, E. L., Martinez, J. L., and Martinez, S. R. (1978). Measure of acculturation for Chicano adolescents. *Psychological Reports, 42,* 159–170.

Redfield, R., Linton, R., and Herskovits, M. (1936). Memorandum for the study of acculturation. *American Anthropologist, 38,* 149–152.

Skuza, J. A. (2003). *The experience of acculturation for Latina adolescents from Mexico: A phenomenological study*. Doctoral dissertation, University of Minnesota.

Szapocznik, J., Scopetta, M., Kurtines, W., and Aranalde, B. (1978). Theory and measurement of acculturation. *Interamerican Journal of Psychology, 12,* 113–130.

Endnotes

1. According to Berry (1997), *nondominant* is used in place of the word *minority*, which is used by the U.S Census and social scientists. Nondominant is a term that references the power (i.e., numerical, economic, or political) difference that exists among cultural groups. In this study, nondominant is specifically used to describe people from the following U.S. Census data categories: Black or African American, American Indian and Alaska Native, Asian, Native Hawaiian and other Pacific Islander, Hispanic or Latino origin, and multiple race options.

2. According to Berry (1997), *dominant* is used in place of the word *non-Hispanic White*, which is used by the U.S. Census, and the word *mainstream*, which is often used in social sciences. Similar to the term nondominant, dominant references the power differences among cultural groups. In this study, dominant is used to describe people from the U.S. Census data category, One Race: White. European American is also used to describe people from this category.

Chapter 18

What About the Girls?

Karla A. Henderson

> Imagine a world where a girl is not limited by the fact that she was born female. She goes to school confident that her clothes, hair, and weight will not be discussed in the hallways. In class, she raises her hand high, not too intimidated about voicing her opinion. After school, she goes to basketball practice at the local recreation center, where the girls' team is cheered on as loudly as the boys' team. She walks home from practice confidently, without worrying that she might be a target for teasing or harassment. (Fine, 2001, p. 1)

Girls have the right to have this scenario be a reality. Indeed, boys and girls face similar issues as they go from childhood to adulthood including questions about "Who am I?" "Where am I going?" and "How do I get there?" However, males biologically differ from females, and because gender constructions in society are not the same for girls as for boys, different challenges exist for girls as they mature. The contradictions in our society, including the ambiguity of expected gender roles and how one defines one's identity and authenticity, offer situations that may cause problems for girls.

In 1982 Gilligan found in her groundbreaking research that women place emphasis on relationships and on caring for and about others. Over 20 years later, relationships continue to be the primary organizer for girls' lives, including leisure. Whereas boys might ask: "What do I like to do?", girls might be more interested in "What are my friends doing?" While boys might ask, "What am I good at?", girls might speculate "Do I belong?" Girls also may wonder about developing a sense of self within the context of relationships, balancing one's needs with others, and living with the consequences of challenging (or not challenging) traditional gender roles.

The purpose of this chapter is to describe some of the issues salient for understanding the development of adolescent girls and to suggest ways that youth workers facilitating recreation programs can address some of the common needs of young women. These issues include social contradictions, body image, food issues, friendships and relational aggression, health education and sexuality, physical activity expression, and violence in the culture.

Social Contradictions

Although girls and women in North American societies generally have been given "permission" to choose any career they want or pursue any leisure interests they wish, the reality is that many of these career and leisure opportunities also have related consequences and contradictions. For example

- Girls who are intelligent may also be perceived as frigid.
- Girls perceived as nurturing may also perceived as having no needs.
- Girls perceived as strong might be equated to being masculine.
- Girls who are assertive might be considered overbearing or aggressive.

In addition, a girl who proclaims that she is a feminist may be portrayed as a "femi-nazi."

These contradictions in girls' lives can make identity development problematic. Girls receive mixed messages about whether or not it is okay to equal or outperform males in school, on the playing field, or at home. The male model is still held as the "norm" for behavior and the degree to which girls' behavior is consistent or inconsistent with that norm may be an issue for identity development.

One's gender, as a psychological and cultural term, signifies different meanings depending on whether one is female or male in our society. Despite the positive influence of the feminist movement, the female gender is still associated with a certain set of expectations. For example, between the ages of 8 and 11, girls tend to be androgynous (American Psychological Association, 1996). However, as girls cross into adolescence, they often are pressured to conform to more rigid conceptions of how women are supposed to behave. This pressure may cause psychological stress for girls. In fact, while both girls and boys show a drop in self-esteem after elementary school, the change is more dramatic for girls than for boys (Pipher, 1994).

Many girls are also socialized to believe that a conflict exists between being feminine and being successful. Sensitivity to failure can also limit girls' willingness to take risks for higher rewards. At the same time, some girls do resist negative cultural messages and liberate themselves from stereotypes that hinder their development. One of the great challenges in working with girls is to help them to understand how to resist the pervasive cultural messages that can impede or damage their development.

Some of the contradictions girls experience are due to the influence of the media, such as TV, CDs, tapes, radio, newspapers, magazines, and online interactions (e.g., the Internet, instant messaging). When girls are online they are most likely sending or receiving e-mail or looking for dieting, health, and fitness information (Girls Inc., 2003). When girls watch television they will most likely see messages that have inflated the perception of violence in the world, which in turn creates a perception that the world is dangerous no matter what actions one undertakes to protect oneself. Additionally, the magazines that young women read are predominated by messages about body appearance (such as diet, exercise, beauty enhancements) and advice (including cosmetic surgery and "how to attract a boyfriend"). Then many times these magazines present conflicting messages to girls, such as an article about the need to lose weight next to a cookie recipe.

Music videos give messages about body image and some popular music has lyrics that are degrading to girls and women. For example, one of the top hits on the R&B/hip-hop charts in 2003 had the following lyrics:

> . . . Most girls lookin' right some lookin' a mess. That's why they spilling drinks all over ya dress. But Louis Vuitton bras all over your breasts. Got me wanting to put hickies all over ya chest-ahh..." (Ludacris, 2003)

Advertisements of all kinds send messages that the most important thing in life for girls is their clothing, bodies, and beauty. Together media messages, along with negative perceptions girls may develop about their rights in society, can create contradictory ideas about what it means to be a physically and emotionally healthy woman. Unfortunately, many girls are unaware of the barrage of explicit and implicit messages they receive each day telling them what they ought to be and how they ought to behave.

Technically the world of work is wide open to girls. Many girls, including girls of color, are going to college and subsequently securing good jobs. However, although progress in equal rights has broadened the vocational choices available to girls, many employed women are still concentrated in lower paying professional jobs (e.g., teaching) while men predominate in the highest paying professions. Even in careers traditionally dominated by men, such as medicine and law, gender segregation occurs with women being predominant in lower paying areas of practice (e.g., family medicine, public defenders).

A backlash against women and other nondominant groups continues to exist even though many positive changes have occurred for young women growing up in the 21st century. Contradictions can be found in everyone's life, but young people may not understand how the inconsistencies in messages, access, and opportunities influence their behavior. The social contradictions that permeate girls' lives cannot be ignored as we examine how recreation and leisure opportunities may lead to the healthy development of young women.

Body Image

Adolescence is marked by the development of secondary sex characteristics for both boys and girls. The development of breasts and the onset of menstruation are obvious physical signs of maturity for girls. The female body is portrayed in numerous ways in society. Girls receive strong messages from the mass media and popular culture that certain types of physical appearance are desirable and efforts should be made to conform to this "normal" image (Frederick, Havitz & Shaw, 1994). Unfortunately, acceptance of media messages about physical appearance is often negatively related to feelings about the self (Polce-Lynch, 2001). The development of the female body may generate status for some girls, but also may be a source of negative consequences regarding their behavior.

In addition to body image, skin color can also make a difference. Ethnicity may impact a sense of belonging in a world that often determines inclusion and exclusion on the basis of skin color (American Psychological Association, 1996).

Bordo (2003) described the postmodern female body as fed on fantasies of rearranging, transforming, and correcting with limitless potential for improvement and change. Girls are pressured in many ways to alter their bodies, which can result in adopting a false self or a self inconsistent with how a girl truly wants to lead her life. Many young women and men have body tattoos and unusual piercings. Billions of dollars are spent on cosmetics and TV reality shows reinforce the idea that an ugly duckling can be turned into a swan. According to Bordo, in 2001 over 8.5 million plastic surgery procedures were performed. Adults who take steps to transform their bodies send important messages to girls about how bodies can (and should) be changed.

Attention to attractiveness through grooming, reading fashion and teen magazines, and shopping often serves as a source of leisure for adolescent girls but also can generate stress and feelings of inadequacy (Henderson, Bialeschki, Shaw & Freysinger, 1996). James (2001) found that the reason Australian girls spent as much time as they did in their bedrooms was what she called "situational body images" (p. 82). Some girls used their bedrooms as a place they could be themselves or for physical recreation since it was a place where they did not experience ridicule for the way their bodies looked.

The challenges that girls face about body image are related to other concerns, including the choice of food and the type and amount of physical activity. The social standard of beauty, the images projected by Barbie dolls, the value placed on being thin (in a country where obesity is currently epidemic), and understandings of where girls can feel safe in their bodies can influence the recreation opportunities that girls choose and undertake.

Food Issues

Food is the sustenance of life and reflects the cultures in which we live. Eating disorders in girls often reflect the image of thinness projected by the fashion, advertising, and media industries (Henderson, Bialeschki, Shaw & Freysinger, 1996). Articles and advertisements in popular magazines read by girls seem to encourage the perception that female happiness and success are tied to physical appearance. Girls who are not attempting to lose weight seem to be in the minority in our culture. In fact, more than one in four girls have used diet pills (Girls Inc., 2003).

Being obese and overweight is caused by taking in more calories than are expended in daily living. Therefore, sedentary lifestyles and a lack of physical activity exacerbates diet-associated problems. Anorexia and bulimia, which were once thought to be problems of white, middle-income girls, are increasingly becoming issues for Latina and African American girls as well. The meanings of media images for body image and food intake are insidious not only in the United States, but in many other countries as well. For example, prior to 1995, when television was introduced in Fiji, no cases of eating disorders had been reported. Three years later 62% of the girls surveyed were dieting (Bordo, 2003).

The importance of food in girls' lives cannot be overestimated. Eating disorders have implications for choices about recreation and its value. Food is often associated with recreation activities whether it is popcorn at the movies or cookies served at a meeting. The use of food as a part of structured recreation programs may have implications for the quality of girls' leisure experiences. Girls who are "on diets" may not want to be associated with activities where food (usually high calorie food) is being served. Additionally, these same girls may not have the energy to participate in various activities. Therefore, the challenge to youth workers is to recognize the meanings food may hold for girls and how those meanings may influence their activity involvement.

Friendships and Relational Aggression

Close friendships appear to be important for the social and emotional health of all adolescents, but friendships are particularly salient for girls regardless of their ethnicity or sociocultural status. Girls seem to make important distinctions between the types of friends they have and the nature and quality of those friendships (American Psychological Association, 1996). For example, many girls "know" what it means to have "best" friends and place great expectations on how best friends are supposed to interact.

Indeed, all peer relations are central for most girls. While friendships can be a source of strength for adolescent girls, they can also be a source of struggle and confusion. Relationally aggressive behaviors, such as spreading rumors or threatening withdrawal of affiliation, seem to arise as girls try to negotiate their power and resist or comply with traditional gender expectations. The role of attractiveness and popularity also play into the "drama" that emerges in girls' lives as they attempt to understand who they are and whether they do or do not fit. Groups of girls or cliques representing different images, expectations or interests often emerge (e.g., Jocks, Cheerleaders, Brains, Goths, Freaks).

As noted previously, many girls may be more concerned with who is doing something than what the activity is. Therefore, recreation professionals cannot ignore the importance of friendships, and how some friendship groups can be exclusionary. Sometimes girls can be their own worst enemies in terms of how they act toward one another. Recreation settings may supply inclusive places where relational issues can be nurtured as well as mediated.

Health Education and Sexuality

Adolescence is a demanding and challenging time as young people strive to become fully functioning adults. Changing bodies, accompanied by changes in emotions, relationships, and experiences, result in awareness of sexual health and sexuality.

Girls' experiences with puberty occur in a regular sequence, but begin at different ages and proceed at different rates. Girls who mature early may experience distress concerning expectations that may not be congruent with their psychological development, while "late-bloomers" worry about not being attractive to males. Unfortunately, much of the research on female adolescent sexuality has focused on negative risk-taking resulting in disease or pregnancy. Further, a tendency exists to "blame" girls when these issues arise, even though the decisions resulting in negative consequences are usually made by both partners (American Psychological Association, 1996).

Traditional views of sexuality can create contradictions for both girls and boys. Girls, however, frequently experience a range of mixed messages. The idea that boys want sex and girls want relationships is too simplistic a dichotomy. Increased understanding of how girls experience their sexuality may be a way to empower girls to make decisions about their sexual behavior that will have fewer negative consequences. Girls need assistance in making active and safe choices about their sexual behaviors, ought to have the opportunity to develop a sense of entitlement about their pleasures and desires (e.g., sex is about more than just reproduction and relationships), and should be able to negotiate the unequal power typical in male-female relationships (American Psychological Association, 1996). Providing these opportunities is critical to enabling girls to achieve physical, sexual, and emotional health.

It is also important to recognize that adolescence is often understood as entry into compulsory heterosexuality. Lesbian, bisexual, or transgendered girls may face particular challenges, especially when they have little support or few role models. Leisure opportunities, especially programs aimed at gay and lesbian youth, may provide an important place for young people to examine their identity as a sexual human being (see Chapter 20).

Sexuality, particularly for girls and women, has not been an easy topic to address for parents, schools, or communities. For example, most of the policymaking actions related to adolescent girls have dealt with sexual behavior issues, such as preventing teen pregnancy, promoting sexual abstinence, limiting autonomy in making reproductive health decisions, and providing sexuality education, which primarily focuses on sex information and in some cases contraception. However, reviews of research have shown that adolescents are not affected positively or negatively by their participation in sex education (American Psychological Association, 1996). Indeed, many adolescents are curious and misinformed about sex and want to know more about how it is a normal part of life rather than something to fear and avoid. For example, some young people believe that only sexual intercourse is defined as sex and activities such as oral sex do not count, even though sexually transmitted diseases can result. On the positive side, it appears that a greater use of contraceptives has lowered the teenage pregnancy rate (Girls Inc., 2003).

Although sexuality education is not necessarily the purpose of most recreation programs, recreation professionals can provide support to help girls understand a range of knowledge and behaviors. Recreation programs for teens can help girls understand how to express their sexuality and to maintain their health through structured social activities.

Physical Recreation Expression

Sports have traditionally been associated more with men and boys than women and girls. Therefore, girls interested in sports may face barriers such as lack of skill or being channeled into "feminine" activities. Additionally, some girls thrive at being able to excel at sports while other girls may not be comfortable in competitive programs. Sports, exercise, and other physical recreation activities emphasizing fun, health, and social involvement, regardless of the level of skill, seem to be especially important for girls.

Statistics concerning the involvement of girls in sports are encouraging. In 1971, before the passage of Title IX (the federal law that prohibits sex discrimination in educational institutions receiving federal funds), only 7% of high school athletes were women. In 2001, this percentage had increased to 42% (National Coalition for Women and Girls in Education, 2002). In a study conducted by the Centers for Disease Control and Prevention (2002), 57% of the young women in Grades 9 through 12 said they engaged in vigorous activity (e.g., sweating, breathing hard) for 20 or more minutes, three times a week. Unfortunately, White girls were more likely than Hispanic and Black girls to report involvement in vigorous activity.

Several years ago, a Nike commercial provided a list of benefits that can occur for girls if we "let them play." Indeed, research has shown that girls who are athletes are less likely to smoke or consume alcohol and more likely to have a positive body image (Miller, Sabo, Melnick, Farrell & Barnes, 2000). Further, female athletes are less likely to get pregnant and more likely to use birth control than nonathletes (Girls Inc., 2003). Physical activity for girls and women also results in lower instances of cardiovascular disease, adult onset diabetes, and some forms of cancer (U.S. Department of Health and Human Services, 1996).

However, involvement in physical activity can also have other positive outcomes, such as stress reduction, amelioration of mid-to-moderate depression, enhancement of psychological well-being, and encouragement of prosocial behaviors. In fact, girls generally know that physical activity is good for them. However, as is true with women in our society, attitudes and behaviors do not necessarily equate (Henderson & Ainsworth, 2000).

Many girls do not participate in sports and vigorous physical activity as they enter into middle adolescence (Smale & Shaw, 1994). Constraints to participation include lack of time, money, and/or resources; disinterest; and concerns about safety. In addition to being highly influenced by their friends, girls are also influenced by what they perceive that boys value. Hultsman (1993) found that constraints to leisure for girls included lack of opportunities, activities offered at the wrong time of day, and location of activities. Involvement in physical activity can also be related to what other people in girls' lives are doing and thinking (James, 2000).

A new generation of female athletes offers hope for changing the image of women involved in sports. For example, when girls see images such as Mia Hamm (soccer) or Serena Williams (tennis), they see that being strong and respected does not mean having to be ultra thin. In the past 30 years, girls and women have had access to more opportunities to be involved in sports. However, recreation professionals must be careful not to assume that opportunities for women have achieved optimum levels. For girls, it is particularly important that there should be multiple levels of physical activity expression, with elite athletic participation being only one aspect.

Violence in the Culture

Violence in American culture has become commonplace and may range from verbal violence, such as sexual harassment, to physical violence, including death. For many young people, and for girls in particular, violence in schools may also be commonplace. Sexual harassment is common and lesbian, gay, bisexual, and transgendered youth report a wide range of verbal and physical threats. Unfortunately, bullying done by girls to other girls also occurs. James (2001) found that one of the reasons girls considered their bedrooms a safe leisure site included being free from physical harm, sexual assault, or abuse.

Physical violence against girls can occur in the form of rape or sexual abuse. Dating violence has been reported to affect 10% of high school girls and 22% of college women (American Psychological Association, 1996). Date rape often has a low incidence of reporting because many girls do not think this type of assault fits the definition of rape. In addition, girls may be made to feel guilty or responsible for being with the attacker and thus feel powerless. Many girls do not realize the serious consequences of dating violence on their psychological development such as later sexual dysfunction, flashbacks, and other symptoms of posttraumatic stress disorder, not to mention the possibilities of sexually transmitted diseases and pregnancy. However, despite the prevalence of date rape, adolescent girls are much more likely to be raped by friends and family members than by strangers (Bordo, 2003).

Self-inflicted violence is another issue that cannot be overlooked. The incidence of "self-cutting" has risen in recent years. Self-mutilators are often single females who report that they feel extremely tense and anxious before the self-injury and calm afterward (Polce-Lynch, 2001). Depression and major adjustment problems can also result in contemplating suicide or turning to substance abuse as another form of violence.

Adolescent female involvement in gangs is increasing. About 10% of gang membership is female (Girls Inc., 2003). The gender structure might be a female autonomous gang, a female auxiliary for a male gang or a gender-integrated gang. Indeed, most studies have shown that females join gangs to achieve friendship, solidarity, self-affirmation, and a sense of new possibilities—the same reasons why a girl would join a club or a sorority. Being in a female gang may also provide a refuge from physical and sexual abuse at home (Juvenile Justice Bulletin, 2001).

Girls' sense of psychological and physical safety is central to their involvement in any type of activity. In recreation programs, we are generally concerned about the safety of participants when they are actively engaged in programs, yet safety concerns for both girls and boys can include what happens in locker rooms and in going to and from the recreation venue. Violence or abuse can occur in recreation settings unless professionals are conscious of the entire breadth of the recreation experience.

Taken Together

For girls, adolescence is an important time to achieve independence and self-awareness. Because of the way that being female is viewed in our society, girls may have different developmental experiences than boys. Many girls evolve into well-adjusted young women due to the support and opportunities they experience. Some girls, however, face major struggles.

The contradictions in girls' lives offer challenges as well as areas for resistance. Girls who recognize the contradictory or demeaning messages they receive can consciously make decisions to resist negative social messages and to choose positive behaviors. Recreation programs for girls ought to focus on affirming girls' strength and resilience. Focusing on relationships and creating an environment that supports and engages girls, while reinforcing their collective attempts to resist the negative impact of the media and other societal forces, is important in helping girls to find their identities through leisure.

Girls Inc. (2003) has developed a "Girls' Bill of Rights" (see Box) Consideration of the delineated rights are important for recreation professionals to consider when designing and facilitating programs.

Addressing these rights so that girls may remain healthy and become strong women requires the efforts of many institutions, including the family, schools, churches, and recreation and other youth-serving organizations. After all, to fully develop, all youth need a cadre of active and involved adults who can provide guidelines, expectations, and boundaries.

Some of the issues impacting the development of adolescent girls may be out of the direct control of individual girls and the adults who work with them. Individuals alone, for example, cannot change the pervasive impact of the media, although a great deal can be done to help girls to challenge the messages they receive. Opportunities that girls have through structured recreation experiences may provide opportunities for them to understand, engage, and change potentially harmful circumstances. Recreation providers can offer relational networks that create social worlds where girls can experience power and meaning. "Schools and communities that engage girls in social critique and in activist experiences appear to be particularly effective, as do adults who demonstrate commitment, respect for youth and a willingness to involve them in making change within their communities" (American Psychological Association, 1996, p. 11).

Girls' Bill of Rights

- Girls have the right to be themselves and to resist gender stereotypes.
- Girls have the right to express themselves with originality and enthusiasm.
- Girls have the right to take (positive) risks, to strive freely, and to take pride in success.
- Girls have the right to accept and appreciate their bodies.
- Girls have the right to have confidence and to be safe in the world.
- Girls have the right to prepare for interesting work and economic independence.

Considerations for Recreation Youth Leaders

Whether working with girls in single-sex or coed groups, professionals must keep in mind some of the issues salient to girls relative to the contradictions in society, including body and food issues, friendships and relationships, sexuality, the role of physical activity, and violence. Some of these issues may be addressed with programming, while dealing with others requires changes in leadership or facility design and maintenance. In most cases, girls can provide input to facilitate their recreation experiences if they are given the opportunity. Changing society is a monumental task but small changes in recreation programs can have positive long-range benefits.

One option to consider is to offer all-girl recreation programs. Some adolescent girls prefer only mixed groups but some do not want all of their activity experiences to be with boys. An all-girl environment may provide opportunities for fun and being with friends in activities without girls having to worry about boys looking at them either as attraction objects or subjecting them to harassment. Girls working together may also find that it is okay to make mistakes and that they can learn to depend on other females (On the Move, 2003). Despite some of the advantages of same sex groups, girls should be given options to decide about the gender makeup of their recreation programs in which they participate.

Following are some basic issues to consider when programming for girls. These provide some guidance when developing all-girl or mixed-sex programs.

Leadership Matters

Providing appropriate leadership is important. The gender of program leaders needs to be consistent with the goals and expected outcomes of the program.

For example, male leadership provides opportunities for girls to have healthy, respectful relationships with men. Male leaders can model a range of gender roles that can be an example for girls as well as for boys. Recreation opportunities can also provide a positive, safe experience where girls can learn that they are valued by men for their competency rather than their bodies.

On the other hand, female leaders can be role models for girls and may relate to important aspects of girls' lives better because these women leaders have had some of the same experiences. Mixed staff probably offer the greatest potential for girls' development since this gives girls choices regarding whom they want to trust or leader gender choices depending on the circumstances. It is essential, however, that all leaders understand the ways that girls' needs are both similar to boys' needs and/or unique to girls.

Do Not Perpetuate Discrimination

It also is important for staff to understand that even though they have never experienced discrimination or treated girls inequitably does not mean that these issues are not present in the lives of program participants. Phrases like "boys will be boys" and "throwing like a girl" should be eliminated from the leader's vocabulary and biases.

The use of inclusive language, including nonsexist and nonracist references, is critical to affirming the lives of girls. All youth serving organizations should have policies about sexual harassment related to the workplace, conduct that occurs among youth in the gym or at the recreation center, and how leaders are to deal with boy-to-girl or girl-to-girl harassment.

Competition in Its Place

Although competition can be a great motivator, recreation leaders need to recognize that competition should be downplayed in some activities, especially for some girls. Leaders must focus on how they can empower girls by teaching decision-making skills as well as nonstereotyped roles.

Know the Salient Issues

Understanding physical and mental health issues faced by girls is also important. Safe and healthy physical and emotional boundaries must be clear when interacting with girls. Being an advisor and a resource rather than an authority figure is also useful.

Sexuality and sexual issues are present in all activities that are undertaken. Staff can help girls deal with these issues and also provide contacts for organizations and institutions that can render assistance.

Helping girls feel good about their body image is essential. Although girls are aware that beauty comes in different sizes, shapes, colors, and abilities, in today's society, this concept is hard to accept. If girls can focus on health, flexibility, and strength, they may be able to make sense of the beauty clichés. Praising girls for their skills and efforts should predominate over praising them for their appearance.

Relationships and Emotions Matter

The focus that girls place on relationships must be respected in any kind of recreation programming. Singing, dancing, and journaling may be important ways for some girls to emote feelings. Recreation facilitators need to be comfortable with the emotional expression and conversations that girls exhibit. Affirming girls' feelings and encouraging them to channel their anger, enthusiasm, or frustration into positive actions should be encouraged. Girls need to be given the opportunity to speak up and speak out. Recreation staff cannot assume they know what individuals are thinking or feeling without getting input from them.

Promote Self-Efficacy

Staff, especially males, need to avoid "rescuing" girls. Girls need to know that it is okay to get dirty or get sweaty and that making mistakes is not harmful when they learn from them. Helping girls learn to say "I'll try" rather than "I can't" may be essential to their development.

Pay Attention to Details

Little things, such as the way that food is used in relation to recreation activities, may be important in working with girls. Food should be emphasized as fuel, with healthy foods provided and efforts made to encourage positive eating habits. In addition, recreation staff should monitor girls to see if there are signs of eating problems, such as food deprivation or eating too much.

Promote Healthy Living

Youth workers must be able to deal with the stress adolescents feel in the process of navigating pathways to adulthood. Many girls are aware of the level of stress in their lives and willingly admit that they need to find ways to deal with it. On the other hand, some girls may lack positive means for dealing with stress and may turn to tobacco, alcohol, or other negative behaviors as ways of handling it. Youth workers should encourage healthier ways to deal with stress, such as involvement in exercise and artistic endeavors, punching a pillow, or quiet relaxation. Staff can provide the resources for helping girls find creative outlets for their stress through the provision of a wide range of recreation opportunities.

Develop Cultural Literacy

Cultural literacy is another area that should be addressed in recreation programs. Talking to girls about media images of girls and women and the messages and contradictions these illicit could be valuable. An understanding of one's culture can be a means for empowerment. Girls should be encouraged to tell one another both their success stories and their struggles. They can also be shown how understanding what it means to be female in our society could foster a sense of solidarity and compassion for the female experience. Encouraging girls to respect one another and establishing symbols or rituals to affirm their sisterhood and togetherness can also be useful. In mixed-sex groups, girls need to learn how to sustain their leadership without deferring to boys. Because boys often demand and get more attention and because many girls are socialized to be pleasing to others, girls are sometimes unaware how they acquiesce in the presence of males.

Empower Girls

Some recreation programs seem to be successful at empowering girls. For example, On the Move, a national female-only program sponsored by the Canadian Association for the Advancement of Women in Sport, provides positive recreation experiences for nonactive girls. The top 10 success factors that have been identified for this program include the following (On the Move, 2003):

1. The program is fun.
2. There is a mix of physical and social activities.
3. Participants have input into program design.

4. There are opportunities for girl-only activities.
5. A safe and supportive environment is provided.
6. Peer age groupings are provided.
7. There are opportunities for basic skill development.
8. A role model leader is available.
9. Food is provided.
10. Participants have a choice of clothing and music.

Staff working with On the Move recognize that traditional activity programs for girls typically involve high costs and extensive time commitments and appeal to only a small number of girls. This organization focuses on issues such as income level, family commitments, and safety concerns in introducing girls and women to a wide variety of individual and team as well as traditional and nontraditional activities.

Summary and Concluding Remarks

This chapter has provided some background information to help you to understand how girls differ from boys developmentally, as well as guidance to facilitate appropriate recreation programming to meet girls' needs. The challenge in providing environments where girls can grow and develop is evident. A variety of recreation programs facilitated by staff who are aware of the issues that girls face as they grow up can help develop strong and resilient girls who become mature and confident women. Recreation contexts, both formal and informal, can provide an excellent place for girls to understand who they are as females, and who they are as females in a male world.

References

American Psychological Association. (1996). *A new look at adolescent girls: Strengths and stresses*. Retrieved on October 26, 2003, from http://www.apa.org/pi/cyf/adolesgirls.html

Bordo. S. (2003, December 19). The empire of images in our world of bodies. *Chronicle of Higher Education*, B6–B9.

Centers for Disease Control and Prevention. (2002, June 28). Youth and behavior surveillance—United States, 2001. *Morbidity and Morbidity Weekly Report, 51* (SS-4). Retrieved from http://www.cdc.gov/mmwr/pdf/ss/ss5104.pdf

Fine, C. (2001). *Strong, smart, and bold: Empowering girls for life*. New York, NY: HarperCollins.

Frederick, C. J., Havitz, M. E., and Shaw, S. M. (1994). Social comparison in aerobics exercise classes: Propositions for analyzing motives and participation. *Leisure Sciences, 16*, 161–176.

Gilligan, C. (1982). *In a different voice*. Cambridge, MA: Harvard University Press.

Girls Inc. (2003). *Girls and sports*. Retrieved December 8, 2003, from http://www.girls-inc.org

Henderson, K. A. and Ainsworth, B. E. (2000). The connections between social support and women's physical activity involvement: The cultural activity participation study. *Women in Sport and Physical Activity Journal, 9*(2), 27–53.

Henderson, K. A., Bialeschki, M. D., Shaw, S. M., and Freysinger, V. J. (1996). *Both gains and gaps*. State College, PA: Venture Publishing, Inc.

Hultsman, W. (1993). The influence of others as a barrier to recreation participation among early adolescents. *Journal of Leisure Research, 25*, 150–164.

James, K. (2000). "You can *feel* them looking at you:" The experiences of adolescent girls at swimming pools. *Journal of Leisure Research, 32*, 262–280.

James, K. (2001). "I just gotta have my own space!" The bedroom as a leisure site for adolescent girls. *Journal of Leisure Research, 33*, 71–90.

Juvenile Justice Bulletin. (March, 2001). *Taking female gangs seriously: Areas for further research*. Retrieved November 26, 2003, from http://www.ncjrs.org

Ludacris. (2003). Stand up. On *Chicken 'n beer* [CD]. New York, NY: Def Jam South.

Miller, K. E., Sabo, D. F., Melnick, M. J., Farrell, M. P., and Barnes, G. M. (2000). *The Women's Sports Foundation report: Health risks and the teen athlete*. East Meadow, NY: Women's Sports Foundation.

National Coalition for Women and Girls in Education. (2002). *Title IX at 30: Report card on gender equity*. Washington, DC: Author.

On the Move. (2003). *What girls want*. Retrieved December 11, 2003, from http://www.caaws.ca/onthemove/e/index.htm

Pipher, M. (1994). *Reviving Ophelia: Saving the selves of adolescent girls*. New York, NY: Ballantine.

Polce-Lynch, M. (2001). Adolescent self-esteem and gender: Exploring relations to sexual harassment, body image, media influences, and emotional expression. *Journal of Youth and Adolescence, 30*(2), 225–244.

Smale, B. J. A. and Shaw, S. M. (1994). *Teenage drop-outs: Explaining the decline in physical activity and participation during adolescence*. Paper presented at the 10th Commonwealth and International Scientific Congress, Victoria, British Columbia, Canada.

U.S. Department of Health and Human Services. (1996). *Physical activity and health: A report of the Surgeon General*. Atlanta, GA: Centers for Disease Control and Prevention, National Center for Chronic Disease Prevention and Health Promotion.

Chapter 19

What About the Boys?

Megan Kelly Cronan and Peter A. Witt

In today's society, males are often thought of as the "norm." As a result, much of the recent attention and literature on gender has focused on the problems that women face living in a male-dominated culture. While this focus has been useful, it means that we often think that because society is centered on men and manhood, boys grow up without significant challenges. This chapter discusses some of the opportunities and barriers that boys experience in their quest to successfully navigate adolescence, and then outlines some of the steps that might be taken to help boys deal with these issues.

The needs, values, attitudes, and behaviors of males have been considered the standard by which the actions of women are judged. For example, despite a rule to the contrary from the American Psychological Association writing standards (2001), people often write or say "he," when referring to both sexes. Additionally, accounts of history mostly explore the actions of men, and until recently, most social science research has been done on males, thus rendering the body of knowledge one-sided. Given this societal norm, most media and literary attention on gender-related challenges have been focused on the experiences of women and girls (i.e., the "other" to the male "norm") and the issues that they face while trying to live in a male-dominated world. However, this recent attention to and focus on girls and women to make up for past wrongs has left the needs of boys and men relatively invisible. Therefore, an explanation for this seemingly contradictory statement is needed.

To do this, one must understand that keeping the majority of societal and cultural attention on men and boys in some ways ignores their issues and needs, just as it ignores the issues and needs of females. That is, when research was done on males, it was meant to represent all people in all situations—an impossible task. Therefore, along with the inherent unfairness of that practice, what it also meant was that the unique needs of neither males nor females were addressed. Men represented us all, but in doing so, neither male nor female differences were understood or valued. Of course, men have held the power and prestige in society for so long that the effects of this practice were much less problematic for boys than for girls. (See Chapter 18 for a discussion on recreation and girls.)

Nevertheless, and given the preceding discussion, the circumstances of boys should be considered for several reasons. For example, with the increasing interest in the lives and circumstances of women comes a challenge to the male norm. Although our culture seems to place men in dominant positions in families, government, and business, we often fail to ask if the resulting societal expectations for men exact emotional consequences or restrictions on them. While on the surface it may appear that men have more choices than women, the roles they are expected to fill also restrict their lives in important ways. Indeed many of these issues faced by men can be traced to their childhood years, and relate to how young boys are raised and what is expected of them.

The Boy Code

Like their female counterparts, young males often lack the resources they need to grow into healthy, fully functioning adults. Also like females, societal attitudes and standards may force boys to adopt behaviors that do not represent their authentic selves. For example, society often controls the growth and development of young men through strictly prescribed gender roles, overdramatized male stereotypes, and rules about expected male behavior. William Pollack, the author of *Real Boys* (1998), attributes this control to a "gender straightjacket" imposed by what he calls the Boy Code. The Boy Code is a set of rules and expectations that stem mainly from traditional gender stereotypes, and encompasses several "rules" about how boys should behave and interact with their surroundings and with other people. The Boy Code states the following:

- Boys should not show emotion.
- Violence is an acceptable response to emotional upset.
- Power is important and self-esteem relies on having power.
- It is important for boys to reject "feminine" qualities and to maintain a masculine image.

The Boy Code is learned on playgrounds and in schoolrooms, camps, religious organizations, and other places that boys hangout. Peers, coaches, teachers, and even parents reinforce the code. From these adults, young boys learn that they must "Keep a stiff upper lip, not show their feelings, act real tough, not act too nice, be cool, [and] just laugh and brush it off when someone punches you" (Pollack, 1998, p. 97). According to Pollack, the Boy Code is first imposed by society but then is perpetuated by parents, peers, and friends as the accepted "way" to be male. For example, the gendering of sports (e.g., football is for boys, dance is for girls) and even the use of sayings such as "boys will be boys" all work to impose controls on the ways in which young boys view and interact with the world.

What are some consequences of the Boy Code for the well-being of boys? While we might think of boys as benefiting from their superior status, the Boy Code imposes a heavy burden for many young men. For example, despite common assumptions to the contrary, one study has shown that boys do not generally have higher levels of self-esteem than girls (Foon, 1989). The similarities in self-esteem levels for young boys and girls may be due to the fact that boys, like their female counterparts, are given conflicting messages about how to behave and express themselves in society. For example, boys are expected to be both tough (especially in sports and with each other) and compassionate (especially with women and children). These experiences of being pulled in different directions create internal conflicts in young men and may lead to creating barriers to their full positive development and formations of healthy self-esteem levels. In other words, it may be difficult for male adolescents to feel good about who they are and what they do if they are not sure if they are doing the right and accepted thing.

The feminist movement has recognized this dilemma for young girls and has made strong inroads toward identifying and dealing with some of the societal messages faced by girls. For example, Mary Pipher, in her 1994 book *Reviving Ophelia*, identifies some of the powerful messages and issues that girls must deal with and overcome to successfully navigate their adolescent years, some of which you have read about in Chapter 18. Yet the same concern and attention to developmental issues have not been as widely extended to boys.

Boy Culture

The Boy Code is connected to and reflective of a *boy culture*, where peer groups reinforce many aspects of the code, often with unfortunate results. Often ridicule and competition serve as major forms of "code reinforcement." Some have even suggested that few codes are more rigid than the standards of acceptable behavior that males impose on one another (Muuss & Porton, 1999). For example, boys are often reprimanded when they stray too far from the expected male ideal, when they do not overtly display their sexuality ("Why don't you have a girlfriend?"), or display the wrong type of sexuality ("You don't like boys, do you?"). In these cases, they are warned not to "be such wimps" (Browne & Fletcher, 1995).

Violence in the form of initiation rites (Rotundo, 1993), bullying, threats, fights, and violent or physical sports and games may also be used to uphold the Boy Code. Inflicting pain on one another (Rotundo 1993) or encouraging and fostering violence allows boys to prove their manliness to one another. In fact, boys may be encouraged to engage in risky behavior and even to hurt themselves to validate their masculinity to others (Browne & Fletcher 1995).

The result of this enforced violence is that males are often viewed by society as aggressive (Muuss & Porton, 1999) or even dangerous to others (Browne & Fletcher, 1995). These problems in perception are further compounded by the fact that boys spend much of their time with their peers engaged in "boy's culture," so much so that they are involved with their peers even more than are their female counterparts (Muuss & Porton, 1999).

"Becoming Male"

Boys spend a lot of time together during their adolescent years. Adolescence itself is a time of transition as young people leave childhood and begin their journey toward adulthood. While girls in our society gradually "become" women through natural processes of physical and emotional changes, boys are expected to quickly become men and so they must "earn" their manhood through concrete, identifiable behaviors. For example, movies and popular literature portray sexual intercourse, a successful deer hunt, or a well-fought fight as some of the socially acceptable ways in which a boy may earn his passage into manhood. The expectation that maleness and manhood be earned adds emotional stress to the process of identity development and further enforces the Boy Code. As long as these expectations exist, and more specifically as long as only certain rigid ways exist for boys to earn their manhood or be successful males, male adolescents will have a difficult time finding their own unique and healthy pathways to manhood.

Violence, Masculinity, and Competitive Sports

In many aspects of male life, competition, winning, and toughness are emphasized and valued. For many boys, a major pathway to success is through sports and other competitive involvements. Many young boys' lives are organized around athletic activities: they go to sports practices; read sports magazines; talk about scores, coaches, and players; and emulate their sports heroes. Much of this is fun and contributes to healthy development. However, problems arise when media that is directed at young boys (e.g., young men's sports magazines) stresses the need to compete and win and presents boys with role models who are hypermasculine, sometimes involved in illegal activities, and often exceedingly wealthy (Drummond, 2001). These media outlets, as well as society itself, enforce the societal message that being ultra-masculine, tough, impenetrable and exceedingly strong is the only acceptable form of "maleness." Pollack finds in *Real Boys* (1998) that "We hold up a mirror to our boys that reflects back a distorted and outmoded image of the ideal boy—an image that our boys feel under great pressure to emulate" (p. 103). One of the ways that boys seek to emulate the "right" image is through competition in sports.

Competitive sports have been likened to the peacetime equivalent of war (Rotundo, 1993). Consider some of the terminology used in sports: "battle in the trenches," "We're gonna kill 'em," "fighting for the ball" and the ways these terms are conducive to a war-like atmosphere. What sort of message are we sending to our young men when we tell them that their leisure time should be full of violence and should simulate war?

Less active forms of male leisure may also embrace violence. Video games, for example, are one of the modes through which boys learn about the need to be prepared for violence as well as gain knowledge about how to engage in strong physical acts. While some controversy exists regarding just how influential video games are in young people's lives, it appears that boys in particular are both drawn to these violent games and often learn and imitate the violent scenarios portrayed in the games (Anderson & Gill, 2000). Although we do not know for sure or to what extent young boys act out this violence in real situations, we do know they are nonetheless attracted to these types of games. Therefore, we are compelled to understand the factors that have molded boys such that they find violence so captivating and necessary.

Interestingly, in other ways, the violent and tough images presented in video games often conflict with the rules that society sets for young people. For example, in our schools we teach young children that they need to sit still, be quiet and polite, and listen to authority figures. Compare that message with the messages available in the media (e.g., those messages promoting violence as a natural behavior) and you can see the conflicting messages a young man faces. In one instance they are to be active, tough, and capable of violence, but in the other instance they are to remain submissive, quiet, and polite. In fact, the Boy Code itself may stem from societal fears regarding the right way to educate boys to lead the appropriate masculine life.

"Feminized" Boys and Gender Role Development

One of the reasons that the Boy Code may exist is in response to the societal fear that female caretakers have *feminized* boys (Rotundo, 1993), meaning that boys are in danger of taking on female roles and behaviors and showing female emotions because of the prevalence of female and not male caretakers. This fear of feminization was one of the reasons for the founding of the Boys Scouts, the YMCA, and other young men's groups in the late 19th and early 20th centuries (see Chapter 2). The founders and leaders of these organizations all sought to enhance and reinforce the gender roles which society deemed important.

Gender roles become obvious in children by the time they reach the 6th grade (Malcolm & Mobily, 1990). As children progress through high school, adults and other children help to further establish firm gender roles through the use of ridicule (or affirmation of correct gender role behavior), behavior modeling (e.g., showing children how to behave according to societal standards for their gender), and peer acceptance of children who follow the "rules" (Muuss & Porton, 1999).

Gender roles extend beyond the classroom as adolescents engage and are interested in activities characterized by their sex-stereotyped nature (Garton & Pratt, 1987). Thus, male adolescents are more likely to engage in stereotypical "male" activities, such as roughhousing, and female adolescents are more likely to engage in "female" activities, such as quietly drawing or talking in small groups. These gender role stereotypes also extend into sports.

Sex-Stereotyped Sports

Sports with a lot of on-field or on-court violence and heavy body contact are often thought of as sex-appropriate for males, while sports that emphasize flexibility and de-emphasize strength are commonly considered more feminine and therefore sex-inappropriate for males. These are constraining labels, although they are very commonly employed and reinforced. Peer groups play a significant role in encouraging these sex-stereotyped behaviors. After all, students who participate in sex-appropriate sports have higher social status among their peers than students who participate in sex-inappropriate sports (Holland & Andre, 1994). Thus, if a young boy is in ballet class, he is likely to be less popular with his classmates than if he participated in football. A question to ask then becomes: What are we teaching young boys about their developing masculinity when we encourage them to participate in certain types of sports with certain qualities and discourage them from participating in other types of sports? (Drummond, 2001).

Although a boy's classmates and parents may reinforce his participation in sex-appropriate sports, *only* participating in so-called sex-appropriate sports may not be the healthiest option for a boy. One study has shown that male adolescents who participate in *both* sex-appropriate and sex-inappropriate sports have been found to have significantly higher self-esteem levels than boys who do not participate in sports at all (Holland & Andre, 1994). Moreover, contemporary research is finding that androgynous (i.e., having the ability to act adaptively in any situation regardless of gender constraints) persons are often the healthiest and most well-adjusted (Pipher, 1994).

Male Sport Choice

Males are significantly more likely to engage in sports, sports teams, and sports-related activities than their female peers (Foon, 1989). However, because of pressures to "earn" their masculinity, boys often do not have a true choice about which sports they participate in. The sex-appropriateness of sports, as discussed previously, as well as other pressures often influences boys' choices of activities.

More than mere athletic participation, competitive sports specifically provide an arena for boys to test their emerging manliness and for adults to review their progress. Being successful in sports translates into being successful in manhood (Muuss & Porton, 1999). For many boys, sports serve as a tool for fostering "moral force" and building character (Rotundo, 1993). In addition, sports that encourage the Boy Code also encourage boys to remain reserved, detached, and hardened (Pollack, 1998).

One might question whether the competitive aspects of athletics simply enforces many of the negative aspects of the Boy Code. In these instances, young men are encouraged to show unchecked aggression and even to hurt one another in the name of winning. Sportsmanship is often abandoned and simple courtesies such as helping a fallen player to his feet are seen as a sign of weakness. This type of involvement in sports rarely helps to build character (Pollack, 1998) and may even serve to enforce the more negative aspects of male socialization. However, since boys typically seek out competitive sports as a way to confirm or earn manhood, they are thought of as simply competitive by nature (Muuss & Porton, 1999), with competitiveness seen as a male virtue (Rotundo, 1993).

Often, success or failure in sports will have a significant impact on a boy's passage into manhood or acceptance by the "boy's culture" (Drummond,

2001). Participation in sports, especially in competitive situations, may create pressure, performance anxiety, tension, and confusion for boys (Browne & Fletcher, 1995). These negative impacts may be exacerbated by coaches, parents, or other boys who have little or no tolerance for mistakes (Browne & Fletcher, 1995). In fact, the pressures may be so great that if boys are unsuccessful in sports (e.g., they do not win or perform at a high level) or feel that their bodies, abilities, or personalities may prevent their success, they might not participate in sports at all (Drummond, 2001). According to the Boy Code, failure in sports may develop into failure as men.

Nonparticipation, however, also may be socially dangerous for young boys. After all, being an athlete usually translates into popularity among a young man's male peers (Thirer & Wright 1985) and with members of the opposite sex. For example, a recent study showed that being an athlete was the number one trait that adolescent females found desirable in adolescent males (Thirer & Wright, 1985).

Of course, boys are not oblivious to these social pressures. One study showed 90% of 8th graders indicated they would like their career to be in professional sports (Fisher & County, 1979) despite the evidence that one has a greater chance of being struck by lightning than eventually becoming a professional athlete. As boys grow older, there is no evidence to suggest that this outlook on sports changes. For example, when polling high school males, "athletic star" was chosen as the number one way that males would like to be remembered by their peers after graduation. Females chose "athletic star" last (Holland & Andre, 1994). From this data, it appears that we equate sports and sport success with masculinity.

Male Body Image

Participation in sports, and the peer and societal expectations that accompany that participation, also lead boys to develop certain ideas about the male body and how it should look. Television, magazines, and popular culture all increase a boy's awareness of his body (Drummond, 2001). Anorexia, long thought of as a female disease, is spreading faster among males than females (Muuss & Porton, 1999). Additionally, 5% to 10% of current bulimics are male—a number that includes only diagnosed and reported cases (Muuss & Porton, 1999). Unfortunately, many practitioners and even many men themselves are unaware of the existence of male body image disorders and the ways in which these disorders manifest themselves (Drummond, 2001). No clinical guidelines have been established for diagnosing male body image problems (Drummond, 2001), therefore male rates of body image disorders are conceivably much higher than have been reported.

To further the problem, many boys, even if they are presenting symptoms of an eating disorder, will not seek professional help. Eating disorders are officially labeled as mental illnesses, and our society's ideas about masculinity often disallow men from admitting to any mental or emotional difficulties. Additionally, eating disorders are also unofficially labeled as a girls' problem and not something that would affect men. As a result, research, programs, and community assistance for young males with body image concerns is lacking (Drummond, 2001).

Another obstacle to the diagnosis of male body image disorders is that body image concerns in men may become apparent in quite the same way as they do in women. For example, our society is more accepting of a lean and muscular man than a very thin man or a man with high body fat. Due to these societal ideals, many male body image disorders often manifest themselves during sports. For example, men often use overexercise as a weight loss technique, and the cultural expectation that men are "supposed" to be involved in sports makes what may be "disordered" physical activity seem to be normal and expected male behavior. Ultimately, for men suffering from body image problems, the excessive training involved with some sports and not the competition itself may provide the greater incentive for participation (Drummond, 2001).

However, along with the other contradictory societal messages we have discussed, men are also told that being "bigger" (i.e., more muscular and "ripped") is more masculine. Therefore, the perfect male body must be thin enough to appear strong and able, but not so thin that it appears weak and delicate. This balance is often difficult for men to achieve.

Compounding this problem is the fact that male athletic potential is often measured in muscle mass (Drummond, 2001). In North American society's version of masculinity, the male body must both be large enough to deter physical violence and fit enough to be able to win physical contests should the need arise. Thus, based solely on their body type, men often feel that they can only play certain sports (Fisher & County, 1979). In some situations, boys and men try to alter their bodies via performance enhancing drugs, such as steroids or Creatin. In fact, coaches may even recommend these drugs. Other boys feel pressure to engage in excessive weightlifting, often inappropriate amounts for their age, in a desperate effort to live up to society's expectations for the ideal male body. Drugs and the overuse of weightlifting facilities may intensify feelings of aggression and agitation and exacerbate body image and other problems discussed in earlier sections of this chapter.

So What Does This All Mean?

It is important to consider whether boy's activities, as they are currently constructed, reinforce the Boy Code or help to break it down. Using sports as an example, we have discussed how society exerts a lot of pressure on young men to participate successfully, and that certain types of involvement in sports may prove detrimental to boys. On the other hand, there is some evidence that sports participation for males is positively related to high self-esteem and favorable affiliation with school and family (Foon, 1989). Some types of sports may even offer a break from the Boy Code by allowing young men a "chance for openness, expression, and intimacy" and allowing them to engage in typically discouraging activities, such as expressing feelings, showing emotion, and revealing their need for connections to others (Pollack, 1998). Nevertheless, we must ask ourselves if males have been channeled into participation in certain sports because of society's values and whether males therefore define sport in a somewhat distorted and gendered fashion (Thirer & Wright, 1985). Importantly, males who participate in "sex-inappropriate" sports have reported even higher self-esteem scores than males in "sex-appropriate" sports, even though the sex-appropriate athlete received higher social desirability ratings by peers (Holland & Andre, 1994). This finding should provide youth workers with a rationale for increasing males' access to and feelings of acceptability about traditionally unmasculine sports. We must find solutions that allow boys alternate ways of feeling masculine, whether it is through nongendered sports or through avenues completely unrelated to sport, such as the arts, hobbies, or varied gender roles within the family and school structure.

How Do Youth Workers Help?

Along with increased awareness about the issues boys face today comes an obligation to help them to overcome obstacles and to live happier and less restricted lives. One way to do this is through a broad and conscious change in the way that our culture perceives and interacts with boys (Browne & Fletcher, 1995). Several approaches have been proposed. Many of these solutions must begin in the schools and therefore will require some changing of the basic school structure (Browne & Fletcher, 1995), but refining out-of-school time youth development practices are also called for. Possibilities for change include the following:

- Youth workers and teachers should compliment boys and welcome them into classrooms and activity settings instead of dreading their presence. As a part of this welcoming process, boys need to feel comfortable asking for help and allowing help to be given.

- Youth workers and teachers should encourage boys to pursue subjects traditionally gendered as female (e.g., writing, reading, home economics) and expand the activity settings in which it is okay for boys to participate.
- Schools and communities may want to consider using drama classes and programs as settings for boys to explore gender roles in a comfortable environment.
- Media studies classes, traditionally used to question the media's role in society, may also be used to challenge stereotypes and the ways that society perpetuates them.
- Fathers could be encouraged to become involved in nontraditional roles in schools and community programs (e.g., volunteering as teachers' assistants).
- Teachers may want to discuss sexuality with their classes and mandate a homophobia-free learning environment to promote the acceptance of the many ways of being male. However we approach it, we need to let boys feel comfortable displaying their masculinity and sexuality beyond the ways fostered by the Boy Code. Youth programs may also be appropriate settings for exploring other meanings of sexuality.
- The Boy Code should be used as a starting place for interaction with boys. Youth workers need to understand the pressures boys feel and the expectations of them. Small movements away from the Code should be taken as signs of success. At the same time, understand that there are some biological reasons for boys' behavior that need to be supported.
- Health education classrooms should focus on helping boys understand natural changes to their bodies, such as semenarch (Muuss & Porton, 1999). In specific classes or programs, teachers and other youth workers should provide materials on the importance of avoiding sex-role stereotyping (Abigail, 1984).
- Organizers of recreation programs should be encouraged to emphasize team and noncompetitive activities like ropes courses as well as the traditionally offered sports. Additionally, incorporating programs on power sharing may prove valuable.

- Youth workers need to be able to recognize bullying versus other behaviors (Browne & Fletcher, 1995). A single-sex school approach might allow boys to feel more comfortable in school and would remove the necessity of their competing with girls in certain subjects (Browne & Fletcher) and visa versa. Single-sex programs are already widely available and promoted in community-based youth programs.

Conclusions

North American society has come a long way in recognizing gender stereotypes, unequal gender roles, and unhealthy media pressures. The natural next step is to take this information and apply it to youth development practices, including those we use with boys. To successfully work with boys, we must first increase our own and society's awareness of the pressures and problems that young men face as they follow pathways to adulthood, and then encourage youth workers in educational and youth development agencies to become involved in finding and implementing solutions.

Boys and girls have many similar needs that cut across adolescent development, but they have gender-unique needs as well. It is time for youth workers to recognize crucial differences in needs and to deliberately work toward meeting them for both sexes.

References

Abigail, J. (1984). Girls and physical education. *New Zealand Journal of Health, Physical Education, and Recreation, 17*(1), 1–4.

American Psychological Association. (2001). *Publication manual of the American Psychological Association*. Washington, DC: Author.

Anderson, C. A. and Gill, K. E. (2000). Video games and aggressive thoughts, feelings, and behavior in the laboratory and in life. *Journal of Personality and Social Psychology, 78*(4), 772–790.

Browne, R. and Fletcher, R. (Eds.). (1995). *Boys in schools*. Sydney, Australia: Finch Publishing.

Drummond, M. (2001). Boys' bodies in the context of sport and physical activity: Implications for health. *Journal of Physical Education New Zealand, 34*(1), 53–64.

Fisher, D. and County, H. (1979). To what degree does a father's interest in sport affect the interests of his adolescent son? *Maryland Journal of Health, Physical Education, and Recreation, 30*(3), 4–6.

Foon, A. E. (1989). Sport participation among adolescents: Sex differences and effects on academic achievement, self-esteem, affiliation patterns and locus of control. *Journal of Applied Research in Coaching and Athletics, 4*(3), 157–175.

Garton, A. F. and Pratt, C. (1987). Participation and interest in leisure activities by adolescent schoolchildren. *Journal of Adolescence, 10*(4), 341–351.

Holland, A. and Andre, T. (1994). Athletic participation and the social status of adolescent males and females. *Youth and Society, 25*(3), 388–407.

Malcolm, S. M. and Mobily, K. E. (1990). Gender differences in the meanings of play and work. *Journal of Applied Recreation Research, 15*(3), 179–196.

Muuss, R. E. and Porton, H. D. (Eds.). (1999). *Adolescent behavior and society: A book of readings*. Boston, MA: McGraw-Hill.

Pipher, M. (1994). *Reviving Ophelia: Saving the selves of adolescent girls.* New York, NY: Putnam.

Pollack, W. (1998). *Real boys: Rescuing our sons from the myths of boyhood.* New York, NY: Henry Holt and Company, Inc.

Rotundo, A. (1993). *American manhood: Transformations in masculinity from the revolution to the modern era.* New York, NY: Basic Books.

Thirer, J. and Wright, S. D. (1985). Sport and social status for adolescent males and females. *Sociology of Sport Journal, 2*(2), 164–171.

Chapter 20

Lesbian, Gay, Bisexual, and Transgender Youth

Arnold H. Grossman

Human sexuality is a complex phenomenon that has been examined from a variety of perspectives—from physical, reproductive, psychological, and sociological, to psychiatric, legal, and religious. It has been studied across the human lifespan, beginning with hormonal influences in the womb to sexual activity in the golden years. Clinicians and researchers have inquired into the causes of various patterns of sexuality (e.g., sexually compulsive behaviors) and effective ways to modify these behaviors (e.g., sexual conversion therapy). As well, scientists and educators have investigated ways to make sexuality healthier (e.g., prevention of sexually transmitted diseases) and ways to make it more pleasurable.

The purpose of this chapter is to examine two additional aspects of sexuality: sexual orientation and gender-variant behavior. These topics are often considered taboo, and many professionals have had difficultly discussing and understanding them. Our discussion is limited to youth and focuses on sexual and gender identities and their developmental trajectories. We also focus on the implications of these understandings for creating youth development programs for lesbian, gay, bisexual, and transgender (LGBT) youth.

Definitions

To effectively discuss human sexuality, it is important to understand the meanings of various concepts and terms. It is also important not to use terms indiscriminately because this may result in inaccurately conveying thoughts and meanings, as well as offending and stigmatizing people, or labeling them in ways that they do not define themselves.

To help avoid erroneous terminology, consider the following definitions:

1. *Sexual orientation* is a broad term that describes the *attraction* (i.e., sexual or affectional) of individuals to other individuals. Sexual orientation itself may be further specified as follows:

a. *homosexuality*, when men or women are sexually attracted only to others of the same sex as themselves.

b. *heterosexuality*, when men or women are sexually attracted only to others of the opposite sex.

c. *bisexuality,* when men and women are sexually attracted to others of the same as well as to those of the opposite sex.

Although there is extensive research exploring the causes of sexual orientation, there are no conclusive results regarding the origins of homosexuality, heterosexuality, or bisexuality (Westheimer & Lopater, 2002).

2. *Lesbian* (for women) and *gay* (for men) are the terms preferred by those who are attracted only to members of the same sex. These terms are favored because the word *homosexuality* was previously used to describe same sex attraction as a "mental illness." Although homosexuality was removed from the American Psychiatric Association's list of mental disorders in 1973, the stigma of the word remains.

3. *Sexual identity* and *sexual behavior* describe the ways in which individuals verbally or behaviorally present their sexual orientation. Some people who are attracted to and/or engage in sexual behaviors with others of the same sex or both sexes may openly identify themselves as lesbian, gay, or bisexual. Other individuals, for various reasons (such as avoiding shame, rejection and discrimination), do not assume any of these identities even though they engage in same-sex behaviors. While hiding their same-sex attraction, these individuals choose to *pass* as heterosexual. Other individuals, who do not want to assume a sexual identity limited by a defining label, such as lesbian, gay, or bisexual, decide to identify themselves as *queer.*

4. *Coming out* describes the processes used by lesbian, gay, bisexual, and transgender people to disclose their sexual orientation or gender identity. "Coming out of the closet" (or revealing one's self-discovery) is often an ongoing process that can occur at any stage of life. It is ongoing, as people have to continually identify themselves in situations when they are presumed to be heterosexual.

5. *Passing* is when LGBT people decide not to disclose their sexual orientation or gender identity. Some lesbian, gay, bisexual,

and transgender people find hiding their same-sex attraction or gender identity easier than claiming it; therefore, they continue to present a heterosexual orientation, and gender identities that are consistent with their birth sex and the cultural expectations associated with it.

6. *Gender* stems from an individual's birth sex as female or male and refers to the roles (i.e., *gender role expectations*) that society imposes on people, as a result of their birth sex (i.e., *feminine* or *masculine*). These roles include a stereotypical cluster of psychological traits and social behaviors, such as nurturance and dependence for females and independence and assertiveness for males.

7. *Gender identity* is how people see and describe themselves, for example, as a woman, as a man, or as transgender.

8. When individuals do not fulfill the roles linked to their sexual anatomy and gender, they are considered to be *gender variant.*

9. *Transgender* is an umbrella term that describes individuals who consistently exhibit gender variant behaviors and who live full-time or part-time as other than their birth sex. The groups described by this term include people who describe themselves as follows:

   a. *Transsexuals* are those who are making or have made a transition to living in the gender other than their birth sex, and who commonly identify as trans-women (MtF) or trans-men (FtM). These individuals make this change after discovering that their *core gender identity* is incongruous with their sexual anatomy.

   b. *Cross-dressers* include drag queens, drag kings, and others who derive sexual pleasure from dressing privately or publicly as a member of the other sex.

   c. *Gender benders* or *gender blenders* are those who incorporate the physical and cultural characteristics of both genders in a way that feels comfortable and appropriate to them.

   d. *Gender queer* are people within these groups who do not want to assume any specific label.

10. A *stigma* is anything that discredits individuals and leads to their being assigned a "spoiled identity" (Goffman, 1963).

> Although stigmas have frequently been attached to a physical deformity or to members of a particular class, race, or religion, they may also be attached to the characteristics of LGBT people. One stigma of LGBT people is that they are considered to have underlying moral failings because of genetics or environmental influences in their development (Grossman, 1997a). Stigmatization may lead to homophobic or transphobic behavior in others.

Heteronormativity, Homophobia, and Transphobia

Youth who grow up to realize they are heterosexual and who identify their gender as congruent with their sexual anatomy are *not* required to give any explanations for their sexual orientation or gender identity. In fact, heterosexually identified youth are provided with many opportunities to pursue social activities, learn dating skills, and explore amorous and intimate relationships (e.g., have steady girlfriends or boyfriends). They have the support of their families, schools, and churches in their attempts to explore their gender identities, gender role expectations, and sexual norms and behaviors. They feel comfortable in after-school programs, recreational centers, and youth clubs, which typically reinforce the expectations of a heterosocial society.

On the other hand, youth who realize they are sexually attracted to members of the same sex or both sexes or who discover that their core gender identity is discordant with their birth sex are either ignored or considered inferior and abnormal. They learn that heterosexuality is the expected sexual orientation and is accepted as the "default" or reference category. Those youth who discover they are not attracted to members of the opposite sex soon discover that they are always assumed by others to be heterosexual in their orientation and gender conforming in their behaviors—that is, if they do not disclose themselves otherwise (Grossman, 2001).

Because of society's *homophobia* (i.e., fear and hatred of lesbian, gay, and bisexual [LGB] people), *transphobia* (i.e., fear and hatred of transgender people), and *heterosexism* (belief that heterosexuality is superior to other sexual orientations), LGBT youth frequently give up many heterosexual privileges by disclosing their sexual orientation or transgender identity. For example, they lose opportunities to learn social skills, to date their peers, to experiment sexually, to develop intimate same-sex and opposite-sex relationships, and to share their innermost feelings and crushes with peers. LGBT youth are frequently deprived of support networks in their homes, schools, and communities. This deprivation often leads to feelings of isolation and loneliness and creates barriers that prevent youth from constructing authentic personal and social identities (Grossman, 2001). Those LGBT youth who are resilient grow to adulthood unscathed, while others become emotionally deprived and scarred (DeCrescenzo, 1994). For young LGBT youth, all aspects of their lives come to be defined by and to depend on their sexual orientation or gender identity.

Like other forms of discrimination, such as racism and anti-Semitism, those who are homophobic and transphobic tend to attribute undesirable (and inaccurate) characteristics to LGBT individuals. Often homophobic and transphobic individuals may claim that LGBT people are trying to seduce heterosexuals (especially children) to their lifestyles. As a result, homophobic and transphobic people may go out of their way to declare how much they hate LGBT people. In fact, they may feel that if they act sympathetically toward the LGBT community, someone may think that they themselves are LGBT. When their fear becomes extreme, they may even try to harm LGBT people. Many, but not all, such acts become classified as *hate crimes.*

LGBT people experience various types of stigma. *Direct stigma* describes the actual experiences of discrimination or oppression encountered by LGBT individuals, while *perceived stigma* delineates those experiences of discrimination or oppression not expressed directly or overtly. Allies of LGBT people frequently experience *associative stigma* because they are voluntarily attached to or acquainted with people who are LGBT. For example, heterosexual students who are members of a "Gay-Straight Alliance" in a school may experience associative stigma. Almost all LGBT individuals experience *internalized stigma*, also known as *internalized homophobia* or *transphobia.* These individuals come to accept (i.e., internalize) the discrediting of their sense of worth, self-esteem, or prestige as a result of the potential threat of society's censure or rejection of homosexuality and transgenderism.

For example, one of the places in which youth spend much of their day and experience many forms of homophobia and transphobia is at school. Bullying, harassment, and name-calling are characteristic of many school climates, and this is especially true in the areas of athletics and sports. Two researchers, when examining sports, sexual orientation and school climate, asked a student who was being bullied in school what he would do if he could change one thing about his school. His response was: "That everyone would get treated the way the athletes get treated; that the drama club would get the same attention as the football team" (Perrotti & Westheimer, 2001, pp. 73–74). Perrotti and Westheimer affirmed that boys learn early if they are unskilled at sports, they face being called sissies and fags, and girls who excel at sports are sometimes assumed to be lesbians and labeled dykes. These stereotypes in athletics perpetuate the school's established pecking order, with male athletes who are most masculine on top. Perrotti and Westheimer, in addressing the challenges of this pecking order with regard to LGB students, stated:

> Our efforts to make schools safe and affirming for gay, lesbian, and bisexual students include increasing awareness regarding the privileged status of male athletes and the way gender roles are perpetuated in sports. By challenging the attention bestowed on certain male students and the marginalization of other students, we strive to create a playing field where all students are valued equally. (p. 74)

Developmental and Gender Expression Milestones of LGBT Youth

Similar to other discussions in the section on diversity, LGBT youth are in many ways similar to their non-LGBT peers in their developmental needs and life goals. There is also considerable diversity among LGBT youth. This is evident when one listens to LGBT youth's life histories (Savin-Williams, 1998). There is diversity among LGBT youth based on their feelings from childhood, personal histories of attachment, and opportunities to meet other LGBT youth in safe spaces. Some LGBT youth are sexually active with only members of their own sex; some have experiences with both sexes over time. Some practice celibacy or monogamy, while others may be involved with multiple partners or experience serial monogamy (i.e., many short-lived relationships with one partner at time; Grossman, 2001).

Sexual Orientation Development of Lesbian, Gay, and Bisexual (LGB) Youth

Savin-Williams (1998) compared the mean age of sexual orientation developmental milestones found in earlier studies of same-sex attractions with the results of a study he conducted with gay/bisexual male youth. Most pronounced among the findings were the ages at which these developmental milestones were reached. For example, while the mean age of awareness of same-sex attractions was at the onset of junior high school in the 1970s studies, Savin-Williams found it to be at an average of third grade among the gay/bisexual male youth in his 1998 study. In the earlier studies, the labeling of oneself as gay or lesbian occurred at an average age of 21, but it dropped to ages 15 to 16 in studies conducted in the early 1990s.

The younger ages of the sexual orientation developmental milestones are reflected in findings of a major longitudinal study of the role of victimization related to sexual orientation and the mental health of LGB youth conducted by D'Augelli and Grossman (in press).[1] The youth, ages 15 to 19, were interviewed three times over a two-year period (June 1999 to December 2001) about their sexual orientation developmental milestones. The youth were recruited from three recreation and social agencies in New York City and its suburbs.

The findings from the first panel of 528 self-identified LGB youth provide the information for this discussion (D'Augelli, Grossman & Starks, in press). Fifty-two percent of the youth in this study were males and 48% were females, and the mean age was 17 years. Racially and ethnically, the sample was quite diverse. For example, 45% (*n* = 234) were of Hispanic/Latino background and include White (86%) and Black (11%) youth. Of the non-Hispanic/Latino youth, 43% were White, 36% Black, 4% were Asian, and two youth were American Indian/Alaskan Native. The remaining youth were of mixed ethnicities and races.

Analysis of the youths' responses indicated the following:

- About three quarters of the youth said they felt "different" from other youth when they were growing up (**Table 20.1**, p. 446). They first experienced this difference at about 8 years of age. Sixty percent of the males and 52% of the females said someone had suggested they were "different." Differences were pointed out to young people when they were about 8 years old.

- For 18% of the youth, acquaintances (either friends, teachers, mothers, or other family members) were the first persons that pointed out their difference from other children. For 17% of the youth, several people pointed out the difference.

- Sixty percent of the youth indicated they had been called a "sissy" or "tomboy" before they were 13 years old. The first time this occurred was around age 8 for both males and females.

- Males first became aware of their same-sex attraction at about age 12 and females about age 13. Both males and females identified themselves as LGB at approximately age 14.

- Both males and females first disclosed their sexual orientation at about age 15. About 65% of the youth told a female and 32% told a male. About half (51%) of the people to whom the youth disclosed their sexual orientation were LGBT; 44% were

Table 20.1: Sex Differences in Sexual Orientation Development for Lesbian, Gay, and Bisexual Youth

Milestone	Males (N = 274)					Females (N = 254)				
	n	%	*M*	*SD*	Range	*n*	%	*M*	*SD*	Range
Age First Felt Different From Others	208	76	7.74	2.95	3–17	179	70	8.09	3.02	5–18
Age Others Said Youth Was Different	165	60	8.33	2.95	2–15	133	52	8.08	2.67	1–17
Age First Called "Sissy" or "Tomboy"	155	57	8.13	2.26	2–13	165	65	7.81	2.34	1–14
Age of Awareness of Same-Sex Attraction	274	100	11.82	3.13	3–18	252	100	13.02	2.54	4–19
Age of Identification as LGBT	274	100	13.63	2.57	5–18	254	100	14.40	1.98	5–19
Age of First Disclosure	273	100	14.53	2.12	6–19	254	100	14.63	1.78	9–19
Age of First Disclosure to Mother	175	64	14.73	2.38	3–19	141	56	15.10	2.06	2–19
Age of First Disclosure to Father	75	27	14.88	2.15	5–19	69	27	15.02	2.06	5–18
Years of Awareness of Sexual Orientation	271	99	7.25	3.54	0–16	254	100	6.77	3.46	0–16
% of Life Aware of Sexual Orientation	271	99	42.38	20.21	0–89	254	100	39.41	19.44	0–89

heterosexual; and 5% of the youth were unsure of the person's sexual orientation.

- 35% of the youth first told a female friend about their sexual orientation, 18% told a male friend, 8% told their mothers and 1% told their fathers. Girls were more likely to tell their female friends and boys were more likely to tell their male friends. Both males and females who had disclosed their sexual orientation to their parents first told them on average at age 15. At the time of the study, these youth had been aware of their sexual attractions for about seven years, or approximately 40% of their lives.

In summary, the LGB youth in this study felt "different" and were told that they were "different" from other kids early in their development, about age 8. They became aware of their same-sex attraction around puberty, and identified as LGB about one year later (age 14). They disclosed their sexual orientation to someone else (most frequently a friend) about one year after that. At the time of the study, 60% of the youth had disclosed their LGB identities to their mother, while only 27% had told their fathers. Those who had disclosed their orientations to their parents did so at about age 15.

Gender Expression Milestones of Transgender Youth

To date, much of the information about transgender individuals has been obtained from transsexuals who have sought counseling and other professional services from gender identity clinics (see Lewins, 1995; Ryan & Futterman, 1998) or from gender variant children referred to therapists (see Bailey, 1996, 2003; Green, 1987; Zucker, 1990). However, there are also retrospective anecdotal reports by transgender individuals and their family members (e.g., Boenke, 1999; Bornstein, 1994). From these retrospective studies, Lewins extracted four themes:

1. a long history of tension between the person's birth sex and his or her preferred gender
2. an awareness and experience of being "different" as a child (i.e., feeling like an outsider) accompanied by bullying and teasing at school
3. an internal struggle to reconcile the conflict between the psychosexual identity and birth sex

4. the need for continued coping with the negative social responses to the disclosure of these feelings

Although stage models describing the identity formation of lesbian and gay adults have been put forth (Cass, 1979; Troiden, 1989), and identity developmental milestones of lesbian, gay, and bisexual youth have been examined (see Savin-Williams, 1998, for a review), comparable studies of developmental milestones of transgender youth did not exist until Grossman and D'Augelli's (2003) study that examined the role of victimization related to gender expression and the mental health of male-to-female and female-to-male transgender youth.

Between 2001 and 2003 the researchers interviewed 55 transgender youth ages 15 to 21. The youth were recruited from the drop-in centers or recreational programs of one social and recreation service agency and one group home, both serving youth in New York City. Of the 55 youth, 31 (56%, mean age = 17.5) were male-to-female transgender (MtF) youth and 24 (44%, mean age = 19.5) were female-to-male transgender (FtM). Not only were there significant age differences between the two groups, but there were also racial, ethnic, and educational differences. Most of the FtM youth were in college ($n = 18$) and identified themselves as White/non-Hispanic ($n = 18$), while most of the MtF youth were in high school ($n = 24$) and the majority ($n = 14$) identified themselves as Puerto Rican ($n = 14$) and Black/African American ($n = 8$). Since there were important differences between the two groups with regard to age, ethnic and racial diversity, and educational levels, their gender development milestones were examined separately.

The transgender youth were asked questions about their sexual gender expression developmental milestones as well as some additional questions related to their transgender identities.

MtF Youth

- All but two of the MtF participants said they felt "different" from other youth when they were growing up (**Table 20.2**). They first experienced this difference at about 8 years of age. About two thirds reported that someone had suggested they were "different" while they were growing up and they were about age 9 when this difference was pointed out to them. Approximately four fifths of the youth indicated they had been called a "sissy" before they were age 13, and this first occurred around age 8.

Table 20.2: Differences in Gender Expression Development for Male-to-Female and Female-to-Male Transgender Youth

Milestone	Male-to-Female (N = 31)					Female-to-Male (N = 24)				
	n	%	*M*	*SD*	Range	*n*	%	*M*	*SD*	Range
Age First Felt Different From Others	29	94	7.62	3.11	1–14	24	100	7.46	3.13	3–12
Age Others Said Youth Was Different	20	65	9.25	3.28	4–16	16	67	6.81	1.60	5–10
Age First Called "Sissy" or "Tomboy"	25	81	8.28	2.42	4–12	23	96	6.70	2.64	3–13
Age of Awareness of Same-Sex Attraction	30	100	8.53	2.81	4–14	24	100	9.08	2.54	4–15
Age of Identification as Transgender	31	100	13.35	2.80	7–18	24	100	15.17	4.55	3–20
Age of First Disclosure	31	100	14.19	2.60	8–19	24	100	17.00	2.73	9–20
Age of First Disclosure to Mother	26	87	14.88	2.01	12–18	17	71	17.8	3.05	9–20
Age of First Disclosure to Father	13	45	14.69	2.56	10–18	13	54	16.54	3.33	9–20
Years of Awareness of Being Transgender	30	97	9.03	3.56	3–14	24	100	10.96	3.65	5–17
% of Life Aware of Being Transgender	30	97	50.67	17.75	18–78	24	100	53.02	16.54	25–81

- Almost all of the MtF youth reported finding other males attractive. They first became aware of their same-attraction at about age 8.5; however, it was not until an average age of 13 that they would first identify themselves as transgender.
- By 14, all of the MtF youth disclosed their transgender identification to someone else. Approximately two thirds first disclosed their transgender identity to a female—mostly to their mothers and female friends. Four youth first told male friends, one told his parents, and three told professionals. They first told their parents at an average age of 15, which was the same for both mothers and fathers.
- The youth provided a number of reasons for currently describing themselves as transgender. Three fourths of the youth said they "identify as another gender or as trans," and they "dress like another gender." All but four of the participants indicated "taking hormones" as a reason, with 21 taking them and another 6 planning to take them. Approximately two thirds of the youth "plan to have an operation to change their body," while four indicated they had such an operation. At the time of the interview, 24 of the youth reported being very or somewhat comfortable with their gender identity, while 5 said they were neither comfortable nor uncomfortable, and only 2 indicated they were uncomfortable.

FtM Youth

- All 24 of the FtM youth said they first felt "different" from other youth when they were growing up. They first experienced this difference at about 8 years of age. Two thirds reported that someone had suggested they were "different" and the age at which this difference was pointed out was when they were about 7.
- When asked if they were called a "tomboy" under the age of 13, all but one of the youth ($n = 23$) indicated this happened; this first occurred around age 7.
- Almost all of the FtM youth reported finding other females attractive. They first became aware of their same-sex attraction at about age 9; however, it was not until an average age of 15 that they would first identify themselves as transgender.

- Within two years, all of the FtM youth disclosed their transgender identification to someone else. Approximately four fifths of the youth first disclosed their transgender identity to a female, mostly to their friends or female sex partners, with the others first telling a male friend or a professional person. At the time of the interview, 17 youth reported disclosing their gender identity to their mothers and 13 to their fathers. They first told their parents at average age of 17.
- The youth provided a number of reasons for currently describing themselves as transgender. The two most frequent reasons, cited by almost 23 of the youth, were they "identify as another gender or as trans" and "dress like another gender."
- Sixteen of the participants indicated "taking hormones" as a reason, with 7 "taking or have taken hormones" and another 9 "planning to take hormones."
- Eight of the youth "plan to have an operation to change their body," while 7 indicated they had such an operation. At the time of the interview, 19 youth reported being very or somewhat comfortable with their gender identity, while 4 said they were neither comfortable nor uncomfortable, and only 1 indicated being uncomfortable. None of the youth reported being very uncomfortable.

In summary, both groups of transgender youth felt "different" and were told they were "different" from other kids, usually between ages 8 and 9. A large majority of the youth in both groups was called "sissy" or "tomboy" during their childhood, but did not identify themselves as transgender until their early teens, with the female-to-male group identifying themselves approximately two years after male-to-female youth. A similar pattern followed with the age of disclosure, with the female-to-male youth first disclosing their transgender identity approximately three years after the male-to-female group. A large majority of both groups described themselves as transgender because they identify and dress as the other gender, and they report feeling comfortable or very comfortable with gender identity.

Most people in society recognize that some individuals eventually identify as LGBT, gender variant, or gender queer. Individuals who so identify grow up in a culture that stigmatizes their nonheterosexual identities, behaviors, relationships, and communities. These individuals internalize society's ideology of sex and gender at an early age, so when they discover their own sexual and gender identities, they usually experience some degree of negative feelings toward themselves (i.e., internalized homophobia or transphobia). These experiences create unique challenges that they must confront during their psychosocial development, most notably, overcoming internalized homophobia and coming out (Garnets, Herek & Levy, 2003).

Becoming a Visible or Nonvisible Minority Group Member

After discovering their sexual orientation and gender identity, LGBT youth have to learn how to manage the stigma associated with these identities against a background of cultural heterosexism. The large majority of LGBT youth manage the stigma of their same-sex attractions and gender identities by hiding them (Mallon, 1999; Martin, 1982). The rewards for not being LGBT are so great that the youth would rather have identities (using Goffman's [1963] terminology) of being "discreditable" rather than "discredited." LGBT youth are aware that even though they pass for heterosexual in the present (i.e., being discreditable); they may become discredited in the future. In the short term, however, they are avoiding acts of prejudice, oppression, and rejection by maintaining an unblemished identity. However, this becomes an unending and extremely stressful chore.

For others, hiding is not an option, and they "come out," by disclosing their sexual orientation and/or gender identity to others. These LGBT youth are transformed from individuals with difficult information to manage (i.e., coming out to themselves) to people with difficult situations to get through, and from people who are discreditable to ones who have become discredited. They become a member of one or more minority groups, and suffer unjustified negative attitudes and actions, ranging from verbal victimization and scapegoating to physical assault and murder.

Being a member of a minority group not recognized as a legitimate minority deserving equal constitutional protections (at the federal level and by the large majority of states) not only leads to feelings of marginalization and experiences of discrimination and violence but also has a direct impact on one's physical and mental health (DiPlacido, 1998). Furthermore, the minority status of being LGBT imposes enormous adaptive tasks on one's developmental trajectories (Mallon, 1999). Everything about an LGBT youth comes to be understood in terms of the stigma attached to his or her minority group status; this overshadows all of their other social identities, such as sons, daughters, peers, friends, and family members.

Additionally, minority group status produces *minority stress,* which some studies have linked to mental health problems, emotional distress, and depressive mood among gay men, and excessive cigarette smoking, heavy alcohol consumption, excessive weight, and high-risk sexual behaviors among lesbians and bisexual women. Some LGB individuals, however, have dealt successfully with minority stress so that it does not lead to negative health outcomes. Social support and certain personality characteristics, such as hardiness and high self-esteem, have been found to moderate the negative effects of stress (DiPlacido, 1998).

The coming out process for LGB and transgender young people has been conceptualized as a developmental step toward healthfulness and a way to cope with minority stress, although societal or familial responses to an individual's disclosure may not be constructive (Mallon, 1999). Most coming-out models (e.g., Cass, 1979; Coleman, 1981/1982; Troiden, 1989) propose an orderly and linear series of stages. Sophie (1985/1986) reviewed six models of gay/lesbian identity development and distinguished the following four essential stages:

1. *first awareness*—cognitive and emotional realization that one is "different" and that homosexuality may be relevant, as well as a feeling of alienation from oneself and others

2. *test and exploration*—testing to determine if one is LGB, and having limited contact with LGB communities, as well as experiencing alienation from heterosexuality

3. *identity acceptance*—preference for interactions with other LGB individuals, a positive LGB identity replacing a negative one, and an initial disclosure to heterosexuals

4. *identity integration*—view self as LGB, publicly come out as LGB, and develop identity stability as an LGB individual

LGBT youth know that coming out has many potential consequences, and it is the weighing of these as well as the "push and pull" of psychological needs that determine the ultimate decision, which gets repeated many times each day, when one is in a new situation. Some of the reasons given for disclosing one's sexual orientation or gender identity include the following:

- to stop living a lie (i.e., the desire for honest and open communication)

- to avoid isolation and loneliness

- to provide opportunities for mutual support and to deepen love

- to strengthen family bonds

- to decrease the "price of passing," which may involve feeling invisible or sadness due to the loss of intimacy

For some LGBT youth, the reasons for nondisclosure of their sexual orientation or gender orientation remain potent, such as fear of rejection, fear of hurting or disappointing parents, fear of criticism and ridicule, protection of the family from shame or crisis, increased vulnerability, and fear of being forced into conversion therapy to change one's sexual orientation or gender identity.

Building Resiliency Through Recreation and Social Programming

The visibility of LGBT people's lives continues to increase in North America, most recently because of actions such as the U.S. Supreme Court's decision *Lawrence v. Texas* (June 26, 2003) that struck down antigay sodomy laws, expansion of the first public high school for predominantly LGBT youth in New York City (September 8, 2003), consecration of the first openly gay Episcopal bishop in any of the world's major Christian denominations (November 2, 2003), and issuing of legal marriage licenses to same-sex couples in the Canadian provinces of Ontario (June 10, 2003), British Columbia (July 8, 2003), and Quebec (March 19, 2004). California became the fourth state in the nation to outlaw discrimination against transgender people (August 2, 2003), and it gave same-sex couples in the state nearly all of the rights that married couples enjoy (September 19, 2003). Additionally, protests advocating for same-sex marriage and same-sex marriage ceremonies have taken place in various cities of the United States (February and March, 2004) with Massachusetts being the only state in which same-sex marriage is legal. These actions not only indicate an increasing visibility and social acceptance of LGBT people (while also recognizing that there are many backlashes: for example, promoting a constitutional amendment that defines marriage as only between a woman and a man) but also help LGBT youth and adults to begin or continue the processes of reclaiming the devalued parts of themselves and fully integrating their sexuality and gender into their self-identities.

Psychosocial adjustment and building resiliency against stigmatization are enhanced by increasing self-esteem; identifying with and seeking role models in the larger gay community; and experiencing support from peers, family members, teachers, recreation specialists, sports coaches, and community services. Recreation programs and social services have some of the best opportunities to enhance the psychosocial development of LGBT youth. For example, sexual identity is a major issue for some people in making their leisure choices (Kelly, 1996) and leisure can become a site in which gay and lesbian people can construct identities and build resistance to oppression (Henderson, 1996). Recreation and leisure service professionals have opportunities to break the cycle of anguish, despair, and victimization that some LGB, as well as transgender, youth come to know as everyday feelings (Grossman, 1997b). In addition, individual recreation experiences can assist LGBT youth in enhancing skill development and promoting feelings of achievement while enhancing self-concept and self-worth. Group recreation activities have the potential of helping LGBT youth to learn social skills, to promote their sense of acceptance, to develop feelings of self-confidence, and to make the transition to adult life with a strong sense of personal identity and independence. Youth programs that focus on youth empowerment, peer education, leisure counseling, and cooperative activities can help LGBT youth and their heterosexual counterparts learn about living in a diverse society and accepting differences.

A recent qualitative study by Johnson (1999/2000), conducted with 19 gay and lesbian young adults (ages 19 to 25), explored how these young adults assigned meaning to their leisure and the role leisure plays in their identity development. The following three major themes were identified:

- the experience of homophobia in leisure
- a desire for group enclosure in leisure
- negotiation of comfort in leisure

These LGB young adults cited acts of discrimination; however, their major concern with homophobia was the fear of potential discrimination in leisure, which would mirror their experiences in other contexts. Their fear of discrimination caused great anxiety and distress about the possible consequences of revealing their sexual identity, and they were afraid of pursuing additional leisure opportunities because of possible negative feedback.

Group enclosure was the conscious effort of these individuals to protect themselves in homogeneous groups—ones with other gay and lesbian people. While group enclosure limited their friendships and leisure activities to other gay men and/or lesbians, it also allowed them to minimize differences within the group and maximize differences outside the group. These young people reported that these strategies helped to raise self-esteem, to promote a positive gay identity, and to create a form of social support not available in their general homophobic and heterosexist environments. However, group enclosure often limited their leisure choices, access to knowledge, facility use, and patterns of participation.

Comfort levels with their own identities of these gay and lesbian young adults determined what, with whom, when, where, and how leisure occurred in their lives. To deal with their comfort levels, they sometimes used negative negotiation strategies, including avoiding activities and not disclosing their sexual orientation (e.g., most of the participants in the study indicated that they had avoided activities because they might feel uncomfortable as a result of being identified as gay or lesbian). While passing as heterosexual allowed these participants to avoid negative reactions associated with disclosing their sexual identity, it also led to protecting a nongay façade by lying or misleading others, which resulted in strained and distant social relationships. Some of these young adults found comfort in their leisure by not hiding their sexual identity, thereby eliminating ignorance and stereotypes about same-sex attractions and establishing pride in their sexuality. "By establishing pride in one's sexual orientation, gay and lesbian young adults created an opportunity to use leisure as a context for power, to create social change, and in many instances, overcome their oppression" (Johnson, 1999/2000, p. 271).

All of the young adults in Johnson's study avoided an activity or passed as heterosexual at some point in their leisure experiences. In other words, they did not always feel free to be open and honest about their sexual identity because they did not have safe and supportive leisure opportunities. While some people can negotiate comfort without group enclosure in their lives, others need safe and separate leisure opportunities to resist the dominance of heterosexism and homophobia. Some communities have created such social and recreation programs for LGBT youth and their allies (Grossman, 1998).

Support, Social, Educational, and Recreational Programs for LGBT Youth and Their Allies

Talking about sexuality makes most youth and adults feel uneasy, and conversing about homosexuality, transsexualism, and other gender-bending topics remains unacceptable in many private and public forums. For example, in some school districts, policies forbid teachers to raise these topics; if the topics are raised by students, only certain prescribed responses are permissible. However, as mass media and the Internet have made information about same-sex and transgender issues readily available, youth have become much more knowledgeable about sexuality than those of previous generations. In some communities, support, social, educational, and recreational programs for LGBT youth and their allies have been established by adults or by the youth themselves. These programs have a number of common elements as well as distinct features. All of the programs provide some type of support to help LGBT youth have safe spaces in which to explore and to solidify their sexual and gender identities. While most of these programs are dominated by LGBT and questioning youth, heterosexual allies or other gender-blending youth are usually not excluded. The following are some of essential components of these programs, and a few specific programs are described for illustrative purposes.

Social Support

Social support programs tend to focus on providing support for youth to negotiate their identities in comfortable and safe spaces without having to lie about or hide their authentic selves. In these groups, LGBT youth learn that others have feelings and questions similar to their own and they have a place to go where people like themselves can gather. For example

- BAGLY (Boston Alliance of Gay, Lesbian, Bisexual, Transgender and Questioning [LGBTQ] Youth) is well-known and respected for its dedication to creating a safe-space where youth are free to explore their identities (http://www.bagly.org).
- "Out Youth Austin" (http://www.outyouth.org) provides support services to LGBTQ youth ages 12 to 19 in Austin and Central Texas. It offers peer support groups counseling, educational programs, social activities and community outreach. But most of all, it offers a safe place for LGBT youth to be themselves and helps make the community safe for LGBTQ youth.

Provision of Social and Recreation Activities

In response to the need for LGBT youth to avoid the fear of being identified or harassed, many programs specifically provide opportunities for LGBT youth to engage in social and recreation with LGBT peers. These programs are designed to combat the isolation and loneliness that a large majority of LGBT youth experience and to provide them with opportunities to engage in age-typical activities, such as sports, hanging out with friends, arts, and dancing. The youth also have opportunities to learn social and dating skills and develop trusting relationships with their peers. Two examples include the following:

- The Youth Services Department of the Los Angeles Gay and Lesbian Center (http://www.laglc.org) focuses on LGBTQ youth who do not always experience safety in a predominantly heterosexual environment and whose unique needs are sometimes overlooked at other agencies. While self-empowerment services are the ultimate goal of the Youth Services Department, it offers supportive services, as well as various social, recreation, and self-development groups.

- The Youth Enrichment Services (Y.E.S.) program of the New York City LGBT Community Center (http://www.gaycenter.org) offers creative arts workshops, social activities, discussion groups, and leadership training to LGBT young people. It focuses on building and strengthening community, creativity and confidence among LGBTQ youth and their allies in a safe, affirming, alcohol-free, and drug-free environment.

Provision of Educational Opportunities

Many of these types of programs also have educational components and a few schools have been established primarily to educate LGBT youth. While the educational foci of programs vary, many tend to examine issues pertinent to LGBT youth not addressed in other settings, such as

- high-risk sexual behaviors that may lead to sexually transmitted infections (including HIV)
- high rates of smoking, alcohol use, and other drug use among LGBT individuals
- risks of using black market hormones by transgender youth

Other programs assist youth to learn to cope with verbal harassment and physical assault in educational environments. In this regard, a growing number of Gay-Straight Alliances of students have been established in junior high and high school settings. A small number of communities provide schooling for LGBT youth who dropped out of school or are at risk for doing so because they can no longer endure the bullying and assaults they experience from their peers while their teachers and school administrators look the other way. For example

- The Hetrick-Martin Institute in New York City has an After-School Services Department (http://www.hmi.org) that provides an alternative safe space on weekday afternoons and evenings for LGBTQ youth to engage in education and training, recreation activities, counseling, and the kinds of socialization and skill-building experiences that most adolescents take for granted. It also serves as the home of the Harvey Milk High School. This four-year, fully accredited public high school provides an education program for at-risk youth who often find it difficult or impossible to attend their home schools due to continuous threats, physical violence, or verbal harassment usually based on their perceived sexual orientation or identity.

- In California, the Hillcrest Youth Center (http://www.thecentersd.org), a program of the San Diego LGBT Center, offers cyber/computer training, health education, basic financial education, diversity and cultural awareness workshops, HIV prevention education, social activities, discussion groups, and group counseling services.
- The Gay, Lesbian, and Straight Education Network (GLSEN; http://www.glsen.org) is an education organization working to ensure safe and effective schools for all people, particularly lesbian, gay, and bisexual students. GLSEN envisions a future in which children learn to respect and accept people regardless of their sexual orientation and gender identity or expression. GLSEN focuses on making bullying and harassment unacceptable in schools and seeks to develop school climates where difference is valued for the positive contribution it makes in creating a more vibrant and diverse community. GLSEN supports students as they form and lead Gay-Straight Alliances that allow students to fully participate in school life, not only in the classrooms but also in after-school activities and clubs. Currently, there are over 2,000 Gay-Straight Alliances in U.S. junior high and high schools.

Recreational Activities

A number of municipal recreation programs, after-school programs, and community centers have created recreational activities designed for LGBT youth, including drop-in centers, volleyball and softball leagues, arts programs, and libraries.

- The San Francisco LGBT Community Center (http://www.sfgaycenter.org) sponsors a Youth Resource Room that provides youth access to services and programs resulting from collaboration with 10 youth service agencies, including the municipally financed Lavender Youth Recreation and Information Center

(LYRIC), Eureka Valley Recreation Center, the Youth Gender Project, and the Queer Youth Training Collaborative. These centers provide LGBTQ youth with social and recreation programs, arts programs, discussion groups, health services, legal counseling, and access to employment information.

Other Services

Some social agencies provide additional services to youth who are "throwaways" or "runaways" because of their sexual orientation or gender identities. These services include the provision of clothing, meals, transitional housing, HIV/AIDS testing and counseling, legal consultation, and personal hygiene items. Other organizations work with city and other community agencies to provide LGBT homeless youth with case management services, access to shelters, mobile health units, individual and group counseling, and weekly independent living skill groups. For example, the Los Angeles Gay and Lesbian Center (http://www.laglc.org) coordinates with a wide range of private and public agencies in the Los Angeles and Hollywood areas to provide a continuum of care specifically for homeless and runaway LGBTQ youth including free clinics, health services, shelters, counseling and case management services, and drop-in and outreach programs.

Implications for the Delivery of Recreation Services

Several strategies are available for use by recreation specialists so homophobia and transphobia do not make LGBT youth invisible in recreation and leisure settings. These include the following:

- Advocate that a nondiscrimination clause based on sexual orientation and gender identity or expression be included in the agency's overall nondiscrimination policy statement of the organization (if it does not already exist).
- Understand the significant impact that the socially constructed roles of gender and gender role expectations have on the development of LGBT youth.
- Comprehend the developmental trajectories and milestones of LGBT youth and the cultural context of heterosexism that frames them. LGBT youths' participation in recreation programs not only provides opportunities to normalize nonhet-

erosexuality but also gives all youth chances to learn about differences that prepare them for the diverse world they will live in as fully functioning adults.

Two cautionary notes are appropriate here. First, recreation specialists should not fall into the trap of "blaming the victim." Some professionals say to LGBT youth: "It's your fault! If you kept your identity to yourself, you would not be harassed," which is certain to alienate LGBT youth—as they have heard that statement for most of their lives.

Second, LGBT youth should be integrated into all programs, while at the same time having opportunities for separate support groups to talk about their unique issues, if they so desire. However, such support groups should also be available to others (e.g., groups for girls, boys, youth who are hard of hearing or deaf) so as not to stigmatize LGBT youth for needing a group when no other youth have one.

Additionally, individual facilities (e.g., rest rooms, changing rooms, and shower rooms) may also be required for transgender youth as well as those with other special needs. Many individuals do not like to change their clothes and shower in public, and most LGBT youth have had their worst experiences in unsupervised locker rooms.

Recreation specialists must do more than provide leadership and programming to contribute to the positive development of LGBT youth. They also need to create safe, welcoming, and supportive environments that will attract LGBT youth and encourage them to access recreation and leisure activities through which they will thrive. Because of the stigma LGBT youth experience daily, recreation specialists need to convince LGBT youth that their recreation and leisure interests, needs, and preferences will be addressed, they will be supported, and they will have input into programming, including rule-making, that will make them feel safe in the space. Many LGB young adults (because of previous experiences) bring perceived notions of homophobia to recreation and leisure settings (Johnson, 1999/2000). These perceptions may require recreation specialists to facilitate cosponsorship of recreation and leisure programming with other agencies that have a proven track record in working with LGBT youth.

Since most services fail to stop the harassment and other types of victimization LGBT youth experience, recreation specialists may also need to develop outreach programs to assist LGBT youth who feel systematically excluded from all services or have found them to be unreceptive. A number of youth who have disclosed their LGBT identities have become runaways or throwaways, and they form a meaningful percentage of the homeless youth in some cities (DeCrescenzo, 1994). They are high-risk youth who feel marginalized from all services: If they were not protected and supported by their families, whom can they trust? The answer must be the availability of professional staff members who are not only skilled and nurturing but also who are accepting and supportive of the youth's sexual orientation and gender identities and who are willing to model appropriate behaviors and work to create accepting communities. It is important that these high-risk youth have ongoing programs that will foster their involvement and gain their sense of trust—a challenging but most worthwhile task.

Positive youth development for disclosed or undisclosed LGBT youth requires programs that do not ignore, negate, or misinterpret their feelings, as such programs will only create

> unnecessary pain and shame that hinder their development of a vibrant, authentic sense of self…Few individuals concerned with the well-being of youths would advocate that being thus marginalized, especially during the vulnerable years of childhood and adolescence, is desirable. (Savin-Williams, 2004, pp. 290–291)

References

Bailey, J. M. (1996). Gender identity. In R. C. Savin-Williams and K. M. Cohen (Eds.), *The lives of lesbians, gays, and bisexuals: Children to adults* (pp. 71–93). Forth Worth, TX: Harcourt Brace College Publishers.

Bailey, J. H. (2003). *The man who would be queen: The science of gender-bending and transsexualism.* Washington, DC: Joseph Henry Press.

Boenke, M. (Ed.). (1999). *Transforming families: Real stories about transgender loved ones.* Imperial Beach, CA: Walter Trook Publishing.

Bornstein, K. (1994). *Gender outlaw: On men, women, and the rest of us.* New York, NY: Vintage.

Cass, V. C. (1979). Homosexual identity formation: A theoretical model. *Journal of Homosexuality, 4,* 219–235.

Coleman, E. (1981/1982). Developmental stages of the coming out process. *Journal of Homosexuality, 7,* 31–43.

D'Augelli, A. R. and Grossman A. H. (in press). Researching lesbian, gay and bisexual youth: Conceptual, practical and ethical considerations. *Journal of Gay and Lesbian Issues in Education.*

D'Augelli, A. R., Grossman, A. H., and Starks, M. T. (in press). Gender atypicality and sexual orientation development among lesbian, gay, and bisexual youth: Prevalence, sex differences, and parental responses. *Journal of Gay and Lesbian Psychotherapy.*

DeCrescenzo, T. (1994). Helping gay and lesbian youth: New policies, new programs, new practice. *Journal of Gay & Lesbian Social Services, 1*(3/4), xix–xxiv.

DiPlacido, J. (1998). Minority stress among lesbians, gay men, and bisexuals: A consequence of heterosexism, homophobia, and stigmatization. In G. M. Herek (Ed.), *Stigma and sexual orientation: Understanding prejudice against lesbians, gay men, and bisexuals* (pp. 138–159). Thousand Oaks, CA: Sage.

Garnets, L. D., Herek, G. M., and Levy, B. (2003). Violence and victimization of lesbians and gay men: Mental health consequences. In L. D. Garnets and D. C. Kimmel (Eds.), *Psychological perspectives on lesbian, gay, and bisexual experiences* (2nd ed., pp. 188–216). New York, NY: Columbia University Press.

Goffman, E. (1963). *Stigma: Notes on the management of a spoiled identity.* Englewood Cliffs, NJ: Prentice Hall.

Green, R. (1987). *The "sissy boy syndrome" and the development of homosexuality.* New Haven, CT: Yale University Press.

Grossman, A. H. (1997a). Growing up with a "spoiled identity:" Lesbian, gay, and bisexual youth at-risk. *Journal of Gay & Lesbian Social Services, 6*(3), 45–56.

Grossman, A. H. (1997b). Lessons from Greg Louganis in relating to gay, lesbian and bisexual youth. *Journal of Leisurability, 24*(4), 14–21.
Grossman, A. H. (1998). Queer youth and urban space: The case for a place of their own. In C. Aitchison and F. Smith (Eds.), *Gender, space, and identity: Leisure, culture and commerce* (pp. 127–136). Eastbourne, England: Leisure Studies Association.
Grossman, A. H. (2001). Avoiding HIV/AIDS and the challenge of growing up gay, lesbian, and bisexual. In A. R. D'Augelli and C. J. Patterson (Eds.), *Lesbian, gay and bisexual identities and youth: Psychological perspectives* (pp. 155–180). New York, NY: Oxford University Press.
Grossman, A. H. and D'Augelli, A. R. (2003). [The role of victimization related to gender expression and the mental health of male-to-female and female-to-male transgender youth.] Unpublished raw data.
Henderson, K. A. (1996). One size doesn't fit all: The meanings of women's leisure. *Journal of Leisure Research, 28*(3), 139–154.
Johnson, C. W. (1999/2000). Living the game of hide and seek: Leisure in the lives of gay and lesbian young adults. *Leisure/Loisir, 24*(3/4), 255–278.
Kelly, J. R. (1996). *Leisure.* Needham Heights, MA: Allyn & Bacon.
Lewins, F. (1995). *Transsexualism in society: Sociology of male-to-female transsexuals.* South Melbourne, Australia: Macmillan Education Australia.
Mallon, G. P. (Ed.). (1999). *Social services with transgendered youth.* New York, NY: Harrington Park Press.
Martin, A. D. (1982). Learning to hide: The socialization of the gay adolescent. In S. C. Feinstein, J. G. Looney, A. Schwartzberg, and J. Sorosky (Eds.), *Adolescent psychiatry: Developmental and clinical studies* (Vol. X, pp. 52–65). Chicago, IL: University of Chicago Press.
Perrotti, J. and Westheimer, K. (2001). *When the drama club is not enough: Lessons from the safe schools programs for gay and lesbian students.* Boston, MA: Beacon Press.
Ryan, C. and Futterman, D. (1998). *Lesbian and gay youth: Care and counseling.* New York, NY: Columbia University Press.
Savin-Williams, R. C. (1998)*...And then I became gay: Young men's stories.* New York, NY: Routledge.
Savin-Williams, R. C. (2004). Boy-on-boy sexuality. In N. Way and J. Y. Chu (Eds.), *Adolescent boys: Exploring diverse cultures of boyhood* (pp. 271–292). New York, NY: New York University Press.
Sophie, J. (1985/1986). A critical examination of stage theories of lesbian identity development. *Journal of Homosexuality, 12,* 39–51.
Troiden, R. R. (1989). The formation of homosexual identities. *Journal of Homosexuality, 17,* 43–73.
Westheimer, R. K. and Lopater, S. (2002). *Human sexuality: A psychosocial perspective.* Philadelphia, PA: Lippincott, Williams & Wilkins.

Zucker, K. J. (1990). Gender identity disorders in children: Clinical descriptions and natural history. In R. Blanchard and B. W. Steiner (Eds.), *Clinical management of gender identity disorders in children and adults* (pp. 1–23). Washington, DC: American Psychiatric Press.

Endnote

1. The longitudinal study of victimization and mental health among LGB youth by Anthony D'Augelli and Arnold Grossman addressed in this chapter was funded by the National Institute of Mental Health (MH51855). The Grossman and D'Augelli study of male-to-female and female-to-male transgender youth study was funded by the New York University Research Challenge Fund.

Chapter 21

Inclusion of Youth With and Without Disabilities: More Than Just Sharing the Same Space

Mary Ann Devine

Irene is used to being stared at, as well as getting looks of pity. As a 14-year-old girl with cerebral palsy she understands that people think she acts, looks, and talks "funny." But all she wants them to do is accept her for who she is and treat her like they would other girls her age. Right now she is on summer vacation and simply wants to play basketball in the summer recreation league and hang out with her friends.

Irene is just one example of the many youth who have some type of condition that results in mental or physical limitations. Unfortunately, even in today's society, many people (including recreation professionals) do not really understand youth like Irene. They do not know how to appropriately and effectively include them in recreation programs and services, and they do not understand the developmental implications of growing up with a disability or chronic illness.

As part of the set of chapters on diversity, this chapter discusses foundations and principles of inclusive recreation services for youth with and without disabilities. Theoretical perspectives that have been used successfully as the foundation for providing inclusive recreation will be presented with examples of how they may be applied. A model that can serve as a framework from which to design, implement, and evaluate inclusive recreation for youth is presented and discussed. Best practices, based on over a decade of research, are presented in conjunction with other practical considerations for providing inclusive recreation for youth with and without disabilities. Applied examples are incorporated throughout the chapter to increase the salience of the concepts, principles, and theories presented.

Introduction to Inclusive Recreation Programming

In the early 1990s Sylvester (1992) challenged recreation professionals to view leisure opportunities for individuals with disabilities as a right—not an occasional privilege. His intent was to reform and to revolutionize not only the concepts and role of therapeutic recreation but also the entire leisure services field. According to Sylvester, the right to leisure is the "unifying principle bonding the diverse profession of leisure services" (p. 19) and is a human right for all. Around this same time, many professionals were debating the role of therapeutic recreation specialists relative to community recreation participation. Specifically, people asked the question, "Whose job is it to promote and to facilitate recreation participation in community settings for individuals with disabilities?"

Much of this debate was spurred by significant changes that were beginning to occur in health care, most notably decreased lengths of stay in hospitals and rehabilitation facilities. For instance, people who had experienced a spinal cord injury had their average length of stay in rehabilitation facilities reduced by 10 weeks between the years 1990 and 1996 (National Institutes of Health, n.d.). There was also a growing recognition that individuals with disabilities lived in communities, not hospitals, and most who lived in communities did not require therapy or wish to be stigmatized as being recipients of *therapeutic* recreation services (Smith, Austin & Kennedy, 2001).

Along with philosophical challenges presented by scholars such as Sylvester, legislative changes were occurring that would impact individuals with and without disabilities. The passage of the Americans with Disabilities Act (ADA) in 1991 (U.S. Department of Justice) mandated that individuals with disabilities have full and equal access to services and programs. Prior to 1991, recreation opportunities for individuals with disabilities were predominantly segregated and limited (e.g., Special Olympics, Very Special Arts, Challenger Little Leagues). Furthermore, virtually no opportunities for individuals with disabilities to recreate with their peers without disabilities existed.

The passage of the ADA has enabled the current generation of youth to grow up being schooled in nonsegregated classrooms. Their expectation is to be included in all aspects of daily life, including recreation opportunities. In sum, the combination of philosophical challenges to service provision, changes in the healthcare industry, the advent of antidiscrimination laws, and changing expectations have spurred the movement to include individuals with disabilities in community life, including recreation.

Benefits to Participating in Inclusive Recreation

The benefits of participation in recreation activities for youth in general have been explored from many perspectives over the past two decades, but it has only been in the past 10 years that researchers have begun identifying the benefits of participation in inclusive recreation programs. Overall, studies have demonstrated that both youth with and without disabilities experience benefits from engagement in inclusive recreation. As discussed previously in this book, all youth, including those with disabilities, benefit by increasing self-determined behaviors (Devine, Malley, Sheldon, Dattilo & Gast, 1997), developing friendships (Schleien, Fahnestock, Green & Rynders, 1990), and developing socially appropriate behaviors (Modell, 1997). For youth with disabilities in particular, inclusive recreation environments build important life skills (e.g., age-appropriate social skills) and improve physical functioning (e.g., cardiovascular endurance; Green & DeCoux, 1994). Another benefit of recreation participation unique to youth with disabilities is that inclusive recreation environments are a forum to dispel myths and stereotypes about their limitations (Devine & Wilhite, 2000).

Other researchers have noted additional benefits of inclusive recreation participation. Henderson, Bedini, Hecht, and Schuler (1995) reported that individuals with disabilities expressed a heightened freedom of choice when inclusive recreation programs were options in their leisure repertoire. In a study on social acceptance and the leisure lifestyle of people with disabilities, Devine and Dattilo (2000) found the frequency of participation and level of satisfaction experienced by individuals with disabilities were positively correlated with perceptions of social acceptance, an important part of inclusive recreation.

In the early years of inclusive programming, some stakeholders (e.g., parents, participants, staff) were concerned that the benefits of participation for youth without disabilities in recreation activities would be negatively impacted by including youth with disabilities. Studies examining inclusive recreation contexts have found this sentiment to be unsubstantiated. For instance, Schleien, Hornfeldt, and McAvoy (1994) identified improved communication, physical fitness, and social skills for youth with and without disabilities as the result of participation in inclusive leisure programs. In their study on inclusive physical education classes, Obrusnikova, Valkova and Block (2003) found no significant difference in sport skill or knowledge acquisition between members of a class that included a student who used a wheelchair and those in a class that had no students with a physical disability. Devine and O'Brien (n.d.) reported that inclusive participation in a residential camp environment provided youth with and without disabilities the opportunity to develop a host of problem-solving skills as well as an appreciation for each others similarities and differences.

Issues Related to Inclusive Recreation for Youth With and Without Disabilities

Since the ADA, inclusion of youth with disabilities has not always been readily available. The inability of recreation professionals to design and evaluate inclusive services has been shaped by several issues, including: (a) not recognizing that the responsibility to provide inclusive services must be shared among stakeholders, and (b) the inconsistent desire and guidance available to meet the mandate of the ADA.

Inclusion of youth with disabilities in recreation programs requires the involvement and commitment of all stakeholders. Parents, teachers, therapeutic recreation specialists, inclusion specialists, general recreation service providers, and the participant must be involved and share responsibility. No longer is inclusive recreation program design or delivery solely the responsibility of a therapeutic recreation specialist. No longer should programs focus on having the individual with a disability conform and make adjustments to fit in with his or her peers without disabilities, which is what happened in the past. Today it is everyone's obligation to make changes to accommodate all youth—changes not only focused on the individual but also on peers, staff, and facility.

Consider Irene in the opening scenario. In the past, recreation staff may have modified the rules such that Irene was not allowed within the three-point shooting area. That put the focus of change on Irene rather than on everyone. A more inclusive approach would be if other players used wheelchairs to play the game and all players using wheelchairs stayed outside the three-point line. That way Irene wouldn't stand out and be the only one for whom the rules had to change.

Undertaking the modifications necessary to share responsibility for inclusive programming have challenged therapeutic recreation specialists and general recreation professionals to consider factors and issues they previously could ignore. For instance, community recreation professionals now have to consider attitudes of the people in the community toward including individuals with disabilities in programs. In Irene's case, her peers may have rebelled if they had to use wheelchairs to play ball just to accommodate Irene. Thus, the recreation staff would have to design a plan as to how to work with the youth to come to a consensus of how to best accommodate

Irene's differences. They also would have to be skilled in responding to all the youth in the league.

Because recreation programs are increasingly more inclusive than segregated, therapeutic recreation specialists have taken on more of an indirect than direct service provision role in relation to the inclusion of youth with disabilities. Often their roles are more related to consulting and developing rather than actually implementing inclusion plans themselves. Thus, inclusive recreation provision is new territory for most community recreation professionals. As service providers address the challenges of inclusive programming, they must not only be open to programmatic changes and appropriate accommodations, but also astute at examining and addressing the culture and climate of an inclusive environment for effective service options for youth with disabilities.

The ADA has provided only some guidance for parameters of service provision that would apply to the delivery of recreation services, and a more closely honed framework is in progress. The uncertainty of exactly how and what to provide, as well as the evolution of professional roles and the need to assume new responsibilities, has left some recreation professionals uncertain about how to provide inclusive leisure services. As more research is conducted, more help will be available to guide recreation professionals in effectively including youth with disabilities in programs.

Some research does exist, however, and has helped to identify important characteristics and elements of inclusion. For example, inclusion involves more than providing an accessible space or piece of equipment; inclusion happens when social acceptance, interdependence, and support are present (Bedini & Henderson, 1994; Devine & Dattilo, 2000; Devine & Lashua, 2002; Wilhite, Devine & Goldenberg, 1999). Five principles of inclusion are provided later in this chapter. Before these are presented, however, it helps to understand some of the main theories used in conducting research on inclusion.

Theoretical Perspectives and Inclusive Recreation

"Theory ought to create the capacity to invent explanations" (Stinchcombe, 1968, p. 3). Inclusive recreation processes and techniques derived from theories are beneficial because they contribute to an understanding of the inclusive recreation environment. Theories guide recreation professionals in determining what may be occurring in particular inclusive situations and what may occur in the future, if similar situations are replicated. The application of theory in inclusive leisure practices and research is critical for professional growth and quality services. Theories also serve as a framework from which to design services, as discussed in Chapter 10.

This section will describe four theories useful in understanding inclusion: *contact theory, social construction theory, ecological theory* and *self-determination theory*. Each of these theories facilitates generalizations and predicts future events concerning psychological, sociological, and environmental phenomena related to inclusion of youth in recreation services. In addition, these theories are potentially applicable to a wide range of inclusive leisure situations (see Devine, 1997; Devine & Dattilo, 2000; Devine & Lashua, 2002; Goodwin & Watkinson, 2000; Hewitt, 1991; Sable, 1995; Schleien, Hornfeldt & McAvoy, 1994; Tripp, French & Sherrill, 1995).

Contact Theory

Contact theory asserts that the quality of interactions between people with differences tends to influence changes in attitudes toward one another (Allport, 1954; Tripp & Sherrill, 1991; Tripp, French & Sherrill, 1995). Specifically, the theory suggests that prejudice, stereotyping, and discrimination may be reduced by creating a context in which contact and interactions are positive (Allport, 1954). Thus, contact theory suggests that it is possible to change one group's perceptions or attitudes toward another group (Roper, 1990b), although contact alone is not enough to result in positive attitudinal changes. Furthermore, contact also can be a source of embarrassment, irritation, and escalation of conflict (Amir, 1969; Sherif, Harvey, White, Hood & Sherif, 1961; Wilhite, Devine & Goldenberg, 1999).

The type of change depends primarily on the conditions under which contact has taken place. According to Roper (1990a), the form of contact and experiences that occur determines its success or failure. For example, Allport (1954) suggested that favorable conditions tend to improve attitudes whereas unfavorable conditions tend to foster harmful attitudes. Minimal or infrequent contact tends to reinforce negative perceptions people with and without disabilities have of each other (Allport, 1954; Archie & Sherrill, 1989). Favorable conditions that tend to foster positive attitude changes involve contacts that

- produce equal status as well as promote contact
- are mutually rewarding to those with and without disabilities
- are personal rather than casual, allowing individuals to get to know each other well
- persist over time

- focus on establishing common rather than individual goals
- receive strong support from relevant authorities (Allport, 1935, 1954; Cook, 1962; Tripp et al., 1995)

Contact theory suggests that to set the stage for positive contact, no one person should be more or less important than another, contact should be ongoing, everyone should gain something from the experience, and everyone should be working toward a similar goal. In inclusive recreation environments, contact theory can be applied by designing programs that promote meaningful interdependence across time. To promote interdependence a recreation professional may select activities where participants are mutually dependent to accomplish a goal (i.e., all participants painting together to create a mural). In these situations, how youth with and without disabilities accomplish the goal (e.g., painting using one's hands, painting using a device attached to one's hand) is less important than everyone learning to create the mural to the best of his or her ability.

Based on contact theory, programmers should also facilitate youth getting to know each other on a personal level. This requires creating an atmosphere where youth can communicate interests, needs, and concerns. Personal contact can also be promoted by focusing on shared interests between youth. For example, in a day camp setting, recreation professionals could group participants according to common interests, such as aquatics, adventure activities, or arts.

Social Construction Theory

Social construction theory seeks to explain the process by which knowledge is created and assumed as reality. This theory asserts that people construct meaning through social interactions, and that the behaviors, objects, and language associated with social interaction contribute to how one creates meaning (Berger & Luckmann, 1966). That is, behaviors, objects, and language in the specific context help one to understand "what is going on" and create a perception of the reality of the situation (Douglas, 1970; Shogan, 1999). For example, if youth associate the use of a wheelchair by someone with cerebral palsy to reflect "independence in participation," then the behaviors toward, objects used in relation to, and language about the wheelchair will reflect independence. In a dance class, for instance, the use of a wheelchair could be viewed as a tool to create freedom of expression rather than an object to which the individual is negatively "bound."

Context is an important component in understanding social construction theory because context establishes meaning. In different contexts, meanings associated with the same behavior, objects, and language may change. A comparison of two different sports contexts illustrates this point. Let us say Irene uses a wheelchair to get around. She is interested not only in basketball but also in playing tennis with her able-bodied peers. In this case, basketball and tennis are two different contexts.

One day Irene went to the recreation center and approached the tennis and basketball coaches about playing in each league. Initially, both coaches expressed a lack of knowledge as to how to accommodate the use of a wheelchair in the respective sports. But, the basketball coach portrayed a sincere interest in trying to accommodate her, expressing his lack of knowledge but willingness to do what it would take to include her. On the other hand, the tennis coach reluctantly agreed to attempt to include her, but expressed doubt that it could be done without negatively influencing the level of play of the other players. The basketball coach used a variety of strategies and techniques to accommodate her wheelchair during basketball play with the overall sentiment that her wheelchair is an object that promotes instead of impedes her independence. He also encouraged Irene's fellow players to view her use of the wheelchair as the tool she needs to play basketball.

The tennis coach took a different approach. She expressed frustration with Irene's inability to rush the net to return a shot because she was too slow moving her wheelchair, how her wheelchair got in the way of her ability to play doubles tennis, and how she slowed down play for the other players because she had to make multiple turns in her wheelchair to get to the other side of the court. In this situation, her wheelchair was viewed and treated as an object of nuisance, something that got in the way of playing tennis. Thus, Irene's wheelchair had different meanings depending on the context. In the basketball context, the use of a wheelchair was viewed as a means to facilitate participation, whereas in the tennis context the wheelchair was perceived as a barrier to participation.

The social construction theory also addresses the meaning of disability. The social construction of disability refers to the meaning ascribed by society to physical, mental, cognitive, and emotional impairments (Oliver, 1996). In certain contexts disability may have a positive meaning; however, traditionally disability has been associated with a negative meaning (Bogdan & Taylor, 1992). For example, often youth with disabilities are perceived as being incapable of meeting societal standards, which tend to emphasize physical attractiveness, reciprocity in relationships, capabilities, and independence. By not meeting these standards, youth with disabilities are perceived to be inferior and disadvantaged (Taylor & Bogdan, 1993). They are often stereotyped as not being capable of functioning as independently, accomplishing as much, or having relationships that are as reciprocal as people without disabilities (Wilhite, Devine & Goldenberg, 1999).

The application of social construction theory to inclusive recreation participation suggests that we should try to promote positive interpretations of behaviors, objects, and language associated with disability, thereby reducing negative meanings and stereotypes. For example, recreation professionals could create opportunities for individuals with disabilities to challenge the notion that they cannot participate in high adventure types of recreation activities (e.g., whitewater rafting, rock climbing) by presenting wheelchairs as vehicles for movement and adventure, not as something constraining.

Ecological Theory

Ecological theory is based on the concept that people and their environments are interconnected. That is, there is a reciprocity and interaction among systems within which we live (Howe-Murphy & Charboneau, 1987). Recall in Chapter 6 this theory was important to understanding risk and resiliency, and these concepts are certainly applicable to our current discussion. Systems can be defined as social organizations (e.g., family, schools, religious affiliations, society) that people interact with directly as well as indirectly. Bronfenbrenner (1979) stated that an individual is nested in a complex web of interconnected systems where each system and each component within a system is related to the other. Ecological theory asserts that if a change occurs within the community, the change will not only impact that system but also directly or indirectly influence individuals. In addition, if something occurs to an individual, there will be a reciprocal influence on another system (e.g., family). For instance, when the ADA was written into federal law, that change impacted state and local governments, communities, families, and individuals with disabilities. Conversely, when individuals with disabilities began to demand full inclusion in society that impacted families, local communities, state systems, and federal systems.

Ecological theory provides a structure for analyzing the complexity and intricacy of relationships between individuals and their environments. In modeling these reciprocal relationships, ecological theory operates under the following four fundamental assumptions:

- Building relationships among people based on mutual respect and reciprocity, authenticity, and openness enables maximal growth and interdependence.
- Recognizing the total person—including their abilities, limitations, interests, needs, and environment—creates a focal point for addressing needs and providing services.

- Viewing problems, limitations, deficits, boundaries, and constraints as the result of a multitude of variables rather than a single causal factor minimizes the effects of individual limitations.
- Designing environments to be least restrictive and providing maximum support empowers people to attain optimal interdependence within a specific setting. (Munson, 1991)

Examining constraints to inclusion for youth with disabilities from the multidimensional perspective adopted by ecological theory suggests that recreation professionals should explore individuals' adaptational needs in relation to the context of their social and physical environment. For example, if youth exhibit inappropriate behavior in an inclusive recreation setting, then their interaction as part of a family, neighborhood, social group, peer network, and community also must be considered in attempts to change their behavior.

Self-Determination Theory

In Chapter 7, the opportunity for self-determined behavior was considered one of the most important aspects of leisure's contribution to healthy human functioning. Self-determination theory (e.g., Ryan & Deci, 2000) suggests that one is healthier and happier to the extent that one enacts behaviors willfully (i.e., one is in control of one's actions). But the theory is a bit more complex than that. Self-determination theory also means that if one is unable to or chooses not to make decisions, as long as one endorses the decisions of others and perceives decisions or choices as being consistent with one's values, one is self-determined. Irene, for example, may have been initially encouraged by her parents to join the basketball league. If Irene felt pressure from them and did not want to join at all because she hated sports, but still had to go because her parents thought it would be good for her, she would *not* experience self-regulation. But if she knew it was good for her to join the team and really understood her parent's point of view, that would be considered a type or degree of self-determination. In this latter case, Irene *internalized* her parent's wishes and willfully joined, even though it was not her choice initially.

Another word often used to describe this phenomenon is *autonomy.* Thus, external influence or interference in making choices or decisions would be considered contrary to promoting self-determination, unless those external influences have been internalized (i.e., accepted as one's own) and valued by the individual. Being self-determined is very intrinsically motivating, as we have already discussed in this book, but externally motivated behaviors often create apathy and boredom.

Inclusive recreation programmers should provide multiple leisure opportunities for youth so meaningful choices appropriate to their age and developmental stage can be made. To provide meaningful opportunities for self-determined behavior, programmers need to understand youth's needs and preferences. One of the best ways to do this is by increasing youth voice, as described in Chapter 13. Promoting communication, asking for input and ideas from all participants, and responding to ideas are all important ways to increase self-determination and empower youth with disabilities. Active participation and engaging in decision making promotes feelings of competence and can further one's sense of freedom from constraints.

In summary, we reviewed four theories that provide a lot of guidance concerning how successful inclusion might occur. Given what we know from research, theory, and best practices, we now discuss a set of five principles that may be helpful in guiding recreation professionals in offering effective inclusive programs.

Principles of Inclusive Recreation Services

The principles of inclusive recreation services are founded on the same need to understand and to celebrate diversity as discussed in other chapters in Section IV of the book. Here, the goal is to develop an awareness of, an appreciation for, and the ability to facilitate the involvement of individuals with disabilities in recreation services.

Principle 1: Understand Multidimensionality of Constraints to Inclusion

The first principle of inclusive recreation services addresses the multidimensionality of constraints to inclusion. Thus, we need to view problems, limitations, deficits, boundaries, and constraints as the result of a number of causal factors rather than a single factor (Howe-Murphy & Charboneau, 1987). This means that recreation professionals must understand situations from an ecological perspective. Specifically, constraints and limitations to inclusive recreation participation should focus not only on characteristics of youths' disabilities but also on ways programs are designed, buildings are built, and staff are trained. This principle requires looking beyond the disabilities and taking into account environmental factors, such as negative attitudes toward inclusion held by the general public. Thus, a thorough analysis of the peers, programs offered, facilities, and attitudes of staff and participants should be undertaken to make sure youth with disabilities are welcomed and feel included in program offerings.

What constraints to inclusion might Irene experience? We described some already, such as the attitude of the tennis coach. Maybe to get on the basketball court Irene has to go through the back door of the building. Maybe her parents do not think it is appropriate for her to play ball, or are too busy to transport her to the recreation center. She may possibly experience each of these constraints. As a recreation professional, it will be important to identify and to work toward overcoming constraints that can inhibit participation.

Principle 2: Create the Optimal Environment

Creating the optimal environment to facilitate inclusion is also necessary (Sylvester, Voelkl & Ellis, 2001). Sylvester and colleagues described the optimal environment as a situation where adaptations would be made only when there is evidence indicating that an individual with a disability needs changes to function in an inclusive setting. Thus, we want to offer the "least restrictive environment." Environments should provide youth with maximum support for engagement in inclusive recreation and not overly rely on adaptations if they are not necessary.

One purpose of modifications or adaptations to programs or services should be to provide youth with disabilities the opportunity to attain an optimal experience or flow, where one's abilities are positively challenged by the activity (Csikszentmihalyi, 1990). The concept of flow was discussed in Chapter 8. Recall that optimal experiences are those where one's skills are compatible with the challenge, resulting in a positive experience and avoiding anxiety or boredom. This is a particularly important concept and means that recreation professionals need to be experience engineers—they need to construct the environment and activity such that youth with and without disabilities have optimal experiences. Inclusion will not work if youth with disabilities are overly challenged, leading to anxiety, or if youth without disabilities are underchallenged, leading to boredom. This engineering can be quite a challenge for the recreation professional. Experience, talking with stakeholders, understanding youths' needs and expectations, and trial and error will be needed. What do you think could be done in Irene's situation to engineer optimal experiences?

One way to help engineer optimal experiences is to make sure adaptations are transitional and individualized. Adaptations allow youth with disabilities to optimally and actively participate with peers who do not have disabilities. To individualize means

- to make adjustments according to the youth's abilities and limitations

- to make only the adjustments needed—no more or less
- to view the changes made as potentially temporary; as the youth's skills improve, adaptations may no longer be needed (Dattilo, 2002; Schleien, Ray & Green, 1997)

The goal is to make changes based on the person's individual strengths and limitations. Some typical areas to consider for individualization include materials, activities, rules, equipment, skills, and instructional strategies. For instance, recreation equipment may need to be larger or smaller, lighter or heavier, or color-coded for recognition. As people learn and change, however, their skills and knowledge may change, eventually rendering adaptations unnecessary (Dattilo, 2002). As the person's skills change, an adaptation or accommodation may restrict rather than facilitate participation.

Two other factors to take into account in engineering an optimal environment include facilitating interdependence and making sure adaptations are age appropriate. Interdependence implies relationships among youth with and without disabilities, as well as the staff they cooperate with to accomplish tasks and achieve common goals. We previously gave the example of youth working together to create a mural, which is an excellent example of interdependence. Cooperatively making decisions and working with others toward a goal is very motivating and healthy.

Age appropriateness is also an integral part of an optimal environment. Age-appropriate recreation options should include participating in activities typically associated with that youth's age group. In Irene's case, it would not have been age appropriate to lower the basketball net to make it easier for her to make baskets—that is something done for younger ages and is something her peers would find juvenile. Or imagine if Irene was taking an art class, and because of her cerebral palsy, the art instructor gave her small, blunted scissors and gave everyone else "grown-up," pointed scissors. That also would be age inappropriate. Unless there were clear safety issues associated with Irene using regular scissors, she should be afforded the same opportunity and equipment as everyone else. All youth should be allowed to take appropriate and acceptable risks.

Principle 3: Facilitate Social Inclusion

Creating a satisfactory inclusive recreation experience takes more than assuring facility accessibility, purchasing adaptive equipment, or changing policies. Social inclusion is also important and includes sharing of common experiences, valuing the participation of all individuals, and providing support for participation (Devine, 2004; Goodwin, 2003). Youth with disabilities describe social inclusion as more than the number of friends they have. Social inclusion is a sense of belonging to a group, feeling that participation is valued, and not being ridiculed when skills look different from one's peers without disabilities (Devine & Lashua, 2002).

Social inclusion is critical because lack of social acceptance in inclusive recreation environments is more constraining than architectural or programmatic constraints (Bedini, 2000; Bedini & Henderson, 1994; West, 1984). Moreover, studies have found that individuals with disabilities take an emotional, social, and psychological risk when they chose to participate in inclusive rather than separate (i.e., disability only) recreation programs (Bedini & Henderson, 1994; Devine & Lashua, 2002). Several variables tend to influence the social inclusion of youth with disabilities. One is the severity of the youth's disability. The more severe a youth's disability, the less likely he or she will feel accepted and included (Devine & Lashua). The nature of the disability also appears to play a role in social inclusion. Youth with disabilities involving behavioral characteristics that differ greatly from the norm (e.g., Asperger's syndrome, where although there is no cognitive deficit, but autistic-like behaviors and marked deficiencies in social and communication skills are common) report greater problems with social acceptance than those who have only physical limitations (e.g., spina bifida).

Another influence on social inclusion is context. The context, including the setting, atmosphere, group dynamic, and type of activity, plays a fundamental role in determining social acceptance and individuals taking risks and being willing to debunk stereotypes and myths. Lack of familiarity with the context, little personal contact from staff or other participants, being in very competitive sport environments, or experiencing a high degree of pity or curiosity can thwart social acceptance and inclusion (Devine, 2004). For example, if Irene was the only one in a wheelchair and the basketball league was highly competitive, it is doubtful she would feel included or socially accepted. If the league was set up such that the competitive aspects were downplayed and a number of participants used wheelchairs, social inclusion and acceptance would be more likely. Therefore, the challenge for recreation service providers is to create a context where the social acceptance comfort zone is not a barrier to participation and facilitates interaction.

Let us take a closer look at Irene for a moment. Although she uses a wheelchair to be mobile, she considers herself to be very active in sports, in school life, and with her friends. Last summer Irene attended a six-day overnight camp. The camp served youth with and without disabilities, offering typical summer activities such as swimming, horseback riding, ropes courses, arts, drama, and hiking. Irene did not know anyone attending the camp and was a bit anxious about the experience since she had never spent a night away from her family and had never participated in activities in which she did not know anyone. She was particularly apprehensive about the degree of social acceptance she would experience from her peers without disabilities. Specifically, she was concerned that they may make fun of her, ignore her, not include her in social interactions, or see her as an object of curiosity instead of a person. Fortunately, Irene's concerns did not occur at this camp. She reported feeling very included in the entire camp experience by peers and staff. In the formal, organized activities (e.g., canoeing lessons) Irene stated that she felt encouraged to try new things and it didn't matter to what degree she participated or whether her skills looked exactly like those of her peers. Irene said what was most important to her was her inclusion in the spontaneous, informal activities (e.g., spending free time with her cabin mates). She stated that her cabin mates and group peers included her in conversations, invited her to eat lunch with them, and asked her for her e-mail address so they could correspond after camp ended. Thus, social inclusion is a forum for developing relationships. Facilitating opportunities for input, building social relationships, and providing supports are fundamental for creating inclusive recreation services.

Principle 4: Address Attitudinal Constraints

Attitudes are beliefs coupled with emotion about an aspect of life (Fishbein & Ajzen, 1975). Historically, North Americans have displayed a variety of attitudes toward individuals with disabilities. For instance, some perceive individuals with disabilities as "objects of pity," someone you should feel sorry for, but never want to aspire to be like (Bullock & Mahon, 1997; Shapiro, 1993). At times, individuals with disabilities are treated with ambivalence and simply tolerated (Devine & Lashua, 2002; Wilhite, Devine & Goldenberg, 1999). On the other hand, some individuals with disabilities are considered heroic and treated as "objects of admiration" (Schleien, Ray & Green, 1997; Shapiro, 1993), because of a belief that there is something extraordinary about being able to live with a disability. These attitudes are powerful constraints to inclusive recreation services, not only because they so strongly affect how a person feels but also because attitudinal constraints are very slow to change (Bullock & Mahon, 1997; Goodwin & Watkinson, 2000).

Training staff is an important way to address attitudinal constraints and is an important component in the inclusion process (Wachter & McGowan, 2002). Over the past 10 years various staff training workshop formats have been empirically tested and recommended by recreation inclusion experts. Training workshops may focus on the effects stereotyping or stigmatizing has on a recreation experience. Another topic for an inclusion workshop is how staff assumptions and expectations of youth with disabilities may prevent effective inclusion. The basketball coach certainly had a better set of assumptions and expectations of what Irene could do than the tennis coach did. If both coaches had attended a staff training workshop on inclusion, they may have been better equipped to individualize accommodations for Irene.

Based on contact theory, Herbert (2000) found that a combination of training and contact with individuals with disabilities may be the optimal way to promote a positive attitude toward inclusion. Disability awareness programs can include learning about disability characteristics, participating in simulation activities, reading about accessibility, and conducting site accessibility surveys. Encouraging interdependence to promote prolonged contact between youth with and without disabilities is also a way to change attitudes (Dattilo, 2002; Schleien, Ray & Green, 1997).

Principle 5: Provide Opportunities to Challenge Myths

Providing opportunities to challenge myths and stereotypes and to counter stigmas is the last principle of inclusive recreation services. This principle is particularly important because it can be a powerful way to change attitudes. One way to counter stereotypes and stigmas about youth with disabilities is to provide opportunities to show peers their skills and abilities. Through this process, nondisabled peers should be able to see them as more than a person with a disability.

The role played by recreation staff is critical to challenging myths about youth with disabilities. Staff attitudes and approaches to inclusion can set the tone for challenging assumptions about those with disabilities (Hutzler, Fliess, Chacham & Van den Auweelle, 2002). Devine (2004) reported that when the recreation staff emphasized abilities of participants with disabilities, focused on similarities between participants, and challenged stereotypes, the inclusive recreation experience was a connecting force between youth with and without disabilities. In addition, when staff provide assistance to all youth, not just those with disabilities, emphasis on the disability decreases and perceptions of social acceptance are more positive (Devine & O'Brien, in review; Slininger, Sherrill & Jankowski, 2000; Wilhite, Devine & Goldenberg, 1999). All youth need supports when faced with challenges and all youth need assistance with skill development. These studies suggest that engineering experiences where staff and peers with and without disabilities have opportunities to be challenged and to engage in recreation experiences are positive for everyone.

Each of the five principles we have just discussed is important because inclusion does not happen by itself. To include youth with disabilities requires a deliberate process and skill and training on the part of the recreation professional. The final part of this chapter provides you with an overall framework for facilitating inclusion, pulling all of the pieces together in one model, the Supportive Recreation Inclusion Model (SRI).

Supportive Recreation Inclusion Model: A Framework for Service Provision

The supportive recreation inclusion (SRI) model is designed to identify supports and constraints to including youth with disabilities in recreation programs with peers without disabilities (Devine, 2002). An analysis of each of the model's components will bridge the gap between constraints and needs, and identify necessary support services. The SRI model consists of four components or systems: (a) individuals with disabilities, (b) support services, (c) recreation service providers, and (d) the community at large (see **Figure 21.1**).

The model is based on ecological theory, which we discussed earlier. The primary assumption of the SRI model is that systems (e.g., families, schools, recreation departments) are interconnected webs in which each has a reciprocal influence on the other. The philosophy behind the SRI model is that a healthy community will be created if individuals with disabilities are active and vital members of that community. Thus, if youth with disabilities are actively participating in community recreation programs, civic activities, or using parks, the community as well as the individual will benefit.

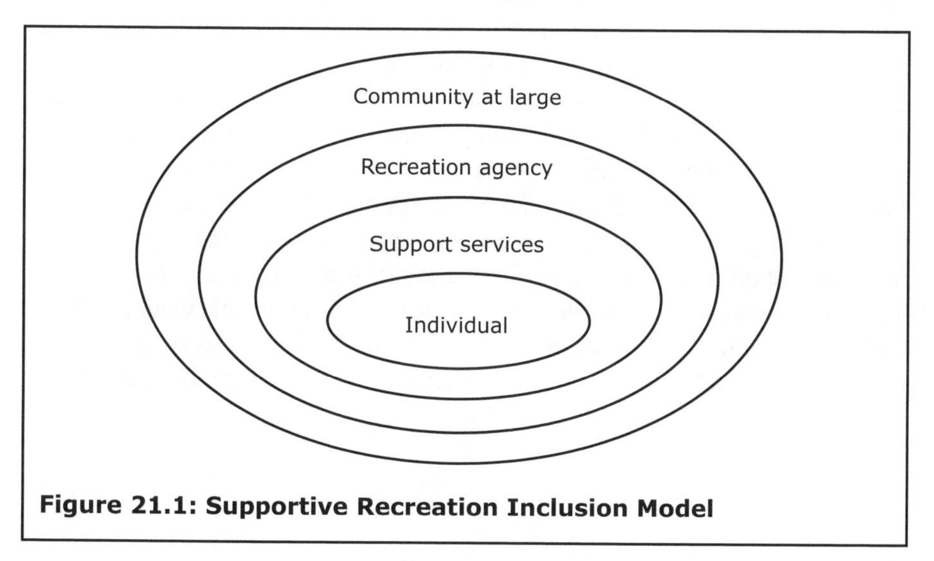

Figure 21.1: Supportive Recreation Inclusion Model

A second premise of this model is that youth with disabilities who are active in community life (a) will have a higher quality of life because they will feel less socially isolated, (b) will have a greater sense of belonging, and (c) will be more likely to be physically and mentally healthier than those who are not active in the community. For example, a recent study on a residential camp experience of youth with and without disabilities found that youth who were actively involved in camp life reported less stress, a greater sense of belonging, and greater physical endurance compared to their nonactive peers (Devine & O'Brien, in review).

The SRI model allows one to consider the way constraints, obstacles, and limitations influence inclusion. For example, in the model it is easy to see how constraints and limitations are a result of a multitude of factors associated with the systems of concern. For example, constraints may be operative in the following components of the system: community (e.g., accessible transportation), recreation organization (e.g., lack of training for recreation staff), support system (e.g., lack of parental support) and individual (e.g., lack of leisure skill training). We now address each of the components in the model.

Individuals With Disabilities

The primary focus of the SRI model is meeting the needs of the youth with a disability who is interested in participating in recreation programs with peers without disabilities. Because the individual's choices and preferences are the main concern, the youth should be included in the identification of potential recreation programs as well as the design, revision, and evaluation of an inclusion plan. The role of the recreation professional is to assist in matching the individual's interests and choices with recreation opportunities in the community, assessing constraints to inclusion, and in conjunction with the individual, designing an inclusion plan. A therapeutic recreation specialist may be consulted, as he or she is specifically trained to conduct such assessments and to design individual plans, although with experience, recreation professionals may be able to undertake the processes themselves. The inclusion plan may consist of support activities, such as transportation training (i.e., to get to and from the program), assisting with the registration process, or facilitating learning prerequisite recreation skills. Recreation professionals would assist with initial implementation of the inclusion plan and discuss accommodations with the individual to evaluate and possibly revise the plan (Devine, 2002).

Support Services

The recreation professional also needs to work with the important people who form a youth's support system (e.g., family, friends, caregivers, caring adults). Understanding a youth's support system will help a recreation professional to more effectively address the youth's needs. For example, when designing an inclusion plan for a youth who has autism, understanding behavior management plans used at home and in school, knowing the composition of a young person's circle of friends, and understanding the family's or caregiver's attitudes toward inclusion will help the recreation professional to address issues that may arise during the inclusion process.

Recreation Service Providers

Recreation service providers are a vital linking mechanism in the inclusion process. Thus, professionals would undertake an analysis of a recreation organization's philosophy and mission statement, administrative processes, program planning system, and resource components. For instance, knowing the level or degree of staff's skills to implement adaptations, their attitudes toward inclusion, and their knowledge of disability characteristics are helpful when assessing staff strengths and any limitations to inclusion. Knowing the organization's philosophy toward inclusion is useful because the philosophy will influence the belief system of the recreation professionals.

After an analysis of the youth's needs, social supports, and agency and staff strengths and weaknesses, an inclusion plan may include providing activities such as staff training on how to make adaptations and accommodations to promote optimal experiences, securing a volunteer inclusion companion to assist the individual with participation in the program, or purchasing adaptive recreation equipment to facilitate participation. Implied in the SRI model, a recreation professional would assist with initial implementation of the inclusion plan as well as conduct observations and follow-up visits to evaluate and possibly to revise the plan.

Community at Large

Individuals, their support systems, and recreation organizations are part of the larger community. The community represents the macrosystem of the SRI model and includes educational, governmental, healthcare, human service, transportation, and commercial organizations. Analyzing the community includes examining things like people's overall attitudes toward inclusion, general compliance levels with the Americans with Disabilities Act among community organizations, existing physical accommodations, and services that support inclusion. This analysis will inform a recreation professional about potential constraints or facilitators to inclusion.

In summary, the SRI model was created by Devine to serve as a framework for identifying the strengths and limitations relative to inclusion of individuals, support systems, recreation service providers, and the community (Devine, 2002). Understanding and analyzing the systems that influence inclusion, as well as adopting the principles of inclusion, will serve to provide the least restrictive environment and maximum support, empowering people to attain optimal interdependence within an inclusive recreation setting (Munson, 1991).

Concluding Remarks

Inclusion of youth with disabilities is an emerging reality. The inclusion movement has evolved from efforts being the responsibility of the person with the disability to make changes, adjustments, and concessions to the perspective that it is everyone's responsibility to make accommodations so youth with disabilities can recreate with those who do not have disabilities. In the future, we would expect to see further advances and more evidence of society's acceptance of social inclusion as the norm.

ADA and other legislation have had a strong influence on the inclusion of youth with disabilities, family members and caregivers, and recreation professionals. For the most part, youth with disabilities prefer to be included in recreation activities with their nondisabled peers (Devine & O'Brien, in review). An entire generation of youth with and without disabilities have known and experienced inclusion in educational settings, and they have come to expect the same opportunities in their recreation choices. Unfortunately, however, stigmas, stereotypes, and negative attitudes toward the inclusion of youth with disabilities in recreation services continue to be a significant constraint to inclusion (Bedini, 2000; Devine, 2004; Devine & Lashua, 2002). Sadly, society in general has been slow in responding to the rights of individuals with disabilities to actively participate in all that communities have to offer.

Despite the general stigmas and negative attitudes, youth with disabilities continue to learn more about and to exercise their right to inclusion. Future generations of youth will seek to have more input and greater involvement in designing inclusive recreation experiences. Thus, inclusive and accessible recreation opportunities must expand. Recreation organizations have begun to respond to the needs for inclusion of youth with disabilities, but a strong sentiment of not being properly prepared to meet this challenge still exists

(Devine & McGovern, 2001; LaMaster, Gall, Kinchin & Siedentop, 1998). For example, too often recreation professionals assume that individuals with disabilities are an occasional special consumer instead of regular participants. Unless that assumption is changed, progress in offering inclusive services will be inadequate. More research is needed to address the needs and desires of youth with disabilities as well as the best way to design inclusive services. Better information and techniques will help recreation professionals to feel more confident about providing these services and regarding these youth with disabilities as regular participants. Finally, armed with increased implementation skills, recreation professionals will be in a better position to be advocates and help change the general societal attitudes toward individuals with disabilities. As society changes its perceptions of individuals with disabilities from "sick and in need of medical attention" to "healthy and living with a disability," including youth with disabilities in a wide variety of recreation options will become more commonplace.

References

Allport, G. W. (1935). Attitudes. In C. Murchinson (Ed.), *Handbook of social psychology* (pp. 802–827). Worchester, MA: Clarke University Press.

Allport, G. W. (1954). *The nature of prejudice*. New York, NY: Addison-Wesley.

Amir, Y. (1969). Contact hypothesis in ethnic relations. *Psychological Bulletin, 7*(5), 319–342.

Archie, V. W. and Sherrill, C. (1989). Attitudes toward handicapped peers of mainstreamed and nonmainstreamed children in physical education. *Perceptual and Motor Skills, 69*, 319–322.

Bedini, L. A. (2000). "Just sit down so we can talk:" Perceived stigma and community recreation pursuits by people with disabilities. *Therapeutic Recreation Journal, 34,* 55–68.

Bedini, L. A. and Henderson, K. A. (1994). Women with disabilities and the challenges to leisure service providers. *Journal of Park and Recreation Administration, 12*(1), 17–34.

Berger, P. L. and Luckmann, T. (1966). *The social construction of reality: A treatise in the sociology of knowledge.* Garden City, NJ: Doubleday.

Bogdan, R. and Taylor, S. J. (1992). The social construction of humanness. In P. M. Ferguson, D. M. Ferguson, and S. J. Taylor (Eds.), *Interpreting disability* (pp. 275–296). New York, NY: Teachers College Press.

Bronfenbrenner, U. (1979). *The ecology of human development.* Cambridge, MA: Harvard University Press.

Bullock, C. C. and Mahon, M. J. (1997). *Introduction to recreation services for people with disabilities: A person-centered approach.* Champaign, IL: Sagamore.

Cook, S. W. (1962). The systematic analysis of socially significant events: A strategy for social research. *Journal of Social Issues, 18*(2), 66–84.

Csikszentmihalyi, M. (1990). *Flow: The psychology of optimal experience.* New York, NY: Harper & Row Publishers.

Dattilo, J. (2002). *Inclusive leisure services: Responding to the rights of people with disabilities* (2nd ed.). State College: PA: Venture Publishing, Inc.

Devine, M. A. (1997). Inclusive leisure services and research: Consideration of the use of social construction theory. *Journal of Leisurability, 24*(2), 3–11.

Devine, M.A. (2002). *The supportive recreation inclusion model: A framework for providing inclusive recreation services.* Las Vegas, NV: National Institute on Recreation Inclusion.

Devine, M.A. (2004). From connector to distancer: The role of inclusive leisure contexts in determining social acceptance for people with disabilities. *Journal of Leisure Research, 35*(2), 137–159.

Devine, M. A. and Dattilo, J. (2000). The relationship between social acceptance and leisure lifestyles of people with disabilities. *Therapeutic Recreation Journal, 34,* 199–218.

Devine, M. A. and Lashua B. (2002). Constructing social acceptance in inclusive leisure contexts: The role of individuals with disabilities. *Therapeutic Recreation Journal, 36*, 65–83.

Devine, M. A., Malley, S., Sheldon, K., Dattilo, J., and Gast, D. L. (1997). Promoting initiation of community leisure participation for adults with mental retardation. *Education and Training in Mental Retardation and Developmental Disabilities, 32*(3), 241–254.

Devine, M. A. and McGovern, J. (2001). Inclusion of individuals with disabilities in public park and recreation programs: Are agencies ready? *Journal of Park and Recreation Administration, 19*(4), 60–82.

Devine, M. A. and O'Brien, M. B. (in review). Perceptions of youth with and without disabilities on an inclusive residential camp: What works and what doesn't. *Therapeutic Recreation Journal.*

Devine, M. A. and Wilhite, B. (2000). The meaning of disability: Implications for inclusive leisure services for youth with and without disabilities. *Journal of Park and Recreation Administration, 18*(3), 35–52.

Douglas, J. D. (1970). Understanding everyday life. In J. D. Douglas (Ed.), *Understanding everyday life: Toward the reconstruction of sociological knowledge* (pp. 3–43). Chicago, IL: Aldine.

Fishbein, M. and Ajzen, I. (1975). *Belief, attitude, intention, and behavior: An introduction to theory and research.* Reading, MA: Addison Wesley.

Green, F. P. and DeCoux, V. (1994). A procedure for evaluating the effectiveness of a community recreation integration program. *Therapeutic Recreation Journal, 28*(1), 41–47.

Goodwin, D. (2003). The meaning of social experiences in recreation settings. *Impact,16*(2), 4–5.

Goodwin D. L. and Watkinson, E. J. (2000). Inclusive physical education from the perspective of students with physical disabilities. *Adapted Physical Activity Quarterly, 17,* 144–160.

Henderson, K. A., Bedini, L. A., Hecht, L., and Schuler, R. (1995). Women with physical disabilities and the negotiation of leisure constraints. *Leisure Studies, 14,* 17–31.

Herbert, J. T. (2000). Therapeutic adventure staff attitudes and preferences for working with persons with disabilities. *Therapeutic Recreation Journal, 34,* 211–226.

Hewitt, J. P. (1991). *Self and society: A symbolic interactionist social psychology* (5th ed.). Boston, MA: Allyn & Bacon.

Howe-Murphy, R. and Charboneau, B. (1987). *Therapeutic recreation intervention: An ecological perspective.* Englewood Cliffs, NJ: Prentice Hall.

Hutzler, Y., Fliess, O., Chacham, A., and Van den Auweele, Y. (2002). Perspectives of children with physical disabilities on inclusion and empowerment: Supporting and limiting factors. *Adapted Physical Activity Quarterly, 19,* 300–317.

LaMaster, K., Gall, K., Kinchin, G., and Siedentop, D. (1998). Inclusion practices of effective elementary specialists. *Adapted Physical Activity Quarterly, 15,* 51–63.

Modell, S. J. (1997). *An examination of inclusive recreation and leisure participation for children with trainable mental retardation.* Unpublished doctoral dissertation, Florida State University, Tallahassee.

Munson, W. W. (1991). Juvenile delinquency as a societal problem and social disability: The therapeutic recreator's role as ecological change agent. *Therapeutic Recreation Journal, 25*(2), 19–30.

National Institutes of Health. (n.d.). *Healthy people 2010.* Retrieved May 20, 2004, from http://www.nih.gov/news

Obrusnikova, I., Valkova, H., and Block, M. (2003). Impact of inclusion in general physical education on students without disabilities. *Adapted Physical Activity Quarterly,* 20, 230–245.

Oliver, M. (1996). *Understanding disability: From theory to practice.* London, England: MacMillan Press.

Roper, P. (1990a). Changing perceptions through contact. *Disability, Handicap & Society, 5*(3), 243–255.

Roper, P. (1990b). Special Olympics volunteers' perceptions of people with mental retardation. *Education and Training in Mental Retardation, 25*(2), 164–175.

Ryan, R. M. and Deci, E. L. (2000). Self-determination theory and the facilitation of intrinsic motivation, social development, and well-being. *American Psychologist, 55*, 68–78.

Sable, J. R. (1995). Efficacy of physical integration, disability awareness, and adventure programming on adolescents' acceptance of individuals with disabilities. *Therapeutic Recreation Journal, 29,* 206–227.

Schleien, S. J., Fahnestock, M., Green, R., and Rynders, J. E. (1990). Building positive social networks through environmental interventions in integrated recreation programs. *Therapeutic Recreation Journal, 24*(4), 42–52.

Schleien, S. J., Hornfeldt, D., and McAvoy, L. H. (1994). Integration and environmental outdoor education: The impact of integrating students with severe disabilities on the academic performance of peers without disabilities. *Therapeutic Recreation Journal, 28*, 25–34.

Schleien, S. J., Ray, M. T., and Green, F. P. (1997). *Community recreation and people with disabilities: Strategies for inclusion.* Baltimore, MD: Paul Brookes.

Shapiro, J. P. (1993). *No pity.* New York, NY: Random House.

Sherif, M., Harvey, O. J., White, B. J., Hood, W. R., and Sherif C. W. (1961). *Intergroup conflict and cooperation: The Robbers Cave experiment.* Norman, OK: University Book Exchange.

Shogan, D. (1999). *The making of high-performance athletes: Discipline, diversity, and ethics.* Toronto, ON, Canada: University of Toronto Press.

Slininger, D., Sherrill, C., and Jankowski, C. M. (2000). Children's attitudes toward peers with severe disabilities: Revisiting contact theory. *Adapted Physical Activity Quarterly, 17,* 176–196.

Smith, R. W., Austin, D. R., and Kennedy, D. W. (2001). *Inclusive and special recreation: Opportunities for persons with disabilities* (4th ed.). Dubuque, IA: Brown & Benchmark.

Stinchcombe, C. (1968). *Constructing social theories.* New York, NY: Harcourt, Brace & World.

Sylvester, C. (1992). Therapeutic recreation and the right to leisure. *Therapeutic Recreation Journal, 26*(2), 9–20.

Sylvester, C., Voelkl, J. E., and Ellis, G. D. (2001). *Therapeutic recreation programming: Theory and practice.* State College, PA: Venture Publishing, Inc.

Taylor, S. J. and Bogdan, R. (1993). Promises made, promises to be broken. In P. Wehman (Ed.), *The ADA mandate for a social change* (pp. 255–268). Baltimore, MD: Paul H. Brookes.

Tripp, A., French, R., and Sherrill, C. (1995). Contact theory and attitudes of children in physical education programs toward peers with disabilities. *Adapted Physical Activity Quarterly, 12,* 323–332.

Tripp, A. and Sherrill, C. (1991). Attitude theories of relevance to adapted physical education. *Adapted Physical Activity Quarterly, 8,* 12–27.

U.S. Department of Justice (1991). *Americans with Disabilities Act* (P.L. 101-336).

Wachter, C. and McGowan, A. (2002). Inclusion practices of special recreation agencies in Illinois. *Therapeutic Recreation Journal, 36,* 172–185.

West, P. C. (1984). Social stigma and community recreation participation by the physically and mentally handicapped. *Therapeutic Recreation Journal, 26*(1), 40–49.

Wilhite, B., Devine, M. A., and Goldenberg, L. (1999). Self-perceptions of youth with and without disabilities: Implications for leisure programs and services. *Therapeutic Recreation Journal, 33,* 15–28.

Chapter 22
Endings

Peter A. Witt and Linda L. Caldwell

We hope you have enjoyed reading this book and have become inspired to use the knowledge you gained to make a difference for youth through recreation and leisure. There are many ways to make a difference and to contribute to positive youth development. The knowledge and perspectives we offered reflect the current state of the art in terms of promoting positive youth development and at the same time reducing the risk of engaging in risky behaviors. Recreation and leisure contexts provide rich opportunities through which development can occur—especially if youth are supported, guided, and given opportunities to engage with life in positive ways.

You may want to reread Chapter 1, which provided and discussed 10 principles to youth development. These principles provided a framework for the rest of the book, and they may make more sense to you now that you have finished reading the chapters.

To end this book, we offer a number of common themes that have occurred as the book evolved. Although we began with the set of 10 principles to guide us as we constructed and wrote the book, as the book evolved and as we worked with other authors, it was clear that there are some main themes that should be recognized as they compliment and extend the original 10 principles.

Cross-Cutting Themes

Ecological perspective. One of the major cross-cutting themes was the usefulness of viewing youth development from an ecological perspective. An ecological model helps to identify the supports, opportunities, programs, and services needed by youth. It is based on how the individual, peers, family, caring adults, institutions and agencies (e.g., schools, churches, recreation departments, YMCA, YWCA), community resources (e.g., transportation systems, facilities), and cultural contexts (e.g., race and ethnicity, community norms and values) interact to promote or detract from positive youth development. Stemming from this model, some noteworthy highlights cut across chapters.

Youth engagement. Youth have many skills, have a lot of potential, are innately motivated to learn, and desire to be engaged with their environments.

Approaches to youth development that capitalize on this positive approach (in concert with risk reduction approaches if needed) are considered to be most effective.

Youth voice, self-determination, and initiative. Youth need to take an active voice in shaping their development; this process takes place in a variety of contexts and is influenced by a variety of factors. Guidance, education, and support are needed for youth to learn self-determination and responsible autonomy.

Adults as supports. Adults can have both positive and negative influences in adolescents' lives, and represent important risk and protective factors to healthy development. Despite the possibility of having a negative influence, adults, in the form of parents, youth workers, coaches, teachers, spiritual leaders, and so forth, can have enormous positive influence on how a young person develops. But this effort has to be deliberate and foster a young person's innate drives and capacities.

Adults as advocates. Adults are also important because they serve an advocacy role. Unfortunately we did not address this area as much as we could have due to space limitation, but we want to make the point that adults must, in concert with youth, advocate for appropriate supports, opportunities, programs, and services for youth. Essentially this means adults and youth should have an influence on policy development (e.g., mandatory leisure education in the schools) through advocacy and political action.

Context and diversity. Although trite sounding, youth share many similarities as well as differences. These manifest themselves in different ways in different contexts. Differences and similarities are both good, but differences should not be ignored, should be embraced, and need to be understood. Often differences are evident in one context and not another. Not all programs and services serve all youth's needs in the same way.

Be deliberate. Deliberate efforts by youth, adults, programmers, and policy makers are essential. While a lot of life "just happens," healthy and positive youth development occurs in contexts where the supports, opportunities, programs, and services are deliberately constructed and deliberately led. This means knowing where you want to go, why you want to get there, how you'll get there, why you were successful, and how you are going to demonstrate you got there.

Finally, we want to reiterate how important recreation and leisure are to youth development. Although youth engage in risky behaviors during recreation and leisure, it is a rich context for healthy development. Recreation and leisure, more than most other contexts in a youth's life, provide the opportunity to actively engage, to develop competence and skills, to make decisions (and mistakes), to have voice, to experiment with identity and gender roles, to connect with others, to contribute to community, and to develop initiative. The inherent qualities of a leisure context and experience suggest that self-determination and initiative are more possible than in work, school, or home contexts.

Throughout this book we hope you have been have been provided with more tools and knowledge to make a difference in young people's lives. Now we challenge you to use those skills to positively enhance the life experiences of young people.

Author Bios

Cheryl K. Baldwin is an Assistant Professor in the Human Services program at Aurora University where she teaches courses in youth development and nonprofit management. Cheryl received her Ph.D. in Leisure Behavior from the University of Illinois at Urbana-Champaign. Her research examines the motivational processes and developmental benefits associated with preferred and meaningful hobbies and youth development programs. She is currently involved in projects designed to advance the use of theory-based practice. She serves as an Associate Editor for *Child and Youth Services*. Cheryl enjoys reading, music, art, and being outdoors.

Jason N. Bocarro is an Assistant Professor in the Department of Recreation Management and Policy at the University of New Hampshire. He received his BSocSc. from the University of Birmingham in England, his MA from Dalhousie University, and his Ph.D. from Texas A&M University. Before working at the University of New Hampshire, Jason was involved with youth programs in a variety of places and settings, including London, Nova Scotia, Texas, and New Hampshire. His current research investigates how healthy relationships develop between youth and adults in community-based programs. He is a regular speaker at conferences on youth and adolescent issues. In 2004 he was awarded the University of New Hampshire School of Health and Human Services Good Stewards award for his work within the communities of New Hampshire. He was also given the University of New Hampshire Young Investigator of the Year award. Outside of work Jason enjoys spending time hiking, biking, running, and most other outdoor activities, catching up with how his beloved Arsenal are doing, and spending time with his wife, Melanie.

Linda L. Caldwell is a Professor of Recreation and Park Management in the Department of Recreation, Park, and Tourism Management at Penn State University. Linda received her PhD at the University of Maryland (1986). Her research interests center on the intersection of youth, leisure, and health, both domestically and internationally, primarily focusing on developing youth competencies and healthy lifestyles and reducing risky behavior in leisure. She is the author of a new school-based curriculum, *TimeWise: Taking Charge of Free Time* (ETR Associates). She has also coauthored *HealthWise South Africa: Life Skills for Young Adults*, which is being evaluated in Cape Town, South Africa. Linda has been an associate editor for a number of journals, including the *Journal of Leisure Research* and the *Therapeutic Recreation Journal*. She served as guest editor for the *Journal of Park and Recreation*

Administration special issue on youth and leisure (2000) and a special issue of *Therapeutic Recreation Journal* on youth (2001). She was also a guest coeditor of a special issue of children and adolescent's leisure for *World Leisure Journal* (2003). She sits on the Board of Directors for the Canadian Association of Leisure Studies, and is secretary of the Children and Youth working group of the World Leisure and Recreation Association. Linda loves traveling, gardening, cooking, photography, being in nature (especially scuba diving and camping), and spending time with her husband and cats.

Megan Kelly Cronan is a graduate student in the Department of Recreation, Park and Tourism Sciences at Texas A&M University. Megan holds a BA in Cultural Anthropology with a minor in Spanish from The University of Texas at Austin. She began her parks and recreation career at the age of 15, and has held management positions for the City of College Station as well as for Rec Sports at the University of Texas at Austin. Her major interests are the empowerment of women and young girls through recreation, the relationship between body image and recreation, and cultural diversity. She has participated in several research studies related to youth development and has been a teaching assistant for a course on *Recreation and Youth Development*. She was named a Future Scholar at the NRPA Congress in 2004. When not working, Megan enjoys reading, live music, outdoor recreation activities, and spending time with her husband, Andrew, and their dogs.

Mary Ann Devine is currently an Associate Professor at Kent State University. She received her Ed.D. from the University of Georgia in 1997. Her research and practice expertise is in the area of inclusion of individuals with disabilities in leisure contexts. Inclusion is not only her vocation, it is her avocation as she believes individuals with disabilities have the right to be included with their peers in all the opportunities a community has to offer. Mary Ann was a member of the founding APRS/NTRS Joint Committee on Inclusion that established the National Institute on Recreation Inclusion. She has done numerous studies examining aspects of the inclusion process such as social acceptance, best practices, stigma, and attitudinal barriers. She can often be found hiking, skiing, biking, reading, and spending quality time with her husband, Craig, and sons, John and Patrick.

Jesse M. Ellis enjoys trying to play softball and golf, cheering for his black lab, Allie, in doggie ice cream eating contests, and goofing off with his wife, Anna, and daughter, Paige. To support these endeavors, he is currently the Supervisor of Community Use for the Fairfax County, Virginia, Department of Community and Recreation Services, where he oversees the scheduling of nearly 1,000 athletic facilities, conducts needs assessments and program evaluations, writes grant proposals, and engages the community in developing and implementing programs. He has created and led youth programs for recreation departments in Fairfax County (VA), Montgomery County (MD), and Ocean City (MD). Jesse has a BS in Recreation and Leisure Studies from Ithaca College and an MS in Leisure Studies from Penn State University, where he focused on youth development and wrote his thesis on youth voice.

Arnold H. Grossman is a Professor in the Department of Applied Psychology, The Steinhardt School of Education at New York University. In 1994 he was named the School of Education's Professor of the Year. Arnold's current teaching and research activities focus on individuals who experience alienation and stigmatization with an emphasis on lesbian, gay, bisexual, and transgender (LGBT) people. He currently serves as chair of the Advisory Council of The Hetrick-Martin Institute, which is the home of the Harvey Milk High School—the first public high school for LGBT students. Arnold has served as chair of NYU's Department of Recreation, Leisure, Physical Education and Sport, and as a member of the Board of Directors of World Leisure and Recreation Association and the Society of Park and Recreation Educators. He is a regular speaker at national and international conferences and the author of numerous chapters and articles. When not working, he can be found attending the theater in New York City or London, reading mysteries, and spending time with his close friends.

Karla A. Henderson is a Professor in the Department of Parks, Recreation, and Tourism Management at North Carolina State University. She was formerly Professor and Chair in the Department of Recreation and Leisure Studies at the University of North Carolina—Chapel Hill. She holds a Ph.D. from the University of Minnesota. Her research focuses primarily on gender and diversity issues pertaining to physical activity, although most recently she has been involved in examining the outcomes of organized camps and youth development. Karla is a Certified Parks and Recreation Professional and currently serves as Chair of the NRPA Forum Research Task Force. She is on the National Advisory Committee of the Robert Wood Johnson Foundation's Active Living Research unit. She has served as President of the Society of Park and Recreation Educators, Academy of Leisure Sciences, and Research Consortium of the American Alliance of Health, Physical Education, Recreation, and Dance. Karla has authored or coauthored several books as well as numerous professional publications. She currently serves as coeditor of *Leisure Sciences*. For her own leisure, she enjoys running, hiking, snowshoeing, playing a trumpet in the Durham Community Band, and being entertained by her three silly cats.

Susan L. Hutchinson began her professional career in the leisure studies field working as a recreation therapist for 12 years prior to returning to graduate school. Her long-standing interest in coping and adjustment grew from her work with people in rehabilitation and long-term care settings in Victoria, British Columbia, Canada. Susan left work to pursue her master's degree at Dalhousie University in Halifax, Nova Scotia, and then her doctorate at the University of Georgia. Along the way she became a mother to her son, Cole. After graduate school she joined the faculty at the Pennsylvania State University in a newly created position designed to foster interdisciplinary research on children, youth, and families. It is here that she enjoyed the opportunity to work with colleagues Linda Caldwell and Cheryl Baldwin to examine parenting practices associated with adolescent free-time use. Susan recently moved back to Canada to pursue her interest in arts and to spend more time having fun with her son.

Reed W. Larson is the Pampered Chef Ltd. Endowed Chair in Family Resiliency and a professor in the Departments of Human and Community Development, Psychology, Leisure Studies, and Educational Psychology at the University of Illinois at Urbana-Champaign. He is author of *Divergent Realities: The Emotional Lives of Mothers, Fathers, and Adolescents* (with Maryse Richards), which examines the organization of time and emotions within the daily lives of families and how emotions are transmitted between family members. He is also the author of *Being Adolescent: Conflict and Growth in the Teenage Years* (with Mihaly Csikszentmihalyi), which deals with the daily experience of high school students. His current area of interest is adolescents' experience in extracurricular activities, community-based programs, and other structured, voluntary activities in the after-school hours. He holds a BA degree in psychology from the University of Minnesota and a Ph.D. in Human Development from the University of Chicago.

Francis Lobo is an Associate Professor and the Senior Honorary Research Fellow in the School of Marketing Tourism and Leisure at Edith Cowan University in Perth, Western Australia. During the 1990s his research focused on unemployment and he coauthored a book on late career unemployment and its impact on self, family, and lifestyle. He was awarded the Wal Okay prize for outstanding research on older people in 1995. This was followed by research into the unemployment of young people. A second book followed, *Leisure, Family and Lifestyle: Unemployed Young People*, establishing Dr. Lobo as a respected scholar in the field of unemployment and leisure. He has been the Editor-in-Chief of the *World Leisure Journal* and is President of the Research Committee 13 of the International Sociological Association. With schooling in India, teacher education in Uganda, an undergraduate degree from the United Kingdom, two masters' degrees in the United States and Australia, respectively, and a doctorate from the University of Western Australia, Dr. Lobo has been eminently qualified to lead numerous research projects in leisure and tourism studies. In recognition of a career performance, Francis Lobo was awarded The Frank Stewart Prize (2000) for outstanding contribution to the Parks and Leisure Industry of Australia.

Kristi Montandon is currently a doctoral student in the Department of Recreation, Park and Tourism Sciences at Texas A&M University. Prior to beginning her Ph.D., she spent 12 years working with the Navy MWR as a Youth Services Director in Washington State. Kristi has also worked in numerous other youth settings, including sports, special events, teen and youth programs, service learning, and camps. She holds a bachelor's degree in Recreation and Leisure planning from Minnesota State University at Mankato and a master's degree in Youth Development from Concordia University at St. Paul. Kristi is a certified Parks and Recreation Professional and enjoys working with practitioners in the field. She has participated in several research studies and has been a teaching assistant and a course instructor. Kristi enjoys spending time with family and friends and can be spotted on the soccer field or behind the plate playing softball.

Bill Niepoth is Chair of the World Leisure Working Group for Children and Youth. He has participated in various events related to the welfare of young people, including World Leisure Congresses in Bilbao, Spain (2000) and Kuala Lumpur, Malaysia (2002). He represented World Leisure at the 2002 United Nations Special Session on Children and continues to work with the NGO Committee on UNICEF. In 2003 he served as guest coeditor for a special issue of *World Leisure Journal* on children and adolescents. He is an emeritus Professor of Recreation and Park Management at California State University, Chico. Previously, he served as Chair of the Department of Recreation at CSU, Hayward. He has held summer or visiting appointments at several other universities and in the former State College System of Victoria, Australia. He also has held administrative positions in municipal recreation and parks and other settings. His undergraduate and master's degrees are from (the then) Chico State College, and he holds an Ed.D. from Stanford University.

Corliss Wilson Outley is currently an Assistant Professor in the School of Kinesiology at the University of Minnesota. Outley earned her BS in biology at Grambling State University, her MS in forestry from Southern Illinois

University-Carbondale, and her Ph.D. in recreation and resources development from Texas A&M University. Since 1999 her research has focused on understanding the relationship between race/ethnicity and recreational behavior in environmental settings and the meaning of leisure for inner city and rural youth of color. She teaches classes in research and evaluation, leisure in human development and positive youth development and recreation programming. Outley also serves as faculty member and advisor to the Youth Development Leadership Program jointly sponsored by the University of Minnesota Extension Service and the College of Education and Human Development. When not working, Corliss enjoys reading mystery novels, collecting elephants, and spending time with her husband, Eric, and their daughter, Kenya.

Daniel F. Perkins is an Associate Professor of family and youth resiliency and policy in the Department of Agricultural and Extension Education at the Pennsylvania State University. Daniel received a Ph.D. in family and child ecology in 1995 from Michigan State University. He received his MS in human development and family studies and BS in psychology from the Pennsylvania State University. His work involves teaching, research, and outreach through the Penn State Cooperative Extension Service. His scholarship involves the integration of practice and research into three major foci: (1) positive youth development—decrease risks and increase skills and competencies of youth, (2) healthy family development—increase resiliency through strength-based educational programming, and (3) community collaboration—promote strategies for mobilizing communities in support of children, youth, and families. His research and extension work have resulted in numerous publications in journals of the field. Recently, he coedited a book that proposes a community youth development framework that intertwines tenets from the positive youth development model and the community development perspective.

Jennifer Skuza is a faculty member at the University of Minnesota and is the Director of the Minnesota Urban 4-H Youth Development program. She holds a Ph.D. in Education from the University of Minnesota where she specialized in the social and cultural foundations of education and education research methodologies. Jennifer has also studied education policy at the International Study Institute, Charles University in Prague, Czech Republic. Since 1992, Jennifer has been working with and on behalf of immigrant, migrant, refugee, and urban youth as an educator, researcher, and advocate. She was selected as the 1997 and 2001 recipient of the University of Minnesota Dean and Director Distinguished Diversity Award. She also received the

1997 Minnesota Education Association Foundation's Excellence in Teaching and Learning Award and 1997 Minnesota Association of Extension Educators Early Career Award. In 1996, she served as a volunteer teacher within the Proyecto Conservacion (Conservation Project) in San Andres, Guatemala, and annually travels to Nicaragua, Costa Rica, and other parts of Central America and Mexico.

Kathrin Walker has over five years of experience conducting applied research and evaluation with out-of-school programs for youth. Currently, she is the Project Director for a qualitative study on youth development programs at the University of Illinois at Urbana-Champaign where she is also pursuing a Ph.D. in educational psychology, with a specialization in evaluation. Her dissertation research explores the nature of youth development practice, with a focus on the multiple roles adult leaders play in the lives of the youth they serve.

Peter A. Witt holds the Bradberry Recreation and Youth Development Endowed Chair in the Department of Recreation, Park and Tourism Sciences at Texas A&M University. His major interests are evaluating outcomes of out-of-school time programs offered by school districts, recreation and park departments, and nonprofit agencies. He is also involved in efforts to identify best practices and characteristics of successful youth development programs. Most of this work is based on models of risk, resiliency and protective factors, and developmental assets. He has written or edited seven books and authored more than 90 articles on the social psychology of leisure involvement and recreation services for a variety of different user groups. Two of his books (with John Crompton) provide case studies of youth recreation best practices in park and recreation agency settings. He is the editor of the *Journal of Park and Recreation Administration*, and former editor of *Journal of Leisure Research* and *Therapeutic Recreation Journal*. He is an elected member and has served as President of both the Academy of Leisure Sciences and the American Academy of Park and Recreation Administration. He has received numerous awards, including the Theodore and Franklin Roosevelt Award for Recreation Research from the National Recreation and Park Association (1988) and the Distinguished Colleague Award from the National Recreation and Park Association. In 2004 he received the Robert W. Crawford Achievement Award for work in youth development, given annually by the National Recreation Foundation.

Cheryl K. Baldwin
Assistant Professor
Aurora University
347 Gladstone
Aurora, IL 60506-4892
E-mail: cbaldwin@aurora.edu
Phone: 630-844-4227
Fax: 630-844-5532

Jason N. Bocarro
Assistant Professor
Recreation, Management & Policy Department
University of New Hampshire
Durham, NH 03824
E-mail: jbocarro@cisunix.unh.edu
Phone: 603-862-1773
Fax: 603-862-1117

Linda L. Caldwell
Professor
Recreation, Park and Tourism Management
The Pennsylvania State University
201 Mateer
University Park, PA 16802-1307
E-mail: lindac@psu.edu
Phone: 814-863-8983
Fax: 814-863-6103

Megan Kelly Cronan
Grad Student
Department of Recreation, Park and Tourism Sciences
Texas A&M University
College Station, TX 77843-2261
E-mail: megkc@tamu.edu
Phone: 979-845-7324
Fax: 979-845-0446

Mary Ann Devine
Associate Professor
Exercise, Leisure and Sport
Kent State University
P. O. 5190

Kent, OH 44242
E-mail: mdevine@kent.edu
Phone: 330-672-2012
Fax: 330-672-4106

Jesse M. Ellis
Supervisor of Community Use
Fairfax County Community and Recreation Services
12011 Government Center Parkway, Suite 1050
Fairfax, VA 22035-1115
E-mail: jesse.ellis@fairfaxcounty.gov
Phone: 703-324-5704
Fax: 703-222-9792

Arnold H. Grossman
Professor
Department of Applied Psychology
Steinhardt School of Education
New York University
239 Greene Street, Suite 400
New York, NY 10003
E-mail: arnold.grossman@nyu.edu
Phone: 212-998-5615
Fax: 212-995-4358

Karla A. Henderson
Professor
Parks, Recreation, and Tourism Management
Box 8004, Biltmore, North Carolina State University
Raleigh, NC 27695-8004
E-mail: karla_henderson@ncsu.edu
Phone: 919-513-0352
Fax: 919-515-3687

Susan L. Hutchinson
Dalhousie University
6230 South Street
Halifax, Nova Scotia, Canada B3H 3J5
E-mail: slh37@psu.edu
Phone: 902-494-1163
Fax: 902-494-5120

Reed W. Larson
Pampered Chef Ltd. Endowed Chair in Family Resiliency
Department of Human and Community Development
University of Illinois
1105 W. Nevada Street
Urbana, IL 61801
E-mail: larsonr@uiuc.edu
Phone: 217-333-2837
Fax: 217-333-9061

Francis Lobo
3 Ghost Gum Road
Willetton 6155 WA Australia
E-mail: F.Lobo@ecu.edu.au
Phone: 61 8 94574420
Fax: 61 8 63045840

Kristi Montandon
Grad Student
Department of Recreation, Park and Tourism Sciences
Texas A&M University
College Station, TX 77843-2261
Phone: 979-845-7324
Fax: 979-845-0446

Bill Niepoth
19 Sierra Lakeside Lane
Chico, CA 95928
E-mail: bniepoth@csuchico.edu
Phone: 530-343-4375
Fax: 530-898-6557

Corliss Wilson Outley
Assistant Professor
Division of Recreation and Sport Studies
University of Minnesota
1900 University Avenue SE
Minneapolis, MN 55455
E-mail: coutley@umn.edu
Phone: 612-624-8065
Fax: 612-626-7700

Daniel F. Perkins
Associate Professor
Family and Youth Resiliency and Policy
Department of Agricultural and Extension Education
323 Ag Administration Building, The Pennsylvania State University
University Park, PA 16802-2601
E-mail: dfp102@psu.edu
Phone: 814-865-6988
Fax: 814-863-4753

Jennifer Skuza
Associate Professor and Director
Urban 4-H Youth Development
University of Minnesota
495 Coffey Hall
St. Paul, MN 55108
E-mail: skuza@umn.edu
Phone: 612-624-7798
Fax: 612-624-7793

Kathrin Walker
Department of Human and Community Development
University of Illinois at Urbana-Champaign
1105 W. Nevada Street
Urbana, IL 61801
E-mail: kcwalkr1@uiuc.edu
Phone: 217-265-8413
Fax: 217-333-9061

Peter A. Witt
Bradberry Recreation and Youth Development Chair
Department of Recreation, Park and Tourism Sciences
Texas A&M University
College Station, TX 77843-2261
E-mail: pwitt@tamu.edu
Phone: 979-845-7325
Fax: 979-845-0446

Other Books by Venture Publishing, Inc.

21st Century Leisure: Current Issues, Second Edition
by Valeria J. Freysinger and John R. Kelly
The A•B•Cs of Behavior Change: Skills for Working With Behavior Problems in Nursing Homes
by Margaret D. Cohn, Michael A. Smyer, and Ann L. Horgas
Activity Experiences and Programming within Long-Term Care
by Ted Tedrick and Elaine R. Green
The Activity Gourmet
by Peggy Powers
Advanced Concepts for Geriatric Nursing Assistants
by Carolyn A. McDonald
Adventure Programming
edited by John C. Miles and Simon Priest
Assessment: The Cornerstone of Activity Programs
by Ruth Perschbacher
Behavior Modification in Therapeutic Recreation: An Introductory Manual
by John Datillo and William D. Murphy
Benefits of Leisure
edited by B. L. Driver, Perry J. Brown, and George L. Peterson
Benefits of Recreation Research Update
by Judy M. Sefton and W. Kerry Mummery
Beyond Baskets and Beads: Activities for Older Adults With Functional Impairments
by Mary Hart, Karen Primm, and Kathy Cranisky
Beyond Bingo: Innovative Programs for the New Senior
by Sal Arrigo, Jr., Ann Lewis, and Hank Mattimore
Beyond Bingo 2: More Innovative Programs for the New Senior
by Sal Arrigo, Jr.
Boredom Busters: Themed Special Events to Dazzle and Delight Your Group
by Annette C. Moore
Both Gains and Gaps: Feminist Perspectives on Women's Leisure
by Karla Henderson, M. Deborah Bialeschki, Susan M. Shaw, and Valeria J. Freysinger
Client Assessment in Therapeutic Recreation Services
by Norma J. Stumbo
Client Outcomes in Therapeutic Recreation Services
by Norma J. Stumbo
Conceptual Foundations for Therapeutic Recreation
edited by David R. Austin, John Dattilo, and Bryan P. McCormick
Constraints to Leisure
edited by Edgar L. Jackson
Dementia Care Programming: An Identity-Focused Approach
by Rosemary Dunne
Dimensions of Choice: A Qualitative Approach to Recreation, Parks, and Leisure Research
by Karla A. Henderson
Diversity and the Recreation Profession: Organizational Perspectives
edited by Maria T. Allison and Ingrid E. Schneider
Effective Management in Therapeutic Recreation Service
by Gerald S. O'Morrow and Marcia Jean Carter
Evaluating Leisure Services: Making Enlightened Decisions, Second Edition
by Karla A. Henderson and M. Deborah Bialeschki
Everything From A to Y: The Zest Is up to You! Older Adult Activities for Every Day of the Year
by Nancy R. Cheshire and Martha L. Kenney
The Evolution of Leisure: Historical and Philosophical Perspectives
by Thomas Goodale and Geoffrey Godbey
Experience Marketing: Strategies for the New Millennium
by Ellen L. O'Sullivan and Kathy J. Spangler
Facilitation Techniques in Therapeutic Recreation
by John Dattilo

File o' Fun: A Recreation Planner for Games & Activities, Third Edition
by Jane Harris Ericson and Diane Ruth Albright
Functional Interdisciplinary-Transdisciplinary Therapy (FITT) Manual
by Deborah M. Schott, Judy D. Burdett, Beverly J. Cook, Karren S. Ford, and Kathleen M. Orban
The Game and Play Leader's Handbook: Facilitating Fun and Positive Interaction, Revised Edition
by Bill Michaelis and John M. O'Connell
The Game Finder—A Leader's Guide to Great Activities
by Annette C. Moore
Getting People Involved in Life and Activities: Effective Motivating Techniques
by Jeanne Adams
Glossary of Recreation Therapy and Occupational Therapy
by David R. Austin
Great Special Events and Activities
by Annie Morton, Angie Prosser, and Sue Spangler
Group Games & Activity Leadership
by Kenneth J. Bulik
Growing With Care: Using Greenery, Gardens, and Nature With Aging and Special Populations
by Betsy Kreidler
Hands On! Children's Activities for Fairs, Festivals, and Special Events
by Karen L. Ramey
In Search of the Starfish: Creating a Caring Environment
by Mary Hart, Karen Primm, and Kathy Cranisky
Inclusion: Including People With Disabilities in Parks and Recreation Opportunities
by Lynn Anderson and Carla Brown Kress
Inclusive Leisure Services: Responding to the Rights of People with Disabilities, Second Edition
by John Dattilo
Innovations: A Recreation Therapy Approach to Restorative Programs
by Dawn R. De Vries and Julie M. Lake
Internships in Recreation and Leisure Services: A Practical Guide for Students, Third Edition
by Edward E. Seagle, Jr. and Ralph W. Smith
Interpretation of Cultural and Natural Resources, Second Edition
by Douglas M. Knudson, Ted T. Cable, and Larry Beck
Intervention Activities for At-Risk Youth
by Norma J. Stumbo
Introduction to Outdoor Recreation: Providing and Managing Natural Resource Based Opportunities
by Roger L. Moore and B. L. Driver
Introduction to Recreation and Leisure Services, Eighth Edition
by Karla A. Henderson, M. Deborah Bialeschki, John L. Hemingway, Jan S. Hodges, Beth D. Kivel, and H. Douglas Sessoms
Introduction to Therapeutic Recreation: U.S. and Canadian Perspectives
by Kenneth Mobily and Lisa Ostiguy
Introduction to Writing Goals and Objectives: A Manual for Recreation Therapy Students and Entry-Level Professionals
by Suzanne Melcher
Leadership and Administration of Outdoor Pursuits, Second Edition
by Phyllis Ford and James Blanchard
Leadership in Leisure Services: Making a Difference, Second Edition
by Debra J. Jordan
Leisure and Leisure Services in the 21st Century
by Geoffrey Godbey
The Leisure Diagnostic Battery: Users Manual and Sample Forms
by Peter A. Witt and Gary Ellis
Leisure Education I: A Manual of Activities and Resources, Second Edition
by Norma J. Stumbo
Leisure Education II: More Activities and Resources, Second Edition
by Norma J. Stumbo

Leisure Education III: More Goal-Oriented Activities
by Norma J. Stumbo
Leisure Education IV: Activities for Individuals with Substance Addictions
by Norma J. Stumbo
Leisure Education Program Planning: A Systematic Approach, Second Edition
by John Dattilo
Leisure Education Specific Programs
by John Dattilo
Leisure in Your Life: An Exploration, Sixth Edition
by Geoffrey Godbey
Leisure Services in Canada: An Introduction, Second Edition
by Mark S. Searle and Russell E. Brayley
Leisure Studies: Prospects for the Twenty-First Century
edited by Edgar L. Jackson and Thomas L. Burton
The Lifestory Re-Play Circle: A Manual of Activities and Techniques
by Rosilyn Wilder
The Melody Lingers On: A Complete Music Activities Program for Older Adults
by Bill Messenger
Models of Change in Municipal Parks and Recreation: A Book of Innovative Case Studies
edited by Mark E. Havitz
More Than a Game: A New Focus on Senior Activity Services
by Brenda Corbett
Nature and the Human Spirit: Toward an Expanded Land Management Ethic
edited by B. L. Driver, Daniel Dustin, Tony Baltic, Gary Elsner, and George Peterson
The Organizational Basis of Leisure Participation: A Motivational Exploration
by Robert A. Stebbins
Outdoor Recreation for 21st Century America
by H. Ken Cordell
Outdoor Recreation Management: Theory and Application, Third Edition
by Alan Jubenville and Ben Twight
Planning Parks for People, Second Edition
by John Hultsman, Richard L. Cottrell, and Wendy Z. Hultsman
The Process of Recreation Programming Theory and Technique, Third Edition
by Patricia Farrell and Herberta M. Lundegren
Programming for Parks, Recreation, and Leisure Services: A Servant Leadership Approach, Second Edition
by Debra J. Jordan, Donald G. DeGraaf, and Kathy H. DeGraaf
Protocols for Recreation Therapy Programs
edited by Jill Kelland, along with the Recreation Therapy Staff at Alberta Hospital Edmonton
Quality Management: Applications for Therapeutic Recreation
edited by Bob Riley
A Recovery Workbook: The Road Back from Substance Abuse
by April K. Neal and Michael J. Taleff
Recreation and Leisure: Issues in an Era of Change, Third Edition
edited by Thomas Goodale and Peter A. Witt
Recreation Economic Decisions: Comparing Benefits and Costs, Second Edition
by John B. Loomis and Richard G. Walsh
Recreation for Older Adults: Individual and Group Activities
by Judith A. Elliott and Jerold E. Elliott
Recreation Programming and Activities for Older Adults
by Jerold E. Elliott and Judith A. Sorg-Elliott
Reference Manual for Writing Rehabilitation Therapy Treatment Plans
by Penny Hogberg and Mary Johnson
Research in Therapeutic Recreation: Concepts and Methods
edited by Marjorie J. Malkin and Christine Z. Howe
Simple Expressions: Creative and Therapeutic Arts for the Elderly in Long-Term Care Facilities
by Vicki Parsons
A Social History of Leisure Since 1600
by Gary Cross

A Social Psychology of Leisure
by Roger C. Mannell and Douglas A. Kleiber
Special Events and Festivals: How to Organize, Plan, and Implement
by Angie Prosser and Ashli Rutledge
Stretch Your Mind and Body: Tai Chi as an Adaptive Activity
by Duane A. Crider and William R. Klinger
Therapeutic Activity Intervention with the Elderly: Foundations and Practices
by Barbara A. Hawkins, Marti E. May, and Nancy Brattain Rogers
Therapeutic Recreation and the Nature of Disabilities
by Kenneth E. Mobily and Richard D. MacNeil
Therapeutic Recreation: Cases and Exercises, Second Edition
by Barbara C. Wilhite and M. Jean Keller
Therapeutic Recreation in Health Promotion and Rehabilitation
by John Shank and Catherine Coyle
Therapeutic Recreation in the Nursing Home
by Linda Buettner and Shelley L. Martin
Therapeutic Recreation Programming: Theory and Practice
by Charles Sylvester, Judith E. Voelkl, and Gary D. Ellis
Therapeutic Recreation Protocol for Treatment of Substance Addictions
by Rozanne W. Faulkner
The Therapeutic Recreation Stress Management Primer
by Cynthia Mascott
The Therapeutic Value of Creative Writing
by Paul M. Spicer
Tourism and Society: A Guide to Problems and Issues
by Robert W. Wyllie
Traditions: Improving Quality of Life in Caregiving
by Janelle Sellick

Venture Publishing, Inc.
1999 Cato Avenue
State College, PA 16801
Phone: (814) 234-4561
Fax: (814) 234-1651